HISTORICAL DICTIONARY

The historical dictionaries present essential information on a broad range of subjects, including American and world history, art, business, cities, countries, cultures, customs, film, global conflicts, international relations, literature, music, philosophy, religion, sports, and theater. Written by experts, all contain highly informative introductory essays on the topic and detailed chronologies that, in some cases, cover vast historical time periods but still manage to heavily feature more recent events.

Brief A–Z entries describe the main people, events, politics, social issues, institutions, and policies that make the topic unique, and entries are cross-referenced for ease of browsing. Extensive bibliographies are divided into several general subject areas, providing excellent access points for students, researchers, and anyone wanting to know more. Additionally, maps, photographs, and appendixes of supplemental information aid high school and college students doing term papers or introductory research projects. In short, the historical dictionaries are the perfect starting point for anyone looking to research in these fields.

HISTORICAL DICTIONARIES OF INTELLIGENCE AND COUNTERINTELLIGENCE

Jon Woronoff, Series Editor

Historical Dictionary of Russian and Soviet Intelligence

Second Edition

Robert W. Pringle

ROWMAN & LITTLEFIELD
Lanham • Boulder • New York • London

Published by Rowman & Littlefield
A wholly owned subsidiary of The Rowman & Littlefield Publishing Group, Inc.
4501 Forbes Boulevard, Suite 200, Lanham, Maryland 20706
www.rowman.com

Unit A, Whitacre Mews, 26-34 Stannary Street, London SE11 4AB

British Library Cataloguing in Publication Information Available

Library of Congress Cataloging-in-Publication Data

Pringle, Robert W.
Historical dictionary of Russian and Soviet intelligence / Robert W. Pringle. — Second edition.
pages cm
Includes bibliographical references.
ISBN 978-1-4422-5317-9 (cloth : alk. paper) — ISBN 978-1-4422-5318-6 (ebook)
1. Intelligence service—Russia—Encyclopedias. 2. Military intelligence—Russia—Encyclopedias. 3. Spies—Russia—Biography—Encyclopedias. 4. Intelligence service—Soviet Union—Encyclope-dias. 5. Military intelligence—Soviet Union—Encyclopedias. 6. Spies—Soviet Union—Biography—Encyclopedias. 7. Intelligence service—Russia (Federation)—Encyclopedias. 8. Military intelli-gence—Russia (Federation)—Encyclopedias. 9. Spies—Russia (Federation)—Biography—Encyclo-pedias. I. Title.
UB252.R8P75 2015
327.1247003—dc23
2015008634

Printed in the United States of America

Contents

Editor's Foreword

Russia was a pioneer in the rather murky field of intelligence and counterintelligence, going back to tsarist times when it spied on enemies both abroad and at home. It became even more essential under the Soviet Union, more to rid itself of (real or imaginary) foes at home than abroad, then came into its own in opposition to Nazi Germany and Imperial Japan. Although the field appeared to be relegated to history when the Soviet empire crumbled and economic concerns became uppermost, it is back with a vengeance with an ex-KGB apparatchik in the Kremlin and intelligence operatives undermining governments in nearby countries. So we are once again studying the efforts of the Oprichina, Okhrana, CHEKA, GPU, NKVD, and FSB.

This second edition of *Historical Dictionary of Russian and Soviet Intelligence* reaches back to the time of Ivan the Terrible and amply covers the even more ruthless regime of Joseph Stalin before reaching Vladimir Putin. Varied intelligence agencies are known best by their Russian names, so the acronyms and abbreviations list will be of great help. The core dictionary section contains entries on major agencies and organizations, tradecraft, major events such as wars and revolutions, acts of internal repression and revenge abroad, top leaders, prominent agents and spies, dissidents, defectors, and traitors. Readers who are interested in further research can consult the bibliography.

Both the first edition and the expanded second edition were written by Robert W. Pringle, whose experience in this field is substantial and varied. After studying Russian history, he went into government service, working for the Department of State and the Central Intelligence Agency for 25 years. During his career, he focused frequently on the then–Soviet Union, serving in analytical positions. Among his service abroad was from 1977 to 1979 as consular and human rights officer at the U.S. embassy in Moscow. On retiring from government service, he was awarded the Career Intelligence Medal. He then turned to academia and taught history and political science at the Patterson School of Diplomacy and International Commerce at the University of Kentucky. He later taught at the Virginia Military Institute and Christopher Newport University in Virginia. Pringle has also written a number of papers and articles on these topics. This book, the result of decades of practical experience and teaching, is both informative and exciting.

Jon Woronoff
Series Editor

Reader's Notes

The book covers intelligence and security services during three periods of Russian history: tsarist/imperial (1590–1917), the Soviet era (1917–1991), and the post-Soviet period. A study of the Russian intelligence service is difficult enough without the frequent changes of names and initials of the Soviet and post-Soviet services as well as of the names of major personalities and cities, not to mention the problem of transliterating Eastern Slavic, particularly Russian, names and places into the Latin alphabet.

The question of the names and initials of the Soviet services is dealt with in appendices A, C, E, and F. I have tried to limit confusion by choosing to use *Smersh*, the Russian acronym for *Smert Spiyonam* (Death to Spies), rather than its full legal title, GUKR/SMERSH, for the Chief Directorate of Counterintelligence/SMERSH, in the text. The post-Soviet services have also gone through periodic name changes.

Many of the early Soviet leaders took revolutionary pseudonyms. Vladimir Lenin was born Vladimir Ulyanov, but he was never "Nikolai" Lenin. (He once signed an editorial "N. Lenin," meaning "not Lenin.") Many security officers, especially those from a Jewish background, changed their names and patronymics. For example, Mikhail Ivanovich Belkin was born Moisei Yelnovich. Whenever possible, I have included both their birth name and their "political" name.

Russian cities and regions deserve a better fate: names changed in 1917–1920, again in 1956–1960, and finally in 1988–1992. St Petersburg has been Petrograd, Leningrad, and now, as before 1914, St. Petersburg. Likewise, Stalingrad, once Tsaritsyn, is now Volgograd, and the Battle of Stalingrad has become the Battle on the Volga.

Cyrillic-to-Roman transliteration is difficult. There are many systems. I have chosen to use the British Standard (BGN/PCGN), which is used by Oxford University Press as the method of transliterating Russian Cyrillic texts into the Latin alphabet. There are a few exceptions: for example, I have used "Trotsky" rather than "Trotskiy."

In order to facilitate the rapid and efficient location of information and to make this book as useful a reference tool as possible, extensive cross-references have been provided in the dictionary section. Within individual entries, terms that have their own entries are in **boldface type** the first time they appear. Related terms that do not appear in the text are indicated in the *See also*. *See* refers to other entries that deal with the topic.

Acronyms and Abbreviations

Abwehr	Literally, "defense." The German Intelligence Service under the High Command of the Armed Forces
AK	Armija Krajowa (Polish Home Army)
AMTORG	American–Russian Trading Company
AOD	Administrative Organs Department of the Communist Party Central Committee
ATTs	Antiterroristicheskiy tsentr SNG (Antiterrorist Center of the Commonwealth of Independent States)
AVH	Hungarian internal security/counterintelligence service
BfV	Bundesamt für Verfassungschutz (Office for the Protection of the Constitution, West German counterintelligence service)
BND	Bundesnachrichtendienst (West German foreign intelligence service)
BO	Boevaya Organizatsia (Battle Organization)
BSS	British Security Service. *See* MI5
CCPC	Central Committee of the Communist Party
ChK or Cheka	Chrevzuychanaya Komissiya po Borbe s Kontrarevolutsei i Sabotazhem (Extraordinary Commission to Combat Counterrevolution and Sabotage)
CIA	Central Intelligence Agency
CPSU	Communist Party of the Soviet Union
CPUSA	Communist Party of the United States of America
Dalstroi	Far Northern Construction Trust
Enormoz	Literally, "enormous." NKVD code name for the Anglo-American nuclear weapons program
FAPSI	Ferderalnoe Agentstvo Pravitelstevennoi svyazi i informatatsii (Federal Agency for Government Communications and Information)
FBI	Federal Bureau of Investigation

FHO	Fremde Heere Ost (Foreign Armies East, unit of German Army High Command responsible for intelligence on the Soviet Army during World War II)
FSB	Federalnaya Sluzhba Bezopasnosti (Federal Security Service)
FSO	Federalnaya Sluzhba Okhrani (Federal Protective Service)
GCHQ	General Communications Headquarters (British signals intelligence service)
GKO	Gosudartsvenniy Komitet Oborony (State Defense Committee)
Glavlit	Glavnoe Upravlenieniye po delam literatury i izdatv (Main Directorate for the Issues of Literature and the Press)
Gostekhkommisia	State Technical Commission. *See* GTK
GPU	Gosudarstvennoye Politicheskoe Upravleniye (State Political Directorate)
GRU	Glavnoe Razvedvitelnoe Upravleniye (Chief Intelligence Directorate)
GTK	Gosudarstvennaya Tekhnicheskaya Komisiya (State Technical Commission)
Gulag	Glavnoye Upravleniye ispravitelno-trudovykh Lagerei (Chief Directorate of Corrective Labor Camps)
GUPVI	Glavnoye Upravleniye po delam Voennoplennikh i Internirovannikh (Chief Directorate for Prisoners of War and Internees)
HVA	Hauptverwaltung Aufklärung (Chief Directorate of Intelligence of East German MfS)
INO	Inostranniy Otdel (Foreign (Intelligence Section of the Cheka, GPU, OGPU)
Instantsiya	"The Authorities." The leadership of the Communist Party and the Soviet Union; the address for important Soviet intelligence cables
KGB	Komitet Gosudarstvennoi Bezopastnosti (Committee of State Security)
KHAD	Department of State Information Services (Afghan secret police)

Khozyain	"The Boss," Joseph Stalin
KI	Komitet Informatsii (Committee of Information)
Komsomol	Young Communist League
KRU	Kontrrazvedyvatelnoye Upravlenie (Counterintelligence Directorate)
MfS	Ministerium für Staatssicherheit (East German Ministry for State Security)
MGB	Ministerstsvo Gosudarstevennoi Bezopasnosti (Ministry of State Security)
MI5	British Security Service. *See* BSS
MI6	British Intelligence Service. *See* SIS
MNVK/2	Hungarian Military Intelligence Service
MSS	Ministry of State Security (China)
MVD	Ministerstsvo Vnutrennikh Del (Ministry of Internal Affairs)
NATO	North Atlantic Treaty Organization
NEP	New Economic Policy
NKGB	Narodniy Kommissariat Gosudarstvennoi Bezopastnosti (People's Commissariat of State Security)
NKVD	Narodniy Kommissariat Vnutrennikh Del (People's Commissariat of Internal Affairs)
NSA	National Security Agency (American signals intelligence service)
OGPU	Obyedinennoe Gosudarstvennoe Politicheskoe Upravleniye (Unified State Political Directorate)
OMSBON	Otdelniy Motorstrelskovoi Brigadi Osobovo Naznacheniya (Independent Motorized Rifle Brigade for Special Operations)
OO	Osobiy Otdel (Special Section)
OSS	Office of Strategic Services
PGU	Pervoye Glavnoye Upravleniye (First Chief Directorate, KGB foreign intelligence component)
RSDLP (B)	Russian Social Democratic Labor Party (Bolshevik)
SB	Polish Security Service

SIS	Secret Intelligence Service, British Foreign Intelligence Service
SLON	Northern Camps of Special Designation (GPU forced labor camps located on the White Sea, ca. 1920)
Smersh	Smert Shpiyonam (Death to Spies), military counterintelligence component of the People Commissariat of Defense
SPETSSVYAZ	Special Service of Communications
Spetznaz	Soviet military and KGB special forces
Stasi	Ministerium für Staatssicherheit (East German Ministry for State Security). *See* MfS
STB	Statni Tajna Bezpecnost (Czechoslovak Secret Intelligence Service)
SVR	Sluzhba Vneshnei Razvedki (Service of Foreign Intelligence)
VM or VMN	Vyshaya Mera (Supreme Measure) or Vyshaya Mera Nakazaniya (Supreme Measure of Punishment), capital punishment
ZK	Zakluchoniy chelovek (prisoner)

Chronology

1564 Ivan IV ("the Terrible") creates *Oprichnina* to purge the country of his enemies. Tens of thousands perish in massive purges sustained by the tsar's hunt for dissidents.

1649 Russian Law Code drafted by court of Tsar Aleksei Mikhailovich defines criticism of the sovereign as treason. The statute "To Protect the Sovereign's Honor" gives government wide latitude to pursue all religious and political critics.

1699 Petr I ("the Great") creates the Preobrazhenskiy Prikaz to combat subversion.

1775–1778 Revolt of dissident peasants and Cossacks led by Emelyan Pugachev shakes the regime; last major peasant revolt before Revolution of 1905.

1790 Authorities arrest Aleksandr Radishchev for his book *Journey from Moscow to St. Petersburg*. Radishchev is initially sentenced to death but later pardoned.

1803 Aleksandr I creates the Committee of General Security to monitor dissent. Though initially interested in the ideals of the enlightenment, Aleksandr refused to consider seriously political reform.

1810 An intelligence branch is founded within the Imperial General Staff.

1825 Decembrists Revolt: dissident officers attempt to unseat Nicholas I. Revolt is put down by the authorities in St. Petersburg and in southern Russia. Five of the revolt's leaders are executed; others are sentenced to exile in Siberia.

1826 Nicholas I creates Third Section of the Imperial Chancery to combat subversion.

1845 A new Criminal Code is drafted at the order of Nicholas I; dissent is narrowly defined.

1848 M. V. Petrashevskiy and his circle are arrested and tried for treason for engaging in sedition under Code of 1845. Most are sentenced to death but pardoned by the tsar at the last moment. All receive sentence of exile.

1863 4 April: Dmitry Karakazov attempts to assassinate Tsar Aleksandr II.

1870–1875 Populist (*Narodnichestvo*) opposition grows in intellectual circles but lacks support among the peasantry; interest in revolution grows among students. The Third Section arrests and exiles numerous revolutionaries, but none are executed.

1881 13 March: Narodnaya Volya assassinate Tsar Aleksandr II. Shortly thereafter, the *Okrannoye Otdelenie* (*Okhrana*) is created within the MVD (Ministry of Internal Affairs) to protect the tsar and regime from subversion.

1904 Russo–Japanese War begins with Japanese surprise attack on Russian fleet at Port Arthur, a massive Russian intelligence failure.

1905 January: Imperial troops fire on peasants peacefully demonstrating at the tsar's palace in St. Petersburg. (Demonstration was organized by Father Georgi Gapon, a Russian Orthodox priest in the pay of the *Okhrana*.) The incident sparks massive urban and rural violence.

1914 August: Russia declares war on Austria; World War I on the Eastern Front is a military, political, and social disaster for the Romanov regime.

1917 March: Riots become revolution in St. Petersburg. Nicholas II abdicates, ending Romanov dynasty. Provisional Government of liberal and socialist parties assumes power. **Spring:** The German General Staff finances the return of Bolshevik leader Vladimir Lenin to Petrograd. **7 November:** "October" Revolution establishes Bolshevik power and sparks civil war. **20 December:** Soviet leader Lenin establishes Cheka.

1918 16–27 July: Cheka execution squad murders the Romanov family. **30 August:** The attempted assassination of Vladimir Lenin is used by Cheka chief Feliks Dzerzhinsky to institute a massive Red Terror.

1920 20 December: To pursue enemies abroad, a Foreign Intelligence Section is founded within Cheka.

1921 Vladimir Lenin institutes the New Economic Policy. Lenin insists on greater Communist Party control on Cheka and an end of the Terror.

1922 8 February: Cheka is transformed into GPU (State Political Administration).

1923 2 November: GPU renamed OGPU (Unified State Political Administration).

1924 Vladimir Lenin dies, and long succession crisis begins. Joseph Stalin, who has the support of the OGPU, is the eventual victor.

1924–1925 Boris Savinkov and Sidney Reilly lured back to the Soviet Union by Trust counterintelligence operations; both are put to death. Trust operations disrupt efforts by hostile foreign intelligence services to operate inside the Soviet Union.

1926 Feliks Dzerzhinsky dies and is succeeded by Vyacheslav Menzhinsky as head of OGPU.

1928 Leon Trotsky is banished from Moscow to Alma Ata.

1929–1932 Joseph Stalin consolidates power in rural areas with the collectivization of agriculture.

1932 Circulation of Riutin Program causes Joseph Stalin to call for execution of political dissidents within the Communist Party; the demand for a political purge is rebuffed by Communist Party Politburo.

1934 10 May: Vyacheslav Menzhinsky dies and is succeeded by Genrykh Yagoda as head of OGPU. **19 July:** OGPU is absorbed into NKVD (People's Commissariat of Internal Affairs). **1 December:** Leningrad Party boss S. M. Kirov is murdered. **2 December:** New antiterrorist laws allow NKVD to arrest, try, and execute "enemies of the people." **Late December:** Trial and execution of those implicated in Kirov murder.

1936 19–29 August: The first Moscow Trial results in death sentences for Lev Kamenev, Evgenii Zinoviev, and 14 others. **25 September:** Joseph Stalin dispatches telegram to Central Committee calling for replacement of Genrykh Yagoda with Nikolai Yezhov. **27 September:** Yezhov is appointed head of NKVD; Yagoda is demoted and later arrested.

1936–1939 Soviet intelligence services are deeply engaged with Republican forces in the Spanish Civil War. NKVD pursues leftist enemies in Spain, murdering more than 10,000.

1937 23–30 January: Second Moscow Trial results in death sentences for all but two of the accused. **25 May:** Purge of Red Army begins with arrest of Marshal Mikhail Tukhachevskiy and others. **11 June:** Tukhachevskiy and other military officers are tried and shot. **June–July:** Massive purge ("Yezhovshchina") of Communist Party and society begins.

1938 2–12 March: Third Moscow show trial ends with conviction of Nikolai Bukharin and 19 defendants; most are shot immediately following trial. **21 August:** Lavrenty Beria is appointed head of NKVD; Nikolai Yezhov is demoted and appointed minister of water transport.

1939 April–May: Nikolai Yezhov is arrested and interrogated. (He will be shot in 1940.) **17 September:** Soviet forces enter eastern Poland, following signing of Nazi–Soviet Pact. Over the next 18 months, more than 1,000,000 Poles are arrested or deported.

1940 GRU activates "X Group, major source of scientific and political intelligence. **5 March:** Joseph Stalin orders the murder of 26,000 Polish officers and civilians in Soviet prison camps. **May:** Mass murder of Poles is conducted at Katyn and other sites. **20 August:** Leon Trotsky is murdered by NKVD agent Roman Mercader.

1941 NKVD is divided into two organizations: NKVD and NKGB (People's Commissariat of State Security). **22 June:** Germany and Axis allies invade Soviet Union (Operation Barbarossa); Joseph Stalin institutes the GKO (State Defense Committee) to manage war effort. **December:** Soviet foreign intelligence produces critical intelligence for major Red Army counterstroke at Moscow.

1942 NKVD and *Smersh* begin a series of "radio games," deceiving the German high command on Soviet strategic priorities. **November:** *Maskirovka* (Strategic Deception) is a critical factor in major Soviet victory at Stalingrad.

1943 2 February: Last German troops surrender at Stalingrad. **4 February:** NKVD executes 46 general officers and senior defense managers. **April:** Joseph Stalin creates *Smersh* (Death to Spies), a parallel counterintelligence organization with General Viktor Abakumov as chief within the People's Commissariat of Defense. **13 April:** Germans report discovery of murdered Polish officer at Katyn. **July:** Soviet intelligence and partisan successes lead to victory in the Battle of Kursk.

1944 June: Foreign intelligence and strategic deception are major factors in Red Army victory in Operation Bagration. **August–October:** Polish Home Army uprising in Warsaw is suppressed by German military, SS, and paramilitary formations. *Smersh* and NKVD units begin purge of noncommunist Polish forces.

1945 April: Red Army begins assault on Berlin. Adolf Hitler's body discovered in early May. **9 May:** Germany surrenders to Allies. **August:** Konstantin Volkov, an NKGB officer, tries to defect in Istanbul. He is betrayed by Kim Philby and executed. **September:** Igor Gouzenko, GRU code clerk, defects to Canada. **December:** Elizabeth Bentley defects to Federal Bureau of Investigation in New York.

1946 NKGB and NKVD are renamed MGB (Ministry of State Security) and MVD (Ministry of Internal Affairs); V. Merkulov demoted and V. S. Abakumov named minister of state security.

1947 October: Lieutenant Colonel Grigori Aleksandrovich Tokaev becomes the first senior Soviet official to defect to the West.

1948–1949 First Berlin crisis ends with major American victory. MGB investigates Leningrad case and arrests Aleksei Kuznetsov, Nikolai Voznesenskiy, and more than 200 of their colleagues from the Leningrad party apparatus.

1950 June 25: Korean War begins with North Korean invasion of South Korea. **September:** Leading officials of Leningrad party apparatus are executed.

1951 June-July: Purge of security services. Viktor Abakumov is arrested; Semyon Ignatiev is appointed head of the MGB.

1952 12 August: 13 prominent Jewish writers executed, " the night of the murdered poets." **October:** 19th Communist Party Conference begins as Joseph Stalin signals that preparations for a purge of old leadership are in place. Arrests are made in alleged "Doctors' Plot" by Jewish physicians in the pay of American intelligence, a signal that Stalin is preparing to move against enemies in party and security apparatus.

1953 1 March: Joseph Stalin suffers massive stroke. **5 March:** Stalin's death sparks succession crisis. Lavrenty Beria exposes some of Stalin's crimes and releases more than a million prisoners. **26 June:** Beria is arrested at Presidium meeting. **23–24 December:** Beria and several subordinates are tried and executed.

1954 13 March: KGB (Committee of State Security) is created, attached to the Council of Ministers. **December:** Viktor Abakumov and subordinates are tried and shot in Leningrad.

1955 Moscow releases the remaining German, Italian, Hungarian, Spanish, and Polish citizens and prisoners of war captured during World War II.

1956 February: Communist Party First Secretary Nikita Khrushchev delivers speech denouncing Joseph Stalin's "Cult of Personality" at the Communist Party's 20th Party Congress. **June:** Riots in Poznan, Poland, are suppressed by police, with 80 killed. **October:** Soviet tanks ring Warsaw, but war is avoided. Soviet forces intervene to crush Hungarian independence.

1957 KGB chair Ivan Serov helps Nikita Khrushchev win victory over party opponents in Antiparty Group.

1958 25 December: A. N. Shelepin named head of KGB; Ivan Serov moves to GRU.

1961 August: Soviet military and East German authorities close the inter-German border and begin construction of the Berlin Wall.

1961–1962 U.S. Central Intelligence Agency and British Secret Intelligence Service successfully run Colonel Oleg Penkovskiy as an agent within the Soviet military establishment. Penkovskiy's information plays critical role in American successes in resolving the Cuban Missile Crisis.

1962 June: Novocherkassk riots are repressed by troops of the MVD (Ministry of Internal Affairs) and the Red Army; there are more than a hundred casualties. **October:** Moscow deploys medium- and short-range missiles to Cuba, along with 40,000 troops.

1964 October: KGB plays crucial role in coup that replaces Nikita Khrushchev with Leonid Brezhnev.

1967 May: Yuri Andropov is named head of KGB. **July:** John Walker volunteers in Washington to work for the KGB. (Walker spies for Moscow until 1985 and betrays U.S. government communication programs.) **November:** KGB reconstitutes the Secret Political Directorate of the Joseph Stalin years as the Fifth (Counterintelligence among the Intelligentsia) Directorate.

1968 August: Soviet military and KGB crush the "Prague Spring."

1970 December: Major workers protests commence in Poland.

1971 First Strategic Arms Limitation Treaty (SALT) is signed in Moscow; verification is guaranteed by "national technical means." **Summer:** London expel more than 100 Soviet intelligence officers following the defection of Oleg Lyalin.

1974 Aleksandr Solzhenitsyn is expelled from the Soviet Union.

1978 Canada expels 11 Soviet intelligence officers.

1979 December: Soviet troops enter Afghanistan; KGB Alpha Group storms presidential palace and kills Afghan president Amin and family.

1980 Andrei Sakharov and wife are banished from Moscow.

1981 Solidarity movement increases authority in Poland. Moscow bluffs to convince Polish communist leaders they intend to intervene. **2–13 December:** Polish regime cracks down on Solidarity.

1982 February–March: Yuri Andropov moves to Central Committee Secretariat as Leonid Brezhnev's heir apparent; Vitalii Fedorchuk heads KGB. **November:** Brezhnev dies and is succeeded by Andropov as party chief. **December:** Viktor Chebrikov succeeds Fedorchuk as head of KGB; Fedorchuk is assigned to MVD.

1983 Edward Lee Howard makes first contact with the KGB. Yuri Andropov demands that the intelligence services provide information about American first strike. **October:** The *RYaN* (Nuclear Rocket Attack) program artificially creates a war scare.

1985 March: Mikhail Gorbachev becomes Communist Party general secretary. **April:** Aldrich Ames volunteers to serve as Soviet agent and provides KGB with information about two cases. **May:** John Walker is arrested by the FBI; other members of the ring are arrested shortly thereafter. **June:** Adolf Tolkachev, CIA's most important asset in Moscow, arrested by KGB on information from Howard. **13 June:** Ames provides KGB with the "big dump," the names of 10 Soviets working for the CIA. (All are arrested by 1987.) **August:** Vitaliy Yurchenko defects to the United States and provides leads to Edward Howard and Ronald Pelton. Howard subsequently flees to Moscow. **October:** Robert Hanssen mails letter to KGB offering to provide sensitive information about FBI cases. Hanssen provides information about three KGB officers under CIA/FBI control, as well as technical information. **November:** Yurchenko "redefects."

1986 April–May: Mikhail Gorbachev begins campaign for *glasnost* (openness) and *perestroika* (economic restructuring). **Summer:** In Operation Famish, the United States expels more than 50 Soviet intelligence officers as the Reagan administration moves to restrict Soviet intelligence activities. **December:** Gorbachev permits Andrei Sakharov to return to Moscow to further *glasnost*.

1987 November: Mikhail Gorbachev fires Moscow city boss Boris Yeltsin. Opposition to Gorbachev's agenda increases from the left (Yeltsin) and the right (party bureaucracy). **December:** Gorbachev travels to Washington to sign series of arms control agreements. Vladimir Kryuchkov, head of the KGB First Chief Directorate, attends as senior intelligence adviser.

1988 February: Mikhail Gorbachev announces that Soviet troops will leave Afghanistan within a year. **Spring:** Ethnic and political violence escalates in the Caucasus, Baltic republics, and Central Asia. **May:** Gorbachev names Vladimir Kryuchkov KGB chair. Moscow begins withdrawing troops from Afghanistan.

1989 February: Last Soviet troops leave Afghanistan. **7 April:** Solidarity is legalized and enters Polish national elections. **4 June:** Solidarity wins parliamentary election in Poland, taking 99 of 100 senate seats and all 161 seats in the Sejm. **October:** Demonstrations throughout East Germany lead to the end of the Berlin Wall. Mikhail Gorbachev refuses to authorize force to maintain regime.

1990 November–December: Mikhail Gorbachev moves to the right, firing MVD chief Vadim Bakatin and replacing him with Boris Pugo. Vladimir Kryuchkov openly opposes Gorbachev's agenda and warns of CIA subversion as the root cause of Soviet weakness. **December:** Growing unrest in Lithuania and Latvia begin with demands for independence from the Soviet Union.

1991 January: Violence in Vilnius and Riga leaves 16 dead. KGB chair Vladimir Kryuchkov and MVD chief Boris Pugo begin plotting coup with military and party leaders. **18–22 August:** Putsch by party conservatives attempts to bring down Mikhail Gorbachev regime; when coup fails, Kryuchkov and three other senior KGB officers are arrested. Pugo commits suicide. **September:** KGB is abolished, replaced by new intelligence, security, and signals intelligence services. **December:** SVR (Service of Foreign Intelligence) is created, with Yevgeny Primakov as head. **25 December:** Final day of the Soviet Union, which dissolves into Russian Federation and other states.

1992 January: Kanatzhan Alibekov, senior scientist in biological warfare, defects to United States. Boris Yeltsin administration's massive market reforms lead to inflation and economic decline. Russian organized crime and the new security services become an increasingly important player in the new capitalist economy. MVD proves incapable of coping with criminal violence.

1993 October: Constitutional crisis between Russian President Boris Yeltsin and Communist Party members of the Duma create first post-Soviet political crisis. Troops loyal to Yeltsin storm Russian White House; over 100 killed in the fighting.

1994 February: Aldrich Ames is arrested by the FBI. **December:** Russian troops enter Chechnya.

1995 FSB (Federal Security Service) is established by Boris Yeltsin.

1996 April: Moscow and London trade expulsions of intelligence officers. **June:** Boris Yeltsin fires intelligence chief Aleksandr Korzhakov and several of his allies. **July:** Yeltsin is reelected president.

1997 November: Former army officer Grigori Pasko, who publicized ecological damage on Russian military bases, is charged with releasing classified information to foreign countries. (After several trials, he will be convicted in 2001.)

1998 Following unsolved bombings in Moscow, the second Chechen War begins. **5 October:** FSB is given greater responsibility for economic counterintelligence and counterterrorism.

1999 29 November: Russia expels a U.S. diplomat for espionage. **8 December:** Russian diplomat Stanislav Gusev is expelled from the United States for operating bugging device in the office of the U.S. Secretary of State. **31 December:** Boris Yeltsin resigns; Prime Minister Vladimir Putin becomes interim chief of state. (Putin will win presidency in 2000, 2004, and 2012 general elections.)

2000 19 January: Nine Russian diplomats are expelled from Poland for espionage. **February:** After intelligence from a Russian defector provides information, Hanssen is arrested by the FBI. **March:** FSB arrests Edmund Pope, a former U.S. naval officer, on charges of espionage. **14 June:** Retired U.S. Army Colonel George Trofimoff is arrested for spying for the KGB during the Cold War. **31 August:** Two Soviet diplomats are expelled from Estonia for espionage. **8 September:** A senior Japanese naval officer is arrested in Tokyo for spying for Russia. **October:** Sergei Tretyakov, senior SVR staff officer, defects to the United States. **December:** Pope is released and deported to the United States after 253 days in jail.

2001 Vladimir Putin begins restructuring Russian intelligence community; he appoints many colleagues (*siloviki*) to senior positions in intelligence and national security agencies.

2002 23–26 October: Chechen terrorists seize Nord-Ost theater in Moscow. FSB uses gas to end siege; 170 killed, including all the terrorists and 133 hostages.

2004 Vladimir Putin is reelected president. Chechen war continues with military and civilian casualties. **1 September:** Chechen terrorists seize a school in the town of Beslan in North Ossetia, taking more than 1,000 children hostage. Two days later, FSB and MVD units storm the school, the terrorists commit suicide, and more than 350 hostages perish, most of them children, while more than 700 children are seriously injured. The security service and police are criticized for their handling of the situation. **9 September:** Statue of Feliks Dzerzhinsky, which had been torn down on 21 August 1991, is placed back in front of Lubyanka, the FSB headquarters. **December:** *Spy Handler*, the memoirs of KGB counterintelligence officer Viktor Cherkashin, is published, providing new insight into the Ames and Hanssen cases.

2005 8 March: FSB paramilitary unit kills Chechen nationalist leader in a firefight in Tolstoi Yurt. **April:** Germany expels Russian diplomat for espionage. **May:** British press publishes details of Russian espionage in Great Britain.

2006 Russian press publishes a series of stories on the involvement of Russian nongovernmental organizations with British intelligence. President Vladimir Putin announces in April that the FSB has been given a greater authority for counterintelligence and counterterrorism. Liberal reformers claim Putin's decision reduces the role of courts and new legal system. **6 October:** Journalist and human rights activist Anna Politkovskaya murdered in Moscow by Chechens with ties to security service. **1 November:** Russian FSB Aleksandr Litvinenko poisoned with polonium-210 in London. He died on 23 November.

2007 April: Russian cyberattack swamps Estonian parliamentary, governmental, and economic computer infrastructure during diplomatic dispute. First demonstration of Russian competence in cyberwarfare.

2008 August: Five day Russo-Georgian War, featuring sophisticated Russian cyberattacks; 171 Georgian and 64 Russians killed in action.

2009 19 January: Anastasia Baburova and Stanislav Markelo, dissident journalists, murdered. Both had been investigating FSB ties to neo-Nazi organizations. Their murderers were arrested and convicted in 2011.

2010 June: FBI arrests 10 Soviet illegals operating in the United States. They are later exchanged for four Russian citizens held as Western spies.

2012 Putin is elected president after serving four years as premier. **May:** Peaceful protests at Putin's inauguration broken up; 19 people arrested.

2013 January: Expulsion of U.S. businessman for espionage. **15 May:** Expulsion of U.S. diplomat for espionage. **April:** Conviction of regime critics and FSB critics for slander. **23 June:** Edward Snowden requests political asylum in Russia.

2014 February–March: Russian paramilitary troops aid pro-Russian parties in Crimea and eastern Ukraine. **April:** Russian special services provide arms and support to Russian secessionists in eastern Ukraine. **June–July:** Heavy fighting in region involves Russian volunteers. **July:** Malaysian Airlines Flight 17 shot down by Russian surface-to-air missiles under command of GRU officer. **August:** Edward Snowden given permission to reside in Russia for three years as permanent resident.

2015 January: FBI arrests three Soviet intelligence officers under nonofficial cover in New York. **February:** Lithuanian authorities arrest SVR officers under nonofficial cover. **27 February:** Boris Nemtsov, opposition politician, murdered in Moscow, apparently by Chechens with ties to the Security Service. **April:** Russian press boasts that hackers gained access to the White House's unclassified e-mails.

Introduction

The internal security apparatus and foreign intelligence services of Russia—whether imperial, Soviet, or democratic—have played a far greater role in domestic and foreign statecraft than have similar services in the West. A discussion of Russian history without a discussion of the state security organs would be equivalent to a discussion of South African history without mention of apartheid. Senior Russian internal security professionals have usually been closer to the center of power than their Western counterparts. Whereas the British Secret Intelligence Service goes back to the first decade of the 20th century and the American Central Intelligence Agency (CIA) was established in 1947 as a general overhaul of the defense establishment, Russian internal security dates to the reign of Ivan IV (the Terrible), more than 400 years before the CIA was established.

Internal security and surveillance have long been a concern of Russian rulers. Many notable Russian and Western historians have seen this obsession as one of the characteristics that created Russian "exceptionalism." English explorers and diplomats to the court of Ivan IV noted the omnipresent role of surveillance. One was greeted in northern Russia with the comment "Only spies come to Russia." He later wrote his queen, Elizabeth I, "No other news I bring to thee. The weather cold. The people beastly be." British and American ambassadors would comment in the 19th century how their ciphers and messages were stolen from diplomatic premises by trusted servants. One British diplomat was told before World War I by a Russian colleague that his codes had been broken and his messages easily read in the Imperial Foreign Ministry before they reached London. Surveillance of friends and enemies of Soviet power was a constant of the Soviet services. Following the fall of the Soviet Union, the Russian security and intelligence services have continued to play a more important role in national security decision making than do the services of most European states or of the United States. This is particularly true at present, as many officers and agents of the services, known as *siloviki*, play important roles in government and business, convincing some journalists to refer to Russia as a "spookocracy."

THE INSTITUTIONS

Since Ivan IV created the *Oprichnina* in the 1560s to sniff out treason, Russian security institutions have been given tremendous leeway to discover and destroy enemies of the regime at home or abroad. The *oprichniki*, the men of the *Oprichnina*, were given absolute power to punish Ivan's enemies and their families and their clans. Villages and cities were destroyed in the effort to protect the tsar. Petr I (the Great) created an office to maintain regime stability. The *Preobrazhenskiy Prikaz* acted as an extralegal body with power to destroy the enemies of the regime. Detained in secret, Petr's enemies were often tortured and killed. It is worth noting that Joseph Stalin, who was a student of Russian history, approved much of what Ivan and Petr had done. Some Russian historians have referred to Stalin's secret police as *Oprichniki*, noting that the past did tragically repeat itself.[1]

Russian internal security institutions were strengthened in the 1820s by Nicholas I following the Decembrists' Revolt. His gift to the leader of the Third Section of the Imperial Chancery was a handkerchief to wipe away the tears of orphans and widows. Less poetically, the Third Section was charged with the surveillance of the educated class, later termed intelligentsia, who were seen as the regime's greatest enemies. It is worth noting that between 1826 and 1880, the Third Section harassed, imprisoned, and exiled many of the greatest minds the country produced, including Feodor Dostoyevsky. Yet the service was so feckless that it was unable to protect Tsar Aleksandr II from the assassins of the *Narodnaya Volya* (People's Will).

One of the greatest tragedies of Russian history was the attempt by the last tsars and their chancellors to replace legal reform with police administration and extrajudicial punishment. The *Okhrana*, a secret police formed within the Ministry of Internal Affairs in 1881, could neither analyze the rising revolutionary expectations of the population nor cope with the revolutionary parties. The *Okhrana*, formed to protect the government, created far more enemies than it identified for tsarist courts and field courts-martial to arrest, exile, and execute. By working with the same fervor against moderate parties as it did against revolutionary movements, the *Okhrana* played a part in simultaneously fomenting unrest through covert action while preventing the rise of a moderate political opposition.

While the *Okhrana* is seen today as inefficient and corrupt, it was feared by generations of opponents of the regime from the center to the far left of the Russian political spectrum. The greatest compliment paid to the institution was that much of its tradecraft and tactics were copied by the Bolshevik Party following the Russian Revolution. Within weeks of the great October Revolution of 1917, Vladimir Lenin had created an organization that beggared the *Okhrana* in resources and ruthlessness. The Cheka became a by-word for terror: Lenin often stated that a revolution without a firing squad was doomed.

The Cheka and its successor agencies had far more administrative— one hates to use the word judicial—power. In the last half century of tsarist power, between 10,000 and 14,000 deaths can be attributed to pogroms and political repression, whereas the Cheka sentenced and shot more than 140,000 prisoners between 1918 and 1921. It is worth noting that between 1866 and 1900, there were 94 executions, and the period was notable for 40 assassinations, including that of Tsar Aleksandr II. While the *Okhrana* could open and read approximately 35,000 letters a year, the GPU (the successor of the Cheka) intercepted 3 million letters and 5 million telegrams in 1925.[2]

Soviet intelligence was designed to serve the ruling party. Unlike Western governments, which created competing intelligence and security bureaucracies, the chief of the Soviet service was able to deploy all his resources to protect or avenge the party. The Soviet intelligence and security empire was, from its origins, integrated into one umbrella organization known as the Cheka, covering intelligence, counterintelligence, the security of the military, surveillance of the population, leadership protection, technical intelligence, and border security. Subsequent versions of this security organization were the GPU, OGPU, NKVD, NKGB, MVD, and KGB. Leaders of the service were the secret servants of the Communist Party. The security services were never masters of the Soviet Union.

In evaluating the impact of the services on Russian history, historians have been forced to confront several issues:

Effectiveness. The security service destroyed opposition to the regime during the post-Revolution civil war. During World War II, it prevented any Nazi intelligence service from penetrating the homeland. Following the war, it defeated insurgencies in Ukraine and the Baltic. Nevertheless, the KGB was unable to prevent the dramatic failure of the regime in 1991.

Scope of Activity. Between 1910 and 1917, the *Okhrana* was running approximately 600 informers in Russia, 116 of them in Moscow. Twenty years later, the NKVD had literally millions of informers across the Soviet Union.[3] A historian of Russian counterintelligence during World War II estimated that more than 20 million Russian soldiers and civilians were serving as informants.[4]

Cost. There is no real butcher bill for the Lenin and Stalin years. How many people were executed, died in camps, or were simply murdered at a leader's whim remains unknown and unknowable. The number of imprisoned, exiled, and executed lies in the tens of millions. Between 1929 and 1953, as a recent history of the forced labor camp system shows, 28.7 million people received sentences of prison or exile, of which 2.7 million were executed or died of hunger or overwork in the camps and jails. One former political prisoner noted that the difference between Adolf Hitler and Joseph Stalin was that Hitler killed only his enemies.[5]

In the decades of Soviet power, the KGB built a network of organizations that ensured Communist Party control. The personnel section (*Perviy otdel*, or First Section) of every institution was staffed by KGB alumni who recruited informants and acted as talent scouts for the service. Another critical KGB ally was *Glavlit*, the regime's "ideological KGB," which employed 70,000 censors. The organization worked in concert with the KGB to ensure ideological control of literature and the arts.

In the end, the KGB could no more save the Soviet state than the *Okhrana* could save Imperial Russia. The KGB had no answers to the growth of corruption and ethnic unrest that characterized Soviet society in the 1970s and 1980s. Surveillance of dissidents and punishment of religious believers in the end were largely counterproductive, ruining the reputation of the communist regime abroad and reducing the resources necessary for policing the corrupt.

The KGB took a prominent part in the failed 1991 August putsch. It was ready to arrest thousands, and it had ordered tens of thousands of blank arrest warrants and handcuffs months before the putsch took place. Thankfully, they were never used. The KGB leadership in 1991 had lost touch with its staff as it had lost touch with developments within the country; crucial paramilitary KGB units refused to obey the putschists' orders, citing their lack of legal mandate.

Russia before 2012 seemed to be developing in fits and starts toward a law-based state. Neither Boris Yeltsin nor Vladimir Putin had been tempted as president of Russia to abandon the power that the security services offer their master. While critics believe that legal reform is dead, others see the process as still continuing—albeit slowly and faltering. Putin, a KGB veteran, has built a power base on intelligence veterans. Moreover, he has recentralized the power of the security services in the Office of the Presidency. One major difference critics see between the KGB of the Soviet era and the present is that the security service now has more power to set its own agenda. One cynic told British journalist Benjamin Judah that "Russia does not have the KGB; Russia should be so lucky."

The security service of postcommunist Russia, the FSB, has lost some of the authority of the internal counterintelligence components of the KGB. It is the largest security organization in Europe and the second largest in the world after the Chinese Ministry of State Security. The FSB reports directly to the president of Russia, and there is little parliamentary oversight. While laws have been passed restricting the service's ability to conduct surveillance of the population, many of its leaders are having trouble dealing with the concept of a law-based society, and several military officers and scientists have been arrested on trumped-up charges. FSB officers have also become the "silent partners" of many businessmen, and reformers, journalists, and lawyers seeking to find the extent of such relations have been killed, beaten, or forced into exile. The most noted martyr, Anna Politkovskaya, was shot in her apartment in Moscow in 2006. Some of those who investigated her murder were also murdered.

The other successor states of the former Soviet Union have had mixed success in subjugating the security services to the rule of law. In the Baltic states, reform has gone the furthest, and the security services remain under legal, parliamentary, and media oversight. In other states, legal reform is far from complete. The behavior of the Ukrainian Security Service since the constitutional crisis in late 2003 suggests to some that it sees its future as a servant of a new elite. In Central Asia, the security services very much resemble Cheka. One measure of the change in the former Soviet space is the death penalty: the last executions took place in Ukraine and Russia in 1996. Executions are still taking place in Uzbekistan, Turkmenistan, and Belarus, according to human rights organizations.

Foreign intelligence in the tsarist, communist, and postcommunist periods was well organized and directed. Several foreign intelligence missions of the tsarist period have continued through Russian history. As far back as the reign of Ivan IV, foreign intelligence was directed against Russian opponents of the tsar living abroad. The Third Section and the *Okhrana* targeted enemies of the regime, and the Paris office of the *Okhrana* coordinated efforts across Europe against revolutionary parties. Russian intelligence also targeted the regime's potential foreign enemies. In the final years of the tsarist regime, military intelligence produced reliable information about the German and Austro-Hungarian military. In the years before World War I, a senior officer of the Austro-Hungarian army was blackmailed into providing information about Vienna's war plans. Russian intelligence was also tasked with providing the Russian military with plans for modern weapons. As far back as the 18th century, Russian students and diplomats sought Austrian technology in building good artillery pieces.

In the Soviet era, foreign intelligence was the province of two competing organizations: the foreign intelligence directorate of the security service and military intelligence—usually referred to as the GRU. Often referred to as the "near and far neighbors," from the distance of their headquarters from the Ministry of Foreign Affairs, they attracted the best and brightest in the Soviet bureaucracy. The effectiveness of the foreign intelligence services was high, and the achievements were impressive. In the early years of the Soviet regime, the Cheka's foreign intelligence component penetrated and neutralized émigré groups that threatened the Bolshevik state. Leaders of the Russian and Ukrainian émigré community were kidnapped and murdered in Western Europe and the Americas. Stalin's bête noire, Leon Trotsky, was murdered at Stalin's command in 1940.

In the field of technical intelligence, the service provided quality information on nuclear weapons, strategic bombers, and literally thousands of Western military and industrial programs. From one British agent, Stalin received information about the atom bomb as early as 1941, before the United States had committed billions for the Manhattan Project. Stalin knew more about the Anglo-American atom bomb in 1944 than did U.S. Vice President Harry Truman.

In the field of political intelligence, the services penetrated the British and American political establishments in the 1930s and 1940s. In Great Britain, the Soviet service gained high-level penetration of the Foreign Office and the Intelligence Service. In the United States in 1944–1945, approximately 350 agents were working for the Soviet Union at a time when the United States and the United Kingdom had not an agent within the Soviet Union.

The intelligence services often acted as a "back channel" between Moscow and foreign governments. This channel served as an alternative to normal diplomatic ones and was used effectively in Germany in the 1960s and 1970s. Soviet intelligence also served as a crucial element of Stalin's strategy of projecting power, first into Spain in the 1930s and a decade later into Eastern Europe. The service arrested and killed enemies of Soviet power and trained the newly minted intelligence and security services of pro-Moscow regimes. In 1979, a KGB paramilitary unit stormed the Afghan presidential palace, killing the hapless president and his entourage.

KGB and GRU scientific and technical intelligence collection remained a priority for their services through the history of the Soviet Union. In an official U.S. government document, the Central Intelligence Agency noted, "The Soviets estimate that by using documentation on the US F-18 fighter their aviation and radar industries saved some five years of development time and 35 million rubles (the 1980 dollar cost of equivalent research activity would be $350 million) in project manpower and development costs. The manpower of these savings probably represents over a thousand man-years of scientific research effort and one of the most successful individual exploitations ever of Western technology."[6]

Soviet scientific intelligence collection may have actually hurt the country in the long run. Undoubtedly, millions of hours and billions of dollars were saved. But Soviet science was essentially like skiing down a mountain in another skier's tracks. It seems easy, but the second skier never catches up with the first and in fact is imprisoned by the direction the first skier took.

The Soviet Union maintained robust signals intelligence programs for intercepting messages and breaking codes. Both the KGB and the GRU collected "Sigint." The GRU maintained scores of Sigint units as well as aircraft and more than 60 ships dedicated to the interception of adversaries' communications. Sigint was strengthened by the KGB's recruitment of code clerks of opposing countries. The recruitment of John Walker, a U.S. Navy warrant officer, gave the Soviet services the ability to read American military communications for more than a decade.

Nevertheless, many of the operational successes of the Soviet and Russian services were squandered by the country's political leadership. Knowledge of the Austro-Hungarian war plans in 1914 was not enough to make the tsarist army capable of defeating the combined forces of imperial Germany and Austria. Stalin and his successors often ignored political intelligence and punished intelligence officers who challenged the leader's judgment. The failure of Stalin to heed GRU and NKVD warnings of Operation Barbarossa constitutes the greatest intelligence failure of the 20th century. KGB chair Yuri Andropov in the early 1980s mandated that his service collect information to show that the United States was planning and ready for nuclear war. This campaign, dubbed *RYaN* (for Nuclear-Rocket Surprise Attack), politicized Soviet intelligence activities and artificially created a crisis in the fall of 1983 that took the United States and the Soviet Union to the brink of war.

The Soviet intelligence establishment shared scientific intelligence effectively with consumers in the military industries. However, unlike the "secular" states in the West, political information was often rejected by important consumers: the Russian services never had strong analytical components. Stalin acted as his own intelligence analyst, and in the post-Stalin years the Communist Party Central Committee became a major consumer of raw intelligence. In the post-Stalin years, political reporting often was sent to the relevant components of the Central Committee, which interpreted reporting through a strong ideological prism.

In the post-Soviet years, Russian foreign intelligence remains formidable. The recently established SVR (Foreign Intelligence Service of the Russian Federation) has run agents within the CIA and Federal Bureau of Investigation (FBI). Both the SVR and the GRU continue to play an important role in Russia's war in Chechnya as well as the clandestine Russian intervention in the Crimea and the eastern provinces of Ukraine. In the Crimea and Ukraine, there have been almost no leaks from Russian intelligence officers or policymakers: a far cry from the Western capitals where secrets have a short half-life and are often leaked or given away.

THE PEOPLE

Any study of Russian intelligence has to concentrate on the competence and personality of those who lead the service and their relationship to the country's rulers. The men who directed the *Okhrana* in the first decades of the 20th century thought of themselves as more than police officers or civil servants. Many saw themselves as forging a social and political policy, finding support within the new urban working class that could guarantee the survival of the regime. One finds it hard—if not impossible—to imagine a minor bureaucrat in the British Home Office trying to create a policy to guarantee the survival of King George V.

Thanks to the opening of the Russian archives and some recent memoirs, we have a far better idea about the leadership of the Soviet security services. Lavrenty Beria, once discussed only as a psychopathic "sexaholic" in historical literature, now can be seen as a competent albeit ruthless manager of a complex security empire.[7] The archives also indicate to what extent the leaders lived in fear and isolation because of the counterintelligence state they had created. Beria told Stalin on 21 June 1941 that the intelligence service had heeded the dictator's wise words that war would not come in 1941. A day later, 3 million German troops invaded the Soviet Union. And when Mikhail Gorbachev, newly raised to the Central Committee Secretariat, sought to invite KGB chair Yuri Andropov to dinner, he was rebuffed. "People will talk," said the master of the security service.[8]

The cadre of Soviet intelligence and security professionals changed radically in type during the Soviet era. The first leaders of the Cheka were heavily drawn from non-Russian peoples—Poles, Latvians, Jews, and Germans—who were committed to an international revolution. Those first-generation Chekists who survived the civil war were murdered by Stalin in the 1930s and replaced by Slavs. The Soviet nonofficial cover operatives, dubbed illegals, who recruited important sources from London to Tokyo, also largely failed to survive Stalin. Their success was never replicated despite crash campaigns to send new generations of officers abroad.

The publication of more than 2,000 deciphered Soviet intelligence telegrams from the 1930s and 1940s has also expanded our understanding of the foreign agents who spied for the Soviet Union. These messages, which have the American code name Venona, have given us a better—but not complete—account of the cases of Alger Hiss and the Rosenbergs. These messages confirm memoir accounts in Russian and English that Stalin's greatest spies were volunteers who rarely accepted money for their work for Moscow. The messages also show the professionalism that Soviet case officers demonstrated in monitoring their American charges. An NKVD case officer cabled

Moscow from New York about Julius Rosenberg, "The state of LIBERAL's health is nothing splendid. We are afraid of putting LIBERAL out of action with overwork."

These were not political sycophants: they were brave and competent men doing their duty—if in a bad cause. We also have the memories of many of these case officers. Among the memoirists are Aleksandr Feklisov, the case officer who ran the Rosenbergs.[9] Other former officers have been interviewed and have written articles and books.

Founded in the last years of the Soviet Union, the Memorial organization investigates the crimes of the communist era and seeks to memorialize its victims. Memorial and other Russian nongovernmental organizations have mined the archives to give us a better understanding of the victims of repression. At the local and national levels, chapters of Memorial have valiantly sought the painful truth of their nation's past. Their work has allowed historians to paint a more complete picture of the Stalinist repression.[10] While many of the early histories of Soviet repression centered on the suffering of the Russian intelligentsia, a class with whom many Western intellectuals sympathize, the vast majority of the "injured and insulted," the dead and imprisoned, were peasants. Peasants have had few historians, so far less is known about the fate of Russian villages than about the fate of the Stanislav-sky movement in the Russian theater during the years of repression. Perhaps the best memorial for those who died is the words of Anna Akhmatova, Russia's great poet who lost a husband and a son to Lenin and Stalin's terror:

> During the terrible years of the *Yezhovshchina*, I spent 17 months in the prison queues in Leningrad. One day someone recognized me. Then a woman with lips blue with cold, who was standing behind me and of course had never heard my name, came out of the numbness which affected us and whispered in my ears (we all spoke in whispers there), "Can you describe this?"
>
> I said, "I can!" Then something resembling a smile slipped over what had once been a face.

Akhmatova, who Stalin contemptuously called "our little nun," waited 16 years before she published this vignette of the terror. Her son, for whom she waited months in a prison queue to find news of, survived to fight as a soldier in the Great Patriotic War. He was arrested in the late 1940s when his mother again fell into disfavor.

SECRETS AND MYSTERIES

There are still countless secrets—which the next generation of scholars will probably uncover with the opening of archives—and mysteries—which no amount of research will ever solve. Russian intelligence history is a "live" subject, and those engaged in researching and writing about it are to some extent working on disappearing archaeological sites as they probe the archives and search for witnesses.

In Mikhail Bulgakov's great novel *The Master and Margarita*, the hero claims that "manuscripts don't burn," reflecting the author's belief that the great truths of Russian history would outlive the tyranny of the Stalin age. This poetic aphorism is both true and not true when applied to Russian intelligence history: the archives have many secrets yet to give up. Tragically, however, some of the archives may no longer exist. As far back as the 1920s, Lenin may have ordered the Cheka to destroy its archives, and many Stalinist-era archives were purged in the 1980s and 1990s. According to one KGB officer, whose career began in the 1950s, the KGB began destroying files in 1959 to eliminate evidence of its excesses.[11] The few remaining living witnesses are interesting, but their memoirs have to be handled by scholars with the same care demolition experts use while dealing with unexploded ordnance.[12]

Historians now know that Robert Oppenheimer, the father of the American atomic bomb, was not a Soviet agent during the years he served at Los Alamos. The role of Ethel Rosenberg and the degree of her complicity in her husband's espionage may possibly be understood once scholars have better access to archives. One of the problems for intelligence scholars is the interpretation of partially deciphered Soviet intelligence messages. Take this message on Ethel Rosenberg sent from the NKVD in New York to Moscow on the recruitment of David and Ruth Greenglass:

> Lately the development of new people has been in progress. LIBERAL recommended the sister of his wife's brother, Ruth Greenglass, with a safe flat in view. She is 21 a TOWNS WOMEN (an American), a GYMNAST (member of the Young Communist League) since 1942. LIBERAL and his wife recommended her as a clever girl. Ruth has learned that her husband was called up by the Army, but he has not been sent to the front. He is a mechanical engineer and is now working at the *Enormoz* plant.[13]

Enormoz was Moscow's code word for the Anglo-American nuclear weapons program. Does the message show that Ethel was engaged in espionage, perhaps even "nuclear" espionage? How much did NKVD case officers know about her relationship with her husband or with the Communist Party? How accurately does this isolated message reflect the inner workings of the

Rosenberg ring? The FBI made judgments based on these intercepts, and scholars continue to disagree with the judgment of law enforcement officials caught up half a century ago in the hunt for spies.

On the other hand, it is highly unlikely that we will ever fully understand why Stalin contemptuously ignored warnings of a German invasion. We will never understand why defendants in the Moscow show trials confessed, knowing that Stalin was unlikely to spare their lives no matter what they might do. It is almost absolutely certain that we will never get a full accounting of the loss of life during the Soviet era. Finally, we will never have an answer to questions posed by dozens of Western and Soviet intelligence officers in their memoirs and in official histories as to which side won the intelligence cold war.

As a former officer of the CIA, I believe that intelligence is the handmaiden of policy and that the Western services won because their political masters were more successful and less ideological in their use of intelligence. However, I am willing to agree with those on the other side that the Soviet services won a great many of the battles. Writing of the disparity of won battles and a lost cause, an intelligence officer wrote an interesting epithet for the KGB: "Perhaps no government in contemporary history had intelligence on its adversaries that was accurate as that provided to Moscow. Its often documentary information was obtained with access to information at the highest levels. Western powers, by contrast, received little comparable information on Soviet plans, capabilities, or intentions. Our analysis of the recently released KGB archival material reveals that the Soviet treasure trove of information never shaped Soviet policy as it could have."[14]

We know something of the *siloviki* who are shaping Putin's intelligence community. They are smart, dedicated men who are Russian nationalists with a strong commitment to restoring Russia economically and politically to what they believe is her rightful place in world affairs. They are not afraid to use force, and they are less constrained to kill enemies foreign and domestic than the KGB of the 1970s and 1980s. They also know how to manipulate their system effectively. Note how, since 2012, the regime has been able to persuade the public that Russia is besieged by enemies within and without, manipulated largely by the United States. Note, too, how diplomacy, covert action, and military strategy have been woven together in Georgia, Crimea, and Ukraine.

Petr Stolypin, Tsar Nicholas II's most competent prime minister and with whom Putin is frequently compared, tried a tactical mix of reform and repression. Yuri Andropov, whom Putin admires, sought to rescue the communist regime from social and economic collapse by a similar set of policies. History will tell whether the current Russian president will be any more successful than the tsarist prime minister and the KGB chairman.

A final note. As a former employee of the CIA, I submitted this manuscript to them for a security review. Review does not constitute approval but, rather, is a legal and ethical obligation of former CIA employees.

NOTES

1. Christopher Andrews and Oleg Gordievsky, *KGB: The Inside Story* (New York: Harper-Collins, 1990), 17.

2. George Leggett, *The Cheka: Lenin's Political Police* (Oxford: Clarendon, 1981), 442ff. For intercepted letters, see Donald Rayfield, *Stalin and His Hangmen: The Dictator and Those Who Killed for Him* (New York: Random House, 2004), 123.

3. Yuri Druzhnikov, *Informer 001: The Myth of Pavlik Morozov* (London: Transaction, 1997), 137.

4. Robert W. Stephan, *Stalin's Secret War: Soviet Counterintelligence against the Nazis* (Lawrence: University Press of Kansas, 2003), 61.

5. Andrew Weier, *Black Earth* (New York: Norton, 1983), 208. Figures for death and imprisonments are taken from Anne Applebaum, *GULAG: A History* (New York: Random House, 2003), 578–83.

6. "Soviet Acquisition of Militarily Significant Western Technology," quoted in Christopher Andrews and Vasili Mitrokhin, *The Sword and the Shield: The Mitrokhin Archive and the Secret History of the KGB* (New York: Basic Books, 1999), 218.

7. Amy Knight, *Beria: Stalin's First Lieutenant* (Princeton, NJ: Princeton University Press, 1994), is the best study of Beria. Also available is a biography written by his son as well as memoirs from other members of his professional circle.

8. Mikhail Gorbachev, *Memoirs* (New York: Little, Brown, 1995), 122.

9. Aleksandr Feklisov, *The Man behind the Rosenbergs* (New York: Enigma Books, 2001).

10. See the Memorial website at www.memorial.ru.

11. For the fate of the Cheka's files, see Leggett, *The Cheka*, 360. For the report on purging files in 1959, see Victor Cherkashin and Gregory Feifer, *Spy Handler: Memoir of a KGB Officer* (New York: Basic Books, 2005), 53.

12. See particularly the debate over Pavel Sudoplatov and Anatoli Sudoplatov in Pavel Sudoplatov, *Special Tasks: The Memoirs of an Unwanted Witness—A Soviet Spymaster* (Boston: Little, Brown, 1994).

13. Venona message dated 21 September 1944 in Nigel West, *VENONA: The Greatest Secret of the Cold War* (London: HarperCollins, 1999), 143–44.

14. David E. Murphy, Sergei A. Kondrashev, and George Bailey, *Battleground Berlin: CIA vs KGB in the Cold War* (New Haven, CT: Yale University Press, 1997), 398.

A

ABAKUMOV, VIKTOR SEMENOVICH (1908–1954). Born into a working-class family in Moscow, Abakumov joined the security service in 1932 and rose very quickly during the *Yezhovshchina* to head the regional state security offices at Rostov. In the early days of **World War II**, he served in military **counterintelligence**. In 1943, **Joseph Stalin** appointed him head of an independent military counterintelligence component, Chief Directorate of Counterintelligence/*Smersh*, located within the People's Commissariat of Defense. As chief of *Smersh*, Abakumov met Stalin and wrote on an almost daily basis, providing details of counterintelligence operations as well as information and gossip about Red Army commanders.

In 1946, Abakumov was promoted by Stalin to head the newly minted Ministry of State Security (**MGB**) with the rank of army general to counter **Lavrenty Beria**'s power. As minister of state security, Abakumov used the service to crush armed rebellions in the Baltic states and the western Ukraine. In 1948–1949, in what became known as the **Leningrad Case**, he led the prosecution and eventual **execution** of senior Communist Party, MGB, and military officials. He met personally with Stalin 67 times between 1946 and 1951, far fewer than members of Stalin's inner circle.

The MGB was not a "band of brothers" in the late 1940s. Abakumov often denounced his subordinates to Stalin, accusing them of malfeasance. There is a certain justice, then, that Abakumov was arrested after being denounced by one of his subordinates in July 1951 for fiscal and moral corruption. A search of his home found war booty from Germany worth thousands of rubles. Even more damning in Stalin's eyes was the charge that Abakumov had deliberately failed to find traitors in the party and the police and that he was guilty of protecting Jews. In his own hand, Stalin approved the following indictment of Abakumov shortly before the leader's death: "The accused Abakumov sabotaged the investigation of criminal activity of the arrested American spies and Jewish nationalists, acting under the cover of the Jewish **Anti-Fascist Committee**." His wife, along with their infant daughter, was also detained.

After his arrest, Abakumov was interrogated and tortured by teams of his former colleagues. He remained in jail for the next three years and was not rehabilitated by the post-Stalinist leadership. Rather, he was tried and shot in December 1954 for treason. At his trial, Abakumov had argued that he acted under Stalin's direction and that he "was responsible only to Stalin." Abakumov apparently had not been informed that he was to be shot immediately following the trial. His last words, spoken before a bullet took his life, were, "I am going to write the Politburo . . ."

Abakumov was both a sensationally successful counterintelligence chief and a major coconspirator in Stalin's crimes against the Soviet people. Unlike Beria, he was never personally close to Stalin, but in the years he served as minister of state security, he was arguably the second most powerful man in the country. Abakumov was partially posthumously rehabilitated in 1990 by a Leningrad court that found his sentence and execution to have been decided illegally.

ABEL, RUDOLPH IVANOVICH (1902–1955). A **KGB** officer and close friend **illegal William Genrykhovich Fisher**, "Abel" was an alias that Fisher used when he was arrested by the Federal Bureau of Investigation (FBI). His use of this alias signaled to KGB headquarters that he had not been broken by the FBI.

ABRAMOV, IVAN PAVLOVICH. A career **KGB** officer, Abramov replaced **Filip Bobkov** as head of the Fifth Directorate, responsible for work against political and religious **dissidents** in 1982. A hard-liner, he won the name *Vanya Palka* (Ivan the Stick) from his subordinates. He was later appointed general prosecutor and played a role in the security services position of power in post-Soviet Russia.

ACTIVE MEASURES. *Aktivnoe meropriatia* (active measures) in the jargon of the Soviet intelligence services meant political manipulation and propaganda to influence international opinion. From the beginning of its existence, the Soviet Union sought to use propaganda to defend its legitimacy and malign its enemies on the right and the left. A special bureau was created in the **GPU** in January 1923 for disinformation "to break up the counterrevolutionary schemes of the enemy." The Soviet security service became more active in the 1930s in financing campaigns to explain the **Moscow Trials** and demonize former party leader **Leon Trotsky**. The Soviet party and security service used contacts with foreign communist parties and Soviet sympathizers—once referred to as "useful idiots" by **Vladimir Lenin**—to legitimatize these campaigns.

After **World War II**, the Soviet intelligence service used the term "active measures" to describe covert political action designed to affect the political opinion of unfriendly and neutral countries. From the early 1950s, a constant theme of Soviet active measures was "peace campaigns," designed to portray the United States as a hawkish and irresponsible nuclear power. Active measures often centered on the placement of misleading or false newspaper stories to impact popular opinion. For example, during the **Korean War**, false stories were planted in the press alleging U.S. complicity in spreading plague and smallpox in Korea and China.

KGB Chair **Aleksandr Shelepin** made **Ivan Agayants** head of a Service D (the D apparently stood for *Dezinformatsiya*) in the late 1950s and insisted that the First Chief Directorate, which was responsible for foreign intelligence, expand its campaigns against the American leadership. Shelepin apparently believed that such campaigns could be directed to drive a wedge between the Americans and their North Atlantic Treaty Organization allies. The KGB gave active measures an important role in Soviet diplomacy. In a 1986 report from KGB Chair **Viktor Chebrikov** to **Mikhail Gorbachev**, the KGB chief trumpeted, "Intelligence systematically carried out active measures to aid the implementation of the Soviet state's foreign policy initiatives and to expose the foreign policy of the United States and its allies. Active measures were carried out to discredit the American 'Star Wars' plan, to aggravate and deepen imperialist contradictions, and to step up the antiwar movement in Western countries."

A major target of KGB active measures was the Central Intelligence Agency (CIA). In the 1960s and 1970s, the KGB sponsored "exposures" of CIA operations in many Western and neutral countries. The KGB in the late 1960s paid for the publication of books blaming the CIA for John F. Kennedy's assassination. In Great Britain, these publications were successful enough to lead 32 Labour members of Parliament to sign a petition calling for the expulsion of the CIA station from London. Articles and books were published listing the names and addresses of CIA officers, leading to the assassination of a CIA officer in Greece. In the 1980s, the **KGB** placed a number of stories in Indian and African newspapers claiming that AIDS had been designed by the U.S. government to destroy the population of Africa. The articles were designed to raise anti-American sentiment in African countries where the United States hoped to base naval units. These articles then appeared in the European and American press and were believed by tens of millions of people.

Soviet active measures were carefully coordinated with the International Department of the **Communist Party** Central Committee and were well financed. Within the KGB, covert actions were managed by Service A (the successor of Service D) of the First Chief Directorate. These activities actually backfired as often as they worked. Evidence that the KGB was behind the

AIDS stories emerged in the 1980s and created devastatingly bad publicity for Moscow at a time when the Soviet Union was seeking better relations with Washington.

ADAMS, ARTHUR ALEKSANDROVICH (1885–1969). The longest-serving military intelligence **illegal** in the United States was an Old Bolshevik and colleague of **Vladimir Lenin**. Adams began work for the GRU in the 1920s, collecting information about U.S. military technology. Under a number of aliases, he reentered the United States in 1938 and began working with agents who had access to the American nuclear weapons program. Several of Adams's agents were exposed by the Federal Bureau of Investigation in 1944–1945, but he avoided arrest. In 1946, he was able to board a Soviet ship and disappeared for the last time. He retired as a colonel. In 1999, he was posthumously given the award Hero of the Russian Federation.

ADMINISTRATION FOR SPECIAL TASKS. Beginning in the early 1930s, the Soviet security service had two foreign intelligence divisions: a Foreign Intelligence Department (**INO**), which controlled intelligence officers under legal cover, and the Administration for Special Tasks, which directed **illegal** operations. The Administration for Special Tasks also directed assassinations of enemies of the Soviet state, including **Leon Trotsky** and the leaders of **émigré** movements. Following the death of **Joseph Stalin**, the division was abolished, and many of its leaders were arrested, including **Pavel Sudoplatov**, **Leonid Eitingon**, and **Yakov Serebryanskiy**. Illegal operations were then placed under the control of Directorate S of the **KGB First Chief Directorate**. Support for illegal activities in KGB *rezidenturas* (intelligence stations) was conducted by Line N officers.

ADMINISTRATIVE ORGANS DEPARTMENT (AOD). The AOD of the **Communist Party** Central Committee was responsible after 1953 for the party's management of the security service, the uniformed police, and the judiciary. Oversight of the AOD was conducted in turn by members of the Communist Party Politburo. The AOD vetted important personnel and logistics issues, approving all promotions to general officer in the security service and the police (**MVD**).

AFGHANISTAN. The **KGB** and the **GRU** played important roles in Afghanistan from the mid-1920s to 1991. Both services maintained large *rezidenturas* (intelligence stations) in Kabul beginning in the 1960s, and both services developed considerable expertise on the country. Afghanistan was also an important base for KGB operations in Iran and Pakistan. In the late 1970s, Soviet intelligence apparently reported accurately about the spread of the anti-Soviet movement. The Kabul *rezidentura* also had a number of agents within the Afghan communist movement, which provided Moscow with details about the deadly internecine battle between Afghan communists. Any information suggesting the impossibility of winning a war in Afghanistan was rejected by **KGB** Chair **Yuri Andropov** and Minister of Defense Dmitry Ustinov, both of whom urged the leadership to intervene in the civil war.

Even before the first main force Red Army units entered Afghanistan, KGB paramilitary organizations were conducting operations clandestinely inside Afghanistan to prepare the way for intervention. KGB's **ZENIT** Group began the war by storming the presidential palace on 27 December 1979 and killing Afghan President Hafizullah Amin and his entourage. The group's commander, Colonel **Grigori Boyarinov**, and five *Spetsnaz* (Special Designation) troops died in the assault, which resulted in the killing of approximately 250 Afghan soldiers and civilians. ZENIT Group was successful in decapitating the Afghan leadership and allowing Moscow to set up a puppet government quickly.

During the war, KGB officers were assigned to the Afghan secret police, KHAD, and worked against the insurgents in all provinces of the country. KGB **Border Guards** also took an active role in the war but were unsuccessful in stopping Afghani insurgents from crossing the Soviet–Afghan border and bringing Islamic literature to Soviet villages. In firefights with insurgents, 10 Border Guards were killed, according to a Russian history of the struggle.

AGABEKOV, GEORGE [GEORGI SERGEEVICH ARTUNYAN] (1896–1937). The first **defector** to the West from Russian intelligence, Agabekov served with the **Cheka** and the **OGPU** International Section in Turkey, Iran, and **Afghanistan** before defecting to the French in 1930. Hiding in plain sight in Western Europe, he wrote books about the Soviet intelligence service, the first exposés of their kind. He was murdered in Paris in 1937 by a Turk under the direction of **NKVD illegal Aleksandr Korotkov**.

AGAYANTS, IVAN IVANOVICH (1911–1968). An experienced intelligence officer who served both as an **illegal** and under diplomatic cover, Agayants served as *rezident* (chief of intelligence) in Paris following **World War II**. Agayants established networks of agents in France from among men and women who had begun their service during the war in France in the "Lemoyne" and "Henri" groups. Many of these agents served out of deep ideological commitment and had been recruited as agents from the French Communist Party. During World War II, he served as *rezident* in Iran and later in Algiers, where he maintained contacts with the Gaullist government in exile. Agayants also was successful in running agents within the French **counterintelligence** service. He was so scornful of French counterintelligence that he referred to the service as a "prostitute" in a lecture to new officers.

Agayants was picked by **KGB** Chair **Aleksandr Shelepin** in the 1950s to establish Service D within the **First Chief Directorate** to rebuild the service's **active measures** capacity. Agayants concentrated Service D on finding ways to divide the United States from its North Atlantic Treaty Organization allies, defame politicians seen as anti-Soviet, and link West German politicians to the worst aspects of Nazism. In 1962, for example, Service D spread rumors about then German Defense Minister Franz Joseph Straus aimed at weakening his position within the German government.

AGRANOV, YAKOV SAMULOVICH (1893–1938). An Old Bolshevik who joined the **Communist Party** in 1915, Agranov was one of the most effective and brutal of the early **Chekist** leaders. He advanced quickly in the service as a **counterintelligence** expert to become deputy chief. Agranov set up the first **show trial** in Leningrad in 1921 to publicize and punish resistance to the regime among the Leningrad intellectual elite. An intellectual, Agranov was close to a number of leading writers, including Vladimir Mayakovsky and Maksim Gorky.

Following **Sergei Kirov**'s assassination on 1 December 1934, Agranov took charge of the Leningrad **NKVD** and pursued the conspirators with zeal. Hundreds of men and women were shot in the few weeks he was in Leningrad. Agranov was then given extraordinary power by **Joseph Stalin** and NKVD chief **Genrykh Yagoda** to prepare a major show trial that would implicate the Old Bolsheviks and **Leon Trotsky** in Kirov's death. Agranov forced two of **Vladimir Lenin**'s old comrades, Grigori Zinoviev and Lev Kamenev, to confess that they had planned Kirov's death and that they were Nazi spies and saboteurs. It was a *coup de theatre*: all the defendants at the trial confessed and were then shot. Agranov had not, however, earned Stalin's gratitude; he was arrested in July 1937 as **Nikolai Yezhov** cleansed the security service of enemies. On 1 August 1938, Agranov was tried and immediately shot for treason. His trial was "private." He has not been rehabilitated like so many of the Old Bolsheviks he helped murder.

See also MOSCOW TRIALS (1936–1938).

AKHMATOVA, ANNA (1889–1966). Born Anna Andreyeva Gorenko, Akhmatova was one of Russia's greatest poets and a repeated victim of Bolshevik repression. Her husband, Nikolai Gumilev, was executed in 1921 following the Kronstadt rebellion. Another lover, Nikolai Punin, died in a labor camp.

In 1937, she became a target of **Joseph Stalin**. Her son, Lev, was arrested, and in the winter of 1937–1938, she waited in a line with food packages, knowing that the **NKVD**'s acceptance meant that her son lived. She later wrote one of her greatest poems, "Requiem," about her experience in the line: "One day somebody in the crowd identified me. Standing behind me was a woman with lips blue with cold . . . she stared out of the torpor common to us all and asked me in a whisper (everyone whispered there): Can you describe this? And I said I can. Then something like a smile passed fleetingly over what had once been her face."

The war came as relief. She was published again and lauded for her patriotic verses. Her son was released and fought in the Red Army. However, reports that she received a standing ovation at a poetry reading reached Stalin, who minuted the report "Who organized the ovation?" Her son was rearrested, and she found herself hounded by the police, Andrei **Zhdanov**, the regime's cultural watchdog, referred to her as "half nun-half whore" in an editorial. Her police file showed more than 900 denunciations.

Life improved following Stalin's death; she was published, but her son was not released until 1956. Akhmatova lived to see her poem of the purge, "Requiem," published. She played a key role in the development of the literary talent of Joseph Brodsky, who after arrest and exile to the United States became poet laureate in 1991.

She is seen by many Russians as the tortured conscience of their country. The British philosopher Sir Isaiah Berlin, who knew her, wrote at the time of her death, "The widespread worship of her memory both as an artist and as an unsurrendering human being, has, so far as I know, no parallel . . . not merely in Russian literature, but in Russian history in the twentieth century."

AKHMEDOV, ISMAIL GUSSEYNOVICH (1904–?). Akhmedov, a **GRU** officer under press cover, was serving in Berlin when **World War II** began. Rather than being repatriated to Moscow with other diplomats and intelligence officers, Moscow assigned him to Istanbul, again under press cover. On receiving orders to return to Moscow a few years later, Akhmedov left the Soviet mission and requested political asylum. He apparently feared arrest and **execution** for operational failures. Akhmedov contacted the British after the war. Unfortunately, the British intelligence station commander in Turkey was **Kim Philby**, who made little effort to debrief this important **defector**. Akhmedov later wrote a good autobiography; his information was not appreciated in the West until it was too late.

AKHMEROV, ISHAK ABDULOVICH (1901–1976). A Tatar, Akhmerov had a career in **counterintelligence** before he was dispatched to the United States by the **NKVD** as an **illegal**. He served as deputy *rezident* (intelligence officer) and then "illegal *rezident*" in the United States for over a decade. In the late 1930s, he recruited and ran important sources within the U.S. government, including **Alger Hiss**. Akhmerov worked closely with committed U.S. Communist Party members, including American party boss **Earl Browder**. One American who refused to spy for Moscow described Akhmerov as "affable" with a good command of the English language. Akhmerov was recalled to Moscow in 1940 after being accused of treason. Miraculously, he escaped trial and **execution** and returned to the United States during **World War II** to run agents in Washington.

Akhmerov's cover during his second tour was as the manager of a clothing and fur store in Baltimore. (His father had been a furrier.) Akhmerov's cover was strengthened further when he married Helen Lowry, the niece of Earl Browder. (Akhmerov was one of the few Soviet intelligence officers permitted to marry a foreigner.) Lowry, whose code name was "Nelly," served as a courier between the illegal apparatus and NKVD officers under "legal" cover as diplomats. She also maintained a safe house in Baltimore where Akhmerov could meet agents.

Akhmerov was a clever and careful case officer. During his second tour as an illegal, he ran a number of agents within the Franklin D. Roosevelt administration, including sources in the White House, the nascent American intelligence services, and the State Department. In 1942 and 1943, he transmitted 300 rolls of microfilm with classified documents and assessments to Moscow, while in 1944, more than 600 rolls of scientific and technical intelligence reached Moscow from Akhmerov's agents. One of his most effective couriers was **Elizabeth Bentley**, who turned herself in to the Federal Bureau of Investigation in late 1945, disclosing Akhmerov's operations. Following Bentley's defection, the Akhmerovs served as illegals in Switzerland, taking the name of a famous American millionaire. In the 1950s, they returned to Moscow for good. He was promoted to colonel and served as the deputy chief of the service's illegals department. Helen taught English in Moscow to a new generation of illegals, while Akhmerov instructed them in **tradecraft**. Akhmerov retired in 1955; he was twice awarded the Order of the Red Banner and other medals.

ALFA **(ALPHA)**. **KGB** chairman **Yuri Andropov** created Group ALFA, an elite paramilitary formation, in July 1974 to deal with domestic terrorism and hostage rescue operations. It was modeled on the British Special Air Service regiment. It operated under the supervision of the Seventh (**Surveillance**) Directorate.

AMERASIA **CASE.** One of the earliest investigations of Soviet espionage occurred in 1945 when the Federal Bureau of Investigation raided the editorial offices of *Amerasia* magazine in Washington, D.C.; confiscated several hundred classified U.S. documents; and arrested several people. Of the detained, two pled to minor charges of illegal possession of classified documents and were fined. The others were cleared. One of those involved but never prosecuted was John Service, a foreign service officer who had served in China during the war. *Amerasia* editor Philip Jaffe, who had been a Communist Party member, claimed that he was collecting documents to complete a detailed study of the Chinese civil war. Jaffe received documents from Service, who acted out of a personal desire to expose Washington's alliance with the corrupt Nationalist regime in China. It is not known if any of the information reached Soviet intelligence, but the scandal demonstrated how lax U.S. security was during the war and the unilateral steps some professionals would take to release classified material.

AMES, ALDRICH (1941–). The **KGB**'s recruitment of Aldrich Ames to penetrate the Directorate of Operations of the Central Intelligence Agency (CIA) was one of their greatest **counterintelligence** successes of the **Cold War**. Ames, angered by slow promotion and in need of money, volunteered to the Soviet *rezidentura* in Washington in 1985. He originally planned to provide the KGB only with the names of agents he believed the KGB already knew about. However, tempted by larger payments, Ames was subtly convinced by his handler, **Viktor Cherkashin**, to give up the CIA's "crown jewels," the names of more than a dozen Soviet officials who had been recruited by the CIA and the Federal Bureau of Investigation (FBI). Of the agents Ames betrayed, two were rescued, but 10 were executed in Moscow, and others were imprisoned. Among the agents reportedly betrayed by Ames were Adolf Tolkachev, who worked in the aircraft industry; **Dmitry Polyakov**, a **GRU** major general; and **Oleg Gordievskiy**, a KGB colonel serving in London and working for the British Secret Intelligence Service. Ames's code name was "Lyudmila": the KGB used a woman's name to help disguise his identity. Ames signed his KGB receipts with the name "*kolokol*" (Bell).

Ames provided the KGB with the names of Western agents operating in the KGB and GRU as well as in the military and military industries. He also provided CIA documents and cables that gave Moscow details of how the CIA operated inside the Soviet Union. In exchange, the KGB paid Ames approximately $2.7 million. Ames was arrested in February 1994, as was his wife, who had supported the operation. In exchange for full cooperation and a light sentence for his wife, Ames received a life sentence.

AMTORG. The AMTORG Trading Corporation was established in 1924 to further American trade with the infant Soviet state. In the early 1930s before the United States recognized the Soviet Union, it became Moscow's de facto embassy. AMTORG from its very beginning was a cover platform for the Soviet intelligence service.

ANALYSIS. The Soviet services had a different approach to intelligence analysis than Western states. **Joseph Stalin** told his intelligence chiefs that he wanted factual information and documents, not political analysis, which was to be left to the chief of state and his trusted lieutenants. Stalin rejected efforts by the **NKVD** and **GRU** to provide analysis of Operation **Barbarossa**, Germany's preparations for war against the Soviet Union in 1941, insisting that intelligence officers were easily deceived. **Lavrenty Beria**, who oversaw all intelligence authority for Stalin, threatened to have one intelligence officer "ground into camp dust" for daring to predict a surprise German attack.

Stalin read analyses of American weapons systems with far greater interest. As a result of analytical reporting in 1942 and 1943 concerning the Anglo-American nuclear weapons program by the NKVD and the GRU, he authorized scarce resources for a Soviet nuclear bomb. Through the late 1940s and early 1950s, Stalin asked for reporting on U.S. nuclear developments, which the Soviets code-named *Enormoz*.

The **KGB** had a small analytic service compared to the Directorate of Intelligence of the Central Intelligence Agency. Political information was sent to the **Communist Party**'s Central Committee for action. According to former Soviet intelligence officers and diplomats, senior KGB officers were warned by the political leadership not to present their analysis of current issues—that was the responsibility of the Communist Party. The KGB did have a major center of scientific and technological analysis that allowed them to work closely with the Soviet military industries. Important material was moved quickly from the intelligence service to the military-industrial complex to enhance the construction of Soviet weapon systems.

Directorate I of the **SVR** is responsible for the analysis and dissemination of current intelligence. According to the service's website, a report is prepared for President **Vladimir Putin** every morning.

The GRU had an analytical component responsible for preparing daily analytical reports for the minister of defense and the chief of the general staff. The GRU also prepared detailed analytical reports on the troops and weapons systems of adversaries. Intelligence was integrated into military decision making, and the chief of the GRU also served as deputy chief of the Red Army General Staff. Since the end Cold War, the GRU also has had responsibility for analytical reporting of the newly independent states of the former Soviet Union.

ANDROPOV, YURI VLADIMIROVICH (1914–1984). The most important post-**Stalin** chief of the **KGB**, Andropov rose quickly in the ranks of the **Communist Party** during the years of purges. During **World War II**, he worked with **partisans** on the Finnish front and continued his rise in the party apparatus. In 1954, Andropov was appointed Soviet ambassador to Hungary and cleverly managed his embassy during the 1956 **Hungarian revolution**. Andropov, according to both Soviet and Hungarian sources, manipulated Hungarian revolutionary leaders, repeatedly deceiving them as to Moscow's intentions. The Hungarian revolution had a profound effect on the rest of his life: Andropov's wife suffered a nervous breakdown after the fighting, from which she apparently never fully recovered. The violence and its impact on his personal life apparently convinced Andropov that Moscow had to be especially vigilant about intellectual dissent.

The Soviet leadership gave Andropov high marks for his role in defeating the Hungarian revolution, and he was promoted to chief of the Central Committee's Department for Liaison with Socialist States. During the **Khrushchev** years, Andropov had a public reputation as a liberal and an anti-Stalinist. He cultivated close relations with Hungarian Communist Party chief Janos Kadar, whom he had helped install in 1956. Andropov was admired by members of his staff as an open and cultured man who accepted some measure of ideological diversity within the Soviet Union and the Soviet bloc. In 1967, he was picked to head the KGB by **Leonid Brezhnev** to replace **Vladimir Semichastniy**, and Andropov quickly took on the persona of a **Chekist**.

Under Andropov's 15-year tutelage, the KGB's foreign and domestic missions expanded: his enemies were ideological dissent and corruption, both of which he insisted were to be prosecuted fiercely. He pushed the establishment of the Fifth Directorate within the KGB with responsibility for "**counterintelligence** among the intelligentsia." The new component intensified surveillance of **dissidents** and took an active role in persecuting **Aleksandr Solzhenitsyn** and **Andrei Sakharov**, the latter of whom he referred to as "public enemy number one." Andropov repeatedly warned the Politburo of the threat of dissent. In January 1974, he urged Solzhenitsyn's immediate deportation because *The Gulag Archipelago* "is not a work of creative literature, but a political document. This is dangerous. We have in this country hundreds of thousands of hostile elements."

Andropov also expanded the role of the KGB in combating corruption within the economy and the police. KGB officials brought thousands of cases against men and women for "specially dangerous state crimes," sending many to their deaths. Yet the KGB was forbidden by Brezhnev from inspecting corruption within the provincial or national leadership of the Communist Party. Andropov apparently covertly kept a record of leading malefactors in the leadership that he would later use to purge the party.

As a manager of foreign intelligence, he left much of the work in the hands of the KGB's First Chief Directorate. He selected **Vladimir Kryuchkov** to head the component, an appointment that many intelligence officers thought was disastrous. According to a KGB general, at one briefing on foreign intelligence, Andropov's sole criticism was on the cleanliness of the facilities. Andropov, according to reports from **defectors** and published documents, increasingly adopted a more conservative and neo-Stalinist ideology during the 1970s and 1980s, blaming the West and Western intelligence services for much of what was wrong with the Soviet Union. Under the *RYaN* program, he pushed for evidence of an American surprise nuclear attack, prompting a major crisis in 1983. Nevertheless, under his leadership, the foreign intelligence component expanded, becoming a worldwide intelligence service.

In 1981–1982, Andropov used the KGB to discredit Communist Party General Secretary Leonid Brezhnev, who was in physical and mental decline. Articles were planted in the foreign press citing Brezhnev's senility and corruption within his family. The campaign worked, weakening Brezhnev's control. In the spring of 1982, Andropov was appointed to the secretariat of the Central Committee as Brezhnev's de facto successor. In November 1982, following Brezhnev's death, he reached the pinnacle of political power as the Communist Party general secretary.

Andropov sought to reform the Soviet Union, prosecuting dissidents and corrupt leaders with tremendous ferocity. In the wake of threatened exposure and arrest, the head of the Soviet police and his wife committed suicide, and many senior leaders found themselves retired, in disgrace, or in jail. Andropov used the KGB to break the **Uzbek Cotton Scandal**, the largest criminal case in Soviet history, but Soviet society by 1984 was not to be motivated or frightened into change.

Andropov was a complex figure. He did not enjoy the physical destruction of enemies like **Lavrenty Beria**. In 1973, he visited the dissident Leonid Krasin in prison and promised him a light sentence if he would cooperate. Andropov sought to promote younger and more idealistic cadres in the Communist Party and the KGB. He was a good judge of talent, raising **Mikhail Gorbachev** from the provinces to the Politburo. Andropov died of kidney disease after only 14 months as national and party leader, and within a year, power passed to Gorbachev.

To Russian intelligence and security officers, Andropov was a modern **Feliks Dzerzhinsky**—an honest, hardworking, and party-minded bureaucrat. **Vladimir Putin**, a veteran of Andropov's KGB, put flowers on Andropov's bust at the **Lubyanka** security service headquarters the day he became president. Nevertheless, Andropov failed dramatically as both a security professional and a party and state leader: the KGB could neither scare nor reform Russia into the modern world.

See also ANDROPOV INSTITUTE.

ANDROPOV INSTITUTE. The Andropov Institute, the **SVR**'s training facility for foreign intelligence officers, is located 15 miles east of Moscow and was named after the former head of the KGB, **Yuri Andropov**, following his death in 1984. The school was founded in 1938 as the *Shkola osovogo naznacheniya* (Special Purpose School) to train intelligence officers who were scheduled to serve overseas under official cover to make up for the intelligence professionals purged during the *Yezhovshchina*. It has also been known as the 101st School and the Red Banner Institute. Courses include tradecraft and foreign languages. Retired intelligence officers with a proven record of success have often been pressed into service as instructors.

ANKETA. The security questionnaire filled out by new security officers and then periodically through their careers was a source of important **counterintelligence** information, allowing cross-checking backgrounds, contacts, and political reliability. The *Anketa* was seen by many officers as a threat: many lied, disguising their years in Nazi-occupied regions during the war, Jewish religion, or politically inconvenient relatives. **Sergey Kondrashev**, for example, had to hide the fact of his grandparents' success in business and their status in tsarist Russia. Although he rose to be a general officer in the **KGB**, he always had to worry about the trail of falsehoods in his questionnaire.

ANTI-FASCIST COMMITTEE. The Jewish Anti-Fascist Committee was authorized to raise money and support for the Soviet Union in the United States during **World War II**. Its leaders, including the actor **Solomon Mikhoels**, brought in more than $45 million to strengthen the country's war effort, but its members were privately critical of Soviet anti-Semitism in conversations with Americans. When the news of the criticism reached **Joseph Stalin**, he ordered the **MGB** to murder Mikhoels and to begin an intensive investigation of the committee's leadership. Stalin also authorized a general purge of Jews from high positions in the Soviet Union. In 1945, Jews held 12 percent of senior posts in the government bureaucracy and the media; in 1951, the figure was 4 percent. Articles in the press criticized Jews for lack of patriotism and insisted on greater vigilance by the Soviet people.

As part of his plans for a purge of the **Communist Party** leadership in 1952, Stalin saw many uses for a series of trials in the Soviet Union and Czechoslovakia of "Zionists." The trials would play to Russian anti-Semitism and enrage political opinion. Between 11 and 15 July 1952, 14 Jewish party officials and intellectuals were tried for espionage and treason in Moscow. The most famous of the defendants was Solomon Lozovsky (1878–1952), one of the few Jewish members of the Communist Party's

Central Committee. The defendants' interrogations and trial was the scene of some of the most striking and revolting anti-Semitic denunciations heard outside the Third Reich. In his pretrial interrogation, Colonel Vladimir Komarov screamed at Lozovsky that "the Jews are a foul and dirty people" who wanted to "annihilate every Russian." Lozovsky compared the court to the Spanish Inquisition, which had forced his family to flee Spain three centuries previously.

All 14 defendants were convicted, and 13 (including Lozovsky) were sentenced to death and executed a month later, along with 10 Jewish "engineer-saboteurs" from a Moscow factory. Ultimately, the series of trials resulted in the conviction of 125 Jews. Those who were alive on Stalin's death in March 1953 were released. The executed men and women were posthumously rehabilitated in 1953–1954.

See also DOCTORS' PLOT; SLANSKY TRIAL.

ANTIPARTY GROUP. In the summer of 1957, conservative members of the **Communist Party** Presidium tried to oust party leader **Nikita Khrushchev** from power. After the vote in the Presidium went against him, Khrushchev appealed to **KGB** chair **Ivan Serov** and Ministry of Defense Marshall **Georgi Zhukov** for assistance in bringing the entire Communist Party Central Committee to Moscow for a second vote. Serov and Zhukov complied, and all members of the Central Committee were flown to Moscow in 24 hours. The full Central Committee supported Khrushchev with the votes to overturn his opponents in the Presidium. Khrushchev repaid Serov and Zhukov by demoting the former and forcing the retirement of the latter.

ANTIRELIGIOUS CAMPAIGNS. From the inception of the **Cheka**, the Soviet security services were engaged at the behest of the ruling party in campaigns against all organized religion. The first target of the Cheka was the Russian Orthodox Church. Between 1918 and 1924, the majority of churches were closed; in 1922 alone, 2,691 priests, 1,962 monks, and 3,447 nuns were shot. During the **collectivization** campaign of the 1930s, 98 percent of the Orthodox churches were closed, and more than 40,000 clergy were arrested. Many of these clergy and their families were shot or imprisoned in the **gulag** during the *Yezhovshchina*.

Joseph Stalin allowed the Orthodox Church greater freedom during the war years to rally popular support. **Nikita Khrushchev**, however, moved against the Orthodox and Baptist churches in the early 1960s. The **KGB** arrested scores of church leaders, and the state closed more than half of the Christian churches. About 200 Baptist and Pentecostal believers were sent to the camps every year for refusing to obey the regime's rules on church policy.

Following the incorporation of the western Ukraine and western Byelorussia into the Soviet Union in 1939 and the annexation of the Baltic states in 1940, the security services targeted the Roman Catholic leadership. This campaign intensified with the return of the Red Army to the Baltic and Ukraine in 1944–1945. One Lithuanian bishop was murdered in a Vilnius prison in the 1950s, and others remained in jail or under house arrest for decades. An aggressive anti-Catholic policy was followed by the KGB in the Baltic and the western Ukraine until the collapse of the Soviet Union.

Islam and Judaism also were targets for antireligious campaigns. Stalin mandated vicious anti-Semitic campaigns in the late 1940s, for example, against the **Anti-Fascist Committee**. Jews were purged from the security service, the **Communist Party** leadership, and the professions. Only Stalin's death in 1953 prevented a larger **pogrom** and the deportation of Jews to forced **exile**. While Khrushchev ended this campaign, the KGB continued to prosecute "Zionist" groups until 1988. By the late 1970s, there were only 60 Jewish houses of worship operating in the Soviet Union.

In Central Asia, the Cheka cracked down hard on Islam in the early 1920s to break political opposition. Mosques and Islamic shrines were destroyed or turned into museums. Religious leaders who refused to be co-opted were arrested or silenced. These campaigns continued through the late 1980s, as even **Mikhail Gorbachev** pushed anti-Islamic campaigns in Central Asia. The KGB and the party's effort to destroy organized Islam may have backfired, forcing many Muslim believers to seek more radical forms of religious expression. The growth of militant Islam in Chechnya and other parts of the Caucasus and Central Asia is the heritage of 60 years of persecution.

While the KGB sought to limit organized religion within the Soviet Union, it simultaneously tried to exploit religion to support Soviet foreign policy. Clergy and laypeople were recruited to endorse Soviet peace campaigns in the World Council of Churches and other international forums. Many Orthodox and Baptist clergy agreed to front for the KGB in order to obtain permission to open churches and train clergy. The patriarch of the Russian Orthodox Church, Aleksey II, was once a KGB co-optee with the cover name "Drozdov."

Through the 1980s, religious **dissident** leaders were harassed, arrested, and sometimes killed. In the 1980s, several Roman Catholic priests died under mysterious circumstances in the western Ukraine. In 1980, **Father Dmitry Dudko** was arrested and forced to confess on national television that he had served an anti-Soviet cause. In 1991, Aleksandr Men, an Orthodox priest, was murdered in Russia, according to some at the behest of the KGB. These activities were attributed to the KGB by dissident and foreign observers of the Soviet religious scene. The martyrdom suffered by the faithful did little to break the religious spirit of the people. Following the collapse of the Soviet regime, the Russian Orthodox Church was seen as the most credible national institution, according to some polls. In Lithuania, Roman Catholic clergy and laypeople were the heart of the nationalist movement in the 1970s and 1980s. In Central Asia, Islam has enjoyed a renaissance.

ANTONOVOV-OVSEYENKO, ANTON VLADIMIROVICH (1920–2013). A victim and historian of **Joseph Stalin**'s terror, Antonovov-Ovseyenko was the son of one of the founders of the Soviet state. In the late 1930s, his father was executed, his mother committed suicide while under interrogation, and he then disappeared into the **gulag** for 13 years. Following his release and almost blind, Antonovov-Ovseyenko became one of the most respected historians of the Stalin era, publishing in *samizdat* inside his country and in the West. His *The Time of Stalin* was a brilliant, polemical study of the terror that detailed the crimes of the Stalin era. It was never published in the Soviet Union.

APRESYAN, STEPAN ZAKHAROVICH (1914–1990). Recruited into the **NKVD**'s Foreign Intelligence Department in 1939, Apresyan served in New York and then in San Francisco in 1943–1945. Under the NKVD cover name "Maj" (May), he stood out for his erudition and linguistic skills. In San Francisco, he supported the Soviet mission to the first UN conference.

ARMS CONTROL INTELLIGENCE. In no area of **Cold War** intelligence was there greater asymmetry between the United States and the Soviet Union than in arms control. At the first Strategic Arms Limitation Talks (SALT) held in 1968, U.S. delegates began to give an account of the American and Soviet nuclear weapons programs but were stopped by a senior Soviet military negotiator. Soviet civilian members of his delegation, he stated, were not cleared for such information, even if it was considered unclassified in the West.

Both the **KGB** and the **GRU** collected a vast amount of information about U.S. nuclear weapons from their open contacts with Americans. Political intelligence officers from the KGB *rezidenturas* were responsible for developing relationships with academics and journalists who had contacts in the defense establishment, while GRU officers tended to concentrate on the uniformed military. Both the KGB and the GRU had analytical departments that conducted weapons and arms control intelligence **analysis**.

On several occasions, the KGB leadership grossly exaggerated the threat of war. In 1960, KGB chair **Aleksandr Shelepin** informed **Nikita Khrushchev** that the United States was planning to initiate nuclear war in the near future. In 1983, the KGB leadership exaggerated the threat of an American nuclear strike in its reports to the political leadership. Their information of a

surprise attack did not come from either human or technical intelligence sources. Rather, it was generated by intelligence officers who were responding to demands from Moscow for proof that war was imminent.
See also RYAN (RAKETNO-YADERNOYE NAPADENIE).

ARTEMIEV, PAVEL ARTEMEVICH (1897–1979). During the German assault on Moscow in the fall of 1941, Artemiev, then a **NKVD** lieutenant general, was placed by **Joseph Stalin** as commander of the Moscow Defense Zone, de facto chief of the final defenses of Moscow. Using civilian workers and volunteer divisions, he built and then manned a series of defense lines to the west of Moscow, preparing to defend the capital house by house. Stalin also gave Artemiev responsibility of the 7 November Revolutionary Day parade, informing him to tell no one—not even Stalin—of the start time. On 7 November 1941, Soviet soldiers marched through Red Square directly to the front. The German command never found out about the parade, which went on without a hitch.

ARTUZOV [FRAUCHI], ARTUR KHRISTYANOVICH (1891–1937). A child of Swiss immigrants, Artuzov joined the **Cheka** in January 1919 and rose quickly. He conducted the **Trust** operation that lured enemies of the state to return to the Soviet Union, where they met jail and death. He served as deputy head of foreign intelligence from 1927 to 1930 and as head of foreign intelligence from 1931 through 1934. He was then assigned to head military intelligence (**GRU**). Artuzov played a major role in the deployment of **illegals** in the 1930s and their recruitment of important sources in England, France, Germany, and the United States. An experienced intelligence officer, Artuzov was distrusted by **Joseph Stalin**. He was arrested in May 1937 and tried and executed on 21 August 1937. According to a semiofficial history of the GRU, Artuzov wrote "I am not a spy" in his own blood on the wall of his cell before he was shot. Posthumously rehabilitated in 1956, Artuzov is recognized as a hero of the foreign intelligence service.

ASSASSINATION. **Joseph Stalin** saw assassination as a credible weapon and used it for his decades in power against enemies foreign and domestic. A former bank robber and revolutionary, Stalin ordered intelligence officers to track down and kill his enemies, personally involving himself in their plans. Perhaps the most famous case was the killing of Stalin's archrival **Leon Trotsky** in Mexico City. Stalin also ordered the killing of prominent **émigrés** and defectors, including **George Ababekov** and **Ignace Reiss**. Following World War II, the **MGB** continued to hunt down leaders of Russian and Ukrainian émigré movements. The service's **Administration for Special Tasks** was given responsibility for these actions.

Stalin also ordered the assassination of enemies at home. Among the most famous victims was Kira Kulik, the wife of Marshal Grigory Kulik. Madame Kulik was kidnapped off the streets of Moscow in1940 at Stalin's direction, taken to **Lubyanka** prison, and shot without trial or interrogation by the service executioner **Vasili Blokhin**. He also ordered the murder of Moscow's ambassador to China and his wife in 1939. Stalin also probably ordered the murder of **Raoul Wallenberg**, the Swedish consul in Budapest, who saved thousands of Jews from deportation to death camps. Wallenberg, whose arrest was denied for decades by Moscow, was either shot or poisoned in Lubyanka in 1947. One of the last murders commissioned by Stalin was the killing of Jewish actor **Solomon Mikhoels** in 1948. In his memoirs, **Pavel Sudoplatov** noted five other inconvenient witnesses murdered without trial.

Contrary to modern fiction, the **KGB** rarely engaged in assassination. The defection of **Oleg Lyalin**, a senior officer in the London *rezidentura* responsible for planning extralegal actions, convinced Moscow to limit assassinations. Its two best cases were the killing of Hafizullah Amin, president of **Afghanistan**, in the hours before Soviet military intervention in December 1979 and its support for the murder of a Bulgarian dissident.

The new Russian services has been implicated in at least two infamous murders abroad and several at home. The assassination of Chechen leader Yandarbayev in Qatar in 2004 and the murder of Russian **FSB** defector **Litvinenko** in London in 2006 were tied to intelligence officers, as were the murders of **Anna Politkovskaya** and Boris Nemetsov.

AUGUST PUTSCH OF 1991. Opponents of **Communist Party** General Secretary **Mikhail Gorbachev** began to plot against him in late 1990, believing that his reforms threatened the party and the Soviet state. A coterie of conservative bureaucrats and senior police and military officials sought to replace him quietly and quickly, the way that party conservatives had replaced **Nikita Khrushchev** in 1964. They failed to consider, however, that the tactics of 1964 could not work in 1991 after six years of Gorbachev's reforms had raised the political consciousness of the Russian people.

KGB chair **Vladimir Kryuchkov** and his senior deputies played a critical role in planning the putsch, as did **MVD** chief **Boris Pugo**. Gorbachev and his wife's office and apartments were bugged, thousands of pairs of handcuffs were ordered, and arrest warrants were drafted for thousands of reformers and "troublemakers" across the country. The plan was to be executed on 18 August while Gorbachev and his entourage were on vacation at their summer retreat at Foros in the Crimea. Early that morning, KGB **Border Guard** units surrounded his dacha, and his chief bodyguard took control of the Soviet "suitcase," a computer notebook that contained the codes required to launch a nuclear strike.

The putsch was generally successful across the country but failed in Moscow, where Russian President **Boris Yeltsin** made his way to the Russian White House (the parliament building) and rallied support. Efforts by the coup plotters to convince KGB *Spetsnaz* units to storm the White House, neutralize Yeltsin, and disperse the crowd failed. An abortive effort to storm the building by a small Red Army unit killed three young Yeltsin supporters near the White House, but the plotters lacked the ruthlessness, intelligence, and craft to seize power.

The putsch ended with more of a whimper than a bang on 21 August when airborne troops in Moscow withdrew to their bases. All the plotters could do was to return Gorbachev to Moscow and beg forgiveness. Gorbachev did return to Moscow that day but without the authority to govern his country. The putsch, however, demonstrated the bankruptcy and incompetence of the Communist Party and the KGB. Within three months, power devolved from the Soviet Union to independent republics, and on 25 December 1991, the Soviet flag was replaced by Russian national colors over the Kremlin. The plotters spent more than a year in jail but never stood trial; they were released in 1993.

AVIATORS' AFFAIR. In 1946, at **Joseph Stalin**'s behest, **MGB** chief **Viktor Abakumov** arrested Air Marshal A. A. Novikov, Minister of the Aviation Industry A. I. Shakurin, and 15 other senior officers and plane designers. All were tortured and received heavy sentences. Earlier in December 1945, Abakumov had arrested Air Marshal S. A. Khudyakov, who was shot in 1950.

The Aviators' Affair may have been sparked by charges by Stalin's son, Vasily Stalin, an air force major general, that German fighters were better designed than Soviet counterparts and that poor construction had led to thousands of warplane crashes. Stalin, however, may have seen the purge as a way of further cowing the military establishment.

AZEV, YEVNO FISCHELOVICH (1869–1918). The most infamous double agent in Russian history, Azev served as both "Raskin," a secret agent for the *Okhrana*, and "Comrade Valentine," chief of the **Battle Organization** of the Socialist Revolutionary (SR) Party. From 1902 to 1908, Azev recruited terrorists and planned the **execution** of several senior tsarist officials and members of the royal family. Simultaneously, he betrayed scores of his own recruits to the *Okhrana* for trial, imprisonment, and execution.

Azev's planning of the assassination of Minister of Interior **Vyacheslav von Plehve** in 1904 made him a hero to Russian revolutionaries, and he was elected a member of the SR central committee. During the same period, he was the *Okhrana*'s highest-paid informant, providing information that saved the life of the tsar and doomed countless plots by the Battle Organization. His treachery was uncovered by Vladimir Burtsev, a revolutionary journalist, who convinced his colleagues that only Azev could have been responsible for the arrests that were undercutting the SR's efforts to build a revolutionary organization inside Russia. Azev fled to Germany, where he lived to see the Bolshevik Revolution.

Azev's motivation is unknown. Was the assassination of von Plehve a strike against a notorious anti-Semite? Was it money that led him to betray friends or a desire to play God? Was it his love of notoriety or an interest in being the hero of two elite combat organizations? This much seems clear: he badly disrupted the SR political and paramilitary organization and weakened their ability to compete with the Bolsheviks.

B

BABICH, ISAI YAKOVLEVICH (1902–1948). A career security officer who joined the **Cheka** in 1920, Babich was one of **Viktor Abakumov**'s three senior deputies in *Smersh*. He was responsible for operations behind German lines, and in the summer of 1945, he headed *Smersh* units in the short war against Japan. Following the war, Babich served as head of military counterintelligence in the new **MGB** until his death in 1948.

BABUROVA, ANASTASIA EDUARDOVNA (1983–2009). A left-wing investigative journalist, Baburo and a colleague, Stanislav Markelov, were murdered in daylight in central Moscow by a neo-Nazi thug. While the murderer was arrested, tried, and sentenced to life imprisonment, Baburova's editor noted that she was the fourth reporter from his paper murdered since 2000, claiming that members of the **FSB** facilitated the killing and probably provided the silenced pistol. Like **Anna Politkovskaya**, Baburova was investigating ties between various criminal organizations and the FSB.

BACK CHANNEL. Moscow frequently used intelligence officers and journalists working with the intelligence services as a back channel of communication with other governments. An alternative channel of communications allowed Moscow to speak candidly with politicians and address issues that were off limits to diplomats. This tactic probably developed out of the 1920s and 1930s, when the Soviet government had diplomatic relations with only a few Western governments. In the 1970s, the **KGB** maintained separate channels of communications with West German politicians as the Socialist Democratic administration of Willy Brandt developed its policy of *Ostpolitik*. An American historian of the KGB noted, "The KGB back channel combined the secrecy of 19th century cabinet diplomacy with the speed of 20th century transportation and communications to transform Soviet–West German relations."

Senior KGB officers, including **Yuri Andropov**, were strong supporters of back-channel diplomacy, arguing that the intelligence service was less corrupt and more competent than the Ministry of Foreign Affairs. Andropov, according to a subordinate, believed that he could solve the Soviet Union's international problems with enough back channels to the major powers.

While back channels were undoubtedly useful in many cases, they could also create unintended confusion about Moscow's intentions. During the **Cuban Missile Crisis**, Moscow used Georgi Bolshakov, an intelligence officer under journalist cover, as a back channel between Attorney General Robert Kennedy and Soviet leader **Nikita Khrushchev**. Bolshakov relayed assurances that the Soviet government was not considering placing nuclear weapons in Cuba just as missile units were arriving on the island. Revelations of this deception badly damaged Soviet credibility, and it reduced the effectiveness of Soviet Foreign Minister Andrei Gromyko and the ambassador in Washington, Anatoly Dobrynin.

BAGRATION, OPERATION. One of the most significant victories of the Red Army in the **Great Patriotic War** was made possible by the creative use of intelligence to deceive the Germans. In early 1944, the **GKO** (State Defense Committee) decided to stage a major offensive against the German Army Group Center. The strike was to destroy the German army group, liberate Minsk and Byelorussia, and drive the Nazis from Soviet territory. To accomplish this, the GKO mandated a complicated program of strategic deception (*maskirovka*) to convince Berlin that the strike would fall farther south in Ukraine. German intelligence was fed hundreds of false reports about a Soviet buildup in the south, which had been the center of the war for the previous 18 months. The movement of Soviet reserves was carefully masked, as Soviet infantry, armor, and artillery were moved silently into position for the June offensive. Moreover, Soviet radio silence along the front made German **signals intelligence** efforts fruitless.

Moscow was able to measure and then modify the extent of the deception efforts through **partisans** in Germany and through agents it was running inside the German intelligence structure. The Red Army blow, involving 14 combined arms armies from four different fronts (army groups), was launched on 20 June. Over 2.4 million soldiers, 4,000 tanks, and 24,000 artillery pieces were engaged. In the first two weeks of the campaign, Germany lost 250,000 soldiers, dead or captured. By the end of Operation Bagration, 300,000 to 350,000 German soldiers were dead, wounded, or captured, and 25 German divisions had been destroyed.

BAKATIN, VADIM VIKTOROVICH (1937–). Bakatin, whose father was shot in the Stalin-era purges, was a pro-**Gorbachev** reformer in the **Communist Party**. In 1988, Mikhail Gorbachev drafted Bakatin to reform and modernize the **MVD** (Ministry of Internal Affairs, or police). While originally a close ally of the general secretary and a competent administrator, Bakatin was fired in 1990 as Gorbachev moved to the right and replaced him with **Boris Pugo**, a career **KGB** official.

Immediately following the **August putsch** of 1991, Bakatin was appointed KGB chair. Bakatin made a valiant effort to reform the service, fired officers implicated in the putsch, and cut down on corruption and nepotism. He even fired his own son, a KGB lieutenant colonel. Bakatin also sought to build ties to Western intelligence and security services, providing diagrams of the KGB's bugging of the U.S. embassy to the American ambassador. Bakatin, however, was not a **Boris Yeltsin** loyalist and was fired in January 1992 before he could make significant changes in the **Russian intelligence services**.

BAKER, RUDY (ca. 1890–?). Born in 1898 in Croatia, probably with the name "Rudolph Blum," Rudy Baker had a four-decade career in the Communist Party of the United States (CPUSA). After receiving training in Moscow in the late 1930s, he was assigned to replace **Josef Peters** as head of the CPUSA's secret apparatus, which was the link between the party and the Soviet intelligence services. Baker's cover position was that of a minor party functionary, and he worked so effectively that the Federal Bureau of Investigation never understood his real identity until it was too late.

Baker played several roles simultaneously. He acted as a financier for the intelligence services, moving money to agents in Latin America and the United States. He vetted recruits and found couriers to move personnel, money, and documents around the world. He set up clandestine radio stations, and he advised Moscow on questions of **tradecraft**. Most importantly, Baker acted as a "cutout," isolating the legal CPUSA from **illegal** clandestine activities. In cables, he was referred to as "son," while CPUSA leader **Earl Browder** was "father." One of Baker's cables to Moscow noted that all clandestine activities "were discussed and considered by father and son."

In the late 1940s, Baker returned to his native Yugoslavia. He worked for many years in Belgrade as a translator in the state publishing house. Far more circumspect than Josef Peters, Baker was one of the most effective spymasters in the **Cold War** because of the care he gave to operational security and tradecraft.

BARBAROSSA. Operation Barbarossa was Adolf Hitler's plan for the invasion of the Soviet Union. From the inception of planning in late 1940, **Joseph Stalin** received and ignored good intelligence of Hitler's intentions. In early 1941, Stalin received information from the **Red Orchestra** and **Richard Sorge**, as well as other **NKVD** and **GRU** sources, about German intentions, which he rejected as disinformation. NKVD foreign intelligence chief **Pavel Fitin** vainly tried to warn Stalin, who believed that many of the reports were generated by the British government. The official Russian intelligence history of the war notes, "Only the outbreak of the war saved Fitin from a firing squad."

Besides more than 100 credible human intelligence reports about German intentions, Stalin also received accurate information about German photoreconnaissance flights over Soviet territory and the capture of German spies on the Soviet–German frontier. On the morning of 22 June 1941, just hours before the attack, a German soldier deserted and warned Moscow of the forthcoming attack. That warning was also ignored; the soldier was shot. Stalin's intelligence chiefs were in large part responsible for the intelligence failures. GRU chief **Filipp Golikov** informed Stalin that many of the reports came from British-controlled sources. Intelligence generalissimo **Lavrenty Beria** also confused the picture, punishing intelligence officers who accepted agent reports of German preparations. On 20 June—two days before the war began—he informed Stalin that war would not come until 1942 at the earliest. As the attack on the morning of 22 June began and more than 3 million German soldiers advanced into the motherland, Soviet units were caught unprepared. Thousands of airplanes and tanks were destroyed on airfields and in training commands. Reserve units, which had been identified by German reconnaissance, were destroyed before they could reach the front.

Russian historians since Stalin's death have sought to explain this monumental intelligence failure. Stalin, who acted as his own intelligence **analyst**, was clearly fooled by German disinformation, which played on his distrust of the British leadership. The Soviet leader also wanted at all costs to delay a general war with Hitler's Germany until 1942, when the Red Army would have more fully recovered from the purges of the 1930s. Moreover, Stalin believed that he understood Hitler better than any of his intelligence officers or their agents; he thought Hitler would not move against his country in 1941, and he informed his military and intelligence chiefs that if Hitler did strike, the offensive would be a local one to force the Soviet Union to make diplomatic concessions. The cost of Stalin's dogmatism was the destruction of several Soviet armies clustered on the Soviet–German border and the death of millions of Soviet soldiers. According to Soviet records, in the first 10 weeks of the war, more than 2.5 million Soviet soldiers were killed or taken prisoner.

BATTLE OF MOSCOW. The first—and most important—Soviet victory over the German military and intelligence services during **World War II** came in the Battle of Moscow in the late fall and early winter of 1941. By October 1941, German troops were approaching Moscow on two axes, and on 16 October, most of the government ministries and foreign embassies were evacuated to Kuibyshev (Samara). This evacuation set off an orgy of looting that lasted for 48 to 72 hours. Had **Joseph Stalin** not been able to marshal the **NKVD** and Red Army resources, it is likely that Moscow would have fallen and the war would have had a different outcome.

The NKVD's first task was to make sure the evacuation went off as planned. **Lenin**'s corpse was removed by train to Tyumen in western Siberia, and the secret police began to mine the most important government buildings. A new NKVD special forces group was created called OMSBON (*Otdelniy motorstrelkovoi brigadi osobovo naznacheniya*, or the Independent Motorized Rifle Brigade for Special Operations) to supervise the defense of the capital and organize **partisan** detachments in the enemy's rear. One of the battalion commanders of the brigade, **Stanislav Vaupshasov**, took his unit hundreds of miles into the enemy's rear before returning to his base three months later. OMSBON mined more than 70 kilometers of highways and 19 bridges, and 12,000 antitank and 8,000 antipersonnel mines were planted in front of the attacking enemy. The NKVD also recruited assassins to kill German leaders should the city fall and Adolf Hitler and his entourage visit Moscow. Among those recruited were leading artistic performers in Moscow and such **émigrés** as **Olga Chekhova**, a Russian movie actress living in Berlin who had access to Hitler.

Soviet foreign intelligence also played a critical role in defeating the German army before Moscow. Information from **Richard Sorge** that the Japanese did not intend to enter the war convinced Stalin to shift elite formations from Siberia to take part in a massive counteroffensive. **GRU** and NKVD sources in Europe provided detailed information about German forces as well as intelligence about German military planning.

While German troops reached the outskirts of Moscow, Soviet resistance stiffened and stopped their advance by the end of November. The following month, a massive Red Army offensive drove the Wehrmacht back hundreds of kilometers and destroyed scores of elite units. Never again was Hitler able to command a nationwide offensive. The Battle of Moscow was the NKVD's finest hour; in the wake of victory, 24 members of OMSBON were made Heroes of the Soviet Union. The unit continued its activities in the enemy's rear throughout the war, infiltrating 212 guerrilla units and involving more than 7,000 of its own officers and personnel. It is credited with killing or capturing 137,000 German officers and soldiers, including 87 senior officers, in the course of the war.

BATTLE ORGANIZATION. The *Boevaya organizatsiya*, or Battle Organization, was the central terrorist organization of the Socialist Revolutionary Party (SR). It was responsible for scores of assassinations between 1902 and 1908, including two ministers of internal affairs and members of the royal family. The organization was repeatedly penetrated by agents of the *Okhrana* but remained a formidable force until 1908, when a radical journalist revealed that its chief, **Yevno Azev**, was an informer for the *Okhrana*. The SR continued to see terror as a weapon in the struggle against autocracy. Unlike the **Bolshevik Party**, however, the SR never developed a central apparatus to use terror effectively. After the **Revolution of November 1917**, a group of "left" SR members joined the Bolsheviks in a coalition government. Their lack of discipline and rejection of Bolshevik strategy and tactics led to a break and the **exile** or arrest of the leadership.

BAZAROV [SHPAK], BORIS YAKOVLEVICH (1893–1939). After joining the **OGPU** in 1921, Bazarov served in the Balkans and Vienna. He later served in Berlin and was responsible for the recruitment of a British Foreign Office code clerk. In 1935, he took on the position as illegal *rezident* in New York, where his group included **Ishak Akhmerov**. He was recalled in 1939 and shot. He was rehabilitated in 1956.

BELKIN, MIKHAIL ILIICH (1901–1996). A senior military counterintelligence officer, Belkin rose to become one of **Viktor Abakumov**'s chief subordinates. During the war, he commanded *Smersh* sections at the corps, army, and front level. Following the war, he was made **Joseph Stalin**'s proconsul in Hungary from 1947 to 1950. Belkin, with the help of Soviet interrogators, masterminded the show trial in Budapest of Lazlo Rajk and seven other accused Central Intelligence Agency spies and "Titoists." After a public confession, most were hanged. Belkin and his minions also supervised purge trials and purges in Czechoslovakia, Poland, and East Germany.

Stalin apparently suspected Belkin of disloyalty because of his Jewish heritage: he was born Moisei Yelnovich. When Abakumov fell in July 1951, Belkin was arrested and spent the next two years in pretrial confinement. He was released in 1953 but immediately dismissed from the service. He worked as a motor mechanic from 1955 to 1980 and died in 1996.

See also FIELD, NOEL HAVILAND (1904–1971); SHOW TRIALS.

BELOMOR CANAL. The first great project of the Soviet forced labor camps, or **gulag** system, was the building of a canal 200 kilometers from the White Sea to the Baltic Sea between 1931 and 1933. The canal was supposed to allow the Soviet navy to transfer major warships between the White and Baltic seas. The project employed more than 100,000 prisoners, the vast majority of whom were peasants the **OGPU** had arrested for resistance to **collectivization**. In one of the first **active measures** of the Stalin years, the canal was used to demonstrate the humanity of the Soviet prison system. Books praising the humanity of the OGPU staff in saving desperate criminals by honest labor were widely distributed in the West, but the reality was different. The canal consumed peasant workers by the thousands. According to some sources, as many as 20,000 prisoners perished in the building of the canal, and tens of thousands more were broken by their service. Worse still for the Soviet military, the canal was icebound several months a year and too shallow to accept major warships. It rapidly became little more than a ditch. The Belomor Canal was a model for larger forced labor projects in Siberia and the Far East. A cigarette product named after the canal continues to be sold to this day in Russia.

BENKENDORFF, ALEKSANDR (1783–1844). Tsar Nicholas I appointed Benkendorff to serve as the first director of the **Third Section** in 1826. Benkendorff expanded the authority of the Third Section and its Corps of Gendarmes to monitor public dissent. Benkendorff's most famous case was the persecution of the philosopher Petr Chaadaev, who was officially judged insane for his *Philosophical Letters*, which took a pessimistic view of Russia's past, present, and future. Beckendorff also ordered the surveillance of Russian **dissidents** living aboard, such as Aleksandr Hertzen.

Benkendorff was of Baltic German descent and had fought in the Napoleonic Wars. An extreme conservative, he played a key role in convincing Nicholas I that in the aftermath of the **Decembrist** risings, a modern security service was a vital necessity to protect the autocracy. Like his tsarist and Soviet successors, he tended to exaggerate the threat of dissent while insisting on greater power for the political police.

BENTLEY, ELIZABETH (1908–1963). Bentley, a Columbia University graduate and longtime Soviet agent, became one of the most controversial witnesses of Soviet espionage in the United States. For more than a decade, Bentley served as a courier and agent for the **NKVD** in New York. She had a torrid love affair with the Soviet case officer **Joseph Golos** that ended with his death in 1943. Bentley was highly valued by senior Soviet intelligence officers serving in America and was given the code names "Umnitsa" (Clever Girl) and "Mirna." Among the agents she helped run was **Duncan Lee**, an official of the **Office of Strategic Services** (OSS). In 1945, she found the *rezidentura*, distancing itself from her, and she was informed that her role as a principal agent would be taken over by a Soviet intelligence officer. Whether she was angered by this arbitrary decision, depressed over the loss of her lover, or afraid of being caught, she decided to defect. In November

1945, she approached the Federal Bureau of Investigation (FBI) in New York City, informed them of her role as a Soviet agent, and prepared a 112-page affidavit detailing her life as a Soviet agent.

In 1948, Bentley testified before the U.S. Congress in public hearings, naming a number of prominent officials as Soviet agents, including **Alger Hiss**, former Assistant Secretary of the Treasury **Harry Dexter White**, and OSS Duncan Lee. An FBI agent commenting on the value of her report noted that before she arrived, "we had files, here, there, and everywhere" but that her reporting "pulled it all together." For the first time, the FBI understood the complexity of Soviet espionage in the United States.

Bentley was widely disliked for her willingness to testify at trials and grand juries. She retired to teach at a girls' reform school. She died of cancer made worse by heavy drinking. Her testimony and autobiography were widely discredited by revisionist historians for more than 30 years. However, NKVD cables intercepted by the United States in the **Venona** program indicate that she was an important source and that most of her testimony was accurate.

BERIA, LAVRENTY PAVLOVICH (1899–1953). Born in the Mingrelian region of Georgia, Beria spent the years of the Russian **civil war** working for various intelligence services in the Caucasus. He joined the **Cheka** in 1921 and advanced quickly. He transferred to **Communist Party** work in the early 1930s, and in 1935, he was ordered by **Joseph Stalin** to oversee the editing of his autobiography.

In August 1938, Beria was brought to Moscow as deputy head of the **NKVD** to counter **Nikolai Yezhov**'s power. Later that year, he was named NKVD commissar and on Stalin's orders put the brakes on the terror that had claimed more than a million victims in the previous nine months. (However, Beria's appointment did not mean an end to terror: on 21 November 1938, 292 people were shot, and on 12 December of that year, Stalin signed death warrants for 3,176 people.) Over the next 15 years, Beria had managerial responsibility for the Soviet security police and served as a member of the Communist Party Central Committee as well as the **GKO** (State Defense Committee), which had overall responsibility for running the **Great Patriotic War**. After 1943, he was also responsible for the Soviet nuclear program. Beria was made a full member of the Politburo by Stalin, and in 1945, he was made a marshal of the Soviet Union.

In the early 1950s, Beria became a target of Stalin's suspicion, and only Stalin's death saved him from execution. From Stalin's death in March 1953 until purged in June 1953, Beria served as one of the three de facto rulers of the Soviet Union. Beria sought to bring the foreign intelligence, **counterintelligence**, police, and security services under his sway. It was a fatal mistake and convinced the other members of the leadership that he had to go. He was arrested at a Communist Party Presidium meeting in the Kremlin on 26 June by military officers commanded by Marshal **Georgi Zhukov**. After a lengthy interrogation, he was tried by an ad hoc court on 23 December and shot the same evening with several of his closest colleagues. He was charged with— among other real and fictitious crimes—having spied for Great Britain since the 1920s. At the trial, his massive crimes against humanity were not mentioned.

Beria was both one of Stalin's most odious lieutenants and a formidable security and intelligence generalissimo. He had a violent and depraved sexual appetite. He picked up and raped many young women, threatening them and their families with execution if they refused his overtures. He controlled a prison camp empire of more than 2 million *zeks* (prisoners), oversaw intelligence and security operations throughout Stalin's empire, and managed the Soviet nuclear program. A frightening boss who sent thousands of his own people to their death, he is remembered as Stalin's first lieutenant.

BERGAVINOV, SERGEI ADAMOVICH (1899–1937). After joining the **Communist Party** and the **Cheka** as a teenager, Bergavinov went into party work. In 1930, he was appointed chief of the **Special Settlements**, established for exiled peasants during **collectivization**. In 1930–1933, 381,026 families, almost 2 million peasants, were resettled in Siberia and Central Asia. There is no evidence that he expressed any regrets about the loss of life in the settlements, which he touted as "a wooden Donbas." He was shot in 1937.

BERLIN OPERATIONS. From 1947 to 1962, the German city of Berlin was the front line of the intelligence **Cold War**. The **KGB** and the **GRU** maintained large *rezidenturas* in Berlin. The KGB had between 2,000 and 3,000 staff officers in East Germany. The *rezidentura* in the **Karlshorst** district of East Berlin had a staff of 350 intelligence officers, the largest Soviet intelligence agency outside the Soviet Union. Two KGB components maintained an important presence in Karlshorst: the **First** (Foreign Intelligence) and **Third** (Military **Counterintelligence**) **Chief Directorates**. From Karlshorst, the KGB worked very closely with the East German *Stasi*, which had a large stable of agents in West Germany.

Soviet intelligence objectives in Berlin were to ensure the security of the East German regime and the Group of Soviet Forces Germany, penetrate the West German regime and its allies, and disrupt Western intelligence operations. In the late 1940s and early 1950s, the "battle for Berlin" was violent: **MGB** squads kidnapped Russian **émigré** and anti-Soviet German politicians. With the assignment of **Yevgeni Pitovranov** in 1953 to head the Berlin *rezidentura*, Soviet operations became more sophisticated.

During the struggle for Berlin, both Soviet services used Berlin as a launching pad for **illegals**. In the 1950s, the Soviet services assigned some of their most experienced illegal support officers to Berlin, including KGB Major General **Aleksandr Korotkov**. The Third (Illegal Support) Department was the largest KGB component at Karlshorst, responsible for producing and checking candidates and their documents. The GRU also dispatched illegals from Berlin to Europe and the United States.

The KGB played a critical part in **Nikita Khrushchev**'s decision to build the Berlin Wall. KGB Chair **Aleksandr Shelepin** and his deputy **Petr Ivashutin** repeatedly warned the political leadership that the mass defections of young, educated East Germans weakened the regime. When Khrushchev made the decision to build the wall (code-named "Rose") in August 1961, he gave the KGB, the Red Army, and the East German authorities less than 96 hours to prepare the closing of the interzone barrier. This decision and all the preparations for the division of Berlin were taken without any information leaking to alert the West.

Following the building of the Berlin Wall, Karlshorst remained an important center of Soviet intelligence activity. Soviet cooperation with the *Stasi* became increasingly close, as the East German service delivered 80 percent of all intelligence on the North Atlantic Treaty Organization. In the last decade of the Cold War, the KGB in Berlin was able to recruit and run agents within the U.S. military, such as **James Hall**. KGB/*Stasi* operations paid dividends to the very end of the Cold War.

See also BERLIN TUNNEL.

BERLIN TUNNEL. Faced with a lack of good human intelligence from the Soviet bloc in the early 1950s, the United States and Great Britain attacked the Soviet target with imaginative technical programs. In Vienna (Operation Silver) in the early 1950s and later in Berlin, the Western allies dug tunnels to tap the Soviet landlines. The Berlin Tunnel (Operation Gold), which was completed in February 1955, projected hundreds of meters into East Berlin and tapped the major military phone lines between Moscow and the Soviet headquarters in East Berlin. The tunnel intercept operators recorded 28 telegraphic circuits and 121 voice circuits continuously.

The **KGB** was alerted to the building of the tunnel by **George Blake** but decided to allow it to operate to protect this key agent from discovery. The KGB may have warned a few of its own communication personnel of the possible threat, but it allowed the Red Army as well as its **GRU** colleagues to continue to use the contaminated lines. The tunnel was "discovered" after 11 months and 11 days of operations. Western intelligence services benefited tremendously from the "take" from the Berlin Tunnel. According to a report by a Central Intelligence Agency officer, more than 440,000 conversations were transcribed, producing 1,750 classified intelligence reports. Also important was RUMINT (rumor intelligence, or gossip) about the leadership of the Soviet Union and East Germany gathered from the talk of Soviet general officers in Berlin with their colleagues and families in Moscow. The tunnel also produced especially sensitive reports on the development of Soviet nuclear weapons and delivery systems.

See also BERLIN OPERATIONS.

BERZIN, EDUARD PETROVICH (?–1937). A Latvian, Berzin was one of a number of Balts who joined the Red Army and the **Cheka** in the winter of 1917–1918. Berzin was cleverly used as a political pawn during the **Lockhart Plot**. Berzin played a disaffected and greedy officer, willing to be corrupted. British agent Robert Bruce Lockhart bought the story and incriminated himself. As a result, the Cheka gained insight into the plot. Berzin had a second career managing a forced labor camp in the **Kolyma** River valley. Berzin was sent to Siberia in 1932 to develop a huge complex of camps to mine gold in sub-Arctic northeastern Siberia. Despite an excellent record of production, Berzin was arrested in 1937 and shot as a spy, apparently because of his relationship with British intelligence in 1918. Berzin was replaced by his deputy **Karp Pavlov**, who had a far more notorious reputation than Berzin.

BERZIN, YAN KARLOVICH (1895?–1938). Born Peteris Kuzis in Russian Latvia, Berzin had a career as an underground Bolshevik revolutionary before the **Revolution of November 1917**. In 1917–1918, he commanded Lenin's bodyguards. In 1924, he was appointed chief of military intelligence, and for the next 10 years, he commanded a small corps of **illegal** agents who made important recruitments throughout Western Europe. In 1936–1937, Berzin served in Spain under the name "General Grishin," dispatching agents and saboteurs behind Franco's lines. In June 1937, he was recalled and reinstalled as chief of military intelligence. Like many veterans of the **Spanish Civil War**, however, he was arrested on **Joseph Stalin**'s orders. He was tried and shot in July 1938.

Berzin is credited by many historians as a competent spymaster and one of the fathers of Soviet special forces, or *Spetsnaz*, operations. During his career, he was awarded the Order Of Lenin, two orders of the Red Banner, and the Order of the Red Star. Like many Latvian, Polish, and German revolutionaries, he fell victim to Stalin's paranoia. Their deaths deprived the Soviet Union of its best intelligence officers. Berzin was posthumously rehabilitated during the 1950s.

BESLAN SCHOOL HOSTAGE CRISIS. On 1 September 2004 (the first day of school), militants commanded by **Chechen** warlord Shamil Basayev took more than 1,100 students, parents, and teachers hostage in the town of Beslan. At least 32 terrorists, most apparently from Dagestan and Ingushetiya, including three women, took part in the operation. After three days of sporadic negotiations, explosions were heard in the building, and **MVD** and **FSB** paramilitary forces, as well as Russian army units, stormed the school. Russian forces used rockets and fire from the tanks' main guns in the assault. In the resulting firefight, 385 people died, including 334 hostages and at least 10 members of the security forces and all 31 of the terrorists. At least 78 were wounded.

The response by the Russian authorities showed a distinct lack of professionalism as well as a lack of concern for the hostages and led to changes in procedures in handling terrorist incidents. Another major concern was the ability of a large party of terrorists to move unnoticed outside Chechnya. The crisis allowed President **Vladimir Putin** to establish new and tighter security laws.

See also CHECHEN WARS.

BLACK CHAMBER. A Black Chamber is a facility, often located in post offices, for mail and message interception, decoding, and decryption. Black Chambers began in Russia and reached their apogee in East Germany, where the *Stasi* read virtually all international and domestic correspondence. For the *Okhrana* and Ministry of Foreign Affairs, the Black Chamber provided diplomatic cables and thousands of pieces of raw intelligence from suspected **dissidents** and radicals. The *Okhrana* model was improved by the **Cheka** and its successor services.

BLAKE, GEORGE (1927–). The most important **KGB** penetration of British intelligence in the post-Stalin era was through George Blake, the son of a Dutch mother and a Sephardic Jewish father. He served in Nazi-occupied Holland as a British agent while an adolescent. Following the war, he joined the British Secret Intelligence Service (SIS) and was posted to South Korea. Following the North Korean invasion of South Korea, Blake was captured and spent the remainder of the war in a prison camp in Manchuria. He claims that he volunteered to the KGB during his captivity out of his revulsion with Allied bombing of civilians in North Korea. Whether Blake was truly an ideological recruit is not known for sure, but by the time of his repatriation to Great Britain in the summer of 1953, he was a trusted Soviet source with the code name "Diomid" (Diamond). Blake's handler in London was **Sergei Kondrashev**, an experienced case officer who devised clever **tradecraft** to run Blake in Western Europe. Blake provided the KGB with detailed information on SIS and Central Intelligence Agency operations, including the **Berlin Tunnel**.

Blake was betrayed by a Soviet bloc **defector, Michael Goleniewski**, and arrested in 1961. At his semisecret trial in London, Blake was sentenced to 42 years in prison—one year, the judge asserted, for every person he betrayed and sent to his death. Blake was sprung from prison in 1966 by an Irish Republican Army veteran acting without KGB direction. Blake made his way to Moscow, where he lives today. He is the author of an interesting autobiography.

BLANK SPOTS. Russian reformers in the 1980s often described the difficult issues of the Stalin era as "blank spots" and called for greater historical honesty. Following the collapse of the Soviet Union, archives became more available to researchers, forcing a rewriting of much of the history of the Soviet era. However, many archives remain closed, and many issues still remain off limits to Russian and foreign researchers.

BLOKHIN, VASILY MIKHAILOVICH (1895–1955). Possibly the most prolific executioner of the 20th century, Blokhin acted as chief of the headquarters branch that ran **Lubyanka** prison from the 1930s through 1953. As such, he personally shot leading party members and two former chiefs of his service, **Genrykh Yagoda** and **Nikolai Yezhov**, as well as members of **Joseph Stalin**'s family. According to a recent biography of Stalin, Blokhin often carried out these duties—which Stalin referred to as "black work" (*chornaya rabota*)—wearing a butcher's leather apron. In 1940, Blokhin oversaw the shooting of 14,000 Polish officers at **Katyn**, reportedly personally executing 7,000 men.

Blokhin, a veteran of the tsarist army, joined the **Cheka** in 1921 and rose through the ranks. He was rewarded for his duties, decorated with the Order of **Lenin**, and promoted to major general in 1945. Blokhin retired for reasons of health in 1953. Shortly prior to his suicide in 1955, he was stripped of some of his medals for "discrediting the service."

BLUMKIN, YAKOV (1898–1929). Blumkin joined the **Cheka** at age 19 and was convinced to kill the German ambassador to Russia in 1918 to prevent a German–Russian peace accord by **dissident** members of the Socialist Revolutionary Party. The assassination, planned by the junior member of the political coalition of Bolsheviks and Socialist Revolutionaries ruling the country, was meant to derail the Brest–Litovsk accord with imperial

Germany. Remarkably, he was forgiven and allowed to continue serving in the Cheka. Blumkin was close to **Leon Trotsky** during the Russian **civil war** and admired his domestic and foreign policies.

Following the civil war, Blumkin entered foreign intelligence and in 1929 was serving in Turkey as an **illegal**. He was tasked with selling ancient Talmudic texts that had been expropriated from Jewish congregations in the Soviet Union by the **Communist Party**. Blumkin clandestinely met with Trotsky, who had just been **exiled** to Turkey, and offered to be his channel of communications with his supporters in the Soviet Union. Blumkin was betrayed by his wife, **Elizaveta Zarubina**, and arrested on his arrival in Moscow. He was tried and, at **Joseph Stalin**'s command, executed.

Blumkin was a talented officer with a genius for languages. He spoke Yiddish, Polish, Persian, Hebrew, and Russian. His talent for conspiracy was far more limited. Blumkin was the first member of the party and the police to be executed for political reasons. Stalin used the **execution** to send a signal to the Soviet elite that he would treat Trotskyism as a capital crime.

BLUNT, ANTHONY (1907–1983). A Soviet agent who recruited agents for Soviet intelligence in the 1930s, Blunt survived exposure for more than a decade and was never prosecuted for his treachery. A brilliant art historian, he had become Queen Elizabeth's principal adviser on art. **Arnold Deutsch**, a Soviet **illegal** operating in Western Europe, recruited Blunt in the early 1930s as a talent scout and gave him the code name "Tony." In the late 1930s, Blunt helped recruit **Michael Straight**, **John Cairncross**, and **Leo Long** for Soviet intelligence. During **World War II**, Blunt worked for the British Security Service (MI5) and provided Moscow with information on British strategic planning and **counterintelligence** operations. According to the Soviet intelligence service archives, Blunt met weekly with a Soviet case officer during the war and provided 1,771 documents between 1941 and 1945. Especially important to Moscow were reports of German order of battle intelligence based on **Ultra** intelligence. After the war, Blunt maintained an unofficial relationship with old friends in British intelligence and continued to provide Moscow with reports on developments inside MI5. Perhaps his most important report concerned London's efforts to use the same tactics to penetrate the new East German service that it had used against the Abwehr.

Blunt was uncovered when Michael Straight, an American citizen Blunt had recruited, confessed to the Federal Bureau of Investigation in 1964. Blunt quickly made a deal with MI5 to make a full confession and provide an account of his intelligence activities in return for immunity. Blunt's interviews were miracles of obfuscation; in hundreds of hours of questioning, he never fully admitted his role as a Soviet agent. Blunt was publicly outed by Anthony Boyle, who named Blunt as the "Fourth Man" (after **Donald Macl-**

ean, **Guy Burgess**, and **Kim Philby**) in *The Climate of Treason* in 1979. British Prime Minister Margaret Thatcher confirmed the information in Parliament in November 1979, setting off a media firestorm. Blunt was immediately stripped of his knighthood and lived in semidisgrace until his death in 1983.

BOBKOV, FILIP DENISOVICH (1925–). An experienced intelligence officer whose career in the **KGB** spanned five decades, Bobkov directed KGB activities against **dissidents** for more than 15 years. During **World War II**, he served in *Smersh*, and he entered the security service in 1946. In the late 1960s, he took a prominent role in the Fifth Directorate (**Counterintelligence** within the Intelligentsia). Under his direction, the KGB penetrated underground religious and nationalist organizations. Bobkov oversaw the persecution and eventual **exile** of Nobel Prize laureate **Aleksandr Solzhenitsyn**. He also worked to coordinate **active measures** against Soviet and East European dissidents. Bobkov was described by one KGB colleague as the agency's main ideological watchdog.

Bobkov, whose career was closely mentored by KGB chief **Yuri Andropov**, rose to deputy chief of the service in 1982. During **Mikhail Gorbachev**'s period of leadership, Bobkov refocused the Fifth Directorate from the struggle with dissidents to the suppression of corruption. He oversaw KGB activities during nationalist riots in Alma Ata (1986) and Baku (1990). But in late 1990, Bobkov publicly criticized Gorbachev, noting in a television interview that he had been "disillusioned" with Gorbachev. He also complained at Central Committee meetings about the growth of "informal groups" in the Baltic Republic and Moscow. Bobkov retired from the KGB in 1991. Following the collapse of the Soviet Union, he became a security adviser to MOST Bank chair Viktor Gusinskiy and wrote a revealing memoir about the KGB.

BOCHKOV, VIKTOR MIKHAILOVICH (1900–1981). Bochkov served simultaneously as head of military counterintelligence and chief procurator of the Soviet Union from 1938 to 1941. This was clearly part of an effort by **Joseph Stalin** to extend the writ of the security service. As one of the country's senior military counterintelligence officers, Bochkov stiffened Soviet resistance around Leningrad in the brutal winter of 1941–1942 on the Northwestern Front by ordering the execution of unsuccessful commanders. From 1944 to 1951, he held a series of posts in the **gulag** as a lieutenant general. In 1959, he left the police to work in the civilian economy.

BOGDANOV, IVAN ALEKSANDROVICH (1897–1942). An **NKVD** lieutenant general, Bogdanov was given command of Reserve Army Group in July 1941 to prevent a German breakthrough to Moscow. Along with several other tough NKVD generals, given the command of armies under Bogdanov, he fought a series of defensive battles that probably saved Moscow from capture in the fall of 1941. Bogdanov died of wounds in July 1942.

See also BATTLE OF MOSCOW.

BOKIY, GLEB IVANOVICH (1879–?). An Old Bolshevik who was an active revolutionary for 20 years before the **Revolution of November 1917**, Bokiy is one of the creators of Soviet **signals intelligence**. He joined the **Cheka** in March 1918 and served first in the defense of Petrograd against White armies and then in Central Asia. In 1920, Bokiy became head of the service's cryptological service. Although there had been competition between his service and the **GRU** in the 1930s, Bokiy molded a small component from both the security service and the military intelligence service that became exceptionally competent in breaking codes. With information provided from recruited code clerks, Bokiy's component read the messages of many of Moscow's opponents.

Bokiy, according to one **defector**, had a reputation as an alcoholic and a womanizer whose home was the scene of orgies. What probably sealed his fate, however, was his long association with Old Bolsheviks such as **Leon Trotsky**. He was arrested on 16 May 1937 and tried by a three-member collegium of the **NKVD** on 11 November 1937. He may have been shot the evening of his trial, but there are reports that he continued to work for the service in jail until his death in 1940 or 1941. He was posthumously rehabilitated in 1956.

BOLSHEVIK PARTY. The Bolshevik (Majority) faction of the Russian Social Democratic Labor Party emerged in 1903, following a party dispute over tactics and organization. The Bolsheviks, led by **Vladimir Lenin**, argued for a party led by professional revolutionaries. The Menshevik (Minority) faction supported a mass-based party similar to the German Social Democratic Party or the British Labour Party. But Lenin and his closest associates broke with the majority of European socialists, who believed that the keys to the victory of socialism were control of the electoral process and the parliamentary process. Lenin advocated a more "Jacobean" program. Victory, he argued, would go to the more ruthless. He was willing to raise money through robberies ("expropriations") and argued that capital punishment and terrorism were necessary ingredients of a successful revolution.

Lenin—as dictator of a revolutionary Russia—put his ideas to work. He believed with every fiber of his being that there was no greater cause than victory. For this victory, he first tolerated and then encouraged revolutionary violence in the name of the Bolshevik Party. Nevertheless, Lenin did not run a tight ship from the standpoint of security: the *Okhrana* had repeatedly penetrated the movement with informers, including **Roman Malinovskiy**. Once the tsarist archives exposed the degree of penetration, Lenin called for a strong **counterintelligence** service to protect the party and the regime.

BORDER GUARDS. The Border Guards were part of the structure of the Soviet security service from the Russian **civil war** to the collapse of the Soviet Union in 1991. During its history, the Chief Directorate of the Border Guards had **counterintelligence**, security, and military responsibilities. At the beginning of **World War II**, the Border Guards had a staff of 167,000 troops. In the 1970s and 1980s, the Border Guards were further expanded to cover the Chinese and Afghanistan borders. At the time of the 1991 **August putsch**, the Border Guards had a strength of 240,000.

See also KGB (*KOMITET GOSUDARSTVENNOI BEZOPASTNOSTI*); KGB ORGANIZATION.

BORTNIKOV, ALEKSANDR VASILYEVICH (1951–). A career security official, Borotnikov was made chief of the **FSB** in 2008. Prior to his appointment, he had served as chief of the St. Petersburg FSB Directorate and director of the service's Economic Security Service. Like his predecessor **Nikolai Patrushev**, he made his career in the Leningrad **KGB** and was close to President **Vladimir Putin**.

BOYARINOV, YEVGIY (?–1979). The commander of the elite paramilitary formation **ZENIT**, Boyarinov led the assault on the presidential palace in Kabul, **Afghanistan**, in December 1979. Boyarinov was killed by friendly fire at the conclusion of the attack. Boyarinov was posthumously and secretly decorated with the award Hero of the Soviet Union. A KGB deputy chairman went to his family apartment to present his wife with the award.

BOYCE, CHRISTOPHER, (1953–), AND LEE, ANDREW DALTON (1952–). Made famous by the book *The Falcon and the Snowman* and the movie of the same name, Boyce and Lee provided the **KGB** with detailed information on TRW satellite systems. Boyce, who worked in TRW's "Black Vault," and Lee, his friend and longtime drug dealer, contacted the Soviet embassy in Mexico City. Lee was motivated only by money, while Boyce saw himself as using his exposure of American foreign policy to gain money.

Lee's drug deals brought him to the attention of the Mexican police, and in a ham-handed effort to escape Mexican justice, he exposed their espionage in interviews with the Federal Bureau of Investigation.

Both Boyce and Lee received long jail terms. Boyce escaped and robbed 17 banks in the American Northwest. Both have been freed, and Boyce has been interviewed on his espionage. Boyce has been seen by some sympathetic commentators as an immature whistle-blower. Analysis of his motives and his personal accounts of the espionage suggest some comparison with **Edward Snowden**. He did, for whatever reasons, major damage to U.S. intelligence.

BREZHNEV, LEONID ILYICH (1911–1982). As **Nikita Khrushchev**'s deputy and later as general secretary of the **Communist Party** from 1964 until his death in 1982, Brezhnev artfully used the **KGB** to secure his position. In the end, however, the KGB brought him down and probably hastened his death.

Brezhnev rose in the Communist Party during the 1930s; his base was the party organization of the Ukrainian city of Dneprepropetrovsk. In **World War II**, he served as the political commissar of a brigade and was decorated for heroism. Following the war, Brezhnev served as a senior party official in the provinces and Moscow. In the early 1960s, he became Khrushchev's de facto deputy, but in 1964, with **Aleksandr Shelepin** and other Politburo members, he began to plot against Khrushchev. Brezhnev used the KGB to isolate his patron as he prepared the **October 1964 coup** that unseated the country's leader.

As the new Soviet leader, Brezhnev stocked the KGB with former political cronies from his hometown, including **Viktor Chebrikov**, **Georgi Tsinev**, and **Semyon Tsvygun**. He worked closely with KGB head **Yuri Andropov**, allowing Andropov great sway to broaden KGB operations internally and externally. In 1981, however, Andropov began to plot against Brezhnev. The KGB spread rumors about corruption in the ruling family as well as Brezhnev's declining physical and mental health, creating confusion in party senior ranks and perhaps hastening Brezhnev's death in November 1982. The Brezhnev era is known today in Russia as a period of "stagnation" during which the KGB stifled religious and political dissent and the country fell further and further behind the West.

BROWDER, EARL RUSSELL (1891–1973). A leader of the American communist movement in the 1930s through **World War II**, Browder also played an important role in Soviet espionage. Browder, whose **NKVD** code names were "Helmsman" and "Father," was an important link between the Soviet's intelligence apparatus and communist sympathizers within the

Franklin D. Roosevelt administration. In decoded Soviet intelligence messages from the 1940s, Browder is mentioned 26 times as Moscow's agent. One of his most influential contacts was **Jacob Golos**, who ran an important espionage ring in Washington. Browder also had extensive experience as an intelligence agent. In the 1920s, he traveled to China on a **Comintern** mission with his lover, **Kitty Harris**, who became an NKVD **illegal**.

Browder often acted as a talent scout, passing on potential candidates to NKVD case officers. Despite his activities as party leader and intelligence agent, however, Browder was considered too soft by Moscow. In 1946, he was relieved of his position and expelled from the party. In less than a year, he went from helmsman to pariah, and he retired to Princeton, New Jersey. Browder's role as a Soviet agent was revealed only after his death.

BUDGETS. The Soviet intelligence services never published their budgets. The only benchmark is a statement by **Leonid Shebarshin** that while the Central Intelligence Agency (CIA) had a budget of $30 billion, the **KGB**'s budget was only 5 million hard-currency rubles, about $8 million, at the end of the **Cold War**. Of course, Shebarshin's statement is self-serving: the budget of the entire U.S. intelligence community—not just the CIA—was $30 billion. Moreover, most of the U.S. intelligence budget went to Defense Department technical programs, whereas such programs in the Soviet Union were managed by the **GRU**. Still, the KGB's power did not come from its budget: it could requisition what it needed—personnel, money, or property—to accomplish its missions.

The post-Soviet Russian military suffered financially before 2000. Officers and soldiers went months without salaries. Ships rusted away at dockside, and planes turned to unflyable relics. The **MVD** (Ministry of Internal Affairs) also suffered greatly as well, with limited funds for operations and police officers. Nevertheless, the **Russian intelligence services** remain robust and are the largest in the world.

BURGESS, GUY FRANCIS DE MONCY (1910–1963). A Soviet agent and member of the **Ring of Five**, Burgess was recruited by an **NKVD illegal** shortly after leaving Cambridge in the early 1930s. Kim Philby, who spotted and evaluated Burgess for the NKVD, strongly recommended against his recruitment because of his personal behavior. His initial code name within the Soviet service was "Mädchen" (Maiden), a cynical comment on his sexual promiscuity. A brilliant and witty raconteur, Burgess was an avowed homosexual who worked unsuccessfully for several British bureaucracies between 1938 and 1951. While a disaster as a member of the British governing establishment, Burgess became an asset for the NKVD as both a recruiter and an agent in place, providing detailed information about personalities and policies. Burgess brought a number of prospective agents to the attention of Soviet case officers.

Burgess provided the Soviets with access to a variety of important political and intelligence policymakers. A cynical Soviet case officer noted in his report to Moscow that Burgess was a "cultural pederast who could exploit the mysterious laws of sex in this country." Working in the Foreign Office in the years after **World War II**, he provided his case officers with thousands of classified documents. In 1950, he was transferred to the British embassy in Washington, where he lived with Philby. In Washington, he became more and more of a diplomatic scandal.

Facing exposure in 1951, Burgess left his post as a junior diplomat in Washington and returned to London, warning **Donald Maclean** that the British and American governments had evidence of his treachery. He then defected with Maclean to Moscow. Burgess was resettled in the Soviet Union and nationalized as a Soviet citizen. Despite his desire to return to Britain, he died in **exile** in Moscow. Burgess has often been treated as a joke by a later generation of intelligence historians. He was, however, a good and ruthless spy. On one occasion, he asked his Soviet case officer's permission to murder another British agent he believed was preparing to turn him in.

See also PHILBY, KIM (1912–1988); RING OF FIVE.

BUTOVO. The Butovo firing range (*Butovskiy poligon*) was an **NKVD** execution site during the Purge of 1937–1938. Incomplete records show that 20,765 people were shot at Butovo between 1 August 1937 and 19 October 1938, 562 on 28 February 1938 alone. In 1995, the site was turned over to the Russian Orthodox Church and is the location of a memorial church.

BYKOV [BUKOV], BORIS YAKOVLEVICH. Bykov, who was fluent in German, first served a **GRU illegal** in Germany and then as the GRU *rezident* in New York from 1936 to 1939. When his cover was blown by **Whittaker Chambers** in 1938, Bykov reinvented himself under a new cover and continued to run two agent groups in the United States until his recall in 1939. He later worked in the Soviet General Staff and the Institute of Military Interpreters.

BYSTROLETOV, DMITRY ALEKSANDROVICH (1901–1975). One of the most successful Soviet **illegals**, Bystroletov operated in Western Europe for more than a decade, recruiting agents in Germany, France, Italy, and Great Britain under a **false flag**. He operated at various times as a Czech, Greek, and British citizen; his British passport identified him as Lord Robert Greenville. Among his greatest successes was the running of agents in the

German and French military and the British Foreign Office, which had access to their countries' diplomatic ciphers. For several years, Bystroletov ran Ernest Oldham, a British code clerk, who provided Moscow with British diplomatic ciphers. Bystroletov, a very handsome man, also seduced a French code clerk in Prague and obtained copies of French diplomatic codes.

Bystroletov, like many of the "great illegals," fell victim to Moscow's paranoia in the late 1930s. In 1937, he was recalled to Moscow and arrested as a German spy. He was tortured into making a false confession, convicted, and sentenced to a forced labor camp. Bystroletov survived the purges, but several members of his family were executed or committed suicide. In 1954, he was released, rehabilitated, and allowed to write a classified account of his activity as an illegal.

BYVSHIE. Russian for "formers"—tsarist officials, merchants, priests, and so on—a category of person target by the **NKVD** for arrest, exile, imprisonment, or execution during the purges of the late 1930s.

C

CAIRNCROSS, JOHN (1914–1999). A British diplomat of Scots heritage who served in the British Foreign Office, Cairncross was recruited by **Guy Burgess** in 1937. An ideological recruit to Stalinism, Cairncross despised the British establishment and embraced Marxism–Leninism as a creed. His Soviet code names were "Moliere" and later "Liszt," reflecting his Soviet handlers' respect for his intellect. He passed thousands of pages of classified documents to his Soviet case officers over more than a decade—more than 3,400 in 1941 alone, according to Soviet records. Cairncross provided the Kremlin with thousands of pages of decrypted German military telegrams, classified **Ultra** top secret by London. He also provided Moscow with information about British nuclear research. According to the Soviet archives, it was Cairncross's reporting on the British nuclear weapons program code-named "Tube Alloy" that initiated research into building a Soviet bomb.

Cairncross was exposed in the early 1960s but avoided prosecution by living outside the United Kingdom. In his later years, he wrote his memoirs, portraying himself as a victim of **Cold War** anticommunism and claiming that he was only a wartime ally of an embattled Russia. The book—like his life—was a half-truth.

CARR, SAM (1906–1989). Born Schmil Kogan in Ukraine, he was a Communist Party organizer and a recruiter for the Soviet intelligence services in Canada during **World War II**. Following the **defection** of **Igor Gouzenko** in 1945, an arrest warrant was issued for Carr. After fleeing to the United States, he was tried and found guilty of passport violations and served seven years in prison.

CAUCASUS EMIRATE (*IMARAT KAVKAZ*). One of the principal targets of the Russian security services, the *Imarat* was created in 2007 by Chechen and Dagistani Islamic militants. The organization claims to represent Islam in the Muslim areas of the Caucasus. Its founders were Chechen militants, former commanders in the wars with Russia. The *Imarat* has been responsible for terrorist acts, including suicide bombings of the Moscow subway in

2010 and in Volgograd in 2013. On several occasions, it has used women suicide bombers in terrorist attacks. Some members of the group traveled in 2013 to Syria to fight in the civil war. In 2013–2014, the **FSB** took action to protect the 2014 Winter Olympics from attacks by the militants of the Caucasus Emirate.

See also CHECHEN WARS.

CHAMBERS, JAY VIVIAN [WHITTAKER] (1901–1961). One of the most controversial "witnesses" of the **Cold War**, "Whittaker" Chambers, author, journalist, and self-confessed Soviet spy, set off one of the most important trials in 20th-century American history. Chambers, an ardent communist, was recruited by the **GRU** in the early 1930s and made part of an **illegal** cell responsible for espionage. In this communist underground in Washington and New York, Chambers met **Alger Hiss**, a rising public servant in Franklin D. Roosevelt's New Deal administration. In the late 1930s, Chambers, after much soul-searching, left the GRU and the party and began a new life as a journalist.

In 1939, Chambers gave a senior State Department official an affidavit naming 13 American communists in high government positions. Chambers also confessed his treachery to a number of American friends in the early 1940s. But no use was made of this information for almost a decade. In August 1948, Chambers testified before the House Un-American Activities Committee and then before several federal grand juries about the scope of Soviet intelligence in the United States. In his testimony, he identified Hiss and others as Soviet agents. Hiss denied the charges before the same committee and was later tried and convicted of perjury.

In the last 25 years of his life, Chambers wrote in detail about his life as a Soviet agent and a communist. To many on the left, he was seen as a false witness and a despicable person who had sent an innocent man to jail. Soviet archives and intercepted **NKVD** intelligence messages suggest that Chambers was in most cases an accurate witness and that his portrayal of Hiss and Soviet subversion in Washington in the 1930s and 1940s was accurate. His autobiography is now seen as one of the best books on American society and politics in the 1930s.

CHAPMAN, ANNA VLADIMIROVNA (1981–). One of the 10 "**illegals**" arrested in 2010 by the Federal Bureau of Investigation, Chapman attended Patrice Lumumba University and then began her intelligence career in the United Kingdom. While in London, she married a British subject and acquired British citizenship. She was living her cover as a real estate broker in New York City, where she was reportedly tasked with developing contacts with influential Democratic Party politicians before she was arrested. Along with nine other illegals, she was traded for four Russian citizens imprisoned for spying for the United States and Great Britain. Welcomed home by then premier **Vladimir Putin**, she has become a glamorous television personality in Moscow. In 2013, she humorously proposed marriage to National Security Agency leaker **Edward Snowden**.

CHEBRIKOV, VIKTOR MIKHAILOVICH (1923–1999). Chebrikov, an old political ally of **Leonid Brezhnev**, was promoted from a position as a director of an industrial institute in Dneprepropetrovsk to **KGB** deputy chair for personnel in 1967. The move was an effort by Brezhnev to ensure his control of the KGB. Following **Semyon Tsvygun**'s death in January 1982, Chebrikov was made first deputy chair of the KGB. Apparently well thought of by **Yuri Andropov**, he was made KGB chair that December and continued the prosecution of religious and political **dissidents** in 1982–1985. **Mikhail Gorbachev**, following his promotion to lead the **Communist Party**, brought Chebrikov into the Communist Party Politburo in 1985.

Chebrikov never fully supported Gorbachev's policies of *glasnost* and *perestroika*. In 1987, he took issue with public disclosure of the historic and present abuses of the KGB and began quietly to sabotage Gorbachev's policies. In his 1987 and 1988 top-secret reports to the Politburo, Chebrikov blamed Western agents and **Trotskyite** saboteurs for the growing level of civil disobedience in the Soviet Union. Chebrikov reportedly believed that the fall of the Soviet Union was part of a Central Intelligence Agency plot.

In 1988, Gorbachev replaced Chebrikov with **Vladimir Kryuchkov**, shuffling Chebrikov into the Communist Party bureaucracy, where he continued to oppose Gorbachev. In 1989, Gorbachev forced his retirement, apparently concerned about his ability to effect policies in the security service. Even in retirement, Chebrikov continued to oppose Gorbachev's policies, often speaking to traditionalist and conservative party chapters about Gorbachev's "treason."

CHECHEN WARS. The Chechens are an Islamic people living in the Caucasus. In the 18th and 19th centuries, they stoutly battled Russian occupation. The Chechens never fully accepted Soviet power; **collectivization** was resisted, and Chechen "bandits" were never fully defeated by the **NKVD**. During **World War II**, **Joseph Stalin** ordered the **deportation** of the entire Chechen population to Central Asia for collaborating with the German occupiers; almost a third died of hunger in the first year. The Chechens, like the other Caucasian people deported by Stalin during the war, were "forgiven" and allowed to return in the late 1950s.

The Chechens found on their return that much of their land had been occupied by Russians. Nevertheless, in the last decades of Soviet power, the Chechens rebuilt their villages. The end of the Soviet Union left the tiny Chechen enclave in a dubious political position: political radicals occupied and ran the "country," imposing taxes and raising an army. Moscow seemed to have forgotten about them. But in 1994, Russian President **Boris Yeltsin** decided to reestablish Russian rule. When several efforts by the Russian security services failed to overturn the rebel regime, Russian troops sought to seize the capital of Grozny by force.

The Soviet intelligence community had not prepared the government for the level or intensity of the resistance they would meet. The 1994 battle for Grozny was a major embarrassment for the Russian army, and a Russian armored brigade was destroyed in several hours of intense urban combat. Faced with military failure, the Russian army destroyed Chechen villages, forcing people to flee into the mountains or accept internment in camps. The situation rapidly became a "dirty war," with atrocities on both sides. The **FSB**, in a major test of its competence, was unable to prevent raids by Chechen battle groups deep into Russia. The FSB was also blamed for the torture and **execution** of civilians.

An armistice in the summer of 1996 ended only a phase of the struggle. The FSB proved incapable of cutting the rebels' ties with Islamic fundamentalists such as Al Qaeda or intercepting the movement of Islamic revolutionaries, funds, or weapons into Chechnya. By 1998, radical Islamicists were well armed and itching for another test.

The second phase of the Chechen wars began in the summer of 1998 with a series of bombings that killed several hundred people and shook Russia. These bombings were blamed on Chechen rebels, although no convincing evidence has been presented that a Chechen organization was responsible. As in the first war, the security services proved to be in equal measure incompetent and brutal, and international human rights agencies accused the Russian government of condoning atrocities. The Chechen rebels resorted to terrorism, bombing bus stations and schools, and sabotaging aircraft. In 2004, FSB and army efforts to take a school occupied by Chechen terrorists ended in a massive tragedy that took hundreds of lives.

See also BESLAN SCHOOL HOSTAGE CRISIS; CAUCASUS EMIRATE (*IMARAT KAVKAZ*); COUNTERTERRORISM; DUBROVKA THEATER SIEGE.

CHEKA. The Extraordinary Commission for Combating Counterrevolution and Sabotage (*Chrevzuychanaya komissiya po borbe s kontrarevolutsei i sabotazhem*), or Cheka, was founded on 20 December 1917, only six weeks after the Bolshevik Revolution. **Bolshevik Party** leader **Vladimir Lenin**

appointed **Feliks Dzerzhinsky**, a Polish Bolshevik, to head the infant service. From its first days, Lenin saw the Cheka as the avenging sword of the party, ordering it to take immediate action against "enemies."

Dzerzhinsky grew the Cheka into a massive security empire with responsibility for **counterintelligence**, oversight of the loyalty of the Red Army, and protection of the country's borders as well as the collection of human and technical intelligence. By the end of the **civil war**, the Cheka had a staff of 250,000. (The total complement of the *Okhrana* and tsarist Corps of Gendarmes was 15,000 in the years immediately prior to the Bolshevik Revolution.) Under Dzerzhinsky, the Cheka became the shield and avenging sword of the revolution. Beginning in 1918, the Cheka arrested and executed hostages, including women and children. One Cheka leader noted that the Cheka's raison d'être was destruction of enemy classes. A recent study estimates that the Cheka was responsible for 143,000 **executions** between 1917 and 1921.

Along with the executions came an orgy of torture and killing not seen in Europe in hundreds of years. Mass drowning of prisoners, the random shooting of hostages, and the use of physical torture were commonly practiced by the Cheka. The rank and file of the Cheka were drawn largely from the lumpenproletariat. Most of the new recruits were in their 20s or late teens. Few had more than a village education, and many had no formal education at all. According to recent academic studies, many came from the Red Guards, which had been organized in 1917, while others came from the underworld. Given authority by the Bolshevik Party to arrest, torture, and execute, they did so with gusto. Part of the cruelty of the Cheka can be explained by the revolutionary times, but part of the explanation lies in the raw material of the new staff.

The Bolsheviks could not have won the civil war without the Cheka, but an issue for the Leninist leadership was how to control the secret police after victory. In late 1921, the Cheka lost much of the power of carrying out executions. Between 1921 and 1922, executions for political offenses dropped from 9,701 to 1,962. In 1923, the number dropped even further to 414. The Cheka also lost some of its bureaucratic clout when it was folded into the **GPU** in February 1922. The decision to reduce the terror was a tactical one as the Soviet leadership began its **New Economic Policy** to help the country recover from the ravages of war and famine.

The Cheka was originally devised by Lenin and Dzerzhinsky as a domestic counterintelligence service. Its foreign operations were an extension of its domestic security and counterintelligence missions. The Cheka did not establish a foreign intelligence component, the *Inostranniy otdel*, until December 1920, three years after the organization's founding. Since its primary responsibility was rooting out subversion, foreign intelligence operations were directed against **émigré** White Russian organizations and the Western states that supported them. During this period, most Cheka foreign intelligence operations were directed by non-Russians because of their extensive revolutionary experience outside the Russian empire.

Under Dzerzhinsky, the Cheka became a major player in Soviet politics. The security service became the prime source of information about developments within and outside the country for the political leadership. Moreover, beginning with Lenin, Soviet leaders used the service to intimidate and silence enemies of the revolution and the state. These years were portrayed as a period of heroic revolutionary sacrifice, and the Cheka's heritage was important for succeeding generations of Soviet intelligence and security officers. They received their pay on the 20th of the month—the service's anniversary.

CHEKHOVA, OLGA KONSTANTINOVNA (1895–1980). Married to the nephew of Anton Chekhov, Olga Konstantinovna immigrated to Germany during the Russian **civil war**. She was almost immediately contacted by members of her family, who had been co-opted by the **Cheka**, and convinced to work as an agent for the security service. In return for exit visas for members of her family, she promised to act as an agent within the **émigré** community and the rising Nazi establishment. In the 1930s, Chekhova became a major movie star in Nazi Germany and a personal favorite of Adolf Hitler and Nazi propaganda boss Joseph Goebbels. The Russian archives suggest that she was a "sleeper agent," maintained first to report on the Nazi leadership and later, during the **Battle of Moscow**, as part of the **NKVD**'s plans to assassinate German leaders. Following **World War II**, she was flown to Moscow and debriefed by *Smersh* director **Viktor Abakumov**. Chekhova's reputation as a femme fatale was greatly exaggerated by Western journalists after the war, some of whom styled her as Hitler's lover.

CHEKIST. Beginning in the 1920s, Soviet security and intelligence officers referred to themselves as Chekists. (The Russian plural is *Chekisty*.) This has continued to some extent since the collapse of the Soviet Union and the disbanding of the **KGB**. Russian intelligence officers continue to use the honorific.

CHEREPANOV, ALEKSANDR NIKOLAEVICH (1915–1964). In late November 1963, Aleksandr Cherepanov, a disgruntled **KGB** officer, persuaded American tourists to carry sensitive documents about KGB operations against the American embassy to the Central Intelligence Agency chief of station (COS) in Moscow. When the chargé d'affaires was informed of the incident, he ordered the COS to hand over the documents so they could be returned to the Soviet Foreign Ministry: the U.S. State Department would not traffic in stolen material. Despite the COS's vehement protests, he was granted only one hour to copy the documents.

The documents were soon handed over to the Soviet Ministry of Foreign Affairs, and the KGB predictably began hunting their sender. It did not take long to identify him. Aleksandr Cherepanov, a 20-year veteran of the security service, had fought in the **partisan** war against the Nazis. Assigned to the First (American) Department of the Second (**Counterintelligence**) Chief Directorate, he had become disillusioned with his jobs and sought to volunteer to the Americans. Cherepanov, realizing that something was wrong, sought to escape. After an intense monthlong manhunt, he was captured near the Turkish border. He was tried and shot shortly thereafter.

The Cherepanov affair illustrated how little Americans understood the Soviet Union, even in 1963. In order to curry favor with the Soviets, secret documents were to be handed back and a person's life was to be endangered. The documents provided by Cherepanov provided insights into how the KGB conducted operations against the American embassy, including the use of a tracking chemical called *metka*. The hunt for Cherepanov and his subsequent **execution** showed how deadly serious the KGB played the game.

CHERKASHIN, VIKTOR IVANOVICH (1931–). One of the most successful case officers in modern **KGB** history was Colonel Viktor Cherkashin, who served as the deputy *rezident* for **counterintelligence** in Washington from 1979 to 1986 and was responsible for the recruitment and initial handling of **Aldrich Ames** and **Robert Hanssen**. Cherkashin's career in the security service began in 1952 and lasted for four decades. He began with the Second (English) Department of the KGB's Second Chief Directorate and took part in the arrest of **Oleg Penkovskiy**. He then served several tours abroad as an officer in the foreign counterintelligence component of the First Chief Directorate.

Cherkashin's greatest accomplishment was his handling of Ames and Hanssen. First, he had to verify the bona fides of the two potential agents: Ames volunteered to the Washington *rezidentura*, and Hanssen contacted the KGB by mail. Second, he had to devise ways to run the agents in Washington under the watchful eyes of the Federal Bureau of Investigation. Finally, he had to convince Moscow of the value of the information—proof that more than a dozen highly placed Soviet citizens were working for American and British intelligence.

Cherkashin received the Order of **Lenin** for his success but was never promoted to general officer or given a responsible position in the KGB again. Because of his relationship with **Oleg Kalugin**, he was not fully trusted by KGB Chair **Vladimir Kryuchkov**, and he was assigned to a minor post. In later years, he was blamed for the loss of Ames and Hanssen, and articles appeared in the Russian press accusing him of being a "super mole" in the pay of the Central Intelligence Agency.

CHIEF INTELLIGENCE DIRECTORATE. *See also* GRU (*GLAVNOE RAZVEDIVATELNOE UPRAVLENIYE*); GRU ORGANIZATION.

CHINA. China from the early 1920s was an important intelligence target for Soviet intelligence both to track the strategy of Imperial Japan and to monitor the activity of hostile **émigré** organizations. Both the civilian service and the **GRU** had **illegal** stations in China, with case officers operating under journalist and commercial cover. Important agents such as **Richard Sorge** and **Ruth Werner** ran Japanese and Western agents in Shanghai in the 1930s. Information from Japanese sources developed by Sorge were critical to intelligence strategy during the **Khalkin Gol** crisis of 1939 and the **Battle of Moscow** in 1941.

During the late 1930s and 1940s, the GRU reported on both the Communists and the Kuomintang from sources within China. According to one biography, Mao Zedong's physician was a GRU officer. Joseph Stalin distrusted his China watchers in the intelligence and diplomatic services. Many were purged between 1949 and 1953, effectively blinding Moscow. Following the creation of the People's Republic, Moscow helped Beijing establish an integrated security service, the Ministry of State Security (MSS), similar to the **KGB**. However, as relations cooled in the early 1960s, China became an important intelligence and counterintelligence target: according to *Tower of Secrets*, the memoirs of a former KGB officer, Moscow was surprised at the sophistication of the Chinese electronic attack on their mission.

Both the GRU and the KGB prepared a cadre of Chinese linguists to serve as case officers against the Chinese target. Because of the almost impossible counterintelligence environment in China, the KGB and GRU conducted operations against the Chinese target from Japan, Mongolia, and the Soviet Central Asian republics. A former KGB officer, **Konstantin Preobrazhenskiy**, and a GRU **military attaché**, **Stanislav Lunev**, who have defected to the United States, have written of the frustration the Russian services had in recruiting intelligence sources.

The Chinese intelligence services are apparently active in Russia despite agreements in 1994 between the **SVR** and the GRU with the MSS. In 2007, Igor Reshetin , the chief executive of Tsnimash, and three researchers were sentenced to prison for passing dual-purpose technology. Analysts speculated that the stolen technology could help accelerate the Chinese ballistic missile program. In 2010, the FSB arrested two scientists involved in classified engineering projects. Finally, in 2013, the Russian security service detained a

Chinese citizen who had been collecting information about Russian military and scientific issues. The Russians are also reportedly concerned about Chinese **signals intelligence** operations.

See also LUNEV, STANISLAV (1956–); PREOBRAZHENSKIY, KONSTANTIN GEORGIYEVICH (1953–).

CHORNAYA RABOTA **(BLACK WORK).** The **Communist Party** leadership in **Joseph Stalin**'s time used the term *chornaya rabota* to refer to legal and extralegal **executions**. Stalin ordered the service to carry out extralegal executions of associates, friends, and unwanted witnesses, such as Kira Kulik, the wife of Marshal Grigory Kulik, and Zinaida Raikh, the wife of Vsevold Myerhold, as well as a number of famous Jewish intellectuals. These killings apparently were commissioned out of personal spite by Stalin and his security generalissimo **Lavrenty Beria**. In the 1970s, the **KGB** also used the term *mokroye delo* (wet work) to refer to executions or assassinations.

CIVIL WAR (1918–1921). The **Cheka** played a critical role in the Bolshevik victory in the Russian civil war that left millions dead by bullet, hunger, and cold. **Feliks Dzerzhinsky** and his subordinates provided critical intelligence on the Bolsheviks' White and anarchist opponents, put backbone in the Red Army, and crushed all opposition to communist rule. The Cheka used the **Red Terror** to destroy real and imaginary enemies of Soviet power, executing more than 140,000 men and women.

The Cheka put cadres into every military formation in the new Workers and Peasants' Red Army. These sections kept an eye on tsarist specialists the Bolsheviks had pressed into serving as military commanders. Military power in commands was shared between the Red Army commander, the party's representative, and a **Chekist**. This division of authority in military commands lasted until the collapse of the Soviet Union. The Cheka officers were the bureaucratic ancestors of the officers in the **Third Chief Directorate** of the modern **KGB**. During the civil war, Cheka representatives took over command of major Bolshevik formations after executing the military commander.

A little-known but critical component of the Red victory over the White resistance was the Cheka's role in the Russian and Ukrainian countryside, where **counterintelligence** targeted clergy and peasant rebels for arrest and **execution**. There were more than 100 peasant risings in the winter of 1920–1921 alone, and rebels controlled large sections of western Siberia and Ukraine. During the Antonov revolt in Tambov province (1920–1922), the Cheka identified rebel leaders for liquidation and carried out 2,500 executions of rebels and the **deportation** of 80,000 families. Cheka gangs, disguised as rebels, lured clandestine supporters of Anatoly Antonov into the open for arrest and elimination.

Cheka units also played a critical role in breaking the revolt of Ukrainian anarchists led by Nestor Makhno in Ukraine during the same years. According to a British scholar, Red forces killed more than 200,000 peasants in crushing Makho's revolt. The Cheka was also instrumental in crushing rebellions in Central Asia and the Caucasus. In 1921, when a revolt by anarchist sailors at the naval base at Kronstadt near Leningrad threatened Soviet power, Cheka units led the assault and forced recalcitrant Red Army units to assault the fortress. Following the victory, Cheka units helped the **Communist Party** reestablish power and shot 2,103 rebels captured in the storming of the naval base.

The secret to the Cheka's success was ruthless efficiency and the use of prophylactic Red Terror to destroy all enemies of the regime. While the tsarist regime never mastered the tools of counterterrorism, the Cheka establish a nationwide ring of surveillance to identify enemies of the people. Moreover, the Cheka had no qualms about destroying the "innocent": as Cheka deputy director **Martyn Latsis** said, "We are not waging war against individuals. We are exterminating the bourgeois as a class."

CHILDS, MORRIS (1902–1991). A Soviet intelligence agent who was recruited by the Federal Bureau of Investigation (FBI), Childs accomplished an important penetration of the American **Communist Party** and the **KGB**. Born Moishe Chilovsky, he joined the Communist Party and was recruited by the **OGPU** in 1929. Caught up in the interparty fights of the postwar years, Childs and his brother Jack were recruited by the FBI in 1952. Over the next three decades, he served as a courier, helping Moscow move $28 million to the American party. He made 52 secret trips to Moscow for the American and Soviet parties. For his efforts, Childs received the Order of the Red Banner personally from Communist Party General Secretary **Leonid Brezhnev** in 1977 and the Presidential Medal of Freedom from President Ronald Reagan in 1987.

COHEN, MORRIS (1910–1992), AND COHEN, LONA (1913–1992). Two of Moscow's most important **illegals** in the first decade of the **Cold War**, Lona and Morris Cohen played a critical role in the **Julius Rosenberg** and **Konon Molody** cases. Morris Cohen, a communist since his high school years, served in the Republican Army in Spain, was wounded, and was subsequently recruited there by the **NKVD**. On his return to the United States, he married Lona Petka, a communist activist. During **World War II**, Lona served the NKVD *rezidentura* in New York as a courier between

Soviet intelligence officers and their agents in Los Alamos, New Mexico. She traveled to New Mexico to meet agents and take nuclear weapons information to Soviet case officers in New York. On one occasion when she was being searched by a **counterintelligence** officer, she gave a box of tissues containing the documents to the officer to hold. Since tuberculosis was common in New Mexico, the officer never inspected the box or found the documents. The Cohens later became important players in the Rosenberg spy network in the late 1940s and were forced to flee to Moscow via Mexico when their roles were discovered.

In 1954, under cover as Peter and Helen Kroger, they traveled to London to support Soviet intelligence. Operating from an antiquarian bookshop in a London suburb, they worked closely with Konon Molody (Gordon Lonsdale), who was running important agents within the British navy. They served as clandestine radio operators for several years with the KGB code name "dachatniki" (the vacationers). In 1961, they were arrested with Molody and sentenced to 20 years' imprisonment. Eight years later, they were exchanged for a British agent. The Cohens' life after their release from prison is a mystery. They may have served in Japan as illegals, and they almost certainly worked to train a new generation of Soviet illegals in Moscow.

Following the collapse of the Soviet Union, the Cohens surfaced in Moscow and gave interviews to both the American and the Soviet press. They were of a generation of ideological recruits who had served Moscow and **Joseph Stalin** without question. Morris Cohen was decorated for service to Russia by President **Boris Yeltsin** shortly before his death.

COLD WAR. The Cold War—an ideological struggle between the Bolshevik regime and its enemies—lasted from 7 November 1917 until the collapse of the Soviet Union in August 1991. It has been more narrowly defined as lasting from 1947 until 1991 between the Western democracies and the Soviet Union. The Soviet security and intelligence services played critical offensive and defensive roles in that struggle: they were the "sword and shield" of the **Communist Party**. The security services, beginning with the **Cheka**, pursued enemies of the regime at home and abroad. The Cheka and its successors, as well as the **GRU**, provided four generations of party policymakers with intelligence and the capability of conducting **active measures** against all opponents.

Marxist–Leninist ideology was a key **motivation** in the recruitment of the first generation of Soviet intelligence officers and their agents. Agents like **Kim Philby** saw themselves in a romantic battle for the future. Philby compared himself in later life to English Catholics who in the 16th century decided to serve Spain against their own country in the wars of the Reformation. But ideology was a double-edged sword in the Cold War: when **KGB** and GRU officers like **Petr Popov** and **Dmitry Polyakov** rejected their country's official ideology, they looked for a replacement.

The greatest impact of Cold War ideology was not, however, on the intelligence services. The Soviet political leadership—the Central Committee and the Politburo of the Communist Party—tended to be blinded by Marxist–Leninist thought. The decision to control academic thought through **First Sections** and *Glavlit*, which limited researchers access to foreign books and other publications, delayed the Soviet Union's entrance into the second industrial revolution and its acquisition of computer technology. The decision to prosecute religious and political **dissidents** in the name of ideological conformity undercut Moscow's desire for legitimacy and commercial ties.

See also KONDRASHEV, SERGEI ALEKSANDROVICH (1923–2007); PHILBY, KIM (1912–1988).

COLLABORATORS. The question of Soviet collaboration with the German invaders in the **Great Patriotic War** remain sensitive to this day. Hundreds of thousands of Soviet citizens were pressed into service by the German authorities, and tens of thousands of prisoners of war volunteered or were pressed into the **Vlasov Army**. The **NKVD** and *Smersh* hunted down collaborators after areas were liberated, be they prison camps or Soviet-occupied Eastern Europe. Filtration camps were established to interview people drafted for labor in Germany. Statistics on those condemned are not completely trustworthy. Almost 370,000 civilians were convicted of collaboration following the war. In the western Ukraine, more than 200,000 were **exiled** to Siberia, and probably more than 150,000 were deported to Siberia from the former Baltic states. The leaders of the Vlasov movement were hanged in 1946. The full extent of the butcher bill, however, is unknown. Collaborators were still being uncovered, tried, and executed as late as 1977.

COLLECTIVIZATION. The decision by the Soviet leadership to force the Soviet peasantry into collective and state farms between 1928 and 1932 was executed at a terrible price. More than half the farm animals in the country were killed by peasants refusing to surrender their livestock. Peasant resistance was fierce: according to **OGPU** statistics, in 1930 alone, there were more than 14,000 massive disturbances, resulting in the death of more than 1,000 officials. These riots, often called "grandmother riots" because many were instigated by older peasant women, involved more than 2 million people.

The human cost was incredibly high: in 1930–1931, 381,000 peasant households, or 1.8 million people, were **deported** to Siberia and Central Asia, where many perished in special settlements. In 1932–1933, another

241,000 peasants were deported. Moreover, 5 million to 7 million died in famines that followed collectivization in the early 1930s. The total human cost to the peasantry may have reached 10 million dead. It was the greatest peacetime human tragedy in European history and one remarkably poorly reported at the time.

The OGPU played a critical role in the execution of **Joseph Stalin**'s agricultural policy. The OGPU and Red Army military units put down thousands of peasant revolts, 6,528 in March 1928 alone. To control peasant villages, the security service recruited **informants**, arrested, tried, and executed rebels and opened hundreds of new **gulag** and **exile** communities. According to the Soviet archives, in 1929–1932, 954,000 people were arrested for counterrevolutionary crimes and more than 36,558 executed. Under the law of "seven-eights," so called because it was passed on 7 August 1932, more than 54,000 peasants were convicted and more than 5,400 shot for gleaning more than five shocks of wheat from collective farm fields. As in the case of the most famous informant **Pavlik Morozov** case, some people sent their own parents into exile or labor camps.

During the great Ukrainian famine of 1932–1933, the OGPU and military units stripped peasant households of grain so that the Soviet Union could continue to export it. OGPU troops prevented peasants from fleeing starving villages; peasants who had reached cities were forcibly escorted back to their villages, where they starved. According to one survivor, it was "Auschwitz without the ovens."

The prisoners and the exiles arrested by the OGPU were the basis of the Soviet penal camp empire. Thousands of former peasants were set to work building railroads, lumbering, and mining for gold. Thousands perished building the **Belomor Canal**. Collectivization had another important impact on the security service: the need to monitor and punish the rural population and to expand the gulag system meant that the security service had to expand rapidly. The OGPU had become by 1934 a major player in Soviet politics at every level, from Stalin's Politburo to the collectivized village.

COMINTERN. The Communist International, or Comintern, was founded in Moscow in March 1919 to serve as the general staff of the world revolution. The second conference of the Comintern in 1920 laid out 21 conditions that socialist and **communist parties** had to adhere to for membership; foremost among them was loyalty to the Soviet Union. Created by **Vladimir Lenin** to mobilize support for the Bolshevik Revolution and spread revolution, the Comintern became as well a critical component of Soviet intelligence for the 24 years of its existence. The **OMS** (Comintern Foreign Liaison Department) acted as an adjunct for the Soviet intelligence service. Both

Soviet services used the Comintern as a cover for **false flag** operations for the recruitment and running of agents. Many of the best Soviet agents in the 1930s believed at first that they were working for the Comintern.

The Comintern developed clandestine radio networks to allow Moscow to maintain contact with foreign communist parties and intelligence officers. During the 1930s, the Comintern maintained three radio links with the Communist Party of the United States (CPUSA). Radio links were also maintained with Western and Central European communist parties. These links allowed the Soviet intelligence services to vet prospective agents and to convince party officials to support intelligence operations. For example, **Pavel Fitin**, chief of **NKVD** foreign intelligence during **World War II**, requested information about Communist Party members who were being considered for recruitment in the United States, Mexico, and Canada.

Soviet leader **Joseph Stalin** used the Comintern to control foreign communist parties. He also purged its leadership of **dissidents** and suspected enemies. During the *Yezhovshchina*, the Polish, Hungarian, Austrian, and German parties were decimated. The entire leadership of the Polish party and most of the leadership of the Hungarian, Austrian, and German parties were shot or perished in the **gulag**. Over 1,100 German communists were arrested by the NKVD, and 132 were eventually handed over to the Gestapo as a gesture of goodwill following the Nazi–Soviet Pact.

While the Comintern was initially established to foment world revolution, it evolved into an extension of the **Communist Party of the Soviet Union** and was seen by the Stalinist leadership as a tool for Russian strategic interests. One leader of the Comintern put it succinctly and cynically: "Since Russia is the only country where the working class has taken power, the workers of the world should become Russian patriots." Stalin abolished the Comintern in 1943 as part of a diplomatic effort to win support for the Soviet Union during World War II. Its functions were transferred to the International Department of the Communist Party's Central Committee. At almost the same time, NKVD officers abroad were cautioned about open contacts with Communist Party members and Comintern officials; in the United States, the handling of especially important agents was switched from CPUSA personnel to Soviet agent handlers. Nevertheless, by the 1940s, the link between communist parties and Soviet intelligence services was clear.

COMMUNIST PARTIES (FOREIGN). Between **World War I** and **World War II**, foreign communist parties tamely accepted the directions of Moscow. The **Comintern**, with its offices in Moscow, controlled the parties through the assignment of special Comintern representatives, financial subsidies, and discipline. Failure to accept the party line meant excommunication. Before 1945, the Soviet intelligence services had a close and symbiotic relationship with foreign communists. Communist Party members became a pool of recruits for the services: the code word for party members in Soviet intelligence traffic was "fellow countrymen." After 1945, Soviet intelligence had greater luck in recruiting communists in France, Italy, and Germany on ideological grounds. The American and British pools had pretty much dried up.

The Comintern and then after 1943 the international department of the Communist Party's Central Committee used the security service to deliver cash to foreign communist parties. As late as the **Mikhail Gorbachev** years, the **KGB** delivered an annual stipend of $2 million to the Communist Party of the United States (CPUSA). The Soviet archives reveal that the KGB brought similar stipends to many North American and European parties. In the case of the CPUSA, it was a waste of funds. The CPUSA barely attracted 20,000 voters in presidential elections and had no impact on American culture or society.

See also COMINTERN.

COMMUNIST PARTY OF THE SOVIET UNION (CPSU). The Soviet security services had a symbiotic relationship with the ruling Communist Party. The **Cheka** styled itself as the "sword and shield" of the party, and the successive services maintained this relationship. Indeed, the identification cards of **KGB** officers had embossed on them a sword and shield. When **Joseph Stalin** served as party leader from 1924 to 1953, he managed the service through a **Special Department**. Stalin paid close attention to the assignment of senior officers and often communicated with them through telegrams and personal letters. He encouraged **Chekisty** to bring their concerns to him, and he became the prime consumer of gossip and denunciations from officials in the field. Stalin also stayed close to the leaders of the service: both **Nikolai Yezhov** and **Lavrenty Beria** were frequent guests at his apartment and vacation homes.

After Stalin's death in 1953, **Nikita Khrushchev** reduced the authority of the KGB in relation to the Communist Party. KGB officers could not arrest senior party officials without the permission of the Central Committee. The party's **Administrative Organs Department** vetted all senior police appointments. For Khrushchev, the KGB was the servant of the party—as well as its avenging sword and shield. Under Khrushchev's successor **Leonid Brezhnev**, the KGB was even further restricted from reporting on developments in the party. The years of Brezhnev's rule were often referred to as "stagnation," as the party leadership in Moscow and the provinces became more entrenched and corrupt. KGB officers reported on gross economic malfeasance to chair **Yuri Andropov** but were well aware that their reports would rarely be acted on. In the years of stagnation, in the provinces and in the center, KGB generals were co-opted by the party. By the 1970s, senior KGB officials were appointed to the Communist Party's Central Committee.

At the local level, senior KGB officers were appointed to the Communist Party's leadership bodies. This interlocking directorate of party and police gradually eroded the effectiveness of the KGB as a guarantee of political and social cohesion, and it corrupted the KGB at the local level.

The Communist Party that **Mikhail Gorbachev** inherited in 1985 was a very dull tool for change. Efforts to raise political consciousness by his twin programs of *glasnost* and *perestroika* were opposed by both the party and the police, which saw it as endangering their prerogatives. In a major speech in 1987, KGB chair **Viktor Chebrikov** attacked reform efforts as undercutting party authority. The Communist Party elite sourly accepted changes in the late 1980s, predicting as they did that any reduction of party authority would lead to chaos. KGB officers watching history unfold before them in the last years of the Gorbachev administration knew they were witnessing the loss of the Soviet empire that Stalin had created. The **August putsch** in 1991 was the last desperate act of these traditionalists to change history.

See also COMINTERN.

CONRAD, CLYDE LEE (1944–1998). Conrad was recruited and run by the Hungarian military intelligence service (MNVK/2) for their Soviet allies for more than a decade. As an active-duty and recently retired army senior sergeant, Conrad had access to highly classified information about the North Atlantic Treaty Organization and American war plans. He also was able to recruit a number of other American noncommissioned officers. Conrad and other members of his ring were paid over $1.5 million for division, corps, and army-level operational plans. The first lead to Conrad's ring came from Vladimir Vasilev, a **GRU** officer serving in Budapest. Vasilev informed his Central Intelligence Agency (CIA) case officer of the danger of the spy ring, noting with little exaggeration that it was the biggest Soviet military intelligence case in the **Cold War**. Conrad became the target of a joint CIA and military intelligence investigation that led to the arrest of 11 men and women working for MNVK/2 in Germany, Sweden, and Austria. Conrad was tried for espionage in a German court; the post-Soviet Hungarian government provided some evidence for the prosecution. He was sentenced to life imprisonment and died in a German prison in 1998. Because Conrad was not convicted by an American court, he continued to receive his military pension until he died in jail.

CONSTANTINI, FRANCESCO (ca. 1900–?). An Italian employee of the British embassy in Rome, Constantini served as a Soviet agent for more than a decade. Under the code name "Duncan," he provided his Soviet handlers with British code material and diplomatic dispatches. In 1935, more than 100 British documents that he stole were translated and presented to **Joseph**

Stalin. Francesco's brother Secondo also spied for the Soviet Union with the code name "Dudley." Like his brother, he was highly valued by the British diplomatic community and in 1937 was given an all-expenses paid vacation to London to witness the coronation of King George VI.

The British embassy in Rome did not have a security officer in the years between **World War I** and **World War II**. Local employees, such as the Constantinis, were given access to the ambassador's safe. They were even given responsibility for locking the embassy at night. The benefit to Moscow from the Constantinis' spying was immense: it gave Soviet **signals intelligence** the ability to read British coded material for more than a decade. The Constantinis were, however, more entrepreneurial than Moscow would have liked: they also sold British diplomatic dispatches and codes to the Italian government.

COPLON, JUDITH (1922–2011). Born into a middle-class Jewish family in New York and educated at Barnard College, Judith Coplon joined the U.S. Justice Department as a clerk in 1943. Her background investigation disclosed that she had been a member of several pro-communist groups while a student, but this fact was ignored. Coplon, who had access to Federal Bureau of Investigation (FBI) information about Soviet intelligence activities, was recruited by a Soviet intelligence officer under journalist cover. In a cable to Moscow, **Vladimir Pravdin** wrote that she was "a serious person who is politically well developed." She was rapidly promoted at Justice and was equally appreciated by the **NKVD** *rezidentura*, which assigned an experienced case officer, Valentin Gubitchev, to work with her. Coplon was identified through **Venona** intercepts and became the object of an intense FBI investigation. She was arrested in 1949 with Gubitchev, who was under cover as a UN employee and was permitted to return to Moscow.

The trial of Coplon was one of the first espionage scandals of the **Cold War**. Filled with dramatic evidence of espionage and Coplon's love life, it ended with her conviction and a 10-year sentence. The sentence was overturned on appeal, as was her second espionage conviction. Coplon never served a day in prison, though evidence of her espionage activities was devastating. She later married one of her defense attorneys and raised several children. Her case demonstrated the problem that American authorities had in proving espionage in open courts, and it raised doubts about the FBI's handling of spy cases.

COT, PIERRE (1895–1977). Cot, who served in six French cabinets as minister of aviation, was first recruited by the **NKVD** in the 1930s. The relationship was renewed in 1943 in Washington, where Cot reportedly approached American Communist Party boss **Earl Browder** and was put in contact with Soviet intelligence officers. An intercepted message indicated that Browder contacted NKVD foreign intelligence chief **Pavel Fitin** about the approach. NKVD *rezident* **Vasily Zarubin** personally ran Cot, a member of Charles de Gaulle's Free French administration. Cot, code-named "Daedalus," provided Moscow with details about the Gaullist movement. He also collaborated with agents of the French Communist Party and the **Comintern**. One cable to Moscow read, "Daedalus will obey unquestionably." In 1944, Cot was sent to Moscow as de Gaulle's personal emissary to **Joseph Stalin**. Following the war, Cot served again as minister of aviation and remained a staunch supporter of strong Soviet–French relations. In 1953, he received the Stalin Peace Prize. He was never prosecuted for espionage.

COUNTERINTELLIGENCE. The principal raison d'être of the Soviet intelligence services was counterintelligence. From the formation of the **Cheka**, the services sought to deceive, penetrate, and destroy all enemy services and **émigré** movements, which were seen as a threat to Moscow. In the first days of the regime, the Cheka copied much of the **tradecraft** of the tsarist *Okhrana*: double agents were run to penetrate émigré movements, and agents provocateurs were used to entrap enemy agents. These operations were run by the Cheka's counterintelligence arm, the KRU (Counterintelligence Directorate), which identified the enemy apparatus inside the Soviet Union and abroad and took steps to end the threat. One of the steps used was assassination, but more often enemy agents were the target of recruitment efforts.

From the 1950s on, the **KGB** had several components dedicated to counterintelligence. The Second Chief Directorate (SCD) was responsible for counterintelligence operations inside the Soviet Union. To defeat enemy intelligence operations, the KGB ran operational games to engage intelligence officers. These games usually involved **double agents**. The SCD was seen as the single most important component of the service and had offices in every republic and oblast in the Soviet Union. It also trained allied services in counterintelligence tradecraft.

The **Third Chief Directorate**, inheriting many of the responsibilities once held by *Smersh*, was responsible for counterintelligence within the military as well as the **GRU** and the police. During the Russian **civil war**, the Cheka had created a component to ensure the loyalty of the military, which included tsarist officers. (The military counterintelligence directorate was established in December 1919, a year before the formation of the Cheka's foreign intelligence component.) These *Osobiy otdel* (Special Sections) had broad power of arrest, prosecution, and **execution**. Until the collapse of the regime in 1991, the Third Chief Directorate had agents in every battalion and ran agents within the police and the GRU.

Directorate K of the First Chief Directorate was responsible for running counterintelligence operations abroad. Its target was the intelligence and security services of enemy states. Under General **Oleg Kalugin**, Directorate K had a number of major successes. This success continued into the 1980s and 1990s with the recruitment of **Edward Howard, Aldrich Ames**, and **Robert Hanssen**. Directorate K was also responsible for the security of foreign missions abroad. Every KGB report from 1985 on had details of Directorate K work in thwarting the defection of Soviet citizens.

The Seventh Directorate was responsible for the physical and technical **surveillance** of known and suspected intelligence officers and their Soviet contacts. Other directorates had responsibility for counterintelligence in the economy, the transportation bureaucracy, and the intelligentsia. In effect, these components of the KGB were more responsible for sniffing out corruption and dealing with anti-Soviet elements than for detecting foreign spies. Nevertheless, the KGB saw these "political" responsibilities as part of its broad counterintelligence mission of protecting the party from subversion and corruption.

Following the fall of the Soviet Union, the Russian foreign intelligence and counterintelligence services continue to run operations against foreign intelligence services. Since 1991, the **SVR**, the new Russian foreign intelligence service, has run two officers of the Central Intelligence Agency and two special agents of the Federal Bureau of Investigation. It would seem from an examination of these cases that the foreign counterintelligence responsibilities of the KGB transferred seamlessly to the successor services.

The **FSB**, the new security service, has been no less busy. The FSB's official website reported the arrest and prosecution of 87 Russian civilian and military personnel for spying or revealing state secrets in 2002 alone. In the last five years, the FSB has identified agents from the United States, the United Kingdom, and China, to name only its major targets. The FSB also pursues political **dissidents** as part of its counterintelligence mission and has arrested several for revealing "state secrets" to foreign governments and nongovernmental organizations. Since the collapse of the Soviet Union, however, convicted spies are no longer shot but receive jail terms.

COUNTERTERRORISM. Until the death of **Joseph Stalin** in 1953, the Soviet Union broadly defined opposition to the Soviet state as terrorism. Millions went to the **gulag**—or the grave—for terrorism offensives such as owning a book of Nikolai Bukharin or telling a joke about Stalin. Post-Stalin legal reforms drastically redefined treason to make it closer to the accepted Western legal definition. The post-Stalin **KGB** had to cope with some political terrorism in the Caucasus and Central Asia. In the late 1970s, three young Armenians were executed for planting a bomb on the Moscow subway.

Since the collapse of the Soviet Union in 1991, Moscow has had to face terrorism from Chechnya and other Muslim enclaves, and Russia has faced a plague of terrorist incidents since 1994. Incidents have included the bombing of buses, bus stations, and schools; hostage taking; and the suicide bombing of Russian aircraft. Civilian casualties have been heavy: a database maintained by the University of Chicago shows that between 2000 and 2011, Chechen terrorist conducted 60 suicide attacks inside Russia that claimed 781 lives and wounded more than 2,300. The **FSB** has primary responsibility for the field of counterterrorism in Russia. It has also broadened its search for international allies in the fight against terrorism. In January 2005, the FSB signed an agreement with the Federal Bureau of Investigation.

In June 2000, the Russian government created the *Antiterroristicheskiy tsentr* (Anti-Terrorist Center), or ATTs, of the Commonwealth of Independent States, drawing its cadre from many of the republics of the Soviet Union. The Russian component of the ATTs is under the National Security Council. The first head of the center, Colonel General Boris Melnikov, and his two chief subordinates were KGB veterans from Kazakhstan and Kirghizstan. The center has both operational and **analytical** components and is headquartered in Moscow. Special force components (*Spetznaz*) of the security services and military also have responsibility for counterterrorism operations. The ATTs website proudly notes that the combined services have sought assistance from Germany, Japan, and Austria as well as the "special services" of the United States.

Presidents **Boris Yeltsin** and **Vladimir Putin** have been critical of their country's counterterrorism operations. In the first of the **Chechen wars**, Chechen rebels seized towns inside Russia and held buildings against determined assaults by *Spetznaz* units before withdrawing to safe havens in Chechnya. Russian special forces also badly botched a hostage situation in a school in **Beslan** in southern Russia in 2004, suggesting that the service would expend more resources for additional training and equipment. Terrorist incidents in Volgograd in late 2013 showed that the FSB and other counterterrorist elements faced an enemy that has not been defeated.

CRIMEAN CRISIS. Following the political crisis in the Ukrainian capital in early 2014, Russian militia quickly took control of the Crimean provincial and local governments. These militias were well armed and led by senior **GRU** *Spetznaz* officers. Ukrainian governance was quickly ended, and a pro-Moscow government, supported by Russian intelligence officers, took control.

Crimea's status remains in dispute. Ukrainian authority has ceased to exist, and Moscow has yet to try to incorporate it legally into Russia. The GRU played a critical role in the crisis, acting as both a political and a military arm of President **Vladimir Putin**. The relatively easy success of the GRU-led coup clearly emboldened Moscow to try similar tactics in the eastern **Ukraine**.

See also GIRKIN, IGOR VSEVOLODOVICH (1970–); UKRAINIAN CRISIS

CRIMEAN WAR. Russian diplomacy in the early 1850s played a critical role in isolating Russia in the first general European war since Waterloo. Disputes over European issues and the question of which country controlled sites in the Holy Land precipitated a war that left Russia alone against an Anglo-French entente assisted by Sardinia. Even Russia's friend Austria stayed neutral. The struggle between Russian and Anglo-French forces on the Crimean Peninsula—the war's main front—between 1854 and 1856 demonstrated the woeful state of the Russian army. In the four decades since the Napoleonic Wars, the Russian army had been the "gendarme of Europe," crushing national revolts in Poland and Hungary. The army had not been modernized and was accustomed to fighting wars against Muslim rebels in the Caucasus and poorly armed Polish and Hungarian rebels.

Russian military intelligence was ill prepared to fight a war against major European powers. There was, for example, no system for interrogating prisoners of war or deserters. (A few Irish and Corsican prisoners apparently deserted to the Russians during the course of the war.) Nevertheless, military intelligence did provide accurate information about the British and French armies, tactics, and leadership. Military intelligence information on the enemy may also have played a role in the inventive way the Russian army, under the direction of E. I. Totleben, built fortifications at Sevastopol to cope with the Anglo-French forces.

The Crimean War cost Russia 600,000 casualties. It also demonstrated to the new tsar, Aleksandr II, that social and political reform would be needed if Russia were to remain a great European power. Many believe that the disastrous performance of the Russian forces in the Crimean War caused Aleksandr to emancipate the Russian serfs. The war also led to major reforms in the Russian army and general staff. The tsar realized that the fabled army that had terrorized liberal Europe after Waterloo was a paper tiger.

CUBAN MISSILE CRISIS. American intelligence won a critical victory over the Soviet services in the Cuban Missile Crisis by its ability to collect, **analyze**, and use intelligence information. Using *maskirovka* tactics, the Soviet military and the **KGB** deceived the West in the movement of 40,000 troops and nuclear-tipped missiles to Fidel Castro's Cuba in the summer of 1962. Moreover, through the use of Georgi Bolshakov, an intelligence officer under journalist cover, Moscow deceived the Kennedy administration as to

Soviet intentions. Moscow used Bolshakov as a **back channel** to President John F. Kennedy and his brother, Attorney General Robert Kennedy, to provide assurances that the Soviet government was not going to deploy nuclear missiles to the island nation.

The Soviet's international position was undone through findings picked up by U-2 aircraft and information provided by Colonel **Oleg Penkovskiy**, a **GRU** officer who volunteered to work for British and American intelligence. Penkovskiy provided detailed information from top-secret publications on Soviet missiles, while the U-2 flights gave the Kennedy administration detailed evidence of the Soviet buildup in Cuba. The information from technical and human intelligence sources showed that the Soviets had not married nuclear weapons to the missiles and thus were not immediately prepared to launch a nuclear strike; it also showed that the Soviets were far behind the United States in missile technology. Using the intelligence information, President Kennedy was able to call Soviet leader **Nikita Khrushchev**'s bluff and demand the pullout of the missiles.

Moscow used its KGB *rezident* **Aleksandr Feklisov** as a back channel to end the crisis. Feklisov, who had served in Washington as a case officer during the 1940s, presented Soviet policy options to ABC News correspondent John Scali, who had connections to the Kennedy administration. Feklisov, operating in Washington under the name "Fomin," probably did more to confuse the Kennedy administration, which was by then wary of any new channels.

The Cuban crisis taught Soviet intelligence officers and diplomats a number of lessons. Soviet Ambassador Andrei Dobrynin, who would go on to serve another 24 years in Washington, insisted that he would henceforth control all back channels to American policymakers, explaining that the actions of Bolshakov and Feklisov had badly compromised the embassy. The Soviet army and the intelligence services presumably learned a great deal about American technical collection and analysis, prompting the creation of a massive deception program.

CURRIE, LAUCHLIN (1903–1993). One of the most disputed cases of **Cold War** espionage revolves around the life of Lauchlin Currie. Born in Canada, Currie immigrated to the United States, received a PhD from Harvard University, and became an American citizen in 1934. A brilliant economist, he joined the White House staff of President Franklin D. Roosevelt in 1939. Soviet intelligence messages from the 1940s show that Currie met on several occasions with two **NKVD** *rezident*s, **Vasily Zarubin** and **Anatoli Gorskiy**. In the intelligence messages, he is referred to by the cover name "Page." **Elizabeth Bentley** informed American **counterintelligence** in 1945 that Currie was an important agent of the **Silvermaster Group**.

Currie became the focus of a series of investigations in the late 1940s. He admitted that he had met with Gorskiy "to discuss Soviet culture," but he denied all charges that he was a Soviet agent. He left the United States in the early 1950s, moved to South America, and took Colombian citizenship. For years, Currie was portrayed as a victim of a witch hunt who had been forced to flee his adopted country. The opening of the **Venona** documents, however, indicated that the NKVD considered Currie an agent, and a retired KGB major general classified him as a "sub-source of the Silvermaster group" who provided valuable information. As in the case of **Harry Dexter White**, scholars still argue over how seriously to take the information from Cold War "witnesses" like Bentley and the Venona material.

CYBERWAR. The first years of the 21st century have demonstrated the competence of the Russian Federation's **intelligence community** in the field of cyberwarfare. In 2006–2007, utilizing a mixture of electronic warfare, computer denial of service, and *maskirovka*, Moscow has extended its strategic reach against potential opponents within the former Soviet Union. Intelligence specialists believe that cyberwarfare is a military trump card that could be played in other international crises. In April 2015, the Russian press boasted that hackers had accessed the White House's unclassified e-mails.

DALSTROI. *Dalstroi* is the Russian acronym for "Far Northern Construction Trust." *Dalstroi* ran the **Kolyma** River complex of forced labor camps in the **gulag** system.

DECEMBRISTS' REVOLT. In 1825, following the death of Tsar Aleksandr I, a group of Imperial Army officers moved to rebel against Aleksandr's brother Nicholas, heir to the throne. The plotters, all drawn from the nobility and veterans of the Napoleonic Wars, sought a confrontation in Senate Square in St. Petersburg on 14 December, when the troops were to take the oath of allegiance to the new autocrat. A second confrontation between rebels and imperial troops took place in southern Russia. The confrontation ended with troops loyal to the new tsar firing on the rebels, many of whom were peasant soldiers who did not even know the cause of the confrontation. For example, rebel troops chanted *"Konstantin i Konstatutsiya"* (Constantine and constitution), but when asked what this meant, the soldiers told the authorities that Konstantin was the legitimate tsar and that Konstatutsiya—a female noun in Russian—was his wife.

The leaders of the revolt were arrested in the capital and the provinces. Five of the conspirators were hanged, and 121 were sentenced to **exile** or imprisonment in Siberia. The Decembrists' Revolt was an important watershed in the history of the Russian internal security service, convincing the new tsar that the threat to his regime came not from a peasant revolution but from young officers contaminated with the virus of liberalism. It also convinced the new autocrat to form a security police, the **Third Section**, to conduct **surveillance** of those suspected of disloyalty and treason. Russians honor the Decembrists as the first Russian revolutionaries.

Joseph Stalin was very conscious of the Decembrists' example. He believed that just as the Decembrists had been impressed with the West during 1812–1814, so Soviet officers exposed to the West during **World War II** could also be seduced into rebellion and treason. For this reason, Stalin and his major security lieutenants carefully monitored the attitude of soldiers who had served in Germany, from the rank of marshal down. Shortly after victory over Nazi Germany in 1945, several leading officers were arrested, and Marshal **Georgi Zhukov** was banished to a military district to rusticate.

DEFECTORS. During the history of the **Cold War**, intelligence officers, diplomats, military personnel, and ordinary citizens crossed to the other side. However, for the most part, it was Soviet citizens who fled westward. The Soviet intelligence services suffered a plague of defections, as hundreds of intelligence officers went over to the West between 1930 and 1991. In the late 1920s, approximately 60 Soviet officials concerned about the purge of **Leon Trotsky**'s followers sought contact with Western governments or with Trotsky himself. In the late 1930s, Stalin's purge of the **NKVD** led several senior officers to defect, along with two Soviet ambassadors. Unfortunately for the West, much of their information was not acted on for a decade. During **World War II**, more Soviet officials defected rather than return to Moscow. Among them were **Walter Krivitsky, Alexander Orlov**, and **Ignatz Poretsky**.

Despite defections to the West during the **Great Patriotic War**, no regular intelligence officer collaborated with the Nazis. During the war, a **GRU** officer of Turkic nationality, **Ismail Akhmedov**, refused to return to Moscow and remained in Turkey, fearing punishment for operational errors. Other officials sought to remain in the United States. The most important of these early defections occurred in September 1945, when **Igor Gouzenko**, a GRU code clerk in Canada, defected, providing critical information about the scope of Soviet intelligence operations in Canada and the United Kingdom.

Defections continued through the post-Stalinist period as GRU and **KGB** officers crossed the lines. Often they came because of concerns about party or service bureaucratic rivalries. In January 1954, a week after **Lavrenty Beria**'s **execution, Yuri Rastvorov**, a KGB officer serving in Tokyo, defected to avoid recall to Moscow. Most of these men and women were also motivated by personal concerns—charges of poor performance, unhappy marriages, or simply a desire to live better in the West. Some, like **Oleg Gordievskiy**, defected for ideological reasons. The Western intelligence services also harvested defectors from Moscow's East European satellites as military attachés, diplomats, and case officers sought sanctuary in the West through the course of the Cold War. The most important of these East Europeans was **Michael Goleniewski**, who exposed KGB operations throughout Europe. A number of Czech intelligence officers defected in 1968 following the Soviet intervention.

Defectors provided Western **counterintelligence** services with important sources of information on Soviet intelligence agents and their **tradecraft**, as well as political and military information. They often, however, created major problems for their hosts, who found the handling of former intelligence officers difficult. **Anatoli Golitsyn**'s misleading information about KGB operations destroyed the careers of several senior Central Intelligence Agency officers and led to the illegal incarceration of another defector, **Yuri Nosenko**.

The care and feeding of defectors was not easy for either the United States or the Soviet Union. Some of the British defectors, such as **Kim Philby** and **Donald Maclean**, believed they did not receive the respect or the work in Moscow that they deserved. A number of Soviet defectors in the West returned to the Soviet Union, most notably **Vitaliy Yurchenko**. Dealing with the egos and fears of those who changed sides was an art form neither side totally mastered.

See also AGABEKOV, GEORGE [GEORGI SERGEEVICH ARTUNYAN] (1896–1937); AKHMEDOV, ISMAIL GUSSEYNOVICH (1904–?).

DEKANOZOV, VLADIMIR GEORGEVICH (1898–1953). One of the better educated of the early **Chekists**, Dekanozov attended school in Baku in 1915–1916 with **Lavrenty Beria** and **Vsevold Merkulov**, for whom he later worked in state security. After serving in the security police in Azerbaijan and Georgia, Dekanozov worked in **Communist Party** posts under Georgian party boss Beria in 1931–1938. In November 1938, Beria brought Dekanozov with him to Moscow, where he served briefly as chief of **counterintelligence** and then foreign intelligence. In May 1939, Dekanozov transferred to the Ministry of Foreign Affairs and served in Berlin as ambassador from November 1939 to the outbreak of war on 22 June 1941. Prior to Operation **Barbarossa**, Dekanozov repeatedly if ineffectually warned Beria about German preparations for war.

Following **World War II**, Dekanozov served as Beria's man in a number of critical positions. Following **Joseph Stalin**'s death in March, Beria brought Dekanozov back into the security police and assigned him to Georgia to coordinate internal security. Dekanozov was arrested a week after Beria's fall. He was tried with his longtime mentor and executed with him on 23 December 1953. In 2000, the Russian Supreme Court reversed the sentence to 25 years' imprisonment, allowing Dekanozov's heirs to claim his estate.

DEPORTATIONS. Prior to **World War II**, the **NKVD** experimented with the mass deportation of suspected peoples. In 1935, NKVD commissar **Genrykh Yagoda** ordered the deportation of 40,000 Finns, Poles, and Germans from the Leningrad oblast as a reaction to the murder of **Sergei Kirov**. Between May and October 1937, 172,000 Koreans living in the Soviet Far

East were deported to Kazakhstan and Uzbekistan. The NKVD also moved several Polish settlements in Ukraine and Byelorussia in 1937 and 1938 as part of a purge of Polish enemies.

During World War II, the NKVD deported to the **gulag** and internally **exiled** millions of Soviet citizens. Between 1939 and 1941, more than 1 million Poles and 200,000 Balts were deported, 5 percent of the population of the three Baltic republics. In August 1941, following the outbreak of war, 1.2 million Soviet Germans, including all 600,000 German inhabitants of the Volga Autonomous Republic, were deported. In 1943–1944, **Joseph Stalin** ordered the deportation of Islamic peoples from the Caucasus and the Crimean Peninsula to Siberia. More than 1.5 million Chechen, Ingush, Balkars, and Crimean Tatars (just to mention the larger groups) were deported.

The **Communist Party** and the police used deportations to reduce the native populations of Lithuania and the western Ukraine following the end of World War II. In fighting insurgencies in these two republics, the **MGB** deported hundreds of thousands of villagers to Central Asia. Mikhail Suslov, who was Stalin's man in Lithuania in 1944–1946, said that the way to keep Lithuania quiet was to have enough boxcars ready. Stalin also insisted on the ethnic cleansing of Islamic peoples along the Soviet–Turkish border, who were presumed to be future traitors in a war with Turkey, a member of the North Atlantic Treaty Organization.

Deportations were conducted under inhuman conditions by armed security forces showing no mercy for men, women, and children who were considered traitors to the motherland for their suspected support of Nazi Germany or Poland. Thousands of deportees were murdered by NKVD special troops or died in transit. Crimean and Chechen historians estimate that one-third of those deported died in transit or in their first year of exile. **Lavrenty Beria** rewarded his officers responsible for the deportations: in 1944, 413 NKVD officers received decorations for their role in the deportation of Chechen and Ingush peoples.

Following the war, most of the Ukrainians and Lithuanians returned from exile. In the 1950s and 1960s, the Muslim peoples of the Caucasus were "forgiven" and allowed to return to their mountain homes. For the Volga German and Crimean Tatars, forgiveness was not immediately forthcoming, and most remained in exile until the 1980s. Today, the majority of Volga Germans and Koreans continue to live in Kazakhstan. For the Chechens, memory of exile and their hatred of Russian occupation spurred resistance to Moscow in the two **Chechen wars** of the late 1990s.

DERYABIN, PETR SERGEEVICH (1921–1992). One of the first important **KGB defectors**, Deryabin was a war hero who was wounded three times as a young officer in **World War II**. Recruited into the **MGB**, he first served in the Ninth (Guards) Directorate and then was posted to Vienna with the

First Chief Directorate. In the early 1950s, he defected to the Central Intelligence Agency, which safely exfiltrated him out of Austria. Deryabin later wrote a number of books on KGB operations.

DÉTENTE. Détente lasted from 1972 to 1981 and is seen as a success for both American and Soviet diplomacy. American President Richard Nixon saw détente as a means of reducing the tensions of the **Cold War** and expanding commercial ties with the Soviet bloc. The Soviet understanding of the process of détente was different. Soviet party leader **Leonid Brezhnev** told the Politburo, "We communists have to string along with the capitalists for a while. We need their credits, their agriculture, and their technology. But we are going to continue massive military programs, and by the mid-1980s we will be in a position to return to a more aggressive foreign policy." Brezhnev's tactics may have been influenced by **analysis** from the Central Committee that capitalism was weakened and that the Soviet Union was in the driver's seat.

The **KGB** saw détente as a golden age in which to collect technical and industrial intelligence. Throughout the 1970s, the KGB strengthened Directorate T of the First Chief Directorate and its **Line X** (Scientific Intelligence) officers in *rezidenturas* abroad. More than 200 Line X officers were operating in Western states in the mid-1970s. The **GRU** also increased its scientific and technical collection. Détente often gave Soviet intelligence officers access to sensitive plants, and they took advantage of almost every collection opportunity. For instance, a KGB officer visiting the Boeing plant in Seattle, Washington, put adhesive tape on his shoes to collect metal samples.

Détente also provided the **Communist Party** and the KGB with a challenge. A policy of even partial openness seemed to encourage dissent, which the Brezhnev leadership was determined to stifle. In the 1970s, the KGB cracked down very hard on religious and political **dissidents** to show that détente did not mean liberalization. Nevertheless, in the Baltic republics and Ukraine, détente did spur nationalist and religious dissent. In Moscow, Soviet human rights organizations and critics like **Andrei Sakharov** emerged, only to be quickly crushed by the KGB.

Détente is often seen as a setback for the naive Western democracies in the intelligence Cold War. It is true that the Soviet economy benefited from the collection of industrial intelligence. But the period forced the Soviet Union to become more dependent on Western foreign credits, foreign food, and pilfered technology. In 1980, after a decade of détente, the Soviet economy was stagnant, its growth barely at 1 percent. Moreover, détente also spurred intellectual diversity inside the Soviet bloc despite the best efforts of the KGB and its allies.

DEUTSCH, ARNOLD (1904–1942?). One of the most gifted of the Soviet **illegals**, Deutsch received a PhD from the University of Vienna at the age of 24. While a graduate student, Deutsch was active in Austrian Communist Party and **Comintern** business. A brilliant student who mastered French, English, and other languages, Deutsch was recruited by the **NKVD** to act as an illegal recruiter and agent handler in the early 1930s.

Operating under the pseudonym "Otto," Deutsch recruited and ran 16 agents in Great Britain, including **Kim Philby**, **Guy Burgess**, and **Anthony Blunt**, during the mid-1930s. Deutsch had a reputation as a skillful street case officer, capable of both inspiring and teaching his agents. In 1938, he was pulled out of contact with his British agents and recalled to Moscow. Unlike so many of the illegals who were summarily executed, Deutsch was relegated to a desk job. He reportedly perished in 1942 when his ship was torpedoed by a German U-boat while he was on the way to an undercover mission in the United States, where he would have acted as illegal *rezident*. He reportedly died heroically trying to save other passengers on the ship. A more recent account of the Philby case maintains, however, that Deutsch was executed in the purges.

DEZA. Disinformation, or *deza*, was used as a tool of Soviet **active measures** during the **Cold War**.

DICKSTEIN, SAMUEL (1885–1954). The only known member of the U.S. Congress on the Soviet intelligence service's payroll, Samuel Dickstein spied for money. Dickstein, who served 22 years in the U.S. House of Representatives, had the derogatory code name "Crook" in the Soviet files. He was paid $1,250 a month for information his committee gathered on anti-Soviet refugees in the United States. His information was useful to the Soviets for targeting **Trotskyites**. The **NKVD** *rezident* in New York, **Gaik Ovakimyan**, had no illusions about his agent, characterizing him in a telegram in 1938 to Moscow as "a complete racketeer and a blackmailer." Dickstein told his Soviet handler that he was also working for Polish intelligence because of the high cost of political campaigning.

DISSIDENTS. In the tsarist period, intellectual dissent originated with Russian military officers who had served in the Napoleonic Wars as well as with a small group of nobility exposed to radical French, English, and German philosophy. This culminated in the **Decembrists' Revolt** of 1825. Despite Nicholas I's repressive regime, some political dissent emerged in the 1840s, such as the publication of Aleksandr Hetzen's *Kolokol* (The Bell), which questioned tsarist authority. In the 1860s, a new generation of intellectuals—many the children of the clergy and the middle class—became more vocal and radical in opposing autocracy. From these radicals came two streams of political opinion: populism (*narodnichestvo*), with its belief in the peasant villages as the engine of change, and Marxism.

The tsarist authorities never understood dissent. The **Third Section** and later the ***Okhrana*** only poorly comprehended their opponents. They never really understood that the threat to the regime was not ideas but rather the living conditions of the peasantry and the new urban working class. All too often, moderate liberals were considered no less dangerous to the regime than anarchists. **Vladimir Lenin** and the other Bolsheviks were descendants of these dissidents. Lenin's older brother, a radical populist, was hanged for plotting the death of tsar Aleksandr III. Lenin was introduced to both populism and Marxism at Kazan University in the late 1880s and early 1890s. One of the major reasons for the survival and flourishing of dissent in Russia was its strong base in Europe. Both Marxists and populists lived abroad with the tolerance of Western governments and the support of liberal and socialist political parties.

The greatest force for dissent in early 20th-century Russia was the Bolshevik Party. However, after seizing power, both Vladimir Lenin and **Joseph Stalin** were committed to the annihilation of political diversity. Before his death, Lenin demanded the arrest of all potential dissenters, including fellow socialists in the Menshevik Party and anarchists. Dissent in Soviet society was harshly punished, and the archives of the security services bear stark witness to the fate of those who challenged the regime. In the last two years of Stalin's life, unsanctioned reading groups at universities were broken up; their leaders were arrested and in a few cases executed.

In the 1950s, the Soviet intelligentsia began to demonstrate political courage. The publication of *Not by Bread Alone* and *One Day of Aleksandr Denisovich* marked a Soviet thaw and slightly greater literary freedoms. Beginning in the early 1960s, a small group of Soviet intellectuals moved to disagree intellectually with the system. Some were motivated by religious opinions, more by a demand that the Soviet system live up to its own laws. These were not revolutionaries; like the men and women of the 1860s, they sought to meet, talk, read, and publish their ideas. They were few in number and totally harmless politically, but they attracted the enmity of the **KGB** and its powerful chair, **Yuri Andropov**.

In 1964, Joseph Brodsky was tried in Leningrad for being a parasite. Brodsky, who later won the Nobel Prize for Literature, was condemned for acting as an independent (not state-employed) intellectual. In 1965, Andrei Sinyavsky and Yuri Daniel were convicted of anti-Soviet agitation for publishing their manuscripts abroad. The **détente** of **Leonid Brezhnev** and the thaw of **Nikita Khrushchev** were clearly over. Other themes galvanized the creative intelligentsia (and concerned the KGB): during the next two years, there was growing interest in immigration to Israel and America by Jews and

Pentecostals. Moreover, **Aleksandr Solzhenitsyn** was preparing his first great novel for publication in the West, with its denunciation of Soviet history. Andropov, reacting to these trends, told the **Communist Party** Central Committee that the service had lost its control of events inside the country.

Beginning in 1967, Andropov moved to crush intellectual dissent. He mandated the creation of the Fifth Directorate for **counterintelligence** within the intelligentsia and moved to break the movement. Andropov, who had witnessed the **Hungarian revolution** as the Soviet ambassador, believed that dissent could lead to counterrevolution in Moscow as it had in Budapest. Andropov also ensured that the Soviet penal code include new laws that harshly punished anti-Soviet agitation with seven years in prison plus a term of internal **exile**. Andropov insisted that the leadership take dissent seriously: from 1967 to the fall of the Soviet Union, the Politburo received scores of memos on dissident activities. These memoranda encompassed subjects as serious as the treason trial of a Jewish dissenter and as relatively minor as the meetings of clubs and even an unauthorized funeral memorial service for John Lennon. For example, the 1985 report of the KGB chair to **Mikhail Gorbachev** revealed that in the previous 12 months, the KGB had broken up 25 illegal nationalist groups in Ukraine and the Baltic republics as well as 28 Zionist organizations, suppressed 170 underground religious schools, prosecuted 97 authors of illegal manuscripts, warned 15,274 individuals in prophylactic meetings, and arrested 661 Soviet citizens for political dissident activity. Nevertheless, dissent was never quashed. Andrei Almarik, the author of *Will the Soviet Union Survive until 1984*, wrote, "Dissidents did the impossible. They behaved as free men."

Similar details of KGB repression are found in every top-secret annual summary. The KGB's First Chief Directorate also made pursuing and discrediting dissidents a major objective. Reports of Solzhenitsyn's speech at Harvard University in 1975 were circulated to the leadership. When Yuri Orlov, a leading dissident, did not receive the Nobel Peace Prize in 1979, the KGB *rezident* in Oslo called Mikhail Suslov, the Communist Party Central Committee secretary for ideology, in the middle of the night to announce the "success." The arrest, imprisonment, and exiling of dissidents, however, was counterproductive for Moscow. It did the reputation of the Soviet state tremendous harm and raised questions about its legitimacy in the West.

See also SAKHAROV, ANDREI DMITRYEVICH (1921–1989).

DOCTOR ZHIVAGO. Boris Leonidovich Pasternak (1890–1960) wrote his great novel *Doctor Zhivago* in secret over many years. In the mid-1950s, several copies of the manuscript was smuggled to the West, where it quickly found publishers in Italy and the United Kingdom. In 1958, Pasternak, one of the greatest Russian poets and a translator of Shakespeare, received the Nobel Prize for his novel and life's work. The **KGB**'s reaction to the novel and its author was volcanic. The security service bombarded the **Communist Party** Central Committee with reports of the book's anti-Soviet themes. Pasternak immediately came under tremendous pressure to denounce his novel. Despite threats to friends (his mistress was arrested), Pasternak refused to bow to pressure from the party and the Writers Union. He was isolated and threatened. He died two years later. An excellent account of the book's publication in the West, subsequent translation into Russian, and distribution in the Soviet Union by the Central Intelligence Agency is the subject of a new book by Petr Finn and Petra Couvee.

The KGB's reaction to *Doctor Zhivago* reflected the worldview of the service even during the "liberal" years of **Nikita Khrushchev**. One party critic denounced Pasternak as worse than a pig "because a pig doesn't defecate where it eats." The virulence of the attacks suggested that the police and the party feared any challenge to their authority.

The name "Zhivago" comes from the Russian Orthodox Church's Easter Mass. (*Ty est voistinu Khristos; syn Boga zhivago.* Thou are the risen Christ. The son of the living God.) The novel and its attached poetry remain a symbol of the victory of ideas over the power of repression. The novel was first published in the Soviet Union in 1987, almost three decades after it won the Nobel Prize.

DOCTORS' PLOT. In 1952, 14 important Soviet doctors, almost all of whom were Jewish or had Jewish connections, were arrested on charges of murdering members of the leadership, planning the murder of **Joseph Stalin**, and working for British, American, and Israeli intelligence. Among the doctors detained was Stalin's cardiologist, who had advised him to retire. The doctors were brutally tortured on Stalin's orders to confess their crimes and name their accomplices in the **Communist Party** and the police. Only one physician, Sophia Karpai, was able to hold out against torture and refused to confess. In February and March 1953, the Soviet press announced that there would be a series of trials and **executions**. The press also hinted of a possible banishment of all Jews from Moscow and a new series of purge trials. Stalin's death on 5 March ended the affair. The 11 doctors who survived interrogation were released, and the security officers involved in investigating the conspiracy were arrested in 1953 and shot in 1954–1956.

The Doctors' Plot and public trials of Jews in Moscow and Czechoslovakia in 1952 were initiated by Stalin to create public support for a new series of purges. Stalin, always suspicious of Jews, had received the initial denunciation of the doctors as early as 1948 but chose to act four years later. His target was the senior members of the party leadership. In late 1952, Stalin hinted in public speeches that Minister of Foreign Affairs **Vyacheslav Molotov** and Minister of Foreign Trade Anastas Mikoyan were enemy agents. In

February 1953, all Jews were dismissed from the security services. Only the supreme leader's death prevented a new round of political violence that would have rivaled the *Yezhovshchina* of the late 1930s in terror.

See also ANTI-FASCIST COMMITTEE; SLANSKY TRIAL.

DODD, MARTHA (1908–1990). Certainly the richest American to spy for the Soviet Union, Martha Dodd was literally seduced into espionage in 1934 in Berlin, where her father was serving as American ambassador. Dodd became the lover of Boris Vinogradov, an **NKVD** officer who was recalled to Moscow, arrested, and shot in 1937. Dodd, undeterred by her lover's death, returned to New York, where she married Alfred Stern, a multimillionaire and a communist, and resumed her intelligence career. She recruited Stern into the NKVD, insisting that he be accepted as an agent.

Dodd, whose code name was "Lisa," had social entrée to the White House of Franklin D. Roosevelt but was less than successful as an agent. She did spot agents for the NKVD and provided a considerable amount of gossip about Democratic Party politics. However, she was difficult to control. When the Sterns were identified as Soviet agents by several Federal Bureau of Investigation sources in the late 1940s, they fled the United States. They were found guilty in absentia of espionage on behalf of the Soviet Union. They lived in **exile** first in Mexico, then applied for political asylum in the Soviet Union. They lived in Moscow, then Prague, and finally Havana. They were never happy in exile but were afraid to return to the United States.

DOLGIKH, IVAN ILYICH (1904–?). The last chief of **Joseph Stalin**'s **gulag**, Dolgikh commanded a guard force of more than 150,000 men and controlled more than 2.6 million prisoners. During the post-Stalinist thaw, he was dismissed from the service in 1956, deprived of his rank of lieutenant general, and given a reduced pension of 840 rubles a month. Dolgikh served in the security service for 28 years, most of them in the gulag.

DOUBLE AGENT. For the Soviet services, a double agent was a controlled asset who was allowed to be recruited by a hostile service. (**Kim Philby** was, therefore, not a double agent; he was a Soviet penetration of British intelligence.) The **KGB**, for example, might know that a Western intelligence service was interested in one of their agents and would allow the person to be recruited and run by the hostile service. KGB "operational games" using double agents were run to allow them to understand the target and **tradecraft** of other services and to identify intelligence officers. They also allowed the KGB to tie up foreign intelligence officers with useless cases. They were also often used as a venue for recruiting opposing intelligence officers. The adversary's case officer would be confronted with evidence that he or she had been duped and would be offered a chance to avoid exposure by working for the KGB.

Rarely did the KGB "dangle" one of its own officers. But in the late 1980s, a senior KGB officer approached the Central Intelligence Agency (CIA) chief of station on a train and volunteered to work for the United States. Dubbed "Prologue" by the CIA, Aleksandr Zhumov provided misleading information about the arrest of spies betrayed by **Aldrich Ames** and **Robert Hanssen**. The KGB risked Zhumov because of their desire to protect those two agents. It was a rare incident; movies and novels to the contrary, the KGB did not relish risking one of their officers as a double agent.

Western services ran similar operational games against the KGB and the **GRU**. The Federal Bureau of Investigation (FBI) artfully ran a military non-commissioned officer for several years. The case allowed the FBI to identify several Soviet intelligence officers. On another occasion, U.S. **counterintelligence** authorities used a young Russian-speaking army sergeant as a double agent. The KGB used a 67-year-old East German professor as his courier. She was arrested and served three years before being traded for 17 East German citizens. A less successful double agent case was that of **Nicholas Shadrin**.

The worth of double agents is difficult to measure. Double agents do not produce valuable foreign intelligence; they are difficult and expensive to run. In his memoirs, a former KGB counterintelligence officer noted that double agents were not worth the cost of running them and "were scarcely more than balls in the games played by intelligence agencies." Yet many professionals on both sides of the Berlin Wall believe there really is no other way to catch spies than to use double agents.

DUBROVKA THEATER SIEGE. On 23 October 2002, 40 to 50 militants from the **Chechen** Islamic separatist movement seized the Dubrovka Theater in Moscow and took 850 hostages. After three days of negotiations failed and after two female hostages were killed, the **FSB** and **MVD** stormed the theater after an aerosol anaesthetic was pumped into the theater through the ventilation system. All the terrorists were killed by the gas or in the assault, and 130 hostages died as a result of gas poisoning.

The Chechen organizations, which provided the militants, had links to Al Qaeda. **Chechen** warlord Shamil Basayev took responsibility for the assault. The Russian authorities were attacked for poor negotiation tactics and for the callous use of the gas. Days after the assault, President **Vladimir Putin** intensified military operations in Chechnya, and the Russian Duma approved a broad range of antiterrorist legislation.

FSB defector **Aleksandr Litvinenko** and human rights activists believe that FSB agents may have manipulated the terrorist group into the assault. They note that the reported FSB agents provocateur left the theater alive before the gas was used. Numerous questions about the gas used, the tactics of the assault force, and the role of the FSB remain unanswered.

DUDKO, DMITRY (1922–2004). One of the most famous evangelists of the Russian Orthodox Church, Father Dudko was broken by the **KGB** in 1980 after months of imprisonment. Before becoming a priest, Dudko had been imprisoned in the **gulag** for writing a derogatory poem about **Joseph Stalin**. In the 1970s, he became an internationally known dissident priest, supporting a more active role for the church. After confessing on national television in June 1980 to spreading anti-Soviet propaganda, he was allotted a minor parish. In later years, he became a supporter of far-right anti-Semitic and nationalist causes.

Dudko's arrest and humiliation came at a time when the KGB was determined to destroy all vestiges of dissent. Jewish emigration was closed off in the late 1970s, and in 1980, **Andrei Sakharov** was exiled to Gorky. While the KGB were successful in breaking Dudko and humiliating many of his supporters, reports of the television interview became a major embarrassment for the **Leonid Brezhnev** regime.

DUNLAP, JACK (1928–1963). A U.S. Air Force noncommissioned officer, Dunlap committed suicide when he believed himself to be under investigation by the Federal Bureau of Investigation (FBI). He had served as a courier for the National Security Agency in the Washington, D.C., area and had passed hundreds of documents to his **GRU** case officer between 1960 and 1963. His widow found evidence that Dunlap had been working for Soviet intelligence when she went through his private papers following his death and turned the information over to the FBI. Dunlap is buried in Arlington National Cemetery.

DZERZHINSKY, FELIKS EDMUNDOVICH (1877–1926). Born into a family of Polish landowners, Dzerzhinsky joined the Socialist Democratic Party of Poland and Lithuania while a student. As a political activist, he was arrested and imprisoned by the tsarist authorities on several occasions, and the February 1917 revolution found him in a Moscow prison cell. As a revolutionary and a prisoner, Dzerzhinsky took great interest in operational **tradecraft** and the **counterintelligence** operations of the tsarist secret service, *Okhrana*. Dzerzhinsky specialized in ferreting out informants from among revolutionaries.

Following the Bolshevik coup of 7 November 1917, **Vladimir Lenin** asked Dzerzhinsky to form a security service that took the name All Russian Extraordinary Commission for Combating Counterrevolution and Sabotage (*Chrevzuychanaya komissiya po borbe s kontrarevolutsei i sabotazhem*). Dzerzhinsky's **Cheka**—as it was referred to by most citizens—became a secret police empire responsible for the security of the state and the party. Dzerzhinsky described the Cheka as "the party's fighting detachment." Most of his deputies were not Russians but came from the Polish, Latvian, and Jewish minorities. Many had served in the Bolshevik underground inside and outside the tsarist state.

During the Russian **civil war**, Dzerzhinsky often traveled as the party's representative to various military fronts as a troubleshooter, and he was instrumental in ordering and managing the **Red Terror** in 1918 that followed the attempted assassination of Lenin. On the first day of the Terror, the Cheka executed without trial more than 500 men and women. During its short existence, the Cheka executed close to 150,000 Soviet citizens and imprisoned tens of thousands in forced labor camps. Dzerzhinsky publicly noted that the Cheka stood for terror and that, regretfully, sometimes the sword of the revolution fell on the innocent as well as the guilty.

Given his long political apprenticeship outside the Bolshevik Party, Dzerzhinsky kept out of party politics as long as Lenin was alive. However, following Lenin's death in 1924, Dzerzhinsky supported **Joseph Stalin** in his struggle with **Leon Trotsky**. As a result, the Cheka, which Dzerzhinsky created, became the Stalinist **NKVD**, a weapon that the leadership could use against **dissidents** within the party. The interrogators who had destroyed countless intellectuals, clergy, and refractory peasants showed little disinclination a decade later to purge the party of enemies.

In 1922, as part of the **New Economic Policy**, the Cheka was folded into the new **GPU** (State Political Administration). The GPU lost none of the power of the Cheka. Moreover, Dzerzhinsky was rewarded for his work in building the security service by being made chair of the Council of the National Economy. This appointment led to greater participation by the security service in the Soviet economy and the employment of thousands of prisoners in logging, gold mining, and manufacturing. Dzerzhinsky died in 1926 following a speech to a party meeting. He was remembered by security professionals as a knight of the revolution. His statue at the service headquarters at **Lubyanka** was torn down immediately following the failed 1991 **August putsch** but recently has been placed back in its position of honor.

Following Dzerzhinsky's death, an admirer noted that his two most striking qualities were fanaticism and mercilessness. Dzerzhinsky was an aesthetic and workaholic who lived in his office the first year he managed the Cheka, subsisting on the meager rations fed his troops in the field. He sought to mold a service of revolutionary priests, describing his **Chekist** colleagues as having "clean hands and warm hearts." He was also a formidable manager who controlled a security service with a staff of 250,000. He had little real interest in foreign intelligence, and the foreign intelligence section was directed mainly at the penetration of **émigré** movements. Under Dzerzhinsky's leadership, the Cheka organized the **Trust** operation to lure émigrés to return to the Soviet Union. By the time of his death, the security service had eliminated the threat of émigré political action against the infant Soviet state.

EITINGON, LEONID ALEKSANDROVICH [NAUM ISAKOVICH]
(1899–1981). Eitingon was an experienced **illegal** who took part in a number of political assassinations. He was also one of the founders of Soviet *Spetsnaz* troops and tactics, working in Spain during the **Spanish Civil War** to train republican **partisans**. In the late 1930s, when **Pavel Sudoplatov** was tasked with organizing the assassination of **Leon Trotsky**, Eitingon masterminded recruiting agents to penetrate Trotsky's inner circle and murder him. During **World War II**, he served as the deputy chief of the **NKVD**'s partisan directorate and took part in an attempted assassination of the German ambassador to Turkey. He was promoted to general's rank in 1945.

Following the war, Eitingon was purged by **Joseph Stalin** and briefly imprisoned. In 1953, he was rearrested in a purge of **Lavrenty Beria**'s subordinates and sentenced to 15 years in prison, of which he served 12. He was posthumously rehabilitated in 1992. Eitingon had a legendary romantic life and an unusually ready wit. He was married to several women, more than one at the same time. When he was asked about survival during the purges, he told a subordinate the way to stay out of jail was "don't be a Jew or a general of state security." Eitingon was both.

ÉMIGRÉS. The initial priority for the **Cheka**'s foreign intelligence component was to neutralize the threat from émigré "White" organizations. Initially, *rezidenturas* were ordered to organize "White Lines" and concentrate on the émigré target. Operations such as the Syndicate and the **Trust** lured émigrés back into the country so they could be jailed or executed. In the 1920s and 1930s, Soviet foreign intelligence penetrated Russian and Ukrainian émigré organizations and assassinated their leaders with impunity. For example, in 1930 and 1936, the **NKVD** kidnapped and murdered two of the leaders of the White Russian movement in Paris. Moscow also recruited agents in communities from Berlin to Shanghai to report on the threat of émigré political movements.

Moscow also recruited émigrés for sources of foreign intelligence. Efforts were made to find émigrés who had access to their host countries' policies and leaders. During **World War II**, agents such as **Olga Chekhova** were seen as important sources on foreign politics and as potential assassins. In the United States, Canada, and Western Europe, émigrés became important agents of NKVD and **GRU** *rezidenturas* in the collection of scientific and technical intelligence. After the war, **KGB** and GRU case officers continued to target émigrés, especially those in the Ukrainian and Baltic communities.

Since 1908, the Russian services have been active in the "near abroad," the states of the former Soviet Union. Two recent **defectors** have written about the new Russian intelligence services to find support in émigré communities. One, **Konstantin Preobrazhenskiy**, has recently written and been interviewed of the **SVR**'s efforts to find agents in the émigré community. Journalists have also written of GRU and SVR efforts to find agents in the Russian populations of the successor states of the former Soviet Union. This has been obvious in the eastern Ukraine, where GRU officers have gathered support from Russian populations.

See also UKRAINIAN CRISIS.

ENEMIES OF THE PEOPLE. The term "enemies of the people" was employed by the Jacobins during the French Revolution for those they wished to kill with a minimum of judicial process. **Vladimir Lenin** and other Bolsheviks were attracted to the term and began using it in 1918. The Soviet press during the rule of **Joseph Stalin** used the term to dehumanize opponents of the regime. When Helen Bonner, **Andrei Sakharov**'s wife, and her little brother saw their father arrested, the boy said, "Imagine, some enemies of the people masquerade as fathers!" During the *Yezhovshchina*, women and children classified as members of the family of enemies of the people were subject to arrest and **exile**. Children were sent to special orphanages established by the security services. When a writer asked Stalin's foreign minister **Vyacheslav Molotov** why it had been necessary to punish the wives of political prisoners, he casually replied that "people would have talked" had the spouses and children been allowed to discuss their husbands' fate.

ENORMOZ. The **NKVD** code name for the Anglo-American nuclear weapons program, *Enormoz*, which is Russian for "enormous," reflected Moscow's obsession with the atomic bomb. The service's code name for the bomb itself was "Funicular." As early as 1941, **John Cairncross** provided the London *rezidentura* with information about the British nuclear program. **Joseph Stalin** initially believed that this intelligence was British disinformation, but in early 1943, he directed the Soviet intelligence *rezidenturas* in Great Britain, the United States, and Canada to collect information on the

Allied nuclear weapons program. Within a year of this order, Soviet intelligence had provided over 280 classified documents on the program. In 1944, the director of the Soviet nuclear weapons program, Igor Kurchatov, wrote **Lavrenty Beria** that information from the United States "was of enormous interest and great value" and pleaded for additional information.

Information on nuclear weapons was collected in Great Britain, the United States, and Canada by both the NKVD and the **GRU**. The Soviet service created **Line X** within the London, Ottawa, Washington, and San Francisco *rezidenturas* to collect scientific, specifically nuclear, intelligence. In 1944–1948, the London *rezidentura* was running 15 agents with access to the nuclear program. In New York, Washington, and San Francisco, the NKVD had at least six agents working within Los Alamos as well as at other classified facilities. In Canada, the GRU was running **Allan Nunn May**, who had access to nuclear secrets as well as agents inside the Manhattan program in the United States.

Stalin personally monitored the collection of information by agents in the United States, Canada, and Britain. The Soviet leader picked Beria to head a committee of the **GKO** (State Defense Committee) to oversee the nuclear program. On 23 January 1946, Stalin met with Beria and Kurchatov to discuss the next steps in building a Soviet atomic bomb. Stalin encouraged Kurchatov to ask for whatever was needed. Acting like a Dutch uncle—a side of the dictator few saw—he told Kurchatov that he was to build a bomb "in the Russian style." In 1949, when Kurchatov had built the uranium "pit" for the first bomb, he presented it (properly shielded in lead) to Stalin. Stalin was impressed but asked when it was to be exploded.

While Stalin and Beria rewarded Kurchatov and the other scientists who had built the Soviet bomb, intelligence officers received scant praise. No mention of their success was allowed in the media for decades, and several of the people who carried out operations in the United States and Britain died in disgrace. In 1992, the surviving members of the intelligence service's nuclear intelligence work finally received their due in articles in the Russian press. At least one of them traveled to the United States to discuss operations with the families of his agents.

See also FITIN, PAVEL MIKHAILOVICH (1907–1971); KVASNIKOV, LEV ROMANOVICH (1905–1993); SEMENOV, SEMEN MARKOVICH (1911–1986).

ETINGER, YAKOV GILYARYEVICH (1887–1951). A famed doctor and military officer, Etinger was one of the first physicians arrested as part of the **Doctors' Plot**. He was arrested on 20 November 1950 and subject to months of intense interrogation to provide evidence that he was part of a Jewish nationalist plot financed by American intelligence and linked to men whom **Joseph Stalin** considered enemies. He died in prison on 2 March 1951 of a heart attack, a result of torture and extensive confinement in an unheated cell. **MGB** chief **Viktor Abakumov** was blamed for not obtaining a confession that could be used to implicate other Jewish doctors and was subsequently arrested.

EVDOKIMOV, EFIM GRIGORYEVICH (1891–1940). One of **Joseph Stalin**'s favorite **Chekists**. He worked first in the northern Caucasus and then was assigned the job of preparing the first major **show trial**, the Shakhty trial of foreign engineers. He was later assigned to obtain a "confession" from former **NKVD** chief **Genryk Yagoda**. He was transferred out of the security service in 1938, arrested, and shot in 1940. Evdokimov was later rehabilitated in 1956.

EXECUTIONS. The last three decades of the tsarist regime experienced intense persecution of political rebels and anti-Semitic **pogroms**, which were often commissioned by agents of the *Okhrana*. During 1881–1914, approximately 11,000 subjects of the tsar were hanged for political crimes, killed in clashes with the security forces in urban and peasant risings, or murdered in pogroms. The term "Stolypin necktie" came from the willingness of Minister of Interior **Petr Stolypin** to sanction execution of rebels following the **Revolution of 1905**.

During the Soviet period, capital punishment was officially referred to by the acronym VM or VMN, for *Vyshaya mera nakazaniya* ("supreme measure of punishment"). Executions were carried out by shooting; usually the condemned was shot in the back of the head. However, during **World War II**, German war criminals and Soviet collaborators were often publicly hanged. Our information on executions during the Soviet period is incomplete. During the first four years of the regime, more than 140,000 people were executed by the **Cheka**. Figures for the late 1920s and 1930s are incomplete because the security service did not include peasants shot resisting **collectivization** or killings in forced labor camps. Information submitted by the security service to the **Communist Party** Central Committee after the death of **Joseph Stalin** indicates that there were 747,772 executions between 1922 and 1939. This figure is rejected by most Soviet experts, including former party leader **Nikita Khrushchev** and Politburo member **Aleksandr Yakovlev**, who put the figure three to 10 times greater. For scholars of Russian history, major lacunae remain in the records of the security services, preventing any accounting of the bloodletting during the **Lenin** and Stalin years.

During the **Great Patriotic War**, between 157,000 and 240,000 Soviet soldiers were sentenced to be shot, the equivalent of 15 to 25 infantry divisions. The NKVD and Red Army executed approximately 13,500 during the

Battle of Stalingrad. The records show that another 25,000 officers were sentenced to penal battalions, where the overwhelming majority were killed in action. Those punished officers would have been sufficient to command the troops of 25 additional infantry divisions.

Following Stalin's death, execution by shooting was used to combat a number of criminal acts, including large-scale theft of state property and embezzlement. According to recently opened Soviet archives, there were 25,000 death sentences and 21,000 executions between 1962 and 1990, most for civil criminal activities. In 1962–1963, approximately 3,000 executions took place as Khrushchev demanded that the security service and police crack down on the illegal economy.

Despite the collapse of the Soviet Union, capital punishment continued in most of the former Soviet republics. Russia legally abolished capital punishment in 1998; the last execution took place in 1996. Popular opinion supports restoring capital punishment, and even former Nobel laureate **Aleksandr Solzhenitsyn** has publicly spoken in favor of renewing capital punishment for murder.

EXILE. The tsarist regime used Siberian exile as a punishment for **dissidents**. Following the **Decembrists' Revolt** in 1825, hundreds of officers were exiled to Siberia by Tsar Nicholas I. Most of these officers took their wives and children with them. The writer Feodor Dostoyevsky was sentenced to exile for his role in the **Petrashevskiy circle**. It is clear that both the police and local authorities used exile as a way of removing troublesome people from society. Political exiles were often treated with compassion as men and women of principle: **Vladimir Lenin** was allowed to take his revolutionary books into exile. He was even allowed to go hunting.

During the Soviet period, exile was also used as a punishment for political prisoners. Millions of peasants were exiled during **collectivization**, and many of them perished in settlements in Siberia. From 1939 until 1953, peoples suspected of collaboration with enemies of the Soviet Union were exiled to Siberia by the hundreds of thousands. The secret police also used exile to keep political prisoners who had been released from the **gulag** in the inhospitable regions. In 1949, Minister of Internal Affairs **Sergei Kruglov** informed **Joseph Stalin** that there were 2,562,830 people living in exile. Five years later, the **MVD** reported that the total had grown to 2,819,776, of whom 884,057 were children.

In the post-Stalin era, Soviet courts continued to use both internal and foreign exile as forms of punishment. **KGB** chair **Yuri Andropov** argued forcefully for the exiling of certain dissidents, such as **Aleksandr Solzhenitsyn**, from the Soviet Union. People convicted of minor civil crimes were often sentenced to internal exile. The Soviet criminal code also had provisions for a sentence of imprisonment plus a term of exile for political offenses. These sentences continued until 1988.

EXTRAORDINARY COMMISSION. Both the **NKVD** and *Smersh* played an important role in the Extraordinary Commission, established in February 1942, for ascertaining and investigating crimes perpetrated by the German–Fascist invaders. The services hunted down Soviet **collaborators** and German war criminals. They also prepared false and misleading documents justifying the Soviet invasion of Finland in 1939 and the **Katyn** massacres.

F

FALSE FLAG. Intelligence services often recruited agents under the "false flag" of other countries or political movements. The Soviet services used this gambit in two creative ways. A Soviet case officer recruited the British communications clerk **John King**, for example, under the false flag of international business. King, the Soviet intelligence officer insisted, was not hurting his country by providing information to an international cartel. In the 1930s and 1940s, NKVD officers often pretended to be "**Comintern** representatives." Information that was going to Moscow to help the international communist movement could not be considered espionage. Rather, it was solidarity with the working class and the struggling Soviet people.

See also MOTIVATION.

FAMISH. Beginning in the early 1980s, the administration of U.S. President Ronald Reagan searched for ways to reduce the Soviet intelligence presence in the United States. The "Famish" action was precipitated in September 1986, when the **KGB** arrested Nicholas Daniloff, an American journalist, in response to the Federal Bureau of Investigation's arrest of Gennadiy Zakharov, a KGB agent who lacked diplomatic cover. At first, Moscow sought an exchange of the Soviet spy for the American journalist, and Soviet leader **Mikhail Gorbachev** and President Ronald Reagan traded charges about the arrests. Reagan and his chief Soviet hand, Ambassador Jack Matlock, decided on a radical reaction to break the Soviets of hostage taking. Soviet diplomatic missions in New York and Washington were informed that they had to drastically reduce their staff, and 80 KGB and **GRU** officers were specifically deemed persona non grata and ordered to leave the United States. The list of those expelled included all the *rezidents* and key intelligence personnel in the United States, including 61 from Washington, 26 from New York, and 13 from San Francisco. While Moscow retaliated by expelling some U.S. diplomats and withdrawing Soviet employees from the American embassy, the Soviet services had suffered a major defeat. Daniloff and Zakharov were later exchanged.

See also SPY SWAPS.

FAPSI. As part of President **Boris Yeltsin**'s efforts to reform and restructure the Russian intelligence community, the Eighth (Government Communications) and Sixteenth (Signals Intelligence) Chief Directorates were removed from the **KGB** in December 1991 to form the *Federalnoe agentsvo pravitelstevennoi syvazi i informatsii* (Federal Agency for Government Communications and Information). In an effort to concentrate the power in a single intelligence service, FAPSI was first transferred to the **FSB** in 2003 and in 2004 was incorporated into the **Federal Protective Service** of the Russian Federation.

See also FEDERAL PROTECTIVE SERVICE; SIGNALS INTELLIGENCE (SIGINT).

FEDERAL PROTECTIVE SERVICE. The *Federalnaya Sluzhba Okhrani* (FSO) is responsible for the protection of the Russian political leadership, the function of the **KGB**'s Ninth and Fifteenth Directorates. Its chief also has responsibility for the Kremlin Regiment and the **Special Communications Service of Russia**, which includes the signals intelligence directorates of the former KGB. Control of the Service of Special Communications (*SPETSS-VYAZ*) gives the service and the Office of the President enormous power to control communications as well as the collection and dissemination of intelligence.

The FSO is also responsible for the "black box," which controls the Russian nuclear arsenal. Its directors have served in the KGB and have long-standing ties to President **Vladimir Putin**.

FEDORCHUK, VITALII VASILYEVICH (1918–2008). Born into a Ukrainian peasant family, Fedorchuk entered the security service in 1939. During **World War II**, he worked in *Smersh* and in 1946 was transferred to the **Third** (Military **Counterintelligence**) **Chief Directorate**. Fedorchuk rose quickly in the **KGB** and in 1970 was made chair of the Ukrainian KGB. After the **Prague Crisis** of 1968, Moscow apparently feared that Ukrainian nationalism was a threat to the Soviet system, and Fedorchuk was given wide latitude to stamp out all religious or political dissent.

The Ukrainian **émigré** press reported that the KGB murdered a number of **dissident** Ukrainian Catholic leaders in an effort to quash political opposition in the western Ukraine during the 1970s, when Fedochuk headed the service. As chief of the Ukrainian KGB, Fedorchuk earned a reputation in Moscow for toughness and ideological orthodoxy. In May 1982, when **Yuri Andropov** entered the Central Committee Secretariat, Fedorchuk was brought to Moscow to head the KGB. According to most scholars, Fedorchuk's appointment represented a compromise within the aging **Leonid Brezhnev** leadership; Fedorchuk apparently had no political ambition and was seen as a competent and loyal senior KGB officer.

In December 1982, Fedorchuk was replaced by **Viktor Chebrikov** and transferred to the **MVD** (Ministry of Internal Affairs). As MVD chief with rank of army general, Fedorchuk worked first with Andropov and then with **Mikhail Gorbachev** to purge and reform the police. His efforts were not successful, though a number of senior MVD officers were arrested and tried for corruption and malfeasance. In 1986, Fedorchuk was offered honorable retirement and assigned to the Group of General Inspectors of the Ministry of Defense.

FEDOTOV, PETR VASILYEVICH (1900–1963). After 16 years of service in the provinces, Fedotov was brought to Moscow by **Nikolai Yezhov** to head the **NKVD**'s Secret Political Department in 1937. During **World War II**, he headed the NKVD's **counterintelligence** directorate and was promoted to lieutenant general in 1945. From 1946 to 1949, he served as **Joseph Stalin**'s chief of foreign intelligence in the *Komitet Informatsii* (Committee of Information). From 1949 to 1959, Fedotov held a series of senior positions in the **MVD** and **KGB**. He retired in 1959, after having served on the faculty of the KGB's Higher School. Fedotov was one of the very few senior **Chekists** of Yezhov's generation to survive promotion to the center in 1937. Of the more than 120 promoted in this period to important posts in Moscow, barely 20 survived.

FEKLISOV, ALEKSANDR SEMENOVICH (1914–2007). As a student in one of the first classes at the **NKVD**'s foreign intelligence school (later named the **Andropov Institute**), Feklisov was prepared to serve as a case officer under legal cover. From 1941 until 1946, he served in New York, where he was **Julius Rosenberg**'s case officer, and he produced some of the most important scientific and technical intelligence to reach Moscow during the **Great Patriotic War**. Through Feklisov, Rosenberg managed several engineers with access to top-secret military and scientific information. Feklisov had great admiration for the Rosenbergs and other American volunteers who worked for Moscow out of ideological affinity. He believed that Moscow should have made more of an effort to save the Rosenbergs from execution.

Following service in New York, Feklisov served in London, maintaining contact with **Klaus Fuchs**, his service's most important source of nuclear intelligence. As the Soviet services lost contact with many of their most productive agents in the British and American nuclear programs, Fuchs's information became increasingly critical. Feklisov was a careful street case officer. He first met Fuchs in a British pub. Longer meetings took place in pubs and on the streets of the British capital, where the case officer and Fuchs could walk and talk with little fear of being overheard. Feklisov was later informed by Moscow that Fuchs's information saved the Soviet Union 200 million rubles. Feklisov served a tour in Prague as an adviser to the Czechoslovakian intelligence service and then for many years was head of the American department of the First Chief Directorate.

Feklisov's next incarnation as an intelligence officer came in the early 1960s, when he served as **KGB** *rezident* in Washington under the name "Fomin." Feklisov's *rezidentura* was very successful in collecting scientific and intelligence information. He was unable, however, to replicate the success of Soviet intelligence chiefs during the 1940s, when they had spectacular sources of political intelligence. During the **Cuban Missile Crisis**, Feklisov was used as a **back channel** between Moscow and the John F. Kennedy administration. His role in the crisis is still controversial: while some believe it opened a channel of communications at a difficult time, others believe it further confused a perilous situation.

In retirement, Feklisov wrote one of the best memoirs of a **Cold War** intelligence officer. Originally published in French as *Confessions d'un agent sovietique*, it was published in the United States as *The Man behind the Rosenbergs*. The book, which deeply angered some in Moscow, confirmed that Julius Rosenberg had indeed been a Soviet agent—though, the author claimed, he had had little to do with nuclear espionage—and that the Anglo-American decryption of the Soviet intelligence messages was genuine. Feklisov remains deeply proud of his and his service's achievements, especially the collection of nuclear intelligence.

See also ENORMOZ; VENONA.

FELFE, HEINZ PAUL JOHANN (1918–2008). After joining the Gestapo, Felfe served in the Netherlands, working against the Dutch underground during **World War II**. Following the war, the British Secret Intelligence Service recruited Felfe as their agent to identify communists and former Nazis in the British zone of occupied West Germany. Felfe was quite effective and was allowed to join the nascent German intelligence organization run by **Reinhard Gehlen**. In 1955, Felfe followed Gehlen into the *Bundesnachrichtendienst* (BND), the West German intelligence service.

Felfe was recruited in 1951 by the **KGB**, which was able to supply money to maintain his lavish lifestyle. Over 10 years, he was paid 178,000 marks ($44,500). The KGB also played on Felfe's hatred of the United States for its bombing of his hometown, Dresden, in 1945. For 10 years, Felfe was an important intelligence source for Moscow, providing information on North Atlantic Treaty Organization operations in Eastern Europe. He provided the KGB with over 15,000 pages of classified documents as well as 20 audiotapes of classified meetings. His position in the BND allowed the KGB to manipulate the German service's operations. He was betrayed by **Michael Goleniewski** and arrested in 1961. In 1963, he was sentenced to 14 years in prison. He was exchanged six years later for 21 men and women, three of whom had served as American and West German agents, and 18 East German political prisoners. In later years, Felfe became an instructor of apprentice spies in East Germany, reportedly using actual radio traffic from Moscow to him during his years as an agent.

The Felfe case shows the KGB at its best. Felfe and two confederates were targeted by the Soviet services because of their previous service in the SS and their common hatred for the American bombing of Dresden. As agents, they were given excellent training in avoiding **surveillance** and were supplied with money and equipment. Felfe received messages inside jars of baby food, supposedly bought for an infant child. Moreover, the KGB realized that when Felfe was finally caught, the news would cripple the BND and poison relations between Bonn and Washington.

FIELD, NOEL HAVILAND (1904–1971). One of the most confusing stories of the **Cold War** is the saga of Noel Field and his wife, Herta. An idealist Quaker, Field joined the U.S. Department of State and was recruited by Soviet intelligence. During the war, he worked in Switzerland to rescue refugees from Nazism, cooperating with the **Office of Strategic Services** chief in Bern, Allen Dulles. After the war, the Fields sought to settle in Eastern Europe, claiming to have been members of the American Communist Party and Soviet agents (which they were).

Noel and his wife were arrested in 1949 and interrogated by the Hungarian and other East European services for several years. Manuscripts from these interrogations seem to implicate **Alger Hiss** as an agent of Soviet intelligence, and evidence gathered by his torturers led to the arrest and execution of hundreds of men and women, many of whom the Fields had rescued from German concentration camps. Analysis of these trials shows that the majority were Jewish communists, of whom Moscow was very suspicious.

Conspiracy theorists have had great interest in the Fields' case. Were they unwilling tools of the Central Intelligence Agency? Were they simply naive beyond human understanding? How much did they know of Hiss? They were loyal communists in any case. The Fields emerged from prison in 1954 and decided to remain in the East. Reportedly, Noel's first words to his wife were, "Have you remained faithful to the Party?"

FIRST CHIEF DIRECTORATE (*PERVIY OTDEL*). One of the keys to the **KGB's** control of Soviet society was First Section, the personnel directorate at every plant and educational institution in the country. The section, always headed by active-duty or retired KGB officers, served as an instrument of bureaucratic control over dissent. The chief of the First Section also had responsibility for the flow of paperwork within Soviet institutions. Material from the West was kept in special repositories (*spetskhran*); the head of the first section decided who could and could not have access to the material and determined what could and could not be photocopied.

Retired KGB officers were often offered positions as head of a First Section as a sort of honorarium. They were useful to the KGB in recruitment of **informers** and in the search for young staff officers. In these positions, the retired officers often received higher academic or bureaucratic rank than they enjoyed in the security service. According to the memoirs of a number of Soviet academics and scientists, First Section heads had and abused considerable power. Yelena Kozeltseva served as a colonel in the **NKVD** before and during **World War II**. Later, as a retired officer, she headed the First Section at Moscow State University for more than two decades. In interviews, she noted with pride that she had been able to "protect" students from their bad judgment by preventing them from attending demonstrations and becoming marked as **dissidents**.

See also KGB ORGANIZATION.

FISHER, WILLIAM GENRYKHOVICH (1903–1971). One of the most famous Soviet **illegals**, Fisher was born in England of German Baltic parents who were clandestine members of the **Bolshevik Party**. Following the revolution, the family returned to Soviet Russia. Fisher joined the Red Army in the 1920s and served in northern Europe as a **GRU** illegal for more than 15 years. During the *Yezhovshchina*, Fisher was purged from the military but not arrested.

Recalled to the **NKVD** during **World War II**, Fisher served as an officer training radio operators, and he was involved in **radio game** deceptions against the Germans. Following the war, Fisher entered the United States in early 1949 with a passport of a deceased American citizen of Baltic descent. For the next seven years, Fisher served effectively as the illegal *rezident* under the alias "Emil Goldfus" in New York City. According to a declassified Central Intelligence Agency study, "Fisher worked diligently to meet the agents he was responsible for and apparently worked to develop some new agents."

Fisher was a careful and professional operations officer who almost certainly would not have been caught had it not been for the defection of his assistant, **Reino Hayhanen,** who was an incompetent alcoholic. Fisher was arrested on 20 June 1957, at which time he identified himself to the Federal Bureau of Investigation as Colonel **Rudolph Ivanovich Abel**, the name of an old friend that he and the **KGB** had agreed he should use should he be arrested to show that he had not been broken and compromised his agents.

He was subsequently tried under federal espionage statutes and sentenced to 30 years' imprisonment. While in prison, he taught French to his cell mate, a Mafia soldier, and painted landscapes that were prized by prison officials and his lawyer. Fisher was exchanged for U-2 pilot Francis Gary Powers in a **spy swap** in February 1962.

Fisher returned to a hero's welcome in Moscow but was never used operationally after his exchange. He told one of his KGB colleagues that he was "a museum exhibit." He was widely admired by both American **counterintelligence** and KGB professionals. He died in 1971 and was identified in an editorial in the Soviet press as "Colonel Abel." His widow, enraged that he had not received his just deserts in death, convinced the KGB to allow a new stone to be placed on his grave finally identifying him as William Genrykhovich Fisher.

FITIN, PAVEL MIKHAILOVICH (1907–1971). Fitin was drafted into the **NKVD**'s foreign intelligence directorate in 1938, following the purge of the component. Within months of completing the Soviet Union's first course for foreign intelligence officers, he was promoted to general's rank. At the age of 34, Fitin took over the foreign intelligence directorate and led it through **World War II**. While untrained and unprepared for the responsibility, Fitin was an exceptionally effective intelligence chief, supervising the penetration of both enemy and Allied governments as well as the collection of critical scientific information on the American and British nuclear weapons program, code-named *Enormoz*.

The KGB's official history notes that Fitin provided accurate documentary reporting of German plans to invade the Soviet Union. **Lavrenty Beria** quashed these reports and repeatedly threatened Fitin with a firing squad for his audacity in contradicting the party leadership. NKVD cables from the war show that Fitin was a demanding but knowledgeable boss. He also appeared to have the moral courage to intercede with Beria in the case of senior officers who were recalled unfairly. When **Vasily Zarubin** and his wife were hastily brought back from New York on charges of disloyalty and malfeasance, he supported them, and they were cleared of all charges.

Beria, never one to forgive or forget, moved Fitin out of foreign intelligence at the end of the war. As a lieutenant general, Fitin served first in Germany and then in the provinces. Beria insisted that he be removed from the service in 1951 for "incompetence." While never prosecuted, Fitin lost his rank, medals, and pension. After Beria's **execution**, work was found for Fitin, but he died in obscurity in 1971.

FORCED LABOR CAMPS. *See* GULAG.

FOREST BROTHERHOOD. In all three Baltic states, opposition by nationalist partisans to Soviet occupation began in 1944 and reached its heights in 1947–1948. The struggle between the **MGB** paramilitary forces and the "forest brothers" continued into the early 1950s, with the last partisans killed in July 1965. Security force casualties testified to the brutality of the struggle: Soviet military losses in 1945–1947 alone were 8,700.

FOURTH DEPARTMENT OF THE GENERAL STAFF. *See GLAVR-VEDUPR*; GRU (*GLAVNOE RAZVEDIVATELNOE UPRAVLENIYE*).

FRADKOV, MIKHAIL YEFIMOVICH (1950–). Fradkov was appointed deputy minister of foreign economic relations in 1992. In 1995, he was made minister of foreign trade, and in 2001, President **Vladimir Putin** made him director of the Federal Tax Police and deputy chief of the National Security Council. He served as prime minister from 2004 to 2007. In 2007, Fradkov was made chief of the **SVR**.

Fradkov has been described in the Russian media as independent of the various clans surrounding the president. Putin's decision to nominate him as premier, however, suggest that he was not an "outsider" but a man trusted and respected by the president for his ability to work with the *siloviki*. Further proof of this assertion is that he has survived several major scandals since 2010, including the arrest of **illegals** in the United States and **defections** by senior officers.

FRENKEL, NAFTALII ARONOVICH (1883–1960). One of the most odious of the first generation of **Chekists**, Frenkel went from prisoner to security service general in less than a decade. His early life is shrouded in mystery. According to most accounts, he was a petty criminal in the Odessa underworld. Following the **Revolution of November 1917**, he was arrested several times for theft and robbery. In May 1927, he emerged from prison to take an important post in the labor camp directorate, apparently because he sold the **OGPU** leadership on the long-term economic benefits of prison labor. In the 1930s, he supervised the work on the **Belomor Canal**, the first massive slave labor project of the **gulag** system. He was promoted to lieutenant general in 1943 and awarded the Order of **Lenin**. He retired in 1947 and died peacefully in 1960.

FRIEDMANN, LITZIE (1910–1991). Kim Philby rescued Friedman from Vienna in 1934 in the aftermath of the government's crackdown on the left. Friedman played a role in Philby's recruitment by Soviet intelligence and was possibly his link to the Soviet agent spotter **Edith Tudor Hart**. To preserve his cover, Philby first distanced himself from Friedman and then divorced her. She later married and moved to East Berlin, where her daughter wrote her biography.

FRINOVSKIY, MIKHAIL PETROVICH (1898–1940). Raised in a middle-class family before the Russian Revolution, Frinovskiy attended a theological seminary for a short period of time, as had **Joseph Stalin**. Frinovskiy's early career was spent in the **Border Guard** Directorate. He took part in the repression of peasant risings in the Kuban, the homeland of the Cossacks, during the **collectivization** of agriculture. As one of **Nikolai Yezhov**'s chief deputies during the **Red Terror**, Frinovskiy took part in the purge of the party and the **NKVD**. Following the purge of the armed forces and the **execution** of many senior naval officers, Frinovskiy was made people's commissar of the navy in September 1938. In April 1939, he was stripped of this post and arrested. He was shot after a short trial in February 1940 on the same day as his mentor, Nikolai Yezhov.

FROZEN CONFLICT ZONES. In international relations, a frozen conflict zone is a situation in which active armed conflict has ceased but no peace treaty has ended the conflict. On the periphery of Russia, there are several such zones, where the Russian intelligence and security services have aided secessionist Russian groups to destabilize neighboring governments. Moscow has artfully used covert paramilitary action to strengthen its surrogates and may be conceivably used in the Baltic states in the future.

FSB *(FEDERALNAYA SLUZHBA BEZOPASNOSTI)*. The FSB (Federal Security Service) was created by Russian President **Boris Yeltsin** on 21 December 1995 to place all the domestic and **counterintelligence** and security components of the former **KGB** under one roof. The FSB took on the domestic duties of the KGB and reports directly to the president of the Russian Federation. The chiefs of the FSB have been close associates of Russian President **Vladimir Putin** and a veterans of the KGB. The FSB is the largest security service in Europe and the second largest in the world.

The FSB remains a formidable counterintelligence service. The Russian press and the FSB website have noted FSB arrests of espionage agents and the expulsion of foreign diplomats, including some from the United States, China, Great Britain, Poland, and Japan. The FSB also arrested a number of foreign terrorists inside Russia who had connections with Islamic fundamentalist organizations, and it conducted covert paramilitary operations in Chechnya against nationalist bases and headquarters. In March 2005, the Russian press announced the death of Aslan Maskhadov, a leader of Chechen nationalists, in an action with an FSB task force.

The FSB is continuing the KGB's responsibility for the prosecution of "especially dangerous state crimes." President Putin has given the service great latitude in investigating some of the "economic empires" that flourished in the Yeltsin period, and several of the new Russian capitalists who flourished during the Yeltsin administration are in custody or have fled the country. At the same time, FSB officers have become vested in many businesses as security officials, in effect silent partners.

But the FSB has had considerable difficulty adjusting itself to the rule of law. In 1995, the FSB arrested a former naval officer, Aleksandr Nikitin, for revealing secrets about the Russian navy. Nikitin had written about certain ecological abuses committed by the navy, which were in fact common knowledge in the West. He was tried several times on charges of treason and acquitted on each occasion. Other whistle-blowers have been tried for treason, and some were also acquitted. In one of its most notorious acts, in 2000, the FSB arrested an American businessperson, retired U.S. Navy commander Edmund Pope, and held him for 253 days. In 2004, based on FSB evidence, a Russian court convicted a Russian researcher of treason for revealing state secrets to Western intelligence. The material released actually was from open sources, but the researcher received a lengthy term in jail.

Putin once described the FSB as "our new nobility" and has allowed the service tremendous latitude in crushing political opposition. As a result, the FSB has apparently acted as "a gun for hire" in crushing businessmen and political figures infringing on Putin's party's turf. According to most scholars and observers, the FSB, unlike the KGB, operates without political supervision and has detained perceived opponents with little regard for law.

FUCHS, KLAUS-EMIL (1910–1988). A gifted physicist, Fuchs fled to London from Nazi Germany in the early 1930s. While he was involved in the early British nuclear weapons program code-named "Tube Alloy," he volunteered to work for Soviet intelligence. In Great Britain, Fuchs originally was run by a **GRU illegal**, but his case was transferred to the **NKVD** after Fuchs moved to the United States to work at Los Alamos. Fuchs was probably the most important of several Soviet penetrations of the nuclear weapons program code-named *Enormoz*. He was run by a series of illegals. His NKVD code names were "Rest" and "Charles."

On his return to Britain after **World War II**, Fuchs maintained contact with Soviet intelligence, passing on information about the British nuclear weapons program for four years. Under suspicion, Fuchs was arrested and confessed to a British **counterintelligence** interrogator in 1950. He was tried and sentenced to 14 years' imprisonment. Released after nine years, Fuchs returned to East Germany, where he worked as a nuclear physicist. He was a member of the **Communist Party** Central Committee, and he died in 1988, a year before the collapse of the system he served.

Of the spies within the American nuclear program, Fuchs and **Ted Hall** were probably the most important sources of information about both the progress of the Anglo-American project and the solutions to the problems facing American and British bomb makers. According to nuclear physicist and Nobel Prize laureate **Andrei Sakharov**, Fuchs provided the Soviet nuclear program with critical intelligence gathered from Los Alamos and later from London. He also provided the first information Moscow received about the "super" H-bomb.

G

GAI, MARK ISAYEVICH (1898–1937). After service in the Red Army, Gai joined the **Cheka** in 1920 at the age of 21. In the 1930s, he played an important role in the establishment of **military counterintelligence** and the **OO** (Special Departments) that provided **NKVD** checks on military commanders. He was chief of military counterintelligence from June 1933 to November 1936. He was arrested in January 1937 as the **Great Purge** began and was shot in June of the same year. According to one story, Gai initially escaped from captivity and hid with friends in the countryside. He was later persuaded to surrender, convinced that party chief **Joseph Stalin** was unaware of his arrest. He was not rehabilitated.

GAPON, GEORGI APOLLONOVICH (1870–1906). Father Gapon ran a large working-class parish in St. Petersburg in the first years of the 20th century and was respected for his defense of workers' rights. He was recruited as an agent by **Nikolai Zubatov,** *Okhrana*'s chief in the capital city. Gapon became deeply embroiled in Zubatov's "police socialism" strategy, a clandestine effort to win working-class support for the tsarist regime. Gapon organized a massive and peaceful march on the Winter Palace in January 1905 that was brutally put down by troops, resulting in the loss of a hundred lives. The "Bloody Sunday" repression ended any hope of police socialism and revolutionized the St. Petersburg working class.

Following Bloody Sunday, Gapon fled abroad, trading police socialism for revolution. He met with **Vladimir Lenin,** as well as other Bolsheviks and the Socialist Revolutionary **Battle Organization** leaders, to obtain weapons and financial support for revolution. In early 1906, Gapon entered Russian Finland, where he was murdered, apparently by members of the Socialist Revolutionary Party who had discovered his relationship with the *Okhrana*. Gapon was a tragic pawn caught between the *Okhrana* and the revolutionary parties. He died a priest without a church and a revolutionary without a party.

GAUCK COMMISSION. Following the collapse of the East German state, the German government in Bonn established a commission under Joachim Gauck to collect, declassify, and release the records of the Ministry of State Security (*Stasi*). The records, more than a million linear feet, documented the history of a **Leninist** state through the eyes of the police and their agents. No such publication has appeared in Russia, though in Latvia and Lithuania, many of the KGB's records have been released. While the publication of the documents sparked more than a few divorces and assaults as spouses, lovers, and friends discovered who had been working for the *Stasi*, it did allow some degree of closure in Germany. Along with Bishop Desmond Tutu's Truth and Reconciliation Commission in South Africa, it demonstrated the need for countries to face the truth of their past. There has been no Gauck Commission in Russia. Most of the research on repression has therefore been carried out by nonprofit organizations, such as **Memorial**.

GEHLEN, REINHARD (1902–1979). Gehlen served as the German military high command chief of intelligence on the Soviet Union from 1942 until the defeat of Nazi Germany. As chief of Foreign Armies East (*Fremde Heere Ost*), Gehlen was repeatedly fooled by *Smersh*, which used **radio games** and **double agents** to misinform German intelligence and deceive the Nazi war machine. He miscalled the Soviet offensive near Stalingrad in November 1942. In 1944, his organization totally missed the Red Army's offensive against Minsk, an error that contributed to the defeat of Army Group Center and more than 300,000 German casualties. Nevertheless, Gehlen was a conscientious intelligence officer whose estimates of the Red Army order of battle angered Adolf Hitler. In early 1945, Hitler fired Gehlen for his estimates of Soviet military strength.

Gehlen sensed by 1945 that the end of the war would bring a cold war between the victors. Prior to the German surrender in 1945, he buried the records of his organization. He then approached the British and the Americans as the expert on the Red Army and the Soviet Union. The Western allies needed intelligence on the Red Army and agreed to finance Gehlen. In the late 1940s, the Gehlen apparatus ran operations inside the Soviet bloc with the same lack of success that they had half a decade earlier. There was little criticism of Gehlen, who was allowed to transform his organization into the *Bundesnachrichtendiest*, West Germany's foreign intelligence service. Gehlen produced important order-of-battle information for the North Atlantic Treaty Organization; he was the only source of human intelligence on the Red Army.

Gehlen's greatest failing, however, was his unwillingness to vet his sources and his deputies. Believing that he could not be deceived, he invariably was. Following revelations in 1961 that a key deputy, **Heinz Felfe**, was a **KGB** agent, Gehlen was forced into relinquishing much of his power over the organization. Neither in Hitler's court nor later in work with the Western allies did Gehlen ever admit he was wrong, which he was on a great many occasions.

See also *MASKIROVKA*; BAGRATION, OPERATION.

GERHARDT, DIETER (1935–). Gerhardt's German family was interned in South Africa during **World War II**. Despite his seething resentment of this "injustice," he joined the South African navy and was commissioned as an officer. In 1960, Gerhardt walked into the Soviet embassy in London and volunteered to work for the **GRU**. A short time later, he divorced his English wife and married Ruth Johr, a Swiss woman who shared his interest in working against the South African government and getting rich in the process.

For the next 23 years, Gerhardt was successful as a South African naval officer and a Soviet agent. He rose to the rank of commodore and in 1983 was the commander of the Simonstown Naval Base. He and his wife received training in Moscow, as well as sophisticated communications equipment, and the Gerhardts provided their Soviet handlers with details about the South African defense establishment and its nuclear weapons program and information about North Atlantic Treaty Organization armed forces.

The Gerhardts were arrested in 1983. Dieter was sentenced to death by a military court-martial, but the sentence was later commuted to life in prison. His wife was sentenced to life by a civil court. Following the collapse of the apartheid government, the Gerhardts were released and settled in Switzerland. In 1994, Gerhardt told the South African press that he had told the Soviets that the South Africans and Israelis had tested a nuclear weapon in 1979 in the South Atlantic. This charge has never been fully substantiated, and some believe that his interview was an effort to excuse 23 years of treason.

GIRKIN, IGOR VSEVOLODOVICH (1970–). The biography of **GRU** Colonel Igor Girkin is linked with Russian *Spetsnaz* operations over the past two decades. He reportedly fought in Chechnya and took part in covert paramilitary operations in **Moldova** on the side of pro-Russian separatists. He also reportedly fought as a volunteer in the early 1990s in the Bosnian War with Serb forces. He was accused in the Bosnian media of participation in the Višegrad massacres, in which thousands of Muslim Bosniaks were killed.

With the nom de guerre "Igor Ivanovich Strelkov," Girkin became the "defense minister" of the self-proclaimed Donetsk People's Republic in the eastern Ukraine in June 2014. Girkin previously had been an adviser to pro-Moscow, Russian irregular battalions in the **Crimea**. He has been identified by the **Ukrainian** government and the international media as the chief of the Kremlin's military effort. As the commanding officer of rebel forces, he was reportedly responsible for the pillaging of Ukrainian arsenals and the storming of police stations and Ukrainian government communication facilities as well as the downing of Ukrainian aircraft and a Malayan aircraft. The government of Ukraine has charged Girkin with terrorism, and the U.S. Department of the Treasury placed financial sanctions on Girkin and six others for their role in attempting to destabilize Ukraine.

Girkin has been identified by Russian human rights activists as having participated in the forced disappearance and presumed murder of Chechen civilians. His pseudonym "Strelkov" can be translated as "shooter." The Ukrainian press has published accounts of the execution of Ukrainian civilians ordered by Girkin/"STRELKOV" (he has reportedly signed death sentences with his pseudonym and then printed underneath the signature his real name).

GKO (*GOSUDARSVENNIY KOMITET OBORONY*). The State Defense Committee was created by **Joseph Stalin** on 30 June 1941 with a basic membership of eight senior party, military, and security police officials to manage the Soviet war effort against Nazi Germany. In effect, the GKO was the government of the Soviet Union during **World War II** (1941–1945) with power to issue decrees with the force of law to all state, party, military, and police organizations. It oversaw military strategy, supervised military production, and directed all matters relating to state security. The leaders of the **NKVD** and **NKGB** reported to **Lavrenty Beria** and Stalin on a daily basis. A major reason for the Soviet Union's success in the war was the creation of political and military unity of command through the GKO. Whereas Adolf Hitler enjoyed watching his underlings fight, Stalin built a coordinated center of political and military operations. While the German intelligence and security services often battled for Hitler's ear, the GKO structure allowed intelligence to be funneled into military strategy.

Beria served as a member of the GKO responsible for all issues of state security and intelligence. Under Beria's direction, the intelligence services provided intelligence on the Nazi enemy and kept the dictator aware of developments in Soviet society. The GKO was a major consumer of foreign intelligence during the course of the war. More than 3,000 raw intelligence reports were circulated to the GKO by the NKGB. Probably no fewer were issued by the **GRU**. Beria and Stalin singled out intelligence officers for medals and promotions. They also mandated criticism and punishment for lack of work or suspected treachery. Senior intelligence officers were recalled from foreign postings for punishment on a few occasions. The GKO was abolished by decree in September 1945 following the defeat of Japan. In the next few years, Stalin permitted the security service to punish many of the most successful GKO's staff officers, including the commanders of the Soviet air force and navy.

GLASNOST. *Glasnost* (openness, transparency) was an effort by **Communist Party** General Secretary **Mikhail Gorbachev** to use information about Soviet history, as well as current political, social, and economic conditions, to modernize the Soviet Union and build a political base. *Glasnost* began after the Chernobyl nuclear reactor disaster in April 1986. The unwillingness of the Soviet bureaucracy to inform the Soviet people of the scope of the disaster until 10 days afterward convinced Gorbachev that radical change was necessary. Critical to the campaign was a reexamination of the crimes of the **Stalin** era. History was rewritten, some archives were opened, and hundreds of thousands of the Stalin's victims were rehabilitated.

Glasnost allowed Soviet citizens a much more honest—though hardly complete—account of the past. It also led to demands for greater freedoms, the establishment of an independent press, and a full accounting of the crimes of the Stalin period. However, *glasnost* also enraged the more reactionary members of the Communist Party, who believed that Gorbachev's policy would destroy the political authority of the party and the **KGB**. *Glasnost*, in the opinion of many historians, was indirectly responsible for the rise of Russian reformer **Boris Yeltsin**. Yeltsin and his supporters saw information as a key weapon in the struggle for political power. They supported new journals, such as *Argumenty i Fakhti* (Arguments and Facts), *Literaturnaya Gazeta* (Literary Journal), and *Ogonek* (The Little Fire), that researched the Soviet past and pushed the envelope in the debate on Soviet politics.

Under the **Vladimir Putin** regimes, *glasnost* has been incomplete. While some archives have been opened and we have more raw information about the Soviet period, access to the old intelligence archives remains limited. **Blank spots** remain.

See also COLD WAR.

GLAVLIT. The "ideological **KGB**" of the Soviet system was *Glavlit*, an acronym for *Glavnoe upravlenie delam literatury i izdatv* (Main Directorate of Literature and the Press). It was founded in 1922 with a **Cheka** officer as its vice director. By 1970, it had become the regime's chief censor with a staff of 70,000. Nothing could be released for publication without its imprimatur. Some Western specialists believe that at least one of *Glavlit*'s deputy chiefs was a KGB official and that the KGB assisted in *Glavlit*'s annual compilation of its *Censor's Index*, a thick volume listing all military, technical, statistical, and other subjects that could not be publicized without specific permission from the Central Committee of the **Communist Party**.

Another of *Glavlit*'s duties was to ensure that there were no mistakes or misprints in the party press. In the Stalin period, even misprints could cost a printer or an editor his freedom. For example, they made sure that the city of Stalingrad never appeared as *Stalin grad* ("Stalin is a reptile"). They also made sure that the publications of **enemies of the people** disappeared from bookstores and libraries and that they were never quoted, except to show their errors. For example, in 1938–1939, 24, 138,77 books were destroyed for political reasons.

Glavlit worked closely with the KGB's Fifth Directorate (**Counterintelligence** within the Intelligentsia) in monitoring the illegal publication of anti-Soviet material. Authors whose material was rejected by *Glavlit* for political or ideological reasons were reported to the KGB and were kept on a watch list.

GLAVRVEDUPR. A Russian acronym for Chief Intelligence Directorate (**GRU**).

GOGLIDZE, SERGEI ARSENYEVICH (1901–1953). A protégé of **Lavrenty Beria**, Goglidze rose quickly with his mentor and became one of the most powerful **Chekists** in **Joseph Stalin**'s Soviet Union. Goglidze left the tsarist army in 1917 and joined the Red Army two months after the Bolshevik Revolution. He joined the **Cheka** in 1921 and served at posts in Central Asia and in Georgia, where he came to Beria's attention.

When Beria was appointed to the leadership of the **NKVD**, Goglidze was assigned to purge Leningrad of enemies. In 1941, he was sent by Beria to oversee developments in the Far East. He held positions in both **counterintelligence** and labor camp administration during the next decade. Goglidze was promoted to colonel general in 1945 and was appointed by Stalin to the **Communist Party** Central Committee. Following Stalin's death in March 1953, Goglidze was responsible for security arrangements for the dictator's funeral. He was then appointed by Beria to a series of important posts, but with his mentor's fall four months later, his fate was sealed. He was arrested on 7 July and tried and shot with Beria on 23 December 1953.

GOLD, HARRY (1910–1974). Born in Switzerland to Russian Jewish parents, Gold was brought to the United States as a small child. He was recruited by the Soviets in 1935 to provide information on American industrial and scientific technology. Gold's service to Moscow was paid for, though he later claimed that he was an ideological recruit. The **NKVD** gave Gold funds to finish his postgraduate education in chemistry. During **World War II**, Gold was assigned by the NKVD's New York *rezidentura* to maintain contact with **Klaus Fuchs**, serving as a courier for documents on the Anglo-

American nuclear weapons program. Gold traveled to New Mexico, New York, and Boston a total of nine times to meet with the German **émigré**, who was the Soviet Union's most important source within the Manhattan Project.

Five years later, in an interview with agents of the Federal Bureau of Investigation (FBI) in London, Fuchs identified Gold as the man he knew as "Raymond." Gold further ensured his own arrest by sloppy **tradecraft**: the FBI found copies of New Mexico maps in Gold's apartment after the accused spy assured them he had never been west of Chicago. After his arrest, Gold provided critical information to the FBI about the Rosenberg ring by identifying David Greenglass, **Julius Rosenberg**'s brother-in-law, as another key agent. Gold was tried with the Rosenbergs and received a 30-year sentence. He was released in 1966, having served half his sentence.

See also ENORMOZ; VENONA.

GOLENIEWSKI, MICHAEL (1922–1993). In March 1958, the American ambassador in Switzerland received a letter from an individual code-named "Heckenschutze" (Sniper) who offered to work for U.S. intelligence. For the next three years, the Central Intelligence Agency (CIA) ran "Sniper" clandestinely, never knowing who the source was but receiving from him 27 letters with a host of **counterintelligence** leads. In January 1961, the source defected in Berlin with his mistress and 1,000 pages of classified information. The CIA could finally put a name to the source.

Michael Goleniewski had been conscripted as a slave laborer by the Germans in 1939. After **World War II**, he was recruited into Polish military counterintelligence, where he was mentored by Soviet officers. The **KGB** ran Goleniewski as a liaison contact and as a penetration of the allied Polish service. It placed Goleniewski in a position where he could do tremendous damage to both his service and the KGB. His information from the KGB and the Polish intelligence services was thus explosive: he could identify **Heinz Felfe** and **George Blake** as Soviet spies. He could also provide information about how the KGB and other Warsaw Pact services operated in the West. Goleniewski was debriefed for several years. He later claimed to be the real Russian tsarevitch, Mikhail Romanov, who had somehow escaped assassination with his parents and siblings in 1918. Despite his eccentricities, Goleniewski was one of the most important of the CIA's counterintelligence agents of the **Cold War**. He provided the West with important details of KGB operations and the Soviet service's ability to recruit and run agents in the West. His information, which compromised Blake badly, damaged KGB operations.

GOLIKOV, FILIPP IVANOVICH (1900–1980). Golikov followed **Ivan Proskurov** as military intelligence chief. Five of his predecessors had been executed for treason in the previous three years. As chief of the **GRU** in 1940 and 1941, Golikov bears considerable responsibility for the Soviet initial response to Operation **Barbarossa.** Despite warnings from agents with access to Nazi war plans, Golikov repeatedly watered down his service's reporting on Nazi military preparation to **Joseph Stalin.** Aware that Stalin did not believe that Adolf Hitler would invade the Soviet Union in 1941, Golikov often labeled accurate intelligence submitted to Stalin as unreliable, dubious, or British disinformation. Miraculously, Golikov was not punished for his gross malfeasance but was assigned first as a liaison officer with the British and then to a troop command. During the war, Golikov commanded armies and fronts. In 1961, he was promoted to marshal of the Soviet Union.

See also FITIN, PAVEL MIKHAILOVICH (1907–1971).

GOLITSYN, ANATOLI MIKHAILOVICH (1926–). The most difficult and disruptive **defector** in the history of the Central Intelligence Agency (CIA), Golitsyn defected to the CIA station in Helsinki, Finland, on 15 December 1961. A **KGB** major at the time of his defection, Golitsyn was slated for demotion for lack of performance. While he had a poor record as an operation officer, he had knowledge of KGB operations in Europe from previous tours in Vienna and Moscow.

Golitsyn and his family were flown immediately to the United States for debriefing. Over the next several months, he provided the CIA with information about KGB operations in Western Europe as well as the names of several Soviet agents, including **Hugh Hambleton**, a Canadian employee of the North Atlantic Treaty Organization. He also reportedly told CIA director Allan Dulles that the KGB had not penetrated the CIA. Later, however, Golitsyn changed his story, claiming that the KGB had indeed recruited several sources inside the CIA. Golitsyn's charges were accepted by CIA **counterintelligence** chief James Jesus Angleton and set off a "mole hunt" that destroyed the careers of several officers and tied up operations against the Soviet target. Golitsyn's accusations that **Yuri Nosenko** was a false defector and a dispatched KGB **double agent** convinced the CIA to illegally incarcerate him for three years.

Golitsyn's charges of KGB penetration were eventually proven false, but by that time, he had badly damaged U.S. intelligence operations. While some analysts went so far as to declare Golitsyn a KGB plant, studies of the case suggest that the damage to the CIA was self-inflicted, that senior counterintelligence officials accepted Golitsyn's charges out of fear that the KGB could penetrate their agencies the way it had British, French, and German intelligence.

GOLOS, JOSEPH [RAISEN, JACOB] (1890–1943). After emigrating to the United States as a political refugee from tsarist repression, Golos joined the American communist movement. During the Russian civil war, he returned to his homeland to serve the infant Soviet state and was recruited into foreign intelligence. In 1927, he returned to the United States, where he worked as an **illegal**. His cover was the head of World Tourists, which arranged travel for Americans interested in visiting the Soviet Union. The cover allowed Golos to move money and people into and out of the United States.

Golos was one of the key people in the Soviet intelligence network. His code name was "Zvuk" (Sound). He acted as a recruiter and agent handler as well as the link between agents recruited by the **Communist Party** and the **NKVD**. His most important sources were the agents of the **Silvermaster group**, more than 20 American civil servants who volunteered to work for Soviet intelligence in the 1930s. Golos also managed an operation that forged passports for Soviet agents.

One of Golos's couriers was his lover, **Elizabeth Bentley**, who maintained contact with important sources in the U.S. Treasury Department, the White House, and the Office of Strategic Services. **Julius Rosenberg** contacted Golos in the early 1940s and was referred by him to a Soviet case officer. The strain of managing cover companies, forging documents, and running agents took a terrible toll on his life, and Golos died of a heart attack in late 1943. His death seriously unsettled Soviet intelligence operations in the United States. The NKVD *rezidentura* badly handled some of his agents, and their ham-handedness convinced Bentley to defect.

GOLUSKEVICH, VLADIMIR SERGEEVICH (1899–1964). Marshal **Georgii Zhukov**'s chief of staff, Lieutenant General Goluskevich, was arrested by the **NKVD** in July 1942, possibly in an attempt to incriminate Zhukov. He was held in pretrial confinement for almost 10 years and was condemned to 10 years' imprisonment in February 1952. He was released and rehabilitated in 1953, largely thanks to Zhukov's efforts. Released NKVD documents reveal that Goluskevich was severely interrogated in an attempt to compromise Zhukov. *Smersh* chief **Viktor Abakumov** reported to **Joseph Stalin** that Goluskevich had been a member of opposition groups.

GORBACHEV, MIKHAIL SERGEYEVICH (1931–). While leader of the **Communist Party** and president of the Soviet Union, Gorbachev presided over the dismantling of the Soviet Union. He had been brought into the Politburo by **KGB** chief **Yuri Andropov** and rose to general secretary of the party in 1985. He was president of the Soviet Union from 1988 to 1991 and introduced a period of liberalization. Gorbachev made use of the security services for **antireligious campaigns** in Central Asia. His efforts with **MVD** head **Vitalii Fedorchuk** to purge and reform the police were unsuccessful, and Gorbachev's reform policies, including *glasnost* and *perestroika*, were resisted by KGB figures such as **Viktor Chebrikov** and **Filip Bobkov**. Conservative bureaucrats and senior police officials sought to replace him through the **August putsch of 1991** but were forced to back down, although Gorbachev was left a weakened figure, overshadowed by **Boris Yeltsin**.

GORDIEVSKIY, OLEG ANTONOVICH (1938–). One of the most important defeats for the **KGB** in the **Cold War** was the defection of Colonel Oleg Gordievskiy, who volunteered to work for the British Secret Intelligence Service (SIS) when he was stationed in Denmark. He apparently acted out of deep anger with the Soviet decision to intervene in Czechoslovakia in the summer of 1968. He agreed to work without payment, claiming that he worked for ideological reasons. On his assignment to London in 1983 as deputy *rezident*, Gordievskiy provided the SIS with thousands of KGB documents. Gordievskiy's reporting allowed London and Washington to defuse a crisis in the fall of 1983, when the Soviets, collecting information through their *RYaN* program, suspected the West of planning a covert nuclear strike against the Soviet Union.

In 1985, **Aldrich Ames** provided the KGB with information to identify Gordievskiy as a British agent. (More recently, Russian intelligence officers have claimed that Gordievskiy was identified by other Soviet agents.) Gordievskiy was tricked into returning to Moscow and confronted with evidence of his behavior. The KGB left Gordievskiy a week to consider his treason and confess. He used a danger signal to alert the British, and with the direct approval of Prime Minister Margaret Thatcher, the British service rescued Gordievskiy from certain death.

Gordievskiy's escape was an embarrassment for the KGB, especially when he began appearing on British television to discuss Soviet intelligence operations in London. Gordievskiy was later received by President Ronald Reagan at the White House. He lectured at the Central Intelligence Agency, with Ames in the audience. The Soviet government refused to allow Gordievskiy's wife or children to join him in London. Following the collapse of the Soviet Union, the new authorities permitted his family to emigrate. Gordievskiy settled in London, where he has written widely about the Soviet intelligence services. His books are considered the most authoritative accounts of KGB foreign operations.

GORSKIY, ANATOLI VENIAMINOVICH (1907–1980). After a decade of work in internal security, Gorskiy joined foreign intelligence and was sent to London as deputy **NKVD** *rezident* in 1936 under the name "Gromov."

With the purge of foreign intelligence, Gorskiy took command of the London *rezidentura*, which Moscow had briefly closed, and ran British agents within the establishment. He was reassigned to Moscow in 1944. With the recall of **Vasily Zarubin** from Washington on suspicion of treachery later that year, Gorskiy was dispatched to Washington, where he served as *rezident* for two years. Intercepted Soviet intelligence messages suggest that Gorskiy ran **Lauchlin Currie**, a White House aide to President Franklin D. Roosevelt.

Gorskiy had unique access to the American political leadership for an Allied diplomat or intelligence officer. On 24 October 1945, Gorskiy met for breakfast with former U.S. Vice President Henry Wallace. Wallace sought to explain the new Truman presidency to Gorskiy, noting that the Democratic Party was now divided between "Roosevelt Democrats," favoring entente with Moscow, and the new hawkish advisers of President Harry Truman, whom Wallace characterized as "petty politicos." The information was sent to **Joseph Stalin**.

Gorskiy was not impressive physically. An agent described him as "a short fattish man in his mid-30s with blond hair pushed straight back and glasses that failed to mask a pair of shrewd cold eyes." Gorskiy was, however, an outstanding agent handler. He ran important agents, such as **Kim Philby**, as well as men and women within the British nuclear weapons program. The Soviet intelligence effort in the United States began to collapse during his tenure as chief, but that was not Gorskiy's fault. Rather, the defection of **Elizabeth Bentley** in the United States and **Igor Gouzenko** in Canada provided critical insights into Soviet **tradecraft** and agents. Gorskiy returned to Moscow, where he worked in the foreign intelligence directorate. He left, highly decorated, with the rank of colonel.

GOTT, RICHARD (1938–). A prominent British journalist, he was identified as a **KGB** agent by **Oleg Gordiyevskiy**. Gott later admitted that he took "Red Gold in the form of expenses for himself and his partner." Gott was never prosecuted and is a professor at the University of London.

GOUZENKO, IGOR (1919–1982). A **GRU** communications clerk, Gouzenko was the first important Soviet **defector** of the **Cold War**. After having served at the front and in Moscow as a code clerk, Gouzenko was sent to Ottawa to the GRU *rezidentura* in 1943. In September 1945, he took more than 100 classified documents out of the Soviet embassy and requested political asylum for himself and his family. Gouzenko's action flummoxed the Canadian government, but Prime Minister McKenzie King ordered that Gouzenko be protected and granted him political asylum. Canada was poorly prepared to deal with Soviet espionage: at the time of Gouzenko's defection, the Royal Canadian Mounted Police had a grand total of two **counterintelligence** specialists.

Gouzenko's debriefing by the Canadian and British governments produced leads to 20 Canadians working with Russian intelligence, including Fred Rose, a member of Parliament. This led to 12 convictions, including Kay Willsher, the secretary to the British high commissioner in Canada, and officials involved in nuclear weapons development. Gouzenko's information illustrated the reach of Soviet networks: another important Soviet spy uncovered by the British from his information was **Allan Nunn May**, who was tried and convicted in London.

Gouzenko was a difficult defector to manage. Despite writing two best sellers, he was constantly in debt. He sued a number of magazines that dared to refer to him as a defector. Nevertheless, Gouzenko's defection marks the public beginning of the intelligence cold war between the Soviet Union and the West.

GPU (*GOSURDARSTVENNOE POLITICHESKOE UPRAVLENIE*). The GPU, or State Political Directorate, was the immediate successor of the **Cheka**. It was formed on 6 February 1922 and was replaced by the **OGPU** in November 1923.

GRAVES, MASS. A major question for modern Russian society has been the resting place for the victims of **Joseph Stalin**. Mass graves are to be found at **Kuropaty** in Belarus and Bykivnia near Kiev, as well as in western Siberia, in Karelia, and at Kommunarka near Moscow—to name only a few. A mass grave site at Butovo in Moscow, now a Russian Orthodox Church property, holds more than 20,000 bodies of men and women shot in 1937 and 1938. Still, most of the mass graves remain unknown and perhaps unknowable, as the **KGB** destroyed records that could implicate surviving officials, but human rights groups persist in documenting the extent of the Soviet holocaust. As late as September 2002, the Russian human rights group **Memorial** discovered a mass grave near St. Petersburg, where as many as 30,000 people are interred.

Mass graves exist at many former forced labor camps. Hundreds of thousands perished from cold and overwork as well as **execution**. According to **gulag** records, for example, 600,000 prisoners perished in labor camps during **World War II**. Yet camp records are at best sketchy and incomplete. Another problem facing the history of the Soviet terror are the graves of those murdered by the security service without any trial or judicial process.

In 1939, Kira Kulik, the wife of Marshal Kulik, was abducted by the **NKVD**, held at **Lubyanka**, and then shot without interrogation or trial. She is but one of a host of people whose fate and final resting place need documentation.

See also YEZHOVSHCHINA (THE TIME OF YEZHOV).

GREAT PATRIOTIC WAR. The war against Nazi Germany, known in the Soviet Union as the Great Patriotic War, cost the Soviet people more than 27 million dead, of whom almost 20 million were civilians. The war could not have been won without the total victory of the Soviet intelligence and **counterintelligence** services over their Nazi enemy. But a proportion of the losses were self-inflicted by the Soviet security service on the people they protected in an effort to ensure the security of the rear area.

Joseph Stalin often ignored good intelligence; his refusal to heed intelligence about the forthcoming German assault was one of the reasons for massive Soviet casualties in the opening battles of the war. Nevertheless, Stalin and his subordinates in the military and intelligence services were able to use the **NKVD** and *Smersh* to defeat the German intelligence services, to support a **partisan** movement behind German lines, and to collect military secrets through human and technical intelligence means. Within six months of the Nazi invasion, the NKVD played a critical role in the **Battle of Moscow** in defeating the Wehrmacht.

As the war progressed, the Soviet services were able to deceive the Nazi enemy repeatedly because of the mastery of the invisible front—the intelligence war between the Nazis and the Soviets. Control of their own rear and penetration of the German military and intelligence establishments allowed Stalin's military commanders to repeatedly deceive the Nazis: the massive Soviet victory in Operation **Bagration** in June 1944 was one of a number of victories made possible by strategic deception. The Soviets also made use of *maskirovka* and **radio games** deception strategies. According to a recent study of Soviet counterintelligence at war, "The Soviets forged counterintelligence—albeit ruthlessly and certainly not efficiently—into a formidable strategic weapon."

The NKVD played a critical role in the first six months of the war on the battlefield. As the situation worsened in the late summer of 1941, **Joseph Stalin** ordered NKVD internal security and **border guard** formations stripped of their officers and noncommissioned officers to form the cadres for nine new rifle divisions. Moreover, of the 15 Soviet army commanders engaged in the fighting of the fall of 1941, five were NKVD generals. While Marshal **Georgy Zhukov** found these men brave, he graded their tactical abilities as poor, and in fact three were relieved for cause by the end of the campaign. NKVD casualties during the war were high, more than 150,000 killed in action. The Internal Troops lost 94,000, while the **Border Guards** suffered 61,000 killed in action, most of the casualties occurring in the first days of the war.

Lavrenty Beria served as Stalin's security and intelligence generalissimo during the war. He and his subordinates were also deeply involved in the partisan movement. Stalin and Beria also used the NKVD to prevent any possible political or ethnic dissent. **Deportations** began before the first round of the war: hundreds of thousands of Soviet Poles and Germans were deported in 1939–1941 to **exile** in Siberia by the security service. Moreover, in 1941–1944, more than 2 million Soviet citizens from the Baltic states, the Crimea, and the Caucasus were deported to Siberia by the security service.

Beria used the security services to punish the incompetent and the weak. In early 1943, the NKVD took control of the railroad network behind Marshal Rokossovskiy's Central Front and executed several managers for inefficiency under the guise of "sabotage." Countless more Soviet citizens were executed under various pretexts: a document submitted to Stalin in the first months of the war indicated that more than 10,000 people were executed in the summer and fall of 1941. The NKVD also shot hundreds of political prisoners in jails across the Soviet Union rather than let them fall into the hands of the advancing Germans. In 1945, with victory in sight, military tribunals sentenced to death or terms in the camps 135,056 members of the military for "counterrevolutionary crimes." Among those condemned to execution or imprisonment were 273 senior officers.

The **GRU** and the NKVD also spied on wartime allies. Both services collected information about Anglo-American strategy, intelligence, and diplomatic services. Another focus was the nascent nuclear weapons program, which the Soviets code-named *Enormoz*. The Soviet services also knew about the British **Ultra** program, which had broken the codes of the Enigma machine. In 1945, 18 Soviet intelligence officers in the United States were running more than 300 sources. Soviet accomplishments in Canada and the United Kingdom were no less impressive.

The war created an "ideological truce" within the Soviet Union. All Soviet citizens were made to feel that they were in the struggle against Nazi Germany together. The Soviet poetess **Anna Akhmatova** noted the strange freedom many felt in those days: "In mud, darkness, hunger, grief, / where death followed our heel like a shadow / we felt such happiness / we breathed such stormy freedom." To Stalin and his police, the end of **World War II** presented the challenge of how to regain control of the country. The year of victory was thus a year of repression in the Baltic republics and the western Ukraine, and it was marked by the arrest of countless men and women who had been captured or forced to work in Hitler's camps or factories.

The Great Patriotic War shaped the strategy and priorities of Soviet intelligence during the **Cold War**. A major issue for both the KGB and the GRU from 1945 to 1991 was the threat of a surprise atomic attack by the North Atlantic Treaty Organization (NATO), leading to the *RYaN* program, which gathered information about possible attack plans. **Yuri Andropov**, first as KGB boss and then as head of state, insisted that the services provide reporting of a possible "nuclear 22 June," forcing intelligence officers to provide highly exaggerated information about a possible NATO strike in the fall of 1983.

GRIGORENKO, GRIGORY FEDOROVICH (1918–2007). Described in Russian intelligence literature as the "father of modern Soviet **counterintelligence**," Grigorenko entered the **NKVD**'s **military counterintelligence** component in 1941 and transferred to *Smersh*. He later served in the KGB as chief of the **Second Chief (Counterintelligence) Directorate** and then as deputy chairman, retiring with the rank of colonel general.

Prior to the **Hungarian revolution** of 1956, Grigorenko warned then ambassador **Yuri Andropov** and KGB headquarters of the possibility of political violence. The warning was not heeded in Moscow, and Grigorenko was reportedly recalled. During fighting in Budapest, Grigorenko was assigned to work with Soviet troops and was wounded seriously. His experience in Budapest earned him Andropov's respect, and he rose rapidly to become a three-star general in the KGB afterward.

GRIGULEVICH, IOSIF ROMUALDOVICH (1913–1988). A Lithuanian Jew, Grigulevich was recruited into the Soviet service as an **illegal** and operated for two decades in Latin America and Europe. In the late 1930s, he established networks that supported the **NKVD**'s assassination of **Leon Trotsky**. During **World War II**, Grigulevich, who was stationed in Argentina, organized the sabotage of neutral ships carrying cargo to Germany. Following the war, he was naturalized as a Costa Rican citizen and was appointed that country's ambassador to Italy and the Vatican. **Joseph Stalin** planned to use Grigulevich to murder Yugoslav leader Josef Broz Tito, but the plan apparently ended with Stalin's death. In 1953, Grigulevich was recalled to Moscow and disappeared from the Costa Rican diplomatic service. He resurfaced in Moscow in the 1960s as an academician, ending his career as a corresponding member of the Academy of Sciences.

GRU (*GLAVNOE RAZVEDIVATELNOE UPRAVLENIYE*). The GRU, the Chief Intelligence Directorate, oversees military intelligence. Russian military intelligence was always formidable in providing human source intelligence on the tsar's adversaries. Russian military intelligence can trace its heritage to 1810, when Tsar Aleksandr I mandated an intelligence bureau within the general staff. In the wars against France (1812–1814), military intelligence provided information on the French adversary and on the country where the Russian army was operating. Many of the intelligence officers had extensive engineering experience, allowing them to translate information from sources on roads, cities, and fortresses into material for a general staff moving hundreds of thousands of military personnel across central Europe.

Tsar Nikolai I reportedly told the general staff at the time of the Crimean War, "We have no need of spies, we have *The Times*. Nevertheless, in the last decades of the 19th century, Imperial Russia developed a core of experts on Western and Central Europe.

Before **World War I**, Russian military attachés were the key players in military intelligence. They also worked with military intelligence officers in Warsaw, Moscow, and St. Petersburg. A major success for military intelligence was the recruitment of Colonel **Alfred Redl**, an Austrian officer who was a promiscuous homosexual. Redl was blackmailed into providing detailed information on Austrian military planning for war against Russia and its ally Serbia, as well as **counterintelligence** information about Austrian agents.

Soviet military intelligence was founded on 5 November 1918 by Commissar of War **Leon Trotsky**, who appointed Semyon Aralov its first chief. While the name changed repeatedly, it is known in Soviet history usually as either the Fourth Department of the General Staff or the Chief Intelligence Directorate (GRU) of the General Staff. The GRU and its predecessors were not political services like the **Cheka** or the **KGB**. Chiefs of military intelligence almost never served on the **Communist Party** Central Committee, and its officers did not have the role of protectors of the party—a role assumed by the Cheka.

In its first two decades of Soviet history, military intelligence's most striking success came from the use of **illegal** officers and agents who were directed by **Yan Berzin**, the service chief for more than a decade. Illegals began operating in Western Europe and Asia in the early 1920s and in the United States in 1923. Illegal agents, including **Maria Polyakova**, **Richard Sorge**, and **Leopold Trepper**, organized intelligence rings in China, Japan, Nazi Germany, France, and Switzerland. GRU illegals in Great Britain and the United States, including **Ruth Werner** and **Arthur Adams**, recruited and ran important sources in the nuclear weapons program, as well as in the military and defense industries.

In the late 1930s, over half the cadre of the GRU was arrested and shot during the *Yezhovshchina*, including Berzin and several of his senior colleagues. Following Berzin's arrest, four other GRU chiefs were purged and shot in the next three years. The **NKVD** especially targeted foreigners who had been GRU illegals. Leopold Trepper wrote in his memoirs, "As a Polish citizen, as a Jew who had lived in Palestine, as an expatriate, and as a journalist on a Jewish paper, I was ten times suspect in the eyes of the NKVD."

The contribution of the GRU during the **Great Patriotic War** was impressive. Sorge, Trepper, and other illegals produced detailed information on German military planning. During this period, GRU *rezidenturas* produced military, scientific, and industrial intelligence from a score of countries. In Canada, **Nikolai Zabotin** and his staff of 13 ran agents in the Canadian Parliament, the British High Commission, and the Anglo-American nuclear weapons program. GRU officers also collected thousands of pieces of unclassified information for the Soviet war effort. According to a study by the Federal Bureau of Investigation, the GRU *rezidentura* in Washington acquired 41,800 American patents.

Following **World War II**, the GRU expanded its network of military attachés and reduced its dependency on illegals. One of the service's greatest successes was the recruitment and running of **Stig Wennerstrom**, a Swedish military intelligence officer. The GRU suffered a massive loss of prestige in the 1950s and 1960s, however, due to the decision of two officers, **Petr Popov** and **Oleg Penkovskiy**, to spy for the United States. As a result of the latter's defection, the chief of the GRU, General **Ivan Serov**, was fired and reduced in rank by three grades. He was replaced by General **Petr Ivashutin**, a KGB veteran who remained as head of the GRU for the next 23 years. Under Ivashutin, the GRU became a sophisticated, all-source intelligence service, conducting **signals intelligence**, space reconnaissance, and human intelligence operations. The GRU prepared daily briefings on military and political issues for the chief of the general staff and the Ministry of Defense, and it controlled several *Spetsnaz* units to conduct long-range military reconnaissance.

GRU headquarters are located in a nine-story building on the Central Military Airfield (also known as Khodinka Field). GRU officers usually have a combat arms background. They are trained at the Military Diplomatic Academy in Moscow, where they receive a postgraduate education in languages and intelligence **tradecraft**.

Following the collapse of the Soviet Union in 1991, the GRU continued its operations abroad and from Russian territory. In July 2003, GRU chief **Valentin Korabelnikov** noted that the GRU continued to have a worldwide mission and both an **analytical** and an operational mission. Korabelnikov noted that GRU units had suffered approximately 300 casualties in the ongoing war in Chechnya.

In the first decade of the 21st century, the GRU appeared to lose prestige. The military intelligence service saw its funding reduced, and according to the Russian media, several senior officers were retired, while many midlevel officers were reassigned to combat formations. Moreover, *Spetsnaz* battalions were reassigned from the GRU to the combined strategic commands. This changed radically, however, in early 2014, when *Spetsnaz* formations, now GRU commanded, won an almost bloodless victory in the Crimea. GRU officers armed and led local militias in taking over civil government in towns and cities and forcing the redeployment of Ukrainian military units.

In the late spring of 2014, *Spetsnaz* units were active in the eastern Ukraine. This was not to be a bloodless victory, however. Major firefights occurred between Ukrainian army units and rebels led and armed by the GRU. Russian and Western observers noted in June that more and more Russian troops entered the fight, now with armored fighting vehicles and sophisticated surface-to-air missiles (SAMs). In June and July, these SAMs shot down several Ukrainian military aircraft and a Malaysian civilian airliner with 298 civilians on board. According to a British newspaper report from Moscow in August 2014, 12 GRU officers killed in Ukraine were given a military funeral in Moscow. A journalist covering the story found that several of the casualties were listed as "on vacation."

The GRU has embraced its recent successes. In the Russian social media, GRU officers have boasted of their successes, including the shooting down of the Malaysian airliner. The Russian media have speculated that the GRU has recovered its prestige and is seen by the administration of **Vladimir Putin** as an important player in national security policymaking.

See also GRU ORGANIZATION.

GRU ORGANIZATION. Far less has been written about the GRU than the **KGB.** The GRU's major components deal with human intelligence, space reconnaissance, and **signals intelligence**. The GRU is divided into numbered directorates, each led by a general officer.

During the **Cold War**, the First Directorate was charged with human intelligence collection and had components responsible for important countries. GRU officers preparing for assignments in *rezidenturas* abroad frequently served a tour as a desk officer in the First Directorate. The Fifth Directorate produced operational-tactical intelligence and worked closely with Red Army and Air Force commands. The Sixth Directorate was responsible for the collection of technical intelligence. This included intelligence collected from space, ground stations, and military signals intelligence units. The Seventh Directorate concentrated on the North Atlantic Treaty Organization. Within the directorate were six components targeted against individual countries. The Ninth Directorate was responsible for questions of military technology and worked closely with the Military-Industrial Commission (VPK) in the collection, **analysis**, and distribution of scientific and industrial intelligence information. Like Directorate T of the KGB's First Chief Directorate, the Ninth collected proprietary secrets as well as classified information. The 11th Directorate dealt with sensitive nuclear questions, including analysis of other states' nuclear weapons programs.

The GRU *rezident* in foreign states was the senior military attaché in the embassy. Other GRU officers were either military attachés or under cover in other diplomatic posts in the Soviet mission or semiofficial posts in the larger Soviet community. For example, a GRU officer might be under cover as the representative of a Soviet shipping line or Aeroflot, posts that gave the officers wide access to military-related information. GRU officers were tasked with the collection of open-source information about the country to which they were accredited. The GRU *rezidentura* in Washington in 1959, for example, subscribed to 44 newspapers and 58 magazines on technical, scientific, and military topics, according to a letter from Federal Bureau of Investigation Director J. Edgar Hoover to President Dwight Eisenhower.

GTK (*GOSTEKHKOMISSII*). The State Technical Commission, or GTK, is one of the least-known components of the Soviet and **Russian intelligence services**, with the responsibility to foil foreign intelligence collection. It was founded 5 January 1992 out of the Soviet-era State Technical Commission to Counter Foreign Intelligence. Its first director was General Yuri Yashin, an experienced **KGB** officer. The GTK draws expertise from both the military and the intelligence services. Its first chief in the Soviet era, Marshall Nikolai Ogarkov, who built the organization, was concerned about the ability of U.S. intelligence satellites to penetrate the Soviet military and military industries.

See also MASKIROVKA.

GUILLAUME, GUNTER (1927–1995). One of the **KGB**'s greatest successes in the **Cold War** was the infiltration of an agent of influence into the West German chancellor's inner circle. Guillaume, whose cover was that of a dedicated socialist who had defected from East Germany, became Willy Brandt's personal assistant and alter ego. His wife, Christl, was a no less important agent, serving as Brandt's private secretary. As Brandt, who served as chancellor from 1968 to 1974, moved the West German regime toward full diplomatic relations with East Germany, the Guillaumes reported every move to their masters in Moscow.

To what degree Guillaume influenced Brandt is open to debate: the German chancellor had already decided to push rapprochement with the East before his association with the Gillaumes. There is no doubt, however, that they were important agents with access to German and North Atlantic Treaty Organization secrets, and their information helped Moscow carefully craft its policy toward Germany. Following their betrayal by a Soviet **defector**, Guillaume was sentenced to 13 years in prison, his wife to nine. Both were later traded for Western agents.

The Guillaume case became—paradoxically—a defeat for the KGB. Following the Guillaumes' arrest, Brandt was forced to resign, and his policy was attacked as naive at best and treasonous at worst by his opponents on the right. The net result was that Moscow lost the one West German politician able to push rapprochement with the East.

GULAG. The term "gulag" is derived from *Glavnoye upravleniye ispravitel'no-trudovykh lagerei*, or Chief Directorate of Corrective Labor Camps, a sector of the Ministry of Internal Affairs (**MVD**). Nobel laureate **Aleksandr Solzhenitsyn** described the network of forced labor camps as an "archipelago" dotting the Soviet Union. At the height of the gulag system in the early 1950s, there were 476 labor camp clusters scattered across the territory of the Soviet Union. According to **Nikita Khrushchev**, 17 million people passed through the camps between 1937 and 1953.

While camps were established in the early 1920s at **Solovetsky** in northern Russia on the White Sea, the use of mass prison labor for economic projects was established by a **Communist Party** Politburo resolution of 27 June 1929. Party leader **Joseph Stalin** and his colleagues saw the opportunity to use imprisoned and **exiled** peasants on projects in the far north and Siberia. The number of prisoners grew from 179,000 in 1930 to 1.6 million in 1938, and they were employed in the building of railroads and canals (such as the **Belomor Canal**), in timbering in Siberia, in mining gold in the **Kolyma** River camps, and in building major mining and industrial centers at **Pechora**, **Norilsk**, and **Vorkuta**. During and after **World War II**, prison labor was engaged in building military airfields, electro-power plants, and facilities for the nuclear weapons program. **Lavrenty Beria** created a "nuclear gulag," a network of camps mining uranium and building secret nuclear sites. Under a secret declaration, no prisoners were released from these camps; rather, they were exiled to the Kolyma River area in northeastern Siberia.

At the time of Stalin's death in 1953, 2.5 million Soviet citizens were in the camps, and another 2.75 million lived in enforced **exile**. Life in the camps during the Stalin era was Hobbsean: at least 2.5 million died of hunger and overwork in the camps between 1930 and 1953, and the real figure may be twice that. (A study of the camps indicated that more than a million prisoners died during the war years.) While prison labor was available as long as the Stalinist terror continued, it was by all accounts expensive and inefficient. In 1952, gulag projects used approximately 10 percent of the capital construction budget of the Soviet Union, but many projects were unfinished or abandoned. Most of the industrial and mining enterprises run by labor camps were transferred to industrial ministries in 1953 within six months of Stalin's death. The post-Stalin leadership canceled many of the major projects, such as the canal between the Volga and Don rivers.

Following Stalin's death, the Soviet Union used labor camps for criminal and political convicts. Between 1955 and 1987, 10,000 to 15,000 political offenders passed through the camps, as well as thousands of religious believers who refused to conform to Soviet law. While these camps were not as brutal as those of the Stalin era, a number of political and religious **dissidents** died of overwork and medical problems.

GUPVI. The Chief Directorate of Prisoners and Internees (*Glavnoye Upravleniye po delam Voennoplennikh i Internirovannikh*) was the **NKVD** component responsible for prisoner-of-war camps during World War II and in the postwar years. During the war, more than 3 million Axis prisoners passed through the camps. Its cover name was "Institute 99."

In 1955, the last prisoners were released, including several thousand German military prisoners and 9,562 Poles who had fought both the German and the Soviet occupiers. Also held were Spanish, Hungarian, and Italians captured in 1942–1945.

GVISHIANI, MIKHAIL MAKSIMOVICH (1905–1966). After joining the Red Army at age 16, Gvishiani entered the **OGPU** in 1928. Like other Georgians in the security service, Gvishiani rose quickly after **Lavrenty Beria** moved to Moscow. Gvishiani was posted in 1938 to the Soviet Far East, where he remained for almost a decade. He took part in the **deportation** of the Chechen people, reportedly ordering mass **executions** of the old and infirm, according to a recent study. During Red Army operations against Japan in 1945, he was decorated for success in repatriating Manchurian industrial plants to the Soviet Union. In 1945, he was promoted to lieutenant general.

In August 1953, Gvishiani seemed in deep trouble. His patron and boss, Beria, had fallen and was destined for execution. But although Gvishiani was removed from the **MGB**, he never was arrested, and apparently he kept his rank. He was married to the daughter of **Communist Party** Central Committee member (and later premier) Aleksei Kosygin, and this connection apparently saved him.

HALL, JAMES (1957–). An important chapter of the **KGB** and *Stasi* partnership was the recruitment and running of James Hall. He volunteered to the KGB in Berlin and was run by the *Stasi*. The East German service also recruited a Turk whom Hall had known in Berlin to act as a courier. Hall was **motivated** to spy by both money and ego, and he received approximately $300,000 for his espionage. He told a KGB case officer, "I wasn't terribly short of money. I just didn't want to worry about where my next dollar was coming from. I am not anti-American. I can wave the flag as well as the next guy." Hall had access to highly classified U.S. technical intelligence secrets as a warrant officer, enabling the KGB's 16th (Signals Intelligence) Chief Directorate to understand the strengths and weaknesses of American **signals intelligence**. Moscow even dispatched a signals intelligence officer from Moscow to debrief Hall. Both the KGB and *Stasi* rated Hall's information as of critical importance.

Hall was identified by an East German agent of the Central Intelligence Agency, arrested in 1988, and tried by a military court-martial in March 1989. Hall pled guilty, agreed to cooperate with the U.S. authorities, and received a 40-year sentence. The Turkish courier received a life sentence for his part in several other operations. According to a senior American **counterintelligence** officer, the Hall case was a textbook illustration of KGB doctrine. "When recruiting Americans, ego is second only to money as a motivator."

HALL, THEODORE ALVIN (1926–2003). One of the most important Soviet penetrations of the American nuclear weapons program was through Ted Hall, who volunteered to work for the Soviet intelligence service while still an undergraduate at Harvard in 1944. While a researcher at Los Alamos, he passed critical weapons information to the Soviet service. Hall was introduced to Soviet intelligence by his friend Saville Sax. Because of the slight difference in their ages, Sax was code-named "Star" (Old), while Hall was "Mlad" (Youth). Hall maintained contact with Soviet intelligence for several years. Although under suspicion, he was never formally charged with espionage because the Federal Bureau of Investigation (FBI) refused to reveal that their evidence against Hall came from deciphering Soviet intelligence telegrams. Hall was able to emigrate to England, where he taught until his death. After his death, his wife admitted that Hall had been a Soviet agent.

Soviet accounts of nuclear espionage usually rank Hall as the second most important—after **Klaus Fuchs**—of their agents within the Manhattan Project. While Hall and his wife tried to portray their intelligence activity to historians as simply a wartime flirtation with Soviet intelligence, they did continue to help Moscow develop intelligence nets for at least three years after the war ended. Their decision to cease working for Moscow was not an act of conscience; it came out of fear of arrest by the FBI.

See also ENORMOZ; VENONA.

HAMBLETON, HUGH (1922–). The **KGB**'s most important Canadian agent was Hugh Hambleton, who spent parts of four decades working for the service in Canada and Europe. A committed communist, Hambleton was recruited in 1945 with the help of members of the Canadian **Communist Party**. For over three decades, he provided information about the North Atlantic Treaty Organization (NATO), British, and Canadian defense planning, including five years in NATO headquarters in Belgium. In 1979, the Canadian security services discovered Hambleton's role as a Soviet spy but were unable to bring the case to court. In 1981, Hambleton traveled to London, where he was arrested under provisions of the Official Secrets Act and sentenced to 10 years' imprisonment.

HANSSEN, ROBERT (1944–). Along with **Aldrich Ames**, Hanssen was one of the greatest **KGB counterintelligence** successes in the **Cold War**. A special agent of the Federal Bureau of Investigation (FBI), Hanssen worked in counterintelligence against the KGB for years. Like Ames, Hanssen volunteered to the KGB in 1985. Unlike Ames, who made an approach in person, Hanssen never had a face-to-face meeting with his KGB handlers. All contact was carried out by notes, letters, and dead drops. His initial message was addressed to the chief of counterintelligence at the *rezidentura* in Washington, **Viktor Cherkashin**, and read in part, "Dear Colonel Cherkashin: I will send a box of documents to your colleague. They are from certain of the most sensitive and compartmented projects of the U.S. Intelligence Community." In the letter's concluding sentence, Hanssen demanded $100,000 for the names of three Soviet intelligence officers run by the FBI. Two of the three were later arrested and executed. In this and later messages, Hanssen adroitly hid any information that could be used to identify him. He signed letters "Ramon."

Hanssen sent the KGB a total of 27 letters and left 22 caches in dead drops in the Washington area. His **tradecraft** was very professional: dead drops were established where he could leave documents and pick up his Soviet handlers' money and instructions. The most important of these dead drops was located under a bridge in a park near his home in Vienna, Virginia. The Soviets did not know of his identity until his arrest.

Hanssen provided much of the same material that Ames did, but he also provided detailed information on FBI operations against the KGB *rezidenturas* in Washington and New York. According to an official U.S. government history of the case, Hanssen advised the KGB as to specific methods of operating that were secure from FBI **surveillance**. Hanssen also provided the KGB with information about classified military projects. If Ames was the "bloodiest" spy of the Cold War, with 10 lives on his conscience, Hanssen may have been the costliest. He provided the KGB with computer discs with thousands of pages of information on U.S. military and technical intelligence programs. He was betrayed to American counterintelligence by a Soviet **defector** known only by the code name "Avenger," who provided critical intelligence that allowed the FBI to identify him.

In 1979, Hanssen had approached the **GRU** and received money in exchange for working for it. When his wife discovered his treachery, she and their Catholic parish priest persuaded him to stop. Hanssen's later decision to approach the KGB was **motivated** by his contempt for the service he served and the need for adventure. A devout Roman Catholic and married with six children, Hanssen lived a double life, apparently seeing spying as the ultimate adventure as well as a way to become rich. Some of the money went to support a platonic affair with a prostitute; other funds went for camera equipment to photograph him and his wife having sex (his wife was not aware of the filming). Hanssen was arrested and in 2001 sentenced to life imprisonment as part of a plea bargain that allowed his wife to collect his pension. A senior Central Intelligence Agency official likened Hanssen to Dr. Jekyll and Mr. Hyde: Mr. Hyde, in his opinion, simply won out in the battle for Robert Hanssen.

HARNACK, ARVID (1901–1942). A noted academic economist, Harnack and his wife, Mildred, were avowed dissidents in Adolf Hitler's Berlin. (Mildred Fish came from a noted midwestern American family.) In 1935, Harnack was recruited by the **NKVD** and with a few colleagues and friends became the first recruits of the famed *Rote Kapelle* (**Red Orchestra**) network. His initial code name was "Balt," but this was later changed to "Corsican." Under Moscow's directions, Harnack joined the Nazi Party and found a job as an economic planner. Harnack and **Hugo Schulze-Boysen** provided the Soviet government with detailed information about the plans for Operation **Barbarossa**, which **Joseph Stalin** ignored. Mildred also provided American diplomats some of the same information.

In the year following the Nazi invasion of the Soviet Union, Harnack and his confederates supplied Moscow with a wealth of military, political, and economic intelligence, especially about plans for Operation Blue, the drive on Stalingrad and the Caucasus. In July 1942, German counterintelligence identified the Harnacks through the decoding of several messages. They were arrested in September 1942. While he was immediately sentenced to death, she received a prison sentence. Adolf Hitler personally quashed her sentenced, and she was retried and executed.

The heritage of the Harnacks in Germany was confusing in the **Cold War**. They were heralded as heroes in the East, while in the West their reputation was more controversial. They were seen by some not as true dissenters but rather as agents of Stalin. This debate obscures their bravery as well as their impact on the war on the Eastern Front.

HARRIS, KATHERINE (1900–1966). One the most quixotic of the Soviet **illegals** was Kitty Harris. Born in England, she moved to Canada as a child. Along with her siblings, she became involved in communist politics in her teens and was recruited as an illegal in the late 1920s. Harris served in China with **Earl Browder** and was his lover (and possibly his wife) on a **Comintern** mission. In the 1930s, Harris was entrusted with handling important agents for the **NKVD**. She was **Donald Maclean**'s case officer for two years, a relationship that became romantic. All communications from Maclean to the Soviet service went through Harris in the late 1930s. In the 1940s, Harris was handling agents in the United States and Mexico. Her code name was "Ada."

While Harris was an effective agent handler, her lack of discipline drove her Soviet masters to distraction. She apparently repeatedly had affairs with agents and often disregarded Moscow's direct orders to break off compromising relationships. In 1946, she was exfiltrated to the Soviet Union, where she was detained by the ever-suspicious **MGB**, seeking reasons for the collapse of American networks. After spending 10 years in prison and asylums, she was released in 1956. She died in the Soviet Union in 1966.

See also VENONA.

HAYHANEN, REINO (1919–1961). Hayhanen was born Eugene Maki, a Soviet of Finnish nationality, and was initially recruited by the **NKVD** as an **informer**. In the late 1940s, he assumed the Hayhanen identity to serve as an **illegal** in the United States as **William Fisher**'s courier. He arrived in New York in 1952 and worked with Fisher for almost five years. Hayhanen was an impossible spy: incompetent and often drunk, he repeatedly failed to carry out Fisher's orders. In May 1957, Fisher decided to send him back to Moscow for reassignment, which Hayhanen knew meant punishment. In Paris, where he was to change planes, he defected to the U.S. embassy and betrayed Fisher, who was arrested six weeks later. Four years later, Hayhanen died in a car accident in Pennsylvania.

HEIFETS, GRIGORY MARKOVICH [MANDELOVICH] (1899–1984). Born into a family of revolutionaries, Heifets was an active revolutionary in the Jewish Bund from the age of 16. Joining Soviet foreign intelligence from the **Comintern**, Heifets served as *rezident* in San Francisco from 1941 to 1944 with the code name "Kharon" (Haron). During his years on the American West Coast, his major effort was to penetrate the inner circle of Robert Oppenheimer. On his return to Moscow, he worked in the section responsible for nuclear weapons research. In 1952, Heifets was arrested as part of **Joseph Stalin's** purge of Jews from the military and state security. He was sentenced to 25 years in the **gulag** in November 1952 and was released in December 1953 but not reinstated in foreign intelligence.

HERRMANN, RUDOLF ALBERT (1929–). Dalibar Valoushek was a Czech border guard recruited by the **KGB** in the early 1950s to act as an **illegal** in the United States. He and his wife, Inga, were documented as German refugees, using the **live double/dead double** ploy favored by the Soviet services. In 1957, the Herrmanns "escaped" to West Germany and five years later emigrated to Canada. The Herrmanns were successful in business in Canada and lived a cover that allowed them to have a middle-class lifestyle. Herrmann was also a successful agent handler, working with **Hugh Hambleton**. In 1968, the Herrmanns moved to the United States, where Herrmann worked as a photographer. The Herrmanns were moderately successful as spies: the KGB promoted Herrmann to colonel and made him illegal *rezident* for the United States.

In 1972, Herrmann revealed his identity to his son Peter and recruited him. Peter was encouraged by Moscow to attend McGill University in Montreal, where he could become a member of the Canadian establishment. A year later, Peter transferred to Georgetown University, but by then family life was interrupted by American **counterintelligence**. Agents of the Federal Bureau of Investigation (FBI) arrested the Herrmanns in 1977 and gave them the opportunity to avoid imprisonment by operating under FBI control. In 1979, the Herrmanns were resettled and began a new life. Information gleaned from an **analysis** of the Herrmann case led to Hambleton's initial arrest in 1979.

HISS, ALGER (1904–1996). The fate of Alger Hiss continues to intrigue and divide American political opinion more than 50 years after his conviction for perjury for lying about his role as a Soviet agent. Hiss was one of the most brilliant New Dealers of the Franklin D. Roosevelt administration. He had been a law clerk for Supreme Court Justice Oliver Wendell Holmes, then rose to a senior position in the State Department before the age of 40. But in November 1948, **Whittaker Chambers** testified to the House Un-American Affairs Committee that Hiss had served as a Soviet agent for more than a decade.

Hiss denied the charge in front of a federal grand jury and subsequently was charged with perjury. (The criminal statute on espionage had expired.) He was tried twice in federal court, the first trial ending in a hung jury, the second in conviction. Hiss spent the next 44 months in federal prison. He spent the last 44 years of his life contesting the conviction, claiming that it was the product of perjured testimony by Chambers and the unscrupulous ambition of then Congressman Richard Nixon. Most scholars now believe that Hiss was a Soviet agent: information from former Soviet intelligence officers, a deciphered **Venona** message that appears to refer to Hiss, and considerable physical evidence all point to his guilt. Hiss's supporters believe that the evidence was doctored and that the trial was unfair. Recent research by a Russian scholar, Svetlana Chervonnaya, alleges that another U.S. Foreign Service Officer rather than Hiss was the Soviet mole inside the Department of State. However, this interpretation has been widely rejected by scholars and legal experts.

HITLER'S CORPSE. Adolf Hitler committed suicide with his bride, Eva Braun, on 29 April 1945. Their bodies were burned and then buried in rubble. On hearing news of Hitler's death, Soviet leader **Joseph Stalin** demanded that *Smersh* find out if Hitler was dead and, if he was dead, to produce his corpse. On 5 May, Lieutenant Colonel Ivan Klimenko, *Smersh* chief of the 79th Rifle Corps, found the bodies and brought them to General **Aleksandr Vadis**, chief of *Smersh* for the 1st Byelorussian Front. Vadis ensured strict secrecy about the events, informing only Stalin and his direct superiors of the find. An autopsy was completed to ensure Stalin that the body was really that of Hitler.

Stalin chose not to reveal to the world that the Soviet Union had Hitler's body. (It was not until 1965 that the **Communist Party** informed Marshal **Georgi Zhukov** about the fate of Hitler.) Soviet propaganda hinted rather that Hitler was alive and that the Western Allies were hiding him. Stalin and his foreign policy team raised the issue with senior Anglo-American diplomats, questioning their sincerity in hunting senior Nazis still at large. Stalin told President Harry Truman at the Potsdam Conference in July 1945 that he believed Hitler was alive. Details about the operation the Soviets called *Mif*

(Myth) were not publicized until the early 1990s, though some of the story had leaked to the West. According to a Russian study published after the fall of the Soviet Union, Hitler's remains were first buried under a highway in East Germany and then exhumed and cremated and the ashes dumped into a river. The accounts of the destruction of the Hitlers' corpses still needs further research.

HITLER YOUTH CONSPIRACY. During the purge of 1937–1938, the **NKVD** began an investigation into the teenage and young adult children of leading German communists who had emigrated to the Soviet Union for creating a chapter of the Hitler Youth. Of the young men and women arrested, 40 were shot, two were turned over to the Gestapo following the Nazi–Soviet Pact of 1939, and at least 20 were sentenced to terms in **labor camps**.

While the two NKVD officers responsible for the arrest, torture, and shooting of the young men and women were themselves **executed** in 1939–1940 for treason, the last German prisoners were not released until 1955. The best-known victim was Helmut Damerius, whose book *Under False Accusations* details 17 years in the gulag or exile.

HOLLIS, ROGER (1902–1977). Hollis, who spent several years in China as a businessperson, joined the British security service (MI5) in 1938 as an expert on Soviet subversion. In 1945, he went to Canada, where he interviewed the first postwar **defector, Igor Gouzenko,** to develop **counterintelligence** leads. From 1956 to 1965, Hollis served as director general of MI5. But Hollis became the target of a mole hunt in the late 1960s, as more conservative officials in MI5 and MI6 sought to prove that he was a Soviet agent. There seems to be no evidence that Hollis was in fact a traitor. The mole hunt was **Kim Philby**'s last gift to his Soviet masters: by making it appear that the **KGB** had access to agents at the highest level of the British government, Philby created a climate of distrust within the London establishment that lasted for more than a decade after his defection.

HOLODOMOR **(HUNGER EXTERMINATION).** The man-made famine of 1932–1933 (*Holodomor* comes from the Ukrainian words for "hunger" and "murder" or "extermination") took the lives of approximately 7 million Soviet citizens, of whom more than 3 million were Ukrainians. (A Ukrainian court in a recent decision put the toll at 3.9 million famine deaths and a 6.1-million-birth deficit for the famine years.) The Ukrainian **NKVD**, as well as army units and **Communist Party** detachments, took grain from hungry peasants and sealed villages to prevent people from fleeing to larger cities to beg and find food. A number of NKVD officers were promoted for their role in controlling Ukraine and other regions during the man-made famine, and several appeared on Soviet stamps in the 1980s.

HOWARD, EDWARD LEE (1951–2002). One of three American intelligence officers to volunteer to the **KGB** in 1985, Howard defected after washing out of the Central Intelligence Agency (CIA) course for case officers. Howard, who had been slated for an assignment to Moscow, was fired for drinking and theft. After being arrested for his part in a barroom brawl in New Mexico, he approached the Soviets in Europe, offering information about the agents he had been trained to run inside the Soviet Union. His treachery was revealed by **Vitaliy Yurchenko**, who informed the CIA of a former officer named "Robert" who had agreed to work with the KGB. Howard was placed under surveillance in New Mexico, but using techniques he had learned in CIA courses, he escaped and made his way to Moscow. Howard's information led to the arrest and **execution** of several of the CIA's Soviet agents, including Adolf Tolkachev, an engineer who provided detailed information about the Soviet aircraft industry to the CIA. Tolkachev's loss was a severe one for the CIA; he is described in a recently unclassified article as a "worthy successor to **Oleg Penkovskiy**."

Howard was never a happy **defector** and chafed under the rules and regulations of his hosts. He wrote a book, *Safe House*, which he submitted to the CIA for vetting—making it probably the only book in the **Cold War** to have been approved by both the CIA and the KGB. In the book, Howard emphasized his innocence, claiming that Federal Bureau of Investigation persecution drove him into **exile**. He died in 2002, apparently in an accident in his home.

HUNGARIAN REVOLUTION (1956). The **KGB** was unable to provide the Soviet leadership any warning of the October 1956 revolution that deposed the pro-Soviet Hungarian government. The archives show that both the Soviet embassy and Moscow were stunned by the level of violence and the **execution** of Hungarian party and security police officials. The KGB did play, however, an important role in the restoration of communist power in Hungary. KGB officers identified Hungarian militants for arrest and persecution; more than 300 were executed, including nationalist leader **Imre Nagy**. The KGB also helped reestablish a new Hungarian security organization.

The KGB repeatedly warned the Soviet leadership in the fall of 1956 that the Hungarian revolution could have consequences for Soviet society. The leadership, they argued, could not allow Magyars greater rights than Balts, Ukrainians, and Russians. **Filip Bobkov**, later a deputy chair of the KGB, noted in his memoirs that the Hungarian revolution set off student protests in several Soviet universities, but the KGB squashed the protests and ensured the punishment of their leaders.

Soviet Ambassador **Yuri Andropov** was deeply influenced by events in Budapest. As KGB chair from 1967 to 1982, Andropov often told people that he wanted to ensure that no such explosion could ever happen again inside the Soviet bloc. Andropov's strong support for a crackdown on the **Prague** Spring in 1968 undoubtedly sprang from his experiences in Budapest in 1956. Andropov's decisions to harshly punish Soviet **dissidents** and to push for the **exile** of **Aleksandr Solzhenitsyn** can also be explained by his fear that intellectual dissent could lead to counterrevolution.

I

IGNATIEV, SEMYON DMITREVICH (1904–1983). Following **Viktor Abakumov**'s arrest in 1951 by **Joseph Stalin**, Ignatiev was appointed minister of state security to supervise the arrest, interrogation, trial, and **execution** of Stalin's enemies within the **Communist Party** and the police. In Stalin's last days, Ignatiev supervised the preparation of the **Doctors' Plot**, which was meant to implicate senior members of the political leadership and initiate a massive political purge. Stalin repeatedly insisted that Ignatiev torture prisoners to make them confess, threatening Ignatiev with death should he fail. **Molotov**, who lived in fear of arrest in Stalin's last days, described Ignatiev as "not especially distinguished, in other words a nobody."

Immediately following Stalin's death, Ignatiev ensured a rapid transfer of power to Stalin's successors. Within hours of the leader's death, he ended the **counterintelligence** investigations of Stalin's subordinates and had some of the interrogators arrested. Ignatiev was dismissed from his post as minister of state security on 2 June 1953 "for deception of the Party and Government, gross violations of Soviet legality, and dishonest conduct." However, for his decisions in the last hours of Stalin's life to end the witch hunt, his life was spared. He was demoted and transferred to the party apparatus in the provinces, where he worked for the next two decades.

See also BERIA, LAVRENTY PAVLOVICH (1899–1953); DOCTORS' PLOT; RYUMIN, MIKHAIL (1913–1954).

ILLEGAL. The Soviet intelligence services, like their Western counterparts, placed intelligence officers under "official" cover as diplomats or commercial attachés or under "nonofficial" cover. The Soviets described an officer under nonofficial cover as an "illegal" (Russian *nelegal*), and the Soviet services spent enormous time and energy preparing men and women to live and operate abroad without the protection afforded by diplomatic passports. In the early years, the Soviet services used nonofficial covers because they had only a few diplomatic missions. The United States did not establish diplomatic relations with the Soviet Union until 1933.

In the 1920s and 1930s, Soviet intelligence services dispatched illegals to Europe and North America to gather intelligence and recruit agents. Most of these were not Russians but were recruited from the Polish, Hungarian, and German communist parties. Skilled in revolutionary **tradecraft**, they recruited and ran agents inside the British and American establishment as well as in France, Germany, Japan, and China. They were effective in collecting scientific and technical intelligence and developing sources in Western governments. While most of the human intelligence successes of Soviet intelligence in the 1920s and 1930s were a result of the work of illegals, they were deeply distrusted by **Joseph Stalin** and the men he chose to run the **NKVD**. Almost all were recalled to Moscow in 1937–1939, and more than half were shot as Nazi agents. Use of illegals during this period was so extensive that the NKVD established a senior illegal to act as "illegal *rezident*." In the United States, **Ishak Akhmerov** served in this capacity for many years.

Following **World War II**, Soviet tradecraft mandated that officers assigned abroad as illegals assume non-Soviet nationality and undergo years of language training to master believable "legends" (covers). Illegals were supported by **KGB** and **GRU** officers under diplomatic cover. These officers collected documents to establish cover identities, frequently using a **live double/dead double** strategy, and they maintained contact with illegals by dead drops and other forms of communications. In the KGB, Directorate S of the First Chief Directorate trained and dispatched illegals, while Line N officers in legal *rezidenturas* provided support.

From the 1950s through the 1980s, KGB and GRU illegals were dispatched to Europe, North America, and Asia with mixed success. Illegals were also dispatched during periods of crisis to allied East European states to monitor public opinion and target **dissidents** for arrest. According to one **defector**, illegals provided the KGB with information about developments in Czechoslovakia before Moscow intervened in the 1968 **Prague Crisis**.

The arrest of 10 SVR illegals in the United States in the summer of 2010 demonstrated the extent of the Soviet services illegals program. One of the illegals was documented as a South American citizen, using a birth certificate of a child who died at the age of two. Since the roundup of illegals in the United States, other illegals were arrested in Western Europe. One couple, living in a provincial town in Germany arrested in 2013, were responsible for running an important agent within the North Atlantic Treaty Organization.

While many American journalists question the utility of illegals, seeing them as a relic of the Cold War, Moscow seems to continue to value them highly for their ability to handle important agents and as a parallel intelligence apparat—a guarantee of an intelligence presence should diplomatic relations be broken and legal *rezidenturas* be closed.

See also FISHER, WILLIAM GENRYKHOVICH (1903–1971); PROGRESS OPERATIONS.

INAURI, ALESEI NIKOLAEVICH (1908–1993). Entering the **KGB** from the Red Army, Inauri served as chief of the Georgian KGB from 1954 to 1986, the longest serving local KGB leader. He played a key role in the **1964 coup** against **Nikita Khrushchev**, escorting the Soviet premier to his fatal meeting with the **Communist Party** Central Committee. Inauri was known as a tough and reactionary security boss quashing dissent. He prevented the release of the Georgian movie *Repentance*, a fictionalized account of Georgia during the Stalin years, arguing that it discredited the Communist Party and the KGB.

INDUSTRIAL ESPIONAGE. Both the **OGPU** and the **GRU** began to collect proprietary and classified industrial information in the late 1920s. As part of **Joseph Stalin**'s plan to modernize the Soviet Union through a series of Five Year Plans, the intelligence service began to recruit agents with access to industrial and technical information. Among the first important agents recruited solely to collect industrial information was **Harry Gold**, an American chemist with access to sugar-refining secrets. He was initially recruited by the OGPU to obtain proprietary information for Soviet industry. During **World War II**, he later became a critical agent in the Soviet nuclear intelligence program.

One of the most famous industrial intelligence rings was one run by **Julius Rosenberg**. Rosenberg, a staunch communist, recruited a number of young left-wing scientists during World War II and passed secrets they gleaned from American industries to the **NKVD** *rezidentura* in New York. Rosenberg and several other American agents were also used to provide information on the Anglo-American program nuclear weapons program, which the Soviets code-named *Enormoz*.

The GRU was also a collector of industrial, scientific, and technical intelligence during the **Cold War**. Within KGB *rezidenturas*, **Line X** officers were responsible for the collection of industrial information. Scientific secrets were passed to Directorate T of the First Chief Directorate, which in turn passed information to the responsible Soviet ministry. The KGB's commitment to industrial intelligence was tremendous. In the early 1980s, the French government expelled more than 40 Soviet intelligence officers engaged in industrial and scientific intelligence collection.

The Soviet services also enlisted the assistance of allied Warsaw Pact services to collect industrial secrets. In East Germany, the KGB worked closely with the *Stasi* to collect industrial secrets from Western business people. Other services contributed as well. For example, in the 1970s and 1980s, Marian Zacharski, a Polish intelligence officer operating as a businessperson in California's Silicon Valley, collected classified information about U.S. defense industries. After his arrest and trial, he was exchanged for more than 20 Soviet bloc political prisoners.

Industrial information saved Soviet industry billions of dollars and hundreds of thousands of hours in research, but it also forced some Soviet industries into copying foreign developments without doing the expensive research necessary for innovations. Industrial espionage contributed to the robust Soviet military-industrial complex from the late 1930s to the end of the Cold War. However, the reliance on industrial espionage may have robbed Soviet industry of the initiative to pursue original research. By the late 1980s, Soviet science lagged behind the West in all the important scientific components of the second industrial revolution.

The **SVR** continues to collect industrial technology. Former SVR boss **Yevgeny Primakov** reported in his memoirs that the SVR "has never hesitated in regards to industrial espionage. Whether we like it or not, it will go on as long as there are military or industrial secrets to be learned." Primakov went on to say that since the collapse of the Soviet Union, most of the Russian service's work in industrial espionage was "analytical." The GRU presumably is also continuing to pursue industrial intelligence.

INFEKTION (INFECTION). The KGB code word for the AIDS **active measure** campaign. Foreign intelligence chief **Yevgeniy Primakov** admitted in 1992 that the campaign had been developed by the **KGB** to embarrass the United States in the Third World.

INFORMANTS. The key to the success of the Soviet security services, from the **Cheka** to the **KGB**, was a huge stable of informants. **Semyon Ignatiev**, chief of state security during **Joseph Stalin**'s last years, stated that his service had 10 million informants in 1952. During **World War II**, it is estimated that 22 million Soviet citizens served as informants. And the KGB is reported to have had more than 10 million informants at the time of the collapse of the Soviet Union.

During the **collectivization** of agriculture, informants were recruited among the poorest peasants to identify rich peasants (kulaks) who had hidden grain and animals and had refused to join collective farms. **Pavel Morozov**, a young boy who informed on his father and was subsequently murdered by his family, became a national hero. Informants who turned in their neighbors received major cash rewards and were selected for **Communist Party** membership. Many suffered Morozov's fate as well. During the *Yezhovshchina*, informing was driven by a demand for the name of traitors and **dissidents**. According to **Nikita Khrushchev**, one woman informer caused the arrest of hundreds of residents of Kiev in 1937–1938.

During World War II, the security service and *Smersh* recruited informers at all levels of Soviet society. *Smersh* was responsible for recruiting informants in every battalion of the Soviet army. Informers were also recruited in every village and housing bloc, as well as in forced labor camps; a recent American study found that 12 percent of Soviet military personnel were informants. Information from informants allowed the security service and *Smersh* to question nearly 7 million people and arrest 2 million during the course of the war. After the war, informers continued to be recruited in every state and nonstate institution, including in the few working churches and the many penal institutions. **Aleksandr Solzhenitsyn**, while serving a sentence in a **gulag**, was approached by a security officer and offered the opportunity to inform. A history of the Russian Orthodox Church identified the majority of the church leadership as active informers.

People informed for a variety of reasons: vengeance, securing privileges such as foreign travel, and patriotism all played a part. It was far harder to refuse offers to inform than westerners realize. In many cases, Soviets informed to protect themselves and their families from more intensive investigations of their private lives. The post-Soviet security services almost certainly continue to recruit informants. While many Russians see the heritage of informants as a sad relic of the Soviet age, it seems inconceivable that any generation of Russian security specialists will abandon this tool.

See also MOROZOV, PAVEL [PAVLIK] TROFIMOVICH (19??–1932); *SEKSOT*.

***INOSTRANNIY OTDEL* (IO).** The Foreign Department of the **Cheka**, the *Inostranniy otdel*, or IO, was created on 20 December 1920. Its first director was a veteran of **Communist Party** underground activity, Yakov Davtyan, who operated under the alias "Davidov." The first *rezidentura* was opened in Berlin in 1922. By the mid-1920s, the IO had established a presence in London, Brussels, Rome, Istanbul, Montreal, and New York. The initial responsibility of the organization was the identification of **émigré** groups operating in the territory of the Soviet Union. From the beginning, the British were identified as the **main adversary**, and efforts were made to recruit sources with access to British policies. Davtyan lasted less than two years as chief of the service before returning to work as a **Comintern** representative. He was executed in 1938, like many of the founders of the IO.

See also ILLEGAL; TRILISSER, MIKHAIL ABRAMOVICH (1883–1938).

IVANOV, EVGENIY (1926–1994). The Soviet naval attaché in London in the late 1950s and early 1960s, "Eugene" Ivanov played a confused role in the "Profumo Affair," which involved important politicians, call girls, and one Soviet spy and resulted in the fall of Prime Minister Harold McMilian's Tory government. Ivanov and Minister of State for War John Profumo shared the same girlfriend, Christine Keeler, and press and then parliamentary inquiries centered on sex and then security issues. Profumo, who first denied the relationship on the floor of Parliament, finally admitted the affair and then resigned.

Ivanov apparently was being used by Soviet intelligence as more than a **GRU** officer. He may have been trying to establish a **back channel** to London during the **Cuban Missile Crisis** of 1962, or he may simply have been caught up in a sordid political tragedy. In any case, he was recalled to Moscow; he later wrote a memoir of the affair and met and apologized to Keeler.

IVASHUTIN, PETR IVANOVICH (1909–2002). The longest-serving chief of any Soviet intelligence service, Ivashutin made the **GRU** the world's largest military intelligence service. Ivashutin entered the **OGPU** in the early 1930s. He served in the **Great Patriotic War** in *Smersh* as the chief of **counterintelligence** in three different Red Army fronts. In 1946, he transferred to the **MGB** and served in Ukraine in 1952–1953 as security chief, then was promoted head of the **Third** (Military Counterintelligence) **Chief Directorate**. Known as a tough counterintelligence officer, he was promoted to the post of **KGB** deputy chair in 1960. In 1962, he was responsible for crushing economic riots in **Novocherkassk**. In 1963, following revelations about the Central Intelligence Agency's recruitment of military intelligence officers, Ivashutin was made chief of the GRU.

During his tenure, the GRU became a full-service intelligence agency. Ivashutin broadened the technical and human intelligence capabilities of the service. The GRU expanded the number of officers under diplomatic cover in Soviet diplomatic and trade missions and became the primary producer of Soviet technical intelligence. During the more than 23 years he led the service, the GRU developed imagery and **signals intelligence** satellites, as well as aircraft and ships to collect intelligence. The GRU also greatly expanded its *Spetsnaz* forces, and by his retirement in 1986, the GRU commanded the largest unconventional warfare force of any army. While most KGB chairs are well known in the West, Ivashutin kept a very low profile. However, he played a key role in the Ministry of Defense in war planning and strategy as well as intelligence. His title at retirement, age 75, was deputy chief of the General Staff.

See also PENKOVSKIY, OLEG VLADIMIROVICH (1919–1963); POPOV, PETR SEMENOVICH (1916–1960); SEROV, IVAN ALEKSANDROVICH (1900–1990).

IVINSKAYA, OLGA VSEVOLODOVNA (1912–1995). Boris Pasternak's mistress and the great love of his life, Ivinskaya was the model of "Larisa" in the film **Doctor Zhivago**. She was targeted by the security police as a weapon to force Pasternak's silence and served two terms in the **gulag**

(1949–1953 and 1960–1964), the latter after the publication of the film and the award of the Nobel Prize to Pasternak. Her daughter was sentenced to forced labor at her second trial. She wrote her memoirs of Russian intellectual life and **KGB** harassment, *A Prisoner of Time*.

IVY BELLS. The code name "Ivy Bells" referred to a top-secret U.S. Navy program to tap undersea Soviet communication lines using submarines. The program was betrayed to the **KGB** by **Ronald Pelton** in 1985. Pelton, in need of money, provided the Soviets with detailed reporting, ending one of the U.S. government's most successful and innovative **signals intelligence** programs. It cost Moscow $35,000 to buy secrets of a program that had cost Washington hundreds of millions of dollars to develop and implement.

J

JAMES, ALBERT (1914–2002). The Australian press, using material from the **Mitrokhin archives**, named Labor Parliamentarian Albert James a **KGB** agent in August 2014. According to material in the archives, James served as a KGB agent from the 1960s to 1980. James, a left-wing Labour member of Parliament from 1960 to 1980, was given the far-from-clever code name "Albert" in KGB cables.

JOHN, OTTO (1909–1997). One of the most bizarre—and still unresolved—stories of the **Cold War** is the defection of Otto John. John was a member of the German resistance and was able to flee to neutral Portugal after the failed assassination of Adolf Hitler in July 1944. John made his way to London and cooperated with British intelligence. Following **World War II**, he helped the Western Allies in their prosecution of German war criminals.

In 1950, John became head of the BfV (*Bundesamt für Verfassungschutz*), West Germany's new counterintelligence service. But he became increasingly discouraged with West German rearmament and the employment of former Nazi officials. He shared his feelings with friends, who happened to be agents of the **MGB**, the Soviet Ministry of State Security. John was offered the opportunity to meet with senior Soviet officials, and on 17 June 1954, he crossed into East Berlin. He appeared at a news conference a few days later to say that he had voluntarily entered East Germany and intended to remain in the East. Over the next few months, he traveled to the Soviet Union to be debriefed by the MGB. John, however, was not a happy **defector**, and the East Germans and the Soviets agreed to allow him to redefect to the West. On 12 December 1954, John was spirited out of East Germany by friends who may or may not have been in the pay of the *Stasi*, the East German security service.

Tried by a West German court, John was sentenced to four years in jail. He spent the rest of his life trying to get his reputation back, claiming that he was not a defector but had been kidnapped and drugged. On five occasions, he unsuccessfully sought to have the German higher courts quash the verdict, and the John case became a West German equivalent of the **Alger Hiss** case in the United States. Shortly before his death, he flew to Moscow in an effort to get documents that would prove his innocence.

The most recent accounts of the case seem to reach a verdict of "not proven." The documents do not definitely prove that John entered the East Zone on his own volition. He did not give the MGB the names of any BfV agents. On the other hand, conservative Germans believe that his work in the war suggested he was a man capable of changing sides all too easily. One also can make the argument that angry about the decisions being made in Bonn, he decided after a few too many drinks to try a little individual diplomacy and that the initiative went horribly wrong.

JOUR. The longest-serving and most productive French agent of the **KGB** was code-named "Jour" (Russian *Zhour*). He is described by a former KGB archivist as a code clerk in the French Ministry of Foreign Affairs who had been recruited in 1945 and worked until at least 1980. Jour, who has never been definitively identified, was paid bonuses almost every year for his services. He was run by the First Chief Directorate case officers, using dead drops to minimize the threat of exposure. His position in the French foreign service reportedly gave Moscow tremendous entrée into French foreign policy and national security decision making.

K

KALMANOVICH, SHABTAY GENRIKHOVICH (1947–2009). A **KGB illegal** who was dispatched to Israel, Kalmanovich was identified by the Israeli secret service, arrested, and imprisoned for several years. He was pardoned in 1993 and returned to Moscow, where he became involved in business and allegedly organized crime. He was murdered in Moscow in 2009 by persons unknown.

KALUGIN, OLEG DANILOVICH (1934–). Kalugin rose quickly in the **KGB**'s foreign intelligence component to become chief of foreign **counter-intelligence** in the First Chief Directorate and the youngest general officer in the service. Kalugin was instrumental in running **Robert Lipka** as well as the **Walker Spy Ring**. Lipka, a young employee of the National Security Agency, was paid $27,000. John Walker was paid more than a hundred times more for information on U.S. cryptological systems. Kalugin was successful as well in the recruitment of a number of Western intelligence officers.

Kalugin was transferred to Leningrad as deputy chief of the city KGB in the early 1980s. Within a short period of time, he made a number of enemies in the party bureaucracy, and his career floundered. He later rallied to **Mikhail Gorbachev**'s policy of *glasnost* and wrote several articles on his career in intelligence. Kalugin was never forgiven by his former colleagues for his decision to break cover, and in the 1990s, he moved to the United States, where he teaches and acts as a business consultant and has become an American citizen. He has since been condemned by Russian President **Vladimir Putin** as a traitor, and he was tried in absentia and sentenced to a prison term.

KAMPELIS, WILLIAM (1954–). An employee of the Central Intelligence Agency (CIA), Kampelis approached the Soviet **military attaché** in Greece in 1977 and provided him with a copy of the operating manual of the KH-11 reconnaissance satellite. Kampelis was immediately in turn betrayed since his **GRU** contact was an agent of the CIA. He was later sentenced to a long term of imprisonment.

KARLSHORST. Headquarters for Soviet intelligence operations in Berlin were located in the city's Karlshorst district. St. Antonius Hospital was originally chosen as the site of the intelligence headquarters soon after Berlin fell to the Red Army in 1945. Karlshorst remained the center of both **KGB** and **GRU** operations until 1992.

KATYN. In April 1943, Nazi Germany announced that it had discovered the mass **grave** of 4,500 Polish officers near Katyn in Byelorussia; Berlin claimed they had been murdered by the Soviets. Moscow immediately denied the charge and used the international debate over Katyn as an opportunity to break diplomatic relations with the London-based Polish government in exile. Until 1992, Moscow denied responsibility for the killings, despite physical and human evidence that the **NKVD** was guilty. Documents presented to the Polish government in 1992 by Russian President **Boris Yeltsin** established conclusively that on **Lavrenty Beria**'s recommendation, **Joseph Stalin** authorized the murder of 25,800 Polish military officers, civil servants, and religious figures captured in 1939. Beria's recommendation was that "examination of the cases is to be carried out without summoning those detained and without bringing charges." The verdict in all cases was death by shooting.

The killings took place at several locations in Byelorussia and Ukraine and were carried out by NKVD **execution** teams. Directing the execution of the Poles was **Petr Soprunenko**, who sent a telegram to Moscow every day, detailing progress in executing Polish officers and civilians. Beria drafted a special order on 26 October 1940, rewarding every member of Soprunenko's team with a sum of money equal to a month's pay "for the successful execution of special assignments." So carefully were the execution sites hidden that not all the graves have been found.

Katyn demonstrated the lengths to which the Stalin regime would go to purge Soviet society and Soviet satellites of suspected **enemies of the people**. In a macabre way, it demonstrated the efficiency—as well as the brutality—of the security service. But its history lives on, for Katyn and the other massacres continue to poison relations between Poland and Russia. The duplicity of Soviet leaders from **Nikita Khrushchev** to **Mikhail Gorbachev** still troubles Poles who lost family members.

KEDROV, MIKHAIL SERGEEVICH (1878–1941). An old Bolshevik, Kedrov joined the **Cheka** in 1918, soon after its establishment, and was appointed the first head of Soviet military **counterintelligence** by **Vladimir Lenin**. He later established the first Soviet concentration camps on the **Solovetskiy Islands**. Although Kedrov left the security police, he was deeply distrusted by party leader **Joseph Stalin** and was arrested in April 1939.

Although he was one of the very few acquitted during the **Great Terror**, he was kept in jail on order of **Lavrenty Beria**. In October 1941, he and 22 other unwanted witnesses to history were shot and buried in an unmarked grave. He was posthumously rehabilitated in 1953. His letter from jail defending his innocence was read at the 20th Congress of the **Communist Party** in 1956.

KENNEDY ASSASSINATION. Probably the most contentious controversy in American history is the assassination of President John F. Kennedy by Lee Harvey Oswald. Oswald defected to the Soviet Union and lived under tight **KGB surveillance** in Minsk. He later approached KGB officers under diplomatic cover in Mexico City. This has been the kindling that has fueled the publication of books implicating the KGB and the Central Intelligence Agency (CIA) in the assassination. While evidence is incomplete, the mass of interviews with former KGB counterintelligence officers as well as Soviet and American records suggest that the KGB was very wary of Oswald after he left Minsk to return to Texas. This dictionary's bibliography lists a number of books implicating and defending Soviet intelligence. The most recent study of Oswald in Minsk suggests that the KGB knew that it was dealing with a difficult and probably uncontrollable loner.

KGB (*KOMITET GOSUDARSTVENNOI BEZOPASTNOSTI*). The KGB was created on 7 March 1954 as one of **Nikita Khrushchev**'s major reforms of the Stalinist system. The complete title of the organization, *Komitet gosudarstvennoi bezopastnosti pri sovete ministrov*, "Committee of State Security under the Council of Ministers," suggested that the security police reported to the government, but in effect, it remained under the tutelage of the **Communist Party** leadership. Under Khrushchev, the KGB chair was not a member of the Communist Party leadership; beginning with the appointment of **Yuri Andropov** in 1967, senior KGB officers moved into the party leadership at the national and local levels.

Data on KGB staffing are incomplete. In 1991, the KGB was reported to have had 486,000 personnel. Of these, approximately one-half were in the Chief Directorate of the **Border Guards**. The KGB had more officers dedicated to internal security and **counterintelligence** functions than any other security service, save that of the People's Republic of China. There is no reliable information on the number of **informants** employed by the KGB, but several former officials put the number slightly in excess of 10 million.

While Khrushchev's reforms sought to reduce the role of the security police in the **surveillance** of the Communist Party leadership, every party leader from Khrushchev to **Mikhail Gorbachev** relied on the KGB for close surveillance of the population, as well as for foreign intelligence and counterintelligence. While never obtaining the reputation for ruthlessness of the Stalinist service, the KGB was a highly effective security service, with informants in every corner of Soviet society. Former KGB officers like Russian President **Vladimir Putin** believe the KGB was the least corrupt of all Soviet institutions. At the national level, this may have been true. In the provinces, however, the KGB often protected corrupt party officials.

See also KGB ORGANIZATION.

KGB ORGANIZATION. The **KGB**—like its predecessors—was managed by a collegium composed of the organization's most important leaders. In the 1970s, the collegium was chaired by the KGB chair and included two first deputy chairs, the heads of the **First** and **Second Chief Directorates**, and the chiefs of the Moscow and Leningrad KGB offices, as well as other officials. The KGB, like its predecessors, was an integrated intelligence community packed into one organization: it conducted foreign intelligence, domestic **counterintelligence**, **signals intelligence**, and border security operations. It was also responsible for the security of the Red Army as well as the protection of the party's leadership and important government installations. In 1954, the KGB was reorganized into chief directorates and directorates, reflecting the responsibilities of the security police's components dating back to the formation of the **Cheka** in 1917.

The First Chief Directorate had responsibility for foreign intelligence. It operated hundreds of foreign *rezidenturas* abroad and was responsible for intelligence officers under official cover as well as **illegals**. The First Chief Directorate essentially was the Soviet Union's Central Intelligence Agency.

The Second Chief Directorate was responsible for domestic counterintelligence. It operated against foreign agents as well as **émigré** political and religious organizations seeking to penetrate the Soviet Union. It ran agents with access to foreign diplomatic and consular missions. For example, its First Department ran operations against the American embassy; the Second Department focused on the British embassy. The Second Chief Directorate also tried to recruit foreign business people and students who could be developed into assets with access to political and commercial information. It was the Soviet Union's Federal Bureau of Investigation but was far larger and more powerful within the country's bureaucracy than any Western security service.

The **Third Chief Directorate** was established to ensure the loyalty of the military during the Russian **civil war**. It assigned officers to military units at the battalion (1,000 members) level and above. During the **Great Patriotic War**, the Third Chief Directorate operated as *Smersh* and assumed the role of guardian of the Red Army. The Third Chief Directorate also was responsible for the security of the cadre of the **MVD** (Ministry of Internal Affairs), the police.

The Fifth Directorate was created by **Yuri Andropov** in 1967 to monitor developments within the intelligentsia. It was responsible for monitoring dissent in religious organizations and ethnic groups throughout the country. During the Stalin years, the Secret Political Directorate had similar responsibility for **surveillance** of the population. The Fifth recruited **informants** in every church congregation and academic institute in the country. Through its connections with *Glavlit*, it kept its finger on the intellectual pulse of a country of 230,000,000 people. It also issued **warnings** to suspected **dissidents**.

The Seventh Directorate was responsible for physical and technical surveillance operations against enemy agents and dissidents. It used a variety of tracking chemicals, such as *metka*, to track targets.

The Eighth and 16th Chief Directorates were responsible for the security of state communications and the breaking of foreign communications, respectively. After the fall of the Soviet Union, they were folded first into the FAPSI (Federal Agency for Government Communications and Information) and then in 2004 into the **Federal Protective Service**.

The Ninth Directorate was responsible for the security of the party's leadership. Along with the 15th Chief Directorate, it was responsible for the control of sensitive installations ranging from the Kremlin to nuclear weapons facilities. The Ninth was also known as the *Okhrana*, a nickname stemming from the tsarist *Okhrana*. It had many of the same responsibilities as the U.S. Secret Service. The 15th Chief Directorate's role is more shadowed in secrecy, and it was apparently involved in the building and securing of a special subway for the evacuation of the Soviet leadership in time of war. A former Politburo member said the secret metro ran more than 20 kilometers and was one of the single most expensive projects Moscow undertook in the **Cold War**.

The Chief Directorate of **Border Guards** commanded air, sea, and ground military units and was responsible for the control of the country's frontiers. In 1991, the Chief Directorate of Border Guards commanded a force of 240,000 troops with naval patrol craft, helicopters, and armored fighting vehicles.

The KGB and its predecessors had offices at the republic, oblast (state), and city levels. These provincial offices had much the same structure of the central organization. For example, the Moscow KGB had First (Foreign Intelligence) and Second (Counterintelligence) departments, as well as other parallel departments that mirrored the center's organization. One of the great strengths of the KGB was its ability to communicate and react quickly. The Soviet services also maintained extremely complete archives of its operations, agents, and targets. **Andrei Sakharov**'s wife, Helen Bonner, was given over 500 KGB operational files following the collapse of the Soviet Union.

President **Vladimir Putin** served in both the Leningrad branch of the KGB and the First Chief Directorate. Many of his closest associates are former KGB officers and informers.

KHALKIN-GOL INCIDENT. In the summer of 1939, Imperial Japan's Kwantung Army based in Manchuria began a multidivision offensive into the Mongolian People's Republic, a Soviet ally. Moscow, considering a strategic alliance at that moment with Japan's ally, Nazi Germany, received critical reporting on Tokyo's strategy from **GRU** agents in Japan and **China**. **Richard Sorge** provided intelligence that the Japanese offensive was local in nature, lacked the support of the cabinet, and therefore was not the beginning of a general war. Moscow quickly defeated the Japanese attack, regained loss territory, and proposed armistice terms to end the "incident," to concentrate on Europe. GRU intelligence allowed Moscow to concentrate on its détente with Berlin.

KHOKHLOV, NIKOLAI YEVGENIYEVICH (1922–2007). A hero of the **partisan** struggle against the Nazis, Khokhlov was responsible for the assassination of Wilhelm Kube, the gauleiter of White Russia. In 1954, he was selected by the **KGB** to supervise the assassination of Gregory Okokovich, chairman of the National Alliance of Russian Solidarists, who was living in West Germany. Khokhlov, at his wife's urging, warned his target and **defected**. His wife was imprisoned as the spouse of a traitor, and Khokhlov was the target of a KGB poisoning in 1957.

Khokhlov later emigrated to the United States and was resettled in southern California. He earned a PhD in psychology and taught in the California university system. After having been pardoned by Russian President **Boris Yeltsin**, he returned to Russia to see his son and other relatives.

KHRUSHCHEV, NIKITA SERGEYEVICH (1894–1971). Khrushchev used the security service in his rise to power within General Secretary **Joseph Stalin**'s inner circle and in his drive to succeed Stalin in the 1950s. However, his rivals' ability to subvert the **KGB** led to his downfall in 1964.

Khrushchev's career was made in the **Communist Party** apparatus, and he was closely monitored by Stalin from 1930 until the latter's death. Khrushchev's first important experience with the security service came in Moscow in the mid-1930s, when he authorized the arrest of thousands of **Trotskyites**. Khrushchev probably carried out this campaign so ruthlessly because he had flirted with Trotskyism in the early 1920s. In 1938, Stalin assigned Khrushchev to lead the Ukrainian Communist Party with a mandate to purge **enemies of the people**. According to all accounts, he did not disappoint his mentor, ordering the arrest of tens of thousands of officials: a total of 168,000 Ukrainians were arrested during the three years Khrushchev served in Kiev. Of the 86 members of the Ukrainian Central Committee working in Kiev on his arrival, 83 were purged. According to KGB records, Khrushchev personally ordered the arrest of 2,140 individuals—almost all of whom were shot. While in his memoirs Khrushchev portrayed himself as horrified by the excesses of the purges, he rarely hesitated to order the arrest of a suspected enemy.

Khrushchev developed close contacts with senior security officials during and after **World War II**. He was especially close to **Ivan Serov**, a hardened security police official who oversaw the **deportation** of millions of Soviet citizens during the war. Following Stalin's death in March 1953, Khrushchev planned and executed the arrest, trial, and **execution** of Stalin's security chief, **Lavrenty Beria**, with the aid of a cadre of loyal **Chekists** like Serov.

As Communist Party boss, Khrushchev curbed the power of the KGB to ensure the primacy of the party. The service was placed under party tutelage. Khrushchev also oversaw the release and rehabilitation of some of the victims of the Stalin era and permitted some disclosure about the extent of Stalin and Beria's crimes.

In his **Secret Speech** to the 20th Party Congress, Khrushchev admitted to a select circle of party officials that Stalin had used the security service to murder millions of innocents. Khrushchev also ordered the rehabilitation of thousands of men and women arrested during the Stalin period. For many families, the rehabilitation of a loved one came 10 to 20 years after they had been sentenced by a court to death or a term in the camps from which they never returned. Moreover, Khrushchev authorized the publication of **Aleksandr Solzhenitsyn**'s novella *One Day of Ivan Denisovich*, which provided a realistic account of life in Stalin's forced labor camps, and he allowed a far more realistic and honest depiction of modern Soviet history. While these post-Stalin accounts of the recent Soviet past were self-serving and far from complete, they presented a far more accurate account of the **Great Patriotic War**.

There was a limit to reform. Khrushchev was fearful of going too far in reforming the state security empire. He told his children that at Stalin's death, the regime was on the brink. He thus believed that further reform would seriously endanger the Soviet state. Khrushchev became increasingly intolerant of intellectual dissent, and he authorized greater surveillance of **dissident** authors and artists. He allowed the party and the KGB to persecute dissident intellectuals.

Khrushchev—like every Soviet leader—depended on the KGB to maintain power. KGB chair Serov supported Khrushchev when Stalinist members of the Politburo tried to wrench power from him in 1957. During his years in power, Khrushchev received memoranda from the KGB on political developments in the country every week. During those years, Khrushchev ensured that the KGB remained in friendly hands by appointing seasoned party bureaucrats to the **Administrative Organs Department** of the Central Committee, which oversaw the KGB. He also appointed loyalists such as **Aleksandr Shelepin** and **Vladimir Semichastniy** to head the service.

In 1963, **Leonid Brezhnev**, Shelepin, and party ideological watchdog Mikhail Suslov began to plot against Khrushchev. They recruited senior KGB officials chafing under the party leader's tutelage, who in turn subverted Khrushchev's bodyguard detail. In October 1964, the KGB played a key role in removing him from political power. Khrushchev spent the last years of his life under modified house arrest, dying in 1971. He was able to smuggle his memoirs out to the West, where they were well received. The Russian people owe Nikita Khrushchev a great deal for reducing the power of the security police and opening up society. While guilty of some of the most horrible crimes of the Stalin era, he took steps as a national leader to prevent a new terror.

KING, JOHN HERBERT (ca. 1905–?). Captain John King was a British code clerk with an expensive American mistress to support when an **OGPU illegal** approached him in 1933. King, who thought his Soviet case officer was a European banker, said that he was Irish and deeply disliked all things English. For the next four years, King provided the Soviets with British code material and diplomatic dispatches, apparently believing they were being used by an international business cartel. In 1939, **Walter Krivitsky** informed the British security service (MI5) about King's treachery. King was arrested and sentenced to 10 years in prison.

See also CONSTANTINI, FRANCESCO (ca. 1900–?); SIGNALS INTELLIGENCE (SIGINT).

KIROV, SERGEI MIRONOVICH (1880–1934). Born Kostikov, Kirov rose quickly in the **Bolshevik Party** as one of **Joseph Stalin**'s chief lieutenants. As party boss of Leningrad, Kirov assured Stalin's control of the country's second city by purging the party of **Trotskyites** and other **dissidents**. At the 17th Party Congress, Kirov emerged as the favorite of the party, garnering more votes in a secret ballot for Central Committee membership than even Stalin. Kirov, however, made no effort to lead a revolt against Stalin, who some believed had lost control of the country and was responsible for the famine of 1932–1933, which claimed 5 million to 7 million lives.

Stalin, who had previously been close to Kirov, apparently decided to remove him from his power base in Leningrad. He offered Kirov a position in the Central Committee Secretariat in Moscow. More ominously, at Stalin's command, major changes were made in the **NKVD** in Leningrad and in Kirov's security detail. On 1 December 1934, **Leonid Nikolaev**, a minor party official, shot Kirov to death in the Leningrad headquarters of the party.

Stalin left Moscow for Leningrad with an entourage of security personnel almost immediately on hearing of Kirov's death. He personally interrogated Nikolaev and upbraided **Fillip Medved**, chief of the Leningrad NKVD, who was subsequently sentenced to three years in a labor camp. More importantly, he issued a new **counterterrorism** decree allowing the NKVD to try and execute **enemies of the people** without defense counsel or appeal for mercy. In Leningrad, this led to the **execution** and **exile** of 6,501 people in December 1934 alone. This also led to plans for **show trials** of Old Bolsheviks, colleagues of **Lenin** who were accused of complicity in Kirov's murder. Hundreds of thousands of Soviet citizens perished in 1934–1938 as a result of 1 December 1934 and the events that followed.

The Kirov case remains open. Many files have been purged, and several key witnesses were executed in the late 1930s, including Medved. While some scholars believe Stalin played a role in Kirov's murder, more are now predisposed to think that Nikolaev acted alone, angered by his lack of promotion in the Leningrad political apparatus.

KIRPICHENKO, VADIM ALEKSEEVICH (1922–2005). After service in the **Great Patriotic War**, Kirpichenko joined the **KGB** and was quickly recognized as one of its leading Arabists. He served more than a decade in Egypt, including four years as *rezident*. He ended his career as a lieutenant general and deputy chief of the KGB **First Chief Directorate**.

KLEBER, MANFRED [STERN, MANFRED] (1896–1954). One of the mythical and tragic figures of the **GRU** and **Comintern**, Kleber was born as Manfred Stern and joined the Red Army to fight in the Russian **civil war**. After finishing the Frunze Military academy, he joined the GRU. In 1929, he was assigned to New York as the illegal *rezident* and lived under a number of aliases. He had a number of successes in the theft of military secrets. In 1932, he handed off the position to **Aleksandr Ulyanovskiy** and went to China, where he served as the Comintern representative to the Chinese **Communist Party**.

In 1936, he arrived in Spain, where he took the name "Kleber" after one of Napoleon's marshals. Kleber served as the International Brigade's military adviser and took part in the defense of Madrid. In Republican Spain, "General Kleber" had a very public persona, and that was to be his undoing. In 1939, he was recalled to Moscow, arrested by the **NKVD**, and sentenced to the **gulag**. He died of exhaustion and malnutrition in Sosnovka in February 1954.

KLINGBERG, ABRAHAM MAREK (1918–). The most important Soviet spy arrested in Israel, "Marcus" Klingberg was born into a Hasidic family and in 1940 emigrated to the Soviet Union, where he served as a medical officer in World War II. In 1949, Klingberg emigrated to the new Israeli state and established himself as a military officer and a scientist, working on highly classified biological and chemical weapons projects. He also published books and papers and developed an international reputation as an epidemiologist.

Klingberg agreed to spy for the **KGB** in the 1950s for ideological reasons and despite Israeli suspicions served the Soviet service without any pay until his arrest in 1982. He provided the KGB with detailed information about both scientific and military intelligence, as well as detailed information about the Israeli intelligence and counterintelligence services. After his arrest in 1982, he was sentenced to 20 years in prison and was released after having served 16 and allowed to finish his sentence under house arrest. In 2003, he was permitted to emigrate to Paris to live with his daughter and grandson, a **Communist Party** city councilor. He published his memoirs in 2007, *The Last Spy*, in Hebrew.

Klingberg, who lost family members in the Nazi Holocaust, apparently felt greater loyalty to the Soviet Union, which gave him asylum and a medical education than to Israel. His intelligence **tradecraft** was as exceptional as his scholarship. It took years to catch him, and according to the Israeli press, he passed a lie detector test.

KLUGMANN, NORMAN JOHN (1912–1977). One of the Soviet intelligence service's prize recruiters in the mid-1930s with the code name "Mayor," "James" Klugmann later played a critical role in orienting British policy toward Tito during **World War II**. Recruited into the Special Operations Executive (SOE), which claimed it had never received reports of Klugmann's real allegiance, Klugmann lobbied hard for Tito, denigrating his opponent, Chetnik leader Mihailovic. While Klugmann may not have been operating as a Soviet agent, his work benefited Soviet plans in the Balkans.

Recent research suggests that he had a major role in the recruitment and running of the **Ring of Five**. He was a successful recruiter, enrolling John Cairncross. Michael Straight, whom Klugman tried to recruit, described him as "a warm hearted and compassionate intellectual whose commitment to Communism left him no time for such minor preoccupations as taking a bath or cleaning his fingernails." Following the war, he became a leading member of the **Communist Party** of Great Britain and wrote a two-volume history of the party.

KOBULOV, AMAYAK ZAKHAROVICH (1906–1955). Like his brother **Bogdan Kobulov**, Amayak Kobulov was brought into the senior leadership of the **NKVD** by **Lavrenty Beria** in 1938. With no experience in foreign intelligence, he was sent to Germany as NKVD *rezident* in 1939 and served there until the outbreak of **World War II**. Veteran intelligence officers stated that Kobulov was an incompetent intelligence chief who added to the confusion in Moscow surrounding German intentions. Following the assignment to Berlin, Kobulov served as security chief in Uzbekistan and deputy chief of the **gulag** system. He was promoted to lieutenant general in July 1945. Like his brother, he was arrested the day after Beria's fall in July 1953. He was tried for treason in October 1954 and shot the following year.

See also BARBAROSSA.

KOBULOV, BOGDAN ZAKHAROVICH (1904–1953). One of **Lavrenty Beria**'s principal deputies, Bogdan and his brother **Amayak Kobulov** were quickly promoted after their mentor's promotion to head the **NKVD** in 1938. Following **World War II**, Kobulov was sent to Germany to supervise the looting of German industry, and he was promoted to colonel general in July 1945. Following **Joseph Stalin**'s death in March 1953, Kobulov was promoted to deputy minister of internal affairs by Beria. Three months later, he was arrested, tried, and executed with his patron in December 1953.

KOGAN, LAZAR ISAYEVICH (1889–1939). A senior **gulag** official, Kogan was chief of the construction directorate for the White Sea–Baltic Canal in 1930–1932. Kogan received the Order of **Lenin** for his work on the canal in 1933 and was later given responsibility for building the Moscow Volga Canal in 1934–1936, another major gulag project. He was arrested in December 1938 and shot in May 1939.

KOLYMA. The forced labor camps in the Kolyma River region of eastern Siberia were the most frightening islands of the **gulag** archipelago. Beginning in the early 1930s, tens of thousands of imprisoned peasants and political prisoners were transported to the Kolyma camps to mine gold. Under a construction trust named **Dalstroi**, a Russian acronym for "Far Northern Construction Trust," the Kolyma camps were run by experienced **Chekists**, such as **Ivan Nikishov**. In two decades, the Kolyma camps produced hundreds of tons of gold.

The capital of the Kolyma area, the port city of Magadan, was ice-bound several months of the year. The weather in the Kolyma region is severe with winter temperatures frequently below −40 degrees Fahrenheit. Prisoners were transported to the region by ship, and thousands apparently perished on the voyages. The Kolyma camps had the reputation as the Auschwitz of the gulag empire. The death rate was very high: one study found that almost 500,000 died of hunger, overwork, or **execution** in 1935–1953. There are very few memoirs of those who mined gold and timbered. A Polish survivor of the Kolyma camps summed up the experience with the Russian proverb *chelovek cheloveku volk* ("man is wolf to man").

KOMITET INFORMATSII **(KI).** The KI (Committee of Information) was created by **Joseph Stalin** in July 1947 to combine the foreign intelligence components of the **MGB** and **GRU** into one centralized intelligence service. The KI was apparently created to mirror the new American Central Intelligence Agency. The KI was initially placed under the management of Minister of Foreign Affairs **Vyacheslav Molotov**. Some soviet ambassadors were asked to serve as intelligence *rezidents*, a job few of them coveted. Diplomats and intelligence professionals alike hated the KI for confusing the roles of their components. The KI was not a success and was disbanded in 1951.

KONDRASHEV, SERGEI ALEKSANDROVICH (1923–2007). One of the most important **KGB** case officers in the Cold War, Kondrashev handled **George Blake** and served as *rezident* in Berlin and Vienna. In a recent book by Central Intelligence Agency counterintelligence veteran Tennent Bagley, he claimed to have recruited a code clerk in the American embassy in Moscow in 1950, a claim that has not been confirmed by either the Russian or the American government. If Kondrashev and Bagley's story is complete and accurate, **Joseph Stalin** had a window into U.S. decision making in the first year of the **Korean War**.

KOMPROMAT. Russian and **KGB** acronym for "compromising material." It generally referred to the security services' collection of material to be used in a criminal case. During the post-Soviet years, it meant material that could be used to blackmail or silence an opponent.

KOPATZKY, ALEKSANDR GRIGORYEVICH (1923–1982). One of the most intriguing **counterintelligence** cases of the **Cold War** involved "Sasha" Kopatzky. Captured by the Germans while serving as a Red Army officer, Kopatzky elected to remain behind after the war. In 1946, he was invited to join the American-supervised German intelligence service, and two years later he married the daughter of a German army officer. In 1949, Kopatzky, for reasons never satisfactorily explained, volunteered to the Soviet intelligence service and began a long career as a **double agent**.

Kopatzky was recruited by the Central Intelligence Agency (CIA) in 1951 in Germany to work against the Soviet target. In 1957, he emigrated to the United States as "Igor Orlov" and continued to work for the CIA. In the early

1960s, he came under scrutiny by the CIA and left intelligence work to open an art store in a suburb of Washington. In late 1961, **Anatoli Golitsyn** defected to the United States and stated that a CIA employee with the code name "Sasha" was an important **KGB** penetration of the CIA. The CIA spent a great deal of money and time over the next decade looking for Sasha. Kopatzky was never prosecuted. He died in 1982, after he was identified by name in a press article. His art store, run by his widow, was reportedly a hangout for espionage writers for many years.

KORABELNIKOV, VALENTIN VLADIMIROVICH (1927–2009). Chief of the **GRU** from 1997 to 2009, Korabelnikov served in military intelligence for 20 years before being made chief in 1997. He took an active role in military activities in **Chechnya** as a GRU staff officer and was reportedly responsible for the operation that killed insurgent leader Dzhokhar Dudayev in 1996. As GRU chief, he publicized the service's historic successes, noting in a television interview that "smart and well trained people work with us."

KOREAN WAR (1950–1953). According to Soviet-era documents, the **MGB** played an important role in the creation of the communist regime in North Korea. MGB officers helped established a North Korean security service. Moscow even provided film of the **execution** of Polish officers at **Katyn** as a training aid for their new ally.

During the Korean War, the MGB assigned intelligence and **counterintelligence** officers to the Soviet military units assigned to fight alongside the North Korean and Chinese forces. **Joseph Stalin** sent fighter wings and antiaircraft regiments to bolster the war effort. MGB intelligence officers recruited at least one important source, **George Blake**, from among the soldiers and diplomats captured by the North Korean and Chinese forces. The MGB and the **GRU** also collected military intelligence from the battlefront. American jet aircraft, shot down in the sky above Korea, were examined and in some cases shipped to the Soviet Union. Captured American jet fighter pilots were apparently interrogated by MGB officers. There is some evidence that a few of these pilots were transported to Soviet prison camps, where they were never heard from again.

A major MGB effort in the war was a massive peace campaign that it fashioned under the direction of the **Communist Party** leadership. This **active measure** was designed to paint the United States as the aggressor in Korea, and it was largely successful. More than a billion people—most of them living in the Soviet bloc—signed petitions denouncing the United States for its use of biological weapons.

Stalin received MGB and GRU reporting about the course of the war. Apparently, he ignored much of the information dealing with the human cost of the struggle, insisting that the war continue regardless of the costs to his Chinese and Korean allies. Stalin insisted that the Chinese and North Koreans reject UN offers that allowed disaffected prisoners to stay with the side that captured them. As in the aftermath of **World War II** when he demanded the return of Soviet citizens and **prisoners of war** in Allied hands, Stalin insisted that these prisoners would be used as agents against the communist world.

KOROTKOV, ALEKSANDR MIKHAILOVICH (1909–1961). The best known of the **World War II** and postwar **illegals** was Aleksandr Korotkov, often described as "king of the illegals." Korotkov started his career as an elevator operator in the **Lubyanka**; he joined foreign intelligence in 1933. His first posting was to France as **Alexander Orlov**'s assistant. Because he had been mentored by men shot in the *Yezhovshchina*, he was fired in 1938—often the first step to **execution**. Korotkov challenged the decision and demanded a hearing. Somehow, he was cleared.

He was then assigned to Berlin under diplomatic cover; his assignment was to contact a German espionage apparatus that had been abandoned during the purge of foreign intelligence. He traveled to Berlin in 1940 to contact **Arvid Harnack**, a dedicated communist who had been recruited several years earlier. Harnack, whose code name was "Corsican," worked with Korotkov to rebuild a ring of agents that formed the core of the **Red Orchestra**. Karnack surprised Korotkov by revealing that in the two years he had been out of touch with the **NKVD**, his group had grown from 16 to 60 potential agents. He had only been waiting to be contacted by Moscow. On 16 June 1941, five days before Operation **Barbarossa** began, Korotkov reported, "All German military measures for the attack on the Soviet Union have been fully completed, and the blow can be expected to fall at any minute."

Following Berlin's declaration of war on 22 June 1941, Korotkov slipped away from Gestapo surveillance and made his way to contact Grete Kuchkhoff to deliver final instructions. He later served as head of the service's German Department.

The German section of the Red Orchestra was prepared to operate secretly and without the active participation of Soviet intelligence officers after war broke out. It is to Korotkov's credit that it functioned for more than a year with minimum support and supervision by Soviet illegals. It lasted for almost a year before Karnack and the rest of his ring were compromised by the Gestapo. It is clear that the ring could not have operated, let alone survived, in the capital of Hitler's Reich without Korotkov's work.

After the war, Korotkov established **Karlshorst**, an area in Berlin, as a base for KGB illegal activities in Germany. Before his death, he served as chief of Service S, the First Chief Directorate component responsible for illegals, and then as KGB *rezident* at Karlshorst as a general officer. As *rezident*, Korotkov worked closely with the *Stasi*'s young chief of foreign intelligence, Markus Wolf. Korotkov recognized that the *Stasi* had far better access to the West German target, and he encouraged his young colleague and his organization to operate in Berlin, West Germany, and North Atlantic Treaty Organization states.

Korotkov died in 1961 after a series of confrontations with KGB chair **Aleksandr Shelepin**. Shelepin, who had had no experience in foreign intelligence, attacked Korotkov's work in Germany for neglecting the recruitment of agents by Soviet case officers. He apparently subjected Korotkov to an hour of insults and imprecations that brought on a heart attack. Markus Wolf delivered Korotkov's eulogy at the funeral.

KORZHAKOV, ALEKSANDR (1950–). As an officer of the **KGB's** Ninth (Leadership Protection) Directorate, Korzhakov was assigned to protect **Boris Yeltsin**. As Yeltsin's personal bodyguard, Korzhakov played a critical role in the 1991 **August putsch**, encouraging the Russian leader to leave his dacha outside Moscow to go the Russian White House, the parliament building, and rally his supporters.

Korzhakov played a critical role two years later, when communist parliamentarians tried a putsch. Korzhakov encouraged Yeltsin to resist pressure from communists in the Duma interested in overthrowing the infant Russian republic. Once again, Korzhakov saved Yeltsin from disgrace or death. Korzhakov was rewarded for his loyalty and courage by promotion to the head of a new independent guard service, the PSB (*Prezidentskaya sluzhba bezopasnosti*, or Presidential Security Service). Under Korzhakov, the PSB grew into a paramilitary service with a large military component. According to the Russian media, Korzhakov became a modern **Lavrenty Beria** with power over the security establishment. As Yeltsin's gray eminence, Korzhakov had tremendous power inside the president's official "family." With his ally, **FSB** chief Mikhail Bursakov, he dominated the president, setting political policies in both foreign and domestic areas. In July 1996, Yeltsin purged Korzhakov and his allies in the inner circle. Korzhakov got even by writing a "tell-all" book about Yeltsin, and he has since been elected to the Russian Duma.

Korzhakov's rapid raise and even more rapid fall illustrated both Yeltsin's unscrupulous use of the security services and the unbridled way that the Russian president controlled his administration and Russia. The disintegration of the Soviet Union did not, as Korzhakov's career illustrated, mean the rule of law for Russia or its security institutions.

KOVAL, GEORGE ABRAMOVICH (1913–2007). Serving as an agent of the **GRU** within the Manhattan Project, Koval produced intelligence that, according to Russian sources, "drastically reduced the amount of time it took for Russia to develop nuclear weapons." Born in Sioux City, Iowa, into a family of revolutionaries that welcomed the Bolshevik Revolution, Koval emigrated in 1930 to Russia. After being drafted into the Soviet army in 1940, he was dispatched to the United States as an **illegal** with the code name "Delmar." After being drafted into the U.S. Army, he was assigned to the Manhattan Project at Oak Ridge, Tennessee.

According to his account of his experience in the United States, which was published in the Russia after his death, his role as a GRU illegal was probably cut short by the **defection** of GRU code clerk **Igor Gouzenko**, who he believed could expose him. He left the United States in 1948 on the SS *America* and made his way back to Moscow. He became an academic, producing more than 100 academic papers, but received no recognition for his intelligence work. After his death in 2007, he was posthumously awarded the highest state honor, Hero of Russia. The Federal Bureau of Investigation has recently released two volumes of their files on Koval.

KRASSILNIKOV, REM SERGEYEVICH (1927–2003). The most adapt of **KGB** spy hunters, Krassilnikov served as the head of the KGB's department tasked with investigating and disrupting Central Intelligence Agency activities in Moscow. Krassilnikov served in Beirut from 1965 to 1970, operating against British intelligence, according to his autobiography. In the 1970s and 1980s, he was a successful counterintelligence chief, rising to the rank of chief of the American section of the **Second Chief Directorate** with the rank of major general. He disrupted several Western operations, arresting Soviet citizens who were subsequently shot. Never satisfied with the credit he believed his office deserved, he authored two books on KGB counterintelligence. He was referred to by one journalist as the "real Karla," after the fictional spymaster in John Le Carre's novels.

KRIVENKO, MIKHAIL SPIRDONOVICH (1904–1954). Chief of the **NKVD Directorate of Prisoners of War and Internees** in the last years of World War II, Krivenko's directorate managed camps across the Soviet Union with approximately 3 million German, Japanese, Italian, and Hungarian prisoners. NKVD statistics show that 381,067 died in captivity; German estimates are two to three times as high.

Previously, Krivenko, who had been an officer of the **Border Guards** as well as labor and prison camp commander, took part in the **Katyn** massacres of Polish officers in 1940 and later took part in the crushing of the Polish Home Army following the Red Army's victories in 1944–1945.

KRIVITSKY, WALTER (1899–1941). Born Samuel Ginsberg in Russian Poland, Krivitsky joined the **Bolshevik Party** in 1917 and entered military intelligence as an **illegal**. Working first in Eastern Europe and then in Western Europe, Krivitsky became a senior **GRU** officer, recruiting and running agents. He was in effect the GRU illegal *rezident* for Western Europe. In 1937, following the assassination by the **NKVD** of his colleague and friend **Ignatz Poretsky**, Krivitsky decided to defect to the United States in the autumn of 1937.

Unlike other early **defectors**, Krivitsky took a very public stance, meeting with anti-Stalinists and writing articles for the popular press, appearing before a congressional committee, and authoring the popular best seller *In Stalin's Secret Service*. Krivitsky in 1938–1940 came under intense pressure from American communists and fellow travelers who sought his extradition to the Soviet Union. Krivitsky survived due to the support of a small coterie of anti-Stalinist intellectuals. He traveled to Canada and then to London, where he was debriefed in detail by the British intelligence and security services. His information identified important Soviet spies in London and gave the British leads to moles deep within the British establishment, but these were not followed up.

Krivitsky continued to speak and write about the Soviet intelligence services and their threat to the United States. In February 1941, he traveled to Washington and was found dead—an apparent suicide—in his hotel room. Krivitsky had frequently told his supporters that the Soviet services would kill him and try to make it look like a suicide. There still is no convincing evidence to prove whether Krivitsky was murdered or committed suicide. His death silenced an important witness who was providing accurate information about the scope of Soviet intelligence operations inside the United States.

KRUGLOV, SERGEI NIKIFOROVICH (1907–1977). As a member of the **Communist Party** apparatus, Kruglov took part in the ruthless purging of the Komsomol in the mid-1930s. In late 1938, he was laterally transferred into the **NKVD** and made deputy people commissar for personnel, probably at **Lavrenty Beria**'s behest. In the next 18 months, Kruglov efficiently purged the service. During **World War II**, Kruglov was moved through a series of posts, frequently serving as the security service representative with major military formations. He was twice decorated with the Order of **Lenin**. He was responsible for security matters at the Yalta and Potsdam conferences in 1945 and was made a Knight of the British Empire for his questionable services to the British.

From 1945 through 1953, Kruglov served as minister of internal affairs, with the rank of colonel general. **Joseph Stalin** promoted him to Communist Party Central Committee membership as a reward for his work. Immediately following Stalin's death, Beria demoted Kruglov and took the position as chief of both the **MVD** and the **MGB**. In response, Kruglov conspired with **Nikita Khrushchev** and took part in the coup against Beria. He was rewarded with a promotion to head the MVD, a position he held until 1956. Khrushchev reportedly disliked and feared Kruglov and demoted him to a post in economic management. Kruglov retired in 1958 at age 51 on a generous pension.

See also SEROV, IVAN ALEKSANDROVICH (1900–1990).

KRYUCHKOV, VLADIMIR ALEKSANDROVICH (1924–2007). During **World War II**, Kryuchkov worked in a factory and in the Komsomol in his native Stalingrad. He served several years in the **procuracy** and then entered the diplomatic academy and from there was assigned to the Soviet embassy in Budapest. Kryuchkov came to the attention of then Soviet ambassador **Yuri Andropov** during the Hungarian revolution of 1956. Kryuchkov's opposition to the "counterrevolution" and his tireless support of a hard line won Andropov's admiration and later his patronage. When Andropov went to the **KGB** in 1967, he made Kryuchkov head of his personal secretariat and in 1971 made him the number two person in the KGB's foreign intelligence component, even though he had no previous experience in foreign intelligence. In 1974, Andropov promoted Kryuchkov to head the **First Chief Directorate** (FCD).

Kryuchkov was not a popular foreign intelligence chief. Some of his staff thought that too much time was spent on the pursuit of **dissidents** within the Soviet bloc and **active measures** against the West. Other critics believed that during his tenure, the FCD became overly bureaucratized and plagued with **defectors**. Nevertheless, during Kryuchkov's 14 years as chief of foreign intelligence, the service had major triumphs in gathering technical intelligence and managed to penetrate American intelligence and **counterintelligence** services. One evaluation of Kryuchkov's worth to his political masters was his rise inside the party leadership and his close association first with Andropov and then **Mikhail Gorbachev**. In 1981, he became the first Soviet foreign intelligence chief to be made a member of the **Communist Party** Central Committee. During the first years of *perestroika*, he became a trusted adviser of Gorbachev, and in December 1987, he accompanied the Communist Party general secretary on his visit to Washington. In 1988, Gorbachev made Kryuchkov KGB chair in a purge of party hard-liners.

Kryuchkov was a canny bureaucrat, capable of using information and disinformation in political struggles. When the Hungarian government decided to rebury **Imre Nagy** and other leaders of the 1956 revolt, Kryuchkov proposed releasing real and forged documents showing that Nagy had been a covert informant of the **NKVD** and was responsible for the death of scores of innocent Hungarian, German, and Soviet communists. The documents were released and have clouded Nagy's reputation and Russian–Hungarian relations ever since.

Gorbachev came quickly to regret his decision to promote Kryuchkov. In 1990, Kryuchkov became one of Gorbachev's principal critics from within the party and the KGB, condemning many of Gorbachev's allies as servants of Western intelligence. Kryuchkov was the prime mover behind the **August putsch of 1991**, and more than a dozen senior KGB officers took part in planning the abortive coup. Following the failure of the August putsch, Kryuchkov was arrested, but he was amnestied before being brought to trial. He has since written his memoirs, which accuse many of Gorbachev's allies of high treason and responsibility for the collapse of the Soviet Union.

KUBATKIN, PETR NIKOLAEVICH (1907–1950). Kubatkin was one of the few **NKVD** chiefs to survive the fall of **Nikolai Yezhov**. In 1939, he became chief of security of the Moscow office, following five men who had been purged or committed suicide. From 1941 to 1946, he was head of the NKVD in Leningrad, where he played an important role in the defense of the city. Kubatkin was an excellent administrator, as well as a merciless security chief, according to released documents. In the first 18 months of the siege, 5,360 men and women were shot for political crimes, and more than 200 were executed for cannibalism.

Viktor Abakumov made Kabutkin chief of foreign intelligence, a post he held for only a few months. He was then shipped to a Gorky as **MGB** chief. He was arrested in July 1949 and charged with treason, along with the other men who had saved the city during the blockade. He was sentenced to 20 years in prison, a charge that was changed to death by shooting on 27 October 1950. He was executed the same day.

Kubatkin rose quickly during the purges of the late 1930s. His survival as Moscow security chief suggests that he either missed the worst bloodletting or knew how to please his new boss, **Lavrenty Beria**. His fall was due to his close association to the small cadre of party and military officials who defended the city. In the first case, he was the right man at the right moment of Soviet history; in the second case, he was the wrong man at the worst moment of his country's history.

KULAK, ALEKSEY ISIDOROVCH (1922–1984). A war hero and walk-in to American intelligence, Kulak set off one of the most damaging spy hunts in the history of the Federal Bureau of Investigation (FBI). Kulak was made Hero of the Soviet Union for his service as an artillery officer in 1945.

He later joined the **KGB** as a scientific and technical officer and was assigned to the United Nations. In 1962, he approached the FBI and worked for American intelligence for the next several years in New York.

Kulak informed the FBI that one of their special agents had been recruited by the KGB. This set off a "mole hunt" within the bureau that lasted the better part of two decades. The debate about Kulak's bona fides convulsed American intelligence, and material about the case was published in the press in 1978. At this point, the Central Intelligence Agency chief of station in Moscow, disguised as an old woman, went to a public telephone booth and warned Kulak, who had since retired, of the danger. Kulak declined assistance and died in 1984, a year before **Aldrich Ames** provided the KGB with proof that he was an American agent.

In 1990, Kulak was posthumously stripped of his war medals, including the Hero of the Soviet Union award. Recent articles by American journalist have confirmed that the FBI had been penetrated and that the evidence provided by Kulak on this and other cases was accurate. A final question remains: why, with all the evidence available to the KGB, was Kulak left in peace? Possibly because he held the Soviet Union's highest military medal, the equivalent of the Congressional Medal of Honor, or possibly because the KGB was caught up in a mole hunt of their own.

KUROPATY. One of the largest mass **graves** in the former Soviet Union is to be found at Kuropaty in Byelorussia near Minsk. According to archaeologists who examined the site, there are approximately 150,000 people buried there in more than 500 mass graves. Other experts put the number of dead between 250,000 and 300,000. The **NKVD** used Kuropaty as a place of **execution** and burial of thousands of Poles and others considered **enemies of the people** who had been **deported** to the Soviet Union following the Nazi–Soviet Pact of 1939.

KUZICHKIN, VLADIMIR ANATOLYEVICH (1947–). A KGB officer in the Soviet embassy in Iran, Kuzichkin **defected** to the British in 1982, apparently after making a series of operational errors. His biography, *Inside the KGB: Myth and Reality*, is one of the few accounts in the West of Soviet intelligence against the regime of Ayatollah Khomeini.

KVASNIKOV, LEV ROMANOVICH (1905–1993). The founder of Soviet scientific and technical intelligence was drafted into the **NKVD** in 1938 following the purge of the foreign intelligence component. Trained as an engineer, Kvasnikov was one of the first intelligence officers to understand the potential of nuclear weapons, and he personally convinced NKVD chief

Lavrenty Beria in 1941–1943 that nuclear weapons were not British disinformation. Beria personally threatened Kvasnikov with summary **execution** should the information prove false.

In 1943, Kvasnikov was sent to New York to head up a small **Line X** *rezidentura* to collect information on the Anglo-American nuclear project— code-named *Enormoz* by the Soviet service—as well as other weapons programs. Over the next two years, Kvasnikov directed a small team of case officers who ran dozens of sources with access to these programs and produced thousands of key reports. The most important of these agent handlers, **Anatoli Yatskov** and **Aleksandr Feklisov**, ran agents in more than a score of critical defense plants as well as at Los Alamos.

On his return to Moscow, Kvasnikov directed the service's scientific and technical intelligence program and retired a highly decorated colonel. In the KGB, Line X ran scientific and technical intelligence inside *rezidenturas*, while Directorate T managed the effort from within the **First Chief Directorate**.

L

LABORATORY 10. In 1937, the **NKVD** created a laboratory inside Moscow to produce substances to support surveillance operations and poisonings. Professor Grigori Maironovskiy, a respected toxicologist, was ordered first by **Nikolai Yezhov** and then **Lavrenty Beria** to create poisons. According to one former NKVD officer, these poisons were first tested on people under sentence of death. In the 1940s, these poisons were used to kill an American who had spied for the service but who had become an unwanted witness, **Raoul Wallenberg**. In 1953, Marionovsky was arrested and in exchange for his life testified at the trials of Beria and **Viktor Abakumov**. After serving his sentence, he died in retirement. Following the formation of the **KGB**, some of the functions of Laboratory 10 were included in the Operational and Technical Directorate. The KGB assisted the Bulgarian security service in poisoning **Georgi Markov**, a Bulgarian defector.

LASKIN, IVAN ANDREYEVICH (1901–1988). On 31 January, Laskin, a senior staff officer in **Stalingrad**, accepted the surrender of Field Marshal Friedrich Paulus. For this act, he was awarded the Distinguished Service Cross by the United States. Less than six months later, he was arrested at *Smersh* for "fabricating" his account of his escape from a German encirclement earlier in the war and charged with treason. Laskin apparently was the target of a senior *Smersh* officer who resented his decision to not recommend him for the Order of **Lenin**.

Laskin spent almost 10 years in pretrial confinement and in late 1952 was sentenced to 10 years' imprisonment. He was released and rehabilitated in 1953. In 1966, he finally received his American decoration.

LATSIS, MARTYAN IANOVICH (1888–1938). Born Ian Fredrickovich Sudrabis in Russian Latvia, Latsis was arrested for revolutionary activity in 1916 and exiled to Siberia. He escaped and traveled to St. Petersburg and took part in the **Revolution of November 1917**. He joined the **Cheka** in early 1918. Latsis then became one of **Felks Dzerzhinsky**'s key deputies, institutionalizing terror first in Siberia and then in Ukraine. He had a reputation for cruelty and the killing of hostages. Latsis later told a journalist that class terror was dedicated to the eradication of the bourgeoisie as a class and that it was unrestrained by any rules of conduct. In a Cheka publication, he wrote, "During the investigation do not look for evidence that the accused acted in word or deed against Soviet power. The first question you ought to ask is to what class he belongs." Following the **civil war**, Latsis left the Cheka for positions in industry and academics. In 1932, he was made head of the Plekhavov Economic Institute, and he wrote a number of books on the role of the Cheka in the civil war. He was arrested in 1937 and shot the following year. Despite his record in the civil war, he was posthumously rehabilitated.

LEADERSHIP PROTECTION. A major role of the Soviet security service from the 1920s to 1991 was the protection of the party leadership. While **Vladimir Lenin** dismissed the need for a large security detail, **Joseph Stalin** saw two reasons for a new and enhanced component to ensure his personal security. Stalin believed that he was in mortal danger from opponents, and he saw the use of a security detail to collect information and gossip about his colleagues and their families. Stalin's chief bodyguards became his close colleagues. **Karl Pauker** was a family friend who frequently dined with Stalin, while **Nikolai Vlasik** was a close associate for two decades. Stalin had both men arrested: Pauker was shot, and Vlasik would have been had Stalin not suffered a fatal stroke in 1953. Under Stalin, the Guard Service had responsibility for every aspect of the leader's personal and professional life.

The Guard Service also carried out surveillance of other members of Stalin's Politburo. **Vyacheslav Molotov**, Stalin's closest associate for more than two decades, told his biographer that he was under surveillance. "I seemed to have been bugged all my life," said the number two man in the Soviet Union. "At times Stalin was extraordinarily suspicious of everyone around him."

In the **KGB**, the Ninth Directorate had responsibility for protecting the party and state leadership, similar to the American Secret Service. The KGB's 15th Chief Directorate had responsibility for important buildings, such as the Kremlin, as well as sensitive military installations. The security of the leadership—and the capital—was further guaranteed by the Dzerzhinsky Division, a well-armed and well-trained **MVD** unit stationed inside Moscow. The division was reportedly under the direct control of the KGB chair.

The KGB's guards were also a danger to the leadership. In 1964, the Guards Directorate failed to protect **Nikita Khrushchev** from those planning a coup. At the beginning of the 1991 August putsch, the chief of the Ninth Directorate informed **Mikhail Gorbachev** that an emergency commission had taken power and took his "suitcase" with the codes needed to launch a nuclear attack.

On becoming president of the Russian Federation, **Boris Yeltsin** relied heavily on his chief bodyguard, **Aleksandr Korzhakov**, who reestablished leadership protection in the Presidential Security Service (PSB). From 1991 to his dismissal in 1996, Korzhakov was one of the most powerful people in Moscow. Since his fall, the PSB has morphed into the **Federal Protective Service** and is commanded by a close associate of President **Vladimir Putin**. *See also* RUSSIAN INTELLIGENCE SERVICES.

LEHMANN, WILLI (1884–1942). One of the **NKVD**'s intelligence coups during **World War II** was the recruitment and running of Willi Lehmann, a senior Gestapo officer. Code-named "Breytenbach," Lehmann entered the Gestapo in 1933 and became the director of anti-Soviet counterintelligence. He later transferred to the SS. On 19 June 1941, he reported the exact date and details of the forthcoming Nazi invasion of the Soviet Union. Beria minuted the report "disinformation" and did not forward it.

In the Gestapo's investigation of the *Rote Kapelle* (**Red Orchestra**) in 1942, Lehmann was identified as a Soviet agent. He was arrested and shot without trial at the order of SS leader Heinrich Himmler. It is difficult to understand Lehmann's decision to work with Moscow. The Russian archives indicate that he was disgusted by Nazi brutality. Other information suggests that he agreed to work with Soviet intelligence in 1929 while serving in the Berlin police for both ideological and monetary reasons.

LENIN, VLADIMIR ILYICH (1870–1924). Born into a family of the petty nobility, Vladimir Ulyanov became a revolutionary at the university. Rather than becoming a member of the populist revolutionary parties, which saw power coming from a revolutionary peasantry, he embraced Marxism. In **exile** in Western Europe for more than two decades, he adopted the nom de guerre "Lenin" and became the leader of the Bolshevik (majority) faction of the Russian Social Democratic Labor Party (RSDLP), which supported a small, tightly organized party run by a dedicated political elite. Unlike European Marxists and Russian opponents in the RSDLP, Lenin embraced conspiracy and political violence. The Bolsheviks supported political terror as an absolute necessity; for them, a revolution without a firing squad or a guillotine was unthinkable.

Without Lenin, there could not have been a **Revolution** in 1917. As both the ideologue and organizer, he put fire into the belly and built an effective militant party with its own strong paramilitary section. Within weeks of the revolution, Lenin instituted a secret police, the **Cheka**, an acronym for *Chrevzuychanaya Komissiya po Borbe s Kontrarevolutsei i Sabotazhem* (Extraordinary Commission for the Struggle against Counterrevolution and Sabotage), which was placed under the Polish revolutionary **Feliks Dzerzhin-**

sky. From its formation on 20 December 1917, the Cheka was designed to be used against the enemies of the revolution among the former ruling classes, the counterrevolutionary peasantry, and the churches. Lenin saw the need from almost the very beginning for prophylactic violence, arguing for the taking of hostages and **executions** as early as 1918. Following a failed assassination by the anarchist Fanny Kaplan, Lenin supported the mass execution of enemies of the revolution, many of whom he personally knew.

During the Russian **civil war**, Lenin served as the chief executive officer of the Bolshevik Party and the Soviet government. A historian of the French Revolution of 1789–1793, he believed that terror was necessary, and he argued for execution of real and potential enemies. In 1918, he ordered party officials in Penza to "(1) Hang (I mean hang publicly so that people will see it) at least 100 kulak rich bastards and known blood-suckers. (2) Publish their names. (3) Seize their grain. Do all this so that for miles around people will see it all, understand it, tremble." The message ends with the postscript "Find tougher people."

Lenin and the Cheka did find tougher people, and the **Red Terror** was intensified. In 1921, at the height of a major famine, he ordered that the Russian Orthodox churches, which were feeding millions, be looted of their icons and their communion vestments and that recalcitrant priests, monks, and nuns be shot without trial. Lenin, however, believed that terror should never be unleashed on members of the ruling party. He believed that if the Bolsheviks used terror in intraparty disputes, the revolution would end up eating its children, as happened in France.

Years after the death of **Joseph Stalin**, former Foreign Minister **Vyacheslav Molotov** told a young researcher that in comparison to Stalin, "Lenin was more severe," and that he had reproached Stalin for his softness. Soviet archives showed that Lenin had a deep interest in Cheka operations, frequently minuting Dzerzhinsky on official documents about operational details. Lenin was a master tactician and organizer who accepted the need of revolutionary violence. While he was unwilling to use the Cheka against opponents in the party, he paved the way for Stalin's acceptance of terror against political opponents.

LENINGRAD BLOCKADE. The **NKVD** played an important role in the almost 900-day German blockade of Leningrad. It organized the firefighting apparat and caught almost all German agents dispatched by German military intelligence. It apparently controlled cannibalism in the terrible winter of 1941–1942, arresting and executing people for marketing human flesh. It also kept a weather eye on any opposition, real or imagined. Throughout the siege, anything that smacked of disloyalty was punished. More than 5,000 were shot, according to a recent history of the siege, while another 18,000 died of hunger in jails. The ability of NKVD chief General **Petr Kubatkin** to ensure the security of "Lenin's city" did him no good; he was executed in 1950 as part of the **Leningrad Case**.

LENINGRAD CASE. Following victory in **World War II**, competition within **Joseph Stalin**'s entourage grew. **Communist Party** Secretary Georgii Malenkov and security police generalissimo **Lavrenty Beria** especially feared two younger competitors. State economic chief Nikolai Voznesenskiy and Stalin's personal favorite and former Leningrad party boss Aleksei Kuznetzov were the target of rumors spread by the old elite that the two were guilty of fixing a party election; they were also accused of managerial incompetence. Stalin ordered **Viktor Abakumov** to investigate the two in the summer of 1948. In August 1949, Kuznetzov and Voznesenskiy and more than 200 of their colleagues from the Leningrad party apparatus were arrested. They were tried in camera on 30 September 1950, and many were shot the same evening. Abakumov apparently played on Stalin's suspicions that Leningraders sought to build a Russian political party and navigate a separate political course for Russia.

Among the casualties of Stalin's paranoia were party, military, and security officials who had defended Leningrad during the epic 900-day siege. During the siege, Stalin had told Kuznetzov, who had spent the war in Leningrad, "The motherland will never forget you." Yet all were accused of treasonously planning to form a counterrevolutionary Russian government and tortured into confessing that they had betrayed the motherland they had defended during the war. The Leningrad Case also suggests how Stalin in his dotage was both the manipulator and the manipulated. Willing to sacrifice acolytes and associates to maintain the balance of power and terror in his entourage, he struck down the most competent members of the party leadership.

See also LENINGRAD BLOCKADE.

LEONOV, NIKOLAI SERGEYEVICH (1928–). One of the most important **KGB** officers working in the developing world, Leonov served as Moscow's main contact with the Cuban government in the early 1960s. Leonov was a close associate of brothers Fidel and Raul Castro and Che Guevara and played an important role in the **Cuban Missile Crisis**. Leonov later served as chief of the KGB's Information and Analysis Department. After the fall of the Soviet Union, he wrote his memoirs, as well as academic books and articles. He was elected to the State Duma as a member of the Nationalist *Rodina* (Motherland) Party in 2003.

LINE X. The **NKVD** and then the **KGB** name for the component assigned to collect scientific and technical intelligence. This nomenclature was apparently first used for officers assigned to run agents inside the British and American nuclear weapons programs. Later, Line X was an established part of all KGB *rezidenturas*, especially in the United States, Western Europe, and Japan. Information from Line X officers was forwarded to Directorate T of the KGB's **First Chief Directorate** for analysis and distribution.

LIPKA, ROBERT STEPHEN (1945–2013). An National Security Agency employee, Lipka spied for the **KGB** from 1965 to 1967 with the code name "Rook." Charged with the destruction of classified material, Lipka sold material to a KGB handler for $27,000. He later rationalized his betrayal by stating that the money was to finance his college education. He was arrested in 1993 on a tip from a retired KGB general resident in the United States. He later pleaded guilty and was sentenced to 18 years in prison.

LITVIENKO, ALEKSANDR VALTEROVICH (1962–2006). An **FSB** officer who defected to Great Britain in 2000, Litvienko was poisoned with radionuclide polonium-210 after meeting with two FSB officers. Litvienko had a tortured career: FSB counterintelligence officer, adviser to President **Vladimir Putin**, defector, author, and murder victim.

Litvienko served in the FSB in the late 1990s, apparently serving as a cutout between Putin and billionaire tycoon Boris Berezovsky. He defected in 2000 after a falling out with Putin's entourage and wrote several books about Russian corruption and the FSB's links with criminal organizations and Putin's closest allies. His poisoning and eventual death were linked to a former FSB officer close to Putin and raised allegations in the British and Russian press that his murder was a "hit" ordered by the FSB leadership.

LITVIN, MIKHAIL IOSIFORICH (1892–1938). Nikolai **Yezhov** brought Litvin into the **NKVD** from the **Communist Party** apparatus to purge the security service in October 1936. He was head of the personnel department and was then assigned to Leningrad in January 1938 to finish purging the region. He was responsible for tens of thousands of arrests over the next 10 months. In late 1938, Yezhov warned Litvin that he would be arrested as part of **Lavrenty Beria**'s cleansing of the service. Litvin chose to commit suicide rather than face disgrace, trial, and **execution**.

LIVE DOUBLE/DEAD DOUBLE. One of the means used by the Soviet intelligence services in establishing **illegals** was the live double/dead double ploy. Intelligence officers would obtain a birth certificate for a child who had died within the first two years of life. The certificate was then used to obtain further documents, such as a passport. The illegal would be given the dead double's documents, along with other documents to create a legend for the new live double. When **William Fisher** entered the United States as an illegal in 1949, he carried the passport of Emil Robert Goldfus, who had died as a two-year-old child five decades previously.

As it became more difficult to find dead doubles in the United States and Great Britain, the **KGB** and the **GRU** began to document many illegals as Germans who had been born outside the borders of Germany and had to flee to Germany with the defeat of the Third Reich. In Eastern Europe, archives and church records were in shambles, and there were many dead doubles to be exploited. When **Rudolph Herrmann** entered Canada in 1962, his wife was using the identity of a German woman born in Czechoslovakia who had perished in an Allied bombing raid in the last days of the war.

KGB Line N (Illegal Support) officers in *rezidenturas* had the duty of collecting documents to create legends for illegals like Fisher. They sought out agents with sources of legal, school, and military records to buttress these legends. Especially prized were documents from small towns where birth and death records were poorly kept and where school records were nonexistent. The live double/dead double ploy is now used by terrorists and gangsters, as well as other people trying to change their identities.

The **SVR** continues to use the live twin/dead twin method of documenting illegals. Russian agents captured in the United States in 2010 and in Germany in 2012 had documents based on dead children.

LOCKHART PLOT. In the spring of 1918, the British intelligence service dispatched Robert Bruce Lockhart and **Sidney Reilly** to Moscow to stimulate resistance to the new Bolshevik regime. Neither Lockhart nor Reilly were professional intelligence officers, and their actions were first monitored and then controlled by the **Cheka**. Their contacts with other Western embassies caused the Cheka to believe it was facing an all-out offensive. The Cheka let the plot play out to expose the role of foreign embassies and catch their Russian accomplices. Thus, Lockhart and Reilly's principal contacts were Cheka agents to whom they willingly confided their ideas for a plot that would include the arrest and **execution** of **Vladimir Lenin** and **Leon Trotsky**. Crucial to this plot was the corrupting of **Eduard Berzin**, the commander of Lenin's elite Latvian rifle detachment. Berzin played the role to perfection, as did the other Cheka actors.

In the summer, however, a series of events endangered the regime. An attempt on the life of Lenin by Fanny Kaplan, followed by violence in Moscow between Bolsheviks and their junior partners in the coalition, the Left Socialist Revolutionaries, caused the Cheka to act. Lockhart was imprisoned briefly; Reilly escaped using another man's passport. Both Lockhart and Reilly were decorated for heroism by the British government, and the Lockhart Plot became part of the mythology of British intelligence. The Cheka saw the Lockhart Plot as more than a series of blunders or British schoolboy heroics. Since 1918, it has been portrayed in the histories of the Soviet security services—both classified and unclassified—as one of the great moments in Cheka history. For Soviet security officers, it was a victory over a major international plot that came within an inch of overthrowing the infant Soviet government.

LONETREE, CLAYTON (1961–). Lonetree, a U.S. Marine Security Guard at the American embassy in Moscow, was recruited by the **KGB** after being seduced by a Soviet employee of the embassy in the early 1980s. Lonetree provided the KGB with information about embassy personnel and offices. When the KGB sought to blackmail him into providing information about the embassy in Vienna, his next assignment, he confessed to an American intelligence officer. Lonetree was convicted by a court-martial and sentenced to 15 years. He was released after serving nine.

LONG, LEONARD "LEO" HENRY (1917–1985). A student of **Anthony Blunt** at Cambridge, Long was recruited to work for the Soviet service by his old tutor during **World War II**. Long, who was working in the British Security Service (MI5), was given the code names "Ralph" and then "Elli" by the **NKVD** (a pun on the Russian for the plural of two Ls). According to a British academic study, he was run as a subagent by Blunt and **Guy Burgess**. He apparently provided Moscow with information about British **counterintelligence** operations against the Soviets and the Nazi intelligence service. Long also passed material garnered from the decryption of German communications, as well as information on British plans for the occupation of Germany. Long later confessed to MI5 in exchange for immunity from prosecution.

See also ULTRA.

LUBYANKA. For seven decades, the headquarters of the Russian security service was in the Lubyanka, an office building in central Moscow. During the tsarist period, the Lubyanka was the headquarters of the State Insurance Company, whose Russian acronym *Gostrakh* can also be translated as an acronym for "state fear." A Russian joke of the 1930s was that the Lubyanka had gone from *Gostrakh* to *Gosuzhas:* from state fear to state horror. It was also said that the Lubyanka was the tallest building in Moscow because from its cellars one could see Siberia.

During the Stalinist period, the Lubyanka also served as a jail and interrogation center. **Executions** of important prisoners were carried out there and at Lefortovo prison, as well as at **Butovo**, on the outskirts of the city, where there were mass **graves**. Following **Joseph Stalin**'s death, the **KGB** used the building as its headquarters, while prisoners were kept and interrogated at Lefortovo and Butyrka prisons. Following the collapse of the Soviet Union in 1991, Lubyanka became the headquarters of the **FSB**, and the **SVR** moved its headquarters to Yasenevo on the Moscow Ring Road.

LUNEV, STANISLAV (1956–). After serving as a **GRU** officer in Singapore, Beijing, and Washington from 1978 to 1992, Lunev defected. The most senior GRU officer to defect to the United States, Lunev has written widely on Russian military intelligence and the **Vladimir Putin** administration. Among his most important revelations were that the **KGB** had prepared armed caches in Western Europe to be used for sabotage operations in the event of war. While his intelligence did lead to the discovery of several caches, his claim that the KGB possessed portable tactical nuclear weapons ("suitcase bombs') was not confirmed.

LYALIN, OLEG ADOLPHOVICH (?–1995). The defection of Lyalin in London in 1971 seriously compromised **KGB** covert operations in Europe. Lyalin, who had been tasked by Moscow to prepare sabotage operations in the United Kingdom to be activated in case of war, provided the British with detailed intelligence and military information about the Soviet Union. As a result of this information, the British government expelled 90 KGB and **GRU** officers and refused to allow another 15 on leave in the Soviet Union to return to Britain. He reportedly compromised agents throughout Western Europe. Lyalin's information also compromised KGB plans for sabotage and terror in the West. Much of his information was declassified and published in the British press. Another result of his defection was the reorganization of the KGB's components responsible for paramilitary operations: within the **First Chief Directorate**, the Eighth Department of Directorate S, which organized **illegal** work, was given additional responsibility for paramilitary activity.

LYUSHKOV, GENRIKH SAMOILOVICH (1900–1945). One of the first Soviet **defectors**, Lyushkov joined the **Cheka** in 1919 before his 20th birthday and was assigned to a frontline infantry division. Lyushkov rose quickly in the service, and in 1938, he was serving as **NKVD** chief in the Far East. Fearing that he was about to become a victim of his own service, Lyushkov defected to the Japanese on 6 June 1938. For the next several years, he worked for the Japanese military. Following the Soviet invasion of Manchuria in August 1945, Lyushkov was shot by a Japanese officer and buried in a grave as a member of the Japanese military.

MACLEAN, DONALD STUART (1913–1984). One of the most important Soviet agents within the British establishment, Maclean provided the Soviet leadership with insight into British policymaking for 15 years. Maclean was the son of a Liberal Party cabinet minister. A brilliant student at Cambridge, he was converted to communism at the university. Run by a Soviet **illegal**, Maclean was asked to assume the cover of an earnest and intelligent ex-communist and apply for the British diplomatic service. Maclean had little trouble fooling his superiors, and he became a "high flyer" in the foreign service. In the late 1930s, he provided Moscow with thousands of British diplomatic dispatches, a window on British foreign policy during the Munich crisis and the run-up to **World War II**.

During and after the war, Maclean served in Washington, where he provided Moscow with detailed information about U.S. military strategy and nuclear weapons development. According to one former **KGB** officer, Maclean's reporting in 1942 filled 45 volumes. In the late 1940s, Maclean was posted to Cairo as the youngest minister counselor (the equivalent of a deputy chief of mission) in the British foreign service. In Egypt, Maclean's life began to unravel, and he drank heavily. One evening, he and a British colleague smashed up the apartment of an American diplomat in fits of drunken rage. Maclean was returned to Britain in disgrace, but he was made head of the American Department.

In his last few months in the department in 1950–1951, Maclean provided Moscow with detailed information about American and British policy in Korea. By this time, however, he had been pinpointed by American counter-intelligence as a Soviet mole. Decryption of Soviet intelligence cables from 1944 to 1945 identified a Soviet agent code-named "Homer." **Kim Philby**, serving in Washington as the British intelligence representative, was aware of the danger and used **Guy Burgess**, another Soviet agent in the British establishment and serving in the British embassy in Washington, to warn Maclean. On 25 May 1951, Maclean and Burgess traveled to France and disappeared. The KGB resettled Maclean under the name "Mark Petrovich Fraser." He and Burgess surfaced in Moscow in 1956.

Maclean was never truly happy in Moscow despite the KGB's exfiltration of his wife, Melinda, and their children from London to Moscow two years later. The KGB and the Soviet system did not know how to use **defectors**, nor did they fully trust them. Maclean lived in Moscow for the next three decades; disillusioned with Soviet domestic policies, he remained a "stranger in a strange land." After his death, his ashes were returned to Scotland and buried there. Perhaps the best assessment of the damage he caused in the first days of the **Cold War** came from Secretary of State Dean Acheson: "That son-of-a-bitch knew everything."

See also HARRIS, KATHERINE (1900–1966); VENONA.

MAGNITSKIY, SERGEI (1972–2009). A Muscovite auditor for an American firm, Magnitskiy died at the hands of Russian security officials in a Moscow jail. He had been arrested when he investigated the **FSB**'s expropriation of an American investment firm's assets. He had been in pretrial confinement for 358 days when he died of kidney problems aggravated by a devastating beating. The U.S. Congress passed the Sergei Magnitskiy Rule of Law Accountability Act in 2012, imposing "visa and banking restrictions on Russian officials implicated in human rights abuses." The Russian parliament retaliated in December 2012 by passing a law prohibiting adoption of Russian children by Americans.

MAIN ADVERSARY. The Soviet security services considered the British their main adversary (*glavniy protivnik*) until 1945. At the conclusion of **World War II**, the United States was designated as the service's main adversary and major target. The Russian word *protivnik* was frequently mistranslated as "enemy" rather than "adversary," and in some literature, the United States is referred to as the main enemy.

MUKASEI, MIKHAIL (1907–2008). One of the legends of Soviet intelligence, Mukasei served under diplomatic cover and as an **illegal** for more than 40 years. With the code name "Zypher," he served in the United States, Canada, and Western Europe. He was decorated by both the Soviet and the Russian government.

MALINOVSKIY, ROMAN VATSLAVOVICH (1878–1918). One of the *Okhrana*'s greatest successes was placing their agent Roman Malinovskiy, code name *"Portnoi"* (Tailor), in the center of the **Bolshevik Party**. Malinovskiy was highly regarded within the party and was elected to the Russian Duma. Deeply respected by **Vladimir Lenin**, who repeatedly sent him on confidential missions inside and outside Russia, Malinovskiy served as the party's contact with major financial donors. Control of Malinovskiy allowed the *Okhrana* to monitor the party. Malinovskiy was a close friend of **Joseph Stalin** and was personally responsible for the future dictator's exile to Siberia.

Lenin defended Malinovskiy as a loyal comrade and close personal friend even after evidence appeared in the European press and the tsarist archives of his treachery. When Malinovskiy returned to Russia in 1918, he was arrested, immediately tried, found guilty, and shot the evening of his trial, one year to the day after the Bolshevik Revolution had brought his old comrades to power.

The disruption caused by Malinovskiy was seen by Stalin and many of his associates as justifying surveillance of even members of the politburo. **Vyacheslav Molotov** told a young biographer, "We never forgot the agent-provocateur Malinovskiy."

MALLY, THEODORE STEPANOVICH (?–1938). Possibly the greatest of the great Soviet **illegals** of the 1930s, Mally traveled a path that led him from one church militant to another and to a martyr's death. Captured on the Eastern Front during **World War I**, Mally, who had been ordained as a Roman Catholic deacon before entering the Hungarian army as an officer, joined the Bolsheviks and the **Cheka**. Following the **civil war**, he went abroad to recruit and run agents in England. He was fondly remembered by **Kim Philby** as the gentle man who taught him how to spy. Mally was a very careful operations officer, and his frequent complaints to Moscow about his inadequate cover prompted suspicions.

Despite his success in recruiting agents in the British establishment, Mally was recalled to Moscow by **Nikolai Yezhov**. Mally apparently knew he was going to his death; he told a friend who had refused to return, "Don't you see that I must go back? Shall I hide now? If I do, they will tell you the priest was a spy." Mally was arrested on his return and tortured. He was tried on 20 September 1938, convicted of working for several hostile intelligence services, and shot the same evening. Following **Joseph Stalin**'s death, he was posthumously rehabilitated, and his picture hangs in the service's museum.

MAMULOV, STEPAN SOLOMONOVICH (1902–1976). One of **Lavrenty Beria**'s chief assistants first in the **Communist Party** apparatus and then in the **NKVD**, Mamulov followed Beria to Moscow in 1939 and became chief of the NKVD secretariat. From 1946 to 1953, he served as deputy minister of internal affairs. According to some memoir literature, he also served as Beria's chief procurer, finding young women for his boss. He was arrested immediately after Beria's fall and sentenced to 15 years' imprisonment

MARKOV, GEORGI (1929–1978). A Bulgarian **dissident** residing in London, Markov was slated for **execution** by the Bulgarian security service because his broadcasts on the BBC World Service were creating problems for the communist regime. **KGB** chair **Yuri Andropov** agreed to provide both the poison and a specialist in assisting the Bulgarian allies in murdering Markov. On 7 September 1978, while Markov waited for a bus on Waterloo Bridge, he received a lethal dose of ricin fired from an air gun concealed in an umbrella. His assassin was a Bulgarian intelligence officer. He died four days later in a London hospital. **Oleg Kalugin**, a KGB **counterintelligence** specialist, wrote in his memoirs that Andropov had authorized the assassination out of "solidarity" with the Bulgarian intelligence service. Kalugin, who acted as the KGB's representative during the planning stage of the assassination, was later denied entry into Great Britain because of his part in the murder.

MASKIROVKA. The Soviet military and intelligence term for strategic deception is *maskirovka*. Soviet military and intelligence doctrines called for a mixture of denial and deception measures to deceive foreign enemies: this doctrine impacted on Soviet **counterintelligence** operations as well as their military deception and denial activities. Beginning in the early 1920s, the **Cheka** created false White Russian movements and operations, such as the **Trust**, to deceive foreign intelligence services and lure **émigré** leaders back to the Soviet Union. During **World War II**, the Soviet sources used complicated **radio games** to confuse Berlin as to Red Army intentions and capabilities. During the **Great Patriotic War**, the Soviet high command used a mixture of human and technical intelligence denial and deception measures to confuse the Nazi enemy. In preparing for the Stalingrad offensive in the late fall of 1942, the movement of reserves was masked by the careful use of camouflage and the observation of absolute radio silence. At the same time that preparations were being made for the Stalingrad offensive, rumors of a massive counteroffensive in the Moscow region were fed to controlled agents who dutifully misinformed Adolf Hitler's intelligence officers. **Stalin** went so far as to allow Marshal **Georgi Zhukov** to launch an offensive in November 1942 (Operation Mars) in the vicinity of Moscow to further his deception. More than 140,000 Soviet soldiers died to ensure surprise later at Stalingrad.

The Soviet general staff perfected *maskirovka* in later campaigns. Prior to the Kursk counteroffensive in 1943 and the Minsk offensive in June 1944, measures were taken to mislead the German high command. The **GRU** and the **NKGB** provided Stalin with concrete information that the Germans were planning a major offensive near Kursk. With great stealth, the high command prepared for a defensive battle followed by a major counteroffensive against the German flanks. Prior to Operation **Bagration** in the spring of 1944, the

German army intelligence chief on the Eastern Front, **Reinhard Gehlen**, was fed misinformation by human agents that the main blow would fall in the south in Ukraine. Every measure was taken to mask the movement of the Red Army's reserves.

During the **Cuban Missile Crisis** of 1962, the Soviet military and intelligence services spoofed the U.S. military. The operation for the movement of troops, missiles, and submarines was code-named "Anadyr," after a river in eastern Siberia. Troops were issued winter clothes and told they were being assigned to a mission in the Soviet east. Ships bound for Cuba were controlled by intelligence officers, and no Soviet soldiers were allowed on the deck of the ships during daylight hours. So carefully orchestrated was this plan that Moscow moved 40,000 troops as well as short- and medium-range missiles to Cuba without alerting American intelligence.

During the **Cold War**, Moscow developed human and **signal intelligence** resources, as well as open-source and unclassified material for *maskirovka*. For example, cities used for the development of nuclear weapons were not identified in atlases and were given false and misleading post office addresses. Thus, Sarov, the Los Alamos of the Soviet nuclear program, was known as "Arzamas-16." Sarov for five decades disappeared from maps of the Soviet Union. In the 1970s, the Red Army and the **KGB** created the **GTK**, or State Technical Commission, to develop measures to deceive Western satellites. The GTK became the official organ of *maskirovka* for the Soviet military-industrial complex.

MASLENNIKOV, IVAN IVANOVICH (1900–1954). An important soldier and **Chekist**, Maslennikov joined the Red Army at age 18 and the **Cheka** in 1928. For the next 25 years, he moved between the military formations of the security service and the military. During **World War II**, Maslennikov commanded major army units. He was made a general of the army in 1945. Following the war, he served as deputy minister of internal affairs for combat troops. He survived the first purge of **Lavrenty Beria**'s lieutenants in 1953. When later threatened with arrest, he committed suicide in April 1954.

MASSING, HEDE (1900–1981). A woman of mystery who served as one of the most controversial witnesses of Soviet intelligence activity, Massing had three husbands as well as numerous lovers and covers. However, she is best remembered as a member of the **NKVD** apparatus in New York from 1933 to at least 1937, shining as a recruiter. She later defected to the Federal Bureau of Investigation in 1947 and was an important witness in **Alger Hiss**'s trials. Her biography, *This Deception*, remains a controversial account of her relationship with Hiss and—among others—**Richard Sorge**.

Massing's cover name "Red Head" appears in deciphered Russian intelligence messages indicating that she worked with Lawrence Duggan, a senior Department of State officer. There is some mystery as to when Massing stopped working for the NKVD: the *Time* magazine article on her in December 1949 says it perhaps best that she was a "woman with a past."

MAY, ALLAN NUNN (1911–2003). An important British nuclear physicist, May worked for the **GRU** *rezidentura* in Ottawa from 1943 to 1945 for very little money—approximately $500. May's **motivation** is thought to have been both ideological and personal. He believed that it was his duty as a scientist to provide Moscow with scientific intelligence. Moreover, he apparently enjoyed the life of being a spy. When **Igor Gouzenko** defected in September 1945, he brought information that showed May was a controlled Soviet agent. The information provided details about May's contact instruction with the GRU in London, where he had returned at the end of the war. The British Security Service was unable to catch May with a Soviet case officer but did trap him into making a full confession.

May was tried and convicted of violating the Official Secrets Act. His defense was that he had never betrayed the interests of the United Kingdom but had only assisted the work of a wartime ally. He served less than seven years in prison and then taught physics at a university in Africa. Postmortem examinations of Soviet espionage in the nuclear program suggested that May was an outstanding and capable agent and that the information he provided was invaluable to Soviet scientists in building a nuclear bomb.

See also ENORMOZ.

MEDVED, FILLIP DEMYANOVICH (1889–1937). Medved was a protégé of **Feliks Dzerzhinsky**, who sponsored him as a member of the **Bolshevik Party** in 1907. He took part in the **Revolution of November 1917** in Moscow as a party militant and organizer. Medved joined the **Cheka** in 1918 and was notorious for his persecution of **dissident** Russian Orthodox clergy in the late 1920s. He was made chief of the Leningrad **NKVD** in 1930.

In Leningrad, Medved worked closely with party boss **Sergei Kirov**, with whom he became especially close. In October 1934, **Joseph Stalin** recommended that Kirov be moved to Moscow and ordered Medved to make changes in Kirov's security detail. On 1 December 1934, Kirov was murdered by a lone assassin, **Leonid Nikolaev**, who had twice been detained loitering near the party leader's residence by the new security detail. Stalin blamed Medved for the assassination, reportedly slapping him across the face when he arrived in Leningrad to investigate the murder. Medved was almost immediately sentenced to three years' confinement in a labor camp. While he was initially treated more as a guest than a prisoner, he was recalled to

Moscow in May 1937 and rearrested for terrorism. He was shot in July 1937, a victim and a scapegoat of the Kirov case. He was posthumously rehabilitated in 1957.

MEDVEDEV FOREST MASSACRE. On 11 September 1941, 157 political prisoners were shot by the **NKVD** on direct order of **Joseph Stalin** in Medvedev Forest near Orel. Among the dead were the old Bolshevik Christian Rakovsky and Maria Spirdonova, a member of the Left Socialist Revolutionaries and political opponent of **Vladimir Lenin**.

Two months later, **Lavrenty Beria** successfully petitioned Stalin to simplify the procedure for carrying out death sentences in time of war. Henceforth, sentences would not have to be approved by the Supreme Military Court or the Politburo. Rather, the Special Council of the NKVD was given the responsibility to confirm sentences.

MEKHLIS, LEV ZAKHAROVICH (1889–1953). While nominally a **Communist Party** official and then a military officer, Mekhlis was more responsible for scourging the Red Army during the Great Purge of 1937–1938 and again in the first days of **World War II** than any security officer. Working with the **NKVD**, Mekhlis, as chief of the Army's Main Political Administration, sent thousands to their deaths. In the first days of the war, Mekhlis personally ordered the execution of senior officers who failed to perform. When given responsibility for troops under fire, Mekhlis performed badly but was repeatedly forgiven by **Joseph Stalin** and retired a colonel general.

MEMORIAL. Founded in the last years of the Soviet Union to investigate the crimes of the communist era and memorialize its victims, Memorial became one of the most powerful nongovernmental organizations in Moscow. In the years since the collapse of the Soviet Union, Memorial has continued its work to uncover the secret history of the former regime. Memorial chapters in cities and regions have produced detailed information of those martyred by the regime between 1917 and 1953. Memorial's website (www.memorial.ru) and its publications are the best primary source for historians studying the purges.

MENZHINSKY, VYACHESLAV RUDOLOLFOVICH (1874–1934). One of the least-known chiefs of Soviet security, Menzhinsky was born in St. Petersburg of Russianized Polish parents. Well educated (he spoke 16 languages), Menzhinsky joined the **Bolshevik Party** in 1902. In 1907, he emigrated and spent the decade before the revolution in Europe and the United States. Before 1917, he wrote novels and poetry and flirted with Satanism. He returned to Russia following the February Revolution.

Menzhinsky joined the **Cheka** in 1919 and served in Ukraine in intelligence and **counterintelligence** capacities during the Russian **civil war**. In the early 1920s, he led the Cheka's **antireligious campaign** against the Russian Orthodox Church. In 1923, he was made **Feliks Dzerzhinsky**'s deputy and heir apparent. On Dzerzhinsky's death in 1926, Menzhinsky was appointed to lead the service. Menzhinsky, like his patron, was willing to use the service in intraparty struggles, supporting **Joseph Stalin** unconditionally against his opposition. Under Menzhinsky, the service's empire grew: it supervised an expanding empire of forced labor camps, crushed opposition in the countryside during Stalin's program of **collectivization**, and became an even more aggressive and intrusive security service. Menzhinsky played a key role in creating public **show trials** of foreign "spies" and Soviet "wreckers" in the late 1920s and early 1930s to intimidate the population and create a **war scare** mentality in the country. These proceedings became the model of the **Moscow Trials** of the late 1930s. Menzhinsky's death in 1934 allowed Stalin to meddle further with the security service, promote **Genrykh Yagoda**, and take the final steps to make the service a pliant tool of the dictator.

MERCADER DEL RIO, RAMON (1918–1978). As a young man, Mercader took part in the **Spanish Civil War**. His mother, Caridad, was a dedicated Spanish communist, and his older brother was killed in combat in Spain. In 1938, Mercader was recruited by **NKVD illegal Leonid Eitingon** and his mother to penetrate **Leon Trotsky**'s inner circle in Mexico. Documented as "Frank Jacson," Mercader gained entry to Trotsky's circle through a woman he had seduced and who was unwitting of his plans. Following failed efforts on Trotsky's life, Mercader was ordered to kill Trotsky with an ice-climbing ax and to plead before a Mexican court that his act was not political but connected with his love affair with one of Trotsky's associates. The murder was successful, and the cover story survived the Mexican court's scrutiny. Mercader served 20 years in a Mexican prison, then made his way to Moscow. He was decorated by the **KGB** and lived in obscurity in Moscow for 10 years. In the mid-1970s, he traveled to Cuba to serve as an adviser to Fidel Castro.

MERKULOV, VSEVOLD NIKOLAEVICH (1895–1953). Merkulov, whose father was an army officer, received a strong scientific education and served for a short time as a lieutenant in the Imperial Army. After **World War I**, Merkulov taught in a school for the blind. He joined the **Cheka** in 1921 and rose quickly as a protégé of **Lavrenty Beria** in the security service and the **Communist Party** apparatus. By 1938, he was one of Beria's chief lieutenants. When **Joseph Stalin** appointed Beria to head the **NKVD** in late 1938, Beria in turn appointed Merkulov to be his deputy to oversee **counterintelligence** and foreign intelligence. In 1939–1940, he was placed in charge of the sovietization of Polish territory.

In 1941, Stalin divided the NKVD. Merkulov was made chief of the newly minted **NKGB** and given responsibility for intelligence and counterintelligence. He therefore bears some responsibility for failing to provide Stalin with adequate intelligence about Operation **Barbarossa**, the German plan to invade the Soviet Union. Like Beria and other senior intelligence officers, he refused to forward or confirm accurate intelligence reports of German intentions. Nevertheless, Stalin was satisfied with his record as a provider of intelligence on Germany and the Western Allies.

Given his university education, Merkulov was uniquely able among the NKVD elite to recognize the importance of intelligence on nuclear weapons and was better prepared to direct operations to collect intelligence about the Anglo-American nuclear weapons program, which the NKVD code-named *Enormoz*. On 2 October 1944, he detailed in a letter to Beria the cooperation that Soviet intelligence was receiving from important American scientists.

Merkulov was promoted to general of the army in 1945 and made the first deputy minister of state security at the **MGB** the next year. Yet, after receiving these promotions, Merkulov was demoted, apparently an effort of Stalin to minimize Beria's control of state security, and was assigned series of less important posts in the government. In September 1953, Merkulov was arrested. He was tried for treason with Beria in December of the same year and executed immediately following the trial. Intelligent and articulate, he is remembered in the memoirs of the period as the most urbane and perhaps the least odious of Beria's subordinates.

MESHIK, PAVEL YAKOLEVICH (1910–1953). One of **Lavrenty Beria**'s men, Meshik served in a number of important roles in *Smersh* and then in Soviet-occupied Poland and Germany during **World War II**. According to a declassified Central Intelligence Agency study, Meshik was responsible for drafting German nuclear scientists for Moscow's nuclear weapons program. He was promoted to lieutenant general of state security at the end of the war.

Following the war, he was made chief of the **MGB** in Ukraine and made responsible for the struggle against Ukrainian nationalists. He was arrested in June 1953 and tried for treason with Beria on 23 December 1953. He was shot the same evening.

See also ENORMOZ.

METKA. Often referred to as "spy dust," *metka* is a special chemical that was applied by the **KGB** to the shoes of foreign intelligence officers to facilitate tracking by dogs. Its chemical composition was nitrophenyl pentadien, which is potentially carcinogenic. The secret was first revealed to the Central Intelligence Agency station in Moscow in 1963 by **Aleksandr Cherepanov**, a KGB walk-in. In 1984, Sergei Vorontsov, a KGB officer working for the Moscow station, provided a sample of the substance. Vorontsov was later betrayed by **Aldrich Ames** and executed. *Metka* allowed the Seventh Directorate of the KGB to track foreign intelligence officers in an urban setting, and it led to some operational successes.

MGB (*MINISTERSTO GOSUDARSTVENNOI BEZOPASNOSTI*). The Ministry of State Security, or the MGB, was created by **Joseph Stalin** on 15 March 1946, when the Soviet government transformed all "people's commissariats" into ministries. **Viktor Abakumov** was the first minister, and he built a powerful organization out of the intelligence, **counterintelligence**, and security components of the **NKVD** and **NKGB**. In 1954, the MGB was transformed into the **KGB** by party First Secretary **Nikita Khrushchev**.

MIF. *Operatsiya Mif* (Operation Myth) was a Soviet **active measure** designed by **Joseph Stalin** and his chief advisers to place blame on the United States for the disappearance of Adolf Hitler at the end of **World War II**.
    See also HITLER'S CORPSE.

MIKHOELS, SOLOMON MIKHAILOVICH (1890–1948). The greatest Yiddish actor of his generation, Mikhoels was used by the Soviet regime to raise funds and popular support in the United States during **World War II**. Following the war, Mikhoels and his colleagues in the Jewish theater came under suspicion for Zionism. In late 1947, **Joseph Stalin** ordered **MGB** officers to murder Mikhoels and make his death look like an accident. On the evening of 13 January 1948, Mikhoels was beaten to death and his body repeatedly run over by a truck. Mikhoels's death marked an upswing in Soviet anti-Semitism and the beginning of a widespread purge of Jews from the security service, the Foreign Ministry, and the army. In 1953, **Lavrenty Beria** announced that Mikhoels had been murdered by **Viktor Abakumov**, Beria's rival. In 1956, **Nikita Khrushchev** gave further details about Mikhoels's murder, placing the blame where it deserved to be: with Stalin.

MILITARY ATTACHÉS. Military officers were assigned to diplomatic missions as attachés from the time of Petr I (1689–1725) to act as representatives of the Russian army and navy and to collect sensitive military information. In tsarist times, military attachés were expected to collect intelligence on their hosts' military and military technology. Military attachés were encouraged to take sabbaticals to travel inside foreign countries to collect intelligence. (This was the usual practice in the 19th century; for example, British, French, Prussian, and Austrian officers attached themselves to the northern and southern armies during the American Civil War.) They also recruited and ran agents in certain circumstances. **Alfred Redl**, for example, was run from 1908 to 1913 by Colonel Mitofan Marchenko, military attaché in Vienna.

In the Soviet period, all military attachés were officers of the Chief Intelligence Directorate, the **GRU**. Attachés had combat arms experience and were trained at the Military-Diplomatic Academy in languages, history, politics, and intelligence **tradecraft**. From the 1930s, military attachés played an important role in Soviet clandestine human intelligence activities, serving as case officers and running agents. In the 1940s, military attachés recruited and ran agents engaged in penetrating the American, Canadian, and British nuclear weapons labs. Soviet military attachés were also assigned to military diplomatic missions. A special military mission was established in both East and West Germany by the North Atlantic Treaty Organization and the Soviet Union.

MILSHTEIN, SOLOMON RAFAILOVICH (1899–1955). An important member of **Lavrenty Beria**'s political machine, Milshtein served in the **Communist Party** in Georgia and then in Moscow in the **NKVD**. Milshtein was Beria's satrap in a number of critical posts in the security service in Moscow and the provinces. He was repeatedly decorated, and he was made a lieutenant general in 1945. He was serving as deputy chief of the Ukrainian **MGB** when Beria fell. He was arrested in June 1953, tried on 30 October 1954, and shot two days later.

MINISTRY OF FOREIGN AFFAIRS. Initially, the **Bolshevik Party** saw little need for diplomacy. The first commissar of foreign affairs, **Leon Trotsky**, believed that the **Revolution of November 1917** had made traditional diplomacy obsolete and that it would set off a series of European revolutions. "I'll just publish some memorandum, and shut up shop," he reportedly said. The Commissariat of Foreign Affairs was until 1939 the weakest of three foreign policy institutions: the security service and the **Comintern** had far greater authority in the Kremlin. With the appointment of **Vyacheslav Molotov** to the post in 1939, this changed. Molotov had **Joseph Stalin**'s ear, and the Commissariat of Foreign Affairs, which after 1946 was the Ministry of Foreign Affairs, increasingly became a center of foreign policy decision making until Stalin's death. Stalin gave Molotov orders to purge the ministry of Jews, which he did.

Under Molotov, the Ministry of Foreign Affairs became a major consumer of foreign intelligence, and he placed heavy demands on intelligence officers for foreign documents and agent reports. In 1947, Molotov, as head of the Committee of Information, or *Komitet Informatsii*, had control of foreign intelligence.

The Ministry of Foreign Affairs grew in authority after 1953 as the Soviet Union became a major power. While it still had to compete with the **KGB** and the International Department of the **Communist Party** Central Committee (CPCC), it did so after 1953 as more of an equal. Longtime Minister of Foreign Affairs Andrei Gromyko and Ambassador to the United States Anatoly Dobrynin played a far more important role in U.S.–Soviet relations than their colleagues in the intelligence service or the CPCC.

Problems between the KGB *rezident* and the ambassador apparently plagued many embassies as they competed to provide Moscow with information. Moreover, ambassadors and senior KGB officers competed for the same sources. Another problem was the KGB *rezidents'* **counterintelligence** authority. The KGB always had the power to destroy the reputation of any diplomat, including an ambassador. KGB **informers** infiltrated every foreign mission, and any sense of disloyalty or personal weakness guaranteed a diplomat a trip home.

MIRONOV, NIKOLAI ROMANOVICH (1913–1964). Mironov began his career in *Smersh* during **World War II** and served in the 1950s in Moscow and Leningrad as a senior **counterintelligence** officer. In 1959, **Nikita Khrushchev** selected Mironov to head the **Administrative Organs Department** of the Central Committee. As one of Khrushchev's key deputies, Mironov served as the party's watchdog on intelligence and security matters. He wrote a number of articles in the press, emphasizing the party's role in establishing a regime of socialist legality. Mironov was reportedly feared by intelligence professionals: **Oleg Penkovskiy** noted in his journal that "this Mironov is tsar and God over us." Mironov perished in an airplane crash in Yugoslavia in October 1964, just a few days before the anti-Khrushchev coup. His death limited Khrushchev's control over the **KGB**, which took an important role in the coup.

MIRONOV LETTER. One of the most bizarre chapters of the espionage war between the Federal Bureau of Investigation (FBI) and the **NKVD** began in August 1943 with the posting of letters to **Joseph Stalin** and the FBI by Vasili Markov, an NKVD lieutenant colonel serving in the *rezidentura* in New York, whose cover name was "Mironov." The letter to Stalin accused NKVD *rezident* **Vasily Zarubin** of being a German spy. The letter to the FBI—addressed to "Mr. Guver"—identified several NKVD officers in the *rezidentura* by name, noting their collection of political and military intelligence. The letter to Stalin caused Zarubin to be recalled to Moscow in 1944. The letter to the FBI led to greater **surveillance** of Soviet trade and diplomatic facilities.

Zarubin was acquitted on his recall to Moscow. But his removal from the United States hurt Soviet intelligence. Mironov/Markov was recalled to Moscow, tried by a special court, and placed in an asylum. His later attempts to contact the American embassy earned him a death sentence; he was shot.

MITROKHIN ARCHIVE. Vasili Mitrokhin was a 30-year veteran of the **KGB**, spent mostly in the **First Chief Directorate**'s archives. Beginning in 1972, Mitrokhin began to take notes on some of the 300,000 operational files for which he was responsible. These notes, which after 20 years totaled more than 100,000 handwritten pages, he buried under his dacha outside Moscow. In 1992, Mitrokhin approached a British intelligence officer in the Baltic and offered his "archives" to London. The publication of a book based on the archives created a firestorm of publicity in Great Britain in 1999 because it named dozens of British subjects and foreigners who had spied for the Soviet intelligence service between 1917 and 1989. Mitrokhin went on to write a monograph on the KGB in Afghanistan; his coauthor, Christopher Andrews, has been widely interviewed by the British and American press on the "archives."

The book's bona fides were challenged by a number of scholars, though at least two of the long-term agents named in it publicly admitted serving Moscow. Some journalists and scholars compared the book to the infamous **Zinoviev Letter**, accusing Andrews of trying to blacken the British left in a mini–Red Scare. However, the majority of experts on security matters recognized the book as genuine. Mitrokhin apparently had acted like many of the **dissidents** the KGB had pursued during the **Cold War**: he wrote "for the dresser drawer"—not in the hope of publication and fame but out of the need to somehow bear witness to the truth.

MODIN, YURI IVANOVICH (1923–). One of the most successful Soviet intelligence case officers, Modin ran many important British agents in London during the late 1940s, including **Guy Burgess** and **Donald Maclean**. In 1951, Modin stage-managed Burgess and Maclean's escape and defection to the Soviet Union. Following his success in Great Britain, Modin returned to Moscow, where he served on the faculty of the **KGB**'s **Andropov Institute**. His memoirs of his time in London, *My Five Cambridge Friends*, is worth reading.

See also RING OF FIVE.

***MOKROYE DELO* (WET WORK).** The **NKVD** used the terms *mokroye delo* ("wet work," or "wet affair") and *chornaya rabota* ("black work") to describe **executions** and assassinations. Later, the **KGB** used *mokroye delo* for foreign assassinations. In the 1930s, the **NKVD's Administration for Special Tasks** assassinated a number of enemies abroad. Those killed include Ukrainian and Russian nationalists, two leaders of the Russian **émigré** community in Paris, and **Leon Trotsky**. At least one American, Juliette Poyntz, was kidnapped in New York and then murdered for political deviation. After **World War II, Joseph Stalin** ordered the assassination of Josef Tito. In fact, at the last meeting of Stalin's presidium, the Soviet leader demanded information about plans for Tito's death.

The KGB continued to plan assassinations into the late 1950s. Two leading Russian émigrés, Lev Rebet and Stefan Bandera, were killed in West Germany. **Bogdan Stashinskiy**, the assassin of Bandera, was personally decorated by KGB chair **Aleksandr Shelepin**. Plans for further assassinations were disrupted when Stashinskiy and **Nikolay Khokhlov**, who had been selected for assassination missions abroad, defected to the West. Stashinskiy and Khokhlov revealed details about the scope of the KGB's plans in books and media interviews. Embarrassed by the defections, the KGB shut down the organization responsible for assassinations. A further blow to plans for further political violence was the defection of **Oleg Lyalin** in 1971.

MOLCHANOV, GEORGI ANDREVICH (1897–1937). One of the most important of the early **Chekists**, Molchanov entered the service at age 23 and advanced quickly to the head of the **NKVD** in Byelorussia as well as the Secret Political Department. In the latter position, he had access to all the records and details of operations of the service against **Joseph Stalin**'s enemies. He took part in the interrogation of **Martimian Riutin**, who had written a memorandum in 1932 calling for Stalin's replacement. Like many of the early generation of security workers, Molchanov was seen as too close to members of the opposition and was slated for **execution**. In early 1937, Stalin asked **Nikolai Yezhov** why Molchanov had not been arrested. He quickly was. He was shot later that fall "by special arrangement," that is, without interrogation or trial. He was obviously a man who knew too much.

MOLDOVAN CRISIS. Moldovia, once the province of Bessarabia in the Kingdom of Romania, was annexed by Joseph Stalin before World War II. In 1945, it became the Moldovan Soviet Socialist Republic with a majority of Romanian-speaking citizens. Following the collapse of the Soviet Union, the Russian 14th Guards Army took control of an area in the newly independent state known as the Dnestr Republic, or the Transnistrian region, on the border. For the next three years, the 14th Army, supported and rearmed by Moscow, fought an inconclusive war with the Moldovan government, resulting in approximately 3,000 combat casualties.

With covert support, reportedly from the **GRU** and the **FSB**, the Russian enclave, with its own armed forces, has continued, as has the division of the country. The small Russian garrison called the Operational Group of Russian Forces in Moldova is under the command of the Moscow Military District. The Transnistria has a population of 555,000 and is not recognized diplomatically by any state save Russia. Meanwhile, Moldova remains divided and according to European Union statistics is the poorest country in Europe.

See also FROZEN CONFLICT ZONES.

MOLODY, KONON TROFIMOVICH (1922–1970). One of the most famous **KGB illegals**, Molody was educated in the United States. After service in the Soviet army in **World War II**, he was recruited by the KGB and dispatched to London under the cover of a Canadian businessperson, "Gordon Lonsdale." In London, Molody ran several sources, including English agents within the Admiralty. In 1961, as a result of the defection of a Polish intelligence officer to the West, Molody was arrested. He spent three years in a British prison before being exchanged for a British agent in Soviet captivity.

See also GOLENIEWSKI, MICHAEL (1922–1993); PORTLAND SPY CASE.

MOLOTOV, VYACHESLAV MIKHAILOVICH (1890–1986). No one save **Vladimir Lenin** and **Joseph Stalin** cast a longer shadow across the first four decades of Soviet history than V. M. Molotov. Born Skryabin, Molotov joined the **Bolshevik Party** in 1905 and took the pseudonym "Molotov," literally "hammer." He became a member of the **Communist Party** Central Committee in 1921 and supported Stalin in his struggle for power. As a reward, he was made a member of the ruling Politburo in 1926. While Lenin was dismissive of his talents, referring to him as the best file clerk in Moscow, Stalin was a friend and patron, and the two vacationed together several times in the 1930s. Molotov became premier in 1930 and was one of Stalin's chief lieutenants during the purges, cosigning hundreds of "death lists" containing the names of tens of thousands of people sentenced to be shot. These lists bear not only his name but also curses directed at the condemned. A grim Russian joke was that the initials "V. M." stood not for "Vyacheslav Molotov" but rather for "*Vyshaya mera*" ("supreme measure"), or **execution**.

In 1939, Stalin appointed Molotov commissar of foreign affairs and made him the coauthor of the Molotov–Ribbentrop Pact. Molotov was very realistic about German–Soviet relations, believing that the alliance could not last. He had the courage of his convictions and argued with Adolf Hitler during a state visit in 1940 about the future division of Central Europe between Germany and the Soviet Union. It was Molotov whom Stalin selected to announce to the Soviet people the beginning of war with Germany. The statement ended, "Our Cause is just. The enemy will be defeated. Victory will be ours."

During **World War II**, Molotov served as foreign minister as well as a member of the **GKO** (State Defense Committee). He was Stalin's principal negotiator with the United States and Great Britain. Molotov was a consumer of intelligence, and he placed intolerable strain on **MGB** officers for purloined documents during negotiations with the British and Americans during and immediately following the war. As minister of foreign affairs, Molotov was the first head of the *Komitet Informatsii* (Committee on Information), which controlled the foreign intelligence assets of both the MGB and the **GRU**.

Stalin became suspicious of Molotov and in his last days meant to purge his old friend. Molotov was stripped of his ministerial position. His wife, Polina, was arrested in 1948, accused of corruption and sexual wantonness, and imprisoned in Central Asia. At the 19th Party Conference, Stalin attacked Molotov, accusing him of proposing that the Crimea be given to the Soviet Jews as a homeland. Stalin also attacked Molotov's wife, maintaining that she had friends "who were not to be trusted." Only Stalin's death saved Molotov from execution, and he regained his position as foreign minister, representing the Soviet Union at international conferences several times.

Molotov gradually lost power. He fought with **Nikita Khrushchev** over de-Stalinization and was banished to Mongolia as ambassador. In 1962, he was stripped of his Communist Party membership. In his dotage, Molotov and his wife bitterly defended Stalin to any who would listen. He repeatedly petitioned the Central Committee to reinstate his party membership, which they finally acceded to 18 months before his death. Molotov left some interesting biographical notes. A young acolyte copied down their conversations over several years, producing *140 Conversations with Molotov*, one of the most revealing memoirs of the Stalinist period.

MOROZOV, PAVEL [PAVLIK] TROFIMOVICH (19??–1932). Perhaps the most famous **informant** in Soviet history, Pavlik (Little Paul) Morozov denounced his father to the **OGPU** for hiding grain during **collectivization** and was in turn murdered by members of his own family. The trial of the Morozov family resulted in the **execution** of several relatives, including a 90-year-old grandfather. Morozov's father, who was in a labor camp, was also shot. Pavlik Morozov became the poster child for informants in the 1930s. Hundreds of children's books and articles were written about him, and statues of the young hero appeared in most major towns. His "martyr-dom" was used by the regime and the security service in their drive to recruit informants. The recruitment of informants led to a number of intrafamily murders: according to a study of the Morozov case, more than 50 "informant-children" were murdered in 1932.

MOSCOW TRIALS (1936–1938). As part of his effort to acquire total power and stigmatize any real or suspected opposition, **Joseph Stalin** ordered the **NKVD** to prepare a series of major public trials of Old Bolsheviks. In these **show trials** in 1936, 1937, and 1938, former close associates of **Vladimir Lenin** who had led the Russian **Revolution of November 1917** and won the **civil war** of 1918–1921 were tried for treason, sabotage, and murder committed on behalf of Nazi Germany. **Leon Trotsky**, living in foreign **exile**, was indicted as a coconspirator, the archfiend responsible for most of the crimes. With one exception, the defendants confessed in open court, and all were immediately shot or **deported** to the **gulag** (forced labor camps), where they perished.

Stalin saw the trials as political theater, insisting that the NKVD wring confessions out of the accused by appealing to their sense of party loyalty, their concern for their families who faced death sentences, and promises of pardons and rehabilitation. Torture was also used; some men were beaten to a pulp, while others were kept awake for days as a conveyor belt of interroga-tors worked on them. (One Old Bolshevik was kept awake for 90 hours in a marathon interrogation session.) Stalin read the interrogation reports, and he even corresponded and met with a few of the defendants, promising some of them clemency for cooperating with the NKVD. All of these promises were broken, and every prisoner who met with Stalin went to the **execution** chambers. Nikolai Bukharin, whom Lenin had dubbed the "favorite of the party," wrote to Stalin hours before his death: "Koba, why do I have to die?" Stalin, who used the name "Koba" as his party nom de guerre, undoubtedly believed that Bukharin's death was a necessary part of the drama he was directing.

The trials were public spectacles, more akin to medieval morality plays than modern judicial processes. The victims—with the exception of Bukhar-in—confessed to being murderers, traitors, and saboteurs, and they de-manded the death penalty for themselves and their codefendants. The prose-cutor, **Andrei Vyshinsky**, echoed this with demands that "these mad dogs be shot." The judges agreed, sentencing the defendants to execution without the right of appeal. The shootings took place in the **Lubyanka** less than 48 hours after the sentences were passed. Foreign diplomats and journalists, as well as a select audience of Soviet citizens, witnessed the trials. According to a British diplomat who was an observer of the process, Stalin watched the trial from a secret room in the courthouse.

The trials were also designed to convince the Soviet people that the rolling purges of the 1930s were a legitimate hunt for terrorists and saboteurs and that political vigilance was necessary. Soviet public opinion was all but unanimous in demanding the defendants be executed. A secondary audience was foreign political opinion. While most liberal and left-wing journals accepted the verdicts, the American educator and philosopher John Dewey conducted an independent probe of the trials to show that much of the evidence was preposterously false. It was not until Robert Conquest's *The Great Terror* was published in the 1960s that the liberal West realized the causes and consequences of the trials. Moreover, it was not until the late 1980s that the trials' defendants were rehabilitated by the regime of **Mikhail Gorbachev**.

See also YAGODA, GENRYKH GRIGOREVICH (1891–1938); *YEZHOVSHCHINA* (THE TIME OF YEZHOV).

MOTIVATION. Most literature on espionage lists four reasons people betray their country and become spies or defect: money, ideology, compromise, and ego (or MICE). These indeed explain the bulk of **Cold War** espionage cases. While both Western and Soviet intelligence service portrayed their own agents as selfless heroes and their traitors as evil incarnate, some generalizations can be made about what motivated westerners and Soviets to spy against their country.

In the 1930s, 1940s, and 1950s, many westerners agreed to spy for Moscow out of deep ideological commitment. The **Ring of Five** all agreed to betray Great Britain and the ruling establishment out of deep disgust with capitalism and British imperialism. **Julius Rosenberg** told his Soviet case officer that he wanted to be a good soldier of **Stalin**. For them, Moscow was the New Jerusalem. A jaundiced former **KGB** officer who worked in Washington believes that ideology is not the reason people decide to change sides. Rather, retired Colonel **Viktor Cherkashin** argues, ideology helps a person explain after the fact why he or she became a spy.

Revelations about the Soviet system, especially **Nikita Khrushchev**'s **Secret Speech** of February 1956, put paid to the idea that Moscow was the city on the hill. Beginning in the 1950s, therefore, the Soviets increasingly recruited agents through money. **John Walker** went to the Soviet embassy in 1967 to find funds to support his failing bar. **Aldrich Ames** needed money for a divorced wife and a new spouse. Yet it was not simply money that made Walker, Ames, and other Americans spy. Anger, often rage, about their personal lives and their lack of professional success also contributed. They might not be a success in the U.S. armed forces or the Central Intelligence

Agency (CIA), but they could be the greatest spy in the world. Anger tinged with contempt of their superiors led many in the American military and intelligence professions to spy. Both **James Hall** and **Clyde Conrad** had deep contempt for their superior officers, whom they "knew" they could outwit. **Edward Howard** clearly volunteered out of his fear of prosecution for civil crimes committed in New Mexico, but another factor may have been the desire to get even with the CIA, which no longer needed him.

A great deal has been written in spy novels about people being recruited after they were placed in compromising situations. While a few minor agents were recruited after having been compromised by prostitutes—both male and female—far more were recruited for financial or personal reasons. **William Vassall** is one of the most important agents who was blackmailed into serving the Soviets. But in his case, money and ego also played roles. Clayton Lonetree, an American marine serving in Moscow, was literally seduced into serving as a KGB agent in the 1980s. Yet Lonetree's decision to work for the KGB also was a product of his anger with U.S. Marine counterparts who repeatedly humiliated him. In the first years of the Cold War, a number of Soviet intelligence officers defected to the West, but relatively few worked in place for the West. In the West, spying was punished by terms in jail, but in the Soviet Union, conviction almost invariably meant the firing squad. Defections from the Soviet services were caused by personal and professional concerns. However, many officers defected or volunteered out of a deep anger with the system. Both **GRU** colonels **Petr Popov** and **Oleg Penkovskiy** and, later, General **Dmitry Polyakov** were deeply offended by the system they served. Other Soviet intelligence officers defected to have access to the Western way of life they had grown accustomed to.

During the last 15 years of the Cold War, a number of GRU and KGB officers changed sides, and the balance swung dramatically in favor of the West. The factors motivating the second season of **defectors** had a great deal to do with what was seen as the faltering Soviet economy and the corruption of the ruling class. **Oleg Gordievskiy** volunteered to serve the British Secret Intelligence Service out of his anger with Moscow's intervention in the **Prague Crisis** in 1968. Other officers clearly were motivated by hopes of resettlement in the West.

An American psychiatrist, Dr. David Charney, has recently written that spies and leakers often acted following a traumatic act of humiliation. He saw the moment a man or women decided to spy as a "psychological perfect storm," involving a series of financial, personal, and professional crises.

The best classical text on motivation, treason, and espionage may be C. S. Lewis's *The Screwtape Letters*, a work of fiction in which a senior tempter writes letters to a young apprentice devil, arguing that the way to hell is very gradual and that temptation to mortal sin seems very venal and minor at first.

Analysis of many Cold War spy cases suggests that most men and women seduced (and self-seduced) into treason move to the other side for a variety of reasons that impact gradually on their consciousness.

MUKASEI, MIKHAIL ISAAKOVICH (1907–2008), AND MUKASEI, ELIZAVETA IVANOVNA (1912–2009). Code-named "Zephyr," the Mukaseis served as **NKVD/MGB/KGB illegals** from 1943 to 1977. In the 1940s, they served in Los Angeles, where Mikhail was deputy consul general. They were tasked with collecting intelligence on the Japanese threat to the Soviet Union. After leaving the United States, they served more than three decades as illegals in Western Europe. On their return to Moscow, Mikhail served as an instructor at KGB institutes.

MÜLLER, HEINRICH ("GESTAPO MÜLLER") (1900–?). As head of the Gestapo, Müller was one of the most hunted war criminals. Central Intelligence Agency declassified documents show that American intelligence spent several years trying to find what happened to Müller, who disappeared in the final days of the Battle of Berlin. Recently, **KGB** veteran Lieutenant General **Sergey Kandrashev** has claimed that Müller had established contact with Soviet intelligence in 1943. After escaping from Berlin, Müller worked with the KGB for more than a decade, according to Kondrashev. There is very little information from Russian, German, or American sources to support this account, but Müller did have contacts with Soviet intelligence in 1937 and again in occupied Poland in 1939. However, there is certainly evidence to the contrary: a German historian has recently found evidence that Müller died in Berlin in 1945 and was buried in a mass grave in a Jewish cemetery. Kondrashev was not above fabricating war stories to improve his own or his service's reputation.

MUROV, YEVGENY ALEKSYEVICH (1945–). Appointed by President **Vladimir Putin** to head the **Federal Guard Service**, in 2000, Murov is in charge of **leadership protection**. A longtime associate of Putin, Murov joined the **KGB** in 1974 and was director of the security service in St. Petersburg from 1997 to 2000.

MVD (*MINISTERSTVO VNUTRENNIKH DEL*). Both the tsarist and the Soviet regimes used the Ministry of Internal Affairs as the name of the state's police agency. In the tsarist period, the Ministry of Internal Affairs was headquartered at 16 Fontanka Quay in St. Petersburg, and the tsarist police used the term "Fontanka" much as their **Cheka** and **KGB** successors would use **Lubyanka** to describe their headquarters and higher authority.

During both the tsarist and the communist periods, the MVD had a strong paramilitary role in controlling and **surveilling** society. Under the tsarist MVD, the Corps of Gendarmes had this role. During the Soviet period, the MVD had control of "Internal Troops," including the famous Dzerzhinsky Division stationed in Moscow. The Internal Troops were well armed and equipped as motorized infantry formations. During wartime, they were expected to function as infantry divisions.

The Old Bolsheviks detested the capitalist term "police" and decided to name the communist service "militia." Under **Vladimir Lenin**, **Joseph Stalin**, and **Nikita Khrushchev**, the militia was often combined into commissariats and ministries of internal affairs and security. Finally, in the early 1960s, a new Ministry of Internal Affairs was created with authority over criminal questions and the labor camps in the **gulag** system, as well as traffic and more mundane duties. The MVD also expanded the strength and military equipment of its internal troops, which were armed and equipped to put down major political disturbances.

During the **Leonid Brezhnev** era (1964–1982), the MVD became notoriously corrupt. One of **Yuri Andropov**'s first efforts to reform the Soviet state on becoming general secretary in 1982 was to place thousands of KGB officers into senior positions in the MVD, simultaneously purging the police. Andropov placed **Vitalii Fedorchuk**, the KGB chair, into the ministry to stir things up. He was at first successful. Former MVD chief Nikolai Shcholekhov was investigated for corruption but committed suicide before being arrested. Leonid Brezhnev's son-in-law and Shcholekhov's deputy, Yuri Cherbanov, went to prison for several years. All efforts to clean up the MVD in the Soviet period failed in the end. Fedorchuk in his service as interior minister was unable to change the culture of the service. Despite the **execution** of a number of corrupt officials, the MVD remained essentially unreformable. In the late 1980s, the MVD's mission changed to ensuring political stability, and MVD troops were committed to preserve peace in the Caucasus, Central Asia, and the Baltic republics—a mission that continues in Chechnya.

In post-Soviet Russia, the MVD remains unreformed, underfinanced, and unprepared to deal with the heavily armed criminal gangs that control many Russian cities. In the 1990s, an average of 140 MVD officers died annually in firefights with criminals. Liaison with Western police forces has been initiated, but as in the Soviet period, the MVD remains the stepchild of the security community.

N

NAGY, IMRE (1896–1958). A lifelong communist revolutionary and bureaucrat, Nagy became the leader of the short-lived Hungarian regime in 1956. He was later tried and hanged by the Hungarian government for treason. In 1988, the Hungarian government decided to rebury Nagy and the men and women executed for their part in the rising. **KGB** chief **Vladimir Kryuchkov** published several documents showing that Nagy had been an **NKVD informer** in the 1930s with the code name "Volodya" and was responsible for the arrest of Hungarian, German, and Soviet communists. Kryuchkov apparently added some fabricated documents to further blacken Nagy.

Historians and journalists have speculated as to Nagy's culpability. There are two schools of thought. One believes that Nagy—like everyone in **Joseph Stalin**'s Russia—acted as an informant to survive. Others believe that he was a more active collaborator with NKVD chief **Lavrenty Beria**. They posit that Beria protected Nagy on his return to Hungary in 1945 and was responsible for his rise to power.

***NARODNAYA VOLYA* (PEOPLE'S WILL).** The most powerful revolutionary movement of the 1860–1880s was populism, *narodnichestvo*, which saw Russia's future as democratic and village centered. In the 1870s, young, idealistic Russian students took their message "to the people," traveling to the provinces to spread their doctrine of village-centered revolution. The peasantry distrusted these young intellectuals and either ignored them or turned them over to the local authorities. In 1875, the **Third Section**, the tsar's secret police, issued 750 arrest warrants for men and women engaged in populist political activities. Populism was not defeated by the Third Section; rather, it was driven underground and became increasing tempted by violence.

The most revolutionary wing of populism was *Narodnaya volya*, the "People's Will," which believed that only violence against the ruling class could liberate the country. The leadership of *Narodnaya volya* believed that their primary target was Tsar Aleksandr II. Beginning in 1879, the group repeatedly tried to kill the tsar, planting bombs on train tracks and in the Winter Palace, the tsar's residence. The incompetence of the Third Section is nowhere better illustrated than in its failure to protect the sovereign.

On 13 March 1881, *Narodnaya volya* assassins ambushed the tsar and mortally wounded him. The assassins were quickly rounded up. After a trial, five of them were publicly hanged. The tactics of *Narodnaya volya* were adopted by the Socialist Revolutionary Party's **Battle Organization**, which saw political assassination as a crucial ingredient of liberation of the Russian people.

NARUZHKA. **KGB** jargon for "surveillance," derived from *naruzhnoye nabyudeniye*, or "external observation."

NEW ECONOMIC POLICY (NEP). Faced with massive peasant rebellions, **Vladimir Lenin** agreed to an armed truce with the countryside in 1921. The NEP ended the forced expropriation of the peasants' grain crop and allowed them to sell their produce on an open market. The NEP created a period of relative prosperity and intellectual freedom. The NEP also saw a reduction of terror. The number of political arrests and **executions** dropped drastically as the security service was kept on a tighter reign. But from the point of view of the **Communist Party** and the **OGPU**, the NEP allowed the emergence of two enemy classes: a small class of better-off peasants, often referred to as kulaks, and traders who were damned as "Nepmen."

NEP was a compromise that threatened the party's monopoly of power. In the countryside, the Communist Party lost much of its authority; the peasants maintained a monopoly on the cities' food supply, and the Soviet Union was unable to pay for needed industrial technology with grain. **Joseph Stalin**'s answer to the crisis was **collectivization**: the destruction of the kulaks and the total subjugation of the countryside. OGPU chief **Vyacheslav Menzhinsky** and his principal subordinates supported an end to the NEP for political and operational reasons. They warned the leadership of the threat of an independent producing class, and they saw a need to restore control of the population.

NICHOLSON, HAROLD JAMES (1950–). Nicholson, a career Central Intelligence Agency (CIA) officer, volunteered to the **SVR** in 1994 while he was completing a foreign tour of duty with the Directorate of Operations. Nicholson, who was divorced with three children, hacked into the CIA's computer system to gather any information he could on CIA operations, including biographic information on every CIA officer he trained between 1994 and 1996. For this important operational information, he was paid approximately $120,000 between 1994 and 1996. Nicholson was tracked and caught in 1996. After failing his polygraph examination, an internal CIA audit of his finances showed that Nicholson was spending money erratically. A joint Federal Bureau of Investigation (FBI)–CIA task force was able to establish Nicholson's pattern of operations. He was arrested in 1996 at Dulles Airport near Washington, D.C. He was sentenced to 27 years' imprisonment.

That, however, was not the end of the story. From prison, Nicholson recruited his son, Nathan, and through him contacted the SVR. This espionage coda ended badly for both Nicholsons, as the FBI exposed the SVR contacts. The younger Nicholson received a suspended sentence after cooperating with the FBI. Later explaining his role as a spy, the younger Nicholson noted, "I allowed myself to be blindsided. I was like a lobster in a pot, heated slowly until it was too late to escape."

NIKISHOV, IVAN FEDOROVICH (1894–1958). After service in the **Border Guards** and internal troops of the **NKVD**, Nikishov became chief of the **gulag** archipelago's largest and most infamous island—the **Kolyma** River network of labor camps. From 1943 through 1948, he managed the huge slave labor complex, which was the major source of the Soviet Union's gold. In 1943, he convinced the visiting U.S. vice president, Henry Wallace, of the generosity of the Soviet penal system and the humanity of its managers. Wallace's visit to Kolyma was a centerpiece of Soviet propaganda in the United States during the war. Nikishov retired in 1948 after being promoted to lieutenant general. He was awarded the Order of **Lenin** and the Order of the Red Banner multiple times for his management of the Kolyma region.

See also DALSTROI.

NIKOLAEV, LEONID (1904–1934). The most infamous assassin in Russian history, Leonid Nikolaev killed Leningrad party boss **Sergei Kirov**, a murder that provided **Joseph Stalin** with justification to ramp up state terror. Nikolaev was a minor party official who blamed Kirov and the party leadership for his failed life. The Russian archives show that Nikolaev was detained twice with a loaded weapon near Kirov's residence and released. On 1 December 1934, he shot Kirov in Smolny, the Leningrad **Communist Party** headquarters building. Kirov's security detail arrived in time to arrest Nikolaev, who had fainted after firing the fatal shots.

On hearing of the murder, Stalin and his subordinates took a train to Leningrad. Nikolaev was personally interrogated by Stalin the day following the murder. According to some witnesses, he implicated **NKVD** officers. He was then brutally interrogated by NKVD officers, and on 29 December, he and 14 other defendants were shot following a short trial. In January 1935, his wife, sister, and remaining friends were also shot.

Nikolaev most probably was used, but historians are not sure exactly by whom. Most recent historians believe that Nikolaev was protected by senior NKVD officers, possibly service chief **Genrykh Yagoda**, with Stalin's approval. The archives, however, do not contain enough evidence to prove that Stalin and Yagoda planned the killing. Other historians believe that Stalin would never have risked using a man like Nikolaev and that Yagoda would never have acted without Stalin's explicit directions.

NIURINA, FAINA (1885–1938). A brilliant Jewish lawyer, educated before 1917 in a school of liberal jurisprudence, Niurina joined the **procuracy** following the **Revolution of November 1917**. Unlike many Soviet prosecutors, such as **Andrei Vyshinsky**, she refused to allow the **NKVD** to dictate verdicts, insisting on the independence of her office. Her opinions cost her her life. She was arrested on Vyshinsky's personal order in 1938, tried, and shot.

NKGB (*NARODNIY KOMMISSARIAT GOSUDARSTVENNOI BEZO-PASNOSTI***).** The People's Commissariat of State Security, the NKGB, was formed in June 1941 from the foreign intelligence and domestic **counterintelligence** elements of the **NKVD**. In 1946, the NKGB was transformed into the **MGB** (Ministry of State Security).

NKVD (*NARODNIY KOMMISSARIAT VNUTRENNIKH DEL***).** The People's Commissariat of Internal Affairs, the NKVD, was formed on 10 July 1936 from the **OGPU**. It included all the organs of repression and intelligence of the Soviet government in one department, as well as directorates for railroad and installation security and the forced labor camps of the **gulag** system. In 1941, the NKVD had 379,000 personnel. During the purges of the 1930s, the NKVD accumulated tremendous power to arrest, interrogate, try, and execute suspected **enemies of the people**. To the Soviet people of the 1930s, the NKVD was synonymous with terror.

With the German invasion of the Soviet Union in June 1941, the NKVD was divided into the **NKGB** (People's Commissariat of State Security) and the NKVD. During the **Great Patriotic War**, **Joseph Stalin** ordered the NKVD's military role expanded, and NKVD units served along with the Red Army in major defensive battles. By 1943, more than 500,000 people were serving in the NKVD Internal Troops in infantry divisions and regiments. According to a recent study of Soviet order of battle in the war, the NKVD had command of a small army of 53 infantry divisions and nine independent rifle brigades. Senior NKVD officers served as division commanders during the defensive battles of Moscow and Stalingrad, and several later rose to command corps and armies. NKVD units also were used as "blocking formations," which were situated in the rear of Red Army formations to prevent retreat, panic, and desertions.

Following the defeat of Nazi Germany, the NKVD played the leading role in the suppression of nationalist forces in Ukraine and the Baltic states. In 1946, the NKVD was transformed by Stalin into the **MVD** (Ministry of Internal Affairs).

NORILSK. One of the most important islands of the **gulag** archipelago, Norilsk was planned by **Joseph Stalin** to be the country's primary source of aluminum, copper, and platinum-family metals, as well as coal and iron. Despite Norilsk's Arctic location, the Soviet regime planned a complex of 18 forced labor camps to tap the riches of the north. The first prisoners arrived in 1935, and by Stalin's death, more than 100,000 prisoners labored in its mines and smelters. The Soviet security service also created secret cities with forced labor near Norilsk to build nuclear weapons and their delivery systems. Stalin also ordered the building of a secret railroad across the Soviet north to link camp complexes, resulting in a tremendous loss of life. The railroad was not finished, however, and was finally abandoned after Stalin's death. Following Stalin's death in March 1953, the prisoners in Norilsk rioted, as did the prisoners in **Vorkuta** and Kengir. The riots were put down by the regime.

By 1955, Moscow began to replace prison laborers with volunteer workers who were attracted to the Arctic by high salaries and bonuses. Norilsk today has a population of more than 200,000 and is one of the most polluted cities in the world.

NORWOOD, MELIA STEDMAN (1912–2005). Probably the **KGB**'s most productive female agent, Norwood was run within the British scientific establishment for several decades. Norwood, who joined the British **Communist Party** in the 1930s, became a Soviet agent in 1937. For 45 years, she provided scientific and technical intelligence to Moscow. Her code name was "Hola." During **World War II**, she provided information on the Anglo-American nuclear weapons program, referred to as *Enormoz* by Soviet intelligence. In a wartime report to Moscow, Norwood was described by her case officer as a "committed, reliable, and disciplined agent." Norwood's five decades as a spy were revealed in 1999 in **Vasili Mitrokhin**'s *The Sword and the Shield*, an account of the Soviet intelligence service coauthored by a British academic. Confronted with the charge of espionage by the British press, Norwood cheerfully and proudly admitted her treachery. She died in 2005 as her biography, *The Spy Who Came in from the Co-op*, was being written.

NOSENKO, YURI IVANOVICH (1927–2008). One of the most difficult **counterintelligence** cases for the Central Intelligence Agency (CIA) was Yuri Nosenko. Nosenko, whose father was a member of the **Communist Party** Central Committee, worked in the **KGB**'s Second (Counterintelligence) Chief Directorate in Moscow. On temporary duty in Switzerland in June 1962, he volunteered to work for the CIA. In January 1964, he returned to Switzerland with two surprises for his CIA case officer: he had information about President John F. Kennedy's assassination, and he wanted to defect.

Nosenko's bona fides almost immediately came under question. CIA officers caught him in a number of minor lies. More importantly, another **defector, Anatoli Golitsyn**, accused Nosenko of being a mole dispatched by the KGB to destroy the CIA's operations against the Soviet Union. Tragically for Nosenko and the CIA, Golitsyn's charges were believed by the CIA counterintelligence director James Jesus Angleton. Nosenko was hounded and finally jailed illegally in solitary confinement for more than three years.

After several major counterintelligence studies of the case, Nosenko was declared a bona fide defector and resettled. His information on KGB agents and **tradecraft** led to a number of Western counterintelligence successes. Nevertheless, the Nosenko case continued to consume many CIA counterintelligence specialists for decades more. KGB defectors and documents all indicated that Golitsyn's charges were baseless and that Nosenko was a bona fide—if flawed—defector.

NOVIK, ALFONS ANDREEVICH (1908–1996). A Latvian revolutionary, Novik was made head of the Latvian republic's **NKVD** when the Soviet Union occupied Latvia in 1940, and he took part in the massive **deportation** of Latvians **exiled** to Siberia. During **World War II**, he worked with Latvian and Russian **partisans** as part of the NKVD's Fourth Directorate. Following the war, he served as republic security chief. He was promoted to major general and highly decorated for his service to Moscow. In 1953, he became deputy minister of agriculture. Novik's life took a turn for the worse in 1991, however. He was named a war criminal by the newly independent Latvian government for his role in Latvia in the Soviet period. Imprisoned in 1994, he died in confinement. Novik, whose name in Latvian would be "Noviks," was seen as a man who betrayed his country, literally changing his name to please Moscow. He was one of the few citizens of the former Soviet Union who were punished for crimes against humanity.

NOVOCHERKASSK. In June 1962, food riots occurred in the southern Russian city of Novocherkassk. The local authorities were unable to quell the riots, which quickly took on a political character, as posters appeared denouncing the **Communist Party** and demanding meat, milk, and wage increases. One poster reportedly suggested turning party bosses into sausage. Following some clashes with local police, **KGB** and army troops fired into the crowd, killing 23 people and wounding more than 100. The KGB official responsible for repression was **Petr Ivashutin**, who later became chief of the **GRU**. The KGB managed the trials of the main Novocherkassk "conspirators," sentencing 10 dangerous state criminals to death and others to 10 to 15 years' imprisonment. The riots at Novocherkassk were symptomatic of public anger with the failure of **Nikita Khrushchev**'s political and economic reforms in the early 1960s, and in several other cities the KGB and the army employed a very heavy hand to maintain order.

NUCLEAR PROLIFERATION. A major responsibility for both the **SVR** and the **FSB** is nuclear proliferation. The SVR has publicly declared that proliferation is a major target of its foreign intelligence operations. The FSB has been given a far harder task—the protection of Russia's nuclear installations from terrorists, smugglers, and enemy agents. The FSB works in concert with the Federal Agency for Atomic Energy and the Ministry of Defense to protect military bases, storage facilities, and power plants. The FSB has apparently had some successes: in 2002, the FSB announced that it had detained two Chechen terrorists for the act of reconnoitering a nuclear facility. Nevertheless, provincial FSB officers have publicly reported that weapons-grade material has disappeared. The Central Intelligence Agency's National Intelligence Council noted in its pessimistic 2004 report to the U.S. Congress, "We assess that undetected smuggling has occurred, and we are concerned about the total amount of material that could have been diverted in the past 13 years."

OCTOBER 1964 COUP. The **KGB** played a critical role in removing **Nikita Khrushchev** from power in October 1964. Many KGB professionals were concerned with Khrushchev's style of leadership, and senior KGB officers readily agreed with party conservatives led by **Leonid Brezhnev** and Mikhail Suslov that he had to be removed for the good of the **Communist Party** and the Soviet state. The plot took shape over several months as the conspirators built support. Khrushchev's son sought to warn his father, but Khrushchev believed that his colleagues were too incompetent and cowardly to act.

The plot was simple: have the KGB chair isolate Khrushchev on his return from vacation, convene a plenum of the Central Committee to convict Khrushchev of "adventurism," and place the former leader under dignified house arrest. It went exactly as planned: Khrushchev's plane was met by KGB Chair **Vladimir Semichastniy**, who whisked Khrushchev off to the Kremlin to face a humiliating trial. After two days of personal attacks, Brezhnev was anointed party leader, and Khrushchev became a "nonperson."

In 1991, the KGB helped party conservatives in the **August putsch** against General Secretary **Mikhail Gorbachev**. Times had changed, however, and the tactics that worked smoothly in 1964 failed badly in 1991.

OFFICE OF STRATEGIC SERVICES (OSS). The OSS, founded in 1942, was America's first centralized civilian intelligence organization. Unfortunately, it was penetrated by the **NKVD**, who referred to it with the contemptuous code name "Izba" (peasant hut). The Soviet service's most important agent inside the OSS was Duncan Lee, a Yale graduate, well-known lawyer, and member of the American establishment. Lee provided the NKVD with details of American intelligence on China, as well as details on how the service worked with the War Department and the White House. Other OSS agents provided details on U.S. intelligence and policy toward Europe, the Soviet Union, and Asia.

The OSS did not conduct operations against the Soviet intelligence services or try to collect intelligence clandestinely on the Soviet Union. On one occasion, the OSS returned to the Soviets one of their codebooks that the OSS had obtained from the Finns. It is believed that no copy was made of the book. The OSS director, Major General William Donovan, sought a liaison relationship with the NKVD during **World War II**. The Soviets did provide the United States with some important information on Nazi tactics and equipment, but no real liaison relationship developed between the two services.

OGGINS, ISAIAH (1898–1947). After joining the American **Communist Party** in 1923, Oggins and his wife, Nerma Berman (1898–1995), served in France, Germany, and China as **illegals**. In 1939, the **NKVD** arrested Oggins, and in 1940, he was sentenced to eight years in the **gulag**. His wife asked the American embassy in Moscow to investigate his disappearance, and he was able to meet with American consular officers in 1943. He was murdered with an injection of curare at **Lubyanka** prison on the order of **Joseph Stalin**.

Oggins's fate, not dissimilar to that of many Soviet illegals, was sealed by U.S. government intervention. He was seen by the Kremlin and the **MGB** as an unwanted witness; there was no room for an American illegal. An excellent account of his case is *The Lost Spy*.

OGOLTSOV, SERGEI IVANOVICH (1900–1977). Ogoltsov was one of the few "Old **Chekists**" to survive the purges of both **Nikolai Yezhov** and **Lavrenty Beria**. Ogoltsov entered the **Cheka** at age 17. During the purges, he was rapidly promoted, and he served as head of the security service in Leningrad during the hardest months of the 900-day German siege. Ogoltsov ensured that order was maintained during the winter of 1941–1942, when more than 600,000 Leningraders starved and froze to death. He was awarded the Order of the Red Banner and promoted for his effort.

In 1946, Ogoltsov was promoted to lieutenant general and made head of the section for "special questions." He planned the murder of the Jewish actor **Solomon Mikhoels**, whose death **Joseph Stalin** had personally insisted on. Ogoltsov received the Order of the Red Banner for this operation. At the time of Stalin's death, Ogoltsov worked closely with Minister of State Security **Semyon Ignatiev** to ensure that power passed quietly to the next generation. Ogoltsov was arrested following Stalin's death for Mikhoels's murder, but he was released four months later, a reward for having smoothed the transition of power following Stalin's death.

OGORONIK, ALEKSANDR DMITRIEVICH (1939–1977). A Soviet diplomat, Ogoronik was recruited by the Central Intelligence Agency (CIA) and became an important source of information on Soviet **arms control** policy. His code name was "Trigon." He was betrayed by Karl Koecher and arrested. Ogoronik had asked for and received a suicide device, fearing torture if he was arrested. He used the device before he was interrogated. Following his suicide, the **KGB** ambushed his CIA case officer, Martha Peterson, on a bridge in Moscow and after detaining her for several hours declared her persona non grata and expelled her. Peterson has written her account of the story, *The Widow Spy*. The KGB presented their version in a multipart television series, *TASS Is Authorized to Announce*.

OGORODNIKOVA, SVETLANA (1950–). A Soviet immigrant to southern California, Ogorodnikova seduced Richard Miller, a maladroit Federal Bureau of Investigation (FBI) agent. He provided her with some FBI documents in exchange for sex. She was apparently run by a **KGB** officer in the Soviet consulate in San Francisco. She was caught and sentenced to 18 years in jail.

OGPU (*OBYEDINENNOE GOSUDARTVENNOE POLITICHESKOE UPRAVLENIYE*). The OGPU (Unified State Political Directorate) was founded on 2 November 1923 as a successor to the **GPU**, and it was replaced by the **NKVD** in June 1934. Under **Joseph Stalin**'s ever-watchful eyes, the OGPU became an important player in the execution of Soviet foreign and domestic policies. Stalin relied on the OGPU for information on political rivals, such as **Leon Trotsky** and Nikolai Bukharin. The OGPU also played a critical role in the industrialization of the country and the **collectivization** of agriculture. The OGPU crushed resistance to collectivization and **deported** millions of peasants and their families to Siberia and Central Asia. The majority of the **exiled** peasants were imprisoned in the OGPU's growing network of forced labor camps in the **gulag** system.

In the field of foreign policy, the OGPU concentrated on **counterintelligence** operations against **émigré** groups. It also recruited and ran agents with access to political and economic information. The OGPU also acted as Stalin's avenging arms, killing two critical White generals in Paris as well as Ukrainian émigré leaders in Poland. OGPU **illegals** recruited important **signals intelligence** agents as sources of cryptological information.

The leadership of the OGPU was drawn from those who had served in the **Revolution of November 1917** and the **civil war**. Jewish, Polish, and Balt **Chekists**, who were deeply distrusted by Stalin, were heavily represented within the leadership of the OGPU. By 1936, Stalin had begun to purge the security service. Only a few of the service's leaders in 1936 would survive the next two years.

See also YEZHOV, NIKOLAI IVANOVICH (1895–1940); *YEZHOVSHCHINA* (THE TIME OF YEZHOV).

OKHRANA (OKRANKA). The most notorious of the tsarist police agencies was the *Okhrana*. Established on 5 December 1882 by **MVD** ordinance in response to the assassination of Tsar Aleksandr II, the *Okhrana* was composed of subordinate *Okhrannye otdeleniia* (Security Divisions) established in Moscow, St. Petersburg, and Warsaw to conduct secret **counterterrorist** operations. Over the next decade, the *Okhrana* evolved into an empire-wide organization targeted against revolutionaries, terrorists, and militant nationalists. In 1883, the *Okhrana* opened a foreign bureau in Paris to conduct operations against enemies operating outside the Russian empire.

Okhrana operations in Paris and within Russia included close **surveillance** of suspected enemies, penetration of terrorist organizations, and the use of agents provocateurs. The *Okhrana* was a small, elite organization. Its total staff was never more than 1,100, with 200 staff officers at headquarters in St. Petersburg. While it had a reputation as an omniscient security service, the *Okhrana* had a relatively small stable of **informants**. According to recent research, the *Okhrana* employed only 600 paid informants in Russia at any one time. In 1910–1916, the service maintained an average of only 116 informants in Moscow.

The *Okhrana* had a number of spectacular successes. It recruited **Roman Malinovskiy**, a Bolshevik member of the tsarist duma (parliament), and ran him in place for more than a decade. Inspection of the *Okhrana* files following the **Revolution of November 1917** revealed that their penetration of the **Bolshevik Party** was extensive and thorough. Another agent, Yakov Zhitomirskiy, was a close friend of **Vladimir Lenin**. In Moscow, four of the five leading Bolsheviks worked for the *Okhrana*.

The *Okhrana*'s failures at home, however, were devastating. One of the *Okhrana*'s key agents provocateur was **Yevno Azev**, who operated as a well-paid informant for more than a decade while simultaneously planning the assassination of senior tsarist officials. Another agent, Father **Georgi Gapon**, led a demonstration of loyal peasants and workers to the Winter Palace in St. Petersburg in January 1905; it was put down by police and army troops and resulted in more than 100 fatalities.

The *Okhrana*'s Paris bureau, headed by the capable **Petr Rachkovskiy** from 1884 to 1902, had 40 French detectives on its payroll and some 30 agents in Paris and elsewhere. The foreign bureau had access to French police records on terrorists and conducted a mail intercept program in Paris, as they did at home. Agents penetrated all the revolutionary movements in

France, Belgium, and Germany, and thousands of weapons, not to mention printing presses and propaganda material, were intercepted before reaching Russia.

The *Okhrana*, like many security police and intelligence organizations, took on other missions because it was available to the political leadership. Agents of the *Okhrana* in Paris dabbled in secret diplomacy, serving as a clandestine channel of diplomacy between France and Russia. At home, the service helped conservative politicians create **pogroms** in which hundreds of Jews were murdered.

Despite its reputation for ruthlessness, the *Okhrana* and its parent organization, the MVD, were less effective and far less terrible than the **Cheka** or the **NKVD**. During the reign of Aleksandr II (1855–1881), approximately 4,000 people were detained and interrogated for political crimes. Nevertheless, **executions** were rare: from the mid-1860s to the mid-1880s, only 44 executions took place in Russia. By contrast, on the day after Lenin launched the **Red Terror** in September 1918, the Cheka executed 500 people. Moreover, the *Okhrana* was far less terrible in the provinces than in Moscow, St. Petersburg, and Warsaw. In Georgia, **Joseph Stalin** and many of his colleagues received light sentences for crimes that would have sent them to the gallows in Moscow—and perhaps even in London or Paris.

Many of the leaders of the *Okhrana* saw themselves as the bulwark of the autocracy. They observed Russian law by accepting the independence of the **procuracy**. Defendants in political trials had active and competent defense lawyers. Prisoners were generally well treated in jail and in **exile**. Stalin and **Leon Trotsky**, as well as a host of other political prisoners, repeatedly escaped exile in Siberia. But the *Okhrana* did not fail because of its liberalism: by targeting liberals and revolutionaries alike, the tsar's secret police prevented the emergence of a loyal opposition. By encouraging and financing pogroms, it satisfied the base anti-Semitism of members of the royal family but destroyed the legitimacy of the regime at home and abroad.

OMS (*OTDEL MEZHDURNARODNYKH SVYAZEY*). The Foreign Liaison Department of the **Comintern** was used as an adjunct by the Soviet intelligence services: a source of agents who had worked in underground party organizations from Berlin to Beijing. Comintern operations occasionally overlapped with those of the services, leading to confusion and compromises.

OO (*OSOBY OTDEL*). The Special Detachments were **NKVD military counterintelligence** and later *Smersh* cells in military units. OO officers recruited informants, recommended arrests, and informed their security superiors of the loyalty and competence of their unit commanders. They were feared and hated: during the **Great Patriotic War** of the Soviet Union, they were a constant presence in every military unit from battalion to army group.

OPPENHEIMER, JULIUS ROBERT (1904–1967). Often credited as the "father of American nuclear weapons," Oppenheimer had friends and family members who were active **Communist Party** members. Many Soviet and American authors claimed that Oppenheimer was a Soviet agent and passed information on the weapons program to the **NKVD**. Information from the Soviet archives, gathered by **Alexander Vassiliev**, strongly suggest that this was not the case. The evidence suggests that Oppenheimer sought to prevent some noted pro-Soviets scientists and technicians from gaining access to the Manhattan Project.

OPRICHNINA. Russia's first secret service, the *Oprichnina*, was founded in 1564 by Tsar Ivan IV ("The Terrible"). To search out his enemies, Ivan dispatched 6,000 *Oprichniki* who were dressed in black, rode black horses, and carried a dog's head and a broom to symbolize their mission of purging the land of terror. The *Oprichniki* murdered thousands of men and women suspected of disloyalty, purging the once-great city of Novgorod of its leaders and merchants. The *Oprichnina* was abolished in 1572. Some Russian historians compared the **NKVD** of **Nikolai Yezhov** and **Lavrenty Beria** to Ivan's *oprichniki*.

ORGANIZED CRIME. There has always been organized crime in Russia. In the last days of the tsars, criminal gangs flourished. In the first days of the **Revolution of November 1917**, many of their members joined the Red Guards and the **Cheka**. After the **civil war**, they were dismissed or executed. **Joseph Stalin**'s efforts to break the back of organized crime failed. Even in the **gulag**, the gang leaders maintained their organizations. Known as *vory v zakone* ("those who live under thieves' law"), they flourished in the Stalinist camps and built organizations that survive today.

In the 1930s, criminals controlled the forced labor camps. Most of the politicals were no match for the underworld and suffered terribly at the hands of the criminals. Things changed with the arrival of hundreds of thousands of new prisoners from the Baltic states and Ukraine in 1945–1946. In the late 1940s, gang war in the camps broke out between the *vory* ("thieves") and political prisoners. Known as the "Bitches' War," the battle left hundreds dead, as political prisoners, many fresh from the front, fought back and killed thieves they believed to be **informers**.

In the 1960s, organized economic crime made a major comeback in the Caucasian republics, Central Asia, and the European republics. **Nikita Khrushchev** tried to crush the new economic criminal: the death penalty was liberally used against economic criminals, and the **KGB** received the mission of investigating "especially dangerous economic crimes." Crime continued to flourish: the new criminals could provide the "deficit goods" that the market failed to produce. By the 1980s, most Soviet citizens lived *na levo*—literally "on the left"—relying on the criminal sector for everything from certain foods and medicines to building supplies and theater tickets. By the 1980s, the *vory v zakone* had begun to establish an alliance with party bosses. Efforts by KGB chair **Yuri Andropov** to disrupt this alliance failed. The **execution** of the manager of Moscow's best-known food store in 1984 did nothing to slow the corruption of the system.

Russian crime was the element in Soviet society best prepared to take advantage of the collapse of the system. With alliances with party bosses, the police, and even the KGB, crime bosses could legitimatize themselves as businesspeople with the power to move money and to kill. In the 1990s, Russian organized crime went international, and Russian criminals were arrested in Miami, New York, Paris, London, and Brussels. In the United States, Russian organized crime has been engaged in a number of white-collar criminal scams.

Crime was one of the communist system's heritages. In creating a system that was both brutal and massively incompetent, the citizens found a need for suppliers of deficit items, just as Americans of the 1920s found a need for rum runners and bootleggers. The problem for fledgling Russian democracy is that organized crime is now deeply entrenched in the system.

ORGANS (COMPETENT ORGANS). During the post-Stalin period, the **KGB** often referred to itself as the "organs of state security," or the "competent organs."

ORDER 227. A People's Commissariat of Defense order personally edited and signed on 28 July 1942 by **Joseph Stalin**, Order 227 mandated that further retreats should be stopped with the immediate execution of cowards and "panic mongers" and that every Red Army front establish blocking detachments and punishment battalions to stop and punish men deserting their post. **NKVD** Special Detachments (**OO**) and, later, *Smersh*, as well as unit commanders, sent more than 427,000 soldiers to punishment battalions during the last 30 months of the **World War II**.

Stalin's order, often referred to in memoirs and the history of the war by its iconic phrase *Ni shagu nazad!* ("Not a step backward!") was read to Red Army units going into major combat operations. The author of the order,

Marshal Aleksandr Vasilevskiy, wrote in his memoirs that the order was "motivated by rough and dark times." It followed **Order 270**, issued in August 1941, in an effort to establish discipline.

ORDER 270. As the Soviet front collapsed in the summer of 1941, **Joseph Stalin** as chief of national defense issued Order 270 on 16 August 1941, mandating that Soviet troops who surrendered were traitors and that they and their families should be punished: "families are subject to arrest as having violated the oath and betrayed their homeland." It gave commanders, political commissars, and security officers authority to shoot on the spot officers and men who deserted their posts. This meant that units that fought their way out of encirclements were often punished rather than rewarded.

ORLOV, ALEXANDER (1899–1973). One of the most important of the early Soviet **defectors**, Orlov provided information that was long ignored by the West. Born Aleksandr Felbin, Orlov joined the **Cheka** during the **civil war**. In the 1920s and 1930s, he served as an **NKVD illegal** in Western Europe and the United States, recruiting and running agents. In 1936, **Joseph Stalin** sent Orlov to Spain, where he served in a dual intelligence and diplomatic capacity during the **Spanish Civil War**.

As Stalin's *rezident* in Spain, Orlov ruthlessly purged the Republican government of dissident **Trotskyites**. He also arranged for the transfer of the republic's gold supply, worth over $700 million in 1937 dollars, to Moscow, where it remained for four decades. As Stalin's rolling purge of the NKVD intensified in 1938, Orlov realized that he was slated for **execution** and decided to defect. He traveled with his wife and mortally ill child to the United States in the summer of 1938 and was interviewed by a senior State Department official. Orlov identified himself as a general of state security with important information. He was next interviewed some 15 years later by American **counterintelligence**.

Orlov worked closely with the Federal Bureau of Investigation (FBI) in the 1950s and wrote two best-selling books on Stalin's terror. He also testified before U.S. congressional committees as an expert witness. But his story has a dramatic posthumous postscript: in the 1990s, two decades after Orlov's death, the **KGB** released his file and claimed that Orlov had never betrayed key agents but had remained true to his service. A book by Orlov's FBI handler predictably and just as dramatically rejected these assertions, claiming that Orlov had served the FBI as faithfully for 20 years as he had the Soviet service previously. There is no final verdict on this case, but given the incomplete nature of the Soviet files and the desire to protect the reputation of their service, Moscow's claims seem spurious.

OSSO (*OSOBOYE SOVESHCHANIYE*). From 1934 until 1953, the **GPU/ OGPU/NKVD/MGB** OSSO (Special Conferences) had the right to sentence Soviet citizens to up to five years' imprisonment administratively. While political prisoners were infrequently sentenced without the right of judicial process, a more common targets of the OSSO were workers and peasants who were tardy or who stole food for their families. According to the Soviet archives, between June 1940 and 1941, the Leningrad OSSO sentenced more than 140,000 workers to punishment for breaking labor discipline: many were mothers who took off work to mind sick children. Many were allowed to take their children with them to jail or labor camps.

Scholars using Soviet statistics that show the number of people arrested in the Stalin era usually fail to realize that most of the victims were workers and peasants arrested for violating labor laws or for minor crimes at the workplace. **Joseph Stalin** defended the need of the OSSO system repeatedly, arguing that it ensured social discipline. One of the first reforms of the post-Stalin years was to abolish the OSSO.

OVAKIMYAN, GAIK BADALOVICH (1898–1975). Known to the Federal Bureau of Investigation (FBI) as the "wily Armenian," Ovakimyan served as the **NKVD** case officer and **illegal** *rezident* in the United States in the 1930s and early 1940s. Ovakimyan's greatest success was in the recruitment of agents with access to scientific and industrial information. In 1939, Ovakimyan's *rezidentura* sent 18,000 pages of technical documents to Moscow. By 1941, the NKVD network in the United States, for which he laid the basic building blocks, included 221 agents. In May 1941, however, the FBI caught Ovakimyan in the act of espionage. After a brief imprisonment, he was allowed to return to Moscow, where he served as a general officer in the NKVD. Many of Ovakimyan's stable of recruits provided critical information about U.S. military technology during and immediately after **World War II**. Following the war, Ovakimyan left the intelligence service and went back into scientific work.

P

PANYUSHKIN, ALEKSANDR SEMENOVICH (1905–1974). Panyushkin joined the **OGPU** in 1927. At the age of 34, he was dispatched to China as intelligence *rezident* and ambassador, dual roles he later held in Washington and in Beijing. After serving in **counterintelligence** in the **MVD** and the **KGB**, he was appointed chief of the KGB's **First Chief Directorate** (Foreign Intelligence) in 1954. He returned in 1955 to the Ministry of Foreign Affairs, where he served as a senior official until 1973. Panyushkin held the rank of KGB major general and was decorated by the **Communist Party**, the Ministry of Foreign Affairs, and the KGB.

PARTISAN WARFARE, ANTI-SOVIET. Soviet authorities faced a partisan threat from Ukrainian and Baltic citizens from the first days of **World War II**. In Lvov in Ukraine and Lithuania, nationalists fired on retreating Soviet soldiers in 1941. Moreover, some Soviet soldiers deserted their formations and joined these groups. During the war, these partisan formations grew, developed secret governments, and operated against both German occupation forces and Soviet partisan bands.

In 1945, Moscow faced organized military opposition in the Baltic states and the western Ukraine. In Lithuania and in some districts of the western Ukraine, nationalists controlled the majority of the populations. Soviet troops following the Germans into the regions were immediately thrown into battle against new enemies. **NKVD** special groups organized by the Chief Directorate for the Struggle against Banditry (*Glavnoe upravlenie borby s banditizom*) operated in rebel areas against the partisans, while the military controlled large towns and cities. They established **informant** nets and forced the rural areas to form self-defense units to isolate partisan commands from their supporters in the population. The NKVD also formed "false gangs" of partisans that moved into villages to test support for the partisans and the communist authorities. Villages that welcomed these "partisans" were ruthlessly punished. Captured partisans were severely interrogated and sentenced to lengthy prison terms.

Moscow's struggle against the anti-Soviet partisans reflected a set of sophisticated political and social policies. There was an exchange of Polish and Ukrainian populations with Poland that ended the ability of Ukrainian partisans to escape inside Poland. The clergy of the Greek-rite Catholic (Uniate) Church in the western Ukraine were arrested or forced to become Russian Orthodox. In Lithuania, hundreds of Roman Catholic clergy were arrested, and many were deported with their flocks to Siberia. There were positive steps as well: money went into the rebuilding of schools, and some children were selected for secondary and higher education in Kiev and Moscow.

Resistance to Soviet authority in these regions lasted until the early 1950s. Efforts by Western intelligence agencies to maintain contact with anti-Soviet partisans failed. **Deportation** of villagers identified as partisan supporters intensified: more than 8 percent of the population of the western Ukraine was deported in 1946–1950. The hunt for partisan leaders intensified. On 5 March 1950, the Soviets identified the hiding place of the commander of the Ukraine Insurgent Army and killed him. Resistance in the western Ukraine and Lithuania gradually ended in 1952–1955. In the 1960s and 1970s, many of the deportees returned to their native villages, but thousands died in **exile** in Siberia and Central Asia.

PARTISAN WARFARE, SOVIET. In the 1930s, the Soviet Union made preparations to conduct partisan warfare, but **Joseph Stalin**, who had promised the Soviet people that war would be fought on the enemy's territory, canceled plans in 1937–1938 and had a number of experts shot for "defeatism." Nevertheless, on 26 June 1941, four days after the Nazi invasion, **Lavrenty Beria** gave orders for the preparation of a nationwide partisan movement and assigned a number of senior security officers to build a partisan organization. The **NKVD**'s Fourth Directorate had responsibility for partisan operations; its chief was **Pavel Sudoplatov.**

For Stalin and Beria, the partisan movement had several aims: maintaining Soviet power behind German lines, the punishment of collaborators, gathering intelligence about the enemy, and sabotaging the enemy's lines of communications. In 1941 and 1942, progress of the movement was spasmodic, but German atrocities toward Soviet prisoners and civilians drove thousands of Russian, Byelorussian, and Ukrainian peasants into the partisan movement. Many young people in the villages faced a choice of **deportation** to Germany or escape into the forests to join the partisans. As the war progressed, more and more chose the latter.

The partisans had their greatest successes in 1943–1944 in both the political and the military arenas. Large liberated areas were created in Russian, Byelorussian, and Ukrainian territories. Partisan governments were established. Many of these liberated areas had their own airstrips. More importantly, partisan units became bolder in striking German military targets. Senior

German officials were assassinated, and the partisans began a highly success-ful railroad war against German logistical services. Before the July 1943 German offensive at Kursk, the partisans conducted over 10,000 attacks against German railroads. The attacks on the German lines of communication cut the flow of supplies to the front and forced Berlin to assign troops from the front to protect the rear. Stalin personally told one of the leaders of the Ukrainian partisans, "You are the leader of the Second Front."

Intelligence gathering also improved dramatically as the war wore on, and information from partisan groups became increasingly important for military planning. In April 1943, Stalin issued an order expanding the intelligence responsibilities of the partisans, and thousands of **GRU** and **NKVD** officers were assigned to partisan detachments to improve the collection of military information for senior Red Army commanders. *Smersh* also operated in the partisan groups, ensuring that the organizations remained under party control and did not turn into bandit formations. *Smersh* officers collected informa-tion about the local population and the names of collaborators for punish-ment after victory.

The partisan war in the east was fought on different fronts. In the Baltic states and Russia, it often involved battles between Jewish and Slavic parti-sans and in Ukraine between nationalists and communist formations. The Nazi policy of genocide drove thousands of young Jews into the partisan movement. In Vilnius and other cities, an urban partisan movement sprang into being. Following the destruction of many ghettos, young Jewish men and women fled to the forests and swamps. Some were absorbed into existing partisan movements, but many were forced to band together and form Jewish partisan detachments. Moscow made some effort to prevent violence be-tween Jewish and Slavic groups, and NKVD and *Smersh* officers tried to keep the peace between them. In Ukraine, the situation was more difficult, as nationalists and Soviet formations fought each other and the Germans. This struggle continued into the 1950s.

Smersh and NKVD officers in partisan detachments also built contacts with Polish and Slovak partisans in 1944. These contacts produced intelli-gence for Red Army formation, as well as information about political devel-opments in Slovakia and Poland. In 1945–1947, this information helped the Red Army and its Polish communist allies destroy opposition from anticom-munist Ukrainian and Polish forces operating in the region.

See also PARTISAN WARFARE, SOVIET.

PATRUSHEV, NIKOLAI PLATONOVICH (1951–). Beginning his ca-reer in the Leningrad section of the **KGB** in 1974, Patrushev was made director of the **FSB** in 1999, replacing **Vladimir Putin**. Patrushev has pre-sided over the rapid development of the FSB into the second-largest security service—after China—in the world, with a reported staff of more than 300,000. A defender of his service, Patrushev described the FSB staff as "our new nobility."

Patrushev served as director of the FSB until 1999. He was been recognized as one of the closest associate of President Putin and has been given the rank of army general and repeatedly decorated. He is at present secretary of the Security Council of Russia. In 2007, he took part in a Russian Antarctic expedition, joining the expedition of noted polar explorer Arthur Chilingarov.

PAUKER, KARL VIKTOROVICH (1893–1937). Born into a family of hairdressers in the Austro-Hungarian Empire, Pauker served as a barber for the Budapest Opera before **World War I**. He was captured by the Russian army in 1915 and, while in prison, joined the **Bolshevik Party**. During the Russian **civil war**, he joined the **Cheka** and rose quickly to head of the Moscow department. From 1934 to 1936, he was chief of **Joseph Stalin**'s security detail. According to recent research, Pauker—like other senior security police officers—was very close to Stalin personally. He was a drinking companion and confidant for several years, and he arranged a state funeral for the leader's second wife, Nadya, who had committed suicide. He also took part in planning the trial of Lev Kamenev and Grigori Zinoviev in the first of the **Moscow Trials**. Pauker soon afterward fell out with Stalin and **NKVD** chief **Nikolai Yezhov**. He was arrested in March 1937 and tried five months later, on 14 August. He was shot immediately following the trial.

PAQUES, GEORGES (1914–?). A career civil servant, Paques was recruited by Soviet intelligence in 1943 while serving in the Free French government in Algiers and spied for Moscow for the next 20 years. After the liberation of France, Paques served as a senior bureaucrat in several ministries and North Atlantic Treaty Organization (NATO) headquarters. He met with his **KGB** case officer in the woods outside Paris. Arrested in 1963, he was sentenced to life imprisonment, but the sentence was later reduced to 20 years.

Paques was a significant penetration of both NATO and the French cabinet. He provided Moscow and the Vietminh with detailed information about French planning in 1953, including the failed Dien Bien Phu operation.

PAVLOV, KARP ALEKSANDROVICH (1895–1957). Pavlov was deputy chief of the **Kolyma** River forced labor camps in 1937 when the *Yezhovshchina* began. He apparently ensured that his boss, **Eduard Berzin**, would be purged, and he was rewarded with Berzin's job. Under Pavlov's rule, conditions for prisoners worsened dramatically. There were a high number of political **executions**. Deaths due to malnutrition and overwork skyrocketed. The winter of 1937–1938 was the worst in the history of these terrible camps. Pavlov's career took off after 1938. He was given increasing responsibility for **gulag** projects across the Soviet Union during **World War II**. These projects took the lives of hundreds of thousands of *zeks* ("prisoners"). In 1942 and 1943, more than 20 percent of the camps' population perished: a total of 620,368 men and women. Pavlov received the Order of **Lenin** and the Order of the Red Banner. He was promoted to colonel general in 1945 and retired in 1949. He committed suicide in 1957.

PAVLOV, VITALY GRIGORYEVICH (1914–2005). Probably no Soviet intelligence officer had as varied or as successful a career as Pavlov. Joining the **NKVD** in 1938, he served in Washington as an **illegal** with the code name "Klim." In July 1942, he became the service's *rezident* in Canada. He later served as a senior officer in the Illegals Directorate, head of foreign **counterintelligence**, intelligence chief in Austria, and chief of the **KGB's First Chief Directorate**'s training complex (later the **Andropov Institute**). He later served for many years in Poland, being the Kremlin's point man during the rise of Solidarity. He also wrote a well-received memoir (*Operation Snow*) and a history of Soviet foreign intelligence.

PECHORA. Officially the "Northern Pechora Camp," this was one of the more brutal camp complexes of the **gulag**. Founded in 1940, it had a population of 91,664 within 14 months. It was created to build the Koltas–Vorkuta railroad. Its most famous prisoner was the Israeli premier Menachem Begin, who was sentenced to eight years' imprisonment as an agent of the British Empire. He was released in May 1942. Begin wrote of his interrogation and life in Pechora in *White Nights*.

One of the best accounts of life in the gulag is Orlando Figes's *Just Send Me Word*, which is based on 1,246 letters smuggled into and out of Pechora between 1946 and 1955 between Lev Mishchenko and his girlfriend and, later, wife in Moscow.

PELTON, RONALD (1942–). Pelton had worked for the U.S. National Security Agency for more than a decade when he suddenly resigned in 1979. Months later, he initiated contact with the **KGB** by walking into the Soviet mission in Washington. The KGB ran Pelton in Washington through occasional personal meetings and dead drops. He offered the KGB information on a top-secret U.S. Navy program, **Ivy Bells**. Pelton was arrested in 1985 following the defection of **Vitaliy Yurchenko**, who provided U.S. intelligence with enough information to identify him. Pelton was tried and sentenced to life imprisonment in 1986.

PENKOVSKIY, OLEG VLADIMIROVICH (1919–1963). As a soldier in the **Great Patriotic War**, Penkovskiy was rapidly decorated and promoted. A full colonel before he was 30, Penkovskiy joined Soviet military intelligence, the **GRU**, and was posted to Turkey. He apparently was a complete failure in Turkey; only his connections in the military saved his career. Angry about being relegated to the sidelines, Penkovskiy volunteered to the Central Intelligence Agency (CIA) and the British Secret Intelligence Service in Moscow in August 1960, passing a letter through American tourists to the CIA. The letter read, "I ask you to consider me as your soldier. Henceforth, the ranks of your armed forces are increased by one man."

Over the next 22 months, Penkovskiy passed thousands of pages of information about the Soviet military and intelligence services to American and British handlers. The information, code-named "Ironbark" by the CIA, provided President John F. Kennedy with critical intelligence about the capabilities of Soviet weapons systems during the **Cuban Missile Crisis** of October 1962. This information allowed CIA **analysts** to identify Soviet missiles in Cuba and provide the president with accurate information about Soviet capabilities and intentions.

Penkovskiy was caught by the **KGB** as a result of his **tradecraft** errors. However, he had by that time operated for almost two years under the eyes of the KGB in the Soviet capital. He was tried and shot in 1963. Following his arrest, eight British and five American diplomats were expelled from the Soviet Union. Penkovskiy's espionage badly damaged the GRU and caused **Communist Party** leader **Nikita Khrushchev** to fire GRU chief **Ivan Serov** and appoint a senior KGB **counterintelligence** officer, **Petr Ivashutin**, to command the military intelligence service. After Penkovskiy's fall, more than 300 GRU officers were recalled to Moscow. Penkovskiy's **motivation** for betraying the Soviet Union has long been debated. Angry about his position and lack of advancement after the war, he probably acted from personal reasons best known to himself—and his KGB interrogators.

PERESTROIKA. Restructuring (*perestroika*) and openness (*glasnost*) were the most important elements of **Mikhail Gorbachev**'s reform agenda. *Perestroika*, in Gorbachev's view, was a reorientation of the Soviet economy toward limited market reform, much like **Vladimir Lenin**'s **New Economic Policy** of the 1920s. The hope was that reform would lead to a revitalization of the consumer sector of the economy. In effect, however, Gorbachev allowed only tinkering with the faltering Soviet economy; he would not consider any legalization of large-scale private business or the return of private property.

Perestroika did not benefit the Soviet populace. The emergence of small business did not fill the economic needs of the Soviet population for higher-quality food and consumer goods. In the late 1980s, inflation and deficits of consumer goods and quality food continued and even intensified as the system teetered toward total collapse. One class did benefit from *perestroika*: the Soviet Union's criminal gangs were well positioned to act as extortionists in the new economy. The **KGB** was horrified by the excesses of limited reform, especially the resurgence of organized crime; much of the senior leadership believed that Gorbachev's halfhearted reforms had unleashed corruption unseen in Soviet history. *Perestroika* may be remembered as a fatal half step that indirectly led to the **August putsch** of 1991 and the end of the Soviet Union.

***PERS* (PERSEUS).** One of the most important **NKVD** agents in the Manhattan Project remains unidentified to this day. A scientist referred to as "Pers" (Perseus) in Soviet intelligence traffic was a key source for the New York *rezidentura*. He could be identified by this code name by American cryptographers. After the collapse of the Soviet Union, a Soviet historian hinted that the name was chosen because Perseus was the person in Greek mythology who went into the underworld to obtain fire.

See also ENORMOZ; VENONA.

PETERS, IAKOV KHRISTOFOROVICH (1886–1938). At the age of 19, Peters took part in the **Revolution of 1905** and was imprisoned and tortured by tsarist authorities. Released in 1908, he made his way to London, where he became engaged in **émigré** anarchist circles. He took part in a botched robbery of a jewelry store that ended with the killing of three London police officers. Peters was acquitted of the crime, however, and married an English woman. He returned to Russia immediately following the fall of the tsar and joined the **Bolshevik Party**. He was appointed to the first **Cheka** governing council (collegium) in early 1918. During the **civil war**, he often deputized for **Feliks Dzerzhinsky** and gained a reputation for mercilessness. He was given ultimate responsibility for the security of Leningrad, Moscow, and Kiev during the most difficult days of the civil war. A competent administrator, Peters went into party work in the 1920s, serving as head of the Moscow city and regional governments. He was arrested in 1937 and shot in 1938.

PETERS, JOSEF (ca. 1895–?). This man, who left a long shadow across American and Soviet intelligence history, had a number of aliases: "Alexander Goldfarb," "Isador Boorstein," and "Alexander Stevens," as well as "Josef Peters." He was born in Cop, then part of the Austro-Hungarian Empire. He emigrated illegally to America after **World War I** and served as a militant in the **Communist Party** of the United States (CPUSA). In 1931, he was recalled to Moscow and trained to be head of the **Comintern**'s **illegal** section inside the CPUSA. For the next six years, he served as a conduit between the

American party and the Soviet intelligence services, traveling monthly to meet with agents in Washington. During this time, he ran **Whittaker Chambers** and helped establish a number of intelligence rings in Washington and New York. In 1938, when Chambers left the Communist Party and his life as a Soviet agent, Peters was blamed by Moscow and was fired. His replacement, **Rudy Baker**, was even better at managing the sensitive CPU-SA–**NKVD** relationship.

Peters later appeared before the House Committee on Un-American Activities and admitted that he was an illegal immigrant. He refused to answer any questions about his intelligence activities and was deported to Hungary. Peters's heritage was the establishment of tight links between the CPUSA and the intelligence services, making the Soviet successes of the 1940s possible.

See also BROWDER, EARL RUSSELL (1891–1973).

PETRASHEVSKIY CIRCLE. A minor official in the Ministry of Foreign Affairs, M. V. Petrashevskiy came under **surveillance** by the **Third Section** in early 1848 because of a political tract he wrote. Petrashevskiy and 33 other men then quickly came under suspicion for a "plot of ideas" and were arrested and interrogated by the authorities. After a military court-martial of 23 dangerous plotters, 21 were sentenced to death by firing squad in December 1848. Three days before Christmas, the convicted men were prepared for **execution**, but instead of being shot, they heard an imperial decree commuting their death sentence and sentencing them to prison and **exile**. One of the condemned was the writer Feodor Dostoyevsky. Petrashevskiy and his co-conspirators were not revolutionaries. But the waves of revolution sweeping over Europe in 1848 convinced Nicholas I that the Third Section had to nip subversion in the bud to prevent another **Decembrists ' Revolt**. The arrest and punishment of Petrashevskiy and his associates presaged the prophylactic arrests of **dissidents** by the *Okhrana* and the Soviet security services.

PETROV, VLADIMIR (1907–1991), AND PETROVA, EVDOKA (1915–2002). Among the **defectors** most damaging to the **KGB** in the post-Stalin years were the Petrovs, who served in the *rezidentura* in Canberra, Australia. Between them, they had more than 30 years of experience in human intelligence and technical intelligence when they defected in 1954. The Soviets tried to prevent the defection by forcing Petrova onto an aircraft bound for Moscow, but the Australian police pried her away from her KGB escorts. The scenes of a frightened woman escaping the clutches of the KGB were caught by an Australian photographer and were on the front pages of newspapers around the world. The publicity generated by the incident convinced Moscow to close its embassy in Canberra. The Petrovs' defection compromised several Soviet intelligence operations. In the 1940s and early 1950s, Australia had been a relatively easy target, and the Soviet services had been able to operate there against American, British, and Australian targets.

PHILBY, KIM (1912–1988). Probably the most famous **Cold War** spy, Harold Adrian Philby was born in India and given the nickname "Kim" from Kipling's novel of the Indian boy who spied for the British. Philby was converted to left-wing socialism while at Cambridge, and during a visit to Vienna in 1934, he saw the Austrian government's repression of a socialist workers' revolt. Philby left Vienna with a communist wife, **Litzie Friedman**, whom he saved from prosecution and possible **execution**, and a lifetime commitment to communism.

Philby came to the attention of Soviet intelligence through several spotters in Cambridge and London, the most important of whom reportedly was **Edith Tudor-Hart**, and was recruited and run in London by a series of Soviet intelligence service **illegals**. He was given the code name "Sohnchen" (Russian for "Little Son"). Soviet intelligence played a "long game" with Philby, instructing him to break contacts with his left-wing friends and migrate to conservative politicians and journalists. As a correspondent in Spain during the **Spanish Civil War**, he was wounded and later decorated by Spanish dictator Francisco Franco. With the beginning of **World War II**, he entered the British Secret Intelligence Service (SIS). Philby was by all accounts an effective member of both the British and the Soviet secret service. In one of the great ironies of intelligence history, he received the Soviet Order of the Red Banner and the British Order of the British Empire for service during World War II.

Over the next decade, Philby became the most important mole in the Cold War. Rising quickly within British intelligence, he gave Moscow all the secrets of British **counterintelligence** operations against the Soviet Union. In 1946, he betrayed Konstantin Volkov, a Soviet intelligence officer who sought to defect to Britain with the names of Soviet moles serving inside the British government. Both Volkov and his wife were drugged and transported back to Moscow, where they were shot. Philby betrayed as well American and British efforts to drop agents behind the Iron Curtain, ensuring that more than 100 men and women were sent to their deaths. As SIS station commander in Turkey, he betrayed British and American operations against the Soviet southern flank. In late 1949, he was posted to Washington as SIS liaison with the Central Intelligence Agency (CIA) and the Federal Bureau of Investigation, and he provided Moscow with detailed reporting on U.S. intelligence.

Philby's downfall came as he sought to protect **Donald Maclean**, who had been identified as a Soviet agent by **Venona** intercepts. Philby instructed **Guy Burgess**, who was living with him in Washington, to return to London and warn Maclean of danger. When Burgess, against Philby's instructions, defected to Russia with Maclean, it was clear to the CIA and to some of his colleagues in the SIS that Philby was a mole. The British establishment decided, however, to protect Philby, and he was exonerated on the floor of the House of Commons by then Foreign Minister Harold Macmillan. Philby went into retirement in the late 1950s, taking a post in Lebanon as a correspondent for the *Observer* and the *Economist*, and he was reemployed by the SIS. In 1963, the SIS received specific information identifying Philby as a Russian agent. An SIS officer and close personal friend was sent to Lebanon to negotiate Philby's return to London. Philby, however, chose to betray the SIS one last time and was exfiltrated by the **KGB**.

Philby's last years in Moscow as a **defector** were not completely happy. He was never accepted as a commissioned officer in the KGB, and he never entered **Lubyanka** until 14 years after his defection. While he informed foreign journalists that he was a general in the KGB, he never held a commissioned officer's rank, and he was known as "Agent Tom." In retirement, he wrote his memoirs under KGB supervision and began to drink heavily. He was apparently rescued by his fourth wife, who has written interesting memoirs of her own, and **Oleg Kalugin**, KGB chief of foreign counterintelligence, who believed that Philby had been shabbily treated. Philby died at age 76 and was buried in Moscow with full military honors. The Soviet Union issued a stamp with his picture on it.

Philby created havoc within Western intelligence agencies. Not only did he betray scores of agents, as well as intelligence and **tradecraft**, but he sowed distrust between American and British security institutions. American security professionals never completely understood why the British establishment protected Philby, whereas the British deeply resented American criticism of their security and intelligence services. Philby's memoirs and even his final interview with a noted British journalist given just a few months before his death sought to further muddle Allied cooperation. But by that time, he was only an exhibit in a museum of the crumbling system he had served.

An interesting postscript to the story of Philby, Maclean, and Burgess was written by an American historian and novelist, S. J. Hamrick, in *Deceiving the Deceivers: Kim Philby, Donald Maclean, and Guy Burgess*. Hamrick believes that based on a close reading of the Venona material, the British service was on to the traitors years before they were discovered. He believes that the British service allowed Philby to operate in order to pass distorted intelligence about nuclear weapons and Anglo-American defense plans to Moscow. He notes that the reason all three were poorly treated on their arrival in the Soviet Union was that their information was false. Philby has been the subject of more than 150 books and articles; most counterintelligence analysts tend to believe that the damage he did to British interests and the West was incredibly serious.

See also RING OF FIVE.

PILYAR, ROMAN ALEKSANDROVICH (1894–1937). Born into the Polish nobility (his name at birth was von Pilhau), Pilyar joined the socialist parties of Poland and Latvia as well as the Menshevik faction of the Russian Social Democratic Labor Party in his youth. Following the **Revolution of November 1917**, he joined the **Bolshevik Party** and was active in party work. He joined the **Cheka** in 1920 and was active in the Russian **civil war** and **collectivization**. Pilyar was one of a number of talented Poles who joined the security service in the heady days of the Revolution. Like **Feliks Dzerzhinsky** and **Vyacheslav Menzhinsky**, the first two chiefs of the service, he was an internationalist rather than a Polish patriot. His Menshevik past dragged him down, however, as the **NKVD** began to look for traitors in their midst in 1937. Pilyar and other Poles in the service came under suspicion, and almost all perished. He was arrested at the beginning of the *Yezhovshchina* in May 1937. He was tried and shot four months later. Pilyar was posthumously rehabilitated in 1957 and is remembered as the Cheka's last nobleman.

PITOVRANOV, YEVGENY PETROVICH (1915–1999). A **KGB** officer whose experience spanned the years of **Joseph Stalin**, **Khrushchev**, and **Leonid Brezhnev**, Pitovranov had a career with a series of sharp turns. In 1938, he was drafted out of the **Communist Party** higher school into the security service. Due to the purge of thousands of officers, his promotion was rapid, and within five years, he was a major general involved in internal security and **counterintelligence**, first in Russia and then in Uzbekistan.

In 1951, Pitovranov's career further accelerated, and he became chief of counterintelligence. But in 1952, as part of Stalin's rolling purge of the **MGB**, he was arrested. He was quickly released from jail, however, and resumed his career as chief of foreign intelligence. He was apparently seen as too junior for this position and was transferred to Berlin as chief of the KGB in East Germany. He was notably successful in rebuilding the security service's operations in Berlin. He later served as KGB *rezident* in China and then as head of the KGB's training school with the rank of lieutenant general. Following his retirement from the KGB, Pitovranov became the first chair of the Chamber of Commerce.

PITTS, EARL EDWIN (1945–). An agent of the Federal Bureau of Investigation (FBI) serving in New York, Pitts volunteered to work for the **KGB** in a letter that he sent to the Soviet security officer at the United Nations. Pitt then worked for the KGB from 1987 until 1992 and received $240,000 for providing top-secret FBI documents. He met with his KGB case officer,

Aleksandr Karpov, in New York on nine occasions, but for the most part, he communicated with Karpov and other KGB officers through dead drops. Pitt was eventually identified to the FBI by Karpov and by his wife, Mary, who suspected his betrayal. The FBI set up an elaborate sting to obtain legal evidence for a trial. Over more than a year, Pitts met with FBI agents masquerading as Russian intelligence officers, and he provided information for more than $60,000 in payments. Pitts was arrested in 1996 and sentenced to 27 years in prison. Asked about his **motivation** for spying, he said it was "to pay them back," referring to a number of unspecified grievances against the FBI.

PLEHVE, VYACHESLAV KONSTANTINOVICH VON (1847–1904). One of the most reactionary and anti-Semitic of Tsar Nicholas II's advisers, von Plehve was made minister of internal affairs in 1902. As security chief, von Plehve supported draconian internal security practices and supported anti-Semitic organizations known as "Black Hundreds." He was despised by liberal and radical public opinion for his sponsorship of the Kishinev **pogrom** of April 1903 that claimed hundreds of Jewish lives. Von Plehve was an incompetent security chief. He fired his most competent subordinate, **Nikolai Zubatov**, and ignored intelligence about growing urban and peasant radicalism. More importantly, he was seen by many Russians as the single most evil figure in the tsar's court. His death became a major goal of the Socialist Revolutionary Party's **Battle Organization**, and after several failed attempts, he was assassinated in 1904, an act that prompted genuine popular rejoicing in Russia.

PLEKHAVOV, YURI SERGEYEVICH (1930–2002). Director of the Ninth (**Leadership Protection**) Directorate of the **KGB** during the failed **August 1991** putsch, Plekhanov used his men to seal off President **Mikhail Gorbachev** at his Crimean retreat, making it possible for the plotters to take power in Moscow. He was dismissed following the putsch.

POGROMS. Organized anti-Semitic violence, known as pogroms, became a fact of Russian political life beginning in the early 1880s. Russia had in the last decades of the Romanov dynasty the largest Jewish population in Europe. But Russian chauvinists saw the Jewish people as ethnically and politically alien. One of Aleksandr III's chief advisers stated that Russia's policy was to convert one-third of the Jews, see another one-third killed, and force the last one-third to emigrate to America. The tsar and his reactionary bureaucrats believed that violence against Jews would divert the revolutionary drive of the Russian people.

The Ministry of Internal Affairs and the *Okhrana* took part in the financing and planning of pogroms during the reigns of Aleksandr III and Nicholas II. The *Okhrana* also almost certainly commissioned the virulently anti-Semitic *Protocols of the Elders of Zion*, which claimed to be a master plan for a Jewish plot to control the world. (The book survived the fall of the Romanov dynasty, was widely read in Hitler's Germany, and is still quoted by virulent anti-Semites.) Interior Minister **Vyacheslav von Plehve**, one of Nicholas II's chief advisers, encouraged his subordinates to incite racial violence, causing thousands of casualties. Over 1,000 people died in a pogrom at Kishinev that von Plehve had had a hand in designing. His assassination in 1904 by the **Battle Organization** of the Socialist Revolutionary Party was partly a result of a demand for vengeance for these pogroms by political radicals.

The pogroms destroyed the authority of Nicholas II's regime at home and abroad, breeding contempt among moderates and conservatives at home and causing diplomatic protests from a number of states. The first American confrontation with Russia came over the Kishinev pogrom of 1903. That year, the U.S. Congress passed a joint resolution denouncing the tsarist regime. The pogroms also drove many young Jews into the revolutionary parties: the SR, the Bolsheviks, and anarchist fighting groups.

Pogroms are also associated with the Russian **civil war**. Both White and Red forces participated in anti-Semitic outrages, and thousands of Jews perished in organized violence. During the **Great Patriotic War**, the Nazi authorities encouraged pogroms in occupied Soviet territory to win support among the Slavic peasantry. Some of the mass killings in Poland, the Baltic, and the western Soviet Union were conducted by Russian, Byelorussian, and Ukrainian paramilitary units cooperating with the Germans.

POLISH CRISES. Poland was always a problem for Russia. From the 1863–1864 uprising until the collapse of the Warsaw Pact in 1991, Moscow tried in ham-handed ways to dominate its western neighbor. In 1921, the Bolsheviks took their revolution to Poland. Polish communists like **Cheka** leader **Feliks Dzerzhinsky** believed that victory in Poland was the first step to world revolution. The Red Army, however, was defeated on the banks of the Vistula, a battle that one British academic claimed prevented Russian from being the language of instruction at Harvard and Cambridge.

Following the defeat of the Red Army, a large Polish communist movement was based on Soviet soil. Soviet leader **Joseph Stalin**, however, saw the Poles as an enemy nation, and this attitude affected Soviet policy for decades. In the *Yezhovshchina*, a major target of the **NKVD** was the Polish Communist Party. In 1937–1938, the entire leadership of the Polish Communist Party was tried and shot. In 1939–1940, it was Stalin's intention to ensure that an independent Poland could never exist again in the wake of the Nazi–Soviet Pact. Through massive **deportations**, over a million Poles were exiled to Siberia by the **NKVD**; over one-half perished. Stalin also ordered the murder of 26,000 Polish officers, civil servants, and clergy. Mass **graves** were later discovered in places such as **Katyn** and **Kuropaty**.

In 1944–1946, Stalin ensured the destruction of the military-political base of the Polish Home Army (AK) when he allowed the German armed forces to defeat the Warsaw uprising in the fall of 1944. When the Red Army entered Poland in 1944, Stalin ordered the NKVD and *Smersh* to disarm the AK, a **partisan** movement representing the last Polish government. AK leaders were arrested, shipped to Moscow, and tried for imaginary war crimes. Rank-and-file AK soldiers were impressed into the Moscow-oriented Polish army. Thousands of men and women who had fought the Nazis as partisans were arrested and imprisoned in Siberia or Central Asia in the **gulag**.

Moscow took control of Polish politics in 1946–1956 using proxies in the Ministry of State Security to arrest and try enemies. Soviet **MGB** officers were inserted into the Polish security bureaucracy. Special targets of the Polish communists and their Soviet patrons were AK veterans and the Roman Catholic Church. In the late 1940s, the Polish Communist Party tried but ultimately failed to set up an alternative Polish church. In 1956, worker violence in Poznan and growing street demonstrations in other cities brought the Soviet leadership to Warsaw in October to confront their puppets. In a series of meetings, the leadership of **Nikita Khrushchev**'s regime agreed to reduce direct Soviet control of Poland in exchange for Poland's continued membership in the Warsaw Pact. Soviet security and military advisers were withdrawn and sent home.

Beginning in the late 1970s, communist power in Poland was challenged by a new political alliance of workers, clerics, and intellectuals. Solidarity, the most important of the movements, won widespread support across the country. The **KGB** developed sources within both Solidarity and the Polish government, and the Soviet leadership was well informed on developments inside Poland. The KGB helped the Politburo of **Leonid Brezhnev** to pressure the Polish government to crack down on Solidarity in December 1981. The Soviet service spread rumors that Moscow was preparing to intervene, and it convinced its agents of influence that the only way to prevent a Soviet–Polish war was for the Polish communists to break Solidarity. The KGB was unable, however, to keep Soviet plans for Poland secret; the Central Intelligence Agency had important sources within the Polish military, including Colonel Ryszard Kuklinski.

POLYAKOV, DMITRY FEDOROVICH (1921–1988). The highest-ranking Soviet officer to spy for the West, Polyakov was an agent for America from 1961 to 1986. During the period that he was promoted in the **GRU** from captain to major general, he served first the Federal Bureau of Investigation and then the Central Intelligence Agency (CIA) by providing information about 19 GRU **illegals**, more than 150 other GRU agents, and more than 1,000 military intelligence officers serving abroad. According to the Russian account of the case, he also passed hundreds of top-secret documents to the West, including Ministry of Defense war plans. He was betrayed to the **KGB** in 1986 by **Aldrich Ames** and was arrested. He was shot two years later.

The KGB account of Polyakov paints him as someone seduced by the American dollar, but Polyakov did not receive substantial funds from the CIA. He spied primarily out of anger and disgust with the Soviet system. A major **motivation** was deeply personal: when his son fell seriously ill in New York, the GRU *rezident* refused to allow him to seek American medical help. His son died, and Polyakov shortly thereafter sought contact with American intelligence.

The Polyakov case illustrates the rivalry that existed in Moscow between the GRU and the KGB. There had been a spate of reports in the American press and from American sources in the 1970s that Polyakov was an American asset. Yet the GRU leadership defended Polyakov and kept him from arrest. It was only when Ames presented documentary evidence of Polyakov's work for U.S. intelligence that he was finally arrested.

POLYAKOVA, MARIA IOSEFOVNA (ca. 1910–?). As a young member of the **Communist Party**, Polyakova was sent to Switzerland in the early 1930s as an **illegal** to establish an intelligence network for the **GRU**. This network became the basis for **Sandor Rado**'s intelligence operation during **World War II**. Despite the fact that several members of her family were purged in the late 1930s, Polyakova became a Red Army intelligence officer with the rank of major and served as chief of the Swiss desk during the war. She directed Rado's efforts from GRU headquarters in Moscow, and she deserves much of the credit for his success.

POLITKOVSKAYA, ANNA STEPANOVNA (1959–2006). A crusading and independent journalist, Politkovskaya was murdered in the elevator of her apartment block in Moscow in 2006. Politkovskaya had been a bitter critic of **President Vladimir Putin** and the **FSB**'s violation of human rights, especially the torture and murder of civilians in Chechnya. She repeatedly received death threats and on one occasion was poisoned. Her murder was linked to Chechens closely connected to the FSB. Four men were tried for her murder; all were acquitted. Evidence submitted by journalists further strengthened the case against the FSB.

There were tragic postscripts the the trial. In January 2009, two journalists who had investigated human rights documented by Politkovskaya were murdered in Moscow. In July 2009, Natalia Estemirova, a board member of the

Memorial Society and a close associate of Politkovskaya, was also murdered. The independent press, as a result of these and other killings of journalists, stop sending correspondents to the Caucasus.

POPOV, PETR SEMENOVICH (1916–1960). An early victory for the Central Intelligence Agency (CIA) in the **Cold War** was the recruitment and running of Petr Popov, a **GRU** lieutenant colonel who volunteered to work for American intelligence in Vienna in the early 1950s. Popov's **motivations** were personal and ideological: he was disgusted with the regime's treatment of peasant families like his own, he coveted a Western lifestyle, and he was deeply fond of his American case officers.

Popov was run successfully first in Vienna and then in Berlin for more than five years by the CIA, and he provided detailed information about GRU espionage and **illegals**, including the names of more than 650 GRU officers and scores of illegals operating in the West. In 1957, he identified Walter and Margarita Tairov, who had been dispatched to New York as illegals. The Tairovs were able to avoid **surveillance** by U.S. **counterintelligence** and return to the East. The Tairov case may have alerted Soviet intelligence that it had a mole in its officer corps.

Popov also provided hundreds of documents on Soviet military policy toward the North Atlantic Treaty Organization and Germany. A CIA officer involved in the case stated that Popov "produced the most valuable intelligence on the Soviet military of any source in that period." The **KGB** after-action report on the Popov case estimates that his reporting saved the U.S. government more than $500 million in its scientific and technical programs. Popov came under suspicion in 1958—probably as a result of either **George Blake**'s treachery or close KGB scrutiny of the Tairov case. He was arrested in October 1959 and interrogated severely. When the KGB tried to run him under their control to entrap a CIA case officer, Popov showed tremendous presence of mind and courage; he slipped the American officer a note stating that he was under Soviet control. Rumors reached the West that following his trial, Popov was fed into a furnace while still alive. The story, like many Cold War stories, appears to be fiction. Popov was shot in June 1960.

PORETSKY, IGNATZ [REISS, IGNACE] (1899–1937). One of the "great **illegals**," Poretsky and his wife, Elizabeth, operated in Western Europe in the 1920s and 1930s. Elizabeth wrote one of the best accounts of Soviet illegals, *Our Own People*. From 1934 to 1936, Poretsky was the **OGPU** *rezident* in Paris, recruiting and running sources in Paris and Belgium. He was one of the first OGPU officers to receive the combat Order of the Red Banner. In 1937, disgusted by **Joseph Stalin**'s purge of the **Communist Party** and the **NKVD** foreign intelligence component, Poretsky publicly resigned from the service. A letter published in the European press read in part, "He who remains silent at this hour makes himself an accomplice of Stalin, and a traitor to the cause of the working class and of socialism." Poretsky publicly returned his Soviet medals and noted his decision to remain in the West. He was assassinated in Switzerland in September 1937 by gunmen dispatched by Stalin only weeks after the letter was received in Moscow. A participant in the assassination was **Vladimir Pravdin**, an NKVD case officer later posted to New York.

PORTLAND SPY CASE. One of the **KGB**'s major victories in London was the running of spies within the British Navy antisubmarine research facility in Portland. Harry Houghton, a British civil servant working in the naval attaché's office, volunteered in 1951 to Polish intelligence. Over the next year, he gave the Poles and their Soviet allies hundreds of pages of classified material and British codebooks. On his return from Warsaw, Houghton, now working at Portland, was run by the KGB's London *rezidentura* and later by an **illegal, Konon Molody** ("Gordon Lonsdale"). Houghton, whose KGB code names were "Shah" and "Shahmakht" (Chess and Checkmate), copied thousands of documents on British and North Atlantic Treaty Organization policy and technology for the Soviet service. The operation ran until 1961, when Houghton and his lover and associate, Ethel Gee, were arrested with Molody, along with **Morris and Lona Cohen**, two illegals sent by Moscow to London to support the operation. Houghton and Gee married after serving their prison sentences.

POTEYEV, ALEKSANDR (1953–). A colonel and a senior staff officer in the **SVR**'s Directorate S **(Illegals)**, he was tried in absentia for treason. He received a 25-year sentence from the court and was stripped of his military decorations. He currently lives in the United States.

PRAGUE, 1948–1954. The **MGB** played an important role in the coup that brought the Czech **Communist Party** to power in 1947–1948 and an even more important role in the party's consolidation of power. MGB officers acted as clandestine advisers to Czech communists in planning the coup and almost certainly were involved in the "suicide" of Czech Foreign Minister Jan Masaryk. Masaryk, the only noncommunist member of the government, was found dead underneath his open window. Between 1948 and 1952, the Czech secret police, under the direction of the MGB, destroyed political diversity. Men and women, democrats and socialists, went to the gallows after garish public **show trials**. The MGB apparently used the most famous of these, the **Slansky trial** in 1952, as a dress rehearsal for a mass trial of Soviet Jews. Public show trials continued for more than a year after **Joseph**

Stalin's death as the Czech party ensured its complete control of the society. The MGB and, later, the **KGB** used the newly Sovietized Czech foreign intelligence service. Czech officers played an important role in Soviet **active measures** in the 1950s and 1960s.

See also PRAGUE CRISIS, 1968.

PRAGUE CRISIS, 1968. The **KGB** was instrumental in persuading **Leonid Brezhnev** to intervene in 1968 in Czechoslovakia, where a reformist party leadership had reduced press censorship and was publishing details of the political repression of the 1940s and 1950s. KGB chair **Yuri Andropov** was quick to see the danger of the "Prague Spring," and in Politburo meetings in 1968, he called for direct Soviet action. The KGB presented very slanted reporting to the leadership, exaggerating the anti-Soviet tendencies of Czech leader Alexander Dubcek and pointing out that liberalism in Prague was infecting Ukraine, Moldavia, and the Baltic republics with similar viruses. To ensure a bloodless putsch, Andropov dispatched teams of **illegals** to Prague in what were known as **Progress Operations** to develop dossiers on Czech **dissidents** and allow the targeting of enemies.

The KGB played a key role in the coup de main that seized Prague in August as well. KGB teams took control of radio stations, police offices, and the headquarters of the Czech **Communist Party**. Dubcek and his colleagues were detained by KGB teams and shipped off to a secret location inside the Soviet Union where they could first reconsider and then publicly confess their sins in documents published around the world. The Czech security and intelligence services were purged of those suspected of liberalism, which caused a number of good intelligence officers to defect to the West.

The Prague Spring was no threat to either Moscow or the Warsaw Pact. Andropov and party reactionaries apparently feared that Dubcek's gospel of communism with a human face could spread to Moscow and lead to demands for greater intellectual freedom. One of the Czech communists who later defected to the West said that he had expected narrow dogmatists in Moscow but not "vulgar thugs." The KGB continued to work closely with the Czechoslovak services until the "Velvet Revolution" ended Communist Party control in 1989.

See also PRAGUE, 1948–1954.

PRAVDIN, VLADIMIR SERGEEVICH (1902–1962). Born Roland Jacques Claude Abbiate of French and Russian Jewish parents in London, Pravdin grew up in Paris. He was recruited for Soviet intelligence by his sister Mieille, who was an accomplished **illegal**. He joined the **OGPU** in 1932 and served in Western Europe under a number of pseudonyms. As "Vladimir Pravdin," he served in Europe and as an **NKVD** case officer in

New York under journalist cover. In his first creation as an intelligence officer, Pravdin took part in the murder of **Ignatz Poretsky** in Switzerland in 1937. In 1944, Pravdin was assigned to New York as *rezident* under cover as a TASS representative. Under journalist cover, Pravdin was a successful intelligence officer; he recruited and ran **Judith Coplon**, and he managed several other successful operations.

The defections of **Elizabeth Bentley** and **Igor Gouzenko**, plus the Anglo-American success in deciphering Soviet codes, undid Pravdin's relationship with important agents. Fearing arrest by the Federal Bureau of Investigation, many productive agents were not recontacted. Moscow decided that a more conservative posture in the United States was needed; Pravdin was recalled in 1946 to Moscow and replaced with a nonentity. Blamed for the loss of agents, Pravdin fell under a cloud of suspicion. He was fired partly because of his foreign Jewish ancestry in 1947.

Pravdin's fate demonstrated graphically the deterioration and collapse of NKVD networks in the United States. As Pravdin and other talented case officers were recalled, they were not replaced with competent agent handlers. New officers were warned about the new **counterintelligence** environment and became risk averse, choosing to write intelligence reports based on articles in the American press. The intelligence empire that had been built up during **World War II** crumbled.

PREOBRAZHENSKIY, KONSTANTIN GEORGIYEVICH (1953–). From 1980 to 1985, Preobrazhenskiy served in Tokyo as a **KGB** scientific and technical intelligence officer under journalistic cover. He was arrested by the Japanese police during a meeting with a Chinese agent and expelled. In 1991, he left the KGB to write two books about his experiences in Japan and his efforts to recruit Chinese agents. In January 2003, he fled to the United States and has written and lectured on Russian President **Vladimir Putin** and the post-Soviet Russian intelligence community and their efforts to form agent networks in the Russian Orthodox Church and Russian émigré communities.

Preobrazhenskiy is an interesting witness to the changes in Russian intelligence since the collapse of the Soviet regime. He sees both the **SVR** and the **FSB** as more dangerous opponents than the KGB because of their ties to Russian religious and **émigré** institutions.

PREOBRAZHENSKIY PRIKAZ. Tsar Petr the Great created the *Preobrazhenskiy prikaz* (Preobrazhenskiy Office) in 1699 as a secret chancery to prosecute treason and disloyalty. The tsar was concerned about opposition to his modernization policies, which were seen as violating Russian Orthodox religious precepts. The group had the tsar's mandate to seek out, detain, torture, and kill those suspected of disloyalty to the throne. The officials of this secret chancery recruited **informants** to gather intelligence about public animosity toward the tsar among the nobility, clergy, and peasantry. Like the *Oprichnina* of Ivan the Terrible, the *Preobrazhenskiy prikaz* did not survive its founder's death; it was abolished in 1725.

PRIMAKOV, YEVGENY MAKSIMOVICH (1929–). A skilled bureaucrat and academic, Primakov served Soviet and post-Soviet leaders effectively for five decades. After finishing his doctorate degree, Primakov worked as a journalist overseas. In 1970, he returned to Moscow to serve as the director of academic institutes, most importantly the Institute of International Economics and International Relations. During these years, Primakov built up excellent personal and professional contacts with Western academics and journalists. He also developed a reputation as a major voice for political reform inside the Soviet Union.

In 1989, General Secretary **Mikhail Gorbachev** co-opted Primakov into the Central Committee and then the Politburo of the **Communist Party**. During the 1991 **August putsch**, Primakov staunchly supported Gorbachev and was one of the party leaders who went to the Crimea to bring Gorbachev back from house arrest. Almost immediately following the putsch, Primakov was appointed by Gorbachev to head the new Central Intelligence Service, which in December of the same year became the Foreign Intelligence Service of Russia (**SVR**).

As a journalist and academician, Primakov had close contact with the staff of the **KGB**'s **First Chief Directorate** and was a good choice both politically and operationally to head the new foreign intelligence service. According to a former Soviet intelligence officer, Primakov was an enrolled KGB agent with the cryptonym "Maksim." Primakov is widely credited with maintaining SVR morale and operational tempo during his tenure. The SVR suffered relatively few defections during this trying period and continued to run penetration agents in the Central Intelligence Agency (CIA) and the Federal Bureau of Investigation. Primakov visited the CIA headquarters in November 1994 to institute liaison between the Russian and American services on drug trafficking, **nuclear proliferation**, and **terrorism**. As intelligence chief, Primakov also conducted secret diplomatic missions for the **Boris Yeltsin** government, visiting Afghanistan and Tajikistan. During the next four years, Primakov became a national and international spokesperson for Russian intelligence, emphasizing the differences between the KGB of the bad old Soviet days and the democratic SVR.

In January 1996, Primakov was appointed minister of foreign affairs, and in September 1998, he was elevated to prime minister of the Russian Federation. In May 1999, however, Primakov was fired by President Yeltsin. Subsequently, he became chair of the Fatherland Party in the Russian Duma.

PRIME, GEOFFREY ARTHUR (1938–). A major penetration of the British **signals intelligence** establishment, Prime volunteered to the **KGB** in 1968 while serving in Berlin. Prime was a tragic misfit who lived a triple life as a sexual deviant, a British **signals intelligence** officer, and a KGB agent. He volunteered to work for the Soviet Union for ideological reasons, and he was paid relatively little for the information he provided Soviet intelligence. Prime was uncovered in 1983 during an investigation of his sexual assault on young women. Although he had broken with Soviet intelligence, he had kept clandestine communications gear. He also had the names of 2,287 young women he had targeted. He was sentenced to 38 years' imprisonment: 35 years for espionage and three years for his sexual activities.

PRISON MASSACRES. In the summer as the German forces occupied the Soviet Union, the **NKVD** evacuated and executed political prisoners incarcerated in the Baltic, Belorussia, and Ukraine. Figures are not accurate, but respected scholars put the number of prisoners evacuated at 140,000. Figures on executions range from 9,000 to more than 100,000. Reporting on events in the western districts of Ukraine suggests that at least 10,000 died in that area.

At the same time, **Joseph Stalin** and **Lavrenty Beria** authorized the shooting of high-level political prisoners held in pretrial confinement or special prison facilities. Several hundred men and women were shot, including senior air force officers and their wives, a former chief of the **GRU**, and the relatives of purged party officials.

To complete the elimination of unwanted witnesses, Beria sent Stalin a list of 47 generals and defense industrial officials in January 1942 with the recommendation that all be shot. Stalin returned the list, initialed, with the comment "shot them all."

PRISONERS OF WAR, FOREIGN. During **World War II**, the Red Army captured more than 2.5 million Germans and Austrians and held them as prisoners of war. It also took 766,000 soldiers prisoner from the armies of Hitler's Hungarian, Italian, and Romanian allies. Treatment of these prisoners was harsh, in part because of conditions on the Eastern Front and in part because neither the Red Army nor the **NKVD** expected to have so many prisoners. Of the 90,000 German soldiers taken prisoner at Stalingrad in February 1943, 90 percent perished in the first six months of their captivity. Conditions gradually got better, but between 381,000 (Soviet figure) and 1 million (West German research) German soldiers taken prisoner between 1941 and 1945 never saw Germany again.

Soviet intelligence and the Red Army recruited former prisoners to serve with Red Army units to spread propaganda within surrounded or isolated German forces. Most of these men were apprehended and shot by the Wehrmacht, but German officers' accounts of the last days of the war are filled with concerns that these "Seydlitz troops" (after a senior officer captured at Stalingrad) could have an impact on morale. Other German and Soviet accounts report Seydlitz troops fighting with Red Army units in the Battle of Berlin, and on at least one occasion, they disrupted the movement of German units by feeding false information to officers.

Beginning in 1942, the NKVD Institute 99, which was responsible for foreign prisoners of war, began to recruit prisoners to serve as espionage agents and as part of a future pro-Soviet German government. The Free German Committee recruited senior officers, including Field Marshall Friedrich Paulus, who had been captured at Stalingrad, and the German commander of Army Group Center, captured in the summer of 1944. Many of the German officials collaborated with the Soviets to save their lives and the lives of their troops. Others believed that a pro-Soviet Germany would be the best future for their country. German prisoners were also prized as laborers; some of the best-constructed apartment buildings in Moscow were built by German prisoners of war in the late 1940s. The last German prisoners of war returned to West Germany in 1955.

Institute 99, later known as the NKVD's Chief Directorate for Prisoners of War and Internees (*Glavnoye Upravleniye po delam Voennoplennikh i Internirovannikh*) (**GUPVI**), also targeted the officers and soldiers of Hitler's allies. As Moscow began to plan for the occupation of Eastern Europe, the NKVD began a program of recruiting future agents from the prison population. Pal Maleter, who later led the Hungarian revolt against Moscow in 1956, was initially recruited while languishing in a prison camp to serve in a pro-Soviet Hungarian military unit. Despite thousands of words written about American prisoners of war in Soviet camps, there is no evidence that there was any effort to keep Americans who had been in German captivity.

PRISONERS OF WAR, SOVIET. The Wehrmacht captured more than 4.4 million Soviet forces, most in the dark days of 1941–1942. More than 1 million of these died of hunger and disease in 1941–1942. **Joseph Stalin**'s son Yakov, a junior officer, was captured and later killed while trying to escape from a German camp. Many senior Soviet officers formed resistance cells inside prison camps. Major General I. M. Shepetov, captured at Kharkov in the spring of 1942, was executed in a Nazi concentration camp a year later for organizing Soviet prisoners.

The fate of former prisoners of war who returned to their own lines was horrific. The Soviet Union—like Nazi Germany—was not a signatory to the Geneva Convention. Soviet law held that there was no reason for a soldier to be captured by the enemy, and there were strict punishments for the families of those who voluntarily went over to the German side. Those who escaped from German captivity and made their way back to Soviet lines were often treated with suspicion, and some were **executed** for desertion. **Aleksandr Yakovlev**, a decorated war hero, noted, "A serviceman taken prisoner was regarded as having committed a premeditated crime. Soviet soldiers and commanding officers who had broken out of encirclements were treated as potential traitors and spies." The end of the war thus presented a major challenge to the regime: what to do with those who had been imprisoned by the Nazi enemy, and—however unwilling—had seen the West.

More than 1.8 million former prisoners of war and 3.5 million civilians drafted as slave laborers returned to Russian hands in 1945–1947. (Almost 500,000 Soviet citizens remained in the West, including 160,000 former prisoners of war.) All former prisoners and forced laborers were put through "filtration" camps run by *Smersh* and the **NKVD**. Of those in the military, 339,000 were sentenced to death or 25 years' hard labor in the **gulag**. Another 145,000 received six-year sentences in special regime camps. Other soldiers were sentenced to internal **exile** to work in eastern Siberia or the far north. Civilians were not completely forgiven: many had their passports stamped with the note that they were forbidden to live in major European cities.

A harsh fate awaited those who had joined the Vlasov Army, a force comprising several divisions of Russian soldiers armed by Germany to fight against the Red Army. The group had been organized by General Andrei Vlasov, the hero of the **Battle of Moscow**, who had been captured in 1942. Vlasov and several of his chief subordinates were hanged in the **Lubyanka** in 1946. A picture of the executed men hanging from gallows was found in **Joseph Stalin**'s desk after his death.

PROCURACY. In the Soviet Union, the prosecutor's office was known as the procuracy. During the years of **Joseph Stalin**, the procuracy's powers were severely limited in favor of the security services. The **Cheka** during the **civil war** and the **NKVD** in the late 1930s had the right to arrest, try, and execute political prisoners. Following Stalin's death, Soviet law was reformed to give the procuracy far greater authority, along with the ability to conduct semi-independent investigations in some criminal cases. But the Soviet procuracy never had the degree of independence held by British or American prosecution attorneys. Sentences were often dictated by the **KGB** or **Communist Party** leaders.

Since the collapse of the Soviet Union, Russian prosecutors have reexamined their juridical roots. Russian law now recognizes—as tsarist law did—that the procuracy needs to have considerable independence in presenting cases and selecting prosecutions. The new Russian offices have also come under tremendous pressure from Russian **organized crime**, and several prosecutors and members of their staffs have been assassinated.

PROGRESS OPERATIONS. Beginning in 1968, **KGB** chair **Yuri Andropov** authorized the use of **illegals** to check on developments in Soviet East European satellites. Prior to 1968, illegals had been used in Eastern Europe only to recruit westerners. The Progress Operations called for illegals under cover as Western business people and journalists to travel to Prague to gather information about Czech **dissidents**. They were also expected to generate **active measures** that would discredit liberal Czech reformers and create reasons for Soviet intervention. Illegals staged anti-Soviet demonstrations that were reported in the Soviet press. Illegals were deployed after Soviet intervention in August 1968 as a check on diplomatic and party reporting of developments.

See also PRAGUE CRISIS, 1968.

PROSKUROV, IVAN IOSIFOVICH (1907–1941). Proskurov was an aviator and intelligence officer. He served in the **Spanish Civil War** in 1936–1938 as a bomber pilot with the Republican forces and was decorated for attacks on German and Italian formations. On his return to Moscow in 1938, he was promoted to general, and the following year, he was made chief of the **GRU**. Proskurov inherited a demoralized service; hundreds of staff officers had been **executed**, and its elite corps of **illegals** had been decimated. Proskurov is recognized in official GRU histories for rebuilding his shattered service.

Proskurov provided **Joseph Stalin** with accurate briefings on German military strategy and intentions toward Poland and the Balkans in 1939–1940, based on reporting from agents within the Nazi foreign service. But Proskurov quickly lost Stalin's favor. Stalin blamed Proskurov for the failure of the Red Army in the Russo–Finnish "Winter War" of 1939–1940 and had him reassigned to a provincial command. In the first days of **World War II**, Proskurov and several other commanders—many of them veterans of the Spanish Civil War—were arrested. He was shot in October 1941 without a trial, as were more than 150 other "inconvenient witnesses" of Stalin's gross military incompetence. His wife and two daughters were **exiled** to Central Asia. He was posthumously rehabilitated in 1954, and his accomplishments in rebuilding the military intelligence service have been recognized.

See also BARBAROSSA.

PUGO, BORIS IVANOVICH (1942–1991). Born into a family of Latvian Old Bolsheviks, Pugo had a successful career in the Komsomol, the **KGB**, and the party. He joined the KGB and rose to head of the Latvian KGB in the mid-1980s. As Latvia's chief **Chekist**, Pugo had a reputation for prosecuting religious and ethnic **dissidents**. Even within the KGB, he was known as a hard-liner. Recognized as a tough, efficient bureaucrat, he was removed from the KGB and promoted to head of the Latvian **Communist Party** in the late 1980s. In 1990, Party General Secretary **Mikhail Gorbachev** made Pugo minister of internal affairs, responsible for the police and the **MVD**'s paramilitary Internal Troops. The appointment was one of the most disastrous the reformist leader ever made; it left an ideological enemy in charge of a key power ministry. Pugo, who did not accept Gorbachev's reforms, repaid his mentor by joining the cabal planning the **August putsch**. Following the failure of the putsch, Pugo and his wife committed suicide.

PUTIN, VLADIMIR VLADIMIROVICH (1952–). Putin, the current president of the Russian Federation, was an intelligence officer for 15 years. After serving in Leningrad with the **KGB**, he was posted to Dresden, East Germany, where he operated with the *Stasi* in collecting scientific and technical intelligence. Putin returned to Leningrad in 1990 with the rank of lieutenant colonel. He reportedly targeted Western businesspeople who had access to proprietary industrial information.

Putin was downsized out of the KGB in 1990 and worked for a former professor at his alma mater, Leningrad State University, and then in the Leningrad/St. Petersburg government (the city reverted to its pre-Soviet name after the dissolution of the Soviet Union). In St. Petersburg, Putin came to the attention of **Boris Yeltsin**'s presidential administration and was brought to Moscow in 1997. In 1998, he was appointed head of the **FSB**. In August 1999, Yeltsin made Putin prime minister; on the last day of that year, he was made interim president of the Russian Federation. Putin has since then won general elections with solid support from the Russian "silent majority." As president, he has led a second **Chechen War**, promising the Russian people to pursue terrorists without pause. He has also selectively moved to prosecute corrupt businesspeople who dominated Russian politics in the Yeltsin years.

Since becoming president, Putin has relied heavily on the **Russian intelligence services** and former KGB colleagues (the so-called *siloviki*), appointing many to senior posts in his administration. Putin is an admirer of former KGB chair and **Communist Party** General Secretary **Yuri Andropov**. He strongly believes that Russia needs a strong reformer who will use the security and intelligence services to accelerate Russia's reforms. Russian liberals are deeply troubled by the war in Chechnya, Crimea, and **Ukraine** and Putin's apparent willingness to ignore the law in prosecuting political enemies. Perhaps future historians will compare him to tsarist reformer **Petr Stolypin**, who combined repression with economic and political reform in the last decade of imperial power.

On becoming president again in 2012, Putin reinvented himself as an ardent Russian nationalist. Relations with the United States worsened dramatically as the media turned against the new American ambassador, Michael McFaul, in a scripted campaign. The American government was blamed for the dissident movement as the FSB took harder and harder steps against dissidents reminiscent of those of the KGB. Arrests, long periods of pretrial confinement, and jail sentences were doled out. Putin's public statements and those of his supporters in the press portrayed Russia as embattled and surrounded by Western enemies who supported dissidents as well as anti-Russian Georgians, Ukrainians, and Balts.

In 2014, following the defeat of a Putin ally in Ukraine, Russian irregular forces aided secessionist forces first in Crimea and then in the eastern Ukraine. Ukrainian government authority was evicted from Crimea, and **GRU** *Spetsnaz* officers are arming and leading a secessionist force against Ukrainian military forces. The Russian/secessionist forces are armed with modern Russian hardware, including artillery, armored fighting vehicles, and surface-to-air missiles. Observers put the number of Russian military advisers in Ukraine as high as 2,000.

Putin again used the media to portray himself and his country as fighting for the human rights of Russians. Russian dissidents and his critics in the West, however, see Putin's strategy as an effort to use chauvinism to win him support as the economy declines. This strategy has improved his popularity at home, as the recent struggles are seen as a legitimate effort to defend Russian rights in foreign countries and return Crimea and the historic Sevastopol naval base to Russia. Nevertheless, the new policy has had possibly disastrous implications for Russia's economy, as sanctions limit Moscow access to Western capital. While the last chapter of Putin's biography has not been written, it seems likely that a major theme of it will be his adroit use of the intelligence services.

R

RACHKOVSKIY, PETR (ca. 1850–?). One of the *Okhrana*'s most successful agent handlers was Petr Rachkovskiy, who headed the *Okhrana*'s Paris bureau from 1884 to 1902. Working with private detectives and the police in France and Switzerland, he disrupted the operations of socialist and anarchist groups. In 1886, Rachkovskiy's agents blew up a *Narodnaya volya* printing plant in Switzerland, making it appear to be the work of disaffected revolutionaries. He also played an important role in Franco–Russian diplomacy. He became an important contact of French Foreign Minister Theophile Declasse, arranging the clandestine meetings between French and Russian diplomats that led to a treaty between the two countries. Rachkovskiy's role in providing a clandestine diplomatic channel for his country was aped by the **KGB** in the 1960s and 1970s, when it provided **back channels** between Moscow and Bonn.

RADIO GAMES. A critical ingredient in the Soviet **counterintelligence** victory over the Germans in **World War II** was its use of *Radio igra*, or "radio games" (*Funkspiel* in German). The Soviet intelligence services created fictitious German ‚spy rings, often using captured and turned German agents who were placed in contact with German intelligence to feed the enemy misinformation. *Smersh* and the **NKGB** ran 183 operations involving fictitious agents, many of whom deceived German intelligence and operational staffs at key moments of the war.

In the most famous game, code-named "Monastery," the Soviets allowed their principal agent, Aleksandr Demyanov, to be captured and then recruited by the German military intelligence, who then parachuted him into Soviet occupied territory to act as their agent. Demyanov, under Soviet control and operating with the alias "Max," then created a fictitious political resistance movement in Moscow and provided the German armed forces with false and misleading information for years. At critical moments before the battles of Stalingrad and Kursk and the June 1944 Red Army offensive in Byelorussia, Monastery provided misleading "feed" material generated by the Soviet general staff as part of strategic deception. German military intelligence never realized that it had been deceived. In books written by German military intelligence veterans after the war, "Max" is cited as an important and verified source.

Moscow began another radio game in the summer of 1944 to convince German intelligence that a major Wehrmacht command, under Colonel Scherhorn, had survived the Soviet offensive and was operating independently in the forests of eastern Poland. Scherhorn had been recruited by *Smersh* after his capture and convincingly played the role, pleading for assistance from Berlin. Demyanov ("Max") was then used by Moscow to confirm the force's existence and resistance. Berlin believed this information and in the course of the war dropped 13 radio sets, 225 cargo packs, and 25 German staff officers to aid Scherhorn. Adolf Hitler maintained a personal interest in the fate of Scherhorn, who was promoted and decorated by Berlin in the last days of the Third Reich. The deception lasted to the very end of the war. Soviet participants were decorated; Scherhorn was released from captivity in 1949 and returned to Germany.

The **MGB** ran similar radio games with Western intelligence services and **émigré** movements following the war. In Poland, the MGB and its Polish colleagues took control of a resistance movement and enticed Western governments to provide it with financial support. The deception continued until a senior Polish intelligence officer defected to the West. As was the case with the radio games in World War II, the Soviet services showed great sophistication in their understanding of their adversaries.

See also MASKIROVKA.

RADO, SANDOR (1899–1981). Born Alexander Radolfi into a wealthy Hungarian Jewish family, Rado joined the Hungarian **Communist Party** in 1921 in time to take part in a bloody and unsuccessful insurrection. Living as an **émigré**, he joined Soviet intelligence in the early 1930s and was sent to Berlin to report on the Nazi movement. By 1933, with the Nazi victory, he was a wanted man again and was sent to Paris by the **GRU** to create an **illegal** *rezidentura*. Rado operated a left-wing publishing house and book service as a cover that employed six other GRU illegals.

Following the purge of GRU officers and illegals, Rado was sent to Switzerland by military intelligence as the illegal *rezident* to develop German sources. He was a successful spy chief, developing contacts with access to priceless information. He used a number of illegals, including **Ruth Werner**, Rachel Duebendorfer (his most important source), and Alexander Foote. The Rado organization provided thousands of accurate reports of German forces on the Eastern Front. Rado also passed on—apparently without knowing it—information from London that was fed to Alexander Foote. This information, reportedly drawn from **Ultra** reporting, complemented raw information from sources inside Germany.

Rado, whose code name "Dora" was a simple anagram of his name, had an impressive record. Between August 1941 and May 1944, he sent more than 5,500 messages to Moscow, an average of five messages a day. Among his most important sources of intelligence on German order of battle and strategy was Hans Oster, for many years deputy chief of the Abwehr.

In 1944, the Swiss police cracked down on Rado and his crew. Rado went into hiding first in Switzerland and then in France. He tried very hard to avoid being repatriated to Moscow, fearing that he would be blamed for the organization's collapse. On arrival in Moscow, he was convicted of espionage and served eight years of a 10-year sentence. On release, he returned to Budapest where he began a new career as a cartographer. He published several books and became a noted expert before his death in 1981.

RAIKHMAN, LEONID FEDOROVICH (1908–1990). One of the senior Soviet counterintelligence officers of the **NKVD**, Raikhman joined **OGPU** and took part in investigations of political dissent in the 1930s. He was promoted to the rank of lieutenant general by **Joseph Stalin** for, among other things, arranging the **Katyn** killings of Polish officers. A close associate of **Lavrenty Beria**, he was arrested first in 1952 as Stalin purged the service of Jews and then again in 1953 following his mentor's fall and served five years in prison. He was rehabilitated in 2003.

RAPAVA, AVKSENTIY NARIKIEVICH (1899–1955). Like **Joseph Stalin**, Rapava received his education in a Russian Orthodox Church seminary. He joined first the **Communist Party** and then, in 1925, the **OGPU**, becoming part of **Lavrenty Beria**'s team. His career took off when Beria went to Moscow to head the **NKVD** in 1938. Beria used Rapava to murder witnesses whom neither he nor Stalin wanted. He purged the Abkhazian area of Georgia in the late 1930s, arranging the death of Beria's old enemies in the region. In 1939, he arranged the murder of a Soviet diplomat and his wife at Stalin and Beria's command. Promoted in 1945 to lieutenant general, he served as NKVD and **MVD** boss in Georgia until 1948, when his fall began.

In 1948, it was discovered that Rapava's brother, an army colonel, had not perished in **World War II** but had been captured and was living in the West. Rapava was removed from state security and made Georgia's minister of justice. Only his friendship with Beria saved him from **execution**. In 1951, he was arrested as Stalin purged Georgia of Beria supporters. In April 1953, he was released from prison and given a senior party post in Georgia. His life took another turn four months later, when he was arrested as one of Beria's men. He was held in prison for two years, then was tried and shot in 1955.

Rapava was one of a number of Georgians who rose and then fell with Beria. Rapava served as Beria's eyes and ears in the Caucasus for 15 years. This made him vulnerable when Stalin turned against Beria in the early 1950s and again when Beria fell in the summer of 1953.

RASTVOROV, YURI ALEKSANDROVICH (1922–2003). A **KGB** lieutenant colonel stationed under diplomatic cover in Tokyo, Rastvorov **defected** to American intelligence in the fall of 1953. One of the first KGB foreign intelligence officers to defect, he provided details about the degree of Soviet penetration of Western intelligence, especially the scope of operations in Japan. Rastvorov later wrote a three-part series on KGB operations for *Life* magazine in 1954. He lived in the Washington, D.C., suburbs for many years and died only five days shy of the 50th anniversary of his defection. An account of his defection and life in the United States appeared in a two-part article in the *Washington Post*.

RAZVEDCHIK. The Russian word *razvedchik* is generally translated as "spy" or "agent." The word can also be translated as "reconnaissance agent" or "scout."

RAZVEDKA. The Russian word *razvedka* is often translated as "intelligence." A more correct translation would be "reconnaissance."

RED ORCHESTRA. Shortly after the German invasion of the Soviet Union, German radio **counterintelligence** picked up a number of Soviet intelligence stations broadcasting from occupied Europe and Germany itself. Noting how the stations seemed to respond to a director, the Germans called the network the *Rote Kappelle*, or Red Orchestra. This network of spies in Nazi-occupied Europe was organized and run by **GRU illegal Leopold Trepper** from 1938 to 1942. Trepper managed a series of espionage rings that had been cobbled together by the GRU and the **NKVD** in the 1930s. In Germany, the agents included **Harro Schulze-Boysen**, an air force intelligence officer, and **Arvid Harnack**, a senior economist in the German government, and a host of socially highly placed German citizens. When shown the first evidence of the Red Orchestra's work, Adolf Hitler was supposed to have said that Germany was superior to Russia in everything except espionage.

More than 100 ideologically motivated agents and a support staff collected critical military, political, and economic information on the Nazi war machine in Belgium (17 agents), France (35), Switzerland (17), and Germany (48). Prior to the Nazi invasion of the Soviet Union, the Red Orchestra provided dramatic evidence of Hitler's plans. **Joseph Stalin** ignored the warnings. During the first year of the Nazi–Soviet war, the Red Orchestra provided the Red Army general staff with important information about German plans and military industrial production. One report in early 1942 dealt with the movement of German fighters from France to bases supporting Army Group Center. Others dealt with production problems in German industry. **Sandor Rado**, operating from neutral Switzerland, commanded one of the important branches of the Red Orchestra and possessed some impeccable sources of information. Operating from Switzerland, this small organization had less to fear from Nazi counterintelligence.

German counterintelligence uncovered networks in Nazi-occupied Europe and Germany in early 1942. In Berlin, the fall of the organization was swift since many of the spies were friends or lovers and had participated together in **Communist Party** operations in the 1930s. In 1942, the networks in France and Belgium were quickly defeated. Almost all members of the Red Orchestra were arrested and executed. Both Schulze-Boysen and Harnack as well as their wives, who were active in the organization, were put to death.

RED TERROR. Vladimir Lenin and **Cheka** chief **Feliks Dzerzhinsky** ordered local Soviets to take violent "prophylactic measures" to prevent insurrections in early August 1918. These messages were followed by orders establishing concentration camps for right-wing and left-wing enemies of the regime. The terror intensified after 30 August, when Fanny Kaplan wounded Lenin in a botched assassination attempt. Within hours, the Cheka began shooting thousands of prisoners across Russia. Kaplan was shot without a trial in early September. According to recent historical estimates, between 10,000 and 15,000 men and women were shot, hanged, or drowned in the fall of 1918, including members of the former royal family, parliamentarians, and military officers, as well as anarchists and socialists. The number of people incarcerated in camps rose from approximately 16,000 in the summer of 1918 to more than 70,000 a year later.

Terror became a tactic of the embattled Bolshevik government, and prophylactic measures were used to **execute** potential enemies of the regime, from the palaces of the aristocracy to the poorest villages in the land. Whole categories of people became targets: members of the middle class, rich farmers, and clergy were killed because of their pasts. In June 1918, Lenin wrote to the head of the Petrograd Cheka, "We are in a war to the death. We must spur on the energy and mass character of the terror against the counterrevolutionaries." For Lenin, who was a student of the French Revolution and the Paris Commune of 1870–1871, revolutionary terror was a necessity. For the Soviet regime, the heritage of the Red Terror was impossible to erase. For **Joseph Stalin**, the mass killing of enemies in the **civil war** justified a new reign of terror in the 1930s—first against the peasantry and then within the **Communist Party**.

REDENS, STANISLAV FRANTSEVICH (1892–1940). An Old Bolshevik, Redens was a Polish worker who joined the **Bolshevik Party** in 1914 and entered the **Cheka** in 1918. He was **Joseph Stalin**'s brother-in-law, which initially accelerated his career but in the end led to his **execution**. Redens had married the sister of Stalin's second wife, Nadezhda Alliluyeva, and remained for many years a member of Stalin's small inner circle. He served as the chief of the security service in Ukraine during **collectivization** and the famine of 1933–1934, and as a reward he became head of the service in Moscow from 1934 to 1938.

In January 1938, Redens was demoted and dispatched to Kazakhstan. Arrested in November 1938, he moldered in jail for 13 months. He was tried for treason in January 1940 and shot a month later. His arrest and execution have been explained by Stalin's decision to reduce the authority of his in-laws in party politics. Redens's Polish nationality may have hastened his fall as well: almost no Polish or Latvian "Old Chekists" survived the purges. The Russian archives also indicate that **Nikolai Yezhov** denounced Redens under torture and that this convinced Stalin that Redens should be executed. Redens's wife was not formally informed of his death, and she and her children continued to visit Stalin at his Moscow dacha.

REDL, ALFRED (1864–1913). Redl, a colonel on the general staff of the Austro-Hungarian imperial army, was recruited to spy for Russia by a Russian military intelligence officer. He was run by the Russian **military attaché** in Vienna. Redl was in charge of Austrian intelligence operations inside Russia; needless to say, his agents did not do well. He also had access to Austrian war and mobilization plans. The Redl case was a major victory for Russian intelligence in the run-up to **World War I**. It allowed the Russian authorities to detain more than 100 Austrian agents operating inside Russia, and it provided the Russian general staff with detailed information about Vienna's war plans.

Redl's motivation in serving Moscow was complex: he reportedly was compromised as a homosexual while serving in an exchange program in Russia, but he was also paid for information. He also spied for Italy, providing intelligence information under the cryptonym "K.K." According to recent literature about his case, he became increasingly dependent on Russian and Italian money for his lifestyle. Redl, when confronted with proof of his treachery on 25 May 1913, was allowed to commit suicide by his colleagues in the general staff. The story of Colonel Alfred Redl has spawned a number of myths. For Austrians, he was a Judas whose treason hastened the end of the Austro-Hungarian Empire. Former Director of Central Intelligence Allen Dulles described Redl as "the arch-traitor" in his history of intelligence. John

Osborne's play *A Patriot for Me* was based on Redl's treachery. Istvan Szabo's celebrated film *Colonel Redl*, which was based on Osborne's play, won the 1984 Oscar for the best foreign film.

REES, GORONWYN (1909–1979). A noted British academic and military officer, Rees was apparently recruited for Soviet intelligence in the late 1930s by his friend **Guy Burgess**. While Rees claimed that he was never an active Soviet agent and had broken with Moscow at the time of the Molotov–Ribbentrop Pact in 1939, the Soviet archives suggest he was an active agent with the code names "Fleet" and "Gross." Burgess was reportedly so concerned with Rees's ability to inform on the relationship that he asked the **NKVD** controller to have him killed.

REGIME CHANGE. A preoccupation of the regimes of **Vladimir Lenin** and **Joseph Stalin** was the threat of regime change from enemies at home and abroad. First the **Cheka** and later other security services targeted, penetrated, and manipulated **émigré** operations. Stalin, during the *Yezhovshchina*, ordered the **NKVD** to target the Polish Military Opposition, a movement that had ceased to exist some 20 years earlier. Literally tens of thousands of Soviet Poles were executed for belonging to the nonexistent organization.

President **Vladimir Putin** seems likewise centered on the threat of regime change, and this seems to be driving his anti-American policies. It is hard to know whether this comes from his (mis)reading of the Arab Spring, where the "street" precipitated regime change; concern with U.S. ties to known **dissidents**; or his work in the KGB with **Yuri Andropov**. Whatever the root causes, he has adopted a far harsher policy toward dissidents and toward the United States. Regime spokesmen have emphasized the ties between U.S. diplomats and dissidents in interviews reminiscent of the **Cold War**. Moreover, dissent since 2012 has been increasingly punished with fines, long terms of pretrial incarceration, and short prison sentences.

REILLY, SIDNEY GEORGE [ROSENBLUM, SHLOMO ABRAMOVICH] (1873–1925). One of the most mythical enemies of the early Bolshevik regime, Reilly was never the "ace of spies" portrayed in books and films; rather, he was one of the world's greatest con artists, an arms dealer, a murderer, and a three-time bigamist. As an arms dealer, Reilly engineered deals for a variety of German and then Russian companies. In 1918, he was recruited by the British Secret Intelligence Service (SIS) to mount a coup against **Vladimir Lenin**'s government. The coup, which was amateurishly managed, failed and helped generate a massive **Red Terror** that claimed thousands of lives. Following the failure of the plot, Reilly fled Russia and was awarded the Military Cross by the British government.

Reilly was involved in **exile** Russian politics in the early 1920s and became a close friend of exile politician **Boris Savinkov**. Both Reilly and Savinkov became pawns in a **counterintelligence** game that was part of the *maskirovka* tactics used by the Soviets. The **OGPU** had created a fictitious émigré organization, the **Trust**, which purportedly was ready to launch a counterrevolution inside Russia and topple the communist regime. First Savinkov and then Reilly were lured back into the Soviet Union to meet representatives of the Trust. Reilly was captured by the OGPU on entering Russia, interrogated, and then shot. The Soviet intelligence service did not formally acknowledge Reilly's capture and **execution** for decades, keeping alive the myth that he had been a Bolshevik agent from the start.

Reilly's legend as a super spy was kept alive by his former friends in SIS. Ian Fleming, when he sought a model for James Bond, chose Reilly. In reality, Reilly was a far better con man than he was a spy.

REVOLUTION OF 1905. Often referred to by historians as the "dress rehearsal" for the **Revolution of November 1917**, the 1905 action was the product of the tsarist regime's gross incompetence and mismanagement of its military and its total misunderstanding of the mood of the mass of workers and peasants. The regime survived because of Prime Minister **Petr Stolypin**'s ability to rally loyal troops and the revolutionary movement's lack of cohesion and direction.

In 1904, the regime decided to pursue a fight with the emerging Japanese empire: what one minister referred to as "a short, glorious war." But the **Russo–Japanese War** demonstrated the incompetence of the regime and set in motion events that led to a national insurrection. The war opened with a Japanese surprise attack on the Russian fleet at Port Arthur, China. Things went from bad to worse in Manchuria, where the war was fought, and on the streets of Moscow and St. Petersburg. In January 1905, a march to the Winter Palace in St. Petersburg by workers, organized by Father **Georgi Gapon**, an *Okhrana* agent, was suppressed with violence by imperial troops. The reaction was massive urban and rural violence. In St. Petersburg, workers' soviets (councils) took control of much of the capital. Led by the charismatic **Leon Trotsky**, the St. Petersburg soviet seemed to signal a new form of revolutionary democracy. Strikes in many industrial areas were followed by military mutinies, including the revolt on the battleship *Potemkin*.

The violence spread to industrial cities and then to the agricultural heartland; peasants burned manors and seized land. Only the competence of Stolypin saved the regime and prevented the rural riots from spinning totally out of control. Loyal troops reined in the violence; more than 1,300 rebels in rural areas were sentenced to death, and even more perished in fights with troops. After heavy fighting, urban soviets were defeated and their leaders arrested, jailed, and **exiled**. Trotsky established his reputation in his trial, in which he attacked both the prosecution and the regime. He was sentenced to exile in Siberia, from which he quickly escaped.

The tsarist regime learned precious little from 1905. Reform measures were doled out too little and too late. The *Okhrana*, which had organized the disastrous march to the Winter Palace, did not improve as a **counterintelligence** organization. Less than five years later, an *Okhrana* double agent would kill Stolypin, removing the one man possibly capable of saving the regime. However, the 1905 Revolution demonstrated to Bolshevik leader **Vladimir Lenin** that a Russian revolution could succeed only with a competent and tightly organized party. Lenin and Trotsky, who flirted with the **Bolshevik Party** between 1905 and 1917, saw the keys to success as organization and violence. Their model was not totally Marxist; rather, it was more Jacobin, from the Paris of the French Revolution of 1789–1793.

REVOLUTION OF NOVEMBER 1917. The revolution that brought the **Bolshevik Party** to power in Petrograd in November 1917 was little more than a military putsch. The provisional government that had come to power following the March revolution had little credibility in the countryside. Divided among radical and liberal parties, it had lost control of the army garrison in Petrograd and lacked any security service to protect it from enemies on the left and the right. In Petrograd, the Soviet, composed of radical parties but dominated by the Bolsheviks, occupied the power vacuum left by the death of imperial authority.

Vladimir Lenin saw strategic and tactical opportunities in the situation in Petrograd. He ordered that his senior subordinates, including **Leon Trotsky** and **Feliks Dzerzhinsky**, arm Red Guards to form an organized Bolshevik militia capable of seizing power. Lenin also insisted on tight operational security in the run-up to the putsch. Agents of the Bolsheviks, called commissars, worked with naval and army units around the capital. This ensured that the party would not face an organized resistance. The storming of the Winter Palace on the evening of 7 November went off like clockwork in large part because of Lenin's planning and the gross incompetence of his adversaries.

The November revolution did not create Soviet power in Russia; it took five years of **civil war** and several million dead to accomplish that. Rather, the events of 7 November signaled the Bolsheviks' willingness to seize and hold power by any means necessary. Many of the leaders of the November revolution were appointed to the new Soviet security service, the **Cheka**, in December 1917.

REZIDENT. The Russian word for chief of the intelligence presence in a city or country is *rezident* ("resident"). Both the **KGB** and the **GRU** used the term. (The American equivalent is chief of station, or COS). KGB residents had tremendous power in Soviet missions during the **Joseph Stalin** era, often surpassing that of ambassadors. After 1953, there was a gradual change, and "straight" diplomats—as opposed to intelligence officers—gained more authority. The Soviet services often appointed the senior **illegal** in a country as "illegal *rezident*," with the authority to take over existing intelligence networks in case of war or a breakdown of diplomatic relations. **William Fisher**, for example, was the illegal *rezident* in New York City from 1949 to 1957. GRU and NKVD networks in occupied Europe were managed by illegal *rezidents*, many of whom were not commissioned officers in the Soviet services.

See also REZIDENTURA.

REZIDENTURA. The Russian word for intelligence station is *rezidentura* ("residency"). Both the **KGB** and the **GRU** used the term. KGB *rezidenturas* were compartmentalized into "lines." Line PR (Political Intelligence) was responsible for the collection of political and economic intelligence and **active measures**. Line KR (**Counterintelligence**) was responsible for the protection of the Russian diplomatic colony and for penetration of hostile intelligence and security services. Many Line KR officers began their career in the domestic counterintelligence components of the KGB. **Line X** (Scientific and Technical Intelligence) recruited and ran agents with access to scientific and commercial information.

Line N (**Illegal** Support) supported the operation of illegals. It recruited agents with access to official documents and archives necessary for the identity of illegals. Line N officers also maintained contact with illegals through indirect means of communication, such as dead drops.

KGB and GRU *rezidenturas* had large support staffs, including dedicated code clerks. *Rezidenturas* also conducted **signal intelligence** operations from embassies, consulates, and the personal residences of diplomats.

See also REZIDENT.

REZUN, VLADIMIR BOGDANOVICH (1948–). A **GRU** officer serving in Geneva, Rezun **defected** to the West in 1978. He has since written a number of accounts of his life in the Red Army and the GRU under the nom de plume "Viktor Suvorov"; the name was taken from one of the greatest tsarist marshals. The books have been published in a number of languages; his account of life in the military intelligence service, *Aquarium*, has been published in Russian. Rezun was sentenced to death in absentia following his defection.

RING OF FIVE. The Soviet intelligence service referred to **Donald Maclean**, **Guy Burgess**, **Kim Philby**, **Anthony Blunt**, and **John Cairncross** as the Ring of Five or the magnificent five. These five agents had penetrated the inner sanctums of the British establishment and over more than two decades produced tens of thousands of British, American, and North Atlantic Treaty organization classified documents. Their damage to the West, however, far exceeded this production: they sowed deep distrust between the American and British security and intelligence services and disrupted all intelligence efforts against the Soviet Union in the critical first years of the **Cold War**.

RIUTIN, MARTIMIAN NIKITICH (1890–1937). A minor party functionary, Riutin drafted a "platform" in 1932 that called for the removal of party leader **Joseph Stalin** to halt the political violence in the countryside. Riutin also claimed that Stalin had served as an **informer** for the tsarist police. After Riutin's arrest, Stalin called for his **execution** for **terrorism**, a demand that was rejected by the rest of the leadership and the **OGPU**. Riutin was sentenced to a term of 10 years in a prison camp but was shot in 1937 after **Nikolai Yezhov** took control of the security service. His wife and two sons were also executed.

Some scholars believe that the Riutin platform spurred Stalin's decision to purge the Soviet party and society. Evidence that a significant portion of the **Communist Party** had rejected his leadership could have only intensified the Soviet leader's paranoia. Other scholars believe that Riutin's manuscript, which challenged the moral authority of the Stalinist leadership, was a cause of the terror. The party leadership and the OGPU's rejection of his demand that Riutin be shot probably also increased Stalin's determination to make the police a sharper sword for repression. All the members of Riutin's circle were shot, as were hundreds of people convicted of being part of his cabal.

ROMANOV FAMILY, MURDER OF. On the evening of 16–17 July 1918, at the express command of **Vladimir Lenin**, a squad of **Chekists** murdered the deposed Romanov tsar along with his wife and five children in the basement of the Ipatyev House in Yekaterinburg (renamed Sverdlovsk from 1920 to 1991). Lenin ordered their **execution** to preclude their liberation by an advancing White Army. The firing squad included seven Russian and six Latvian Chekists. It was commanded by Yakov Yurovsky, who believed that he was avenging the victims of anti-Semitic **pogroms**. Contrary to legend, there were no survivors.

Yurovsky later gave a revolver used in the murder of the royal family to the Museum of the Revolution in Moscow's Red Square, and he died in his bed without remorse. The Ipatyev House became a shrine for many Russian Orthodox Christians, and at the order of **KGB Chair Yuri Andropov**, it was torn down in the 1970s. Following the collapse of the Soviet Union, the Romanovs' remains were interred in St. Petersburg, and they are now considered martyrs by the Russian Church.

Explaining the murder in his memoirs, **Leon Trotsky** wrote, "The execution of the tsar's family was needed not only to frighten, horrify, and dishearten the enemy, but also in order to shake up our own ranks, to show them there was no turning back, that ahead lay either complete victory or complete ruin." Trotsky's comments explain the **Red Terror** as well: the regime acted not only to terrorize its enemies but also to somehow strengthen the resolve of a small militant party.

ROSENBERG, JULIUS (1918–1953), AND ROSENBERG, ETHEL (1915–1953). The most divisive espionage case of the **Cold War** involved a husband and wife who were either deeply engaged in Soviet intelligence or innocent martyrs of a monstrous Red Scare. Julius Rosenberg approached the **NKVD** for the first time in 1942 through **Jacob Golos**, a Soviet **illegal** responsible for much of the NKVD's espionage on American soil. Over the next five years, Rosenberg managed 10 agents, most of whom were engineers. All willingly provided the Soviets with information about classified weapons programs. Rosenberg also recruited David Greenglass, his wife's brother, a U.S. Army machinist at Los Alamos. Greenglass later provided information on the high explosive lens, a piece of the atomic bomb puzzle. In deciphered Soviet intelligence traffic, Rosenberg had the code names "Antenna" and "Liberal," while Greenglass had the code name "Caliber."

Ethel Rosenberg played a less important role than her husband, according to many studies of the case. She was knowledgeable about his espionage, helped and encouraged his work, and served as a lookout during meetings with Soviet intelligence officers. Her name was not encrypted in Soviet intelligence cables, signifying that the NKVD did not consider her an enrolled agent like her husband. NKVD officers did, however, recognize her as a member of a ring of communists and communist sympathizers who were spying for the Soviet cause.

Material from a variety of reliable sources now conclusively shows that the Rosenbergs were the center of a ring of agents that provided the Soviet Union with technical and military information, including some information on the nuclear program. They were not, however, as important to the Soviet covert intelligence attack on the nuclear weapons program as either **Klaus Fuchs** or **Ted Hall**.

The Rosenbergs were Stalinists who believed they were serving an international movement while betraying the interests of their own country. Other members of the ring, as well as **Morris and Lona Cohen**, who supported their espionage, fled to the Soviet Union. It was the fate of the Rosenbergs to wait too long before fleeing the United States, and they were arrested by the

Federal Bureau of Investigation in June 1950. Their trial became an international cause célèbre, as many liberals and leftists believed the trials were politically motivated. The prosecution relied heavily on the testimony of David Greenglass while refusing to use evidence from top-secret intercepts of Soviet intelligence messages in open court. This decision subsequently raised questions about the trial and the subsequent verdict. The jury's verdict of guilt and the judge's death sentence created an international movement for clemency that the Soviet intelligence services exploited to discredit the United States. The Rosenbergs were executed in 1953.

The Rosenberg case revolves around three distinct issues: Were they Soviet spies? Did they receive a fair trial? Was the death sentence justified? Almost all the documentary evidence indicates they were committed spies. Information on the trial and sentencing procedure suggests there were considerable irregularities, in part the result of an overzealous prosecution, in part due to an incompetent defense. The sentence reflected both the tenor of the times and the desire of the judge and the prosecution team to use the trial to send a political message.

See also ENORMOZ; FEKLISOV, ALEKSANDR SEMENOVICH (1914–2007).

ROZENBLIUM, ANNA ANATOLIEVNA (ca. 1900–?). An **NKVD** doctor at Lefortovo prison, Rozenblium nursed tortured prisoners back to health and shielded many from torture sessions. She documented for the NKVD that 49 prisoners had been tortured to death in the prison in the short time she labored there. In January 1939, she was arrested on **Lavrenty Beria**'s orders, tortured, and sentenced to a forced labor camp for 15 years. Rozenblium somehow survived the **gulag** and returned to testify against her tormentors in trials of members of Beria's circle. Referred to as "the good fairy of Lefortovo," she exemplified the courage of the old Russian intelligentsia, which Beria sought to destroy first in Georgia and then in Moscow. Her fortitude was unusual, and there is little evidence that other officials in the Stalinist system ever demonstrated the moral courage of Anna Rozenblium.

RUSLANOVA, LIDIA ANDREYEVNA (1900–1973). A well-known folksinger, Ruslanova entertained Soviet troops close to the fighting and was close to Marshal **Georgi Zhukov.** In an order of the day, Zhukov awarded her a decoration. **Stalin** saw this as proof of Zhukov's imperial ambition, and in 1949, she and her husband, Lieutenant General Vladimir Kryukov, were sent to the **gulag,** where they remained until well after Stalin's death. The **MGB** under **Viktor Abakumov**'s direction falsified evidence to convict the couple and embarrass Zhukov, who was in the dictator's bad graces. According to witness, she emerged from the camps thin, gray, and stooped. She continued to perform until her death, never mentioning in public her imprisonment.

RUSSIAN INTELLIGENCE SERVICES. Following the 1991 **August putsch**, Russian President **Boris Yeltsin** began to systematically dismantle the **KGB**. Over the next year, several different services were created, all of which reported to the president through a newly established National Security Council. The *Sluzhba vneshnei razvedki* (Foreign Intelligence Service), or **SVR**, was built from the First Chief Directorate. The *Federalnaya sluzhba bezopasnosti* (Federal Security Service), or **FSB**, includes the **counterintelligence** and security components of the KGB. The *Federalnoe agentsvo pravitelstevennoi svyazi i informatatsii* (Federal Agency for Government Communications and Information), or FAPSI, included KGB components responsible for government communications, and **signals intelligence** was initially created as an independent agency but was placed under tighter presidential control in 2003. The *Prezidenskaya sluzhba bezopasnosti* (Presidential Security Service), or PSB, was drawn from the KGB components responsible for leadership protection.

Other security services were created to deal with technical counterintelligence and **counterterrorism**. The new Russian services are robust and well financed. For example, the FSB is by far the largest security service in the world, except for the People's Republic of China. While president of the Russian Federation, Yeltsin maintained control of these organizations through the appointment process. He appointed KGB veteran **Vladimir Putin** to head the FSB in 1998 to intensify **surveillance** of personal opponents. (One wonders if a **Communist Party** general secretary would have acted any differently.)

As president, Putin immediately began to place his mark on the new Russian intelligence community. **Leadership Protection** and signals intelligence components were renamed and reassigned as subunits of the Office of the President. The new **Special Communications Service** was placed within the newly minted **Federal Protective Service** in 2004. Putin from the first took great care in promoting close associates to leadership positions in all the services and using alumni of the services (*siloviki*) to ensure the political reliability of the intelligence service, the government national security bureaucracy, and his political party. The new intelligence services have acquired considerable power at the local, regional, and national levels and have been implicated in several political assassinations, including that of journalist **Anna Politkovskaya**. One critic of the Putin regime told British journalist Benjamin Judah, "Russia doesn't have the KGB. Russia isn't that lucky."

RUSSO–JAPANESE WAR (1904–1905). What started as a "glorious little war" to win support for the tsarist regime ended in catastrophic defeat that almost spelled the end of the House of Romanov. The Russian military intelligence service and the *Okhrana* were poorly prepared for war. The *Okhrana* was unable to counter Japanese intelligence operations in Moscow and St. Petersburg or in Manchuria. The military intelligence department of the general staff had only a very poor understanding of the Japanese enemy, of whom they were totally contemptuous. The best examples of military intelligence incompetence were their failures to foresee the Japanese attack on Port Arthur and the imperial fleet's doom at Tsushima.

The Japanese fleet struck Port Arthur, China, catching the Russian navy unaware and unprepared. Japanese spies inside Port Arthur apparently produced excellent order-of-battle information on the Russian forces. The Japanese specialized in recruiting low-level employees and servants who could provide intelligence about the military. When the fleet left the Baltic to relieve the garrison at Port Arthur, it had been given no information about the Japanese order of battle. The fleet got into its first action with a group of British fishing boats, which Russian commanders believed were Japanese boats. The so-called Battle of Dogger Bank, which caused a major diplomatic crisis with Britain, resulted from the fleet's blindness—a wonderful example of the fog of war.

Russian intelligence poorly prepared the tsarist commanders for war in Asia. With little real knowledge of the Japanese navy or army, it lacked basic data about Japanese military units or warships. Military **counterintelligence** was weak as well. In contrast, the Japanese had agents within the Russian base at Port Arthur who provided critical intelligence for the Japanese surprise attack that began the war. Inside the Russian empire, Japanese agents monitored developments though such mundane means as reading the Russian press. They also liaised with other **military attachés** to initiate contacts with revolutionaries such as Father **Georgi Gapon**. The Japanese were willing to support violence by revolutionary parties to force St. Petersburg to divert troops from the front to quell internal revolution. The *Okhrana*'s dogged interest in the subversion of the domestic enemy blinded it to the greater threat from Japan.

See also REVOLUTION OF 1905.

RYAN (RAKETNO-YADERNOYE NAPADENIE). In 1981, Moscow began a worldwide program for the collection of information about a U.S. nuclear surprise attack. Under the program, named *Raketno yadernoye napadenie* (Nuclear Rocket Attack), or *RYaN*, the **KGB** and **GRU** *rezidenturas* were ordered to collect and submit information about U.S. attack plans. For the next several years, *RYaN* became the Soviet intelligence services' priority, and it created a **war scare** inside the Soviet political leadership. In 1983, misleading information convinced Moscow that Washington was planning a surprise nuclear attack to coincide with a North Atlantic Treaty Organization (NATO) military exercise. The London *rezidentura* was told to look for evidence of British complicity, such as the increasing slaughter of cattle and the movement of the royal family out of London.

RYaN information created a crisis mentality in the Kremlin in the fall of 1983. Soviet chief of state **Yuri Andropov** was convinced that NATO would use a military exercise as cover for a covert nuclear strike. KGB Colonel **Oleg Gordievskiy**, a British source in the *rezidentura*, provided the West with information about *RyaN* that allowed the British and American governments to defuse the crisis. British Prime Minister Margaret Thatcher also used Gordievskiy's information about Soviet foreign policy to persuade U.S. President Ronald Reagan to pursue a more nuanced policy toward the Soviet Union.

The *RYaN* program produced a bimonthly report for the political leadership for another seven years. **SVR** chief **Yevgeny Primakov** finally canceled the *RYaN* program in November 1991, putting an end to a "purely formal but mandatory" report. The *RYaN* crisis, however, demonstrated the weakness of KGB **analysis**.

RYASNOI, VASILII STEPANOVICH (1904–1995). Ryasnoi was transferred from **Communist Party** work to the security service during the height of the *Yezhovshchina*, and he rose quickly in the service. During **World War II**, he served in Ukraine, and he was later given responsibility for the **MVD**'s campaign against "bandits" (anti-Soviet **partisans**) in the western Ukraine and the Baltics. Following **Joseph Stalin**'s death, he served as chief of foreign intelligence and then chief of the security service in Moscow. He was expelled from the service in 1955 and died in obscurity.

RYUMIN, MIKHAIL (1913–1954). Ryumin began his career in the **NKVD** working on massive forced labor projects. During **World War II**, he served in military **counterintelligence** and was transferred to Moscow as an interrogator. Facing personal ruin because of a security lapse, he denounced his boss, **Viktor Abakumov**, as an enemy in a letter to **Joseph Stalin**. Ryumin apparently told Stalin that Abakumov was not pursuing the search for traitors inside the party with zeal. Following Abakumov's arrest, Ryumin was given responsibility for cases of critical importance to Stalin as chief of the Department of Interrogation of Specially Important Cases. He served as de facto deputy chief of the **MGB** as a lieutenant general of state security in 1952, investigating the **Doctor's Plot** and torturing doctors suspected of ties to Western intelligence. Stalin's creature, Ryumin was used by the Soviet leader to create a case that would implicate the senior **Communist Party** leadership and pave the way for a purge. He was arrested immediately following Stalin's death in March 1953, made a full confession, and was **executed** after a secret trial.

S

SAKHAROV, ANDREI DMITRYEVICH (1921–1989). The father of the Soviet hydrogen bomb, Sakharov became one of the two main **dissident** targets of the **KGB** in the 1970s, along with **Aleksandr Solzhenitsyn**. Sakharov, who served unselfishly as a mentor to political and religious dissidents in the 1970s, received the KGB code name "Asket" (Ascetic) for his involvement in dissident causes. In the 1970s, Sakharov and his wife, Helen Bonner, edited the *Chronicle of Current Events*, a *samizdat* publication that chronicled the fate of Soviet dissidents. Sakharov and Bonner had tremendous civil courage. They risked everything to protect the political outcasts of Soviet society.

In 1975, Sakharov received the Nobel Peace Prize, which he was forbidden to travel to Stockholm to receive. Under KGB chair **Yuri Andropov**'s direction, his apartment and dacha were bugged, and agents provocateur were inserted into his inner circle. Andropov at **Communist Party** Politburo meetings went as far as to describe Sakharov as "public enemy number one." In early 1980, following Sakharov's public denunciation of the invasion of Afghanistan, he and his wife were **exiled** to Gorkiy, a closed provincial city to the east of Moscow. His treatment in Gorkiy was atrocious. His wife was denied access to physicians for her eye disease. But in December 1986, the KGB installed a telephone in Sakharov's apartment so that **Mikhail Gorbachev** could call with the news that he could return to Moscow. In the last three years of his life, Sakharov played a critical role in the development of nascent secular political institutions. Until his death, he quietly nurtured political reformers and dissidents interested in creating a law-based state.

Andropov and the KGB's persecution of Sakharov and his wife discredited the Soviet Union in the eyes of westerners and many Soviet intellectuals. The dissident movement in the Soviet Union was at most a small and inchoate group and never presented a danger to the Communist Party. The prosecution of Sakharov and a Nobel laureate like Solzhenitsyn did the Soviet Union far more harm than good.

SAMIZDAT. To avoid Soviet censorship, Soviet **dissidents** produced *samizdat* (self-publishing) political documents, which were handwritten, mimeographed, or photocopied. The most famous *samizdat* publication was the *Chronicle of Current Events*, which tracked the dissident movement in the Soviet Union. *Samizdat* included religious tracts as well as popular literature. Many Russian intellectuals who had written only "for the drawer" used *samizdat* to publish their thoughts. The **KGB** was never totally able to shut down *samizdat*. Nevertheless, the KGB and conservatives in the **Communist Party** leadership reacted strongly to the problem posed for them by the publication of a few thousand pages of material.

SAVCHENKO, SERGEI ROMANOVICH (1904–1966). After almost two decades of service in the **Border Guards** Directorate, Savchenko was transferred to the Ukrainian **NKVD** in 1938 as **Lavrenty Beria** purged the security service. During the **Great Patriotic War**, Savchenko worked behind Nazi lines in Ukraine and was promoted to lieutenant general in 1945. He was highly decorated, receiving the Order of **Lenin** and the Order of the Red Banner, among other decorations. From 1949 to 1953, he served as chief of foreign intelligence and from 1951 to 1953 as deputy minister of state security. Savchenko was a mediocre chief; he had no previous experience in foreign espionage, and he was concerned about arousing the ire of Beria. After **Joseph Stalin**'s death and Beria's purge in 1953, Savchenko was demoted. In 1955, he was ousted from the **KGB** for incompetence.

SAVINKOV, BORIS VIKTOROVICH (1879–1925). As a member of the **Battle Organization** of the Socialist Revolutionary Party, Savinkov carried out a number of terrorist acts under the direction of **Yevno Azev**. After being imprisoned in a Sevastopol prison, Savinkov escaped with the aid of a **dissident** sailor and made his way 300 kilometers in an open boat to Romania. Following the February 1917 revolution, Savinkov returned to Russia to serve as deputy minister of war in the provisional government. The **civil war** forced Savinkov to **emigrate**, and he worked with a number of Western governments against Moscow. As a result of a clever **Cheka** provocation, the **Trust**, Savinkov was lured back into the country in 1924. He was immediately arrested, and he made a full confession of his crimes at a public trial. Shortly after his trial, Savinkov committed suicide or was murdered in the **Lubyanka** prison.

Savinkov was a revolutionary polymath, at home in terrorist planning rooms as well as Winston Churchill's offices. His novel *Pale Horse* is an excellent description of the prerevolutionary terrorist movement.

SCHULZE-BOYSEN, HARO MAX WILHELM GEORGE (1909–1942). As a young man, Schulze-Boysen was arrested and badly beaten by Nazi thugs in the first days of Adolf Hitler's regime. Only his family's position (his father was a naval officer) and the fact that Admiral von Tirpitz was a kinsman saved him from a concentration camp. In 1935, he and his wife, Libertas, made contact with Arvid Harnack and his circle and a year later with Soviet intelligence. Part of the core of the **Red Orchestra** (*Rote Kapelle*), he provided detailed information from his post in the Air Ministry about German plans for Operation **Barbarossa** and the Stalingrad operation.

The Schulze-Boysens were reckless, often putting up anti-Nazi posters in Berlin, at the same time as they were part of a Soviet intelligence network. They were caught following the decoding of some of their messages, but they were already under Gestapo suspicion. They were tried on 19 December 1942 and executed three days later.

SECOND CHIEF DIRECTORATE. *See* KGB ORGANIZATION.

SECRET SPEECH. On the evening of 25 February 1956, in what became known as the Secret Speech, **Nikita Khrushchev** spoke for several hours at the 20th Congress of the **Communist Party** on **Joseph Stalin**'s "Cult of Personality." The speech was not approved by Khrushchev's colleagues, who feared the opening of the historical record. Khrushchev told 2,000 party leaders that Stalin used the security services to imprison and murder millions of party officials and military officers who had aroused his suspicion. He noted that almost all those who perished had been innocent. Khrushchev quoted documents in which Stalin ordered the police to torture confessions out of doctors accused of poisoning party leaders. The Secret Speech, however, did not absolve the Old Bolsheviks shot in the 1930s. It made no mention of **Leon Trotsky**'s life or death, and it did not discuss **collectivization**. Not all enemies of the people warranted forgiveness.

Khrushchev's speech was classified top secret but reached the West through the machinations of the Central Intelligence Agency. It was broadcast back into the Soviet bloc, and the speech was printed in several languages. Nevertheless, Soviet citizens were not legally permitted to read the speech until 1988. Following the speech, the Central Committee mandated severe punishments for party members who questioned the role of the party during the purges. According to a recent account of the immediate post-Stalin period, thousands of people were arrested for "slandering the Soviet system," for discussing the Secret Speech.

Khrushchev intended for the speech to destroy Stalin's reputation and to break the authority of those in the party who wished to continue to use Stalinist methods. Despite his efforts to limit the impact of the speech, it raised the consciousness of a number of young party officials, such as **Mikhail Gorbachev** and **Aleksandr Yakovlev**, who crafted the *glasnost* campaign of the 1980s.

SEKSOT. Russian security service acronym for secret coworker (i.e., informant).

SELIVANOVSKIY, NIKOLAI NIKOLAALEVICH (1902–1997). **Viktor Abakumov**'s most important deputy in *Smersh*, Selivanovskiy began his career in military counterintelligence in 1923 and worked in the 1930s in foreign intelligence. During the siege of **Stalingrad**, Selivanovskiy served as the military counterintelligence chief, reporting on a daily basis to Abakumov and **Joseph Stalin** about the battle. His reports were quite candid about both the military situation and the Red Army commanders, noting arrests and executions of spies and traitors, as well as the establishment of espionage networks in the German rear. Following the battle, he became Abakumov's deputy in *Smersh*.

Selivanovskiy was Abakumov's choice to head military counterintelligence and for deputy minister when he was promoted to head the Ministry of State Security. Following his chief's arrest in 1951, Selivanovskiy was arrested but pretended to suffer from mental illnesses. He escaped prosecution and was allowed to retire on grounds of poor health. He outlived Abakumov by 43 years.

SEMENOV, SEMEN MARKOVICH (1911–1986). Semenov was sent to the Massachusetts Institute of Technology in 1937 after joining the **NKVD** to strengthen his cover as well as to learn engineering. He graduated in 1940 and then adopted a new cover in New York as an engineer assigned to the Amtorg Trading Company. Semenov was one of the most successful Soviet case officers in collecting scientific and technical intelligence. He is described by his colleagues and agents as a warm and sympathetic figure, known to his agents as "Sam." He ran agents within the American nuclear program, code-named *Enormoz*, for which he was decorated. After leaving New York, he served in Paris and in Moscow as a lieutenant colonel. He was fired in 1953 as part of the anti-Semitic purge of the foreign intelligence directorate. He was rehabilitated in the 1970s.

SEMICHASTNIY, VLADIMIR EFIMOVICH (1924–2001). Semichastniy entered the Komsomol (Young Communist League) apparatus and then the **Communist Party**, where he rose quickly as an ally of **Aleksandr Shelepin**. He proved his ideological credentials as chief of the Komsomol by leading a merciless attack on Nobel laureate Boris Pasternak in 1958, accusing Pasternak of writing *Doctor Zhivago* at the behest of Western intelligence. In January 1961, Semichastniy was appointed **KGB** chair—the youngest leader of the security service ever. He worked closely with Shelepin in carrying out the **October 1964 coup**. When **Nikita Khrushchev** returned from the Crimea, Semichastniy escorted him personally to the Central Committee meeting that stripped him of his power and position. Semichastniy never enjoyed the respect of KGB professionals, and he was removed from his position in 1967, as **Leonid Brezhnev** moved to strengthen the KGB. Semichastniy held only minor public posts after this demotion.

SEREBRYANSKIY [BERGMAN], YAKOV ISAKOVICH (1892–1956). One of the most famous of the Soviet **illegals**, Serebryanskiy went from underground work to the condemned cells of Soviet prisons, then to the rank of colonel in the security services, and finally back to a Moscow prison. From 1920 to 1938, Serebryanskiy served as an illegal in Persia, the United States, and Western Europe. He ran agents and was responsible for the kidnapping of General Aleksandr Kutepov, a leader of the **émigré** White Russian community in Paris. In the late 1930s, Serebryanskiy commanded the **NKVD's Administration for Special Tasks**, controlling 212 illegals in 16 countries. Despite his successes and the award for the kidnapping of Kutepov, he was arrested in 1938 and sentenced to death in 1941. After spending a month on death row, he was amnestied and returned to illegal work.

During **World War II**, Serebryanskiy worked in the **partisan** directorate and was highly decorated for his work against the Germans. According to **Pavel Sudoplatov**, he also recruited agents among German **prisoners of war**, who were used in **radio games** or were inserted behind enemy lines. In 1953, he was rearrested under the charges for which he had been sentenced to death in 1938. He died in Butyrka prison three years later under interrogation. In 1996, he was rehabilitated, and his government honors, including two Orders of **Lenin** and two Orders of the Red Banner, were restored.

SERGUN IGOR DMITIEVICH (1957–). Sergun, then a major general (one star), was named chief of the **GRU** in December 2011. His appointment suggested to some analysts that the GRU was in bureaucratic trouble since the director of military intelligence was usually a three- or four-star general. Sergun has played a major role in Russian statecraft over the past two years, as GRU *Spetsnaz* forces have played important roles in **Crimea** and the eastern **Ukraine**. He has since been promoted to lieutenant general (two stars).

Sergun entered military intelligence in 1984, speaks several languages, and served as the **military attaché** in Tirana, Albania. For his role in the Russian intervention in Ukraine, he has been placed on a sanction list by the European Union and the U.S. Department of Treasury.

SEROV, IVAN ALEKSANDROVICH (1900–1990). After service in the **Communist Party** bureaucracy and the military, Serov (like **Sergei Kruglov**) was brought into the **NKVD** in 1938 as part of **Lavrenty Beria**'s efforts to purge the service and establish his own power base. In September 1938, Serov was appointed NKVD chief in Ukraine, where he worked closely with **Nikita Khrushchev**. He inherited a security service deeply traumatized by 18 months of purges, arrests, and killings. His immediate predecessor, **Aleksandr Uspenskiy**, had gone so far as to fake his own suicide and disappear.

In 1939–1941, Serov supervised the sovietization of the western Ukraine and the Baltic states, directing the mass **deportation** of Poles, Latvians, Estonians, and Lithuanians to Siberia. Serov was also implicated in the murder of thousands of Polish officers and civilians in 1940. During **World War II**, Serov, serving as the deputy chief of state security, supervised the deportation of more than 1.5 million Soviet citizens—Volga Germans, peoples of the Caucasus, and Crimean Tatars—of whom approximately one-third perished of cold, sickness, and hunger. For carrying out these deportations, **Joseph Stalin** approved 413 medals for Serov's team.

During the last days of the war, Serov served as Stalin's security chief in Poland and eastern Germany. Serov was instrumental in the arrest of anti-Soviet Polish patriots, members of the AK (the Polish Home Army) in 1944 and 1945. He also acted as the Soviet leader's watchdog on the Red Army and its popular commander Marshal **Georgi Zhukov** in Germany. In July 1945, Serov was rewarded by promotion to colonel general.

Following the war, Serov became one of the most important figures in the security service. Among his responsibilities was oversight of "special prisons," where especially important people were interrogated and **executed**. Following Stalin's death, Serov successfully plotted against Beria, and he maintained his rank and authority in the security service. In March 1954, he was made chief of the newly minted **KGB**, in part because of his close relationship with Khrushchev. As KGB chair, Serov was involved in putting down the **Hungarian revolution** and supporting Khrushchev against the plotting of the **Antiparty Group**, which had sought to remove Khrushchev from the party leadership. In 1958, Khrushchev moved Serov to the **GRU**, where his career was ended by the exposure of **Oleg Penkovskiy** as a spy for the Americans and British. Serov was demoted, stripped of many of his decorations, and sent to a military post in the provinces.

Serov was one of the last of Stalin's **Chekists** to die. Well rewarded by Stalin, he received six Orders of **Lenin** and four Orders of the Red Banner, the same number as Marshal Zhukov. Nevertheless, he was truly a monster, responsible for the execution and **exile** of millions of innocent Soviet citizens.

SEVENTEEN MOMENTS OF SPRING. The most popular Soviet spy thriller, *Seventeen Moments* was a 12-part series about a Soviet intelligence officer masquerading as an SS officer in Berlin at the end of **World War II**. The show was popular with the average Soviet viewer, the intelligentsia, and the party elite: **Leonid Brezhnev** reportedly watched it 20 times and postponed Politburo meetings so as not to miss it.

The series was created by Yulian Semyonov, but its impresario was **KGB** chairman **Yuri Andropov**. Andropov godfathered the series as part of his efforts to humanize the KGB. The hero of the series, Stierlitz, reflected Andropov's image of a KGB agent as modest, patriotic, and professional. The series was popular, streets in major cities were empty, and crime rates dropped during its showing. Until the fall of the Soviet Union, it was shown annually, usually around Victory Day (9 May).

SHADRIN, NICHOLAS [ARTAMONOV, NIKOLAI FEDOROVICH] (1924–1975). After having **defected** from the Soviet navy, Artamonov was resettled in the United States under the name "Nicholas Shadrin." He was sentenced to death in absentia by a Soviet military court. But while working for the U.S. Naval Department as an **analyst**, Shadrin was recruited by the **KGB** *rezidentura* in Washington. He was also working for the Federal Bureau of Investigation (FBI) as a **double agent**. For several years, Shadrin met Soviet case officers in a dangerous game. When the KGB learned they were being duped, they convinced him to meet case officers in Vienna, where he was kidnapped. Shadrin died as a result of a drug administered during the kidnapping. The KGB leadership were delighted with the success of the operation, however, and awarded the officials involved medals for military valor.

Shadrin's role as a double agent and his death remain contentious issues to this day. Many believe that he should never have been run as an agent by the FBI. Moreover, despite rumors that Shadrin redefected to the Soviet Union, evidence from defectors such as **Vitaliy Yurchenko** and **Oleg Kalugin** established that he died as a result of a KGB blunder. President Gerald Ford asked Soviet leader **Leonid Brezhnev** about Shadrin and was told that Shadrin had never met the KGB in Vienna. President Jimmy Carter received the same story.

SHARASKA. The informal name given to research establishments set up within the **gulag** system. **NKVD** chief **Lavrenty Beria** set up a special design bureau in 1938. He further expanded their role in 1941 and again in 1949. The "special technical and design bureaus," their official name, worked on classified military problems, including aviation and rocketry. Among the alumni of the system were aircraft designers Aleksandr Petlyakov and Andrei Tupolev, as well as Soviet rocket designer Sergei Korolyov. **Aleksandr Solzhenitsyn** referred to the *Sharaska* as "the first circle" (of hell), where the condemned received a minimum of decent treatment.

SHEBARSHIN, LEONID VLADIMIROVICH (1935–2012). After joining the **KGB**'s **First Chief Directorate** in 1962, Shebarshin served in India as deputy chief and then in Iran as *rezident* during the Iranian Revolution. In 1989, **Communist Party** boss **Mikhail Gorbachev** appointed Shebarshin to head the First Chief Directorate. According to his own and other KGB memoirs, Shebarshin tried to keep the foreign intelligence directorate neutral during the 1991 **August putsch**. As a reward, he was appointed KGB chair immediately following the coup, but he was forced to resign within a few weeks. Shebarshin was a competent and brave intelligence officer; he met agents on the streets of Tehran during the Iranian Revolution. It was his fate to be promoted to the top of his service when the system he had served for three decades was collapsing. His memoirs, *Ruka Moskvy* (The Hand of Moscow), portrayed the problems of the KGB both operationally and politically. In 2012, going blind and living alone since the death of his wife, he committed suicide with his service pistol.

SHELEPIN, ALEKSANDR NIKOLAEVICH (1918–1994). Shelepin joined the Komsomol (Young Communist League) in 1939 and rose very quickly in the organization during the **Great Patriotic War**. From 1952 to 1958, he was the Komsomol first secretary, and he was a minor ally of **Nikita Khrushchev** in Khrushchev's power struggle with conservatives. On 25 December 1958, Khrushchev appointed Shelepin to head the **KGB** as part of his move to solidify **Communist Party** control of the security service. During his three years as KGB chair, Shelepin had a reputation as a hardliner on domestic and foreign policy issues. He clashed with **Aleksandr Korotkov**, the *rezident* in Berlin, over the recruitment of agents, and he pushed hard for policies that would guarantee the security of East Berlin. His advice was significant in Khrushchev's decision to build the Berlin Wall.

Shelepin also played a key role in the modernization of the KGB's **active measures**. He ordered the creation of Service D within the **First Chief Directorate** to coordinate active measures suggested by KGB overseas components. Shelepin ordered the chief of Service D, **Ivan Agayants**, to target West German and American politicians in an effort to damage the North Atlantic Treaty Organization alliance.

As KGB boss, Shelepin apparently did far more harm than good. He appointed young Komsomol activists to management-level positions in the KGB, replacing experienced **Chekists**. He fought with senior managers in foreign intelligence over **tradecraft** issues, creating problems for the KGB in Germany. Most of all, Shelepin was disliked for using the KGB as part of his ambitious scheme to rise to the top of the Communist Party.

In January 1961, Shelepin left the KGB to work in the Central Committee Secretariat, and he convinced Khrushchev to appoint his protégé and successor in the Komsomol, **Vladimir Semichastniy**, to succeed him as head of the KGB. Shelepin played a key role in the coup that brought **Leonid Brezhnev** to power in October 1964. His efforts to contend with Brezhnev for supreme political power in 1964–1970 failed, however, and he retired in semidisgrace in the mid-1960s. He is remembered as an Iago, a man with an infinite capacity for conspiracy.

SHEYMOV, VIKTOR. An officer in the **KGB** Eighth Chief (Government Communication) Directorate, Sheymov **defected** to the United States in 1980 with his family. His book *Tower of Secrets*, published in 1993, was the first unclassified insider account of KGB **signals intelligence**. Since his defection, Sheymov has become a successful entrepreneur.

SHLYKOV, VITALII VASILYEVICH (1934–2008). In January 1983, Shlykov was arrested by the Swiss police for espionage. A **GRU illegal**, Shlykov traveled to Zurich to meet with his agent, Ruth Gerhardt, whose husband was an important asset. (**Dieter Gerhardt**, who had been a GRU agent for 20 years, had already been arrested by the South African authorities.) Shlykov never revealed his mission and served three years in a Swiss prison. He later wrote widely on Russian defense policy and was made deputy minister of defense by **Boris Yeltsin**.

SHOW TRIALS. Large, public and fabricated judicial proceedings were a constant of the early post-Revolution period. The trial of the Petrograd Fighting Organization was organized by the **Cheka** in 1921 to publicize the link between **dissident** intellectuals and rebellious sailors and **émigrés**. Confessions were beaten out of witnesses, false evidence was presented in court, and the defendants were condemned. In the 1920s and early 1930s, there were series of show trials of "bourgeois specialists," foreign engineers, and Mensheviks. In each proceeding, the security service got better and better at handling witnesses and testimony.

The greatest of the show trials were the **Moscow Trials** in 1936, 1937, and 1938. In the dock were the leaders of Soviet Russia, **Vladimir Lenin**'s closest friends and colleagues. In a series of stage plays produced by **Joseph Stalin** and directed by the **NKVD**, the prisoners confessed, begged for the death penalty, and went to their deaths. The trials were not to be matched. Efforts to hold public show trials of Polish soldiers who fought against the Nazis and the Soviets in 1946 and of Jews accused of serving as American spies in 1952 failed because the prisoners refused to play their roles. The **MGB**, however, taught the services of Eastern Europe how to produce and direct such political theater, and show trials continued until 1954.

The evidence and the verdicts of the show trials were widely believed inside the Soviet Union and among leftist intellectual circles in the West. In the United States, left-wing intellectuals took out space in major magazines to affirm that the Moscow Trials were fair. In France, communist members of the Chamber of Deputies defended the 1952 **Slansky trial** in Prague. Robert Conquest's *The Great Purge* radically changed the public attitude toward the trials among Western intellectuals. It was not, however, until the era of **Mikhail Gorbachev** that the victims of the Moscow trials were pardoned, and the regime admitted they had been convicted on perjured evidence.

SHPIGELGLAS, SERGEI MIKHAILOVICH (1897–1940). One of the few early **Chekists** with a university education was Sergei Shpigelglas, who studied law at the university in Moscow prior to the Bolshevik Revolution. He was drafted out of the university in his final year by the tsarist army and found his way into the Red Army and the **Cheka**. Originally, Shpigelglas worked in the military **counterintelligence** section of the Cheka, but he entered foreign intelligence in the 1920s.

A natural recruiter as a foreign intelligence officer, Shpigelglas, who spoke French, German, and Polish, served as an **illegal** in Mongolia, China, and Western Europe. In 1936, he was made deputy chief of foreign intelligence and undertook missions in Germany, France, and Spain. In February 1938, **Joseph Stalin** promoted him to head the component. One of his most important achievements was the establishment of a school to train foreign intelligence officers. Shpigelglas did not survive **Lavrenty Beria**'s purge of the **NKVD**. He was arrested in late 1938 and shot in 1940. He was posthumously rehabilitated in 1956.

See also ANDROPOV INSTITUTE.

SIGNALS INTELLIGENCE (SIGINT). The tsarist regime maintained a sophisticated signals intelligence capability. Both the *Okhrana* and the Foreign Ministry worked to break the codes of radical groups and foreign powers. A British diplomat was warned by a Russian colleague in the late 19th century that all his diplomatic dispatches were read in the **Black Chamber** of the Russian Foreign Ministry long before they reached London, and he was politely advised to send his messages by surface mail rather than telegraph. The British had a Black Chamber of their own and had been reading Russian diplomatic communications since the Napoleonic Wars.

In the early years of the Bolshevik regime, the Cheka worked diligently but with mixed success to rebuild sigint capability. Cheka code making was so poor during the Polish–Soviet War of 1920–1921 that the Poles read all the Soviet military messages they intercepted. The **defection** of many tsarist sigint professionals following the Revolution made it difficult initially for the Bolshevik regime to maintain the security of its communications and to develop a signal intercept capacity. The British, to name one hostile country, read much of the Soviet diplomatic traffic into the early 1920s.

In the early 1930s, the signals intelligence sections of the **NKVD** and the **GRU** were combined and operated under the direction of **Gleb Bokiy**. Bokiy's success stemmed largely from the recruitment of foreign code clerks who betrayed their countries and provided codebooks to Moscow. In the 1930s, the NKVD was receiving code material from two British code clerks and had access to the British ambassador's diplomatic codes in Rome. And there was an agent inside the British embassy in Paris. This combination of human and signals intelligence that began in the 1930s lasted through the history of Soviet sigint.

Soviet code making and code breaking developed rapidly during the 1930s and 1940s. While the Soviet Union apparently did not break the codes of the German Enigma machines, they did make codes that were unusually secure. In the 1930s and 1940s, the Soviet security services developed a "one-time pad" as a means of encrypting messages. The pad consisted of a list of random five-digit number groups that, when added to already enciphered figures, made a totally secure code. For example, if 12345 in the codebook meant Moscow and the five-digit group was 11111, Moscow would be enciphered as 23456. The system was secure as long as Soviet clerks did not use the one-time pads more than once. When code clerks repeatedly used the same one-time pads during **World War II**, their mistake allowed American and British code breakers to decode messages.

During the **Cold War**, responsibility for Soviet sigint was divided between the Eighth and the 16th Chief Directorates of the **KGB** and the GRU's Space Intelligence Directorate. Major Soviet successes had to do with recruitment of signals intelligence officers and code clerks of Western powers, such as Bernon Mitchell and William Martin in the 1960s and **Ronald Pelton** and John **Walker** in the 1970s and 1980s. In the late 1960s, the KGB scored another major coup against its Western opponents with the recruitment of **Geoffrey Prime**, who worked for the Royal Air Force. Both the

KGB and the GRU collected signals intelligence from installations inside the Soviet Union and abroad as well as from Soviet diplomatic and trade facilities. According to the memoirs of a former KGB archivist, by the early 1980s, all KGB *rezidenturas* possessed an intercept post. The largest foreign installation was located at Lourdes in Cuba, where both of the Soviet services intercepted messages transmitted by satellites. The KGB reportedly forwarded 100,000 intercepted diplomatic and military messages to the **Communist Party** Central Committee every year between 1960 and 1991.The GRU's sigint program was immense, and it targeted potential adversaries' military communications. By the end of the 1980s, the GRU had 40 sigint regiments and 170 sigint battalions. The GRU also had 130 sigint satellites and made use of 20 different types of aircraft and more than 60 surface ships to collect information from the air, according to a study by an Australian academic.

Russia continues to collect signals intelligence. The station at Lourdes apparently has been closed, but the GRU's signals intelligence component has its own sites on the World Wide Web that advertise historic successes and present missions. The KGB components responsible for communication and signals intelligence were first folded into **FAPSI** and later into the **Special Communications Service of Russia (*SPETSSVIAZ*)**.

See also CONSTANTINI, FRANCESCO (ca. 1900–?); HALL, JAMES (1957–); KING, JOHN HERBERT (ca. 1905–?).

SILOVIKI. From *Sila* (Russian for "strength"), a term for men who served in the Soviet intelligence community and are now part of President **Vladimir Putin**'s inner circle. A recent study of senior members of the Russian government found more than two-thirds of them qualified as *siloviki*.

SILVERMASTER GROUP. One of the earliest and most effective Soviet espionage rings in the United States was established in the early 1930s by Nathan Gregory Silvermaster. Born in Imperial Russia in 1898, he came to the United States in 1914 and earned a PhD in economics at the University of California. In 1935, he moved to Washington to take part in President Franklin Roosevelt's New Deal.

Silvermaster acted as one of **Joseph Golos**'s and later **Ishak Akhmerov**'s principal agents. Among the agents he helped the **NKVD** *rezidentura* run were **Harry Dexter White** in the Treasury and **Lauchlin Currie**, a White House aide to President Roosevelt. Silvermaster; his wife, Helen Witte Silvermaster; and her son, Anatole Volkov, worked as agent handlers and as couriers moving between agents in the federal bureaucracies and Soviet intelligence officers. Silvermaster personally handled a number of agents in the War Department. He used these agents to manipulate War Department policies on security to allow other communist agents greater access to information. According to unclassified U.S. government documents, Silvermaster handled 27 different agents in seven departments in Washington.

The Silvermaster ring was undone in the 1940s by a series of events. **Elizabeth Bentley**, who had served the ring as a courier, defected to the Federal Bureau of Investigation (FBI) and made a full confession of her espionage activities. The decryption of Soviet intelligence messages provided the FBI with corroboration for Bentley's statements, identifying Silvermaster as "Robert" and his wife as "Dora" in dozens of messages. The messages also showed that the NKVD paid Silvermaster for managing the espionage ring and carefully monitored the agents he ran in Washington. In November 1944, the NKVD awarded Silvermaster with Order of the Red Star, according to a former KGB officer who had access to Silvermaster's personnel file.

SIMM, HERMAN (1947–). One of the most damaging penetrations of North Atlantic Treaty Organization (NATO), Simm, a senior Estonian defense official, worked for the **SVR** from 1995 until his arrest in 2008. Simm, who had begun his professional life as a policeman in Soviet Estonia, had previously worked as an **informer** of the **Third Chief (Military Counterintelligence) Directorate**. He has initially recruited by **Valeriy Zentsov** and run by him as well as **illegals**. He was arrested in 2008 and in 2009 was sentenced to 12 years' imprisonment.

SKOBLIN, NIKOLAI VLADIMIROVICH (1892–1938?). A tsarist officer, political **émigré**, and Soviet (and possibly) German spy, Skoblin's life has spawned books and movies over the past few decades. After service as a cavalry officer, Skoblin emigrated to Paris, where he became deeply involved in émigré politics. While informally chief of security for the Russian All-Military Union (ROVS), he also was recruited by Soviet intelligence. Skoblin set up the kidnapping and murder of the former White general and ROVS chief Evgenii Miller in 1937 for the **NKVD**. He also may have acted as a point of contact between the Gestapo and the NKVD, providing forged documents to implicate Marshal **Mikhail Tukhachevskiy**.

After Miller's disappearance (he left a note in good Agatha Christie fashion implicating Skoblin as his murderer should he fail to return from a clandestine meeting), he fled. Several stories have him murdered by the NKVD at sea or killed in Spain during a bombing raid. His wife, Nadezhda Plevitskaya (1884–1940), was arrested and convicted of Miller's kidnapping and presumed murder. She died of a heart condition in 1940 in a French prison.

This Soviet mystery has something for every writer of spy fiction—a Mata Hari, murder, disappearances, and letters from the dead—and it has been the source of Russian, French, and English books, plays, and films. The Skobin–Plevitskaya–Miller story was fictionalized by Vladimir Nabokov, who had known Plevitskaya. It has also been the basis of the French film *Triple Agent* and was fictionalized in Nikita Mikhailov's Academy Award–winning film *Burned by the Sun*.

SLANSKY TRIAL. On 22 November 1952, Rudolf Slansky and 13 other former leaders of the Czechoslovak **Communist Party** were tried for treason, charged with espionage for the United States and Israel. All were convicted, and 11 were immediately hanged. Slansky and his codefendants were Jews, victims of **Joseph Stalin**'s decision to scapegoat Jews in the Soviet Union and the East European satellites as part of a rolling purge of the party and police apparatus. Many historians of the period believe that the Slansky trial was a dress rehearsal for a mass trial of Soviet doctors charged with poisoning members of the Soviet Politburo. Scholars believe that these trials were to unleash a massive purge of the Soviet political elite. Within Czechoslovakia, the Slansky trial set off a series of new arrests, trials, and **executions** that lasted until mid-1954.

See also ANTI-FASCIST COMMITTEE; DOCTORS' PLOT; SHOW TRIALS.

SLUTSKIY, ABRAM ARONOVICH (1898–1938). Slutskiy deserted from the tsarist army and joined the **Bolsheviks** in 1917. He joined the **Cheka** in 1920 and in 1930 entered foreign intelligence. According to his official biography, he specialized in the collection of scientific, technical, and industrial intelligence. He was well regarded by his superiors and twice received the Order of the Red Banner for his work.

Slutskiy was deputy chief of foreign intelligence from 1930 to 1936 and chief of the foreign intelligence component of the **NKVD** from 1936 to his mysterious death in February 1938. As NKVD chief **Nikolai Yezhov** began to purge his service of experienced officer and **illegals**, suspicion fell on Slutskiy, a Russian Jew who had been involved in dispatching and managing illegals. On 17 February 1938, he was found dead in his office, an apparent suicide, though many of his colleagues believed he had been murdered. The Soviet press announced that he had died at his "military post." Two months later, he was posthumously expelled from the **Communist Party** as an **enemy of the people**. (Slutskiy's official biography also maintains he was poisoned, but not a single witness to his death survived the purge years.)

Slutskiy's death set off an even more vicious purge of the foreign directorate that claimed four directors in less than one year. More importantly, the purge of the NKVD's foreign intelligence arms left **Joseph Stalin** with little access to foreign intelligence about developments in Europe or the Far East. According to Russian records, for 127 days in 1938, Stalin did not receive a single foreign intelligence report.

SMERSH. In April 1943, **Joseph Stalin** mandated a new **counterintelligence** service for the People's Commissariat of Defense. *Smersh*, an abbreviation of *Smert shpiyonam*, or "Death to Spies," was created to ensure control of the military and the punishment of anti-Soviet elements in the military and the **partisan** movement and as a parallel security service to contend with **Lavrenty Beria**, who had political oversight of the **NKGB** and the **NKVD**. Stalin may have seen *Smersh* as a way to coordinate counterintelligence operations with the planning of offensive military operations.

Stalin appointed **Viktor Abakumov**, a young and competent security officer who had risen quickly during the purges of the 1930s, to head *Smersh* with the rank of colonel general. *Smersh* had an active presence in all military units down to the battalion level. Recent research established that *Smersh* had a staff of 15,000 to 30,000 officers, with a headquarters staff in Moscow of 225. It had five regiments with every Red Army front, as well as detachments with rear area units, partisan formations, and Axis prison camps. *Smersh* officers' major responsibility was the recruitment of **informants** within the army, **prisoner-of-war** camps, and the civilian population to help identify Nazi agents and military deserters. So effective was this web of agents and informers that German intelligence efforts inside the Soviet Union were totally foiled.

Smersh officers closely operated with partisan detachments within Nazi-occupied areas of the Soviet Union as well as in Poland, Hungary, and Czechoslovakia, frequently eliminating those believed to be anti-Soviet. Following the defeat of the Third Reich, *Smersh*'s Vetting and Screening Commissions (*Proverochni-filtrovochnye kommissii*) interrogated former Soviet prisoners of war, as well as Soviet citizens who had been deported to work in Nazi Germany. According to former Soviet archives, over 25 percent of those interviewed were **executed** or sentenced to lengthy terms in a **gulag**.

One of the most infamous chapters of **World War II** history for both the Soviet Union and the Western Allies was the forcible repatriation of more than 40,000 Cossacks by the British to the Soviet Union. *Smersh* officers persuaded British army officers to force men, women, and children on trains bound for the Soviet zone. Worse, at least 10 percent had never been Soviet citizens or had fled Russia during the **Revolution of November 1917.**

Smersh also received British help in arresting Cossack leaders who had fled the Soviet Union in the early 1920s. They were later hanged in the **Lubyanka**.

Following the war, *Smersh* ran foreign intelligence operations in Germany and Austria, recruiting military and civilian sources. Because *Smersh* operations were essentially counterintelligence by nature, these efforts produced little important political intelligence. Following the war, *Smersh* ran foreign intelligence operations in Germany and Austria, recruiting military and civilian sources. Because *Smersh* operations were essentially counterintelligence by nature, these efforts produced little important political intelligence. In Hungary, *Smersh* at Abakumov's orders arrested the Swedish consul, **Raoul Wallenberg**. Wallenberg was reportedly murdered two years later in Moscow.

Smersh was folded into the new Ministry of State Security (**MGB**) in March 1946. Many of its responsibilities were transferred to the **Third** (Military Counterintelligence) **Chief Directorate**. *Smersh*'s fearsome reputation outlived its short bureaucratic life, and it showed up in numerous novels about Russian intelligence, including those by Ian Fleming.

SNOWDEN, EDWARD JOSEPH (1983–). Whether Snowden acted as an agent of Russia or a narcissistic "whistle-blower" is a question that cannot be answered at this moment. The former National Security Agency (NSA) contractor has provided Russian intelligence with details of NSA's capabilities in conducting intercept operations. As several journalists have pointed out, only a handful of the secrets had anything to do with domestic surveillance. Most of the information had to deal with NSA's foreign operations.

Moscow's **signal intelligence** capabilities are excellent and well funded. They are well positioned to take advantage of Snowden's revelations. Future scholars of intelligence will better be able to judge the net advantage Moscow has gained from examining the success that Russian signals intelligence has had against the West and the corresponding lack of success that the West has had against Moscow. It should be noted that the material leaked by Snowden has apparently helped terrorist groups: according to Recorded Future, "al Qaida dramatically changed the way its operatives interact on line." It can be assumed that the Russian security services are no less adroit than Al Qaeda.

Snowden has also helped Moscow in its anti-American campaign. In an interview with President **Vladimir Putin**, he blandly accepted the Russian president's assertion that the security services do not bug private citizens. In August 2014, Snowden received permanent residence in Russia, and this would allow him to travel abroad on a Russian travel document.

SOBLE, JACK (1903–1967), AND SOBLEN, ROBERT (1900–1962). Together with his brother Robert Soblen (the brothers translated their names differently from Lithuania), Jack penetrated **Leon Trotsky**'s entourage for the **NKVD**. The Soble brothers and Jack's wife, Myra, were part of a small nest of illegals initially set up to provide information on Trotsky and his movement. They were exposed by Federal Bureau of Investigation (FBI) agent Boris Morros, and Jack and Myra received relatively short prison terms after agreeing to cooperate with the FBI. (President George H. W. Bush granted Myra a presidential pardon in 1991, shortly before her death.)

Robert Soblen took part in political and military intelligence work. He was convicted of providing the Soviet Union with Office of Strategic Service documents and information about U.S. nuclear tests. After his arrest, Soblen, unlike his brother, refused to cooperate with the prosecution. Out on bail after being sentenced to life imprisonment, Soblen obtained a false passport and flew to Israel. After Israel refused to accept him under the Law of Return, he committed suicide as he transited London on his way to the United States. Jack Soble's code name in Russian intelligence traffic was "Abram"; his brother's was "Roman."

SOLOVETSKY. The first cluster of forced labor camps was located on the White Sea, north of the Arctic Circle. The camps were centered on Solovetsky Island, which had been a Russian Orthodox Church monastery before the **Revolution of November 1917**. The Solovetsky camps, known as Northern Camps of Special Designation, were established to punish political **dissidents**. Prisoners included clergy, corrupt businesspeople, rich peasants, and former tsarist soldiers and civil servants. The camps had a brutal reputation: many prisoners were **executed**, and many starved or were worked to death. Attempted escapes were punished by mass shootings, according to one of the few survivors of the camps. The camps at first had only a relatively minor economic function, but they later became a model for the **gulag** empire that played a historic role in **Joseph Stalin**'s era of terror.

See also BELOMOR CANAL; FRENKEL, NAFTALII ARONOVICH (1883–1960).

SOLZHENITSYN, ALEKSANDR ISAYEVICH (1918–2008). Arrested while serving as an artillery captain at the front in 1945, Solzhenitsyn was sentenced to eight years' imprisonment for his criticism of **Joseph Stalin**. Over the next eight years, he served his sentence in jails and forced labor camps in Central Asia and Siberia. In 1952, he was released and sentenced to internal **exile** in Kazakhstan, where he found work as a mathematics teacher and began to write. After being amnestied, Solzhenitsyn returned to the Moscow region as a teacher and developed as a writer. In 1962, his novella *One*

Day in the Life of Ivan Denisovich was published in *Novy Mir*, the preeminent Soviet literary journal, with the permission of **Nikita Khrushchev**. The novella chronicled one day in the life of an ordinary political prisoner, and it was embraced as a masterpiece of Russian fiction within and outside the Soviet Union. The Soviet political scene in the early 1960s was becoming increasingly reactionary, however, and Solzhenitsyn was able to publish only one more piece legally in the Soviet media.

Beginning in the mid-1960s, Solzhenitsyn began to write about the Stalinist terror and the forced labor camps. Several novels were smuggled abroad and published to critical acclaim, but the author was now under the scrutiny of the **KGB**. KGB chair **Yuri Andropov** and his deputies saw Solzhenitsyn as a major threat to the regime and authorized close **surveillance** of him and his few supporters. The KGB code name for him was "Pauk" (Spider). Solzhenitsyn's few friends were the target of surveillance and torture: the interrogation of one of Solzhenitsyn's secretaries led to the woman's suicide. With rumors that Solzhenitsyn's masterpiece, *The Gulag Archipelago*, a history of the **gulag**, or forced labor camp system, was about to be published in the West, Andropov successfully lobbied the **Communist Party** Politburo for the author's arrest and exile from the Soviet Union.

Solzhenitsyn settled in the United States and continued to write. He was a difficult **émigré**, misunderstood by many liberals who were offended by his criticism of American society. It also was hard for westerners to understand that Solzhenitsyn had not written out of a desire for fame or glory. Rather, as he explained in *The Oak and the Calf*, he was the calf butting his head against the mighty oak. He acted not to dislodge the oak but because he had to act—if nothing else—as a witness against the brutality of the Stalinist system. His three-volume history of the gulag was a literary success for the author and a major ideological defeat for the Soviet Union. The book discredited the communist parties of Western Europe, forcing intellectuals to consider the crimes of the Stalin era with the moral and intellectual rigor they had once reserved only for Adolf Hitler's Germany.

Following the fall of the Soviet Union, Solzhenitsyn returned to Russia in 1994. While respected as a historian and intellectual, he has not played a major role in the development of a new Russia under **Boris Yeltsin** or **Vladimir Putin**. Rather, he has been seen by many as a relic of an ancient and forgotten age. Nevertheless, Solzhenitsyn in his novels and by personal example forced millions of Americans and Europeans to consider the human cost of the Soviet regime. He was one of the few to realize that ideas could shatter a regime's legitimacy.

SOPRUNENKO, PETR KARPOVICH (1908–1992). Soprunenko was transferred from the Red Army to the **NKVD** in November 1938 as **Lavrenty Beria** rebuilt the security service. In April 1940, he was assigned responsibility for the **execution** of 25,700 Polish military officers and civilians held at **Katyn** and other camps. Every day, he submitted a report to Beria detailing the day's killings. Soprunenko was rewarded and promoted for his work as an executioner. He was made a major general in 1945. Soprunenko continued to work as a commander of forced labor camps engaged in military work. He escaped arrest in the aftermath of **Joseph Stalin**'s death in 1953 and retired in 1963.

SORGE, RICHARD (1895–1944). A frontline veteran of **World War I**, Sorge was an ideological convert to Stalinism. In the 1930s, under cover as a journalist, Sorge served as a Soviet military intelligence (**GRU**) **illegal** in China and then in Japan. In Tokyo in the late 1930s, he became close to the German ambassador and had access to official Nazi military and diplomatic dispatches. He also developed a number of important sources in the Japanese establishment who provided detailed information about Japanese military planning and were able to corroborate much of the reporting from the German embassy. His code name in GRU cables was "Ramzei" (Ramsey). In early 1941, he repeatedly provided detailed reporting of German plans for war, including the date of the Nazi invasion of the Soviet Union (22 June).

Joseph Stalin disregarded Sorge's warnings in the spring of 1941 that Hitler was poised to invade the Soviet Union. However, the dictator believed Sorge's reporting in the fall of 1941 that Japan was not planning war with the Soviet Union but was moving toward war in Southeast Asia. As a result of this information, Stalin deployed infantry and tank formations from Siberia to the west in time to win the critical **Battle of Moscow** in December 1941.

Sorge handled sources with sophistication, living his cover in Japan as a jaded journalist. He had a reputation as an alcoholic and a womanizer and apparently paid little attention to **tradecraft**. He was arrested in October 1941 and executed in 1944. The Soviet government disavowed him, and no effort was made to rescue him. When the Japanese government made an effort to trade Sorge, Stalin responded that he "did not know that name." Following the war, Sorge was made one of the Soviet intelligence heroes of **World War II**. Stamps were issued with his picture, and several books were written about his exploits.

SORM (*SISTEMA OPERATIVNO-ROZISKNIKH MEROPRIYATII*). The **FSB**'s domestic audio surveillance system, "System for Operational Investigative Activities," was developed in the early 1990s. It gave the security service an automated nationwide communications intercept system. The system has reportedly been upgraded in 1998 and 2012 to monitor the Internet.

Despite the fact that the Russian Duma gave the FSB the right to monitor telephone communications, President **Vladimir Putin** denied in a television interview with Edward Snowden in 2014 that these activities took place.

SOTSVREDNIKI. In Russian, *sotsvredniki* means "socially harmful." This was the term used by the **NKVD** during the purges in the 1930 to describe enemies in Soviet society that needed to be arrested. According to NKVD records, more than 3 million Soviet citizens were listed as socially harmful, of whom approximately two-thirds were arrested and 700,000 were shot.

SOUTHER, GLEN MICHAEL (1957–1988). A civilian employee of the U.S. Navy with access to highly sensitive technical intelligence, Souther volunteered to work with the **KGB** while serving in Italy. While Souther worked for the Soviet services for a short period of time, he provided important information on U.S. military satellites. He apparently worked for the Soviet Union out of a highly romantic view of Russian culture and espionage. When he felt in danger in 1986, Souther **defected** to the Soviet Union, where he was nationalized under Soviet law as "Mikhail Orlov" and made a commissioned officer of the KGB. He committed suicide three years later, however, for reasons that have never been well explained. The official newspaper of the Red Army reported that "he had a short but full and brilliant life totally devoted to the struggle for removing the threat of nuclear war hanging over mankind and for a better life for ordinary people." The report added, "Over a long period he performed important special missions and made a major contribution to ensuring state security."

SPANISH CIVIL WAR. The Soviet intelligence security services played a critical role in **Joseph Stalin**'s strategy in the Spanish Civil War to create a Soviet satellite state run by a communist party absolutely loyal to Moscow. To achieve this end, the **NKVD** and **GRU** trained Republican intelligence and Special Forces for operations against General Francisco Franco's army. The NKVD was also used to destroy any potential opposition within Republican ranks. NKVD executioners, working with Spanish colleagues, murdered thousands of **Trotskyites**, anarchists, and disloyal communists. NKVD resident **Alexander Orlov** masterminded these terrorist operations and persuaded the Republican government to allow the country's gold supply, reportedly $700 million, to be shipped to the Soviet Union for safekeeping.

Stalin's paranoia and the NKVD's tactics in Spain were a major reason for Franco's eventual victory. Both services kept lists of Spanish officers and international volunteers to be shot: the only reason was their lack of affection for the **Communist Party**. This spasmodic persecution of enemies in the Republican camp reduced the effectiveness of the armed forces. Militants who could have been employed against Franco were murdered in the **execution** chambers of the NKVD. Moreover, as defeat became obvious, NKVD and GRU officers blamed and denounced each other, damaging relations between the services and weakening their ability to serve the Republican cause. The end of the war came in 1939 with a total Franco victory. At the end, 20,000 Spanish citizens left for the Soviet Union. Among them were 2,000 children and many of their teachers. They were able to return to Spain only after 1970.

Stalin deeply distrusted the Red Army, NKVD, and GRU specialists who served in Spain. Many were executed on their return from the battlefield. Among those executed were senior GRU and NKVD officers, as well as Red Army pilots and military advisers. Two of the most famous "Spaniards" to be executed were Vladimir Antonov-Ovsenko, whom **Lenin** had selected to lead the attack on the Winter Palace on 7 November 1917, and Mikhail Koltsov, the "Soviet Hemingway," who was known for his coverage of the war. Both were arrested hours after interviews with Stalin in the Kremlin. Nevertheless, the Soviet experience in Spain benefited Stalin's intelligence services and prepared them for war on a larger front four years later against Nazi Germany. Spain also was a venue for the services to recruit idealistic anti-Fascists for operations in Europe and North America. One Soviet intelligence officer noted in his memoirs, "Spain was sort of a children's playground where we perfected many of our later espionage techniques."

SPECIAL COMMUNICATIONS SERVICE OF RUSSIA (*SPETSSVI-AZ*). Created from the former 8th Chief (Communications) and 16th Chief (**Signals Intelligence**) Directorates of the **KGB**, *SPETSSVIAZ* was initially placed under the operational control of the **FSB**. In 2004, President **Vladimir Putin** mandated that it served as a subunit of the **Federal Protective Service**. This decision further strengthened the power of the Russian president. Its director since 2010 is General Aleksei Mironov.

SPECIAL DEPARTMENT. Joseph Stalin created a special department in the Central Committee Secretariat to manage the security services and the armed forces. The department, occasionally referred to as Stalin's personal secretariat, acted as his watchdog over the secret service. In the early 1930s, **Nikolai Yezhov** established the bureaucracy. For the rest of Stalin's life, the department was managed by Aleksandr Poskrebyshev, whom **Nikita Khrushchev** sarcastically identified in his **Secret Speech** as "Stalin's loyal shield bearer." Following Stalin's death in 1953, Poskrebyshev and Stalin's other secret servants were placed under house arrest and then pensioned off.

Most of the functions of the Special Department were assigned to the **Administrative Organs Department** of the **Communist Party**'s Central Committee.

SPETSNAZ (SPETSIALNOGO NAZNACHENIYA). *Spetsnaz* is short for *Spetsialnogo naznacheniya* (Special Designation). Early in the Soviet era, the Soviet military intelligence (**GRU**) and security services developed the Special Designation forces to operate deep in the enemy's rear and sow terror and confusion with sabotage and assassination. In the early 1920s, the Fourth Bureau of the Soviet General Staff trained terrorists and **partisans** from several nations. German communists were prepared during this period to seize power. Their coup in 1923 fizzled as the German working class stayed out of the fight. Beginning in the 1930s, the Red Army developed a doctrine of unconventional warfare, featuring the use of *Spetsnaz* troops. During the **Spanish Civil War**, GRU and **NKVD** cadres trained Spanish Republican forces in unconventional warfare with great success.

The GRU's success in the Spanish Civil War in partisan warfare convinced senior military officers of the greater need for troops schooled in guerrilla warfare and terrorism. During the **Great Patriotic War**, *Spetsnaz* forces took part in operations on all fronts, and *Spetsnaz* units became integrated into Soviet war planning. Beginning with the **Battle of Moscow**, *Spetsnaz* formations disrupted the German rear areas and logistical networks.

The security service always had an ability to conduct terrorist operations, killing dangerous **émigrés** and **defectors**. It was not until June 1974, however, that the **KGB** created its own *Spetznaz* formation, Group Alpha, which was responsible for operations against terrorism and "extremists" within the Soviet Union. In December 1979, Group Alpha was tasked with capturing the presidential mansion of Afghanistan's President Hafizullah Amin and killing him and his entourage. Alpha's work in Afghanistan, as well as other GRU and KGB *Spetsnaz* successes, created concerns about the threat of Soviet special forces in the West. *Spetsnaz* became a subject of misinformation in the Western press: Soviet *Spetsnaz* forces were reported to have a corps of sinister women killers and credited with operations in Alaska that never took place.

As the Soviet Union slowly disintegrated in the late 1980s, Group Alpha was increasingly used against domestic enemies. In January 1991, Alpha stormed the main television station in Vilnius, Lithuania, killing several civilians. It also operated in Latvia and Azerbaijan. During the **August putsch**, Alpha was ordered to storm the Russian White House (the parliament building) in central Moscow and kill President **Boris Yeltsin**. Alpha commanders, however, refused the order, citing its illegality.

Group Alpha is now subordinated to the **FSB**. GRU and **MVD** special forces units, as well as Alpha, have been engaged in operations against insurgents and terrorists and in Chechnya since the early 1990s. In the summer of 2004, *Spetsnaz* troops stormed a school held by Chechen terrorists in **Beslan** in southern Russia. In the resulting firefight, all the terrorists, hundreds of hostages, and several members of Alpha perished. Russian *Spetznaz* units, reportedly well trained and well armed, continue to play a critical role in Russian security, **counterterrorism**, and war fighting. However, these special forces are still developing new strategies for operating against domestic enemies. Operations inside Russia have generated casualties that in the West would be seen as unacceptable. Liaison with Western services may have an impact on Russian use of deadly force.

GRU *Spetsnaz* operations in 2014 have demonstrated a new role for special forces. Troops in disguise infiltrated the **Crimea** and the eastern **Ukraine**, strengthening Russian nationalist movements and providing covert communications, weapons, and funds. **Igor Girkin,** a senior GRU *Spetsnaz* officer, has been identified as the "minister of defense" of the pro-Moscow Donetsk People's Republic.

SPY SWAPS. In 1962, the United States and the Soviet Union inaugurated a policy of trading captured agents. The first trade involved the exchange of the Soviet **illegal William Fisher** ("Colonel Abel") for U-2 pilot Francis Gary Powers at the Glienicker Bridge in Berlin. A year later, the Soviet Union escalated the policy by arresting a Yale professor in Moscow to exchange for a captured intelligence officer in the United States who lacked diplomatic protection. These swaps continued through the 1970s and 1980s. The United States largely tolerated Moscow's actions, trading to get back American citizens and allowing Moscow to protect its agents. In 1986, the Ronald Reagan administration ended this with the wholesale expulsion of Soviet intelligence officers in an action referred to as **Famish**.

Spy swaps became a major feature in the struggle between East and West Germany. To redeem agents captured by the West German security service, the East German regime traded and sometimes sold its citizens seeking a life in the West. Bonn accepted the policy as part of the price of doing business with the East German regime. Up to 1986, hostage taking benefited Moscow and its German ally, allowing them to tell their agents that they had a "get out of jail" ticket should they be arrested.

In 2010, the Washington agreed to trade 10 Soviet illegals arrested in the United States for four men charged with spying for the United States and the United Kingdom and being held in Russian prisons. It seems likely that spy swaps, now more rare, will continue.

See also CHAPMAN, ANNA VLADIMIROVNA (1981–).

SPETSPOSELENIE. An **NKVD** acronym from the words "special settlement," created for dispossessed and **exiled** kulaks during **collectivization**. According to one document, 381,026 families with 1.8 million people were settled in Siberia and Central Asia. Most settlements had not been prepared, and thousands perished from hunger and cold.

STALIN, JOSEPH VISSARONOVICH (1878–1953). Born into the family of a drunken cobbler, Stalin was educated in a Russian Orthodox seminary. Expelled for reading banned material, he drifted into Marxist revolutionary circles. As a youthful revolutionary, Stalin worked in the Bolshevik underground and may have been co-opted by the *Okhrana*. What is certain is that he was at home with the most extreme and violent members of the party, some of whom were implicated in bank robberies. In his **Communist Party** biography, Stalin gave his profession as "professional revolutionary."

Stalin, unlike other Old Bolsheviks, sought power through key administrative posts. As the Communist Party's general secretary, he served as its chief administrative officer, assigning people to key party and police posts. As general secretary in the early 1920s, Stalin built contacts with the **Cheka** through his role as overseer of the party's personnel directorate, and from 1924, he used the service to keep track of his political opponents. Crucial to Stalin's defeat of his rival **Leon Trotsky** was his ability to use the security service to harass and disrupt his opponent's political movement.

During his three decades in power, Stalin micromanaged the security services, paying particular attention to personnel appointments and assignments. To ensure the loyalty of the leaders of the service, he used as his watchdog the **Special Department** within the Communist Party Central Committee. Using information from this department, he frequently reorganized and purged the security service. Stalin encouraged security officers to write to him with their complaints and denunciations of colleagues and superiors. Stalin replaced and executed senior officers for rumors of immorality and financial impropriety as well as political subversion.

Beginning in the early 1930s, Stalin urged the party leadership to use the secret police against **dissidents** inside the party. Following the murder of **Sergei Kirov** on 1 December 1934, Stalin ordered the institution of draconian laws and then moved to replace **Genrykh Yagoda** with **Nikolai Yezhov** as chief of the **NKVD**. Yezhov brutally used the NKVD against all real and potential dissident elements in the party and Soviet society. In 1937 and 1938, more than 1.5 million Soviet citizens were arrested for counterrevolutionary crimes; more than 650,000 were executed. Stalin oversaw the preparation of cases against Old Bolsheviks in the **Moscow Trials**. When one Old Bolshevik refused to confess, Stalin told his interrogator to ask the prisoner "how much does the Soviet Union weigh," implying that no one could withstand the physical and psychological pressure the NKVD could produce. On another occasion in 1937, he wrote NKVD chief Yezhov, "Isn't it time we squeezed this gentleman . . . where is he, a prison or hotel?" Stalin took a personal interest in the victims of the purge. He signed 362 death lists in 1937–1938, including the names of 39,000 condemned men and women. Only on a few rare occasions did he exercise clemency and pardon someone. Even during the darkest days of the **Great Patriotic War**, Stalin signed execution lists: on 29 January 1942, he minuted a list of 46 generals and senior military industrial mangers, "Shoot all named in the list.—JS."

When Stalin sensed the purge had gone too far, he brought **Lavrenty Beria**, a trusted official from Georgia, to command the security service. From 1938 to Stalin's death, Beria controlled the intelligence and security organs of the Soviet government from positions in the government and the party Central Committee. Stalin kept Beria close; the security generalissimo was a constant guest at Stalin's late-night dinners and visited him when Stalin vacationed in the Caucasus.

Stalin used the NKVD to collect information on all senior members of the party, military, and police leadership. His chief bodyguard, **Nikolai Vlasik**, collected information on members of the leadership and acted as a **back channel** for communications with selected officials in the party and the police. In his last 10 years, Stalin acted on rumors to dispatch senior officials to **exile** or **execution**. For example, in 1946, Marshal **Georgi Zhukov** was sent to a minor military command following information that he had brought back an excessive amount of loot from Germany and had been recruited by British intelligence. Stalin told the marshal, "I don't believe these reports, but people are talking!" During the same period, Stalin condemned three senior military officers to death on the basis of a taped telephone conversation that showed their concern with the country's dismal economic situation.

Stalin's record as a user of foreign intelligence is mixed. In the late 1930s, he oversaw a purge of the foreign intelligence component of the NKVD and the **GRU** that limited critical political and military intelligence reporting on Nazi Germany. Stalin distrusted any intelligence **analysis**. In 1936, he warned a GRU officer, "An intelligence hypothesis may become your hobby horse on which you will ride straight into a self-made trap." Stalin thus rejected analysis of Nazi war preparations and warnings of the German invasion of 22 June 1941, an error that cost the Soviet Union millions of military and civilian casualties. Five days before the invasion, he minuted a report predicting an imminent invasion, "You can send your source on the German air force staff intelligence to his whore of a mother. This is not intelligence but misinformation." It is little wonder that in 1941, the leaders of the GRU and NKVD carefully edited warnings from agents in the field.

Nevertheless, during **World War II**, Stalin used foreign intelligence about Nazi war plans as well as American and British strategy to maximize Soviet gains in Europe and Asia and to develop Soviet nuclear weapons. During the war, the Soviets had more than 300 agents working in the United States, providing Stalin with detailed and accurate information about Washington's plans for the war and postwar world. Stalin insisted on bugging Franklin D. Roosevelt's bedroom at the Tehran (1943) and Yalta (1945) conferences, and he demanded a translation of all conversations the next morning before he met with the American leader. Agents within the British establishment provided documents on British foreign and military policy, and **Pierre Cot**, the Free French minister in Moscow, was a Soviet agent. No generalissimo has had the intelligence assets that Stalin did during the war.

Stalin used his service as the long and vengeful arm of Soviet power. In the late 1930s, he used the NKVD to track and eventually kill **émigré** White generals and his former rival Trotsky. Following the war, the service kidnapped and killed enemies of Moscow in West Germany and Austria. At his last Presidium meeting, Stalin reviewed a program to kill the Yugoslav leader Joseph Tito. In the last years of his life, Stalin prepared a purge of the party and the security service. The centerpiece of the purge was to be the testimony in the case of the **Doctors' Plot** that prominent physicians planned to poison the leadership under the direction of the Central Intelligence Agency and international Jewish organizations. Only Stalin's death prevented another bloodletting.

Stalin—like Beria, his primary intelligence and security lieutenant—was a frightening boss. He often communicated with *rezidenturas* abroad using the pseudonym "Ivan Vasilevich," demanding information and action by his service. Good intelligence officers, as well as incompetents and cowards, often found themselves on trial for their lives for real and suspected omissions. Stalin also awarded intelligence professionals with rank, privileges, and personal attention. When he left for his last vacation in the south in 1952, he made sure that **Yevgeny Pitovranov**, an up-and-coming **MGB** officer, was specially invited to see him off.

Contrary to some recent literature, neither Beria nor the security service was responsible for Stalin's death. But Stalin's decision to replace his chief bodyguard Vlasik in late 1952 may have indirectly played a part in his death. When Stalin's guard detail noticed that Stalin had not awakened on the morning of 2 March, they first waited hours before entering the room and then waited hours more before summoning medical help for the stroke that he had suffered. Stalin's policy of a tight control of his guards may have hastened his painful death on 5 March.

The heritage of Joseph Stalin—like that of his intelligence service—remains mixed in Russia. While there is now a treasure trove of literature on the crimes of the Stalin era in the Russian language, there has also been considerable rehabilitation of the leader and a number of books on the wartime exploits of the security services.

Furthermore, the statue of **Feliks Dzerzhinsky** torn down in August 1991 has been placed back in a position of honor at the **Lubyanka**. In a recent Russian poll, half of the respondents believed Stalin was a positive figure. The speaker of the Russian Duma in 2004 hailed Stalin as a "positive force."

See also BARBAROSSA; BATTLE OF MOSCOW; STALINGRAD, BATTLE OF.

STALINGRAD, BATTLE OF. The **NKVD** played a critical role in the defense of Stalingrad in the autumn of 1942. The NKVD chief **Aleksandr Voronin** took charge of the city's defense in the first days of the siege, and the NKVD 10th Rifle Division took part in the initial firefights in the city, suffering very heavy casualties. **Nikolai Selivanovskiy**, the senior NKVD officer in Stalingrad during the battle, submitted daily reports to **Joseph Stalin**, and **Viktor Abakumov**, chief of military counterintelligence, provided detailed information detailing intelligence operations in the Nazi rear, as well as the capture of German agents, deserters, and traitors. The report included the number of executions of Soviet citizens. The report for 19–20 September read that 184 men had been apprehended and 21 shot: seven for spying, five for treason, two for self-mutilation, and six for cowardice. The report notes that the deputy commander of the Soviet forces artillery had been been detained for anti-Soviet agitation.

STARINOV, ILYA GRIGOREVICH (1900–2001). After fighting in the civil war, Starinov joined the **GRU**. In the 1930s, he became one of the founders of GRU *Spetsnaz* forces, preparing Soviet soldiers and foreign communists to conduct operations behind invaders' lines. In 1936, Starinov was dispatched to train Spanish Republicans in *Spetsnaz* tactics. As "Comrade Rudolfo," he was successful in training a cadre of dedicated saboteurs and partisans during the Spanish Civil War. To his Soviet colleagues in Spain and Moscow, he was known by the code name "Volk" (Wolf). Starinov barely escaped arrest on his return to Moscow, and he continued to work in the GRU. He ran schools for special forces and partisan forces. In the terrible first days of the **Great Patriotic War**, he established bases for partisans behind enemy line. He reportedly also played a critical role in the destruction of Soviet installations as a German.

STASHYNSKY, BOHDAN (1931–). As a student, Stashynsky was an **informer** of the **NKVD** and was later recruited into the service. Trained as an assassin, he murdered two Ukrainian exiles living in West Germany, using a spray gun that fired a jet of poison gas. So sophisticated was the toxin that both men were certified by physicians as dying from heart attacks. After being order to kill yet another Ukrainian politician in exile, Stashynsky **defected** to the United States.

Publicity surrounding Stashynsky's defection and revelations of the murder of exiled politicians convinced Moscow to halt the assassination of enemies living abroad. Stashynsky served a short term in jail and then disappeared, possibly to South Africa.

STASI. The most important **KGB** ally in the **Cold War** was the East German Ministry of State Security (*Ministerium für Staatssicherheit*), known to all as *Stasi*. In 1989, the *Stasi* employed 91,000 men and women—four times as many as the Gestapo in a state one-quarter as populous. Coverage of the population was ensured by more than a million **informants**. The activities of the *Stasi* were later documented by the **Gauck Commission** after the collapse of the East German state.

The *Stasi* foreign intelligence directorate (*Hauptverwaltung Aufklärung*), the HVA, led for more than 30 years by Markus Wolf, provided Moscow with critical military and scientific intelligence. Former KGB officers rated *Stasi* as the best of the satellite intelligence services, and they estimated that 80 percent of their information on the North Atlantic Treaty Organization came from *Stasi*. A large number of KGB officers were stationed at a large *rezidentura* at Karlshorst in East Berlin and in provincial East German cities. Russian President **Vladimir Putin** served for five years as a KGB liaison officer in Dresden, where the *Stasi* and the KGB targeted Western businesspeople to collect scientific, technical, and industrial intelligence. *Stasi* also had a large **signals intelligence** service that also collected intelligence and **counterintelligence** for the KGB.

Stasi and Wolf provided the KGB with detailed reporting of political developments in West Germany. Wolf's service recruited and ran **Gunter Guillaume**, West German Premier Willy Brandt's aide. The HVA also recruited agents in the right-wing Christian Democratic Party to serve as sources of information and clandestine agents of influence. The HVA also used "romeo spies," **illegals** dispatched specifically to seduce and recruit female secretaries of senior politicians, including the president of the German Republic.

Another of Wolf's gifts to his Soviet allies was the penetration of the West German intelligence and security services. Bonn had no secrets from Moscow in the Cold War. The first chief of the West German security service, **Otto John**, was lured into **defecting** in 1954, and senior intelligence and counterintelligence personnel were recruited as agents from the 1950s to the fall of the Berlin Wall. Three of these were particularly important. Gabriele Gast was recruited by a romeo spy in 1973. A brilliant **analyst**, she was at the time of her arrest in 1987 deputy chief of the West German intelligence service's Soviet bloc division. Klaus Keron, of the West German counterintelligence service, offered his services to *Stasi* for money. A senior counterintelligence officer, he was paid 700,000 marks over eight years. Hans-Joachim Tiedge, the chief officer in West Germany's counterintelligence service, the BfV, defected to East Germany in 1985. He was close to being charged with manslaughter in the death of his wife in a household brawl.

Stasi also penetrated the West German political parties: in 1988, it had 368 informants within the Green Party. In the last year before the Berlin Wall came down, *Stasi* received 180,000 reports, 15,000 a month, or 500 a day. While many were certainly of little value, 2,500 were rated as "valuable."

Stasi **tradecraft** was quite sophisticated and reminiscent of the **Cheka, GPU,** and **OGPU** in the first decades of Soviet power. Rather than depend on case officers under diplomatic cover, East German citizens were frequently dispatched as illegals to handle agents. Turning adversity to opportunity, Wolf's *Stasi* seeded the stream of **émigrés** leaving East Germany with dedicated agents. Wolfe was able to use this tactic because he knew that punishment for espionage in West Germany was light and that *Stasi* could use **spy swaps** to exchange political prisoners and suspected **dissidents** for agents captured in the West.

STOLYPIN, PETER ARKADIEVICH (1862–1911). Stolypin was the most successful reformer of the last years of tsardom and an effective and brutal security boss. After serving as governor of Saratov oblast, Stolypin was brought to the capital as minister of internal affairs in early 1906 to deal with growing urban and social violence. Shortly thereafter, he was made prime minister. Stolypin called for a policy of authoritarian reform. He institutionalized a "wager on the strong," making it possible for rich peasants to obtain land at nominal prices. As the empire's security generalissimo, he crushed revolution; in 1906–1908, more than 25,000 rebels received sentences of death, imprisonment, or **exile**. During this period, the noose was referred to as a "Stolypin necktie," and freight cars used to transport prisoners into exile were known as "Stolypin cars." He used the *Okhrana* effectively, breaking up many terrorist organizations. Stolypin was assassinated on 1 September 1911 by an anarchist who was also an **informant** for the *Okhrana*. In an article on Stolypin's death, the *New York Times* noted that the person most responsible for his death was "Stolypin himself."

STONE, I. F. (ISIDOR FINSTEIN) (1907–1989). One of the most noted radical American journalists of the 20th century, he served as a Soviet agent in the late 1930s, according to notes taken in the Soviet archives by **Alexander Vassiliev**. Given the code name "Pancake," the files show Stone acting as a courier and talent spotter for the **NKVD**.

STRAIGHT, MICHAEL (1916–2004). The scion of a wealthy and powerful American family, Straight was recruited for the **NKVD** by **Anthony Blunt** in the mid-1930s at Cambridge. Straight, according to his autobiography, refused to cooperate with Soviet intelligence on his return to the United States. This self-serving account of his life has been challenged by scholars with access to Soviet records. In 1963, Straight, who was being considered for a senior federal appointment, informed the American and British authorities of his recruitment and Blunt's role as a Soviet agent. Straight's testimony opened the door to the prosecution of Blunt for espionage. The British authorities did not believe that the testimony was usable in a court of law and chose to use it instead to force Blunt to confess.

STRELKOV, IGOR IVANOVICH. Cover name for a military officer with a **GRU** background, Colonel **Igor Girkin**, serving since June 2014 as minister of defense of the so-called Donetsk People's Republic in **Ukraine**.

STRONG, ANNA LOUISE (1885–1970). Strong was an early apostle of the Soviet experiment. After being disappointed by the failure of the American progressive movement, she went to Russia in 1921 and worked as an unabashed apologist for **Joseph Stalin** for the next 28 years. In 1935, she was appointed by Stalin as the editor of the English-language *Moscow News*. Strong was in it for more than the ideology; she was richly paid for her articles on Soviet politics and culture. She was also an agent of the **NKVD** with the code name "Lira," presumably for her support of Moscow's **active measures**. In February 1949, Strong was arrested in Moscow by the **MGB** as an American spy. After several days in the **Lubyanka**, she was deported to the United States. She apparently had been arrested because of her travels in Yugoslavia and China. Moscow may have believed that she was forging contacts between Titoists and Maoists. In the mid-1950s, Strong was forgiven and traveled to Moscow. Finding the Soviet Union too tame, she settled in China, where she wrote glowing reports of the great proletarian Cultural Revolution before she died at age 85.

SUDOPLATOV, PAVEL ANATOLEVICH (1907–1996). Orphaned by Russia's **civil war**, Sudoplatov joined the Red Army at age 12 and the **Cheka** in his teens. In the early 1920s, he worked as an **illegal** in operations against Russian and Ukrainian **émigré** organizations. In the 1930s, Sudoplatov personally assassinated a Ukrainian émigré leader with a booby-trapped box of chocolates. In 1938, he was made **Yakov Serebryanskiy**'s successor as chief of the **Administration for Special Tasks** and was given personal responsibility by **Joseph Stalin** to organize the assassination of **Leon Trotsky**.

With the purge of the leadership of the foreign intelligence component, Sudoplatov also served as the head of foreign intelligence for several weeks in 1938.

During **World War II**, Sudoplatov was chief of the **NKVD**'s Fourth Directorate responsible for partisan and terrorist operations behind German lines. He was also made head of Department S, which coordinated all Soviet espionage against the Anglo-American nuclear weapons program, codenamed *Enormoz*. For his work, Sudoplatov was repeatedly decorated by Stalin and made a lieutenant general in 1945. Following the war, he initially was given responsibility for purging collaborators from the Soviet territory that had been occupied by the Germans. He then returned to foreign intelligence, concentrating on operations against North Atlantic Treaty Organization military forces. Along with many of **Lavrenty Beria**'s subordinates, Sudoplatov was arrested in August 1953 and sentenced to 15 years' imprisonment. His sentence was reversed in the 1990s following appeals by military and intelligence veterans.

Sudoplatov's memoirs published soon after his rehabilitation raised a firestorm in the West. His charges of NKVD recruitment of Western scientists, including Robert Oppenheimer, were correctly rejected out of hand by most scholars and counterintelligence professionals. Nevertheless, the book is now more highly regarded and is considered insightful regarding Stalin's management and use of foreign intelligence.

SUMBATOV [TOPURIDZE], YUVELYAN DAVIDOVICH (1889–1960). After a career as a political agitator, Sumbatov joined the Red Army during the Russian **civil war** and commanded an armored train. He joined the **Cheka** in 1920 and advanced in the Azerbaijan Republic service. In the late 1930s, he was transferred by his patron **Lavrenty Beria** to work in the **gulag** program. In 1945, he was promoted to lieutenant general, but two years later, he left the security service to work as deputy premier of the Azeri Republic. He fell along with Beria and was arrested in July 1953. Sumbatov survived trials for treason by pretending to be psychologically ill. He was in and out of institutions several times before his death in 1960.

SURVEILLANCE. For the Russian and security services, physical and technical surveillance was a critical tool. The *Okhrana* conducted surveillance of **dissidents** by intercepting mail and through close physical surveillance of suspects and their associates. In St. Petersburg, the *Okhrana* recruited cab drivers because of their ability to travel anywhere in the capital without raising suspicion. Surveillance allowed the *Okhrana* to keep careful and generally accurate files on dissidents in both radical and moderate parties.

The **Cheka** expanded surveillance of known and suspected enemies of the infant Bolshevik regime. Along with mail interception and physical surveillance, the service perfected the use of **audio surveillance**. **Joseph Stalin** read reports of surveillance of both political enemies and poets. He decided on **Solomon Mikhoels**'s murder when he read in surveillance reports that the actor had made denigrating statements about the **Communist Party** to Americans. When Stalin read a detailed surveillance report on the great poet **Anna Akhmatova**, he reportedly said, "Our little nun is now receiving foreign spies." Akhmatova had met with the British philosopher and diplomat Isaiah Berlin.

The **KGB** and its predecessors developed a number of technical tools to make surveillance easier. *Metka*, or spy dust, was used to allow KGB dogs to follow suspected intelligence officers. The KGB also planted electronic devices in the shoes of North Atlantic Treaty Organization diplomats and small radio transmitters in the cars of diplomats and intelligence officers. The KGB's Seventh Directorate was specifically established to conduct surveillance in cars and on foot. A team of 50 surveillants was dedicated to covering the British embassy. Three cars were assigned to follow the British chief of station Roderick Chisolm wherever he went. His wife was followed too: it was surveillance of Mrs. Chisolm that gave the KGB their first lead to **Oleg Penkovskiy**.

Surveillance had two important benefits for the regime. It provided necessary information on a host of **counterintelligence** and domestic security issues. It also served to intimidate the opponents of the regime, forcing them to consider their powerlessness in the struggle with the state. Within the KGB, the word *naruzhka* was used as insiders' jargon for "surveillance," from *naruzhnoye nablyudeniya*, or "external observation."

See also SURVEILLANCE, AUDIO.

SURVEILLANCE, AUDIO. Party leader **Joseph Stalin** began eavesdropping on his colleagues in 1922, when he ordered telephone taps on members of the Soviet leadership. According to Stalin's private secretary, in the mid-1920s, Stalin listened to the phone conversations of his adversaries to learn of their tactics in the interparty wars that followed the death of **Vladimir Lenin**. Stalin continued the practice of tapping the telephones of his colleagues right up to his death in 1953.

The Soviet intelligence and security services perfected audio **surveillance** to keep track of foreign suspected **dissidents**, diplomats, and intelligence officers at home and abroad. President Franklin D. Roosevelt's offices and bedrooms were bugged at the Tehran and Yalta conferences, where he met with Stalin. According to **Lavrenty Beria**'s son, who translated the material,

Stalin asked for copies of Roosevelt's conversations as well as detailed comments on what the president's talks revealed about his health and state of mind.

One of the most famous incidents of audio surveillance involved a wooden carving of the Great Seal of the United States presented to the American ambassador in 1945. The seal, which was placed on the wall behind the ambassador's desk, contained a bugging device that transmitted any conversations in the office. The device was discovered in 1952 and was put on display at the United Nations several years later during a debate on Soviet and American espionage.

Audio surveillance remained an important tool of the **KGB** to the end of the Soviet regime, and it provided an immense amount of raw information for security officers. In the months before the 1991 **August putsch**, the KGB placed bugging devices in the offices of **Mikhail Gorbachev**, his wife, and his wife's hairdresser.

See also SORM (*SISTEMA OPERATIVNO-ROZISKNIKH MEROPRIYA-TII*); SURVEILLANCE.

SUVOROV, VIKTOR. *See* REZUN, VLADIMIR BOGDANOVICH (1948–).

SVERDLOV, ANDREI YAKOVLEVICH (1911–1969). The son of Yakov Sverdlov, first chief of the Soviet state and a close friend of **Vladimir Lenin**, Andrei Sverdlov was security service interrogator for several decades. He was recruited into the service and then almost immediately arrested during the *Yezhovshchina*. He was again recruited as an interrogator by **Lavrenty Beria**. Sverdlov was frequently given important intellectuals to break and obtain confessions from. After **Joseph Stalin**'s death, Sverdlov retired and worked in the Academy of Sciences as a researcher.

SVR (*SLUZHBA VNESHNEI REZVEDKI*). The Foreign Intelligence Service of the Russian Federation, the SVR, was created from the **KGB's First Chief Directorate** in December 1991 following the failed **August putsch**. Laws on foreign intelligence passed by the Duma in December 1991 made the service directly subordinate to the president of the Russian Federation. The SVR headquarters are located in Yasenevo outside Moscow, the former headquarters of the First Chief Directorate.

Yevgeny Primakov, first director of the SVR, defined its duties in post-Soviet Russia as intelligence collection and **analysis**, as well as **active measures**. For Primakov and his subordinates, all veterans of the First Chief Directorate, the critical targets are terrorist groups that threaten the integrity of the Russian Federation. Other concerns are the economic viability of

Russia, problems from the narcotics trade, **nuclear proliferation**, and international crime. This list is, of course, hardly complete. The SVR is active in a number of countries, collecting political and economic intelligence. Since 1991, SVR officers have been expelled from a number of Western and Eastern European states, as well as the United States.

According to the SVR website, the new foreign intelligence service has kept the bureaucratic structure of the First Chief Directorate. Deputy directorates of the service are charged with bureaucratic oversight of major components, such as geographic departments, and directorates deal with technical collection, foreign **counterintelligence**, and **illegals**. The service remains confident and competent: since its foundation, it has run agents inside the U.S. intelligence community. Like the First Chief Directorate, the SVR is not risk averse: in 1999, an SVR officer was expelled from the United States for placing a bugging device in the secretary of state's conference room. SVR **illegals** have been exposed and arrested on several occasions since 2010, including 10 in the United States and two in Germany. Since 2007, **Mikhail Fradkov** has been chief of the SVR.

SYMONDS, JOHN (1936–). A former Scotland Yard officer, Symonds worked for the **KGB** under the code name "Scot," first as a courier and then as a seducer targeting vulnerable women attached to foreign embassies. According to the **Mitrokhin archives**, he also passed on the name of British officials he believed could be recruited by the KGB.

T

TARASOV, GERMAN FEDOROVICH (1906–1944). One of the many **NKVD** officers called up to command Red Army formations in the fall of 1941, Tarasov commanded first an infantry division and then the 41st Army. Tarasov's performance in the Rzhev offensive in November 1942 was not considered successful, and he was relieved of command and demoted to deputy army commander. He was later given command of the 70th Army, failed, and was relieved once again. He was killed in combat in 1944 in Hungary.

Joseph Stalin relied on NKVD officers to command units from the battalion to the army level in 1941 as the fronts disintegrated. Many of these men, like Tarasov, were young security professionals who had been rapidly promoted in the late 1930s and had no military experience. Western military historians see the rapid promotion of NKVD officers as a mixed blessing: they were brave, and they undoubtedly stiffened the defenses of Moscow, but they were often only marginally competent, and their operations squandered the lives of Red Army men.

TASS IS AUTHORIZED TO ANNOUNCE. One of the most popular Soviet television shows from the late 1970s deals with the **Ogoronikov** case and the subsequent **KGB** detention of Central Intelligence Agency officer Martha Peterson. The Soviet writer changed Peterson into a male officer, amusing **Rem Krassilnikov**, who was in charge of the KGB operation. He later wrote that "women in the CIA often performed just as well as the stronger half of mankind." Peterson's account is told in her book *The Widow of Moscow*.

"TEN YEARS WITHOUT THE RIGHT OF CORRESPONDENCE". One of the cruelest fictions of the purges. Family and friends of victims of the **Stalin** era were told that their loved ones had been sentenced to "Ten Years without the Right of Correspondence" when in fact they had been shot.

TERRORISM. *See* COUNTERTERRORISM.

THEREMIN, LEON (LEV SERGEYEVICH TERMEN) (1896–1993). A Soviet electronic genius who served as a spy, invented sophisticated bugging devices, and survived the **gulag**, Theremin is widely credited as the father of electronic music. After serving as an **illegal GRU** agent in New York, Theremin returned to Moscow, where he was arrested and sentenced to six years in the labor camps in **Kolyma**. He was rescued from certain death by **NKVD** chief **Lavrenty Beria**, who placed him in a special design bureau (*Sharaska*) to build a wireless bugging device. Code-named "Buran" (snowstorm), the device was implanted in the Great Seal of the United States in the office of the U.S. ambassador in Moscow. Theremin was awarded a Stalin prize, worth $20,000, while a prisoner. He appeared in **Aleksandr Solzhenitsyn's** *The First Circle* as Pryanchikov. In his later years, Theremin served as an academician, returning to electronic music.

THIRD CHIEF DIRECTORATE. *See* KGB ORGANIZATION.

THIRD SECTION. Following a failed coup by liberal officers in December 1825, Tsar Nicholas I sanctioned the first modern Russian security service, the Third Section of the Imperial Chancery, in 1826. The **Decembrist** risings indicated to Nicholas and his more conservative advisers that there was a need for greater surveillance of the population. The Third Section worked in concert with the paramilitary Corps of Gendarmes to extend its reach to urban and rural areas. The Russian archives show that Nicholas paid a great deal of attention to the staffing of the Third Section, and he read and commented on its reporting.

From its beginning, the Third Section targeted intellectuals suspected of revolutionary thoughts and deeds. Count **Aleksandr Benkendorff**, head of the section in 1826–1844, and his successors tended to rely on **informers** and agents provocateurs employed by the Corps of Gendarmes. Despite efforts to modernize the Third Section, it failed to defeat populist revolutionary movements, such as *Narodnaya volya* (People's Will), which assassinated a number of senior tsarist officials in the late 1870s. The Third Section had poor relations with other security bureaucracies and was incompetent against an organized terrorist organization. Worse yet, it was often penetrated by the terrorist organizations it was sworn to defeat. In 1880, Tsar Aleksandr II abolished the organization, replacing it with a secret chancery under Count Loris-Melikov. But it was too late: in 1881, *Narodnaya volya* assassinated the tsar, still poorly served by his secret service. The failure of the Third Section to defeat political radicalism, and the escalation of political terrorism in 1880–1882 led to the formation of the Division for the Protection of Order and Social Security, better known as *Okhrana*.

TRADECRAFT. Tradecraft can best be defined as the art or science of spying. The Russian word *konspiratsiya* is usually rendered as either "trade-craft" or "security." Russian intelligence from the late 19th century on has generally practiced outstanding tradecraft. In the last decades of the tsarist regime, the *Okhrana* developed more sophisticated intelligence tradecraft than any other intelligence service. In matters of cover, **surveillance**, safe houses, and clandestine communications, the tsarist service was light-years ahead of the rest of the world. Agents were bought or frightened into collaborating with the service but then were run with care and were paid well. The *Okhrana* ran as an agent **Roman Malinovskiy**, the leader of the Bolshevik faction in the Duma, for several years. So sure were the *Okhrana* of Malinovskiy's bona fides that they allowed him to travel abroad to meet with a journalist whose specialty was "outing" tsarist agents in the revolutionary parties.

Soviet intelligence tradecraft was derived in part from the underground activities of the Bolshevik Party and in part from the *Okhrana*. Many of the initial **Cheka, GPU,** and **OGPU illegals** had served as couriers and political agents in radical underground movements. They had studied the activities of the *Okhrana* and other European services and developed a style of *konspiratsiya* that allowed them to survive on the streets of Europe, Asia, and the United States. Many of these men and women had served time in tsarist prisons and were not intimidated by the **counterintelligence** services of the West.

A critical strength of Soviet tradecraft was mastery of "the street." Soviet case officers were drilled in the arts of surveillance and countersurveillance. When one young Soviet intelligence officer arrived in New York in the 1940s, he was told to look for drugstores with two entrances that would allow him to lose possible surveillance. The same case officer often met his contacts in movie theaters, where it was possible for an agent and case officer to arrive and depart separately and to meet in the dark. When **Yuri Modin** was running agents in London in the late 1940s, he took five hours to make sure that he had no surveillance before he met with agents.

The creation of effective covers was another strength. Intelligence officers, especially illegals, were expected to live their covers. In the United States, **Joseph Golos** operated a tourist company. Decades later, **Morris and Lona Cohen** ran a bookshop in a London suburb. Lona was remembered by her English neighbors as an eccentric New Zealander with a love for gin and an interest in cricket.

Patience and study were also crucial. Potential agents were investigated for years before they were approached by the service. **NKVD** cables from the 1930s showed a great deal of understanding of the **motivation** that led young British aristocrats to betray their country. In the reports are comments about their parents, their education, and their sexuality. NKVD case officers often demanded that agents write a detailed autobiography to get a better understanding of their personality. This autobiography was used extensively in Moscow as well. The Soviet services also gave their case officers time to develop and work with their agents. **Ruth Werner**, the **GRU** officer who ran **Klaus Fuchs**, noted in her biography, "They always gave me plenty of time."

Agents were to be run with care. Ideological spies like **John Cairncross** received Soviet military combat medals. **Elizabeth Bentley** received the Order of the Red Star. **Oleg Kalugin** and his colleagues in the Washington *rezidentura* ran **John Walker**, a U.S. Navy warrant officer who was in espionage for money, with great interpersonal skills. They treated Walker as an equal and made sure that he knew he could retire in the Soviet Union with the rank of admiral. **Viktor Cherkashin** persuaded **Aldrich Ames** that it was time for him to reveal all the secrets he knew. Ames had already provided the **KGB** with the names of two agents, so Cherkashin argued persuasively that Ames had crossed the Rubicon, and it was time for him to provide the KGB with all the information he had. The result was the "Big Dump": Ames turned over the names of 10 important agents.

Another factor was the service's willingness to spend money when necessary. The OGPU paid Italian agents well to burgle the British ambassador's safe in Rome in the 1930s. The KGB provided Aldrich Ames with more than $2 million. Soviet intelligence officers paid **Clyde Conrad** and **James Hall** hundreds of thousands of dollars.

Willingness to take a risk was also important. All the major KGB successes in the 1980s came out of a willingness to risk meeting and running agents who could have been **double agents**. The decisions to run John Walker and Aldrich Ames took no small amount of physical and bureaucratic courage.

Moscow closely vetted KGB and GRU operations. The **Venona** cables show how carefully operations were managed from Moscow. Agents were investigated and reinvestigated; in 1943, when the **Ring of Five** members were providing thousands of reports on the German army, Moscow carefully considered whether they were controlled by the British Secret Intelligence Service (SIS). The intelligence managers were too aware of the consequences of having SIS manage Soviet policy through its agents. The corollary to this carefulness was a willingness to act on intelligence. Scientific and technical information allowed the Soviet Union to build weapons and develop industries. Information from Ames led to the arrest of Central Intelligence Agency and SIS agents in place.

KGB **defectors** since the 1980s have claimed that the KGB's First Chief Directorate became more and more risk averse. They claim that the leadership of the KGB gave only lip service to the principles that had made the service so successful in previous decades. While some of this criticism is true, the KGB was able to run important agents like **James Hall** and **Clyde Conrad** in West Germany, as well as Aldrich Ames and **Robert Hanssen** in the United States.

TREHOLT, ARNE (1943–). A Norwegian politician and diplomat, Treholt was an important **KGB** agent within his country's Foreign Ministry for almost 15 years. Not only did Treholt provide the KGB with confidential information, but he influenced his country's negotiations with Moscow on the Barents Sea border between the two countries. Treholt was identified as a Soviet agent by **Oleg Gordiyevskiy**, a KGB officer who had volunteered to British intelligence. Treholt was arrested and sentence to 20 years in prison in 1985.

Treholt did his country considerable harm and has been called the worst Norwegian traitor since Vidkun Quisling. His **motivation** for espionage has been discussed in the Norwegian media. As a young man, he was very anti-American, and this brought him to the attention of Soviet intelligence. He was well paid by Moscow and lived well. Moscow may also have flattered him, emphasizing the role he was playing in Norwegian–Soviet relations.

TREPPER, LEOPOLD (1904–1982). A Polish Jewish communist, Trepper served successfully as a **GRU illega l** for two decades. In the 1920s and 1930s, he operated in British-occupied Palestine and France. Beginning in 1938, Trepper built and managed a network of agents in Western Europe that the Nazis referred to as the **Red Orchestra**. Using as a cover the director of a raincoat company, Trepper oversaw the work of dedicated communists and antifascists from Paris to Berlin. His network provided **Joseph Stalin** with thousands of pieces of intelligence over the next four years, much of which was ignored prior to Operation **Barbarossa**. In 1941 and 1942, however, the Red Orchestra provided thousands of accurate reports on German military operations and German industrial production.

Trepper was an imaginative and brave operations officer. He once chose an office for his cover company in the same building as the Brussels headquarters of German military **counterintelligence** (*Abwehr*), and he traveled throughout Nazi-occupied Europe to meet with his principal agents and radio operators. Trepper had only contempt for Soviet officers provided by Moscow to help his apparatus. In his memoirs, Trepper noted that there was no way to teach a man or women to be an effective spy. Either one had imagination and courage, he argued, or one did not.

When Trepper was arrested by German counterintelligence in Paris in 1942, he pretended to cooperate with them to save his life. He later escaped and, after years of hiding, was repatriated to the Soviet Union, where he was almost immediately sent to prison. He was released following Stalin's death and later moved to Poland. Due to anti-Semitic campaigns in Poland in the late 1960s, he moved to Israel, where he died in 1982.

TRILISSER, MIKHAIL ABRAMOVICH (1883–1938). Born into a Jewish family in Astrakhan, Trilisser joined the **Bolshevik Party** in 1901 and led the life of a professional revolutionary for the next 17 years. He took part in the **Revolution of 1905** and served six years in tsarist jails and Siberian **exile**. After the **civil war**, he transferred to the security service, becoming head of foreign intelligence in 1926. His initial responsibility was to target **émigré** groups and disrupt their operations against the infant Bolshevik state, as was done successfully through the **Trust** operation. Trilisser's agents were also successful in penetrating exile groups and their foreign sponsors in France, Germany, Poland, and Great Britain. Trilisser traveled to Germany to meet with his intelligence officers and important agents.

In 1935, Trilisser transferred to the **Comintern** and headed its secret apparatus under the name "Moskvin." He was tasked to serve as a link between the Comintern apparatus and the security and intelligence services. In 1937, he was directed to weed traitors and **Trotskyites** out of the organization. As Moskvin, he ruthlessly purged the Comintern of suspected foreign spies and Trotskyites, but he never met **Joseph Stalin**'s expectations of vigilance. He was arrested and executed in 1938. He was rehabilitated posthumously during the **Nikita Khrushchev** years.

Trilisser was one of the creators of Soviet foreign intelligence. Given his long years in the Bolshevik underground, he understood the value of **illegal** agents. During his years as head of foreign intelligence, the service nurtured a corps of officers—for the most part non-Russians—who recruited important sources in Europe and North America. Soviet penetration of foreign governments owes much to Trilisser's management of the foreign intelligence component.

TROFIMOFF, GEORGE (1927–). The highest-ranking American military officer to be convicted of espionage, Trofimoff was recruited by a Russian Orthodox Church clergymen acting as a conduit for the **KGB**. Trofimoff was head of the Joint Interrogation Center in Nuremburg, Germany, and passed thousands of documents to the Soviets. He was awarded the Order of the Red Banner and paid $250,000 by Moscow. He was initially identified by material in the **Mitrokhin archive**. Former KGB general **Oleg Kalugin** testified at his trial. He was sentenced to life imprisonment in 2001.

TROTSKY, LEON (1879–1940). Born Lev Davidovich Bronstein, Trotsky adopted the name of one of his prison guards and had a distinguished career as a revolutionary before the **Revolution of November 1917**. As a Menshevik, he took part in the **Revolution of 1905** in St. Petersburg. Following arrest and trial, he escaped and went into **exile**. Trotsky often argued with **Vladimir Lenin**, but behind the infighting, there was mutual respect and admiration. Trotsky joined the Bolsheviks in 1917 and became first commissar of foreign affairs and later commissar of war in the Bolshevik government. His repeated successes on the battlefield in the **civil war** guaranteed the survival of the Bolshevik state.

Following Lenin's death, **Joseph Stalin** built a series of alliances in the **Communist Party** to isolate Trotsky from his base in the party and the armed forces. Stalin also used his contacts with **Cheka** leaders **Feliks Dzerzhinsky** and **Vyacheslav Menzhinsky** to harass and detain Trotsky's followers. After Trotsky's **deportation**, the security service continued to keep him under constant **surveillance** in his foreign sanctuaries while arresting his supporters in the Soviet Union. By the mid-1930s, Stalin identified Trotsky as his most implacable and dangerous enemy, despite Trotsky's woefully weak support in the Soviet Union and abroad. The **Moscow Trials** sought to identify Trotsky as an ally of Adolf Hitler, a charge that was widely accepted by communists in the Soviet Union and abroad. In 1936–1938, his few supporters were shot in jails and camps where they had been confined for years, and the **NKVD** began a complex plot to kill Trotsky. In the late 1930s, the NKVD would murder one of his sons inside the Soviet Union and another in Paris.

Two NKVD specialists in assassination and *chornaya rabota* ("black work"), **Pavel Sudoplatov** and **Leonid Eitingon**, were personally directed by Stalin to organize Trotsky's murder in his Mexican exile. A number of agents were recruited in Trotsky's entourage, and one of them, **Ramon Mercader**, was assigned the job of killing Trotsky. On 20 August 1940, Mercader asked to meet Trotsky alone to discuss a magazine article he was writing. When Trotsky's back was turned, Mercader struck him with a mountaineer's ax, mortally wounding him.

Trotsky's death was celebrated by Stalin publicly and privately. Sudoplatov and Eitingon were rewarded, and Stalin wrote an editorial for *Pravda* titled "Death of an International Spy." Vengeance was Stalin's. But Trotsky in exile never was a threat to Stalin in exile: in the words of his most prominent biographer, he was the "prophet unarmed."

TRUBNIKOV, VYACHESLAV IVANOVICH (1944–). One of the most influential of modern Russian foreign intelligence officers, Trubnikov entered the **KGB First Chief Directorate** in 1967. In the 1980s, he served as *rezident* in India and Bangladesh. In 1996, he was made chief of the Foreign

Intelligence Service, the **SVR**, succeeding **Yevgeny Primakov**. Two years later, he was promoted to the rank of general of the army. Russian President **Vladimir Putin** used Trubnikov as a special ambassador within the Commonwealth of Independent States. According to the Soviet media, he was an apostle of a very hard line. In 2004, Putin appointed him Moscow's ambassador to India.

Trubnikov was an experienced intelligence officer and a capable administrator. While the Russian military was suffering major budget cuts, the SVR was able to maintain the tempo of its operations, remaining a worldwide intelligence service. In his four years as chief of the SVR, Trubnikov appeared frequently in the media, giving Russian foreign intelligence a human face.

TRUST OPERATION. The most sophisticated **counterintelligence** operation run by the **Cheka** and the **GPU** involved their creation in the early 1920s of a fictitious opposition group within the Soviet Union. The Cheka-created Monarchist Organization of Central Russia created in turn a trust in Paris called the Municipal Credit Organization of Moscow. The Trust was crafted to establish ties with Russian **émigré** groups in the West and lure the leaders of the White movements back into the Soviet Union. Émigrés and some Western intelligence services fell for the ruse: some actually traveled to the Soviet Union, met with dissidents, and returned safely to the West. In August 1924, **Boris Savinkov**, a former revolutionary and minister of war in the transitional Aleksandr Kerensky government, entered the Soviet Union clandestinely to contact the Trust. He was arrested and publicly confessed his sins in a Soviet court. Shortly thereafter, in September 1925, **Sidney Reilly**, sometimes agent of British intelligence, crossed the Finnish–Soviet frontier to contact the Trust. He was captured, interrogated, and then executed in Moscow.

Following the success in capturing Savinkov and Reilly, the Trust disappeared as stealthily as it emerged. It has been studied in the West as well as the Soviet Union as the model of a successful counterintelligence operation. The Soviet and Eastern European intelligence services often engaged in **false flag** organizations such as the Trust to distract émigrés and foreign intelligence services.

TSANAVA, LEVRENTY FOMICH (1900–1955). One of **Lavrenty Beria**'s protégés in the Soviet security service, Tsanava joined the **Cheka** before his 21st birthday and rose quickly in the Georgian **NKVD**. In 1933, he transferred to the **Communist Party** apparatus to work with Beria. In 1938, he followed Beria back into the security service and was appointed chief of the Byelorussian NKVD. During **World War II**, Tsanava worked with the

partisan movement in Byelorussia and then in Moscow as deputy chief of the central partisan staff and in 1945 was made a lieutenant general. After the war, Tsanava was made head of the **MGB** in Byelorussia. He masterminded the murder of the actor **Solomon Mikhoels** in Minsk at **Joseph Stalin**'s behest in 1948. In 1952, he was removed from his senior position and placed on leave. In April 1953, he was arrested for Mikhoels's murder and died in pretrial confinement in 1955, possibly a suicide.

TSINEV, GEORGI (1907–1996). Tsinev attended the same metallurgical institute in Ukraine as **Leonid Brezhnev**, who became a colleague in the Ukrainian **Communist Party**. During **World War II**, Tsinev transferred from party work to the Soviet army and served on several fronts as the chief political adviser. After the war, he served in the **Third** (Military Counterintelligence) **Chief Directorate** of the **KGB**. He was chief of military **counterintelligence** in Berlin in the 1950s, rising quickly to head of the Third Chief Directorate, and then first deputy chief of the KGB. Tsinev was a crucial member of Brezhnev's "Dneprepropetrovsk mafia," which helped him control the service, and served as well as a key link with the military. He was made a general of the army, four stars) in 1978 and served as a member of the Central Committee of the Communist Party of the Soviet Union from 1976 to 1986, a sign of his political power in the KGB.

TSVYGUN, SEMYON KONSTANTINOVICH (1917–1982). A career **KGB** officer who rose to first deputy chief of the service because of his family connections to **Leonid Brezhnev**, Tsvygun was an important member of Brezhnev's "Dneprepropetrovsk mafia." Tsvygun served in Moldavia with Brezhnev in the 1950s and, according to many sources, was a boon drinking companion. Tsvygun wrote several books and movie scenarios on the KGB and **partisan** warfare, as well as a history of the **Cheka**.

In early 1982, Tsvygun was attacked for professional incompetence by Mikhail Suslov, **Communist Party** second secretary responsible for ideology. Suslov blamed Tsvygun for allowing damning information about Brezhnev to reach the West. Later that week, Tsvygun apparently committed suicide. Brezhnev refused to sign his obituary, the first sign that the West had of growing divisions in the ruling elite. Suslov, who was in poor health, died shortly thereafter and was replaced as the number two man in the party by **Yuri Andropov**.

TUDOR-HART, EDITH (1908–1973). One of the most unheralded Soviet spies of the period between the two world wars was the noted photographer Edith Tudor-Hart (née Suchetzky). Born in Austria, she married a left-wing English doctor and moved to London in the early 1930s. Tudor-Hart worked as a spotter and recruiter for Soviet intelligence. She helped enlist **Kim Philby** and other upper-class Britons sympathetic to **Joseph Stalin**'s Russia. She was deeply trusted by the Soviet intelligence service, which came to her for help in 1940 when they lost contact with **Guy Burgess** and **Anthony Blunt**. According to Soviet memoirs of the period, it was through her efforts that Moscow reestablished its intelligence apparatus after losing the **Ring of Five**.

TUKHACHEVSKIY, MIKHAIL NIKOLAYEVICH (1893–1937). Tukhachevskiy was the *wunderkind* of the Red Army. A tsarist guards officer, he was captured in **World War I** and spent time in the same prisoner-of-war camp as Charles de Gaulle. He joined the **Bolshevik Party** and commanded armies in the early 1920s, and from 1925 to 1928, he was chief of staff of the Soviet armed forces. In 1935, he was one of five men promoted to the rank of marshal of the Soviet Union. Unfortunately, Tukhachevskiy had made a mortal enemy in **Joseph Stalin** in 1921 when they served in the war against Poland. Tukhachevskiy had blamed Stalin for malfeasance and publicly rebuked Stalin for gross strategic incompetence. Stalin did not forget the insults.

In the spring of 1937, Stalin decided to move against what he saw as dissent in the army. This was not, as many intelligence historians maintain, a result of secret information provided by the Czechs; it resulted from Stalin's decision to purge the military. People close to Tukhachevskiy were arrested and tortured into confessing that Tukhachevskiy and other senior officials were Nazi agents. On 22 May 1937, Tukhachevskiy and other senior officers were arrested, tortured by the **NKVD**, and confessed. Tukhachevskiy's dossier was splattered with his blood, according to witnesses. On 11 June, Tukhachevskiy and other senior officers were tried by a special military court, convicted, and immediately shot.

Following Tukhachevskiy's **execution**, the NKVD fell on the army, arresting between 30,000 and 40,000 officers. Several thousand senior commanders were shot in 1937–1940, including three of five marshals, 15 of 16 army commanders, 50 of 57 corps commanders, and more than half of the division and brigade commanders. In the Soviet navy, eight of nine four-star admirals were shot, as well as the majority of the navy staff. Party commissars in the army and navy staff suffered the same fate: all 16 army commissars were shot, as were 25 of 28 army corps commissars and 79 of 97 division commissars. All were loyal to Stalin, the state, and the army. More Soviet commanders and political commissars died at Stalin's hands in 1937–1940 than from German bullets and shells.

Tukhachevskiy and almost all his colleagues were formally rehabilitated in 1956 by **Nikita Khrushchev**. The real cost of the Tukhachevskiy affair was the abysmal performance of the Red Army in the "Winter War" against

Finland in 1939–1940 and the opening battles of **World War II**. Incompetent staff officers and commanders were incapable of fighting the German *Wehrmacht*, and millions of Soviet soldiers died or went into prison camps. Some of the Red Army commanders responsible for defeats on the Eastern Front were arrested and shot in the fall of 1941—the final casualties of the Tukhachevskiy affair.

TUPIKOV, VASILII IVANOVICH (1901–1941). Tupikov served as the Soviet **military attaché** in Berlin from December 1940 to 22 June 1941. Tupikov was a strong officer who reported in detail on German preparations for Operation **Barbarossa**, which was rejected by **GRU** chief **Fillip Golikov**. After being exchanged with other Soviet diplomats for their German opposite numbers, he was appointed chief of staff of the Southwestern Front. He died in battle with the front's staff on 20 September 1941 near Kiev.

U

UKRAINIAN CRISIS. Following Moscow's success in displacing the Ukrainian authorities in **Crimea**, violence broke out in the three eastern coal mining region (*oblast*s) of Ukraine in the spring of 2014. These provinces have a majority of Russians, but there had been no previous political conflict between them and Kiev. The struggle was clearly orchestrated from Moscow: Russian paramilitary organizations well armed and organized took control of several small cities, expelled small Ukrainian military garrisons, and proclaimed a Donetsk People's Republic. By the summer of 2014, the war had become a stalemate, with Ukrainian and secessionist forces fighting in several small cities for control. The crisis worsened in July 2014, when the secessionist forces shot down several Ukrainian planes and a Malaysian civilian aircraft.

Several senior **GRU** officers, led by **Igor Girkin**, commanded the rebel forces and served as political advisers to the Russian leaders of the "people's republic." As in the Crimea, the GRU seems to be President **Vladimir Putin**'s weapon of choice in expanding Russian power outside of Russia and into the territories of the successor states of the Soviet Union. The United States has publicly identified Girkin as well as the GRU chief, Lieutenant General **Igor Sergun**, and other Russian officials as war criminals and imposed financial sanctions on them.

ULTRA. The British code name "Ultra" was given to intelligence derived from breaking the codes of Germany's Enigma machine. Sensitive top-secret information decoded from the intercepted messages was referred to as "Ultra top secret." With the exception of the atom bomb, Ultra was the greatest secret of the war: it provided the Western Allies with critical naval, air, and army information. Ultra intelligence also included detailed information on the German military's order of battle and military planning on the Eastern Front. The problem for the British government was how to pass this material to the Soviet Union without revealing its source.

The British government passed Ultra material to Moscow through liaison between the two countries' intelligence services without revealing that it came from signals intelligence. (American and British generals were misinformed as well; they were told that the material with the fictional code name "Boniface" came from a spy ring inside Germany.) The British may also have passed diluted versions of the material to Moscow through a spy ring operating in Switzerland. None of this saved the Ultra secret from Moscow: Soviet agent **John Cairncross** provided his Soviet case officers with thousands of raw Ultra messages during the war. The Soviet military considered this material "very valuable" in preparing to counter the last German strategic offensive of the war at Kursk in 1943. Cairncross's treachery also allowed Moscow to check the material they were receiving from London and to understand British capabilities to break codes, including their own. The British and American public found out about the Ultra secret 30 years after the Soviets did.

ULANOVSKY, ALEXANDER PETROVICH (1891–1970). A revolutionary before he was 20, Ulanovsky was exiled to the same village in Siberia as **Joseph Stalin**. According to one account, he stole Stalin's winter coat during an escape attempt. Following the Bolshevik Revolution, Ulanovsky returned to Moscow and joined the Red Army. In 1932, he came to the United States with his wife, Nadezhda, to take over the post of **GRU illegal** *rezident*, where his responsibility was to obtain scientific and technical intelligence. One of his agents was **Whitaker Chambers**, who described his boss as "the only Russian who was ever to become my close friend."

After serving in Europe and surviving 18 months in a Danish jail for a bungled operation, Ulanovsky returned to Moscow, where he survived the great purge of 1937–1938. When he apparently protested his wife's arrest in 1948, he was in turn arrested and sentenced to 10 years in the **gulag**. Both were released following Stalin's death.

UNSHLIKHT, JOSEPH STANISLAVOVICH (1879–1938). Born into a middle-class Polish Jewish family, Unshlikht joined the underground Social Democratic Party of Poland and Lithuania in 1900 but gravitated to the Bolsheviks. Between 1902 and 1916, he was repeatedly arrested for his work in the Bolshevik underground and spent several years in jail or **exile**. Following the **Revolution of November 1917**, Unshlikht joined the **Cheka** and acted on the Northern Front as the security service's troubleshooter. Unshlikht was **Feliks Dzerzhinsky**'s de facto deputy in 1921–1923, dealing with sensitive dangers, such as the Tambov revolt and rural insurrection in Ukraine. Subsequently, he held important military and party posts and served as the chief of the security service in Moscow. He was a member of the

Communist Party Central Committee for several years and was repeatedly decorated. Unshlikht was described by **Leon Trotsky** as "ambitious but a talentless intriguer." **Joseph Stalin** may have shared Trotsky's opinion, at least about his capacity for intrigue: Unshlikht was arrested in June 1937 and shot on 28 July 1938.

URITSKIY, SEMEN PETROVICH (1899–1938). As chief of the **GRU** from 1935 to 1937, Uritskiy directed **Richard Sorge** in Asia, as well as other talented **illegals**. Despite promotions and rewards, he was never fully trusted by **Joseph Stalin**. He was arrested in November 1937 with most of his staff and shot shortly thereafter. According to a recent GRU history, 200 senior members of the GRU headquarters cadre were arrested in 1937–1938. Most of their replacements had no intelligence experience. In 1964, Uritskiy was posthumously rehabilitated and given credit for Sorge's operations in Japan.

USPENSKIY, ALEKSANDR IVANOVICH (1902–1940). Uspenskiy joined the **Cheka** at age 18 and rose quickly. In January 1938, he was appointed by **Nikolai Yezhov** as head of the Ukrainian **NKVD**, and over the next 10 months, he carried out a merciless purge of the **Communist Party** and the local organs of the NKVD. Sensing Yezhov's fall in November 1938, Uspenskiy faked his suicide and disappeared in hopes of finding a sanctuary. He was captured five months later following an intense manhunt, tried, and convicted of treason on 27 January 1940. He was shot the next day. His wife was executed for her role in his flight. Uspenskiy's flight reflects how the rolling purge of the late 1930s impacted on the NKVD. Even successful NKVD chiefs were sacrificed to the whim of **Joseph Stalin**'s policy. Information from the Russian archives suggest than only 23 of 120 senior NKVD officers appointed by Yezhov survived his fall.

UZBEK COTTON SCANDAL. The greatest single financial crime in Soviet history involved the massive overreporting of cotton production in the Central Asian Republic of Uzbekistan. Uzbek party boss Sharaf Rashidov, who ruled the republic from 1959 to 1983, treated Uzbekistan as his own private fief and created a massive criminal family to run it. Cotton was Uzbekistan's most important resource, and every effort was made to grow it. Beginning in the 1970s, the Uzbek government massively overreported the amount of cotton delivered to the mills in Moscow, and the Uzbek machine received billions of rubles for imaginary cotton.

Rasidov's tactics were well known in Moscow, but his close friendship with party boss **Leonid Brezhnev** protected him from punishment. Following Brezhnev's death in November 1982, **Yuri Andropov** ordered the KGB to begin a massive investigation of the Uzbek party. Rashidov either committed suicide or died of a heart attack or was murdered, and the **KGB** moved to roll up his subordinates. Hundreds of party and police officials were tried, and a number were sentenced to death and shot in 1985–1987. Brezhnev's son-in-law, Yuri Churbanov, deputy minister of the Ministry of Internal Affairs, was tried and imprisoned for his role in protecting Rashidov. The Soviet press devoted thousands of pages to the story, heralding the punishment of the Rashidov gang as a triumph of law and order.

The **MVD** and the KGB's investigation of the "Uzbek mafia," as it was called in the Soviet press, caused major problems for Moscow in the long run. Many Uzbeks believed that their nation had been singled out for racial and religious abuse and that worse crimes were committed in the European parts of the Soviet Union. Rashidov had tolerated Islam, and the investigation of corruption led to the arrests of a number of religious figures. In 1988–1990, there was ethnic violence in Uzbekistan as the Uzbeks sought to maintain control of ethnically divided areas, resulting from their fears that Moscow was again seeking to minimize Uzbek interests.

See also BREZHNEV, LEONID ILYICH (1911–1982); MVD (*MINISTERSTVO VNUTRENNIKH DEL*).

V

VADIS, ALEKSANDR ANATOLEVICH (1906–1968). Vadis was orphaned during the Russian **civil war**, entered the security service from the
Red Army in 1930, and somehow survived the *Yezhovshchina*. In 1942, he
entered **counterintelligence** and was drafted into *Smersh* in 1943. He ended
World War II as a lieutenant general, having served as the *Smersh* commander of the Second Byelorussian Front, which captured Berlin. Vadis was
one of **Joseph Stalin**'s favorite military counterintelligence chiefs. He took
control of **Adolf Hitler's corpse** and Eva Braun's after they were discovered
by a *Smersh* patrol in Berlin on 5 May 1945. Vadis informed Stalin of the
news, had the bodies autopsied, and shipped the corpses to the Soviet Union.
Vadis warned the military and medical personnel that this secret had to be
kept forever. (Marshal **Georgi Zhukov** was not informed about the disposi-
tion of Hitler's remains until 1965.)

Following the war, Vadis held positions in the **MGB** in Moscow and the
Far East. He was purged at the same time as his boss in *Smersh*, **Viktor
Abakumov**, but never imprisoned. He was suspended in 1951, then removed
from the service in 1954 and reduced in rank "for disgracing himself."

VASSALL, WILLIAM JOHN CHRISTOPHER (1924–). The son of an
Anglican clergyman, Vassall went to Moscow in the early 1950s as a clerk in
the Naval Attaché's Office. He was quickly identified as a homosexual by
the **KGB** and blackmailed into working for Soviet intelligence. On his return
to London, Vassall was promoted by the Admiralty and continued to work in
place for the KGB. He was caught in 1962, tried, and sentenced to 18 years
in prison. He was paroled after serving 11 years. Vassall, along with Harry
Houghton, provided Moscow with a tremendous amount of top-secret information about British and North Atlantic Treaty Organization military plans.
It was important to the Soviet Union, which at the time was building a
modern blue-water navy.

VASSILIEV, ALEXANDER (1962–). A former **KGB** officer and dedicated researcher, Vassiliev has contributed to some of the passionate debates on Soviet espionage. In 1990, Vassiliev resigned from both the KGB and the **Communist Party**. Over the next several years, he was granted access to historical files of the Soviet intelligence services, some of which he copied by hand and on others took notes.

Vassiliev emigrated in 1996 and became the coauthor of two well-received histories of Soviet intelligence in the United States: *The Haunted Woods* and *Spies*. On the conclusion of the latter work, Vassiliev donated his notebooks (over 1,150 pages) to the Library of Congress, where they have been translated and can be accessed online from the Cold War International History Project. The books and the archives do much to broaden the story of Soviet intelligence. For example, they provide more evidence for continuing to believe that **Alger Hiss** was guilty of spying, they open an espionage case against the radical journalist **I. F. Stone**, and they indicate that **Robert Oppenheimer** almost certainly was not a Soviet agent.

Vassiliev's books have poured more aviation gas on the debate over the role of Soviet intelligence and its assets. Vassiliev worked under pressure, copied handwritten documents, and had to cope with hundreds of code names. His work is not perfect and, like any primary source, needs to be checked. However, most, in the opinion of major scholars, holds up.

VAUPSHASOV, STANISLAV ALEKSEEVICH (1899–1976). One of the most strikingly successful **partisan** leaders, Vaupshasov joined the Red Army at age 19 and began working as a partisan behind White lines during the **civil war**. He entered the **NKVD**'s foreign intelligence directorate in the late 1930s and served as an **illegal** in Western Europe. During the Spanish Civil War, he served as an adviser to the Republican government in intelligence and sabotage operations.

With the beginning of **World War II**, he commanded a battalion of partisans deep in the enemy's rear during the **Battle of Moscow**. Vaupshasov specialized in deep raids, taking his units on forced marches hundreds of kilometers behind enemy lines. These raids had both political and military purposes: they disrupted German logistics and lines of communication, and they allowed the establishment of liberated areas deep in the enemy's rear. In 1944, after the liberation of Byelorussia, where he had operated for months, Vaupshasov was made a Hero of the Soviet Union. For his career in Soviet intelligence, he was awarded four Orders of Lenin. Following the war, he resigned from the service as a colonel and wrote several accounts of the partisan war, the most important of which was *People with Clean Conscience.*

VENONA. The American code name for the interception and decryption of more than 2,900 Russian intelligence messages in the late 1940s was "Venona." (One of the British code names was "Bride.") The original breakthrough was made possible by errors committed by Soviet code clerks who continued to use the same one-time pads in enciphering messages. In 1946, the U.S. Army **signals intelligence** agency first began reading the Soviet intelligence messages. In 1947–1948, the information was shared with the Federal Bureau of Investigation (FBI) but not the Central Intelligence Agency (CIA). An FBI officer who worked with the information to identify Soviet spies later wrote, "I stood in the vestibule of the enemy's house, having entered by stealth."

The information in the intercepts identified more than 349 American citizens as Soviet agents. Of these, 171 are identified by their true names, and 178 are known only by their cover names in the Venona cables. The messages also identified more than 100 citizens of Great Britain, France, Canada, and other countries as Soviet agents. Information from Venona allowed the American and British security services to identify scores of agents by name, including **Julius Rosenberg**, **Alger Hiss**, and **Donald Maclean**. The information led, however, to few prosecutions because neither the United States nor Great Britain wanted to risk compromising the sources.

The material was a critical **counterintelligence** tool for the British and Americans as they began to cope with the Soviet intelligence services. For example, messages indicated that in 1944, a Soviet agent named "Homer" in the British embassy was meeting his Soviet case officers frequently in New York. When one message noted that Homer was going to New York to be with his pregnant wife, who was living with her mother, it was possible to discern that the agent was Donald Maclean, whose American wife was pregnant and living at the time with her mother.

Venona could have done Moscow far greater harm, but the secret was betrayed by **William Weisband**, an agent serving in the U.S. Army signals intelligence service. Through Weisband, Moscow learned about Venona four years before the CIA did. According to one **KGB** officer's memoir, several **NKVD** and **GRU** code clerks were executed for their errors in constructing one-time pads. Venona almost certainly convinced Moscow to cut ties to some of its most productive agents and led to the disintegration of the Soviet spy apparatus in North America after 1948.

The Venona program was not acknowledged by either Washington or London until 1995. The publication of the messages and supporting documents in the United States by the CIA and the National Security Agency had a dramatic impact on the writing of **Cold War** history. While some historians continue to claim that Venona was created out of whole cloth by Allied intelligence services, most historians and journalists acknowledge that the information proves that the Soviet intelligence services had penetrated the

Allied nuclear weapons program, military and diplomatic services, and intelligence establishments in Washington and London. Recently, the **SVR** allowed the publication of material from its archives that confirms 58 persons identified in Venona as Soviet spies and establishes the identity of nine persons who were hiding behind cover names in the Venona messages.

VETROV, VLADIMIR IPPOLITOVICH (1927–1984). An officer of Directorate T of the **KGB**'s **First Chief Directorate**, Vetrov volunteered to work for France in 1980 and was given the code name "Farewell." Over a few years, Vetrov provided the French Security Service with information to frustrate the Soviet collection of scientific and technical intelligence. Paris used the information to expel more than 40 KGB officers in 1981 and alerted the United States about the scope of KGB scientific and technical intelligence activities. An official U.S. government report noted that Vetrov had alerted the West to Soviet theft of highly classified aircraft technology and prevented the loss of billions of dollars of critical scientific information.

Vetrov's downfall came out of an illicit love affair. In 1982 on his return to Paris, he was confronted by his mistress, who demanded he leave his wife and marry her. Vetrov panicked and stabbed her and attacked a police officer. She lived, but Vetrov was arrested and convicted of murder. He was sentenced to 12 years in prison. Later in letters from his prison cell, he admitted his espionage to friends. He was tried and executed.

VIETNAM WAR. Soviet intelligence played a minor if not unimportant role in the Franco–Vietminh War of 1946–1954. The *rezidenturas* of both the **MGB** and the **GRU** in Paris collected information from agents recruited from the French **Communist Party**, which was passed to the Vietminh. The most important source probably was **Georges Paques**, who served as a senior civil servant in the Mayer, Laniel, and Mendes-France administrations; Paques was recruited in 1946 and served as a Soviet agent until 1963. Soviet military intelligence officers also served with Vietminh headquarters near Dien Bien Phu.

Both the **KGB** and the GRU saw the U.S. involvement in Vietnam as an opportunity to gather information about the U.S. military. In exchange for billions of dollars of military equipment provided to the Vietnamese, the Soviet intelligence services expected a free hand to collect information. According to the Soviet archives, they were disappointed. On at least one occasion, a Vietnamese military officer was prosecuted for providing a Soviet counterpart information about the effectiveness of surface-to-air missiles against American aircraft. North Vietnam was never a Soviet satellite, and billions of dollars of military aid did not buy Moscow as much as it wanted.

The Vietnam War also provided the KGB with the basis for many of its most successful **active measures**. Working through Eastern European communist parties and their intelligence services, as well as front organizations, the KGB planted anti-American issues in the press of the world. The KGB saw the war as a golden opportunity to weaken the U.S. position in the North Atlantic Treaty Organization and to strengthen the Soviet Union's position in international fora.

VLASIK, NIKOLAI SIDOROVICH (1896–1967). Vlasik entered the **Cheka** from the Red Army in 1919. He formed a close personal relationship with **Joseph Stalin** in the 1920s and served as his bodyguard for almost two decades. In 1938, he officially took command of the directorate responsible for leadership protection, and from 1946 to 1952, he served as the commandant of the Kremlin with the rank of lieutenant general. Vlasik also served as Stalin's chief **informer**, gathering information about other members of the leadership. He was by all reports widely hated within the party leadership and the security service. Along with Stalin's unofficial chief of staff Aleksandr Poskrebyshev, he had immense authority. Foreign Minister **Vyacheslav Molotov** believed him to be very corrupt, telling a young biographer that he should have been arrested earlier.

In May 1952, Vlasik was stripped of his command and made deputy head of a forced labor camp as Stalin moved to purge the security service. He was arrested at Stalin's order in December 1952 and spent the next two years in confinement. In 1955, he was sentenced to 10 years in **exile**. An amnesty set him free a year later, but he was condemned to live out the rest of his life under **surveillance**.

VLODOMIRSKIY, LEV YEMELYANOVICH (1903–1953). Vlodomirskiy was one of the most prominent Russian **Chekists** in **Lavrenty Beria**'s official family. He apparently came to Beria's attention in the Caucasus, where he had been assigned by **Genrykh Yagoda**. Beria brought him to Moscow to head the investigations department. In this role, Vlodomirskiy routinely tortured and executed prisoners. In the summer of 1941, Vlodomirskiy was put in charge of the arrest, interrogation, and **execution** of senior officers and their wives who had angered **Joseph Stalin**: among those executed were a former chief of the **GRU** and two former leaders of the air force.

Vlodomirskiy is remembered as one of Beria's hardest men. He took part in a number of extralegal killings for Beria. He was arrested shortly after Beria and executed the same evening. In 2000, a Moscow court reversed the death sentence, substituting one of 25 years. This allowed his heirs to claim his estate, which had been confiscated as part of the 1953 death sentence. This decision angered many of the descendants of Vlodomirskiy's victims, who saw the decision as an effort to efface the terror of the Stalin years.

VOICES. Radio broadcasts from abroad—such as the Voice of America, the BBC, and broadcasts from France, Germany, and the Vatican—were referred to by Soviet citizens as "voices." The official Soviet line was that they were *golos vraga* ("the voice of the enemy"), but the broadcasts reached millions of Soviet citizens every day. By the late 1970s, Iranian and Saudi radio stations were also broadcasting into Soviet Central Asia and the Caucasus, where 40 million Soviet Muslims lived. The **KGB** spent a great deal of time and attention trying to block these stations through jamming but with little success. The "voices" created a problem for the Soviet leadership, challenging the **Communist Party**'s monopoly on information.

VORKUTA. One of the **gulag** system's largest concentration of forced labor camps centered on the northern city of Vorkuta. The city and the camps were established in 1931 in the tundra north of the Arctic Circle for mining coal. The first 23 "settlers" to arrive were prisoners, and approximately a million prisoners and **exiles** passed through the camp system. In July 1953, news of riots in East Berlin led to strikes and riots in the Vorkuta camps. In Camp Number 6, the strikers refused promises from the authorities of better conditions and resisted a blockade by security forces. Moscow then decided to use force, and **MVD** troops fired on the strikers, killing scores. Several of the strike leaders were later executed. Vorkuta today is a city of 200,000.

VORONIN, ALEKSANDR IVANOVICH (1908–1990). After joining the **NKVD** from the **Communist Party** apparatus, Voronin was assigned as security chief for Stalingrad. During the opening days of the **Battle of Stalingrad**, Voronin organized the evacuation of civilians and developed volunteer battalions to support beleaguered Red Army formations. These actions were important in preventing the fall of the city in August 1942. Voronin was promoted to lieutenant general in 1943, served as the **KGB** representative in Albania for several years, but left the KGB in disgrace in 1962.

VYSHAYA MERA NAKAZANIYA **(SUPREME MEASURE OF PUNISHMENT).** Capital punishment during the years of **Joseph Stalin** was referred to as *Vyshaya mera* ("supreme measure") or *Vyshaya mera nakazaniya* ("supreme measure of punishment") or simply as *Vyshaya* or the acronyms VM and VMN. Lists of condemned prisoners were provided to Stalin in 1936–1938 with "VMN" typed next to them. Stalin usually signed the list, giving the **NKVD** authorization to shoot the condemned.

VYSHINSKY, ANDREI YANUARIEVICH (1883–1954). Vyshinsky, a Menshevik in his youth, served a sentence for political radicalism with **Joseph Stalin** in 1907–1908. He apparently befriended Stalin, feeding him from food packages he received from his wealthy parents. In the late 1920s, Vyshinsky entered the **procuracy** and was the lead prosecutor in the three **Moscow Trials**. Vyshinsky gained an international reputation from his rhetoric: he demanded in all three trials that the defendants, "these mad dogs," be shot. He was made procurator general of the country in 1938 and sat on three-person special courts that sent thousands of men and women to their death.

Beginning in 1939, Stalin used Vyshinsky in diplomatic missions to the Baltic and Eastern Europe, promoting him to deputy foreign minister. Over the next five years, he was Stalin's enforcer, shaping governments, crafting agreements, and ordering the arrests of real and suspected enemies. In May 1945, Stalin sent Vyshinsky to Berlin to act as Marshal **Georgi Zhukov**'s "political adviser." Vyshinsky later served at the Nuremberg trials as an adviser to the Soviet judges and prosecutors. He was rewarded by Stalin for his work on the court and in Eastern Europe by promotion to minister of foreign affairs and to chief of the *Komitet Informatsii* (Committee of Information). He died in 1954 of a heart attack.

Vyshinsky was one of Stalin's most successful and long-standing servants. A cultured man from a family of Polish aristocrats with a prerevolutionary legal education, he became the public face of Stalin's justice to Soviet citizens and the world. The Soviet archives show that his speeches at the Moscow Trials were edited and rewritten by Stalin. Yet he apparently lived with dread that the wheels of history could crush him, as they had many of his victims. Vyshinsky, according to longtime foreign minister Anatoly Gromyko, lived in fear of **Lavrenty Beria**. When Beria called, Vyshinsky sprang to attention. Vyshinsky, Gromyko claimed, "cringed like a dog before his master."

WALKER SPY RING. The most significant victory of Soviet intelligence in the **Cold War** may have been the recruitment of four Americans with knowledge of military and intelligence codes. John Walker, a U.S. Navy warrant officer who had served on nuclear submarines and was deeply in debt, walked into the Soviet embassy in Washington in 1967 and volunteered to work for the **KGB**. "I'm a naval officer," he reportedly said. "I'd like to make some money and I'll give you some genuine stuff in return." The KGB deputy *rezident*, **Oleg Kalugin,** recognized the value of Walker's "genuine stuff" and developed **tradecraft** to run him first in the United States and later in Vienna. Over the next 18 years, Walker, his brother, his son, and a close colleague, Jerry Whitworth, provided Moscow with the ability to crack several American codes. The Soviets paid Walker more than $2 million for his role and gave Whitworth over $100,000 to remain at his post as a navy code clerk.

After retiring from the navy, Walker served as spymaster of his little ring of traitors. The KGB met with him in Vienna and used specially designed dead drops in suburban Maryland to pay him and receive raw material from his agents. Walker hid the payments artfully, running a small private detective agency in the Norfolk, Virginia, area that was perfect for laundering money. Walker's detective work gave him access to law enforcement and naval personnel, which may have allowed him to recruit other sources.

In May 1985, the Federal Bureau of Investigation (FBI) arrested Walker and his three confederates after his wife reported his activities to the FBI. All were sentenced to life in prison. Walker later told an American television interviewer that K-Mart, a chain retail store, had better security than the U.S. Navy. One Soviet **defector** later told a congressional committee that had war occurred while Walker was providing coded material, the Soviet military would have won because of its ability to read U.S. communications. The Soviets gained another, perhaps even greater advantage from the Walker ring. The information showed them their submarines' vulnerability in the open ocean, causing them to make changes in their naval weapons and strategy.

WALLENBERG, RAOUL (1913–1947?). As a Swedish diplomat, Wallenberg saved thousands of Hungarian Jews caught between the Nazi authorities in Budapest and the advancing Red Army. He was able to document many Jews as citizens of neutral states and on more than one occasion was able to remove Jews from trains that were bound for the death camps. Following the Red Army's conquest of Hungary, Wallenberg was arrested by *Smersh* on 17 January 1945 and shipped to Moscow on suspicion of being an American intelligence agent. For the next two years, he was interrogated in **Lubyanka** prison. In July 1947, the head of the Lubyanka hospital reported to **Viktor Abakumov** that Wallenberg had died of a heart attack. He was cremated without an autopsy, and the Swedish government was not informed of his fate until 1957. He had been murdered by poison or perhaps shot, apparently at Abakumov's orders.

Wallenberg's death has never been satisfactorily documented for his family or supporters. The Swedish government and international human rights organizations tried for decades to ascertain his fate, and many believed until the fall of the Soviet Union that he was held in a **gulag**. However, recent memoirs by **KGB** officers establish that he was assassinated—a tragic fate for a great hero.

WAR SCARES. On several occasions, the Soviet authorities used the security services to whip up war scares for international and domestic political reasons. In 1927, **Joseph Stalin** spoke of the imminent danger of war with Japan and Great Britain. Stalin used this fear to give the security police far greater power in arresting **dissidents** and **deporting** such figures as **Leon Trotsky**. In 1952, Stalin again used the threat of war with the West to create a domestic hysteria about spies and terrorists. He aimed this campaign domestically at Jews, who were called "rootless cosmopolitanites." The Soviet people were bombarded with accounts of the **Doctors' Plot**, alleging that Jewish doctors were poisoning Russians and spying for America and Israel. Stalin almost certainly would have parlayed this threat into a massive purge of the political leadership had he lived.

Yuri Andropov approved a war scare in 1982–1984. The themes of the campaign were the threat of an American nuclear strike and the need for greater discipline and vigilance at home. Several leading dissidents were arrested, and conditions for political prisoners worsened. Soviet propaganda portrayed the West as led by a "mad" President Ronald Reagan, and the Soviet media blamed the United States for the assassination of Indian premier Indira Gandhi. The war scare infected the **KGB**'s foreign intelligence component: under the *RYaN* program, KGB and **GRU** *rezidenturas* were ordered to look for (and find) proof of an American plan for nuclear war.

Unlike previous war scares, this had the potential of accidentally igniting a nuclear war. The Soviet leadership abandoned this war scare following Andropov's death in early 1984.

War scares may have deceived the Soviet leadership as well, creating a "wilderness of mirrors" where it was impossible to understand the adversary's strategy or intent. Certainly, Andropov believed much of the inflated intelligence that he demanded the KGB and the GRU collect in the early 1980s. In the end, the final war scare may have had the Soviet leadership as its victim.

WARNINGS. One of the key weapons of the **KGB**'s battle against **dissidents** was the "prophylactic warning." In 1967–1975, more than 130,000 Soviet citizens were called into the KGB's offices and warned. The warning may have revolved around an unauthorized meeting with a foreigner, possession of a banned book, or attendance at an unregistered church. Warnings were often conducted by the KGB's Fifth Directorate. Warnings occasionally led to expulsion from a school, loss of a job, removal from an apartment, or even arrest. Warnings also allowed the security service to keep its finger on the pulse of public opinion. According to memoirs written by dissidents, the KGB often used the meetings as an opportunity to recruit informers.

WEISBAND, WILLIAM (1908–1961). The son of Russian **émigrés**, Weisband worked in American military **signals intelligence** during World War II as a translator. He was also an **NKVD** agent, recruited before the war, and he served Moscow as a penetration of the U.S. Army Security Agency. In 1947, he informed his Soviet controllers of the **Venona** program. This critical information alerted Moscow that some of its top-secret messages from the previous decade had been deciphered by the United States and that its spy rings had been compromised. Despite the fact that he was identified in Venona messages as an agent with the Soviet code name "Link," Weisband was never prosecuted for espionage. He was convicted of contempt for refusing to answer questions before a federal grand jury in California and served a year in jail. He died of a heart attack in 1961.

WENNERSTROM, STIG (1907–2006). One of the **GRU**'s signal successes in the **Cold War** was the recruitment of Colonel Stig Wennerstrom, a Swedish military intelligence officer who served in Washington and Moscow as a **military attaché**. He was recruited in 1948 and for the next 15 years provided important intelligence to the GRU. He was arrested in 1964 by the Swedish security service and sentenced to life imprisonment but was released in 1974. Wennerstrom's **motivation** in serving Moscow was personal. He resented the fact that he had not been promoted to general officer. Aware of his anger, his GRU handlers referred to him as "General" and informed him that he held the rank of major general in the GRU.

WERNER, RUTH (1907–2000). One of the **GRU**'s most famous **illegals**, Ruth Werner was born Ursula Kuczynski into a middle-class German family in Berlin and was a committed communist from her teens. After recruitment into military intelligence, she served as a GRU illegal in Manchuria, Shanghai, Poland, and Switzerland. (In Shanghai, she was **Richard Sorge**'s lover.) During **World War II**, Werner served as an illegal in England. The GRU selected a husband for her, a British subject, so that she would obtain British citizenship. Werner's brother, Juergen Kuczynski, was also an important GRU asset; he helped Soviet intelligence mold the German **exile** community in London during the war.

While in England, Werner acted as **Klaus Fuchs**'s case officer, transmitting information about the Anglo-American nuclear weapons program to Moscow. In 1950, following Fuchs's arrest, Werner fled to East Germany, where she was resettled. A decorated Red Army colonel, Werner held a prestigious job in her native Germany, wrote several semiautobiographical novels as well as her memoirs, and raised three children. She remained a communist even after the collapse of the East German regime. At the time of her death, she was an active member of the Party of Democratic Socialism, the successor to the **Communist Party**.

WHITE, HARRY DEXTER (1895–1948). The most senior American civil servant to cooperate with Soviet intelligence, White was one of the most brilliant economists of his age. As a senior official in the Treasury Department, White helped establish American financial policy during the last years of **World War II**. He and John Maynard Keynes were the architects of the historic Bretton Woods Conference in 1944, and he was the first chief of the International Monetary Fund. The evidence from former communists such as **Whittaker Chambers** and **Elizabeth Bentley**, as well as Soviet intelligence messages, indicates that as White progressed through the Treasury Department, he had a long and informal relationship with the **NKVD**.

White evidently never was a member of the **Communist Party**, though he was clearly a sympathizer. He began working with the NKVD in the mid-1930s, but he stopped reporting after Chambers's defection in 1938 became known. In the 1940s, White again provided the NKVD *rezidentura* with information on American foreign and monetary policies. He advised Moscow on America's policy toward the Nationalist regime in China and toward the evolving situation in Poland. He is mentioned in a number of **Venona** messages as an important source with the code names "Lawyer" and "Richard." White, according to these messages, was handled personally by senior Soviet intelligence officers. He apparently never considered himself a spy or agent; he was apparently never paid but cooperated for personal reasons.

In 1948, White was named as·a Soviet spy by Chambers. Following interviews with Federal Bureau of Investigation special agents, he died of a heart attack. To many of his friends and colleagues, White was a victim of a witch hunt. A modern scholar has portrayed him as a radical New Dealer who believed he was furthering American policy through his private diplomatic initiatives. The Russian intelligence traffic suggests that White was a very important agent who provided Moscow with a source of significant political intelligence. More recently, spokesmen for the **SVR** have maintained that White was not a recruited asset but rather an informal personal contact of Russian intelligence officers and diplomats. White's **motivation** is difficult to understand; the damage he did to U.S. interests is not.

WIKI LEAKS. The release of hundreds of thousands of pages of classified American diplomatic and military messages by Private Bradley Manning provided researchers and intelligence services with insight of American diplomats and Federal Bureau of Investigation special agents on the state of the **FSB** and its relationship with the Russian government. While the loss of information was not as drastic as that from **Edward Snowden**'s defection, it did provide Moscow with a very good idea of who American diplomats' contacts were in the opposition.

WOOLRICH ARSENAL CASE. One of the early failures of Soviet intelligence in Great Britain in the late 1930s was the Woolrich Arsenal Case. Soviet **illegals** recruited British **Communist Party** members with access to military secrets at the arsenal. These agents ran in turn several men with access to British military secrets. The operation failed because the British security service (MI5) had inserted an agent, Olga Grey, into the Communist Party, and she was able to provide detailed information about the agents' plans. Percy Glading and two other conspirators were arrested and tried and received short jail terms.

However, the affair gave MI5 an exaggerated sense of its ability to defeat the Soviet services. It may also have convinced MI5 not to place the Soviet mission under **surveillance** during the war, allowing **NKVD** officers to move freely in London. **Anthony Blunt** stole a copy of the official MI5 report of the Woolrich Arsenal Case that provided Moscow with a very good idea about the modus operandi of British **counterintelligence**. The NKVD learned that if they were to recruit and run communists, they must make very sure that their sources had no recent overt contact with the Communist Party.

Part of the intelligence successes in the 1940s and 1950s in London came from the Soviets' ability to convince their recruits to break contact with communist and left-wing organizations.

WORLD WAR I. Neither the *Okhrana* nor Russian military intelligence was prepared for a general European war in 1914. Russian military intelligence had good basic intelligence on the border districts of imperial Germany and the Austro-Hungarian Empire, as well as a great deal of information on the enemies' general staff plans, thanks to an agent within the Hungarian Ministry of War, Colonel **Alfred Redl**. Russia also provided one of the first military intelligence coups of the war. Having retrieved a codebook from a stranded German warship in 1914, the Russians immediately made the contents known to their British ally, who used it to break German military and diplomatic codes throughout the rest of the war.

Nevertheless, in 1914, the *Okhrana* was having difficulty coping with a series of major industrial strikes that had exploded in 1912 and continued for almost two years, while military intelligence was very short staffed. Even more critical for the survival of the regime, neither service was capable of countering German subversion inside the imperial court. German military intelligence had agents inside the army's general staff, and Berlin was well informed of the regime's plans. As the war progressed, German intelligence was able to recruit agents within the Russian court and manipulate policy.

The tsarist regime also lacked basic military communications security. Radio traffic frequently was sent using primitive or very elemental codes. The German general staff's ability to read Russian military traffic in the summer of 1914 allowed it to counter the first Russian offensive of the war and win the battle of Tannenburg. As the war progressed, the Russian military intelligence service did far better in providing information about the Austrian enemy than the German. Even fighting on their own territory, the Russian service had only a limited number of reliable sources with access to German military or political intelligence.

The war stretched the ability of the *Okhrana* and military intelligence to the breaking point. By 1916, troops in many urban garrisons were in a state of mutiny. While frontline troops were loyal, troops in St. Petersburg were under the influence of agitators from a number of left-wing parties. The most successful covert action of the war was Germany's financing the travel of Bolshevik leader **Vladimir Lenin** and a number of his supporters from Switzerland to neutral Sweden in a protected train in 1917 after the March Revolution. Lenin and his entourage then made their way to the Finland Station in Petrograd (St. Petersburg). The German leadership realized how fragile Russia was and believed—correctly—that Lenin might upset the provisional government and bring peace on the Eastern Front.

Demobilized frontline Russian soldiers and deserters played a critical role in the newly minted Workers and Peasants Red Army and the **Cheka**. Many disillusioned noncommissioned and junior officers joined the Bolsheviks. World War I ensured the destruction of the tsarist regime and provided the new revolutionary authorities with many of its most effective military commanders and intelligence agents.

WORLD WAR II. The Soviet regime signed a nonaggression pact with Germany in August 1939, and following Germany's invasion of Poland, the Soviet Union on 17 September sent troops of the Red Army into eastern Poland. The Soviets also gained territory in Finland and the Baltics and from Romania. But the Soviets were not drawn into the war against Nazi Germany until the German invasion of the Soviet Union on 22 June 1941, which began what is known in Soviet history as the **Great Patriotic War**. The Soviet Union declared war on Japan in August 1945, and Red Army troops entered Japanese-occupied Manchuria on 9 August. During the course of the war, the Soviet military suffered more than 8 million killed in action or dead of combat wounds, more than 4 million captured or missing, and more than 15 million wounded. Soviet citizen casualties were far greater: estimates put the total loss of life between 20 million and 27 million.

See also GREAT PATRIOTIC WAR.

WYNN, ARTHUR (1910–2001). A noted Oxford academic and social reformer, Wynn was reportedly recruited by **Theodore Mally** and **Edith Tudor Hart**, the same duo that brought **Kim Philby** into Soviet intelligence. Files discovered in Moscow by former **KGB** officer **Alexander Vassiliev** stated that he had the cover name "Scot" and was active recruiting other sources by 1941. One document suggests that he recommended 25 associates and friends for recruitment. We have little information on Wynn's intelligence activities after the mid-1940s. His role as an advocate for social reform continued almost until his death at age 90.

X

X GROUP. A **GRU** network of British intellectuals was developed in the late 1930s and early 1940s. Its two most famous members were Ivor Montagu, code name "Intelligentsia," and J. B. S. Haldane, a noted Oxford biologist. A GRU message intercepted in July 1940 identified Montagu as "the well-known communist, journalist and lecturer . . . and head of the X Group."

While we have a great deal of information about Soviet intelligence activities at Cambridge in the 1930s, we are yet to have a good account of X Group and the possible links to Oxford in the same period. There are only a few bits of evidence. Christopher Hill, a noted Oxford historian, apparently admitted that he had cooperated with Soviet intelligence in the 1940s, and **Arthur Wynn**, an Oxford academic and noted reformer, was identified as "Agent Scot" in old NKVD files. (Hill and Wynn apparently left the British **Communist Party** in the 1950s.)

YAGODA, GENRYKH GRIGOREVICH (1891–1938). The chief instigator of the purges of the 1930s, Yagoda was eventually replaced for ideological and operational failures. Yagoda grew up in a family of radicals; his father forged documents for left-wing parties. Yagoda joined the anarchists at age 16 and was a member of several anarchist "fighting commands." He joined the Bolsheviks in the summer of 1917 and served in the Red Army for the next two years.

Yagoda joined the **Cheka** in 1919 and proved to be a merciless administrator of the **Red Terror**. In 1920–1921, he took part in crushing a mass peasant revolt in Tambov. Ten years later, he played a critical role in **collectivization**, again employing troops against peasant rebels. Yagoda also established the forced labor empire for building the **Belomor Canal** and other projects. In 1931, he was appointed deputy chief of the service, and in July 1934, he replaced **Vyacheslav Menzhinsky** as head of the **NKVD**. **Joseph Stalin** apparently had a low personal opinion of Yagoda, who had repeatedly been charged with corruption during his years in the security service. But Stalin apparently believed he could control and manipulate Yagoda as he began his purge of the **Communist Party**.

During the next two years, Yagoda at Stalin's behest moved against **dissidents** in the party. Many scholars believe he took an active part in organizing the assassination of **Sergei Kirov** on 1 December 1934, setting off the purges. Following Kirov's death, the NKVD was given power to arrest, try, and execute enemies of the people. Yagoda took advantage of the law to order the arrest and **execution** of thousands of men and women. Yagoda, however, was far too slow in pursuing enemies of the regime for Stalin, who demanded that Yagoda provide confessions from Old Bolsheviks that they were spies and terrorists. In the summer of 1936, Stalin in a public note to the Central Committee called for Yagoda's replacement and an intensification of the purge.

Yagoda was transferred to a minor post and became people's commissar of communications in September 1936. When Stalin saw him at a social function in late 1936, he reportedly asked why "that creature was hanging around." Six months later, in March 1937, Yagoda was arrested. After several months of interrogation, he agreed to play an important role in the trial of Nikolai Bukharin and the Rightists in February 1938, confessing to being an avowed **enemy of the people** and a fascist spy. Despite promises that his life would be spared, he was shot less than 48 hours after the trial ended.

Yagoda saw himself as a secret and terrible servant of Stalin and the regime. He wrote the writer Maksim Gorky, "Like a dog on a chain, I lie by the gate of the republic and chew through the throat of anyone who raises a hand against the peace." His service has not been rewarded by posterity any more than it was by his boss. Unlike the others tried and shot in February 1938, Yagoda has never been rehabilitated. His ultimate failure was an inability to meet the demands of Stalin, not an excess of mercy for those unfortunate enemies of the people who fell into his hands. Following his execution, his wife, mother, father, and two sisters were either shot or perished in the **gulag**.

YAKOVLEV, ALEKSANDR NIKOLAEVICH (1923–2005). A decorated veteran of **World War II**, Yakovlev went into **Communist Party** work after recovering from severe wounds. In 1970, he was purged from his post in the Central Committee and posted to Canada as ambassador because of his opposition to hard-line Russophile and anti-Semitic attitudes within the **Leonid Brezhnev** leadership. During his long **exile** in Canada, Yakovlev met **Mikhail Gorbachev** and influenced his attitude toward reform. From 1985 to 1989, Yakovlev played a crucial role in the Politburo as the architect of *glasnost* and *perestroika*. Yakovlev was a bête noire for traditionalists like **KGB** chair **Vladimir Kryuchkov**, who publicly excoriated him as an American agent. Bowing to pressure, Gorbachev forced Yakovlev out of the leadership in late 1990. Yakovlev was lucky that the 1991 **August putsch** failed; he certainly would have been prosecuted had it succeeded.

Following the collapse of the system he served but in the end despised, Yakovlev took on the mission of rehabilitating those repressed during the Soviet era. His books, which have been published in the United States and Russia, have been the best short studies of Soviet repression. Conservatives and anti-Semites continue to attack him; he has been labeled a secret Zionist whose real name is "Yakobson," and Kryuchkov in retirement continued to blame him for the collapse of the Soviet Union.

YAKOVLEVA, VARVARA NIKOLAEVNA (1885–1941). One of the few women who had a leadership role in the **Cheka**, Yakovleva was born into a bourgeois family and studied math and physics at the university. She was a secretary in the **Bolshevik Party**'s Moscow branch in 1917 and transferred to the Cheka in 1918. She took an active role in the **Red Terror** in

Moscow and had a reputation for enjoying the torture and **execution** of prisoners in her hands. In the 1920s, Yakovleva fell into disfavor because of her **Trotskyite** sympathies. She was arrested in 1937 and sentenced to 20 years in prison. In 1941, **Lavrenty Beria** ordered her shot with a number of other survivors of the early Cheka. She was rehabilitated in 1958.

YATSKOV, ANATOLI ANTONOVICH (1913–1993). Yatskov joined the **NKVD** and entered foreign intelligence in 1939. In 1941, he was sent to New York under consular cover with the name "Yakovlev." He was one of the officers working with **Lev Kvasnikov** in the collection of nuclear weapons intelligence through the *Enormoz* project. He was **Harry Gold**'s case officer and thus was directly responsible for the running of **Klaus Fuchs**, the most important Soviet penetration of the Manhattan Project. After service in New York, Yatskov was one of the pioneers of Soviet scientific and technical intelligence collection and **analysis**. He also taught aspiring foreign intelligence officers at the **Andropov Institute**. He retired as a colonel and received several combat decorations for his work in foreign intelligence.

YELTSIN, BORIS NIKOLAYEVICH (1931–2007). Boris Yeltsin rose quickly in the **Communist Party** to head the Sverdlovsk party apparatus in the late 1970s. He was, however, twice deeply embarrassed by the **KGB** in the 1970s. KGB chair **Yuri Andropov** ordered him to destroy the house in Sverdlovsk in which the **Romanov family** had been murdered in 1918. A few years later, when a biological weapons plant released anthrax spores into the atmosphere in 1979 and 69 people died, he was ordered to cover up the mistake by claiming the problem came from rotten meat.

Catching the eye of reformist party leader **Mikhail Gorbachev** in 1985, Yeltsin was brought to Moscow as party first secretary in 1985, and he gained a reputation of being a reformer willing to take on party officials. But Yeltsin quarreled with Gorbachev in November 1987 and was fired. Gorbachev publicly humiliated his one-time protégé, dragging him before a Central Committee meeting while he was recovering from a heart attack. In 1988, Yeltsin took over the leadership of the reformist movement in the Soviet Union, opposing Gorbachev from the left. Yeltsin called for massive reforms of the party and government, including changes in the KGB. While Yeltsin made enemies of many reactionaries in the security service, others saw him as a necessary champion of change.

At the time of the **August putsch** of 1991, the plotters failed to arrest Yeltsin, allowing him to lead the opposition for three days at the Russian White House, the parliament building in the center of Moscow. Following the failure of the putsch, Yeltsin cemented his role as president of the newly minted Russian Federation. As president, Yeltsin sought to end some of the traditional abuses of the security service and oversaw the division of the service into a number of independent organizations, but he assured that he would maintain control of the services from the president's office. The president's former bodyguard, **Aleksandr Korzhakov**, helped him restructure the security community to make it responsive to him alone.

Once entrenched in power, Yeltsin used the **Russian intelligence services** to guarantee his political power, much like any Communist Party general secretary. During his years in power, the services prevented investigations of major financial crimes and protected his "family" of supporters. The new Russian services are run by experienced **Chekists**, who use many of the same tools as their communist predecessors. Yeltsin's handpicked successor, **Vladimir Putin**, was a KGB officer and served as chief of the **FSB**.

YEZHOV, NIKOLAI IVANOVICH (1895–1940). The most infamous of the Soviet security generalissimos, Yezhov was born into a military family in Russian Lithuania. He later altered his birth certificate to show that he came from a working-class family and had been born in St. Petersburg. Yezhov deserted the tsarist army in February 1917 and joined the Bolshevik Red Guard in May of that year. During the **civil war**, he served as a political officer in the Red Army; after the war, he drifted into party work.

In the 1930s, Yezhov served in **Joseph Stalin**'s political secretariat, supervising the security police for Stalin. In September 1936, at Stalin's behest, Yezhov took over the **NKVD** and directed a massive purge of the **Communist Party** and Soviet society that took his name: the *Yezhovshchina* ("the time of Yezhov"). The Kremlin's archives show that during the 15 months of the *Yezhovshchina*, he met with Stalin 278 times in the Kremlin, spending more than 800 hours in personal conferences with him. Yezhov saw to it that Stalin's plan for a purge of Soviet society was fulfilled, taking part personally in interrogations and **executions**. According to many sources, Yezhov was a sadist who gloried in the suffering of former friends and strangers alike. He was promoted to membership in the party Politburo and for a short period became the hero of the Stalinist media. The Russian root of Yezhov's name is "hedgehog," and the media referred to Yezhov as "Stalin's hedgehog."

Stalin decided to replace Yezhov with **Lavrenty Beria**, who was brought to Moscow from Georgia in the summer of 1938 to serve as Yezhov's chief deputy. In August, Yezhov left the NKVD to assume the post of people's commissar of water transport. At the March 1939 Central Committee plenum, Yezhov was personally attacked by Stalin for not arresting the right **enemies of the people**. He was arrested a month later. After almost a year in prison, he was tried on 2 February 1940 and shot two days later as a Polish, German, and British spy, as well as a traitor who had planned the overthrow of the Soviet government. While Yezhov apparently admitted these crimes under threat of torture, he later denied his guilt at the trial, claiming that he had purged the NKVD of 14,000 enemies. He was dragged kicking and screaming to his execution.

Described by one of his subordinates as a "bloody dwarf," Yezhov stood only five feet tall. He is a mystery to his biographers and to historians. While he was remembered as a quiet and unremarkable bureaucrat before rising to take charge of the great purge, he became addicted to vodka and drugs during his last years. He was also bisexual with a thirst for sexual conquests no less than for vodka.

Yezhov's last letter to Stalin reveals a man confused about the nasty trick that history and fate played on him. To the end, he never realized that he was Stalin's tool. In his last words on the purge, he noted, "My great guilt lies in that I purged so few of them." The statement ends, "Tell Stalin I shall die with his name on my lips." Following the execution, Beria reportedly gave Stalin a list of 346 of Yezhov's associates to be executed. Fifty of them reportedly were Yezhov's male and female sexual partners.

YEZHOVSHCHINA (**THE TIME OF YEZHOV**). Following **Sergei Kirov**'s murder in December 1934, **Joseph Stalin** instituted a law giving the **NKVD** power to try and execute suspected terrorists without recourse to defense lawyers or appeals. In 1936, Stalin made **Nikolai Yezhov** head of the NKVD, citing the security service's lax work in rooting out traitors. In 1936–1937, he urged Yezhov to begin a massive purge of three suspected enemy elements: Poles and other foreign communists, men and women arrested during the previous decade, former kulaks (rich peasants) and petty criminals, and suspected **Trotskyites** and other **dissidents** within the **Communist Party**. The initial planning called for the arrest of 250,000 men and women.

Yezhov and his immediate subordinates drove regional security officers into a frenzy of arrests, torture, and **execution**. The *Yezhovshchina* seemed to take on a life of its own as the controlled media called for greater vigilance and more arrests, and public denunciations of innocent citizens filled the prisons. The NKVD fabricated hundreds of thousands of cases, torturing millions into confessions of spying for foreign states, planning terrorist acts, and wrecking the Soviet economy. The guilty—there were few found innocent—were tried and convicted, often after 15-minute trials. Executions usually took place immediately following conviction.

There is no full accounting of the casualties, but statistics provided to the Communist Party Central Committee by the **KGB** in the 1960s indicate more than 1.5 million arrests and 750,000 executions in less than 15 months. (In the 16 months of the *Yezhovshchina*, 50,000 were executed per month, or 1,700 a day.) Five of 15 members of the ruling Politburo were shot, as were 98 of 134 members of the Central Committee. The Komsomol was equally devastated, with over half its ruling central committee executed in 1937–1938. Arrests and executions in the provinces claimed tens of thousands of party officials. In Byelorussia, only three of 100 senior Communist Party officials survived 1937–1938.

Arrests put almost 1 million men and women in the forced labor camps, and recent research suggests that another 100,000 men and women perished in the **gulag** in 1937–1938. In Leningrad, approximately 40,000 were executed. In Moscow, 21,000 were shot between August 1937 and September 1938 at Butovo. A survey by the **Memorial** organization found that 24 to 28 percent of those executed were manual workers and peasants, while 12 percent were professional workers. Especially vulnerable were men and women who had been previous targets of repression, kulaks, and Russian Orthodox clergy. Moreover, 18,000 wives of **enemies of the people** were imprisoned and 25,000 children dispatched to orphanages.

Yezhov also purged the army and the police, sending 34,000 military officers to the camps or the firing squad. The military leader **Mikhail Tukhachevskiy** and other senior officers were tried by a special military court and then shot. More Soviet generals died during the *Yezhovshchina* than during the **Great Patriotic War**. Several thousand NKVD officers were arrested, as officers in Moscow and the provinces followed their victims to Siberia and execution cellars. In 1938, Leningrad had six different NKVD chiefs. The NKVD's foreign intelligence section was particularly devastated, and five men served as its chief in less than 18 months. The purges ravished the corps of people serving overseas under diplomatic cover and as **illegals**. The *rezidenturas* in both London and Berlin suspended operations for several months. **Theodore Mally** was recalled from England, arrested, tortured, and shot.

A major target of the NKVD was the leadership of foreign communist parties and the **Comintern**. In 1938, the Polish **Communist Party** was liquidated. All 12 members of its Central Committee living in **exile** in Moscow were shot. The Hungarian and German parties were also purged: Bela Kun, the leader of the Hungarian party since 1919, was shot after a 15-minute trial, as were many members of the German communist leadership. The only communists who were safe in Moscow were those from the Western democracies. NKVD executioners were also sent to the Mongolian People's Republic, where almost 4 percent of the male population was executed.

There is no consensus as to why Stalin gave Yezhov his head to terrorize Soviet society. Was it to cleanse society of potential traitors—a political inquisition driven by popular demand for scapegoats or personal vengeance—or did it have more to do with Stalin's personality? Speaking to Comintern leaders in late 1937, Stalin threatened, "We shall destroy every enemy, even an Old Bolshevik, we shall annihilate his kith and kin." Revisionist scholars believe that the purge took on a life of its own—much like the witch hunts of the 16th century. Whatever the root cause, the *Yezhovshchina* traumatized Soviet society, and it stripped the society, party, and Red Army of many of the leaders who would have made defeating Adolf Hitler less costly.

YURCHENKO, VITALIY SERGEEVICH (1936–). One of the strangest stories of the **Cold War** was the **defection** and then redefection of **KGB** officer Vitaliy Yurchenko. Yurchenko, who had served as the KGB security officer in Washington for several years in the 1970s, became disillusioned with the KGB after years of apparently successful service. On 1 August 1985, Yurchenko defected to the United States. His story was widely covered in the media and heralded as a major U.S. intelligence success. Yurchenko was debriefed by the Central Intelligence Agency (CIA) and the Federal Bureau of Investigation, and he identified **Edward Lee Howard**, a recently dismissed CIA employee, and **Ronald Pelton** as Soviet agents. Then, only weeks after coming to Washington, he marched out of a French restaurant in Georgetown and into the Soviet embassy. He returned to Moscow to tell a story of drugging and kidnapping and a thrilling escape from the CIA. He was subsequently decorated by the KGB and retired in 1991.

The KGB chose to "believe" Yurchenko's story, apparently to indicate to other defectors that they could return to the Soviet Union after defecting to the West without fear of punishment. Some observers of the contest between the KGB and the CIA saw Yurchenko as a false defector sent to confuse the West. A more likely explanation is that it was he rather than the KGB who was confused.

Z

ZABOTIN, NIKOLAI (ca. 1910–?). As **GRU** *rezident* in Ottawa from 1943 to 1945, Zabotin had a successful career, managing a staff of 14 officers and running important agents in the Canadian and British governments and within the Anglo-American nuclear weapons program. His *rezidentura*'s most important agent was **Allan Nunn May**, a Canadian nuclear physicist. But when **Igor Gouzenko**, one of Zabotin's code clerks with whom he had very good relations, defected in September 1945, Zabotin's career and life changed forever. His agents were exposed, and several went to prison. Zabotin was blamed for Gouzenko's treachery and recalled to Moscow. A special commission headed by **Lavrenty Beria** and **Viktor Abakumov** was created by **Joseph Stalin** to investigate Zabotin's *rezidentura*. He was found guilty of professional misconduct, and he, his wife, and son were rusticated in a forced labor camp until 1953.

ZAKOVSKIY, LEONID MIKHAILOVICH (1894–1938). A Latvian worker born Henry Shtubis, Zakovskiy joined the **Bolshevik Party** at age 19. He was arrested before the **Revolution of November 1917** but then joined the Red Guards and helped the Bolsheviks build support among the soldiers and sailors in Petrograd (St. Petersburg). Zakovskiy was co-opted into the **Cheka** in December 1917 and served in intelligence and **counterintelligence** in the Russian **civil war**.

Days following **Sergei Kirov**'s death in December 1934, Zakovskiy was brought to Leningrad to take command of the local **NKVD**. Zakovskiy, clearly **Joseph Stalin**'s man, pushed the purge of **dissidents**. Over the next four years, thousands of men and women were arrested, tried, and shot for being somehow connected to the murder of Kirov. There has been speculation that Zakovskiy was sent to Leningrad by Stalin to cover up any evidence that Stalin and NKVD chief **Genrykh Yagoda** had set up Kirov's murder. At a **Communist Party** plenum, however, Zakovskiy played a key role in calling for an intensification of the terror and the arrest of Yagoda.

In 1938, Zakovskiy began a downward spiral. He was given a provincial assignment for a few weeks to get him away from his power base; his inevitable arrest followed. After several months of interrogation, Zakovskiy was tried on 29 August 1938 for treason. He was shot the same day. He has not been rehabilitated.

Zakovskiy was typical of those drafted into the Cheka in the early days of the regime. Poorly educated, street smart, and tough, he was the type of person first **Vladimir Lenin** and then Stalin relied on to maintain power. Yet during the *Yezhovshchina*, people with Zakovskiy's background were at risk, and many perished. They were not Russians or Slavs, they had little idea of how to manage the more complex Soviet society, and they knew the most important secrets of the leadership.

ZAPOROZHSKIY, ALEKSANDR (1957–). A **KGB** and later an **SVR** officer who served in Africa and the American departments of the **First Chief Directorate**, he was arrested in 2003 for treason and espionage and sentenced to 18 years. He was one of the four Russian citizens exchanged in a "spy swap" for 10 Russian illegals in 2010.

ZARUBIN, VASILY MIKHAILOVICH (1894–1974). After military service in the Russian **civil war**, Zarubin joined the **Cheka** in 1920, taking part in the fight against "bandits." In 1925, he joined the foreign intelligence department and spent 13 years as an **illegal** in Europe and Asia. During **World War II**, Zarubin served in Washington as the intelligence services *rezident* under the name "Zubilin." He managed the recruitment and running of American agents within the nuclear weapons program (which the Soviets code-named *Enormoz*), as well as the State and War departments and American security agencies. His official biography notes that his reporting was frequently read by **Joseph Stalin**. He was awarded two Orders of **Lenin** and two Orders of the Red Banner, plus other combat decorations.

Nevertheless, Zarubin was not always an effective or careful intelligence officer, and his lack of street **tradecraft** was a reason for the collapse of the service's networks in the postwar years. His meetings with members of the **Communist Party** of the United States were monitored by the Federal Bureau of Investigation (FBI). These meetings alerted the FBI to the fact that the **NKVD** was using Communist Party members as agents. The FBI also observed Zarubin in operational meetings with other agents, further intensifying **surveillance** against him and his team. He was by the end of his tour well known in official Washington circles as a Soviet spy.

Zarubin and his wife, **Elizaveta Zarubina**, were recalled to Moscow in late 1944. He had been denounced by a jealous and emotionally unstable subordinate and had to face an inquiry by **counterintelligence** officers. Although Zarubin was cleared, decorated once again for his successes, and promoted to the rank of major general, his career as a foreign intelligence operative was over. He worked in Moscow until 1948, then retired for health reasons. Zarubin's daughter, **Zoya Zarubina**, served in the foreign intelligence service during the war as a captain.

See also MIRONOV LETTER.

ZARUBINA, ELIZAVETA YULEVNA (1900–1987). Before her 20th birthday, Zarubina had taken part in underground **Communist Party** activities behind enemy lines in the Russian **civil war**. After serving as a translator for Soviet trade agencies in Vienna, she joined the intelligence service. From 1925 to 1938, she worked as an **illegal** in Turkey, Denmark, Germany, France, and the United States. While in Turkey, she betrayed her first husband, **Yakov Blumkin**, who had formed a personal relationship with **Leon Trotsky**. Blumkin was recalled to the Soviet Union and later executed.

In 1941, she worked in the *rezidentura* in Washington with her husband, **Vasily Zarubin**, and was successful in recruiting and running agents. In order to gather information about the U.S. nuclear weapons program, she persuaded Maria Konnenkova, a female **NKVD** staff officer, to seduce Albert Einstein and recruit him as a source. According to NKVD records, the seduction was successful, although the recruitment was not.

An American **counterintelligence** agent for the Federal Bureau of Investigation remembered Zarubina as a "frail, pretty, middle-aged woman with an aristocratic manner." The agent noted, "She was sort of a Red Joan of Arc, a saint whose faith in the Soviet Union was pure and bottomless." Zarubina was recalled to Moscow with her husband in 1944. She served in Moscow from 1944 to 1946, when she retired from the service with the rank of colonel. She was apparently the first woman to hold that rank in Russian foreign intelligence.

See also ZARUBIN, VASILY MIKHAILOVICH (1894–1974).

ZARUBINA, ZOYA VASILYEVNA (1922–). The daughter of **Vasily Zarubin** and **Elizaveta Zarubina**, Zoya Zarubina entered the service at the time of the **Battle of Moscow** as part of a team of **partisans** established to sabotage the city should the Germans occupy it. She later served as **Joseph Stalin**'s interpreter at the Tehran (1943) and Yalta (1945) conferences, where Stalin met with U.S. President Franklin D. Roosevelt. On one occasion when she was interpreting for Stalin, Roosevelt complained about the frogs keeping him up all night. Having forgotten the word for "frog," Zarubina told Stalin that the American president was bothered by the animal that sits in ponds and croaks. She was forgiven and promoted, and she went on to become one of the country's premier interpreters.

ZAVENYAGIN, AVRAAMI PAVLOVICH (1901–1956). As the director of many **NKVD** industrial programs, Zavenyagin was responsible for the construction of the massive **Norilsk** mining complex, as well as many of the facilities for the Soviet nuclear weapons program. In August 1945, he was one of six senior **Communist Party** and state officials mandated by **Joseph Stalin** to be responsible for the construction of nuclear weapons. He took part in negotiations with the Bulgarian government in 1945 to obtain uranium ore. In the late 1940s and early 1950s, he served as chief of the **MGB**'s directorate responsible for the nuclear weapons program. Following Stalin's death in March 1953, he was appointed first deputy minister in the Ministry of Medium Machine Building, responsible for building and testing nuclear weapons. Zavenyagin died young. According to one history of the Soviet nuclear weapons program, he bravely and perhaps recklessly exposed himself to nuclear radiation in the building of the first Soviet nuclear weapons. Igor Kurchatov, the father of the Soviet bomb, also died young after being heavily exposed while working with Zavenyagin.

ZEK. In **Joseph Stalin**'s **gulag** system, the term for a prisoner was *zek*, short for *zakluchoniy chelovek* ("imprisoned person").

ZENIT. An elite **KGB** paramilitary formation, ZENIT was created in the late 1970s for foreign operations. It, like KGB Group Alpha, was modeled on the British Special Air Services. It was initially stationed in the Soviet embassy in **Afghanistan** to protect the mission, and in December 1979, it took part in the successful storming of the presidential palace in Kabul, Afghanistan. Five members of ZENIT were killed in the assault, including its commander, Colonel **Yevgeniy Boyarinov**.

ZENTSOV, VALERII (1946–). As a **KGB** pensioner, Zentsov recruited and later ran **Herman Simm**, a senior Estonia defense official, as a penetration of North Atlantic Treaty Organization offices. Zentsov had risen to chief of the Estonian republic's KGB before "retiring" and joining the **SVR**. He carefully recruited Simm using a mixture of flattery, blackmail (they had previously worked together in the Soviet system), and money.

ZHDANOV, ANDREI ALEKSANDROVICH (1896–1948). One of the hardest of **Joseph Stalin**'s men was Andrei Zhdanov. In Leningrad, he carried out Stalin's orders to purge the city: between 68,000 and 90,000 were arrested. Of the 383 execution lists circulated within the Politburo, containing more than 30,000 names, Zhdanov signed 177. According to his English biographer, "An unflinching ability to order limitless acts of cruelty became a litmus test for any Stalinist leader."

Zhdanov was Stalin's cultural and ideological commissar following **World War II**. During the **Great Patriotic Wa**r, Zhdanov served as **Communist Party** boss in Leningrad during the siege. Following the war, Zhdanov was Stalin's mouthpiece, attacking modern trends in literature, art, and film in a campaign known as the *Zhdanovshchina* ("the time of Zhdanov"). He denounced the great poet **Anna Akhmatova** as "half nun, half harlot" and railed against anti-Russian and anti-Soviet trends in the arts. Stalin used the issue of ideological conformity to crack down on Jewish intellectuals and order the murder of the actor **Solomon Mikhoels**. The **MGB** also moved to destroy small literary groups that had sprung up during the war. Hundreds of students were arrested for participation in these groups.

Zhdanov, in poor health, died of a heart attack as the campaign he unleashed began to gather speed. A young doctor denounced Zhdanov's primary physicians to Stalin for mishandling his care: Zhdanov had been allowed out of bed prematurely after suffering a series of heart attacks. Stalin paid no attention to the denunciation at the time, but he had the letter placed in a special archive. Four years later, he would use the denunciation as the spark to begin his last great purge, the **Doctors' Plot**. Even in death, Zhdanov served Stalin.

ZHUKOV, GEORGI KONSTANTINOVICH (1896–1974). A highly decorated soldier in the tsarist army in **World War I**, Zhukov joined the Red Army during the Russian **civil war**. He was rapidly promoted to general officer and miraculously survived the *Yezhovshchina*. He did not denounce colleagues and protected several subordinates.

Zhukov was **Communist Party** General Secretary **Joseph Stalin**'s choice to lead the Red Army in the conflict with Japan in 1939. After victory in the Far East, Zhukov directed Soviet forces in battles from the gates of Moscow to Berlin and was made marshal of the Soviet Union. Stalin was deeply suspicious of Zhukov and allowed *Smersh* to intimidate and arrest his subordinates. Following his victories over the Imperial Japanese Army, the **NKVD** began collecting compromising material on Zhukov. In 1942, they established bugs on his personal and official phone lines.

In the late 1940s, *Smersh* provided Stalin with evidence of Zhukov's corruption, much of which was trumped up or based on evidence from senior officers who had been tortured by the **MGB,** including Chief Marshal of Aviation Aleksandr Novikov. (The case had the code name *Gorodetz*, "arrogant man.") Stalin used the evidence as an excuse to rusticate Zhukov to a provincial post. His wife later told friends that he had expected to be arrested at any moment.

Before his death, Stalin "forgave" Zhukov and brought him back to Moscow. In July 1953, Zhukov helped **Nikita Khrushchev** carry out a coup that removed **Lavrenty Beria** from the leadership. In 1957, Zhukov—now minister of defense—helped Khrushchev survive a putsch by reactionaries in the leadership. Nevertheless, several months later, Khrushchev removed Zhukov from his post and sent him into retirement.

Zhukov spent his last years writing his memoirs, which were heavily censored. Until his death, his apartment was bugged, and he was kept under strict surveillance by the **KGB**—testimony to his popularity with the Russia people.

See also ANTIPARTY GROUP; AUGUST PUTSCH OF 1991; RUSLA-NOVA, LIDIA ANDREYEVNA (1900–1973); SEROV, IVAN ALEKSAN-DROVICH (1900–1990).

ZHURAVLEV, MIKHAIL IVANOVICH (1911–1976). After a career in the Red Army and the Komsomol, Zhuravlev was transferred laterally to a senior post in the **NKVD** following the *Yezhovshchina*. Zhuravlev had a seemingly unspectacular career in **Lavrenty Beria**'s service as a manager of major forced labor camp institutions, including those responsible for work on the Soviet nuclear weapons program, for which Zhuravlev played a crucial role. He was one of a handful of NKVD officers directly involved in the program. Zhuravlev was promoted to lieutenant general in 1945 and for several years was in charge of the economic directorate of the **MGB** and the **MVD**. In 1956, he left the security service to work in the Ministry of Medium Machine Building, which was responsible for building and testing nuclear weapons.

ZHURAVLEV, VIKTOR IVANOVICH (1902–1946). During the *Yezhovshchina*, Zhuravlev rose quickly to be head of the provincial branches of the **NKVD** in major cities. Watching the rolling purge of the NKVD leadership, Zhuravlev wrote directly to **Joseph Stalin** warning of a conspiracy within the security service. Stalin rewarded Zhuravlev, making him NKVD chief for Moscow in December 1938 and selecting him to serve on the **Communist Party** Central Committee (CPCC). Zhuravlev's fall was less spectacular than that of those he denounced. He was fired as Moscow's security chief and relieved of his CPCC post in 1939, then assigned to command a forced labor camp. He spent the war in Siberia and was not promoted to general officer in 1945 like most of his contemporaries. In 1946, he was recalled to Moscow from Siberia—reportedly to face charges of corruption—and committed suicide on the way.

Zhuravlev's rise and fall indicates how closely Stalin and his lieutenant **Lavrenty Beria** supervised the security service. They respected and rewarded vigilance (denunciations), but they demanded competence. Zhuravlev, a drunk and a sadist, was not tolerated, and he sank almost as quickly as he rose.

ZINOVIEV LETTER. On 8 October 1924, the British Labour Party lost a vote of confidence in the House of Commons. On 25 October, a letter reportedly from Grigori Zinoviev, the head of the **Comintern**, to the British **Communist Party** was published in the *Daily Mail*, encouraging the British party to prepare for class war. Four days later, Labour lost a general election, and the Conservatives returned to power. Moscow always denied that the Comintern had sent such a letter, but for 75 years, a debate continued about the provenance of the letter. There are several mysteries in the brief outline of the story: was such a letter sent by the Comintern, what was the role of the **OGPU**, was it part of a plot by the Secret Intelligence Service (SIS) to destroy the Labour Party, and did the Conservative Party deliberately use a forged document to bring down Labour?

In 1998, a British historian was given access to British, Russian, and American archives. She found that the Zinoviev letter was a forgery—possibly created by White Russian **émigrés** operating in Riga, Latvia. The OGPU had no role in a plot against the crown. The letter was obtained by SIS officers who believed the information was accurate and passed to the Foreign Office, which accepted the bona fides of the information. There is no firm evidence that the Conservative Party used the letter in the election, although two of the men responsible for leaking it did belong to the Conservative Central Office.

While the evidence of Moscow's innocence in the case is proven, the Comintern did in fact seek a more militant British Communist Party. A letter from Christian Rakovsky, a senior Comintern official, to British comrades in 1924 stated, "Real, objective conditions are being created for a real revolutionary mass communist party in Great Britain." Clearly, the Whitehall civil servants were not able to understand Marxist rhetoric or differentiate between forgeries and real documents.

ZUBATOV, NIKOLAI VASILYEVICH (1863–1917). One of the most clever *Okhrana* leaders, Zubatov sought to undercut support for revolutionary parties by the strategy of police socialism, aimed at garnering support for the monarchy from the working class. Zubatov entered the *Okhrana* as a penetration agent, working against revolutionary parties in Moscow. After his cover was blown, Zubatov entered the police, rising to head of first the Moscow and then the St. Petersburg *Okhrana* offices.

Zubatov believed that the greatest danger to the tsarist regime was a revolutionary marriage between the radical intelligentsia and the working class. His strategy called for regime support of working-class economic demands and the recruitment of deep-penetration agents within the revolutionary movements. He planned to use these agents to "guide" the proletariat away from the radical parties. Among his most famous recruits were the infamous **double agent Yevno Azev** and Father **Georgi Gapon**. Gapon, at Zubatov's direction, managed social programs for the St. Petersburg working class, becoming a major factor in Russian politics. Zubatov believed that his strategy would produce critical intelligence about terrorist cells and allow the security police to manipulate the working-class parties that supported the terrorism.

Zubatov's strategy smacked of revolution to conservative bureaucrats, and he was fired by the arch-reactionary minister of internal affairs **Vyacheslav von Plehve** in 1903. Zubatov was given 24 hours to leave the capital. His successors mismanaged his strategy of police socialism, contributing to the terrible political and social violence at the time of the **Revolution of 1905**. Following the February Revolution in 1917 that ended the **Romanov** dynasty and installed a provisional government, Zubatov returned, but, fearing retribution from the revolutionary parties that he had zealously hunted, he became depressed and took his own life.

Appendix A

The Evolution of Soviet State Security

December 1917	Cheka
February 1922	Incorporated into the NKVD as the GPU
July 1923	OGPU formed
July 1934	OGPU incorporated into the NKVD as the GUGB (Chief Directorate of State Security)
February 1941	GUGB elements incorporated into the NKGB
July 1943	*Smersh* created from the Military Counterintelligence component of NKGB
March 1946	NKGB becomes MGB; *Smersh* reincorporated into the MGB
March 1953	Creation of enlarged MVD by Lavrenty Beria to include NKGB and NKVD
March 1954	Creation of KGB

Appendix B

KGB Chairs, 1917–1991

Feliks Edmundovich Dzerzhinsky	1917–1926
Vyacheslav Rudolovich Menzhinsky	1926–1934
Genrykh Grigoreyevich Yagoda	1934–1936
Nikolai Ivanovich Yezhov	1936–1938
Lavrenty Pavlovich Beria	1938–1941
Vsevold Nikolaevich Merkulov	1941 (February–July)
Lavrenty Pavlovich Beria	1941–1943
Vsevold Nikolaevich Merkulov	1943–1946
Viktor Semenovich Abakumov	1946–1951
Semyon Denisovich Ignatev	1951–1953
Lavrenty Pavlovich Beria	1953 (March–June)
Sergei Nikiforovich Kruglov	1953–1954
Ivan Aleksandrovich Serov	1954–1958
Aleksandr Nikolaevich Shelepin	1958–1961
Vladimir Yefimovich Semichastniy	1961–1967
Yuri Vladimirovich Andropov	1967–1982
Vitalii Vasilevich Fedorchuk	1982 (May–December)
Viktor Mikhailovich Chebrikov	1982–1988
Vladimir Aleksandrovich Kryuchkov	1988–1991
Vadim Viktorovich Bakatin	1991 (August–December)

Appendix C

Russian Foreign Intelligence Organizations, 1920–

20 December 1920	Foreign Intelligence Section, Cheka
6 February 1922	Foreign Intelligence Section, GPU
2 November 1923	Foreign Intelligence Section, OGPU
10 July 1934	Seventh Section of the State Directorate of State Security of NKVD
July 1939	In connection with a reorganization of the NKVD, reformed as the Fifth Section
February 1941	Reformed as the First Directorate of NKGB as part of the division of NKVD into NKVD and NKGB
March 1946	Reformed into the MGB as First Directorate
1947	First Directorate of MGB and GRU combined into the *Komitet Informatsii*
January 1952	Foreign Intelligence placed into the MGB as First Chief Directorate
March 1953	First Chief Directorate transferred to the newly minted KGB
November 1991	Following August putsch, KGB is disbanded, and the First Chief Directorate becomes the Central Intelligence Service (TsSR) of Russia
18 December 1991	Foreign Intelligence Service of the Russian Federation is formed

Appendix D

Chiefs of Soviet and Russian Foreign Intelligence, 1920–

1920–1921	Yakov Davidov (Davityan)
1921	Ryuben Katanyan
1921–1922	Solomon Mogilevskiy
1922–1930	Mikhail Trilisser
1930–1931	Stanislav Messing
1931–1936	Artur Artuzov
1936–1938	Abram Slutskiy
1938	Zelman Passov
1938	Pavel Sudoplatov
1938–1939	Sergei Shpigelglas
1939	Vladimir Dekanozov
1939–1946	Pavel Fitin
1946	Petr Kubatkin
1947–1949	Petr Fedotov
1949–1952	Sergei Savchenko
1952	Vasilii Ryasnoi
1953	Yevgeny Pitovranov
1953–1954	Aleksandr Korotkov
1954–1956	Aleksandr Panyushkin
1956–1972	Aleksandr Sakharovskiy
1972–1974	Fedor Motrin
1974–1988	Vladimir Kryuchkov
1988–1991	Leonid Shebarshin
1991–1996	Yevgeny Primakov
1996–2000	Vyacheslav Trubnikov

| 2000–2007 | Sergei Lebedev |
| 2007– | Mikhail Fradkov |

Appendix E

Russian Security Services, 1991–

Since the August putsch of 1991, the leadership of Russia has sought to realign the internal components of the KGB into different organizations. The rapid changes of names in the years after the August putsch suggest efforts by President Boris Yeltsin to put his own stamp on the service. The major components of the security service are the internal counterintelligence components of the KGB; the most important are the Second and Third Chief Directorates, the Fourth and Sixth Directorates, and the Surveillance Directorate. The security service has gone through a number of name changes.

1954–1991	KGB (Committee of State Security)
1991–1992	AFB (Federal Security Agency)
1992	MB (Ministry of Security)
1992–1995	FSK (Federal Counterintelligence Service)
1995–	FSB (Federal Security Service)

Appendix F

Heads of Military Intelligence (GRU), 1918–

1918–1919	Semen Aralov
1919	Sergei Gusev
1920	Georgi Pyatakov
1920	Vladimir Aussem
1920–1921	Yan Dentsman
1921–1924	Arvid Zeibot
1924–1935, 1937	Yan Berzin
1935–1937	Semen Uspenskiy
1937–1938	Sergei Gnendin
1938–1939	Aleksandr Orlov
1939–1940	Ivan Proskurov
1940–1941	Filipp Golikov
1941–1942	Andrei Panifilov
1942–1945	Ivan Ilichev
1945–1947	Fedor Kuznetsov
1947–1949	Nikolai Trusov
1949–1952	Matvei Zakharov
1952–1956	Mikhail Shalin
1956–1957	Sergei Shtemenko
1957–1958	Mikhail Shalin
1958–1963	Ivan Serov
1963–1986	Petr Ivashutin
1986–1991	Vladlen Mikhailov
1991–1992	Evegeni Timokhin
1992–1997	Fedor Ladygin
1997–2009	Valentin Korabelnikov

2009–2011	Aleksandr Shlyakhturov
2011	Igor Sergun

Appendix G

Venona Code Names and Encryption

The NKVD *rezidenturas* in New York, Washington, and San Francisco used code names to refer to case officers, agents, places, targets, and even personnel in Moscow. For example, a cable from the Washington *rezidentura* to Foreign Intelligence chief Pavel Fitin would be signed Maksim (Zarubin) and would be addressed to Viktor (Fitin). Sometimes humor entered into the designations: Boris Moros, an agent in Los Angeles and later an agent for the Federal Bureau of Investigation, was referred to in code as "Frost." The Russian word *Moroz* means "Frost."

Venona Code Name	Real Name
Ales	Alger Hiss
Babylon	San Francisco
Caliber	David Greenglass
Camp 2	Los Alamos
Clever Girl	Elizabeth Bentley
Liszt	John Cairncross
Carthage	Washington, D.C.
Compatriot	Communist Party member
Enormoz (Enormous)	Nuclear weapons program
Father	Earl Browder
Funicular	Atom bomb
Gus (Goose)	Harry Gold
Helmsman	Earl Browder
Homer (Gomer)	Donald Maclean
Hotel	Secret Intelligence Service (SIS)
Koch	Douglas Chaplin Lee
Izba (Hut)	Office of Strategic Services (OSS)
Kaptan (Captain)	President Franklin D. Roosevelt

Lawyer	Harry Dexter White
Leslie	Leona Cohen
Liberal/Antenna	Julius Rosenberg
Lira	Anna Louise Strong
Mädchen (Maiden)	Guy Burgess
Maksim	Vasily Zarubin
Moliere	John Cairncross
Mlad (Youth)	Ted Hall
Son	Rudy Baker
Star (Old)	Saville Sax
Probationers	Agents
Polecats	Zionists
Raymond	Harry Gold
Rats	Trotskyites
Richard	Harry Dexter White
Rest	Klaus Fuchs
Robert/Pal	Nathan Silvermaster
Sohnchen (Little Son)	Kim Philby
Tyre	New York City
Vardo	Elizaveta Zarubina
Volunteer	Morris Cohen
Wasp	Ruth Greenglass

THE SOVIET SYSTEM OF ENCRYPTION

During the late 1930s, the Soviet Union had designed a sophisticated method of securing its diplomatic communications. Messages were sent by diplomatic pouch, shortwave radio, and international cable. While longer messages and scientific samples could be sent by pouch, it often took three months for them to reach Moscow from the United States. Shortwave radio was seen as having limited viability; messages could be intercepted, and the discovery of a station alerted the host country's counterintelligence service that the Soviet services were active. Learning from the mistakes of the British and French, the NKVD used a complex system to protect intelligence and diplomatic messages sent by international cable.

For example, the NKVD *rezidentura* in New York had to send a message to Moscow that Harry Gold (Gus) was traveling to New Mexico to meet an agent. The initial message would be as follows: Gus traveling to Camp 2 (Los Alamos) to meet probationer (agent). The code clerk would then take the codebook and find the five-digit code group for the words. In the case of proper names or locations, the word was spelled out; the codebook had a five-digit code group for each letter:

Gus	traveling	Camp 2	meet	probationer
45211	14402	34500	14521	22305

To ensure the security of the message, the clerk would then take a one-time pad, a list of random number groups, and would add a five-digit group to each of the code groups from the book. (Numbers were not carried as in "espionage arithmetic.") The clerk ended the message with five-digit code groups from the one-time pad, which would show the recipient what numbers had been used in enciphering the message. Thus,

45217	14402	34500	14521	22305	Codebook
12345	*32503*	*13542*	*33454*	*61234*	*Added numbers*
57552	46905	47042	47975	83549	

As a last step to ensure the security of the message, the numbers would be translated into letters, using an established code (0 = O, 1 = I, 2 = U, 3 = Z, 4 = T, 5 = R, 6 = E, 7 = W, 8 = A, 9 = P). The final message to Moscow would read,

RWRRU TEPOR TWOTU TWPWR AZRTP

Even if an adversary had access to the Soviet codebook, the system was secure if the code clerks used the one-time pads only once. During the first two years of the war, however, the NKVD and GRU code clerks went through existing one-time pads and began to use the numbered groups repeatedly. This allowed American and British cryptographers to see a pattern in the messages; over years of hard work, thousands of messages were decrypted.

Two excellent sources for the layperson on the Venona process are John Earl Haynes and Harvey Klehr, *Venona: Decoding Soviet Espionage in America* (New Haven, CT: Yale University Press, 1999), and Robert Louis Benson and Michael Werner, *Venona: Soviet Espionage and the American Response* (Washington, DC: National Security Agency, Central Intelligence Agency, 1996). Benson worked on Venona as a young cryptographer; Michael Warner is a distinguished historian of intelligence. Good places to begin a study of cryptology are David Kahn, *The Codebreakers* (New York: Scribner, 1996), and Rudolf Kippenhahn, *Code Breaking: A History and an Exploration* (New York: Overlook Press, 1999).

Appendix H

Loss of Life in the Stalin Era

Alexander Yakovlev, in a recent book, *A Century of Violence in Soviet Russia* (New Haven, CT: Yale University Press, 2002), put the number of deaths due to the Soviet system at 60 million. Yakovlev, who along with Mikhail Gorbachev was an architect of *glasnost*, called the Soviet tragedy a "democide." Despite research done over the past decades by Russian and other scholars, there are no exact numbers for those who perished in the years 1928–1953. The following account of repression is taken from a variety of primary and secondary sources; it deals with only 10 major incidents of repression in the Stalinist period.

Collectivization and the Famine of 1933–1934. A figure of 7 million to 10 million deaths is probably as accurate an estimate as can be provided. This includes the loss of 2 million to 3 million peasants during collectivization, the death of approximately 500,000 Kazakh nomads, and the death by starvation of approximately 5 million Ukrainians.

The Yezhovshchina. The KGB provided the Communist Party Central Committee with information during the Nikita Khrushchev years that there had been approximately 1.5 million arrests and 650,000 executions in 1937–1938. This figure is almost certainly too low: the Memorial organization has established that there were more than 40,000 executions in Leningrad alone in that period, and no less than 20,000 people were shot at Butovo near Moscow in just 14 months. Moreover, the figure may not include thousands shot without trial or interrogation or those murdered in provincial jails. In 1953–1956, the newly minted KGB had every reason to provide the leadership with a very low figure.

Incorporation of Western Byelorussia and Western Ukraine. A noted Western historian, Jan Gros, places the loss of life in Poland between 750,000 and 1 million in his *Revolution from Abroad* (Princeton, NJ: Princeton University Press, 1988). This included those shot out of hand, those executed after a trial, and those who perished in Siberia. The large mass grave at Kuropaty in Byelorussia, where tens of thousands were shot in 1939–1940, suggests that the latter figure is closer to the truth.

Katyn. Information provided by Moscow to the Polish government in 1992 showed that Lavrenty Beria had suggested the execution of more than 25,000 Polish military officers and civilian notables. Joseph Stalin and other members of the ruling Politburo signed the order.

Incorporation of the Baltic States. While the loss of life in the Baltic was less than that in eastern Poland, it amounted to more than 5 percent of the population, with approximately 200,000 shot and deported. Combined with heavy losses in 1944–1950 as the Soviet authorities reestablished power, executions and deportations constituted a demographic catastrophe for the people of Lithuania, Latvia, and Estonia.

Executions during the Great Patriotic War. There were approximately 250,000 executions of Soviet soldiers during the war. At Stalingrad, 13,500 men were shot in the course of the campaign that lasted from August 1942 to February 1943. In contrast, there was one execution for desertion in the U.S. Army during World War II and fewer than 10 executions in the British armed forces for mutiny and other military crimes during six years of war. During World War I, more than 300 British service personnel were shot for military crimes; this is seen today as a mark on the honor of the country and the military.

Death during Deportations, 1943–1945. The NKVD and NKGB deported 1.5 million to 2 million Soviet citizens during the war. There are no real morbidity figures for these people. The Chechens and the Crimean Tatars in their accounts state that 20 to 30 percent of the deportees died on the way to Central Asia or perished during the first year. This would lead historians to the conclusion that 300,000 to 500,000 perished in the first year of captivity.

Death in Camps, 1930–1953. A recent study of the gulag system put the number of deaths in the camps during 1930–1953 at more than 2.7 million. The author concludes that this figure is almost certainly too low because prisoners who were mortally ill were often released from penal servitude days before they passed away.

Famine of 1946–1948. There is only very sketchy information on this "unknown" famine. Recent Russian scholars have placed the death toll at 2 million. It is estimated that almost half the population, 100 million people, suffered from malnutrition after World War II. Thousands of peasants were arrested for stealing food for their families during the famine: MVD figures show 53,369 arrests in 1946 alone for theft of food. Most of those convicted were women pilfering food for their children. Almost three-quarters of those arrested went to forced labor camps. They were not reckoned as political prisoners, but they were victims of the system.

Political Arrests during Stalin's Last Years. Approximately 350,000 captured Soviet military personnel received death or 25-year sentences after their repatriation from Germany. In Ukraine and the Baltic states, prophylactic arrests of villagers continued until 1953, as the MGB sought to break the back of nationalist resistance. Arrests of intellectuals and dissident military officers continued as well, though not at the pace of the *Yezhovshchina*: between 1947 and 1953, there were 350,000 arrests for political offenses.

The last mass execution of political prisoners was the shooting of Jewish intellectuals and factory workers following the trial of the Anti-Fascist Committee in late 1952.

These figures are "soft." They do not include those killed in the prolonged partisan war in Ukraine and the Baltic states in 1945–1953 or the peripatetic civil war that existed in the Caucasus in 1925–1935 over collectivization. Nor does the figure include those who were murdered out of hand on Stalin's and others' personal orders. Alexander Yakovlev's *A Century of Violence in Soviet Russia* (New Haven, CT: Yale University Press, 2002) is the best short volume on the costs of the terror. It is not for the squeamish. The Memorial organization is creating a history of the martyrdom of the people, but despite extraordinary courage and persistence, it lacks complete records for the period. It now has lists for many mass graves and still continues to search for other execution grounds. Its website in Russian and English is the best place to follow developments in the history of the Soviet holocaust.

Demographers are now better able to comment on this bloody period in a different way. Their research, like Yakovlev's study and Memorial's research, shows that the countries that once composed the Soviet Union are still reeling from the terrible losses of the Stalin era. The Slavic countries, the Russian Federation, Byelorussia, and Ukraine, as well as three Baltic states, have suffered a demographic catastrophe that will take decades from which to recover.

Appendix I

Agents and Programs Betrayed by Aldrich Ames, Robert Hanssen, and Edward Lee Howard

Sergei Bokhan (Blizzard). GRU colonel serving abroad. Recruited in 1978. Rescued.

Oleg Gordievskiy. KGB political intelligence officer in London. Recruited in 1974. Rescued by the British Intelligence Service.

Valery Martynov (Gentile). KGB scientific and technical intelligence officer serving in Washington. Arrested and shot in 1986.

Sergei Motorin (Gauze). KGB political intelligence officer serving in Washington, DC. Arrested and shot in 1986.

Vladimir Piguzov (Jogger). KGB colonel serving in Indonesia. Arrested and shot 1987.

Dmitry Polyakov (Top Hat, Fedora). GRU major general. Initially volunteered to the Federal Bureau of Investigation in 1961. Provided information about Soviet arms control issues as well as significant counter-intelligence information. Arrested in 1986, shot in 1988.

Leonid Polishchuk (Weigh). KGB lieutenant colonel serving in Nepal and Nigeria. Recruited in 1974. Arrested and executed 1986–1987.

Vladimir Potashov (Median). Research analyst, Institute of the United States and Canada. Recruited in 1981. Arrested and sentenced to 13 years in prison.

Gennady Smetanin (Million). GRU colonel serving abroad. Recruited in 1983. Arrested (with his wife) on his return for home leave in 1986. He was later shot.

Adolf Tolkachev (Sphere, Vanquished). Aircraft designer. Volunteered in 1979. Provided critical information about Soviet aircraft and avionics. Arrested and shot in 1985–1987.

Gennady Varennik (Fitness). KGB lieutenant colonel serving in Bonn under cover as a TASS correspondent. Recruited in 1987. Arrested and shot in 1987–1988.

Vladimir Vasiliev (Accord). GRU lieutenant colonel. Provided lead to Clyde Lee Conrad ring, which led to the arrest of Conrad and 10 others. Arrested and shot in 1987.

Sergei Vorontsov (Cowl). KGB major in the counterintelligence section of the Moscow directorate. Volunteered in 1984. Provided information about the use of *metka*, or "spy dust." Arrested and shot in 1986–1987.

Boris Yuzhin (Twine). KGB lieutenant colonel. Sent to the University of California, Berkeley, in 1975 as a student. Sent back to San Francisco in 1978 under journalist cover. Arrested and sentenced to 15 years in prison in 1986. Two other Soviet bloc sources betrayed by Aldrich Ames were Eastbound, a Soviet radar scientist, and Motorboat, a Bulgarian official.

Appendix J

Maskirovka: Deception on Nuclear Weapons Programs

The Soviet security services played a critical role in building and protecting the Soviet nuclear weapons programs. Protection strategies included *maskirovka*, the Soviet military and intelligence term for a mixture of denial and deception measures. In 1944–1950, more than 100,000 prisoners were engaged in building secret facilities for the Soviet atom bomb. Between 1946 and 1956, 10 secret cities were built for nuclear weapons research and development, plutonium production, and warhead assembly. These cities were surrounded by barbed wire and never appeared in a Soviet atlas. The two most famous secret cities were Sarov, the Los Alamos of the Soviet weapons program, which took the artificial name Arzamas-16, and Ozersk, the first center of plutonium production, which was given the name Chelyabinsk-40.

The NKVD, MGB, and KGB were also engaged in hiding these cities from spies and technical intelligence. All papers leaving the cities were classified; "free workers" were discouraged from leaving the cities even on their vacations; freed prisoners were often exiled to the most distant locations of the far north or Siberia. The security services also vetted all employees, their families, and their contacts. In 1947, the MGB assigned 1,400 security officers to protect the facility at Sarov.

Maskirovka strategies also included building facilities in tunnels to hide the production of highly enriched uranium at Zheleznogorsk (Krasnoyarsk-26), the movement of plants and cities to remote locations, and the design of elaborate denial and deception plans to conceal facilities from American satellites. The KGB insisted that all communications between the cities and Moscow were to be conducted by landline to prevent the interception of radio communications.

The existence of the 10 secret cities was not revealed until after the collapse of the Soviet Union in 1992. A good primer on the maintenance of Soviet nuclear secrecy can be found in Oleg Baukharin, "The Cold War Atomic Intelligence Game, 1945–70," *Studies in Intelligence* 48, no. 2 (1999).

Bibliography

CONTENTS

INTRODUCTION

Any observer of the Russian intelligence and security services is bedeviled by questions of quantity and quality of information. This bibliography is a selection of relevant and important books and articles mostly in English and Russian that deal with the tsarist, Soviet, and post-Soviet Russian intelligence and security services. It does not include histories and memoirs unless they deal with the services directly. It also does not include general Soviet/Russian histories, military histories, or many of the Cold War memoirs by participants on both sides.

Since the first edition of this historical dictionary was published in 2006, there has been the publication of excellent general histories, monographs, and memoirs in Russian and English. We have an outstanding history of *Smersh* by a noted Russian dissident, several studies of the politics of the Soviet security services, and scores of memoirs by former and active intelligence officers, including one by the chief of a forced labor camp. Revelations from the archives have also been exciting, but—and this is a tremendous but—crucial areas remain off limit to researchers.

Until 1991, much of the information on the Soviet services and the most important cases came from dubious sources. Literally thousands of books have been written on the subject of Soviet intelligence—many of which are quite frankly useless to the modern scholar. For example, 12 books were written in Great Britain between 1953 and 1977 about the Soviet agents Donald Maclean and Guy Burgess: most of them frightfully inaccurate. Two of Kim Philby's wives have written memoirs. Even much of the "factual" material on which scholars must rely remains questionable: scholars have recently been able to establish that Stalin was born in 1878, not 1879, and that Nikolai Yezhov was born in Lithuania, not St. Petersburg. The death dates for many eminent Chekists are also in doubt.

Information on the number of victims of the Joseph Stalin era also remains a subject for bitter debate among scholars, as does the relationship between the Soviet security services and left-wing movements in the Western democracies. A French scholar, Stephanie Courtois, noted in a history of the crimes of communism that we have far less evidence of the crimes of Lenin and Stalin and almost no photographs or films of the terrors of their rule: "Alas, we have only a handful of rare archival photographs of the Gulag. There are no photographs of dekulakization or of the famine. . . . The victorious powers could at least photograph and film the thousands of bodies found at Bergen-Belsen. . . . No such record exists in the Communist world, where terror has been organized in strictest secrecy" (Courtois et al. 1999, 36).

Evidence for this study had to be carefully reviewed, and this bibliography therefore had to exclude many interesting books. For example, there have been over a dozen books in Latvian, Lithuanian, Ukrainian, Russian, and German on the riots in the Soviet labor camps in 1953. Nevertheless, for readers interested in the subject, Aleksandr Solzhenitsyn's *Gulag Archipelago* (1974) and Anne Applebaum's *Gulag: A History* (2003) still provide the best accounts. Likewise, Pavel Sudoplatov's *Special Tasks* (1994) is listed but not his *Spets operatsii* (1995) and *Razvedka i Kreml* (1996), which are basically Russian versions of the English best seller.

In the past 25 years, it has been possible to study the tsarist police and intelligence service from archives in the West and Russia. While some of the Russian archives may have been adulterated or purged during the Soviet period, historians are now far better able to gauge the effectiveness of the *Okhrana*'s operations against the revolutionary parties and the professionalism of the tsarist military intelligence service. Another important trove of *Okhrana* material can be found in the Hoover Institute archives in Stanford, California. Articles about Okhrana operations from the Hoover Institute are now available in unclassified editions of the Central Intelligence Agency's *Studies in Intelligence*.

While there have been a staggering number of books on Soviet history since the dawn of the Cold War, few studies address the role of the security services in Soviet domestic and foreign policies. There are hundreds of memoirs of the inmates of forced labor camps as well as almost as many from defectors and émigrés. But general histories of the Soviet Union have little time or space for the security police, and few even try to define the role of the Soviet services in protecting the Communist Party and the Soviet state. As one outstanding Kremlinologist wrote near the end of the Cold War, "The Soviet security police, or KGB, looms as an uncertain variable for scholars, mainly because we have no commonly accepted conceptual framework to explain its role in the system. The KGB has never received much scholarly attention in the West . . . the dearth of serious scholarly research on the KGB has left a deep gap in how the Soviet system works and what factors influence Soviet decision making" (Knight 1988, xvi).

There are some exceptional monographs on Soviet and post-Soviet intelligence: Amy Knight's *Beria: Stalin's First Lieutenant*, Michael Parrish's *The Lesser Terror*, and Robert Conquest's *The Great Terror* and *Inside Stalin's Secret Police* have enriched us with their research, writing, and courage. Conquest's books on repression, beginning with *The Great Terror*, forced both the academic community and the Western intelligentsia to consider the costs of the Soviet experiment. Revisionist histories in the 1980s tried to minimize repression and the number of victims, but the opening of the Soviet archives after 1991 showed that it was Conquest rather than his critics who was closer to the truth. Robert W. Stephan's recent *Stalin's Secret War: Soviet Counterintelligence against the Nazis* (2003), which mined Soviet, former *Wehrmacht*, and American records, is the first Western monograph on the "invisible front," the intense battle between the Soviet and German secret services. Two recent histories of the first days of World War II have also successfully mined Soviet archives: David Murphy, *What Stalin Knew: The Enigma of Barbarossa* (2005), and Constantine Pleshakov, *Stalin's Folly* (2005), are the best accounts in English of Stalin's intelligence failure in 1941. Murphy's book also uses GRU material effectively, detailing the operations of illegals in Europe and Japan.

The status of Russian archives has been a matter of concern to researchers and human rights activists. Many of the KGB archives were reportedly destroyed in 1989–1991. According to a press release, the KGB burned 583 archival files pertaining to Andrei Sakharov. Since the end of the Cold War, some of the former Soviet archives have been opened and are being mined by scholars—Russian and Western. Joseph Brent's *Inside the Stalin Archives* (2008) gives a firsthand perspective of the bitter fight to get access to Russian archives.

The Cold War International History Project, Louise Shelley's *Policing Soviet Society* (1997), and Anne Applebaum's *Gulag* (2002) on the forced labor camps show what can be achieved by scrupulous research. Michael Parish's *The Lesser Terror*, on the role of repression in Soviet politics after the Great Terror, is one of the best examples of how to mine and refine material from the Russian archives. There are several new books in English and Russian on Stalin's relationships with the secret police based on archival research. Donald Rayfield's *Stalin and His Hangmen: The Tyrant and Those Who Killed for Him* (2004) is a passionate account of Stalin's personal and professional relationship with his security chieftains. Marc Jansen and Nikolai Petrov's biography of Nikolai Yezhov is a particularly good monograph. Vadim Birstein's *SMERSH: Stalin's Secret Weapon* (2011) is the first detailed history of Russian counterintelligence from 1918 to 1945. Well researched, it provides the first detailed account of how Stalin managed and won the intelligence struggle with Hitler.

Material in the Russian Soviet archives has also allowed Western and Russian historians to better understand the intelligence war between the Cheka and the foreign intelligence services. Archivists of the Federal Security Service (FSB) have written three histories of Russian special service operations in the Great Patriotic War. V. S. Khristoforov, the service chief archivist, used over 100 top-secret documents to write *Lubyanka in the Days of the Battle of Moscow* (2002). The same team of archivists and historians has also written a history of *Smersh*; while not as complete as Birstein's book, it includes many *Smersh* documents minuted by Stalin.

We also have several books in English that integrate intelligence and security operations into history. Recommended is Christopher Bellamy's *Absolute War* (2007), which is especially good on Soviet prewar and military operations. One cannot recommend too highly Timothy Snyder's *Bloodlands* (2012), about the history of central Europe between 1930 and 1953. Finally, an excellent account of the Leningrad blockade based on NKVD and Communist Party documents is Richard Bidlanck and Nikita Lomagin, *The Leningrad Blockade, 1941–1944*.

The KGB's long struggle against the dissidents is well documented. Particularly recommended are Jay Bergman's *Meeting the Demands of Reason: The Life and Thought of Andrei Sakharov* (2009). His chief persecutor, Filip Bobkov, has also written his memoirs, *KGB Vlast* (*KGB: The Power*). Also interesting is the crackdown on riots and demonstrations in Novocherkassk in 1962, *Bloody Saturday in the Soviet Union: Novocherkassk 1962* (2001), by the noted Russian scholar Samuel H. Baron.

The new generation of Russian archivists and scholars is to be congratulated for taking on difficult subjects such as the Red Terror and collaboration with the Germans during the early days of the war. There remain, however, important limitations for scholars of this field: many of the archives have not been opened or are available only by the whim of the archivists. The archives of the SVR, the FSB, and the GRU generally remain closed, though some documents have been released and published in documentary collections and on websites. While more is known about the Stalinist and post-Stalinist intelligence and security services, there are still major lacunae.

The role of Soviet intelligence in the United States and the United Kingdom remains a contentious issue. The best summary of the debate within academe is John Earl Haynes and Harvey Klehr's *In Denial* (2003). There are two recent bibliographies of Elizabeth Bentley, the "Red Spy Queen," as well as case studies of Judith Coplon and Harry Dexter White. Ethel Rosenberg's granddaughter has recently produced a film biography of her grandmother. The Hiss and Rosenberg cases remain the subject of polemics and histories. A recent study of the Noel Field case, Tony Sharp's *Stalin's American Spy* (2014), is an excellently researched and written account of a critical case. The collection of Venona messages released in 1995—more than 2,400 decrypted and partially decrypted Soviet intelligence messages—indicates that Moscow believed that most of the infamous Cold War spies were in fact Soviet agents. Some historians have continued to challenge this judgment, most notably the Russian historian Svetlana Chervonnaya and her website www.DocumentsTalk.com, and it seems likely that the debate over Soviet espionage will continue.

Post–Cold War memoirs by former Soviet intelligence officers, diplomats, and politicians have added both heat and light to a history of the Soviet Union. There are books by Malenkov and Beria's sons as well as a number of men and women who survived the court of Stalin. Most of these books, while informative, contain some factual errors and do not cite specific documents to allow scholars to check specific claims. There are a number of good books by former Soviet intelligence officers in English and Russian. The FSB website (www.fsb.ru) contains an excellent annotated bibliography for the scholar of Soviet intelligence. Moreover, Christopher Andrews has written several monographs and two general histories of the KGB's foreign intelligence operations using recent Soviet defectors, and we have a history of the Cold War from Moscow's perspective, Jonatham Haslam's *Russia's Cold War*. Haslam's bibliography provides the best source list available of Russian research and archival material on Moscow's Cold War. We still lack a good institutional history of the GRU and good biographies of Viktor Abakumov, Yuri Andropov, Aleksandr Shelepin, and other important security chiefs as well as a new look at Soviet national security decision making in the post-Soviet period.

We have a number of biographies of Vladimir Putin as well as a few insightful journalistic accounts of the Putin period. Ben Judah's *Fragile Empire* uses academic and journalist reporting and also mines the documents released during the "Wikileaks" scandal. The books and articles of the late Anna Politkovskaya cannot be recommended too highly for their coverage of the Chechen War and the FSB's battle against terrorism and dissenters. Her murder at the hands of men alleged to be close to the FSB strongly suggest the accuracy of her work and the degree of irritation it caused people in the Kremlin.

Since the collapse of the Soviet Union, a number of excellent websites have appeared on the Soviet intelligence and security services. The Federation of Atomic Scientists Intelligence Research Program (www.fas.org/irp provides useful though dated information on the Russian services. The best Russian website on intelligence is www.agentura.com, in both Russian and English. Essays in the Russian language on this website provide detailed information on the organization, chronology, and personnel of the Soviet and post-Soviet intelligence and security services. Both the Russian counterintelligence and foreign intelligence services have their own websites (www.fsb.ru.gov and www.svr.ru.gov) that contain sanitized biographies of heroes and agents and accounts of operations against enemies foreign and domestic. Recommended with reservations is www.DocumentsTalk.com. This website provides detailed biographies of Soviet intelligence officers and some of their Western agents as well as documents from Stalin's NKVD.

While the webmaster goes overboard in defending NKVD operations and attacking Western counterintelligence, she has effectively reopened the debate on the Hiss and other Cold War spy cases.

A website with detailed and accurate information on the Stalinist services is managed by Memorial, a Russian human rights organization (www.memorial.com). One entire section of this website is given over to a detailed history of the NKVD between 1934 and 1941, "*Kto Rukovoditel NKVD, 1934–1941*" (*Who Led the NKVD, 1934–1941*). The section includes detailed bibliographies of more than 500 senior security and intelligence officers. There are a number of good English, German, Polish, and Russian websites on forced labor camps: among the more interesting are the Open Societies Archives on the gulag system (www.osa.ceu.ru/gulag), a German site on the northern camps (www.solovki.org), and the Katyn website (www.electronicmuseum.ca/Poland-WW2/katyn). A good website on Russian strategy and tactics in the Great Patriotic War is Russian Battlefield (www.battlefield.ru), which contains scores of documents in Russian and a few in English on Soviet intelligence in 1940–1945.

The best academic websites on intelligence during the Cold War are the Cold War International History Project (www.cwihp.si) and the Harvard Project on Cold War Studies (www.fas.Harvard.edu/~hpsws). Both contain a number of documents from the Russian archives and some outstanding analysis of the role of the Soviet services in both foreign intelligence and Soviet power politics. The Worldwide Socialist Web (www.wsww.org) has an outstanding oral history program, and it often has a number of editorials and interviews with the remaining survivors of the Comintern and Trotsky's Fourth International.

Western intelligence and security services now all have websites that contain details about operations against the Soviet intelligence services and analysis of the Soviet threat during the Cold War. The National Counterintelligence Center (www.nacic.org) has a four-volume history of American counterintelligence on its site, including detailed histories of many famous counterintelligence cases. On the CIA site (www.cia.gov), the Center for the Study of Intelligence publishes studies by in-house historians and former intelligence officers as well as by former Russian bureaucrats and intelligence officers. Among the best of the CIA in-house historians is Ben Fischer, who has produced a study of the *Okhrana* and an account of the Katyn massacre. The National Security Agency (www.nsa.gov) has published all the Venona messages as well as essays by the men and women who worked on this signals intelligence problem.

A bibliography of the Soviet services is an effort to hit a moving target, and information must be used with care. Disinformation remains an issue but is less important in the Soviet worldview. More and more books are being released in Russia and the West about how the Soviet past influences Russian behavior. Beginning with Czeslav Milosz's *The Captive Mind*, written in 1951, efforts have been with mixed success. A very good read for understanding the worldview of the Russian leaders who rose to power after the fall of the Soviet Union is Dicks Combs, *Inside the Soviet Alternative Universe* (2008). More important is that we are dealing with the living, breathing organism: the Russian services are active and competent, especially in disguising their role in events. One of the first posters for the Soviet home front in 1941 showed a woman shushing a conversation, with the words *Ne Boltai!* (Don't Blab!). These remain important watchwords for Vladimir Putin's Chekists.

PUBLISHED ARCHIVAL MATERIAL

Andrews, Christopher, and Oleg Gordievsky, eds. *Instructions from the Center: Top Secret Files on KGB Foreign Operations 1975–1985*. Stanford, CA: Stanford University Press, 1993.

———. *More Instructions from the Center*. London: Frank Cass, 1993.

Brent, Jonathan. *Inside the Stalin Archives: Discovering the New Russia*. New Haven, CT: Yale University Press, 2008.

Central Intelligence Agency. *The Rote Kapelle: The CIA's History of Soviet Intelligence and Espionage Networks in Western Europe, 1936–1945*. Washington, DC: University Publications of America, 1984.

———. *Annual Report to Congress on the Safety and Security of Russian Nuclear Facilities and Military Forces*. Washington, DC: National Intelligence Council, May 2004. www.internet.cia/nic/Specialrussiannuke04.

Cold War International History Project Bulletins. Washington, DC: Woodrow Wilson Center, 1990.

Khronika tekushchikh sobytii (Chronicle of Current Events). Helsinki Group. www.memoria.ru.

Khveniuk, O. V. *Stalinskoe politburo-30e gody: Sbornik dokumentov* (The Stalinist Politburo in the 1930s: Collection of Documents). Moscow: AIR O-XX, 1995.

Knight, Amy. "Russian Archives: Opportunities and Obstacles." *International Journal of Intelligence and Counterintelligence* 12, no. 3 (1999).

Leningradskiy martirolog, 1937–1938 (List of People Martyred in Leningrad, 1937–1938). St. Petersburg: Akademiya, 1995.

National Security Agency. *Introductory History of VENONA and Guide to the Translations*. Fort Meade, MD: National Security Agency, 1995.

Organy gosudartvennoi bezopasnosti SSR v V.O.V.: Sbornik dokumentov (Organs of State Security of the USSR in the Great Patriotic War: Collection of Documents). Moscow: SVR, 1995.

Politicheskie protsessy 30–50 godov (Political Trials of the 1930s to 1950s). Moscow: Nevka, 1991.

Rahr, Alexander. *A Biographic Dictionary of 100 Leading Soviet Officials.* Denver, CO: Westview, 1991.

Rasstrelniye spiski, Moskva 1937–1941 (Execution Lists: Moscow, 1937–1941). Moscow: Memorial, 2000.

Razumov, A. Ya. *Leningradskiy martirolog* (Leningrad Martyrology). Vols. 1–4. St. Petersburg: Nevka, 2002.

Romanian Academy, National Institute for the Study of Totalitarianism. *Totalitarian Archives.* Vols. 1 and 2. Bucharest: Romanian Academy, 2002.

Samolis, T. V., ed. *Veterany vneshnei razvedki Rossii: Kratkiy biograficheskiy spravochnik* (*Veterans of Russian Foreign Intelligence: A Short Bibliographical Account*). Moscow: SVR, 1995.

Sovetskaya voennaya entsiklopediia. Moscow: Voenizdat, 1978.

Stalin's Special Files. Archives of Contemporary Russian History. Pittsburgh, PA: University of Pittsburgh, Center for the Study of Russia and the Soviet Union, 1995. Trotsky Archives. Houghton Library, Harvard University.

U.S. Congress. Senate Committee on the Judiciary. *The Wennerstrom Case: How It Touched the United States and NATO.* Washington, DC: Government Printing Office, 1964.

———. *Soviet Security Services 1964–1970: A Selected Bibliography of Soviet Publications with Some Additional Titles from Other Sources.* 92nd Congress, 1st Session. Washington, DC: Government Printing Office, 1972.

———. *Amerasia Papers: A Clue to the Catastrophe in China.* Washington, DC: Government Printing Office, 1979.

U.S. Department of State. *Soviet Active Measures, Special Report 110.* Washington, DC: Bureau of Public Affairs, September 1985.

VENONA: Decrypted Soviet Intelligence Service Telegrams. www.nsa.gov.8080.

GENERAL HISTORIES

Andrew, Christopher. *Her Majesty's Secret Service: The Making of the British Intelligence Community.* New York: Viking, 1986.

———. *Defend the Realm: The Authorized History of MI5.* New York: Knopf, 2009.

Berlin, Isaiah. *The Soviet Mind.* Washington, DC: Brookings Institution, 2004.

Conquest, Robert. *Reflections on a Ravaged Country*. New York: Norton, 2000.

Courtois, Stephanie, et al. *The Black Book of Communism*. Cambridge, MA: Harvard University Press, 1999.

Cram, Cleveland. *Of Moles and Mole Hunters*. Washington, DC: Central Intelligence Agency Center for the Study of Intelligence, 1993.

Deacon, Richard. *The French Secret Service*. London: Grafton, 1990.

Dunlop, John. *The Rise of Russia and the Fall of the Soviet Union*. Princeton, NJ: Princeton University Press, 1993.

Figes, Orlando. *A People's Tragedy: A History of the Russian Revolution*. New York: Viking, 1996.

Fitzpatrick, Sheela. *Everyday Stalinism: Ordinary Life in Extraordinary Times*. New York: Oxford University Press, 1999.

Furet, Francois. *The Passing of an Illusion: The Idea of Communism in the Twentieth Century*. Chicago: University of Chicago Press, 1997.

Gellately, Robert. *Lenin, Stalin, and Hitler: The Age of Social Catastrophe*. New York:Knopf, 2007.

Hammond, T. T., ed. *The Anatomy of Communist Takeovers*. New Haven, CT: Yale University Press, 1975.

Herspring, Dale. *The Soviet High Command, 1967–1989: Personalities and Politics*. Princeton, NJ: Princeton University Press, 1990.

Hinsley, F. H., and C. A. G. Simkins. *British Intelligence in the Second World War*. London: Her Majesty's Stationery Office, 1990.

Hutchings, Raymond. *Soviet Security and Non-Security*. Totowa, NJ: Barnes & Noble, 1988.

Jeffrey, Keith. *The Secret History of MI6, 1909–1949* . New York: Penguin, 2010.

Khvenyuk, Oleg. *Politburo: Mikhanizmy politicheskoi vlasti v 1930–e gody* (The Politburo: Mechanisms of Soviet Power in the 1930s). Moscow: ROSSPEN, 1996.

Malia, Martin. *The Soviet Tragedy*. New York: Free Press, 1994.

Mayer, Arno J. *The Furies: Violence and Terror in the French and Russian Revolutions*. Princeton, NJ: Princeton University Press, 2000.

McDermott, Kevin, and Jeremy Agnew. *The Comintern: A History of International Communism from Lenin to Stalin*. New York: St. Martin's, 1997.

Merridal, Catherine. *Nights of Stone: Death and Memory in Twentieth Century Russia*. London: Granta, 2000.

Overy, Richard. *Interrogations: The Nazi Elite in Allied Hands, 1945*. New York: Viking, 2001.

Parker, John W. *The Kremlin in Transition: From Brezhnev to Chernenko*. Boston: Unwin, 1995.

Pipes, Richard. *Russia under the Bolshevik Regime*. New York: Random House, 1994.

Porch, Douglas. *The French Secret Service*. New York: Farrar, Straus and Giroux, 1995.

Pryce-Jones, David. *The War That Never Was: The Fall of the Soviet Empire, 1985–1991*. London: Weidenfeld and Nicolson, 1995.

Reddaway, Peter, and Dmitri Glinski. *The Tragedy of Russia's Reforms: Market Bolshevism against Democracy*. Washington, DC: United States Institute of Peace, 2001.

Volensky, Michael. *Nomenklatura*. London: Bodley Head, 1984.

Volkogonov, Dmitri. *Autopsy for An Empire: The Seven Leaders Who Built the Soviet Regime*. New York: Free Press, 1998.

Weitz, Eric D. *A Century of Genocide*. Princeton, NJ: Princeton University Press, 2003.

West, Rebecca. *The New Meaning of Treason*. New York: Viking, 1964.

Wright, Susan, ed. *Biological Warfare and Disarmament*. Lanham, MD.: Rowman & Littlefield, 2002.

Zimmerman, William, *Ruling Russia: Authoritarianism from the Revolution to Putin*. Princeton, NJ: Princeton University Press, 2014.

Memoirs and Biographies

Amis, Martin. *Koba the Dread: Laughter and the Twenty Million*. New York: Talk-Miramax Books, 2002.

Arbatov, Georgi. *The System: An Insider's Life in Soviet Politics*. New York: Times Books, 1992.

Beria, Sergo. *Beria My Father: Inside Stalin's Kremlin*. London: Duckworth, 2003.

Bissell, Richard J. *Reflections of a Cold Warrior: From Yalta to the Bay of Pigs*. New Haven, CT: Yale University Press, 1996.

Bodin, Valery. *Ten Years That Shook the World*. New York: Basic Books, 1994.

Bullock, Alan. *Hitler and Stalin: Parallel Lives*. New York: Knopf, 1991.

Chernayev, Anatoly. *My Six Years with Gorbachev*. University Park: Pennsylvania State University Press, 2000.

Chuev, Feliks. *Molotov Remembers: Inside Kremlin Politics*. London: Ivan R. Dee, 1993.

Cohen, Stephen F. *Bukharin and the Bolshevik Revolution, 1888–1938*. New York: Vintage, 1973.

Dallin, Alexander, ed. *Dmitrov and Stalin, 1934–1943: Letters from the Soviet Archives*. New Haven, CT: Yale University Press, 2000.

Deutscher, Isaac. *The Prophet Armed: Trotsky 1879–1921*. London: Oxford University Press, 1954.

————. *The Prophet Unarmed: Trotsky 1921–1929*. London: Oxford University Press, 1959.

————. *The Prophet Outcast: Trotsky 1929–1940*. London: Oxford University Press, 1963.

Djilas, Milovan. *Conversations with Stalin*. New York: Harcourt Brace Jovanovich, 1962.

Dobrynin, Anatoly. *In Confidence: Moscow's Ambassador to Six Cold War Presidents*. New York: Times Books, 1995.

Gorbachev, Mikhail S. *Memoirs*. London: Doubleday, 1996.

Gromov, Yevgeny. *Stalin, vlast i iskusstvo* (*Stalin: Power and Art*). Moscow: Respublika, 1998.

Ilizarov, B. S. *Tainaya zhizn Stalina* (The Secret Life of Stalin). Moscow: Veche, 2002.

Kaganovich, Lazar. *Tak govoril Kaganovich* (*Thus Spoke Kaganovich*). Moscow: Otechestvo, 1992.

Khrushchev Remembers. Boston: Little, Brown, 1970.

Khrushchev Remembers: The Last Testament. Boston: Little, Brown, 1974.

Lih, Lars T., ed. *Stalin's Letters to Molotov, 1925–1936*. New Haven, CT: Yale University Press, 1995.

Malenkov, A. G. *O moem ottse: Georgii Malenkov* (Concerning My Father: Georgii Malenkov). Moscow: NTTS tekhnoekos, 1992.

Medvedev, Roy, and Zhores Medvedev. *The Unknown Stalin: His Life, Death, and Legacy*. New York: Overlook, 2004.

Montefiore, Simon Sebag. *Stalin: The Court of the Red Tsar*. New York: Knopf, 2004.

Novikov, Viktor. *Beria: Konets karierie* (*Beria: The End of His Career*). Moscow: Polizdat, 1991.

Primakov, Yevgeny. *Russian Crossroads*. New Haven, CT: Yale University Press, 2004.

Putin, Vladimir. *First Person*. New York: Public Affairs, 2000.

Radzinsky, Edward. *Stalin*. New York: Doubleday, 1996.

Overy, Richard. *The Dictators: Hitler's German, Stalin's Russia*. New York: Norton, 2004.

Sagdeev, Roald Z. *The Making of a Soviet Scientist*. New York: Wiley, 1994.

Service, Robert. *Lenin*. New York: Belknap, 2002.

Simonov, Konstanti. *Through the Eyes of a Man of My Generation*. Moscow: Kniga, 1989.

Volkogonov, Dmitry. *Lenin and New Biography*. New York: Free Press, 1992.

————. *Stalin: Triumph and Tragedy*. New York: Prima, 1992.

Yeltsin, Boris. *Against the Grain: An Autobiography*. New York: Summit, 1990.

Reference Works

Johnson, Loch K., ed. *The Oxford Handbook of National Security Intelligence*. Oxford: Oxford University Press, 2010.

Kahana, Ephraim. *The Historical Dictionary of Israeli Intelligence*. Lanham, MD: Scarecrow Press, 2005.

Smith, I. C., and Nigel West. *Historical Dictionary of Chinese Intelligence*. Lanham, MD: Scarecrow Press, 2012.

Turner, Michael. *The Historical Dictionary of United States Intelligence*. Lanham, MD: Scarecrow Press, 2006.

West, Nigel. *Historical Dictionary of British Intelligence*. Lanham, MD: Scarecrow Press, 2005.

———. *Historical Dictionary of International Intelligence*. Lanham, MD: Scarecrow Press, 2006.

———. *Historical Dictionary of Cold War Counterintelligence*. Lanham, MD: Scarecrow Press, 2007.

TSARIST REGIME AND ITS SECURITY SERVICES

Churkarev, A. G. *Tainaya polititsiya Nikolai I* (Secret Politics of Nicholas I). Yaroslav: Pechati Dvor, 2002.

Elwood, R. C. *Roman Malinovsky: A Life without a Cause*. Newtonville, MA: Oriental Research Partners, 1977.

Fischer, Ben B. *Okhrana: The Paris Operations of the Russian Imperial Police*. Washington, DC: Central Intelligence Agency Center for the Study of Intelligence, 1997.

Gapon, G. *The Story of My Life*. London: George Bell and Sons, 1905.

Geifman, Anna. *Thou Shall Kill: Revolutionary Terrorism in Russia, 1894–1917*. Princeton, NJ: Princeton University Press, 1996.

Kennan, George. *Siberia and the Exile System*. New York: Praeger, 1970.

Koropotkin, Peter. *In Russian and French Prisons*. London: Ward and Downey, 1887.

La Porte, Maurice. *Histoire de l'Okhranaka police secrete des tsars, 1880–1917*. Paris: Payot, 1935.

Nicolajevsky, Boris. *Aseff, the Spy*. New York: Doubleday, 1934.

Orlovsky, Daniel T. *The Limits of Reform: The Ministry of Internal Affairs, 1802–1881*. Cambridge, MA: Harvard University Press, 1981.

Pipes, Richard. *The Degaev Affair*. New Haven, CT: Yale University Press, 2003.

Plougin, Vladimir. *Russian Intelligence Services*. Vol. 1, *The Early Years*, translated by Gennady Kashkov. New York: Algora, 2000.

Radzinsky, Edward. *The Last Tsar: The Life and Death of Nicholas II*. New York: Doubleday, 2002.

Raeff, Marc. *The Well-Ordered Police State: Social and Institutional Change through Law in the Germanies and Russia 1600–1800*. New Haven, CT: Yale University Press, 1983.

Rubenstein, Richard E. *Comrade Valentine: The True Story of Azev the Spy: The Most Dangerous Man in Russia at the Time of the Last Tsars*. New York: Harcourt, 1994.

Rudd, Charles A., and Sergei Stepanov. *Fontanka 16: The Tsarist Secret Police*. Montreal: McGill-Queens University Press, 1999. Expanded from Sergei Stepanov, *Fontanka 16*. Moscow, 1994.

Sablinsky, Walter. *The Road to Bloody Sunday: Father Gapon and the St. Petersburg Massacre*. Princeton, NJ: Princeton University Press, 1976.

Savinsky, Boris. *Memoirs of a Terrorist*. New York: Albert and Charles Boni, 1925.

Schimmelpenninck van der Oye, David H. "Tsarist Codebreaking: Some Background and Some Examples." *Cryptologia* 22, no. 4 (1998).

Schleifman, Nurit. *Undercover Agents in the Russian Revolutionary Movement: The SR Party, 1902–1914*. London: Macmillan, 1988.

Schneiderman, Jeremiah. *The Tsarist Government and the Labor Movement: Zubatovshchina*. Berkeley: University of California Press, 1967.

Smith, Edward Ellis. *"The Okhrana": The Russian Department of Police: A Bibliography*. Stanford, CA: Hoover Institution, 1967.

Vasilyev, A. T. *The Okhrana: The Russian Secret Police*. London: George G. Harrap, 1930.

Venturi, Franco. *Roots of Revolution: A History of the Populist and Socialist Movements in Nineteenth Century Russia*. London: Weidenfeld and Nicolson, 1960.

Wolfe, Bertram D. *Three Who Made a Revolution*. New York: Dial, 1948.

Zuckerman, Frederic S. *The Tsarist Police in Russian Society, 1880–1917*. New York: New York University Press, 1996.

The Redl Affair

Alekseev, Mikhail. "Agent No. 25. "*Sovershenno Sekret*, no. 8 (1993).

Asprey, Robert. *The Panther's Feast*. London: Jonathan Cape, 1959.

Deutsch, Harold. "Sidelights on the Redl Case: Russian Intelligence on the Eve of the Great War." *Intelligence and National Security* 4, no. 4 (1989).

Milshtein, M. "Delo polkovnika Redlya (The Colonel Redl Affair)." *Voenno-istoricheskiy zhurnal*, no. 1 (1966).

Schindler, John R. "Redl—Spy of the Century." *International Journal of Intelligence and Counterintelligence* 18, no. 3 (2005).

GENERAL HISTORIES OF RUSSIAN AND SOVIET INTELLIGENCE SERVICES

Albats, Eugenia. *The State within a State: The KGB and Its Hold on Russia, Past, Present, and Future.* New York: Farrar, Straus and Giroux, 1994.

Andrews, Christopher, and Oleg Gordievsky. *Inside the KGB: The Inside Story of Its Foreign Operations from Lenin to Gorbachev.* New York: Harpers, 1986.

Andrews, Christopher, and Vasili Mitrokin. *The Mitrokhin Archives and the Secret History of the KGB.* New York: Basic Books, 1999.

————. *The World Was Going Our Way: The KGB and the Battle for the Third World.* New York: Basic Books, 2005.

Azrael, Jeremy. *The KGB in Kremlin Politics.* Los Angeles: RAND Corporation, 1989.

Ball, Desmond. *Soviet Signals Intelligence (SIGINT).* Canberra: Australian National University, 1989.

Brown, Anthony Cave, and Charles B. Mac Donald. *On a Field of Red: The Communist International and the Coming of World War II.* New York: G. P. Putnam's Sons, 1981.

Burgess, William H., ed. *Inside SPETZNAZ: Soviet Special Operations, a Critical Analysis.* Novato, CA: Presidio, 1990.

Conquest, Robert. *Inside Stalin's Secret Police: NKVD Politics 1936–1939.* London: Macmillan, 1985.

Dallin, David J. *Soviet Espionage.* New Haven, CT: Yale University Press, 1952.

Deacon, Richard. *A History of the Russian Secret Services.* London: Frederick Muller, 1972.

Deriabin, Peter. *Inside Stalin's Kremlin.* Washington, DC: Brassey's, 1998.

Deriabin, Peter, and T. H. Bagley. *The KGB: Masters of the Soviet Union.* New York: Hippocrene, 1990.

Dziak, John J. *Chekisty: A History of the KGB.* Lexington, MA: Heath, 1988.

Hingley, Ronald. *The Russian Secret Police: Muscovite, Imperial, and Soviet Political Security Operations.* New York: Simon and Schuster, 1972.

KGB vchera, sevodnya, zavtra (The KGB Yesterday, Today, Tomorrow). Moscow: Glasnost, 1996.

Knight, Amy. *The KGB: Police and Politics in the Soviet Union.* Boston: Allen and Unwin, 1988.

Kokurin, A. I., and N. V. Petrov, eds. *Lubyanka: VChK-OGPU-NKVD-NKGBMGB-MVD-KGB. Spravochnik (Lubyanka: VChK-OGPU-NKVD-NKGBMGB-MVD-KGB, Reference Book).* Moscow: Memorial, 2003.

Kolpakadi, D. P., and D. P. Prokhorov. *Imperiya GRU Ocherki rossiiskoi voennoi razvedki* (The GRU Empire: Outline of Russian Military Intelligence). Moscow: Olma, 1999.

————. *Vneshnaya razvedka Rossii* (The Foreign Intelligence Services of Russia). Moscow: Olma, 2001.

Levytsky, Boris. *The Uses of Terror: The Soviet Secret Police, 1917–1970.* New York: Coward, McCann and Geoghegan, 1972.

Lure, V. M., and V. Ya. Kochik. *GRU: Dela i liudi* (The GRU: Operations and People). St. Petersburg: Neva, 2002.

Mitrokhin, Vasili. *KGB Lexicon: A Handbook of Chekist Terminology.* London: Frank Cass, 2001.

Myagakov, Aleksei. *Inside the KGB: An Expose by an Officer of the Third Directorate.* Richmond, UK: Foreign Affairs, 1986.

Parrish, Michael. *Soviet Security and Intelligence Organizations, 1917–1990: A Biographical Dictionary and Review of the Literature in English.* Westport, CT: Greenwood, 1992.

Pravdin, A. "Inside the CPSU Central Committee." *Survey* 20, no. 4 (1974).

Rayfield, David. *Stalin and His Hangmen: The Tyrant and Those Who Killed for Him.* New York: Random House, 2004.

Rocca, Raymond, and John Dziak. *Bibliography on Soviet Intelligence and Security Services.* Denver, CO: Westview, 1985.

Rosenfeldt, Niels Erik. *Stalin's Special Departments.* Copenhagen: C. A. Reitzels Forlag, 1989.

Shelley, Louise. *Policing Soviet Society.* New York: Routledge, 1997.

Shultz, Richard H., and Roy Godson. *Dezinformatsia: Active Measures in Soviet Strategy.* Washington, DC: Brassey's, 1984.

Suvorov, Victor. *Soviet Military Intelligence.* London: Hamish Hamilton, 1984.

————. *Spetznaz: The Story behind the Soviet SAS.* London: Hamish Hamilton, 1987.

Tatu, Michel. *Power in the Kremlin.* New York: Viking, 1968.

Thomas, Paul. *Le KGB en Belgique.* Brussels: J. M. Collet, 1987.

Wolin, Simon, and Robert Slusser. *The Soviet Secret Police.* New York: Frederick A. Praeger, 1957.

Wolton, Thierry. *Le KGB en France.* Paris: Bernard Grasset, 1986.

THE SOVIET HOLOCAUST

Soviet Security Services and Governance

Agabetkov, G. S. *GPU: Zapiski chekista* (The GPU: Notes of a Chekist). Berlin: Sterla, 1930.

———. *Cheka za robotoi* (The Cheka at Work). Berlin: Strela, 1931.

Antonov-Ovsyenko, Anton. *The Time of Stalin.* New York: Harper and Row, 1980.

———. *Beria.* Moscow: AST, 1999.

Bazhanov, Boris. *Vospominaniya byshego sekretariya Stalina* (Memoirs of Stalin's Former Secretary). Paris: Tretya Lolna, 1980. Originally published as *Avec Stalin dans le Kremlin.* Paris: Les editions de France, 1930.

Brent, Jonathan, and Vladimir P. Naumov. *Stalin's Last Crime: The Plot against the Jewish Doctors, 1948–1953.* New York: HarperCollins, 2003.

Bugai, L. N. *L. Beria–I. Stalinu, "Soglasno vashemu ukazaniu"* (L. Beria–J. Stalin, "In Accordance with Your Instructions"). Moscow: AIRO XX, 1995.

Chase, William J. *Enemies within the Gates: The Comintern and Stalinist Repression, 1934–1939.* New Haven, CT: Yale University Press, 2002.

Conquest, Robert. *The Harvest of Sorrows.* London: Oxford University Press, 1986.

———. *Stalin and Kirov's Murder.* Oxford: Oxford University Press, 1989.

———. *The Great Terror.* London: Oxford University Press, 1990.

Davies, Sarah. *Popular Opinion in Stalin's Russia: Terror, Propaganda, and Dissent, 1934–1941.* Cambridge: Cambridge University Press, 1997.

Deriabin, Peter S. *Inside Stalin's Kremlin.* Herndon, VA: Brassey's, 1998.

Druzhnikov, Yuri. *Informant 001: The Myth of Pavlik Morozov.* London: Transaction, 1997.

Fainsod, Merle. *Smolensk under Soviet Rule.* Cambridge, MA: Harvard University Press, 1958. Republished with an introduction by Jerry Hough as *How the Soviet Union Is Governed.* Cambridge, MA: Harvard University Press, 1979.

Figes, Orlando. *The Whisperers: Private Life in Stalin's Russia.* New York: Macmillan, 2008.

———. *Just Send Me Word: A True Story of Love and Survival in the GULAG.* New York: Macmillan, 2012.

Garros, Veronique, et al. *Intimacy and Terror: Soviet Diaries of the 1930s.* New York: New Press, 2000.

Getty, J. Arch, and Oleg V. Naumov. *The Road to Terror: Stalin and the Self-Destruction of the Old Bolsheviks, 1932–1939.* New Haven, CT: Yale University Press, 1999.

Graziosi, Andrea. *The Great Soviet Peasant War: Bolsheviks and Peasants, 1917–1933*. Cambridge, MA: Harvard University Press, 1996.

Jansen, Marc, and Nikolai Petrov. *Stalin's Loyal Executioner: People's Commissar Nikolai Ezhov*. Stanford, CA: Hoover Institute, 2002.

Khlevnyuk, Oleg. *1937: Stalin, NKVD, i sovetskoe obshchestvo* (The Year 1937: Stalin, the NKVD, and Soviet Society). Moscow: Republika, 1992.

————. *Master of the House: Stalin and His Inner Circle*. New Haven, CT: Yale University Press, 2009.

Knight, Amy. *Who Killed Kirov: The Kremlin's Greatest Mystery*. New York: Hill and Wang, 1999.

Kopelev, Lev. *The Education of a True Believer*. London: Woldwood House, 1981.

Kuromiya, Hiroaki. *The Voices of the Dead: Stalin's Great Terror in the 1930s*. New Haven, CT: Yale University Press, 2007.

Levytsky, Boris. *The Stalinist Terror in the Thirties: Documents from the Soviet Press*. Stanford, CA: Hoover Institute, 1974.

Medvedev, Roy. *Let History Judge: The Origins and Consequences of Stalinism*. New York: Knopf, 1972.

Orlov, Alexander. *The Secret History of Stalin's Crimes*. New York: Random House, 1953.

Parrish, Michael. *Stalin's Secret War: Soviet Counterintelligence against the Nazis*. Westport, CT: Praeger, 1996.

Rogovin, Vadim Z. *1937: Stalin's Year of Terror*. New York: Mehring, 2003.

Rubenstein, Joshua, ed. *Stalin's Secret Pogrom: The Postwar Inquisition of the Jewish Anti-Fascist Committee*. New Haven, CT: Yale University Press, 2001.

Satter, David, *It Was a Long Time Ago, and It Never Happened Anyway: Russia and the Communist Past*. New Haven, CT: Yale University Press, 2007.

Schapiro, Leonard. *The Communist Party of the Soviet Union*. New York: Random House, 1960.

Tucker, Robert. *Stalin in Power: The Revolution from Above, 1928–1941*. New York: Norton, 1992.

Tucker, Robert, and Stephen Cohen. *The Great Purge Trials*. New York: Grosset and Dunlap, 1965.

Viola, Lynne. *Peasant Rebels under Stalin: Collectivization and the Culture of Peasant Resistance*. Oxford: Oxford University Press, 2000.

Wilmars, Mary-Kay. *The Eitingons: A Twentieth Century Story*. London: Verso, 2009.

Vaksberg, Arkady. *Stalin's Prosecutor: The Life of Andrei Vyshinsky*. New York: Grove and Weidenfeld, 1990.

Yakovlev, Alexander. *A Century of Violence in Soviet Russia.* New Haven, CT: Yale University Press, 2003.

Zubkova, Elena. *Russia after the War: Hopes, Illusions, and Disappointments.* London: M. E. Sharpe, 1998.

The Gulag and Forced Labor Camps

Applebaum, Anne. *Gulag: A History.* New York: Doubleday, 2003.

Bacon, Edwin. *The Gulag at War: Stalin's Forced Labor Camp in Light of the Archives.* New York: New York University Press, 1994.

Bardach, Janusz, and Kathleen Gleeson. *Man Is Wolf to Man.* Berkeley: University of California Press, 1988.

Bollinger, Martin J. *Stalin's Slave Ships: Kolyma, the GULAG Fleet and the Role of the West.* New York: Greenwood, 2001.

Conquest, Robert. *Kolyma: The Arctic Death Camps.* New York: Macmillan, 1978.

Dallin, David J., and Boris I. Nicolaevesky. *Forced Labor in the Soviet Union.* London: Hollis and Carter, 1948.

Ginzburg, Evgenia. *Journey into the Whirlwind.* New York: Harcourt, Brace and World, 1967.

———. *Within the Whirlwind.* New York: Harcourt, Brace and World, 1981.

Gorbatov, A. A. *Years Off My Life.* London: Oxford University Press, 1964.

Gregory, Paul R., and Valey Lazarev, eds. *The Economics of Forced Labor: The Gulag.* Stanford, CA: Hoover Institution, 2003.

Ivanovna, Galina. *Labor Camp Socialism: The GULAG in the Soviet Totalitarian System.* Armonk, NY: M. E. Sharpe, 2000.

Jakobson, Michael. *Origin of the Gulag: The Soviet Prison Camp System, 1917–1934.* Lexington: University Press of Kentucky, 2002.

Kokurin, Aleksandr, and Nikita Petrov. *Gulag, 1918–1960.* Moscow: Memorial, 2000.

Kuusinen, Aino. *The Rings of Destiny: Inside Soviet Russia from Lenin to Brezhnev.* New York: St. Martin's, 1974.

Lengyel, Josif. *Acta Sanctorum and Other Tales.* London: Peter Owen, 1970.

Malsagov, S. A. *An Island in Hell: A Soviet Prison in the Far North.* London: A. M. Philpot, 1926.

Mandelstam, Nadezhda. *Hope against Hope.* New York: Atheneum, 1970.

———. *Hope Abandoned.* London: Collins, 1974.

Naimark, Norman M. *Fires of Hatred: Ethnic Cleansing in Twentieth Century Europe.* Cambridge, MA: Harvard University Press, 2001.

———. *Stalin's Genocides.* Princeton, NJ: Princeton University Press, 2009.

Mochulsky, Fyodor. *GULAG Boss: A Soviet Memoir.* New York: Oxford University Press, 2011.

Roginsky, A. T. *Sistema ispravitelno-trudovykh lagerie v SSSR, 1923–1960* (The System of Forced Labor Camps in the USSR, 1923–1960). Moscow: Avenia, 1999.

Rossi, Jacques. *Qu'elle etait belle cette Utopie!* Paris: Le Cherche Midi Editeur, 2000.

———. *Jacques le Francais: Pour memoire de goulag.* Paris: Le Cherche Midi Editeur, 2002.

Ruder, Cynthia A. *Making History for Stalin: The Story of the Belomor Canal.* Tallahassee: University Press of Florida, 1998.

Shalamov, Varlan. *Kolyma Tales.* New York: Penguin, 1995.

Shifrin, Avraham. *The First Guidebook to the Prisons and Concentration Camps of the Soviet Union.* New York: Bantam, 1982.

Solzhenitsyn, Alexander. *The Gulag Archipelago.* Vols. 1–3. New York: Harper, 1972–1976.

Stejner, Karlo. *7,000 jours en Siberie.* Paris: Gallimard, 1983.

Swianiewicz, S. *Forced Labor and Economic Development: An Enquiry into the Experience of Soviet Industrialization.* London: Oxford University Press, 1965.

Viola, Lynne. *The Unknown Gulag: The Lost World of Stalin's Special Settlements.* Oxford: Oxford University Press, 2007.

Vrantsev, N. N. *Norilsk.* Moscow: Nedra, 1969.

Weissberg, Alex. *Conspiracy of Silence.* New York: Simon and Schuster, 1951.

Werth, Nicholas. *Cannibal Island: Death in the Siberian Gulag.* Princeton, NJ: Princeton University Press, 2007.

LENIN AND THE DEVELOPMENT OF THE CHEKA/GPU, 1917–1924

Agar, Augustus. *Baltic Episodes.* Annapolis, MD: Naval Institute Press, 1963.

Akseneva, N. S., and V. S. Vasileva. *Soldaty Dzerzhinskogo* (Soldiers of Dzerzhinsky). Moscow: Kniga, 1977.

Avrich, Paul. *Krondsadt, 1921.* Princeton, NJ: Princeton University Press, 1991.

Bennett, Gill. *A Most Extraordinary and Mysterious Business: The Zinoviev Letter of 1924.* Historian LRD No. 14. London: Foreign and Commonwealth Office, 1999.

Brook-Shepherd, Gordon. *The Iron Maze: The Western Secret Services and the Bolsheviks.* London: Macmillan, 1999.

Central Intelligence Agency. *The Trust*. Arlington, VA: Security and Intelligence Foundation, 1989.

Cook, Andrew. *Ace of Spies: The Real Story of Sidney Reilly*. London: Tempus, 2004.

Danilov, V., and T. Shanin. *Krestyanskoe vosstanie v Tambovskoi gubernii v 1919–1921* (*The Peasant Rebellion in Tambov Province, 1919–1921*). Tambov: Intertsentr, 1994.

Debo, Richard K. "Lockhart Plot or Dzerzhinsky Plot?" *Journal of Modern History* 43, no. 3 (1971).

Dolot, Miron. *Execution by Hunger: The Hidden Holocaust*. New York: Norton, 2011.

Dzerzhinsky, F. E. *Prison Diary and Letters*. Moscow: Foreign Languages Publishing House, 1959.

Figes, Orlando. *Peasant Russia, Civil War: The Volga Countryside in the Revolution*. New York: Oxford University Press, 1989.

Gerson, Lennard D. *The Secret Police in Lenin's Russia*. Philadelphia: Temple University Press, 1976.

Goncharov, A. K., ed. *Iz istorii vserossiiskoi chrezvychainoi komissii, 1917–1921* (From the History of the Extraordinary Commission, 1917–1921). Moscow: Polizdat, 1958.

Hill, George A. *Go Spy Out the Land*. London: Cassell, 1932.

Leggett, George. *The Cheka: Lenin's Political Police*. Oxford: Clarendon, 1981.

Lockhart, Robert Bruce. *Memoirs of a British Agent*. London: Putnam, 1932.

———. *Ace of Spies: A Biography of Sidney Reilly*. London: Hodder and Stoughton, 1967.

Milton, Giles. Russian Roulette: *How British Spies Thwarted Lenin's Plan for World Revolution*. London: Bloomsbury Press, 2014.

Radkey, Oliver H. *The Unknown Civil War in Soviet Russia: A Study of the Green Movement in the Tambov Region*. Stanford, CA: Hoover Institution, 1976.

Reed, John. *Ten Days That Shook the World*. New York: International Publishers, 1952.

Serge, Victor. *Memoirs of a Revolutionary: 1901–1941*. London: Oxford University Press, 1963.

Sokolov, N. A. *The Sokolov Investigation of the Alleged Murder of the Russian Royal Family*. New York: Robert Speller and Sons, 1971.

Tishkov, A. V. *Perviy Chekist* (The First Chekist). Moscow: Voenizdat, 1968.

Trotsky, Leon. *History of the Russian Revolution*. London: Scribner, 1931.

———. *My Life*. London: Scribner, 1931.

Tsvygun, S. K. *V. I. Lenin i Cheka: Sbornik dokumentov, 1917–1922gg* (Lenin and the Cheka: Collection of Documents, 1917–1922). Moscow: Izdatelstvo Politicheskoi Literaturi, 1975.

Vinogradov, V. K., et al. *Delo Fani Kaplan ili kto strelyal v Lenina* (The Fany Kaplan Affair or Who Shot Lenin). Moscow: Editions OOO XX-History, 2003.

Volkogonov, Dmitry. *Trotsky: The Eternal Revolutionary*. New York: Free Press, 1995.

STALIN'S SECRET SERVICES AND THEIR FOREIGN INTELLIGENCE OPERATIONS, 1924–1953

Agabekov, Georgii. *OGPU*. New York: Brentano's, 1931. Originally published as *GPU: Zapiski Chekista*.

Costello, John, and Oleg Tsarev. *Deadly Illusions*. New York: Crown, 1993.

Dallin, Alexander, and F. I. Firsov, eds. *Dmitrov and Stalin 1934–1943*. New Haven, CT: Yale University Press, 2000.

Deriabin, Peter S. *Inside Stalin's Kremlin*. New York: Brassey's, 1998.

Duff, William E. *A Time for Spies: Theodore Stepanovich Maly and the Era of the Great Illegals*. Nashville, TN: Vanderbilt University Press, 2002.

Gazar, Edward P. *Alexander Orlov: The FBI's KGB General*. Chicago: Carroll and Graf, 2002.

Gross, Babette. *Munzenberg: A Political Biography*. Ann Arbor: University of Michigan Press, 1974.

Hyde, Earl M. "Still Perplexed about Krivitsky." *International Journal of Intelligence and Counterintelligence* 16, no. 3 (2003).

Kearn, Gary, and Nigel West. *A Death in Washington: Walter G. Krivitsky and the Stalin Terror*. New York: Enigma, 2003.

Koch, Stephen. *Double Lives*. London: HarperCollins, 1995.

Krivitsky, Walter. *In Stalin's Secret Service*. New York: Harper and Brothers, 1939.

Nicolaevsky, Boris I. *Power and the Soviet Elite: The Letter of an Old Bolshevik and Other Essays*. New York: Praeger, 1965.

Orlov, Alexander. *The Secret History of Stalin's Crimes*. New York: Random House, 1953.

Poretsky, Elizabeth. *Our Own People*. London: Oxford University Press, 1969.

Radosh, Ronald, Mary R. Habeck, and Grigory Sevostianov. *Spain Betrayed: The Soviet Union and the Spanish Civil War*. New Haven, CT: Yale University Press, 2001.

Rogovin, V. Z. *1937: Stalin's Year of Terror*. Oak Park, MI: Mehring Books, 1998

Romanov, A. I. *Nights Are Longest There*. Boston: Little, Brown, 1972.

Stolyarov, Kirill. *Golgopha* (Golgotha). Moscow: 1991.

Sudoplatov, Pavel. *Special Tasks: The Memoirs of an Unwanted Witness—A Soviet Spymaster*. Boston: Little, Brown, 1994.

Tzouliadis, Tim. *The Forsaken: an American Tragedy in Stalin's Russia*. New York: Penguin, 2008.

Secret Services Operations in Western Europe, 1924–1953

Bovorik, Genrikh. *The Philby Files: The Secret Life of the Master Spy—KGB Archives Revealed*. Boston: Little, Brown, 1994.

Bower, Tom. *Red Web: MI6 and the KGB Master Coup*. London: Aurum, 1989.

Boyle, Andrew. *The Climate of Treason*. London: Hutchinson, 1979.

Brooks-Shepherd, Gordon. *The Storm Petrels*. London: Jonathan Cape, 1984.

———. *The Storm Birds*. London: Weidenfeld and Nicolson, 1988.

Brown, Anthony Cave. *"C": The Secret Life of Sir Stewart Menzies*. London: Macmillan, 1987.

———. *Treason in the Blood*. London: Michael Joseph, 1996.

Cairncross, John. *The Enigma Spy*. London: Century, 1997.

Carter, Miranda. *Anthony Blunt: His Lives*. New York: Farrar, Straus and Giroux, 2003.

Catherwood, Christopher. *The Cuckoos' Nest: Five Hundred Years of Cambridge Spies*. Cambridge: Oleander Press, 2013.

Costello, John. *Mask of Treachery*. New York: Collins, 1998.

Elliott, Nicholas. *With My Little Eye*. London: Michael Russell, 1993.

Friedman, Richard. "A Stone for Willy Fisher." *Studies in Intelligence*. Special edition (Fall 2000).

Hamrick, S. J. *Deceiving the Deceivers: Kim Philby, Donald Maclean, and Guy Burgess*. New Haven, CT: Yale University Press, 2004.

Harrison, Edward. *The Young Kim Philby: Soviet Spy and British Intelligence Officer*. Liverpool: Liverpool University Press, 2012.

Knightley, Phillip. *The Master Spy: The Story of Kim Philby*. New York: Vantage, 1988.

Macintyre, Ben. *A Spy among Friends: Kim Philby and the Great Betrayal*. New York: Random House, 2014.

Milne, Tim. *Kim Philby: The Unknown Story of the KGB's Master Spy*. London: Biteback Publishing, 2014.

Modin, Yuri. *My Five Cambridge Friends*. London: Headline, 1994.

Page, B. D., and P. Knightley. *Philby: The Spy Who Betrayed a Generation*. London: Deutsch, 1968.

Philby, Kim. *My Silent War*. London: MacGibbon and Key, 1968.

Poretsky, Elizabeth. *Our Own People*. New York: Oxford University Press, 1969.

Seale, Patrick, and Maureen McConville. *Philby: The Long Road to Moscow*. London: Hamish Hamilton, 1973.

Sharp, Tony. *Stalin's American Spy: Noel Field, Allen Dulles and the East European Show Trials*. London: Hurst, 2014.

Sobolyeva, Tatyana A. "Some Incidents in the 1930's." Translated by Thomas R. Hammant. *Cryptologia* 25, no. 1 (2001).

Tanenhaus, Sam. *Whittaker Chambers*. New York: Random House, 1997.

Trevor-Roper, Hugh. *The Philby Affair*. London: William Kimber, 1968.

West, Nigel, and Oleg Tsarev. *The Crown Jewels: The British Secrets at the Heart of the KGB Archives*. New Haven, CT: Yale University Press, 1999.

Wolton, Thierry. *Le grand recruetment*. Paris: Grosset, 1993.

Soviet Operations in Asia and Australia, 1920s–1950s

Ball, Desmond, and David Horner. *Breaking the Codes: Australia's KGB Network*. St. Leonards, Australia: Allen and Unwin, 1998.

Johnson, Chalmers. *An Instance of Treason: Ozaki Hotsumi and the Sorge Spy Ring*. Stanford, CA: Stanford University Press, 1990.

McKnight, David. *Australia's Spies and Their Secrets*. St. Leonards, Australia: Allen and Unwin, 1994.

———. "The Moscow-Canberra Cables: How Soviet Intelligence Obtained British Secrets through the Back Door." *Intelligence and National Security* 13, no. 2 (1998).

Wasserstein, Bernard. *Secret War in Shanghai*. New York: Houghton Mifflin, 1999.

Soviet Intelligence and Nuclear Weapons

Albright, Joseph, and Marcia Kunstel. *Bombshell: The Secret Story of Ted Hall and America's Unknown Atomic Spy Conspiracy*. New York: Times Books, 1997.

Chikov, Vladimir, and Gary Kern. *KGB File 13676: Stalin's Atomic Spies*. Paris: Robert Laffront/Fixot, 1996.

"Documents on Soviet Espionage and the Bomb." *Cold War International History Project Bulletin*, no. 4 (1994).

Feklisov, Alexander. *The Man behind the Rosenbergs*. New York: Enigma, 2001.

Holloway, David. "How the Bomb Saved Soviet Physics." *Bulletin of Atomic Scientists*, January/February 1994.

———. *Stalin and the Bomb*. New Haven, CT: Yale University Press, 1994.

Lowenhaupt, Henry S. "On the Soviet Nuclear Scent." *Studies in Intelligence*. Special edition (Fall 2004).

Rhodes, Richard. *The Making of the Atom Bomb*. New York: Simon and Schuster, 1986.

———. *Dark Sun: The Making of the Hydrogen Bomb*. New York: Simon and Schuster, 1995.

Roberts, Sam. *The Brother*. New York: Random House, 2001.

Sobell, Morton. *On Doing Time*. New York: Charles Scribner's Sons, 1974.

VENONA: Soviet Espionage and the American Response. Washington, DC: Central Intelligence Agency, 1996.

West, Nigel. *VENONA: The Greatest Secret of the Cold War*. London: HarperCollins, 1999.

———. *Mortal Crimes: The Greatest Theft in History: The Soviet Penetration of the Manhattan Project*. New York: Enigma, 2004.

West, Nigel, and Oleg Tsarev. *TRIPLEX: Secrets from the Cambridge Spies*. New Haven, CT: Yale University Press, 2009.

Williams, Robert Chadwell. *Klaus Fuchs, Atomic Spy*. Cambridge, MA: Harvard University Press, 1987.

Soviet Intelligence in the United States and Canada, 1920s–1950s

Bentley, Elizabeth. *Out of Bondage*. New York: Ballantine, 1988.

Bothwell, Robert, and J. L. Granatstein. *The Gouzenko Transcripts*. Toronto: Deneau, 1982.

Budenz, Louis. *This Is My Story*. New York: McGraw-Hill, 1947.

Canadian Royal Commission. *Defection of Igor Gouzenko*. Ottawa: HMSO, 1948.

Chambers, Whittaker. *Witness*. New York: Random House, 1952.

Craig, R. Bruce. *Treasonable Doubt: The Harry Dexter White Spy Case*. Lawrence: University Press of Kansas, 2004.

Dainsher, Igor, and Geoffrey Elliott. *Kitty Harris: The Spy with Seventeen Names*. London: St. Ermin's, 2001.

Davis, Hope Hale. *Great Day Coming: A Memoir of the 1930s*. Royalton, VT: Sternforth, 1994.

Donovan, James. *Strangers on a Bridge: The Case of Colonel Abel*. London: Secker and Warburg, 1964.

Evans, M. Stanton, and Herbert Romerstein. *Stalin's Secret Agents: The Subversion of the Roosevelt Government*. New York: Simon and Schuster, 2012.

Haynes, John Earl, and Harvey Klehr. *The Soviet World of American Communism*. New Haven, CT: Yale University Press, 1998.

———. *VENONA: Decoding Soviet Espionage in America*. New Haven, CT: Yale University Press, 1999.

———. "The Cold War Debate Continues: A Traditionalist View of Historical Writing on Domestic Communism and Anti-Communism." *Journal of Cold War Studies* 2 (Winter 2000).

Hook, Sidney. *Out of Step: An Unquiet Life in the 20th Century*. New York: Carroll and Graf, 1986.

Kerschner, Donald S. *Cold War Exile: The Untold Story of Maurice Halperin*. Columbia: University of Missouri Press, 1995.

Kessler, Lauren. *Clever Girl: Elizabeth Bentley, the Spy Who Ushered in the McCarthy Era*. New York: HarperCollins, 2003.

Klehr, Harvey, and Ronald Radosch. *The Amerasia Spy Case: Prelude to McCarthyism*. Chapel Hill: University of North Carolina Press, 1996.

Koch, Stephen. *Double Lives*. New York: Free Press, 1994.

Lamphere, Robert. *The FBI-KGB War*. New York: Random House, 1986.

Mitchell, Marcia, and Tom Mitchell. *The Spy Who Seduced America: Lies and Betrayal in the Heart of the Cold War—The Judith Coplon Story*. New York: Invisible Cities, 2002.

Newton, Verne. *The Cambridge Spies: The Untold Story of Maclean, Philby, and Burgess in the United States*. New York: Madison, 1991.

Olmsted, Kathryn S. *Red Spy Queen: A Biography of Elizabeth Bentley*. Chapel Hill: University of North Carolina Press, 2002.

Radosh, Ronald, and Joyce Milton. *The Rosenberg File*. New York: Holt, Rinehart and Winston, 1983.

Romerstein, Herbert, and Eric Breindel. *The VENONA Secret: Exposing Soviet Espionage and American Traitors*. Washington, DC: Regnery, 2000.

Romerstein, Herbert, and Stanislav Levchenko. *The KGB against the "Main Enemy."* Lexington, MA: Lexington Books, 1989.

Sawatsky, John. *Gouzenko: The Untold Story*. New York: Macmillan, 1984.

Schecter, Jerrold, and Leona Schecter. *Sacred Secrets: How Soviet Intelligence Operations Changed American History*. Washington, DC: Brassey's, 2002.

Shipley, Katherine A. S. *Red Spies in America*. Lawrence: University Press of Kansas, 2004.

Tanenhaus, Samuel. *Whittaker Chambers: A Biography*. New York: Random House, 1997.

Weinstein, Allen. *Perjury: The Hiss-Chambers Case*. New York: Random House, 1978.

Weinstein, Allen, and Alexander Vassiliev. *The Haunted Woods: Soviet Espionage in America—The Stalin Era*. New York: Random House, 1999.

White, G. Edward. *Alger Hiss's Looking Glass War: The Covert Life of a Russian Spy*. New York: Oxford University Press, 2004.

THE GREAT PATRIOTIC WAR

Beevor, Anthony. *The Mystery of Anna Chekhova*. New York: Viking, 2004.
Bellamy, Christopher. *Absolute War: Soviet Russia in the Second World War*. London: Macmillan, 2007.
Bezymenski, Lev. *The Death of Adolf Hitler: Unknown Documents from the Soviet Archives*. New York: Harcourt, Brace and World, 1968.
Birstein, Vadim J. *Operatsiya mif* (Operation Myth). Moscow: Mezduraodnaya Otnasheniya, 1995.
———. *SMERSH: Stalin's Secret Weapon, Soviet Military Counterintelligence in World War II*. London: Biteback Publishing, 2011.
Bradley, Mark A. *A Very Principled Boy: The Life of Duncan Lee, Red Spy and Cold Warrior*. New York: Basic Books, 2014.
Brysac, Shareen Blair. *Resisting Hitler: Mildred Harnack and the Red Orchestra*. London: Oxford University Press, 2000.
Buttar, Prit. *Battleground Prussia*. London: Osprey Publishing, 2009.
———. *Between Giants: The Battle for the Baltic in World War II*. London: Osprey Publishing, 2013.
Central Intelligence Agency. *The Rote Kapelle: The CIA's History of Soviet Intelligence and Espionage Networks in Western Europe, 1936–1945*. Washington, DC: University Publications of America, 1984.
Deakin, F. W., and G. M. Storry. *The Case of Richard Sorge*. New York: Harper, 1966.
Dementyeva, I. A., N. I. Agayants, and Y. Y. Yakovlev. *Tovarishch Zorge* (Comrade Sorge). Moscow: Sovetskaya Rossiya, 1965.
Emelianov, Y. *Prybaltika: Mezhdu Stalinim I Hitlerom* (*The Baltics: Between Stalin and Hitler*). Moscow: Bystrov, 2007.
Erickson, John. *The Soviet High Command*. London: St. Martin's, 1962.
———. *The Road to Stalingrad*. New York: Harper and Row, 1975.
———. *The Road to Berlin*. London: Nicolson, 1983.
Foote, Alexander. *Handbook for Spies*. London: Museum Press, 1949.
Fugate, Bryan. *Operation Barbarossa: Strategy and Tactics on the Eastern Front, 1941*. Novato, CA: Presidio, 1984.
Garlinski, Jozef. *The Swiss Corridor: Espionage Networks in Switzerland during World War II*. London: Dent, 1981.
Gehlen, Richard. *The Service*. New York: World, 1972.
Gisevius, Hans Bernd. *To the Bitter End*. New York: Houghton Mifflin, 1947.

Glantz, David M. *Soviet Military Deception in the Second World War*. London: Frank Cass, 1989.

———. *Soviet Military Intelligence in War*. London: Frank Cass, 1990.

———. *Kharkov: Anatomy of a Military Disaster*. Rockville Centre, NY: Sarpedon, 1998.

———. *Colossus Reborn: The Red Army at War, 1941–1943*. Lawrence: University Press of Kansas, 2005.

Glees, Anthony. *The Secrets of the Service*. London: Jonathan Cape, 1987.

Karner, Stephan. *Gulag GUPVI* (The Gulag of the Chief Directorate for Prisoners of War and Internees). Moscow: RGGU, 2002.

Khristoforov, V. S., et al. *"Smersh": Istorichickie ocherki i arkhivnie dokumenti* ("Smersh": Historical Outline and Archival Documents). Moscow: Izdatelstvo Gravarkhiv, 2003.

Kuznetsov, I. I. "Stalin's Minister V. S. Abakumov, 1908–1954." *Journal of Slavic Military Studies* 12 (March 1990).

Naumov, V. P., ed. *1941 god. Dokument, kniga pervaya* (The Year 1941: Documents, Book One). Moscow: Mezhdunarodny Fond "Demokratiya," 1988.

Nelson, Anne. *Red Orchestra*. New York: Random House, 2009.

Paul, Allan. *Katyn: The Untold Story of Stalin's Polish Massacre*. New York: Scribner's, 1991.

"Perepiska V. A. Molotova s I. V. Stalinym. Noyabr 1940 goda" (Corresponence of V. M. Molotov with I. V. Stalin. November 1940). *Voenno-istoricheskiy zhurnal* 9 (1978).

Perrault, G. *The Red Orchestra*. London: Barker, 1968.

Prange, Gordon. *Target Tokyo: The Story of the Sorge Spy Ring*. New York: McGraw-Hill, 1984.

Reese, Roger R. *Why Stalin's Soldiers Fought: The Red Army's Military Effectiveness in World War II*. Lawrence: University Press of Kansas, 2011.

Roberts, Geoffrey. *Stalin's War: From World War to the Cold War, 1939–1953*. New Haven, CT: Yale University Press, 2006

———. *Stalin's General: The Life of Georgy Zhukov*. New York: Random House, 2012.

Roloff, Stefan. *Die Rote Kapelle*. Munich: Olsten, 2004.

Shtemenko, S. M. *Generalnyi shtab v gody voiny* (The General Staff in the Years of the War). Moscow: Voenizdat, 1973.

Simonov, Konstantin. *Glazami cheloveka moego pokoleniya* (*Through the Eyes of a Man of My Generation*). Moscow: APN, 1988.

Smith, Bradly. *Sharing Secrets with Stalin*. Lawrence: University Press of Kansas, 1996.

Stephan, Robert W. *Stalin's Secret War: Soviet Counterintelligence against the Nazis*. Lawrence: University Press of Kansas, 2004.

Thomas, David. "Foreign Armies East and German Military Intelligence in Russia, 1941–1945." *Journal of Contemporary History* 22 (1987).

Tolstoy, Nikolay. *Victims of Yalta*. New York: Hutchinson, 1988.

Trepper, Leopold. *The Great Game*. New York: McGraw-Hill, 1977.

Watson, Peter, and Alda Petrova. *The Death of Adolph Hitler: Documents from the Soviet Archives*. New York: Harcourt, Brace and World, 1993.

Weeks, Albert. *Stalin's Other War: Soviet Grand Strategy, 1939–1941*. Lanham, MD: Rowman & Littlefield, 2002.

Werner, Ruth. *Sonya's Report*. London: Chatto and Windus, 1991.

Werth, Alexander. *Russia at War*. New York: Dutton, 1964.

Operation Barbarossa

Glantz, David M. *Stumbling Colossus: The Red Army on the Eve of World War*. Lawrence: University Press of Kansas, 1998.

Gorodetsky, Gabriel. *Grand Delusion: Stalin and the German Invasion of Russia*. New Haven, CT: Yale University Press, 1999.

Lukacs, John. *June 1941: Hitler and Stalin*. New Haven, CT: Yale University Press, 2006.

Maslov, A. A. *Fallen Soviet Generals: Soviet General Officers Killed in Battle, 1941–1945*. London: Frank Cass, 1998.

Murphy, David E. *What Stalin Knew: The Enigma of Barbarossa*. New Haven, CT: Yale University Press, 2005.

Nekrich, A.M. *Pariahs, Partners, Predators: German-Soviet Relations, 1922–1941*. New York: Norton, 1997.

Pleshakov, Constantine. *Stalin's Folly: The Tragic First Ten Days of WWII on the Eastern Front*. New York: Houghton Mifflin, 2005.

Whaley, B. *Codeword Barbarossa*. Cambridge, MA: MIT Press, 1973.

Yakovlev, Aleksandr N., ed. *1941 god* (The Year 1941). Moscow: Mezhdunarodny Fond "Demokratiya," 1998.

Zetterling, Nikolas, and Ander Frankson. *The Drive on Moscow, 1941. Operation Taifun and Germany's First Great Crisis in World War II*. Philadelphia: Casemate, 2012.

Partisan War

Andreyev, Catherine. *Vlasov and the Russian Liberation Movement*. Cambridge: Cambridge University Press, 1987.

Andrianov, V. N. *Voina v tyly vraga* (War in the Enemy's Rear). Moscow: Polizdat, 1974.

Armstrong, John A. *Soviet Partisans in World War II*. Madison: University of Wisconsin Press, 1964.

Browning, Christopher R. *The Origins of the Final Solution: The Evolution of Nazi Jewish Policy September 1939–March 1942*. Lincoln: University of Nebraska Press, 2004.

Dallin, Alexander. *German Rule in Russia, 1941–1945*. London: Macmillan, 1957.

Desbois, Patrick. *The Holocaust by Bullets*. New York: Palgrave, 2008.

Fischer, George. *Soviet Opposition to Hitler*. Cambridge, MA: Harvard University Press, 1952.

Grenkevich, Leonid. *The Soviet Partisan Movement*. London: Frank Cass, 1999.

Khristoforov, V. S., et al. *Lubyanka v dni bitvy za Moskvu: Materialy organov gosbezopasnosti SSSR iz tsentralnovo arkhiva FSB* (Lubyanka in the Days of the Battle for Moscow: Material from the Organs of State Security USSR from the Central Archive of the FSB Russia). Moscow: Izdatelskiy Dom Zvonnitsa MG, 2002.

Kovpak, S. S. *Our Partisan Course*. London: Hutchinson, 1947.

Kuodyte, D. *The Unknown War: Armed Anti-Soviet Resistance in Lithuania in 1944–1953*. Vilnius, Lithuania: Genocide and Research Resistance Center, 2004

Ponomarenko, P. K. *Vsenarodnaya borba v tyly nemetsko-fashistkikh zakhvatchikov, 1941–1944* (All People's Struggle in the German-Fascist Invaders' Rear Areas, 1941–1944). Moscow: Nauka, 1985.

Raach, R. C. "With *Smersh* in Berlin: New Light on the Incomplete History of the Führer and the Vozhd'." *World Affairs* 154, no. 2 (1991).

Reitlinger, Gerald. *The House Built on Sand: The Conflicts of German Policy in Russia, 1939–1945*. Westport, CT: Greenwood, 1960.

Shepher, Ben. *War in the Wild East: The German Army and Soviet Partisans*. Cambridge, MA: Harvard University Press, 2004.

Soviet Services in Eastern Europe and the Baltic States, 1944–1953

Berkhoff, Karl. *Harvest of Despair: Life and Death of the Ukraine under Soviet Rule*. New York: Belknap, 2004.

Davis, Norman. *Rising '44: The Battle for Warsaw*. New York: Viking, 2004.

Djilas, Milovan. *Tito: The Story from Inside*. New York: Harcourt Brace Jovanovich, 1980.

Gross, Jan. *Revolution from Abroad: The Soviet Conquest of Poland's Western Ukraine and Western Belorussia*. Princeton, NJ: Princeton University Press, 1988.

Hodos, George. *Show Trials: Stalinist Purges in Eastern Europe, 1948–1954.* Westport, CT: Praeger, 1987.

Krickus, Richard J. *Showdown: The Lithuanian Rebellion and the Breakup of the Soviet Empire.* London: Brassey's, 1996.

Leonhard, Wolfgang. *Child of the Revolution.* London: Collins, 1957.

Naimark, Norman, *Stalin's Genocides.* Princeton, NJ: Princeton University Press, 2009.

Paul, Allen. *Katyn: The Massacre of the Seeds of Polish Insurrection.* Annapolis, MD: Naval Institute Press, 1996.

Rosenburg, Tina. *The Haunted Land: Facing Eastern Europe's Ghosts after Communism.* New York: Random House, 1995.

Scheurig, Bodo. *Free Germany.* Middletown, CT: Wesleyan University Press, 1969.

Snyder, Timothy. *Bloodlands: Europe between Hitler and Stalin.* New York: Basic Books, 2012.

Toranska, Teresa. *"Them": Stalin's Polish Puppets.* New York: Harper and Row, 1986.

Zawodny, J. K. *Death in the Forests.* South Bend, IN: University of Notre Dame Press, 1960.

COLD WAR CRISES

Applebaum, Anne. *Iron Curtain: The Crushing of Eastern Europe, 1944–1956.* New York: Random House, 2012.

Arbel, David, and Ran Edelist. *Western Intelligence and the Collapse of the Soviet Union, 1980–1990: Ten Years That Did Not Shake the World.* London: Frank Cass, 2003.

Beschloss, Michael R. *The Crisis Years.* New York: HarperCollins, 1995.

Braithwaite, Rodric. *Across the Moscow River: The World Turned Upside Down.* New Haven, CT: Yale University Press, 2002.

Central Intelligence Agency. *Analysis of the Soviet Union, 1947–1991.* Washington, DC: Central Intelligence Agency Center for the Study of Intelligence, 2001.

Combs, Dick. *Inside The Soviet Alternative Universe: The Cold War's End and the Soviet Union's Fall Reappraised.* State College: Pennsylvania State University Press, 2008.

Darling, Arthur B. *The Central Intelligence Agency: An Instrument of Government to 1950.* University Park: Pennsylvania State University Press, 1990.

Fischer, Benjamin B. *A Cold War Conundrum.* Washington, DC: Central Intelligence Agency Center for the Study of Intelligence, 1997.

Frolik, Josef. *The Frolik Defection: The Memoirs of an Agent*. London: Leo Cooper, 1975.

Gaiduk, I. V., et al. *Kholodnaya voina: Novye podkhody, novye dokumenty (The Cold War: New Approaches, New Documents)*. Moscow: Otvet, 1995.

Garthoff, Raymond. *Détente and Confrontation: American-Soviet Relations from Nixon to Reagan*. Washington, DC: Brookings Institution, 1994.

Gates, Robert M. *From the Shadows*. New York: Simon and Schuster, 1996.

Gellateley, Robert. *Stalin's Curse: Battling for Communism in War and Cold War*. New York: Random House, 2012.

Gorlizki, Yoram, and O. V. Khlevniuk. *Cold Peace: Stalin and the Soviet Ruling Circle*. London: Oxford University Press, 2004.

Gribianski, Leonid, and Norman Naimark. *The Establishment of Communist Regimes in Eastern Europe*. Boulder, CO: Westview, 1997.

Haslam, Jonathan. *Russia's Cold War: From the October Revolution to the Fall of the Wall*. New Haven, CT: Yale University Press, 2011.

Lashmar, Paul. *Spy Flights of the Cold War*. London: Sutton, 1996.

Mark, Eduard. *Revolution by Degrees: Stalin's National Front Strategy for Europe, 1941–1947*. Cold War International History Project. Working paper 31 (2001).

Mastny, Vojtech. *Russia's Road to the Cold War: Diplomacy, Warfare, and the Politics of Communism*. New York: Columbia University Press, 1979.

Molnar, Miklos. *From Bela Kun to Janos Kadar: Seventy Years of Hungarian Communism*. New York: St. Martin's, 1990.

Moynihan, Daniel. *Secrecy: The American Experience*. New Haven, CT: Yale University Press, 1998.

Parish, Scott D., and Mikhail M. Narinsky. *New Evidence on the Soviet Rejection of the Marshall Plan, 1947*. Cold War International History Project. Working paper 9 (1994).

Pechatnov, Vladimir O. *The Big Three after World War II: New Documents on Soviet Thinking about Relations with the United States and Great Britain*. Cold War International History Project. Working paper 13 (1995).

Robert, Geoffrey. *A Chance for Peace? The Soviet Campaign to End the Cold War, 1953–1955*. Cold War International History Working Paper 57, December 2008.

———. *Molotov: Stalin's Cold Warrior*. Washington, DC: Potomac Books, 2012.

Rosenberg, Tina. *The Haunted Land*. New York: Random House, 1995.

Treml, Vladimir G. "Western Analysis and the Soviet Policymaking Process." In *Watching the Bear: Essays on CIA's Analysis of the Soviet Union*, edited by Gerald K. Haines and Robert E. Leggett. Washington, DC: Central Intelligence Agency, Center for the Study of Intelligence, 2003.

Zubok, Vladimir. *A Failed Empire: The Soviet Union in the Cold War from Stalin to Gorbachev*. Chapel Hill: University of North Carolina Press, 2007.

Zubok, Vladimir, and Constantine Pleshkov. *Inside the Kremlin's Cold War: From Stalin to Khrushchev*. Cambridge, MA: Harvard University Press, 1996.

Afghanistan

Arnold, Anthony. *The Fateful Pebble: Afghanistan's Role in the Fall of the Soviet Union*. Novato, CA: Presidio, 1993.

Bradsher, Henry. *Afghanistan and the Soviet Union*. Durham, NC: Duke University Press, 1985.

Braitwaite, Rodric. *Afgantsy: The Russians in Afghanistan, 1979–1989*. Oxford: Oxford University Press, 2011.

"Cold War in the Third World and the Collapse of Détente." *Cold War International History Project Bulletin* no. 8/9 (2001). Contains Communist Party Central Committee documents on the decision to intervene in Afghanistan, including meeting notes and memoranda.

Ghaus, Abdul Samad. *The Fall of Afghanistan: An Insider's Account*. Washington, DC: Pergamon-Brassey, 1988.

Grau, Lester W. *The Bear Went over the Mountain: Soviet Combat Tactics in Afghanistan*. London: Frank Cass, 1998.

Grau, Lester W., and Michael A. Gress. *The Soviet Afghan War: How a Superpower Fought and Lost*. Lawrence: University Press of Kansas, 2002.

Jalali, Ali Ahmad, and Lester W. Grau. *The Other Side of the Mountain: Mujahideen Tactics in the Afghan War*. Quantico, VA: U.S. Marine Corps Staff Study, 1998.

MacEachin, Douglas. *Predicting the Soviet Invasion of Afghanistan: The Intelligence Community's Record*. Washington, DC: Central Intelligence Agency Center for the Study of Intelligence, 2002.

Mayorov, Aleksandr. *Pravda Afganskoye voine* (The Truth about the Afghan War). Moscow: Prava Cheloveka, 1996.

Mitrokhin, Vasily. *The KGB in Afghanistan*. Cold War International History Project. Working paper 40 (2002).

Berlin, 1947–1989

Adams, Jefferson. "Probing the East German State Security Archives." *International Journal of Intelligence and Counterintelligence* 13, no. 1 (2000).

———. "The Strange Demise of East German State Security." *International Journal of Intelligence and Counterintelligence* 18, no. 1 (2005).

Ausland, John C. *Kennedy, Khrushchev, and the Berlin-Cuban Crisis, 1961–1964*. Oslo: Scandinavian Press, 1996.

Catudal, Honore M. *Kennedy and the Berlin Wall Crisis: A Case Study in U.S. Decision Making*. Berlin: Berlin-Verlag, 1980.

Clay, Lucius. *Decision in Germany*. New York: Doubleday, 1950.

Colitt, Leslie. *Spy Master: The Real-Life Karla, His Moles, and the East German Secret Police*. New York: Addison-Wesley, 1995.

Critchfield, James H. *Partners at the Creation: The Men behind Germany's Defense and Intelligence Establishment*. Annapolis, MD: Naval Institute Press, 2004.

Felfe, Heinz. *Im Dienst des Gegners—10 Jahre Moskaus Mann im BND* (In the Adversary's Service—10 Years as Moscow's Man in the BND). Hamburg: Rasch und Rohring, 1986.

Fischer, Ben B. "'One of the Biggest Ears in the World': East German SIGINT." *Journal of Intelligence and Counterintelligence* 11, no. 2 (1998).

Frischauer, Willi. *The Man Who Came Back: The Story of Otto John*. London: Frederick Muller, 1958.

Harrison, Hope M. *Ulbricht and the Concrete "Rose": New Archival Evidence on Soviet-East German Relations and the Berlin Crisis, 1958–1962*. Cold War International History Project. Working paper 5 (1993).

Hertle, Hans-Hermann. "The Fall of the Wall: The Unintended Self-Dissolution of East Germany's Ruling Regime." *Cold War International History Project Bulletin*, no. 12/13 (2001).

Hoehne, Heinz, and Hermann Zolling. *The General Was a Spy*. New York: Coward, McCann, 1957.

John, Otto. *Twice through the Lines*. New York: Harper and Row, 1972. Originally published in German as *Zweimal kam ich heim* (1965).

Klimov, Gregory. *The Terror Machine: The Inside Story of the Soviet Administration in Germany*. London: Faber and Faber, 1953. Originally published in Russian in West Germany as *Berlinskiy Kreml* (The Berlin Kremlin). Frankfort-am-Main: Possev, 1953.

Miller, Barbara. *The Stasi Files Unveiled: Guilt and Compliance in a Unified Germany*. London: Transaction, 1999.

Murphy, David, Sergei A. Kondrashev, and George Bailey. *Battle Ground Berlin: CIA vs. KGB in the Cold War*. New Haven, CT: Yale University Press, 1997.

Naimark, Norman M. *"To Know Everything and to Report Everything Worth Knowing": Building the East German Police State, 1945–49*. Cold War International History Project. Working paper 10 (1998).

Popplewell, Richard J. "The KGB and the Control of the Soviet Bloc: The Case of East Germany." *Intelligence and National Security* 13, no. 1 (1998).

Reese, Mary Ellen. *General Reinhard Gehlen: The CIA Connection.* Fairfax, VA: George Mason University Press, 1990.

Stafford, David. *Spies beneath Berlin.* New York: Overlook, 2002.

Stiller, Werner, and Jefferson Adams. *Beyond the Wall: Memoirs of an East and West German Spy.* Washington, DC: Brassey's, 1992.

Wolf, Markus. *Man without a Face: The Autobiography of Communism's Greatest Spymaster.* New York: Times Books, 1997.

Wyden, Peter. *Wall: The Inside Story of a Divided Berlin.* New York: Simon and Schuster, 1989.

Zubok, Vladislav M. *Khrushchev and the Berlin Crisis (1958–62).* Cold War International History Project. Working paper 6 (1998).

Cuba, 1959–1990

Allison, Graham T., and Philip Zelikow. *Essence of Decision: Explaining the Cuban Missile Crisis.* 2nd ed. New York: Longman, 1999.

Bright, James, and David A. Welch. *Intelligence and the Cuban Missile Crisis.* Portland, OR: Frank Cass, 1988.

Brugioni, Dino. *Eyeball to Eyeball: The Inside Story of the Cuba Missile Crisis.* New York: Random House, 1991.

Central Intelligence Agency. *Documents on the Cuban Missile Crisis.* Washington, DC: Government Printing Office, 1995.

Frankel, Max. *High Noon in the Cold War: Kennedy, Khrushchev, and the Cuban Missile Crisis.* New York: Ballantine, 2004.

Fursenko, Aleksandr, and Timothy Naftali. *"One Hell of a Gamble": The Secret History of the Cuban Missile Crisis—Khrushchev, Castro, and Kennedy.* New York: Norton, 1997.

Garthoff, Raymond L. *Reflections on the Cuban Missile Crisis.* Washington, DC: Brookings Institution, 1989.

Gribkov, Anatoli, and William Y. Smith. *Operation Anadyr: U.S. and Soviet Generals Recount the Cuban Missile Crisis.* Chicago: Edition Q, 1994.

Huchthausen, Peter. *October Fury.* Hoboken, NJ: Wiley, 2002.

Penkovsky, Oleg. *The Penkovsky Papers.* Garden City, NY: Doubleday, 1965.

Shakhnazarov, Georgi. "Fidel Castro, Glasnost, and the Caribbean Crisis." Cold War International History Project. Virtual Archive.

Poland, 1956–1990

Ash, Timothy. *The Polish Revolution: Solidarity.* New York: Vantage, 1985.

Gluchowski, Leszek W. *The Soviet-Polish Confrontation of October 1956: The Situation in the Polish Internal Security Corps.* Cold War International History Project. Working paper 17 (1999).

Kostrzewa, Robert, ed. *Between East and West: Writings from Kultura.* New York: Hill and Wang, 1990.

Kremer, Mark. *Top Secret Documents of Soviet Deliberation during the Polish Crisis.* Cold War International History Project. Working paper 1 (1999).

Kuklinski, Ryszard. "The Crushing of Solidarity." *Orbis* 32, no. 1 (1998).

MacEachin, Douglas. *US Intelligence and the Polish Crisis, 1980–1981.* Washington, DC: Central Intelligence Agency Center for the Study of Intelligence, 2002.

Mastny, Voytek. "The Soviet Non-Invasion of Poland in 1990–1991 and the End of the Cold War." *Europa-Asia Studies* 51, no. 2 (1999).

Pavlov, Vitalii. *Operatsiya Sneg: Polveka vo vneshnei razvedka KGB (Operation Snow: Half a Century in KGB Foreign Intelligence).* Moscow: Geja, 1996.

Trubnikov, Vadim. *Operation Polonia, 1980–1981* (Operation Poland: The Years 1980–1981). Moscow: Izdatelstvo Pechati Novosti, 1983.

Weiser, Benjamin. *A Secret Life.* New York: Public Affairs, 2004.

Prague, 1948–1990

August, Frantisek, and David Rees. *Red Star over Prague.* London: Sherwood, 1984.

Bittman, Ladislav. *The Deception Game: Czechoslovak Intelligence in Soviet Political Warfare.* Syracuse, NY: Syracuse University Research Corp., 1972.

Dubcek, Alexander. *Hope Dies Last: Autobiography of Alexander Dubcek.* London: Kodansha, 1993.

Frolik, Josef. *The Frolik Defection: The Memoirs of an Agent.* London: Leo Cooper, 1975.

Havel, Vaclav. *Disturbing the Peace.* New York: Knopf, 1990.

———. *Open Letters: Selected Writing, 1965–1990.* New York: Knopf, 1991.

Kusin, Vladimir V. *The Intellectual Origins of the Prague Spring: The Development of Reformist Ideas in Czechoslovakia 1956–1967.* Cambridge: Cambridge University Press, 2002.

Matthews, John P. C. "Majales: The Abortive Student Revolt in Czechoslovakia in 1956." Cold War International History Project. Working paper 24 (1998).

"Memorandum to the Communist Party Central Committee Secretariat Prepared by the Second Secretary of the Moldavian Communist Party." *Cold War International History Project Bulletin*, no. 11 (2002).

Navratil, Jaromir. *The Prague Spring '68*. Ithaca, NY: Cornell University Press, 1998.

Sommer, Mark. *Living in Freedom: The Exhilaration and Anguish of Prague's Second Spring*. San Francisco: Mercury House, 1992.

Tuma, Oldrich. *Srpen '68* (August 1968). Prague: USD-Maxdorf, 1966.

Valenta, Jiri. *Soviet Intervention in Czechoslovakia, 1968: Anatomy of a Decision*. Baltimore: Johns Hopkins University Press, 1991.

THE KGB, 1954–1991

Bitman, Ladislav. *The KGB and Soviet Disinformation: An Insider's View*. London: Pergamon, 1972.

Donovan, James. *Strangers on a Bridge*. London: Secker and Warburg, 1964.

Dzhirkvilov, Ilya. *Secret Servant*. London: Collins, 1987.

Epstein, Edward Jay. *Deception: The Invisible War between the KGB and the CIA*. New York: Allen, 1989.

Kalugin, Oleg. *The First Directorate: My 32 Years of Intelligence and Counterintelligence against the West*. New York: St. Martin's, 1994.

Kuzichkin, Vladimir. *Inside the KGB: My Life in Soviet Espionage*. London: Andre Deutsch, 1990.

Lyubimov, Mikhail. *Dekameron shpionov* (Decameron of Spies). Moscow: Tsentrpoliagraf, 1998.

Martin, David C. *Wilderness of Mirrors*. New York: Ballantine, 1981.

Medvedev, Zhores. *Andropov*. New York: Norton, 1983.

Petrov, Vladimir, and Evdokia Petrov. *Empire of Fear*. London: Andre Deutsch, 1956.

Pringle, Robert W. "Andropov's Counterintelligence State." *International Journal of Intelligence and Counterintelligence* 13, no. 2 (2000).

Sheymov, Victor. *Tower of Secrets*. Annapolis, MD: Naval Institute Press, 1993.

Trimble, Delmege. "The Defection of Otto John." *Studies in Intelligence*. Special edition (Fall 2000).

The KGB as a Political Institution

Bobkov, F. D. *KGB i vlast* (*KGB and the Power*). Moscow: 1995.

Dunlop, John B. *The Rise of Russia and the Fall of the Soviet Union*. Princeton, NJ: Princeton University Press, 1992.

Garthoff, Raymond L. "The KGB Reports to Gorbachev." *Intelligence and National Security* 11, no. 2 (1996).

Gorbachev, Mikhail S. *The August Coup*. London: HarperCollins, 1991.

Murphy, Kenneth. *Retreat from the Finland Station: Moral Odysseys in the Breakdown of Communism*. New York: Free Press, 1992.

Steele, Jonathan. *Andropov in Power*. Oxford: Martin Robertson, 1983.

Taubman, William. *Khrushchev: The Man and His Era*. New York: Norton, 2003.

Zemskov, Ilya. *Partiya ili Mafiya* (Party or Mafia). Paris: Les Editeurs Reunis, 1976.

The KGB versus the Western Intelligence Services, 1954–1991

Ashley, Clarence. *CIA Spymasters*. New York: Pelican, 2004.

Barron, John. *Breaking the Ring*. New York: Avon, 1988.

———. *Operation SOLO: The FBI's Man in the Kremlin*. Washington, DC: Regnery, 1996.

Bearden, Milt, and James Risen. *The Main Enemy: The Inside Story of the CIA's Final Showdown with the KGB*. New York: Random House, 2003.

Blake, George. *No Other Choice: An Autobiography*. London: Jonathan Cape, 1990.

Brennikow, Louise. *Abel*. New York: Ballantine, 1982.

Central Intelligence Agency. *Abstract of Report of Investigation: The Aldrich H. Ames Case*. Washington, DC: Central Intelligence Agency, 1984.

Chalet, Marcel, and Wolton Thierry. *Les visiteurs de l'ombre*. Paris: Bernard Grasset, 1990.

Cherkashin, Victor, and Gregory Feifer. *Spy Hunter: Memoir of a KGB Officer*. New York: Basic Books, 2004.

Daniloff, Nicholas. *Two Lives, One Russia*. New York: Houghton Mifflin, 1988.

Deryabin, Peter. *The Secret World*. New York: Doubleday, 1959.

Drozdov, Yuri. *Nuzhnaya rabota* (Necessary Work). Moscow: VlaDar, 1994.

Earley, Pete. *Family of Spies: Inside the John Walker Spy Ring*. New York: Bantam, 1988.

———. *Confessions of a Spy: The Real Story of Aldrich Ames*. New York: G. P. Putnam's Sons, 1997.

Epstein, Edward. *Deception: The Invisible War between the KGB and the CIA*. New York: Simon and Schuster, 1989.

Finn, Peter, and Petra Courvee. *The Zhivago Affair: The Kremlin, the CIA, and the Battle over a Forbidden Book*. New York: Pantheon, 2014.

Gordievsky, Oleg. *Next Stop Execution*. London: Macmillan, 1995.

Hart, John L. *The CIA's Russians*. Annapolis, MD: Naval Institute Press, 2003.

Headley, Lake, and William Hoffman. *The Court Martial of Clayton Lonetree*. New York: Henry Holt, 1989.

Heaps, Leo. *Thirty Years with the KGB: The Double Life of Hugh Hambleton*. London: Methuen, 1983.

Helms, Richard, with William Hood. *A Look over My Shoulder: A Life in the Central Intelligence Agency*. New York: Random House, 2003.

Herrington, Stuart. *Traitors among Us*. Novato, CA: Presidio, 1999.

Hood, William. *Mole*. New York: Norton, 1982.

Houghton, Harry. *Operation Portland: The Autobiography of a Spy*. London: Rupert Hart-Davis, 1972.

Kahn, David. "Soviet Comint in the Cold War." *Cryptologia* 22, no. 1 (1998).

Kessler, Ronald. *Spy vs. Spy: Stalking Soviet Spies in America*. New York: Scribner's, 1988.

———. *Moscow Station: How the KGB Penetrated the American Embassy*. New York Scribner's, 1989.

———. *The Spy in the Russian Club*. New York: Scribner's, 1990.

———. *Escape from the CIA: How the CIA Won and Lost the Most Important Spy Ever to Defect to the U.S.* New York: Scribner's, 1991.

Kevorkov, Vyacheslav. *Tayniy kanal (Secret Channel)*. Moscow: Geya, 1997.

Keworkow, Wjatscheslaw. *Der geheime Kanal: Moskau, der KGB und die Bonner ostpolitik*. Berlin: Rowohlt, 1995.

Kholkhov, Nikolai. *In the Name of Conscience*. London: Frederick Muller, 1964.

Koehler, John. *Spies in the Vatican: The Soviet Union's Cold War against the Catholic Church*. New York: Pegasus, 2007.

Krassilnikov, Rem. *KGB protiv MI6* (KGB against MI6). Moscow: Tsentrpoligraf, 2000.

Krotkov, Yuri. *I Am from Moscow*. New York: Dutton, 1967.

Kuzichkin, Vladimir. *Inside the KGB: Myth and Reality*. London: Andre Deutsch, 1990.

Levchenko, Stanislav. *On the Wrong Side: My Life in the KGB*. New York: Pergamon, 1988.

Mangold, Tom. *Cold Warrior*. New York: Simon and Schuster, 1991.

Martin, David. *Wilderness of Mirrors*. New York: Ballantine, 1981.

Nechiporenko, Oleg. *Passport to Assassination*. London: Birch Lane, 1993.

Powers, Thomas. *The Man Who Kept the Secrets*. New York: Knopf, 1979.

Reed, Thomas C. *At the Abyss: An Insider's History of the Cold War*. New York: Ballantine, 2004.

Reisch, Alfred. *Hot Books in the Cold War: The CIA-Funded Secret Western Book Distribution Program behind the Soviet Union*. New York: Central European University Press, 2013.

Sakharov, Vladimir, and Umburto Tosi. *High Treason*. New York: Putnam, 1980.

Shainberg, Maurice. *Breaking from the KGB*. New York: St. Martin's, 1986.

Shebarshin, Leonid. *Ruka Moskvi: Zapiski nachalnika sovetskoi razvedki* (The Hand of Moscow: Notes of the Chief of Soviet Intelligence). Moscow: Tsentr 100, 1992.

Shvets, Yuri B. *Washington Station*. New York: Simon and Schuster, 1994.

Suvorov, Victor. *The Victors*. Boston: Berkeley, 1985.

Tarin, Oleg, and Edward Talanov. *TsRU: Gosudarstveniy terrorizm SShA* (CIA: American State Terrorism). Moscow: Planet, 1987.

Verbitsky, Anatole, and Dick Adler. *Sleeping with Moscow: The Authorized Account of the KGB's Bungled Infiltration of the FBI by Two of the Soviet Union's Most Unlikely Operatives*. New York: Shapolsky, 1987.

Vise, David A. *The Bureau and the Mole*. New York: Atlantic Monthly Press, 2002.

West, Nigel. *Mole Hunt: Searching for Soviet Spies in MI5*. New York: William A. Morrow, 1989.

Whiteside, Thomas. *An Agent in Place*. New York: Viking, 1966.

Wise, David. *Molehunt: The Secret Search for Traitors That Shattered the CIA*. New York: Random House, 1992.

———. *The Spy Who Got Away: The Inside Story of Edward Howard, the CIA Agent Who Betrayed His Country's Secrets and Escaped to Moscow*. New York: Random House, 1998.

———. *Spy: The Inside Story of How the FBI's Robert Hanssen Betrayed America*. New York: Random House, 2002.

Wynne, Greville. *Contact on Gorky Street*. New York: Atheneum, 1968.

Zubok, Vladislav M. "Spy vs. Spy: The KGB vs. the CIA, 1960–1962." *Cold War International History Project Bulletin*, no. 4 (1994).

The KGB and the Debate over the Kennedy Assassination

"Defector Study." House Select Committee on Assassinations, no. 180-10147-10238. U.S. National Archives.

Epstein, Edward Jay. *Legend: The Secret World of Lee Harvey Oswald*. New York: McGraw-Hill, 1978.

Holmes, Robert. *A Spy Like No Other: The Cuban Missile Crisis and the KGB Links to the Kennedy Assassination.* London: Biteback Publishing, 2012.

Nechiporenko, Oleg. *Passport to Assassination: The Never-before-Told Story of Lee Harvey Oswald by the KGB Colonel Who Knew Him.* New York: Birch Lane, 1993.

Pacepa, Ion Mihai. *Programmed to Kill: Lee Harvey Oswald, the Soviet KGB and the Kennedy Assassination.* Lanham, MD: Ivan R. Dee, 2007.

Savodnik, Peter. *The Interloper. Lee Harvey Oswald inside the Soviet Union.* New York: Basic Books, 2013.

The KGB and Human Rights: The Dissidents

Adler, Nanci. *Beyond the Soviet System: The Gulag Survivor.* London, Transaction, 2002.

Alexeyeva, Ludmilla, and Paul Goldberg. *The Thaw Generation.* Pittsburgh, PA: University of Pittsburgh Press, 1990.

Almarik, Andrei. *Will the Soviet Union Survive until Nineteen Eighty-Four?* New York: Harcourt Brace, 1968.

———. *Involuntary Journey to Siberia.* New York: Harcourt Brace, 1970.

———. *Notes of a Revolutionary.* New York: Knopf, 1982.

Baron, Samuel H. *Bloody Saturday in the Soviet Union: Novocherkassk, 1962.* Stanford, CA: Stanford University Press, 2001.

Bergman, Joseph. *Meeting the Demands of Reason: The Life and Thoughts of Andrei Sakharov.* Ithaca, NY: Cornell University Press, 2009.

Brodsky, Joseph. *Less Than One.* New York: Viking, 1986.

Bukovsky, Vladimir. *To Build a Castle: My Life as a Dissenter.* New York: Viking, 1978.

Garrard, John, and Carol Garrard. *The Bones of Berdichev: The Life and Fate of Vasily Grossman.* New York: Free Press, 1996.

Grigorenko, Petro. *Memoirs.* New York: Norton, 1982.

Hill, Kent R. *The Puzzle of the Soviet Church.* Portland, OR: Multnomah, 1989.

Kopelev, Lev. *No Jail for Thought.* London: Secker and Warburg, 1977. Published in the United States as *To Be Preserved Forever.*

Krasin, Viktor. *Sud* (The Trial). New York: Chalidze Foundation, 1983.

Labedz, Leopold, and Max Hayward. *On Trial: The Case of Sinyavsky and Daniel.* London: Collins Harvil, 1967.

Laurie, Richard. *Sakharov.* Hanover, NH: Brandeis University Press, 2002.

Orlov, Yuri. *Dangerous Thoughts: Memoirs of a Russian Life.* New York: William Morrow, 1991.

Plyushch, Leonid. *History's Carnival.* New York: Doubleday, 1979.

Reddaway, Peter, ed. and trans. *Uncensored Russia: Protest and Dissent in the Soviet Union (The Unofficial Journal: A Chronicle of Current Events)*. New York: McGraw-Hill, 1972.

Reddaway, Peter, and Sidney Bloch. *Russia's Political Hospitals*. London: Futura, 1978.

Rubenstein, Joshua, and Alexander Gribanov, ed. *The KGB File on Andrei Sakharov*. New Haven, CT: Yale University Press, 2005.

Sagdeyev, Roald. *The Making of a Soviet Scientist. My Adventures in Nuclear Fission and Space from Stalin to Star Wars*. New York: Wiley, 1994.

Sakharov, Andrei. *Memoirs*. New York: Knopf, 1990.

Scammel, Michael. *The Solzhenitsyn Files*. Chicago: Edition Q, 1995.

Shentalinsky, Vitaly. *KGB's Literary Archive*. London: Havill, 1995.

Simis, Konstantin. *USSR: The Corrupt Society*. New York: Simon and Schuster, 1982.

Solzhenitsyn, Aleksandr. *The Oak and the Calf*. London: Collins and Harvil, 1980.

Thomas, D. M. *Alexander Solzhenitsyn: A Century in His Life*. New York: St. Martin's, 1998.

THE POST-SOVIET YEARS

Russian Intelligence, 1991 to the Present

Alibek, Ken, and Stephen Handelman. *Biohazard*. New York: Random House, 1999.

Ebron, Martin. *KGB: Death and Rebirth*. New York: Praeger, 1994.

Friedman, Robert I. *Red Mafiya: How the Russian Mob Has Invaded America*. Boston: Little, Brown, 2000.

Gurov, Aleksandr. *Krasnaya mafiya* (Red Mafia). Moscow: Samozvet, 1995.

Handelman, Stephen. *Comrade Criminal: The Theft of the Second Russian Revolution*. New Haven, CT: Yale University Press, 1995.

Hoffman, David E. *The Oligarchs: Wealth and Power in the New Russia*. New York: Public Affairs, 2011.

Judah, Ben. *Fragile Empire: How Russia Fell in and out of Love with Vladimir Putin*. New Haven, CT: Yale University Press, 2013.

Knight, Amy. *Spies without Cloaks: The KGB Successors*. Princeton, NJ: Princeton University Press, 1994.

———. "The Enduring Legacy of the KGB in Russian Politics." *Problems of Communism* 47 (July/August 2000).

Korzhakov, Aleksandr. *Ot rasveta do zakata* (From Dawn to Dusk). Moscow: Interbuk, 1997.

Laqueur, Walter. *Black Hundreds: The Rise of the Extreme Right in Russia.* New York: HarperCollins, 1993.

Lucas, Edward. *The New Cold War: Putin's Russia and the Threat to the West.* New York: Macmillan, 2009.

———. *Deception: The Untold Story of East-West Espionage Today.* London: Walker Books, 2012.

Odom, William E. *The Collapse of the Soviet Military.* New Haven, CT: Yale University Press, 1998.

Politkovskaya, Anna. *A Russian Diary: A Journalist's Final Account of Life, Corruption, and Death in Putin's Russia.* New York: Random House, 2009.

Pringle, Robert W. "The Heritage and Future of the Soviet Intelligence Community." In *Strategic Intelligence*, edited by Jim Wirtz and Loch Johnson. Los Angeles: Roxbury Press, 2004. Previously published in *International Journal of Intelligence and Counterintelligence* 11, no. 2 (1998).

Shevstova, Lillia. *Putin's Russia.* New York: Carnegie Endowment for International Peace, 2010.

Solnick, Steven L. *Stealing the State: Control and Collapse in Soviet Institutions.* Cambridge, MA: Harvard University Press, 1997.

Stepankov, Valentin, and Yevgeni Lisov. *Kremlevskiy zagovor* (The Kremlin Plot). Moscow: Ogonek, 1992.

Timofeyev, Lev. *Russia's Secret Rulers.* New York: Knopf, 1992.

Vaksberg, Arkady. *The Soviet Mafia.* New York: St. Martin's, 1991.

Waller, J. Michael. *KGB in Russia Today.* Boulder, CO: Westview, 1994.

The Rise of Vladimir Putin and the *Siloviki*

Arutunyan, Anna. *The Putin Mystique: Inside Russia's Power Cult.* New York: Skyscraper Publications, 2014.

Asmus, Ronald D. *A Little War That Shook the World: Georgia, Russia, and the Future of the West.* New York: Palgrave Macmillan, 2010.

Bennets, Marc. *Kicking the Kremlin.* London: Oneworld, 2014.

Felshtinsky, Yuri, and Vladimir Pribylovsky. *The Corporation: Russia and the KGB in the Age of Putin.* New York: Encounter Books, 2008.

Gessen, Masha. *The Man without a Face: The Unlikely Rise of Vladimir Putin.* New York: Penguin, 2012.

Knight, Amy. "The Two Worlds of Vladimir Putin." *Wilson Quarterly* 24, no. 2 (2000).

Politkovskaya, Anna. *A Dirty War.* London: Havrill Press, 2007.

———. *Putin's Russia: Life in a Failing Democracy.* New York: Macmillan, 2007.

Putin, Vladimir. *Ot pervovo litsa: Razgovory s Vladimirom Putinym* (*First Person: Conversations with Vladimir Putin*). Moscow: Vagrius, 2000.

Roxburg, Angus. *The Strongman*. London: I. P. Tauris, 2011.

Van Herpen, Marcel H. *Putin's War: The Rise of Russia's New Imperialism*. Lanham, MD: Rowman & Littlefield, 2014.

About the Author

Robert W. Pringle is a veteran of 25 years of service with the Department of State and the Central Intelligence Agency (CIA). He was educated at Bucknell University and the University of Virginia. After service in Vietnam as a U.S. Army officer, he spent two years at the Department of the Army's Center for Military History. From 1975 to 1982, he served two tours in southern Africa and one in Moscow as a consular and political officer with the State Department. In Moscow and later in Cape Town, he was those missions' human rights officer. From 1983 to 1998, he served as an analyst and manager at the CIA. He was awarded the Career Intelligence Medal on his retirement. From 1998 to 2004, Pringle taught history and political science courses at the University of Kentucky's Patterson School of Diplomacy and International Commerce. While at Kentucky, he wrote a number of articles on Soviet intelligence. He also taught as an adjunct professor at the Virginia Military Institute and Christopher New Port University. He now lives in Williamsburg, Virginia.

All statements of fact, opinion, or analysis are those of the author and do not reflect the official positions or views of the CIA or any other U.S. government agency. Nothing in the contents should be construed as asserting or implying U.S. government authentication of information or CIA endorsement of the author's views. The material has been reviewed by the CIA to prevent the disclosure of classified information.

CPSIA information can be obtained at www.ICGtesting.com
Printed in the USA
BVOW11*1119180715

409205BV00005B/8/P